Cost and Optimization Engineering

Cost and Optimization Engineering

F. C. Jelen, Editor

Professor, School of Engineering
Lamar State College of Technology
Beaumont, Texas

Sponsored by the American Association of Cost Engineers

McGRAW-HILL BOOK COMPANY
NEW YORK, ST. LOUIS, SAN FRANCISCO, DÜSSELDORF,
LONDON, MEXICO, PANAMA, SYDNEY, TORONTO

Cost and Optimization Engineering

Copyright © 1970 by McGraw-Hill, Inc. All rights reserved. Printed in the United States of America. No part of this publication may be reproduced, stored in a retrieval system, or transmitted, in any form or by any means, electronic, mechanical, photocopying, recording, or otherwise, without the prior written permission of the publisher.

Library of Congress Catalog Card Number 76-95811

32323

1 2 3 4 5 6 7 8 9 0 Q B B P 7 9 8 7 6 5 4 3 2 1 0

This book was set in Times Roman by The Universities Press, printed on permanent paper by Quinn & Boden Company, Inc., and bound by The Book Press, Inc. The designer was Richard Paul Kluga; the drawings were done by Joseph Buchner. The editors were B. J. Clark and J. W. Maisel. Stuart Levine supervised the production.

Dedicated to Dr. James Hay Black, Executive Secretary of the American Association of Cost Engineers and Professor of Chemical Engineering at the University of Alabama, whose original conception of the need for this book has led to its realization.

Preface

The book is intended as an introduction to cost and optimization engineering, including engineering economy. It includes all the topics required even for an extensive course, although doubtless some instructors will choose to omit certain chapters. This is one of the few textbooks covering in detail the three major categories of cost comparisons and profitability, optimization, and cost engineering.

The text is at the undergraduate level but is directed as well to continuing education activities and to the practicing engineer who will use it for self-study. Over 100 examples are worked out in detail. The book emphasizes clarity and good delineation so that the student will know where he is at all times. The format, which contains some innovations, has been selected to permit high accessibility of the contents.

Superficial treatments and mere enumerations have been avoided. All topics in the major chapters are presented with sufficient depth for genuine understanding. Problems or questions are supplied at the end of chapters. The appendixes contain extensive tables, in particular for profitability studies, and should be valuable to even the practicing engineer.

Dr. James H. Black originally proposed the book and started the project under the sponsorship of the American Association of Cost Engineers. Unfortunately, he had to withdraw as editor for reasons of health early in the preparation, and the present editor accepted the responsibility of finishing the project.

Besides the editor 16 authors have contributed, making possible the wide coverage. Since a cooperative book runs the peril of being redundant and disorderly, the text has been critically edited to achieve a harmonious presentation. Indeed, the editor must be blamed for any shortcomings inasmuch as he certainly had adequate authority to eliminate them.

A book on cost and optimization engineering should be an example of efficiency and brevity. If the reader considers that the coverage is complete, the presentation clear, and the format pleasant to use, the major ambitions will have been realized.

Acknowledgement is made to the Lamar State College of Technology for granting the editor a development leave to complete the book and to the American Association of Cost Engineers for sponsoring the work.

F. C. JELEN

Contents

PREFACE vii

LIST OF CONTRIBUTORS xxi

Chapter 1 INTRODUCTION 1

1.1 Concern for cost and optimization   1
1.2 Some definitions   2
1.3 Scope   2
1.4 Organization by sections   3
1.5 Nomenclature   3

Part I
MATHEMATICS OF COST COMPARISONS

Chapter 2 EQUIVALENCE AND COST COMPARISONS 11

TIME VALUE OF MONEY AND EQUIVALENCE

2.1 Compound interest as an operator   11
2.2 Uniform annual amount, unacost   15
2.3 Double interest rates—Hoskold's formula   19

COST COMPARISONS

2.4 Comparisons with equal duration   21
2.5 Comparisons with unequal durations—common denominator of service lives   22
2.6 Cost comparison by unacost   25
2.7 Cost comparison by capitalized cost   27

x CONTENTS

2.8 Examples of cost comparisons   31
2.9 Finding the best alternative   34
2.10 Considerations in cost comparison   36
2.11 Nomenclature   37
2.12 Problems   38
2.13 References   41

Chapter 3   DEPRECIATION AND TAXES—EQUIVALENCE AFTER TAXES   42

DEPRECIATION AND TAXES

3.1 Nature of depreciation   42
3.2 Depreciation terms   43
3.3 Straight-line depreciation (SL)   46
3.4 Sinking-fund depreciation (SF)   47
3.5 Declining-balance depreciation (DB)   48
3.6 Double-declining-balance depreciation (DDB)   48
3.7 Sum-of-digits depreciation (SD)   49
3.8 Units-of-production depreciation (UP)   49
3.9 Taxes and depreciation   49
3.10 Comparison of methods   52
3.11 Special considerations   53
3.12 Depletion   54

COST COMPARISONS AFTER TAXES

3.13 Present worth after taxes   55
3.14 Nomenclature   61
3.15 Problems   62
3.16 References   63

Chapter 4   CONTINUOUS INTEREST AND DISCOUNTING   64

4.1 Logic for continuous interest   64
4.2 Continuous interest as an operator   64
4.3 Uniform flow   67
4.4 Flow changing at an exponential rate   69
4.5 Flow declining in a straight line to zero   70
4.6 Discounting with improving performance—learning   72
4.7 Unaflow—capital-recovery factor   74
4.8 Capitalized cost   75
4.9 Income tax   76
4.10 Equivalence   77
4.11 Nomenclature   81
4.12 Problems   81
4.13 References   82

Chapter 5 PROFITABILITY 83

- 5.1 Profit 83
- 5.2 Investment evaluation 84
- 5.3 Four economic guideposts 84
- 5.4 Payout time 85
- 5.5 Payout time with interest 85
- 5.6 Return on original investment 86
- 5.7 Return on average investment 87
- 5.8 Discounted cash flow (DCF) 87
- 5.9 Venture worth 88
- 5.10 Three projects compared 88
- 5.11 Continuous interest 90
- 5.12 Some considerations in profitability studies 92
- 5.13 Classification system for economic appraising 95
- 5.14 Special topics 95
- 5.15 Nomenclature 97
- 5.16 Problems 97
- 5.17 References mentioned in text 100
- 5.18 References—books 100
- 5.19 References—additional articles 100

Chapter 6 TECHNOLOGICAL ADVANCEMENT—INFLATION 102

DISPLACEMENT

- 6.1 Displacement vs. replacement 102
- 6.2 One year more of existent 103
- 6.3 More than one year of existent 106
- 6.4 Uniform-gradient series 108
- 6.5 Best policy with a uniform-gradient cost 109
- 6.6 Delay value of existent 113
- 6.7 A mathematical model for technological advancement 114
- 6.8 The MAPI model 116
- 6.9 Group displacement 120

INFLATION

- 6.10 Cost comparisons under inflation 122
- 6.11 Unaburden 125
- 6.12 High inflation rates 125
- 6.13 Inflation and technological advancement 127
- 6.14 Nomenclature 128
- 6.15 Problems 129
- 6.16 References 131

Part 2
OPTIMIZATION

Chapter 7 BREAK-EVEN AND MINIMUM-COST ANALYSIS   135

7.1 Types of costs   135
7.2 Economic-production charts   138
7.3 Economic-production chart above 100% capacity   139
7.4 Economic-production chart for dumping   141
7.5 Nonlinear economic-production charts   141
7.6 One-product multiple-machine example   145
7.7 Multiple-products one-machine example   147
7.8 Critique in use of break-even and minimum-cost analysis   148
7.9 Nomenclature   149
7.10 Problems   149
7.11 References   150

Chapter 8 PROBABILITY—UNCERTAINTY—SIMULATION   151

DISCRETE FREQUENCY DISTRIBUTIONS

8.1 Distribution functions   151
8.2 Properties of discrete-distribution functions   152
8.3 Cumulative-distribution function   155
8.4 Binomial distribution   156
8.5 Poisson distribution   157

CONTINUOUS FREQUENCY DISTRIBUTIONS

8.6 Continuous distributions   158
8.7 Cumulative-distribution function   159
8.8 Rectangular or uniform distribution   159
8.9 Exponential distribution   160
8.10 Normal distribution in standard form   162
8.11 Normal distribution with arbitrary parameters   163

SPECIAL TOPICS

8.12 Monte Carlo method—simulation   164
8.13 Least squares   166
8.14 Nomenclature   168
8.15 Problems   168
8.16 References   169

Chapter 9 THE LEARNING CURVE   170

9.1 Practice improves performance   170
9.2 The learning curve and learning-curve function   171
9.3 Properties of the learning-curve function   173
9.4 Cumulative values   176
9.5 Learning curve and economic evaluation   177
9.6 The learning-curve function from single-unit data   178
9.7 The learning-curve function from grouped data   178
9.8 Development of learning-curve tables   182
9.9 Nomenclature   183
9.10 Problems   183
9.11 References   184

Chapter 10 INVENTORY PROBLEMS   185

DETERMINISTIC MODELS

10.1 Definitions   185
10.2 General inventory model   186
10.3 Model 1 of Fig. 10.2F2   187
10.4 Model 2 of Fig. 10.2F2   191
10.5 Model 3 of Fig. 10.2F2   191
10.6 Model 4 of Fig. 10.2F2   193
10.7 Model 5 of Fig. 10.2F2   195
10.8 Model 6 of Fig. 10.2F2   195
10.9 Model 7 of Fig. 10.2F2   197
10.10 Model 8 of Fig. 10.2F2   197
10.11 Model 9 of Fig. 10.2F2   198
10.12 Model 10 of Fig. 10.2F2   198
10.13 General analytical method   199
10.14 Graphical or tabular method   199

PROBABILISTIC MODELS

10.15 Optimum stock by incremental analysis   201
10.16 Optimum inventory based on expectation   202
10.17 Monte Carlo simulation in inventory   203
10.18 Nomenclature   205
10.19 Problems   206
10.20 References   206

Chapter 11 QUEUING PROBLEMS   207

11.1 Prevalence   207
11.2 Description of queuing system   207

11.3	Classification of queuing systems	208
11.4	Solution of queuing problems	211
11.5	Model 1 of Table 11.4T1	211
11.6	Model 2 of Table 11.4T1	214
11.7	Model 3 of Table 11.4T1	214
11.8	Model 4 of Table 11.4T1	216
11.9	Model 5 of Table 11.4T1	216
11.10	Model 6 of Table 11.4T1	219
11.11	Finite queuing—Model 7 of Table 11.4T1	219
11.12	General method with certainty	222
11.13	General method with uncertainty	224
11.14	Nomenclature	226
11.15	Problems	227
11.16	References	228

Chapter 12   OPTIMIZATION   229

ONE VARIABLE

12.1	Optimization—a human trait	229
12.2	Nature of optimization	230
12.3	Optimization methods	231
12.4	Analytical method for optimization	232
12.5	Graphical method for optimization	233
12.6	Incremental method for optimization	234
12.7	A cyclic process	234
12.8	An example involving rate of return	239
12.9	A two-step example with recycle	241
12.10	Variocyclic processes	244

MULTIVARIABLE OPTIMIZATION

12.11	Analytical method	246
12.12	Graphical method	247
12.13	Incremental method	247
12.14	A two-variable optimization example	248
12.15	Lagrange multipliers	249
12.16	Sensitivity and response analysis	251
12.17	Simplification of multivariable problems	253
12.18	Nomenclature	253
12.19	Problems	254
12.20	References	257

Chapter 13   LINEAR AND DYNAMIC PROGRAMMING   258

LINEAR PROGRAMMING (LP)

13.1   Optimization of an objective function   258
13.2   Development of linear-programming equations   259
13.3   Slack variables   261
13.4   Quality constraints   262
13.5   Method of solution   263
13.6   Algebraic method   267
13.7   Simplex method   268
13.8   Applications   271

DYNAMIC PROGRAMMING (DP)

13.9   An allocation example   272
13.10   A transportation example   276
13.11   Pros and cons of dynamic programming   278
13.12   Nomenclature   279
13.13   Problems   279
13.14   References for linear programming   280
13.15   References for dynamic programming   280

Chapter 14   SPECIAL MATHEMATICAL TECHNIQUES   281

UNIVARIABLE SEARCH METHODS

14.1   Search techniques   281
14.2   Uniform search   282
14.3   Uniform dichotomous search   283
14.4   Sequential dichotomous search   284
14.5   Fibonacci search technique   285
14.6   Comparison of methods   287

MULTIVARIABLE FUNCTIONS

14.7   One-at-a-time method   288
14.8   Method of steepest ascent   289
14.9   Constrained optimization   292

SUMMATION OF SERIES

14.10   Recurring power series   293
14.11   General term from generating function   294
14.12   Some recurring power series   295
14.13   Nomenclature   296
14.14   Problems   296

14.15 References on search methods 297
14.16 References on series summation 297

Part 3
COST ESTIMATION AND CONTROL

Chapter 15 CAPITAL INVESTMENT COST ESTIMATION 301

15.1 Fixed capital and working capital 301
15.2 Types of estimates 302
15.3 Cost of making estimates 302
15.4 Functions of capital-cost estimates 303
15.5 Representation of cost data 303
15.6 Cost indexes 305
15.7 Cost-capacity factors 310
15.8 Equipment installation cost ratios 311
15.9 Plant cost ratios 316
15.10 Plant component ratios 318
15.11 Plant cost by analytical procedure 319
15.12 Building costs 322
15.13 Engineering costs 326
15.14 Piping costs 326
15.15 Insulation costs 333
15.16 Start-up costs 333
15.17 Nomenclature 333
15.18 Problems 334
15.19 References 334

Chapter 16 OPERATING-COST ESTIMATION 338

16.1 Definitions 338
16.2 Operating-cost estimation—general 341
16.3 Raw materials 344
16.4 Utilities 345
16.5 Operating labor 347
16.6 Maintenance 348
16.7 Indirect payroll cost 348
16.8 Operating supplies 349
16.9 Laboratory and other service costs 349
16.10 Royalties and rentals 349
16.11 Contingencies 349
16.12 Indirect costs 350
16.13 Distribution costs 350
16.14 Avoidance of nuisances 351

16.15   An example   351
16.16   Shortcut methods   351
16.17   Questions   352
16.18   References   353

Chapter 17   COST CONTROL   355

CAPITAL-COST CONTROL

17.1   The nature of control   355
17.2   Elements of cost-control program   356
17.3   Scope definition   356
17.4   Project planning and scheduling   357
17.5   Cost reporting   359
17.6   Corrective action   361

OPERATING-COST CONTROL

17.7   Operating costs are repetitive   363
17.8   Conjunction with cost accounting   363
17.9   Define objectives   364
17.10   Standard costs   365
17.11   Cost reporting   365
17.12   Corrective action   365
17.13   Classification of operating-cost control problems   366

CRITICAL-PATH METHOD (CPM)

17.14   Network diagrams   366
17.15   A simple network   367
17.16   Advantages of CPM   370
17.17   Problems   371
17.18   References on cost control   372
17.19   References on CPM and network methods   372

Chapter 18   TOTAL COST AND PROFIT   373

18.1   Elements of complete cost   373
18.2   Estimating general and selling expense   373
18.3   Start-up costs   375
18.4   Contingencies   378
18.5   Financing   378
18.6   Plant-location studies   378
18.7   Offsite costs   380
18.8   Forecasting   381
18.9   Profit   383
18.10   Questions   383
18.11   References   384

Part 4
ASSOCIATED TOPICS

Chapter 19 COST ACCOUNTING 387

BASIC CONCEPTS

19.1 Cost accounting and the cost engineer 387
19.2 Accounting definitions 388
19.3 The operating accounting system 388
19.4 Types of accounting 390
19.5 Development and objectives of cost accounting 390
19.6 Definitions and classification of costs 391
19.7 Historical against future-directed costs 391

COST-ACCOUNTING CYCLE

19.8 Production cycle and cost cycle 392
19.9 Direct costs against indirect costs 393
19.10 Cost centers, unit costs 394
19.11 Job-order costing and process costing 394
19.12 Techniques of overhead-cost accounting 396

RELATED TOPICS

19.13 Cost behavior against activity volume 398
19.14 Normal volume 399
19.15 Direct costing and absorption costing 399
19.16 Variance analysis 400
19.17 Standard costs and budgets 400
19.18 Joint costs 401
19.19 Relevant and differential costs 402
19.20 Inventory valuation 402
19.21 Depreciation 403
19.22 Questions 403
19.23 References 404

Chapter 20 SOCIAL VALUES AND NONMATHEMATICAL ASPECTS 405

SOCIAL ASPECTS

20.1 Social values 405
20.2 Community relations 406
20.3 Employee relations 406

20.4 Educational activities 407
20.5 Effect of technical developments 408
20.6 Effect of government 408
20.7 Effect of social changes 408

STRATEGIC ASPECTS

20.8 Company policy 409
20.9 Customer relations 410
20.10 Maintaining market position 410
20.11 Raw-material position 410

ETHICAL ASPECTS

20.12 Meaning of ethics 411
20.13 Applications 413

LEGAL ASPECTS

20.14 Contracts 413
20.15 Hedge clauses 414
20.16 Cost engineer's obligation to employer 415
20.17 To bid or not to bid 416
20.18 Starter sheets 417
20.19 Patents and proprietary information 417
20.20 Dealings with administrative bodies 418
20.21 Professional registration 419
20.22 Questions 420
20.23 References on social and nonmathematical aspects 421
20.24 References on legal aspects 421

Chapter 21 REPORTING RESULTS 423

21.1 Presentation counts 423
21.2 Grand plan—scope and audience 423
21.3 The outline 424
21.4 Special considerations 425
21.5 Writing style 427
21.6 Physical form 429
21.7 Oral presentations 430
21.8 Questions 432
21.9 References 432

Appendix 1 DISCRETE COMPOUND INTEREST 435

Table 1 Discrete Compound-interest Table 436
Table 2 Value of $F_{PS} = (1 + i)^n$ for Large i 449

Table 3   Value of $F_{SP} = (1+i)^{-n}$ for Large i 450
Table 4   Discrete Compound Interest with Negative Rate
$F_{PS,-p,n} = (1-p)^n$ 451

Appendix 2   CONTINUOUS COMPOUND INTEREST   452

Table 1   Continuous Compound Interest: Value of $F_{PS,\bar{\imath},n} = e^{in}$ 453
Table 2   Continuous Compound Interest: Value of $F_{SP,\bar{\imath},n} = e^{-in}$ 456
Table 3   Continuous Compound Interest: Value of   459

$$F_{\bar{R}P,\bar{\imath},n} = \frac{1 - e^{-in}}{in}$$

Table 4   Continuous Compound Interest: Value of   463

$$F_{SDP,\bar{\imath},n} = \frac{2}{in}\left(1 - \frac{1 - e^{-in}}{in}\right)$$

Appendix 3   PROBABILITY   466

Table 1   Cumulative Probability for Z or Less for Standard Normal Distribution   467
Table 2   Random Numbers: The First 1,000 Decimal Places of π 468

Appendix 4   LEARNING CURVE   469

Table 1   Values for Exponential Learning-curve Function   470

ANSWERS TO PROBLEMS   473

NAME INDEX   479

SUBJECT INDEX   483

List of Contributors

Ali, A. M., Ph.D., Associate Professor of Industrial Engineering, Lamar State College of Technology, Beaumont, Texas. Chaps. 8, 10, and 11.

Ariet, M., Ph.D., Associate Professor of Industrial and Systems Engineering and Systems Director, Health Center Computer Science Program, University of Florida, Gainesville, Fla. Coauthor Chap. 7.

Bauman, H. C., B.E.E., Assistant Manager of Project Engineering Department, Engineering and Construction Division, American Cyanamid Company, Wayne, N.J., Chap. 181.

Behrens, H. J., Industrial Engineer, Northrup Norair, Hawthorne, Calif. Chap. 9.

Black, J. H., Ph.D., Professor of Chemical Engineering, University of Alabama, University, Ala. Chap. 16 and Coauthor, Chap. 20.

Boas, A. H., Ph.D., Manager, Computer Applications, Engineering Department, Stauffer Chemical Co., Dobbs Ferry, N.Y. Chaps. 13 and 14.

Brauweiler, J. R., M.B.A., Manager, Operations Research, National Dairy Products Corporation, Chicago, Ill. Coauthor Chap. 4.

Carlson, R. O., M.B.A., Amoco Chemical Corporation, Chicago, Ill. Coauthor Chap. 5.

Hirschmann, W. B., M.S., Industrial Economist, Research and Development, American Oil Company, Whiting, Ind. Coauthor Chap. 4.

Horstmeyer, A. L., Chairman of the Board, Horstmeyer Construction Company, San Francisco, Calif. Coauthor Chap. 20.

Jelen, F. C., Ph.D., Professor of Chemical Engineering, Lamar State College of Technology, Beaumont, Texas. Chaps. 1, 2, 3, and 6, and coauthor, Chap. 12.

Lovett, J. F., B.S., Chief Engineer, Industrial Chemicals and Construction Materials, Engineering Department, United States Steel Chemicals, Pittsburgh, Pa. Chap. 17.

Peters, M. S., Ph.D., Dean, College of Engineering, University of Colorado, Boulder, Colo.   Coauthor Chap. 12.

Schweyer, H. E., Ph.D., Professor of Chemical Engineering, University of Florida, Gainesville, Fla.   Coauthor Chap. 7.

Thorne, H. C., M.B.A., Manager, Planning and Commercial Development, Patchogue-Plymouth Company, Atlanta, Ga.   Coauthor Chap. 5.

Weinwurm, E. H., LL.D., Ph.D., Professor Emeritus of Accounting, College of Commerce, DePaul University, Chicago, Illinois; present address: Santa Monica, Calif.   Chap. 19.

Zimmerman, O. T., Ph.D., Professor and Chairman, Department of Chemical Engineering, University of New Hampshire, Durham, N.H.   Chap. 15.

part one
Mathematics of Cost Comparisons

1
Introduction

F. C. Jelen

1.1 Concern for cost and optimization

Although cost considerations and optimization are basic principles that have long been latent factors in economic and engineering decisions, they now have become dominant features for several reasons. First, modern technology is becoming exceedingly complicated, enterprises increasingly larger, competition keener and more widespread, and the time scale for decisions and action greatly reduced. The stakes never were higher. A savings of a mere cent per tire amounts to about $250,000 per year for one automobile manufacturer.

Second, there is an autocatalytic effect brought about by advancing technology releasing personnel from ordinary production tasks and freeing them for more sophisticated studies. The personnel, time, and tools available to study cost and optimization applications are continuously increasing.

Third, as technology advances and predictions are more precise, it becomes necessary to calculate more closely in order to remain competitive. Overdesign is essentially a safety factor for ignorance, but the space age emphasizes the need for exact design. If a rocket is overdesigned, it may be too heavy to achieve orbit. If too light, it may explode on the ground. Thus it is with other engineering projects. A bid based on overdesign may be too high to win the award. If based on underdesign, it may well win the award and then require large additional expenditures at an overall loss to make the project workable.

1.2 Some definitions

Modern analysis of cost and optimization falls roughly into three categories: (1) cost and optimization engineering, (2) operations research, and (3) management science. All are changing rapidly, and there is considerable overlap between the three.

Cost and optimization engineering, which includes the topics of engineering economy, is the basic category. It is engineering-oriented much more than the other two categories and is the subject of this book.

Operations research is mathematics-oriented and is concerned generally with advanced techniques for solving complicated optimization problems using mathematical models. It tends to be aimed toward the computer. As with all knowledge, concepts introduced at one level become the fundamentals of a different level. Some chapters in this book, like those on queuing and linear programming, were (and still are) part of operations research.

Management science is a relatively new category and perhaps may be regarded as a continuation of operations research. It is aimed at overall policy and decision making and attempts to inject analysis and rationale into management problems that were formerly decided by intuition and acumen. Management science is business-oriented but is attracting attention from many engineers. In a broad sense it is cost and optimization engineering at the management level.

1.3 Scope

This book brings together all the topics necessary for a study of cost and optimization engineering either as an end in itself or as prelude for operations research or management science.

The text is divided into three major parts. Part 1 is basic and covers in detail the mathematics of cost comparisons, profitability, and some allied topics. Chapter 4 on continuous interest can be omitted in a short survey, and parts of Chap. 6, particularly on inflation, can be reserved for an extensive course.

Part 2 covers optimization, and Chap. 12 is the basic chapter. Selection from the other chapters can be made on the basis of available time.

Part 3 covers costs, with all chapters of about equal importance. The inclusion of cost engineering, particularly on the same basis as the two other parts, is a feature of the book. The American Association of Cost Engineers was not founded until 1956, but cost engineering has become an established discipline and must now be included in any basic course on optimization. Most of the cost data in this book are from the process industries, which have been foremost in publicizing cost data. However, the data are used for illustrative purposes, and engineers from other fields should benefit from the chapters on costs and perhaps be inspired to publicize cost data better in their own disciplines.

Part 4 covers some associated topics to round out the presentation.

1.4 Organization by sections

The basic unit of presentation in this book is the section. All equations, figures, tables, examples, questions, problems, and references are numbered by sections. The key used is:

(2.1#1)	Sec. 2.1, Eq. 1
13.9F4	Sec. 13.9, Fig. 4
6.5T1	Sec. 6.5, Table 1
5.4E1	Sec. 5.4, Example 1
16.17Q5	Sec. 16.17, Question 5
6.15P20	Sec. 6.15, Prob. 20
[9.11R3]	Sec. 9.11, Ref. 3

Examples are always worked out in the text. Problems, questions to qualitative chapters, and references appear at the end of the chapter.

1.5 Nomenclature

Nomenclature always presents a problem, particularly in books covering a wide range of topics. The nomenclature used is characterized by being highly delineated. In engineering problems use of an orderly system of nomenclature is good discipline, and it becomes a necessity in large problems such as those for computer programming. For example, in comparing two machines A and B on a present-worth basis P, it is not good discipline to write

$$P_A \quad \text{and} \quad P_B$$

If each machine is compared on a 10-year basis it is much more informative to write

$$P_{A_{10}} \quad \text{and} \quad P_{B_{10}}$$

Indeed, this kind of notation will avoid making a false comparison with, say,

$$P_{A_8} \quad \text{and} \quad P_{B_{10}}$$

for the difference in duration is clearly evident.

Perhaps in the end nomenclature will imitate computer language, which manages with capitals and numbers alone but uses a high degree of delineation for distinction and detail. Hence, if the nomenclature and typography seem to be needlessly exact at times, it merely reflects the modern approach to engineering requirements for good characterization.

The nomenclature for a chapter is given immediately following the text of the chapter. A summary of nomenclature is given in Table 1.5T1.

Tables in the appendixes are in the conventional format for computer printout with the numbers following E representing powers of 10. Thus

$$2.8902\text{E} \quad 02 = 2.8902 \times 10^2 = 289.02$$
$$3.4603\text{E}-03 = 3.4603 \times 10^{-3} = 0.0034603$$

INTRODUCTION

Table 1.5T1   Nomenclature

a	Intermediate term for evaluation of Eq. (11.9#2)
a	Sec. 8.14, constant
A	Parameter, as in Eq. (12.16#1)
A	Sec. 8.14, one of k kinds of events in multinomial distribution
A	Total cost of all battery-limit investment in Eqs. (15.11#1) to (15.11#3), \$
A_{ij}	Coefficient in restraint equation, ith row, jth column
A_0	$A/1{,}000$ in Eqs. (15.11#2) to (15.11#4), M\$
A_{t_1}	Amount at time 1, \$
b	Constant in equation for straight line
b	Intermediate term for evaluation of Eq. (11.9#2)
B	Book value
B	Parameter, as in Eq. (12.16#1)
B	Sec. 14.10, constant in scale of relation
B	Cost of all erected equipment in Eq. (15.11#1), \$
B_i	Right side of ith restraint equation
c	Intermediate term for evaluation of Eq. (11.9#2)
C	Cost in Eqs. (15.7#1) and (15.7#2), \$
C	Incremental cost of alloys used for corrosion resistance in Eq. (15.11#1), \$
C_{bx}	Irregular cost at beginning of xth year, \$
C_d	Depreciable cost, \$
C_e	Cost for one idle service facility per period, \$/(facility)(period)
C_{ex}	Irregular cost at end of xth year, \$
C_f	Cost for servicing one unit, \$ per unit
C_F	Fixed cost, \$
C_h	Holding cost per unit per period, \$/(unit)(period)
C_i	Initial or first cost, \$
C_i	Section 13.12, unit cost associated with basic variable in ith row
C_j	Unit cost associated with X_j in linear programming
C_{nd}	Nondepreciable cost, \$
C_0	Initial level of cash flow in Eq. (5.12#1), \$/per year
C_o	Sec. 10.18, cost of placing and receiving an order, \$
$C_{o,p}$	Cost of placing and receiving an order per period, \$ per period
C_q	Cost for one unit in the queue, \$/(unit)(period)
C_r	Reneging cost per unit per period, \$/(unit)(period)
C_s	Storage cost per unit per period, \$/(unit)(period)
C_{sal}	Salvage value, \$
C_t	Total variable cost per period, \$ per period
C_t	Variable cash flow in Eq. (5.12#2), \$ per year
C_T	Total cost, \$
C_u	Purchase price per unit, \$ per unit
C_w	Cost for one unit waiting one period, \$/(unit)(period)
d	Inflation rate, decimal/year
D	Depreciation, \$
D	Sec. 10.18, delivery or replenishment rate per period, unit/period
D	Sec. 14.13, distance from end of interval in Fibonacci search
DB	Declining-balance method of depreciation
DDB	Double-declining-balance method of depreciation
D_f	Fractional depreciation, decimal
DP	Dynamic programming
e	Naperian constant 2.71828 ...
e	Total heat-exchanger cost less incremental alloy in Eqs. (15.11#2) and (15.11#3), \$

Table I.5T1   Nomenclature   (*continued*)

E	In Appendix tables denotes power of 10
E	Indirect cost factor in Eq. (15.11#1), dimensionless
E_N	Effort required to produce the Nth unit, e.g., man-hr/unit
$E(r^2)$	Average of r^2 with respect to time, where r is number of arrivals per period
E_T	Cumulative effort to produce units 1 through N, e.g., man-hr
E_T/N	Cumulative average unit effort, e.g., man-hr/unit
$E(X)$	Expected value of X
f	Total cost of field fabricated vessels in Eq. (15.11#2), \$
F	Objective function to be optimized
F	Intermediate term for evaluation of Eq. (11.9#2)
F_a	Return from project A in dynamic programming
F_{DB}	Factor for declining-balance depreciation, decimal
F_{DDB}	Factor for double-declining-balance depreciation, decimal
F_{GP}	Factor to convert G to P; uniform-gradient series present-worth factor, years
F_i	Fibonacci number
F_L	Cost factor for field labor in Eqs. (15.11#1) and (15.11#2), dimensionless
F_M	Cost factor for miscellaneous items in Eqs. (15.11#1) and (15.11#4), dimensionless
F_P	Cost factor for piping material in Eqs. (15.11#1) and (15.11#3), dimensionless
F_{PK}	Factor to convert P to K; capitalized-cost factor, dimensionless
F_{PR}	Factor to convert P to R; capital-recovery factor, year^{-1}
$F_{P\bar{R},\bar{i},n}$	Factor to convert P to $\bar{R}$ with continuous compounding, year^{-1}
F_{PS}	Factor to convert P to S; compound-interest factor, dimensionless
$F_{PS,\bar{i},n}$	Factor to convert P to S with continuous compounding, dimensionless
$F_{PS,-p,n}$	Compound-interest factor with negative compounding, dimensionless; used with technological advancement
F_r	Fractional ratio of interval left to original interval
F_{RP}	Factor to convert R to P; unacost present-worth factor, years
$F_{\bar{R}P,\bar{i},n}$	Factor to convert $\bar{R}$ to P with continuous discounting, years
F_{RS}	Factor to convert R to S; equal-payment-series future-worth factor, years
F_{SD}	Factor for sum-of-digits depreciation, decimal
F_{SDP}	Present worth of \$1 for sum-of-digits depreciation, decimal
$F_{\mathrm{SDP},\bar{i},n}$	Factor to convert a unit flow declining to zero at a constant rate over n years starting with the reference point and with continuous discounting, decimal; approximates ψ_{SD} for continuous discounting
F_{SLP}	Present worth of \$1 for straight-line depreciation, decimal
F_{SP}	Factor to convert S to P; single-payment present-worth factor, dimensionless
F_{SR}	Factor to convert S to R; sinking-fund factor, year^{-1}
F_{UP}	Factor for units-of-production depreciation, decimal
g	Constant in exponential rate-flow change, decimal
g	Constant in Eq. (5.12#1), dimensionless
G	Uniform-gradient amount, \$ per year
G	Intermediate term for evaluation of Eq. (11.9#2)
H	Number of objects in population with desired property in hypergeometric distribution
H	Intermediate term for evaluation of Eq.(11.9#2)
i	Rate of return, decimal/year
i	The ith row in linear programming
i'	Stipulated rate in Hoskold's formula, decimal/year
i''	Sinking-fund rate in Hoskold's formula, decimal/year
I	Total battery-limits investment in Eq. (15.11#1), \$
j	The jth column in linear programming
k	Empirical constant in learning-curve relationship, decimal

Table I.5T1 Nomenclature (*continued*)

k	Number of kinds of events in multinomial distribution
K	Capitalized cost, $
K	Constant
K	In Eq. (9.2#1) theoretical effort required for first unit, e.g., man-hr
K	Fraction of patient customers, Chap. 10, decimal
$K_{d>r}$	Capitalized cost with $d > r$, $
K_n	Constant for integer values of n in Eq. (5.12#2), decimal
$K_{r>d}$	Capitalized cost with $r > d$, $
L	Number of channels in service facility
L	Range of a variable
L_D	Decimal learning ratio, dimensionless
LE	Lagrange expression
LP	Linear programming
L_P	Percentage learning ratio, dimensionless
m	A number, e.g., mth year or mth term in a series
M	Number of units or objects in population
M	Sec. 3.14, units of production
M	Sec. 4.11, profit margin, $
M	Sec. 10.18, maximum number of units in stock
n	A number, usually a period of years, e.g., life of an article in years
n	Sec. 14.13, nth or last term
n'	Life for tax purposes, years
N	Number, e.g., units produced
N	Sec. 8.14, number of trials or data
N	Sec. 10.18, number of periods per cycle
N	Sec. 11.14, number of units in the queue plus service facilities at time T
N	Sec. 12.18, cycles/month in Example 12.7E1; batches/year in Example 12.14E1
N	The Nth stage in dynamic programming
N	Sec. 14.13, number of experiments or calculations allowed
N'	Number of units of production above 100% capacity
N''	Number of units of production dumped
N_e	Expected value of N
p	Technological advancement rate, decimal/year
p	Secs. 2.11 and 4.11, number of periods per year
p	Probability for success in a single trial in the binomial distribution
p	Total pump plus driver cost less incremental alloy in Eq. (15.11#3), $
P	Present worth, $
P	Power to stirrer in Example 12.14E1, kw
$P_c(X)$	Cumulative probability of X or less
$P_d(X)$	Probability density at X, probability per unit interval
$P(N)$	Probability of N units in system at time T
$P(0)$	Probability of zero units in the service system at time T
$P(X)$	Probability for event with value X
q	Intermediate term for evaluation of Eq. (11.9#2)
Q	Lot size, units
Q	Sec. 4.11, total flow, $
Q	Sec. 13.12, quality coefficient
Q	Capacity in Eqs. (15.7#1) and (15.7#2), any convenient dimensions
Q_c	Cumulative feet drilled in Example 12.7E1
r	Rate of return, generally after taxes, decimal/year
r	Conversion rate, mole D formed per mole B in Example 12.9E1

Table I.5T1 Nomenclature (continued)

R	Uniform end-of-year amount; unacost, $ per year
R	Intermediate term for evaluation of Eq. (11.9#2)
$\bar{R}$	Uniform flow; unaflow, $ per year
R'	Return on original investment in Hoskold's formula, $ per year
R''	Sinking-fund payment in Hoskold's formula, $ per year
R_b	Uniform beginning-of-year annual amount, $ per year
R_D	Unaburden; uniform end-of-year burden with inflation, $ per year
R_0	Initial flow rate, $ per year
R_p	Yearly operating expense subject to improvement by technological advancement, $ per year
R_S	Sinking-fund deposit, $ per year
R_v	Revenue, end of year, $ per year
R_x	Flow rate at time X, $ per year
s	Slope constant, decimal
S	Future worth, $
S	Sec. 7.9, net realizable sales value per unit sold, $ per unit
S	Sec. 10.18, safety stock, units
S	Sec. 11.14, number of service stations in system
S	Capacity of reactor-mixer in Examples 12.14E1, lb
SD	Sum-of-digits method of depreciation
SF	Sinking-fund method of depreciation
SL	Straight-line method of depreciation
S_T	Total realizable sales value
t	Tax rate, decimal
t	Total cost of tower shells less incremental cost of alloy, in Eq. (15.11#4), $
T	Time, generally years
T	Secs. 8.14 and 10.18, time in periods
T	Residence time in Example 12.9E1, hr
T	Total time required for batch in Example 12.14E1, hr
T_a	Time between arrivals, periods
T_d	Drilling time from start of cycle in Example 12.7E1, days
T_l	Procurement or lead time, period
T_s	Time in periods to service 1 unit, periods/unit
U	Demand or use rate, units/period
U	Sec. 14.13, factor $1/(1+i)$
UP	Units-of-production method of depreciation
v	Intermediate term for evaluation of Eq. (11.9#2)
V	Variable cost per unit of production, $ per unit
V	Volume of reactor in Example 12.9E1, cu ft
V'	Variable cost per unit of production above 100% capacity, $ per unit
W	Dependent variable
W	Sec. 8.14, number of objects withdrawn from population in hypergeometric distribution
W	Sec. 10.18, lead-time demand, or demand during lead time, units
X	Independent variable
X	Sec. 15.17, total cost-capacity factor in Eq. (15.7#1), dimensionless
X_a	Investment in project A, $
X_j	Variable input in linear programming
X_N	Decision variable associated with Nth stage
Y	Independent variable
Y	$(1 - 0.48 F_{\mathrm{SDP},r,25}) F_{PR,r,25}$ in Example 12.8E1
Y_N	Output from Nth stage

Table I.5TI Nomenclature (*continued*)

Z	Independent variable, particularly in standard normal distribution measured from mean value
Z	Sec. 10.18, factor connected with utilization of warehouse space (see Sec. 10.3)
Z	Sec. 13.12, objective function
Z_g	Gross profit before tax, $
Z_j	$\sum_{i=1}^{m} C_i A_{ij}$ in linear programming
Z_t	Net profit after tax, $
Δ_j	$Z_j - C_j$ in linear programming
θ_N	Theta of N; factor connected with probabilities in finite queuing, dimensionless
λ	Lagrange multiplier
λ	Secs. 8.14 and 11.14, average or expected arrivals per period
λ'	Specific values of λ in Eq. (11.7#6)
μ	Mean or average value
μ	Sec. 11.14, average or expected servicing rate, units per period
μ'	Optimum values of μ in Eq. (11.7#6)
σ	Standard deviation
σ^2	Variance
σ^2	Sec. 11.14, variance of a service distribution, period^2
$\sum_{1}^{N} E_N$	Same as E_T
$\sum_{1}^{N} E_N/N$	Same as E_T/N
χ	Load factor or ratio of arrival rate to potential service rate, λ/μ, dimensionless
ψ	Psi; general symbol for present worth of $1 of depreciation, decimal
ψ_{SD}	ψ factor for sum-of-digits depreciation
ψ_{SL}	ψ factor for straight-line depreciation

2
Equivalence and Cost Comparisons

F. C. Jelen

TIME VALUE OF MONEY AND EQUIVALENCE

2.1 Compound interest as an operator

Investments are spread over a period of time, and time has a monetary value. An investor expects his investment, with due allowance for dividends, to increase with time in the form of appreciation. The appreciation of one year becomes an investment of the next and in turn should earn appreciation of its own. The increase in investment should be compounded with time, much like the increase of a deposit in a bank, but the time value of money in a practical problem applies without an actual banking transaction.

Suppose a present amount, or *present worth*, P earns at the rate i per year expressed as a decimal. Also let S be the value or *future worth* at some later time. Then at the end of 1 year

$$S_1 = P + iP = P(1 + i)$$

$P(1 + i)$ becomes the starting value at the beginning of the second year, and at the end of the second year

$$S_2 = P(1 + i) + iP(1 + i) = [P(1 + i)](1 + i) = P(1 + i)^2$$

12 MATHEMATICS OF COST COMPARISONS

Repeating for another year gives

$$S_3 = P(1+i)^2 + iP(1+i)^2 = [P(1+i)^2](1+i) = P(1+i)^3$$

The form of the relationship is obvious and for n years is

$$S = P(1+i)^n \qquad (2.1\#1)$$

or
$$S = PF_{PS} \qquad (2.1\#2)$$

Future worth = (present worth)(compound-interest factor)

The relationships above are the *compound-interest law*. Factors in this book are designated by the letter F with suitable subscript. The symbol F_{PS} is read "factor for converting P to S." It is more completely designated as $F_{PS,i,n}$, where i is the rate of return and n is years. Thus

$$F_{PS,i,n} = (1+i)^n \qquad (2.1\#3)$$

$(1+i)^n$ or F_{PS} is the *compound-interest factor*, values for which are given in Appendix 1, Tables 1 and 2. It should be noted that P is a single payment and that compounding is carried out periodically in steps.

In engineering economy, a year is usually taken as a unit period of time. Equations (2.1#1) and (2.1#2) are used with n in years and i the yearly rate of return expressed as a decimal, although i is usually stated as a percentage. If compounding occurs p times per year, the relationship is

$$S = P\left(1 + \frac{i}{p}\right)^{np} \qquad (2.1\#4)$$

where np is the number of periods and i/p is the rate of return per period, inasmuch as i always refers to the rate of return per year. The last equation can be written

$$S = P\left[\left(1 + \frac{i}{p}\right)^p\right]^n$$

where the expression in brackets is the value of 1 at the end of 1 year. The *increase* in value for 1 year is

$$\left(1 + \frac{i}{p}\right)^p - 1 = \text{effective rate of return} \qquad (2.1\#5)$$

The *effective rate of return* can be used as if the compounding were done once a year instead of p times per year. For distinction i is referred to as the *nominal rate of return*.

The compound-interest law is used in engineering economy if the time is over 1 year. If the time is less than 1 year, *simple interest* can be used, with interest charged only on the original amount

$$S = P(1 + ni) \qquad (2.1\#6)$$

where n may be a fractional part of a year.

Example 2.1E1 How long will it take for money to double if compounded annually at 6% per year?

By Eq. (2.1#2)

$$S = PF_{PS,6\%,n}$$

and for $S = 2P$

$$2P = PF_{PS,6\%,n} \quad \text{or} \quad F_{PS} = 2$$

From Appendix 1, Table 1,

$$F_{PS,6\%,11} = 1.8983$$
$$F_{PS,6\%,12} = 2.0122$$

By interpolation

$$F_{PS,6\%,11.9} = 2.0000$$

That is, money will double in about 11.9 years at 6% per year.

Example 2.1E2 If $10,000 compounds to $14,120 in 4 years, what is the rate of return?

By Eq. (2.1#1)

$$14{,}120 = S = P(1+i)^n = 10{,}000(1+i)^4$$
$$(1+i)^4 = 1.412$$

Taking logarithms,

$$4\log(1+i) = 0.1498$$
$$\log(1+i) = 0.0374$$
$$1+i = 1.090$$
$$i = 0.09, \text{ or } 9\% \text{ per year}$$

Equation (2.1#1), the compound-interest law, can be written as an expression for P, present worth, in terms of S, future worth, and becomes

$$P = \frac{S}{(1+i)^n} \tag{2.1#7}$$

or
$$P = S(1+i)^{-n} \tag{2.1#8}$$

or
$$P = SF_{SP} \tag{2.1#9}$$

Present worth = (future worth)(present-worth factor)

The factor $(1+i)^{-n}$, or F_{SP}, which converts S to P is the single-payment present-worth factor. It will be referred to as the *present-worth factor* and is tabulated in Appendix 1, Tables 1 and 3. The complete designation of F_{SP} is

$$F_{SP,i,n} = (1+i)^{-n} \tag{2.1#10}$$

It will be noted that F_{SP} and F_{PS} are reciprocal relationships, i.e.,

$$F_{SP} = \frac{1}{F_{PS}} \tag{2.1#11}$$

Equations (2.1#8) and (2.1#9) show that a future amount is reduced when converted to a present amount. The procedure of reducing a future amount to

14 MATHEMATICS OF COST COMPARISONS 2.1

a present amount is known as *discounting*. Discounting is merely an application of the principle that because of the time value of money the future is not worth as much as the present when viewed from the present.

Equations (2.1#1) and (2.1#8) can be written as:

Moving with the calendar: $S = P(1 + i)^n$

Moving against the calendar: $P = S(1 + i)^{-n}$

and can be combined in a single relationship

$$A_{t_2} = A_{t_1}(1 + i)^n \qquad (2.1\#12)$$

Amount time 2 = (amount time 1)(compound-interest operator)

where n positive = with the calendar
n negative = against the calendar

The student should become familiar with Eq. (2.1#12), the *time-value conversion relationship*. The compound-interest factor $(1 + i)^n$ can be regarded as a mathematical operator which moves a unit value n years, with or against the calendar depending on the sign of n.

In engineering economy, receipts and disbursements occur at different instants of time. They can be combined only after conversion to a single common instant. The time-value conversion relationship defines the mathematical operator that makes this possible. It is convenient in solving problems to diagram expenditures and receipts as vertical lines positioned along a horizontal line representing time. Expenditures and receipts can point in opposite directions. The problem can be visualized in this manner and each amount moved by a routine technique to some common instant for consolidation.

Example 2.1E3 A boy is celebrating his sixteenth birthday and will need $3,000 on each of his seventeenth, eighteenth, nineteenth, and twentieth birthdays for his college education. His father agrees to lay aside a certain amount now and each year thereafter until the boy is twenty years old; moreover the contributions will form an arithmetical progression for all years, increasing by 20% after the first year. If money is worth 4% per year, what is the father's first contribution?

If x is the first contribution, succeeding contributions are $1.2x$, $1.4x$, etc. The diagram is:

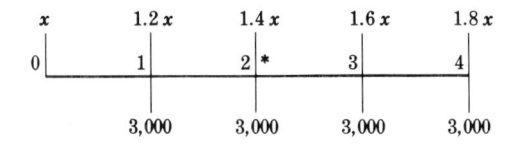

```
      x      1.2x    1.4x    1.6x    1.8x
      |       |       |       |       |
      0       1       2  *    3       4
                      |       |       |
                    3,000   3,000   3,000   3,000
```

Take 2 years from now as the reference instant. Use the time-value conversion relationship, Eq. (2.1#12), noting that contributions must equal withdrawals:

$x(1.04^2) + 1.2x(1.04^1) + 1.4x(1.04^0) + 1.6x(1.04^{-1}) + 1.8x(1.04^{-2})$

$\qquad = 3,000(1.04^1) + 3,0000(1.04^0) + 3,000(1.04^{-1}) + 3,000(1.04^{-2})$

Use Appendix 1, Table 1, to obtain $1.04^n = F_{PS,4\%,n}$ and $1.04^{-n} = F_{SP,4\%,n}$. Numerical substitution in the previous relationship leads to

$6.9323x = 11,778$

$x = \$1,700$ first contribution

2.2 Uniform annual amount, unacost

Consider a uniform end-of-year annual amount R for a period of n years. The diagram is:

```
        R    R    R              R        R
0    1|   2|   3|      ...   (n-1)|     n|
```

where R will be referred to as *unacost*. The terms can be replaced by a single present worth P by moving all terms to zero time using time-value conversion relationship Eq. (2.1#12)

$$P = R\left[\frac{1}{1+i} + \frac{1}{(1+i)^2} + \cdots + \frac{1}{(1+i)^n}\right] \qquad (2.2\#1)$$

The terms in the brackets can be condensed by the Σ (sigma) notation to

$$\sum_{1}^{n} \frac{1}{(1+i)^n}$$

and represent a geometrical series of n terms with first term $1/(1+i)$ and ratio $1/(1+i)$. For a geometric series

$$\text{Sum of geometric series} = \frac{1 - \text{ratio}^{\text{no. of terms}}}{1 - \text{ratio}} \text{ first term} \qquad (2.2\#2)$$

The previous summation becomes

$$\sum_{1}^{n} \frac{1}{(1+i)^n} = \frac{1 - \left(\frac{1}{1+i}\right)^n}{1 - \frac{1}{1+i}} \frac{1}{1+i} = \frac{(1+i)^n - 1}{i(1+i)^n} \qquad (2.2\#3)$$

so that Eq. (2.2#1) is

$$P = R\frac{(1+i)^n - 1}{i(1+i)^n} \qquad (2.2\#4)$$

or $\qquad P = RF_{RP} \qquad (2.2\#5)$

Present worth = (unacost)(unacost present-worth factor)

F_{RP} must be called by its full name, *unacost present-worth factor*, to avoid confusion with F_{SP}, which is called simply the present-worth factor. F_{RP}, which

16   MATHEMATICS OF COST COMPARISONS

converts R to P, has for its complete designation

$$F_{RP,i,n} = \frac{(1+i)^n - 1}{i(1+i)^n} \qquad (2.2\#6)$$

and is tabulated in Appendix 1, Table 1. It is also known as the equal-payment-series present-worth factor and as the annuity present-value factor.

Example 2.2E1   Find the equivalent value of the following series of receipts as of the end of the third year if money is worth 6% per year:

```
      100  100  100  100  100  100   50  100  100  100
 0     1    2    3    4    5    6    7    8    9   10
```

The series has an irregularity at the end of 7 years but with 50 added and subtracted at that time becomes:

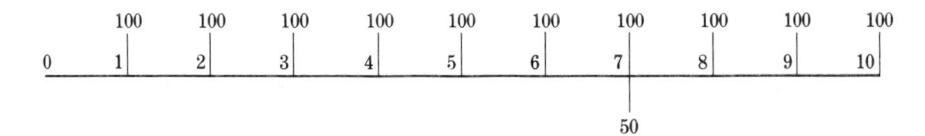

```
      100  100  100  100  100  100  100  100  100  100
 0     1    2    3    4    5    6    7    8    9   10
                                      |
                                     50
```

The present worth of all the ascending lines is given by Eq. (2.2#5), and Eq. (2.1#9) gives the present worth of the single descending line

$P = 100 F_{RP,6\%,10} - 50 F_{SP,6\%,7}$

$P = 100(7.3601) - 50(0.66506) = 7{,}027$ zero time

Move 3 years with the calendar

$7{,}027 F_{PS,6\%,3} = 7{,}027(1.1910) = \$8{,}369$ end of third year

Equation (2.2#4) written as an expression for R in terms of P becomes

$$R = P \frac{i(1+i)^n}{(1+i)^n - 1} \qquad (2.2\#7)$$

$$R = P F_{PR} \qquad (2.2\#8)$$

Unacost = (present worth)(capital-recovery factor)

These relationships are very important in engineering economy. The *capital-recovery factor* converts a single zero-time cost to an equivalent uniform end-of-year annual cost, unacost. The unacost repays the initial expenditure with interest, hence the name capital-recovery factor. The factor has the complete designation

$$F_{PR,i,n} = \frac{i(1+i)^n}{(1+i)^n - 1} \qquad (2.2\#9)$$

and is tabulated in Appendix 1, Table 1. F_{PR} and F_{RP} are reciprocal relationships

$$F_{PR} = \frac{1}{F_{RP}} \qquad (2.2\#10)$$

2.2 EQUIVALENCE AND COST COMPARISONS 17

Relationships between R and P have been established by Eqs. (2.2#4) and (2.2#5). Relationships between R and S, the future amount, are easily established. Noting that $P = S(1 + i)^{-n}$ from Eq. (2.1#8) and placing this expression for P in Eq. (2.2#4) gives

$$S = R\frac{(1 + i)^n - 1}{i} \qquad (2.2\#11)$$

or $\quad S = RF_{RS} \qquad (2.2\#12)$

Future amount = (unacost)(equal-payment-series future-worth factor)

The factor

$$F_{RS,i,n} = \frac{(1 + i)^n - 1}{i} \qquad (2.2\#13)$$

called the *equal-payment-series future-worth factor* is not tabulated in the Appendix but can be obtained from the corresponding F_{RP} factor

$$F_{RS} = F_{RP}(1 + i)^n = F_{RP}F_{PS} \qquad (2.2\#14)$$

Also Eq. (2.2#11) can be written as

$$R = S\frac{i}{(1 + i)^n - 1} \qquad (2.2\#15)$$

$$R = SF_{SR} \qquad (2.2\#16)$$

Unacost = (future amount)(sinking-fund factor)

The factor

$$F_{SR,i,n} = \frac{i}{(1 + i)^n - 1} \qquad (2.2\#17)$$

called the *sinking-fund factor*, is not tabulated in the Appendix but can be obtained from the corresponding F_{PR} factor

$$F_{SR} = (1 + i)^n F_{PR} = F_{SP}F_{PR}$$

F_{SR} and F_{PS} are reciprocal relationships

$$F_{SR} = \frac{1}{F_{RS}}$$

Instead of unacost, which is a uniform end-of-year annual amount, one might consider R_b, a uniform beginning-of-year annual amount. R and R_b are connected by the relationship

$$R = R_b(1 + i) \qquad (2.2\#18)$$

and substitution of this relationship for R in Eqs. (2.2#4), (2.2#7), (2.2#11), and (2.2#15) gives various relationships between R_b and P and between R_b and S.

18 MATHEMATICS OF COST COMPARISONS

Table 2.2T1 Summary of S, P, R, and R_b Relationships

Item	Conversion	Algebraic relationship	Relationship by factor	Name of factor
1	P to S	$S = P[(1+i)^n]$	$S = PF_{PS,i,n}$	Compound-interest factor
2	S to P	$P = S[(1+i)^{-n}]$	$P = SF_{SP,i,n}$	Present-worth factor
3	R to P	$P = R \dfrac{(1+i)^n - 1}{i(1+i)^n}$	$P = RF_{RP,i,n}$	Unacost present-worth factor
4	P to R	$R = P \dfrac{i(1+i)^n}{(1+i)^n - 1}$	$R = PF_{PR,i,n}$	Capital-recovery factor
5	R to S	$S = R \dfrac{(1+i)^n - 1}{i}$	$S = RF_{RS,i,n}$ $S = RF_{RP,i,n}F_{PS,i,n}$	Equal-payment-series future-worth factor
6	S to R	$R = S \dfrac{i}{(1+i)^n - 1}$	$R = SF_{SR,i,n}$ $R = SF_{SP,i,n}F_{PR,i,n}$	Sinking-fund factor
7	R_b to P	$P = R_b(1+i)\dfrac{(1+i)^n - 1}{i(1+i)^n}$	$P = R_b(1+i)F_{RP,i,n}$	
8	P to R_b	$R_b = \dfrac{P}{1+i}\dfrac{i(1+i)^n}{(1+i)^n - 1}$	$R_b = \dfrac{P}{1+i}F_{PR,i,n}$	
9	R_b to S	$S = R_b(1+i)\dfrac{(1+i)^n - 1}{i}$	$S = R_b(1+i)F_{RS,i,n}$ $S = R_b(1+i)F_{RP,i,n}F_{PS,i,n}$	
10	S to R_b	$R_b = \dfrac{S}{1+i}\dfrac{i}{(1+i)^n - 1}$	$R_b = S\dfrac{1}{1+i}F_{SB,i,n}$ $R_b = S\dfrac{1}{1+i}F_{SP,i,n}F_{PB,i,n}$	

So far four amounts have been introduced:

P = present worth, a single amount at zero time
S = future worth, a single amount at the end of n years
R = unacost, a uniform end-of-year annual amount for n years
R_b = a uniform beginning-of-year annual amount for n years

The various relationships between these amounts are summarized in Table 2.2T1. The student should become familiar with the first four items of the table and understand fully the meaning of equivalence. The other relationships in the table are less important.

There are numerous applications of the relationships of Table 2.2T1 in the mathematics of finance. An *ordinary annuity* is a series of equal end-of-year annual payments R for n years. An *annuity due* is similar, but the payments are at the beginning of the year R_b. Amortization implies the substitution of a number of equal end-of-year annual payments R for a present obligation P. A *sinking-fund payment* is a uniform end-of-year annual payment which will amount to an amount S at the end of n years. Bonds present some interesting applications, as illustrated in the next example. Interest is usually compounded more than one period per year in the mathematics of finance.

Example 2.2E2 A $1,000 face value bond bearing 4% per year interest, coupon rate, payable semiannually, and due in 6 years is to be bought so as to yield the purchaser 8% per year, yield rate. What price should be paid for the bond?

There are 12 semiannual periods involved with a 2% per period coupon rate. The 12 coupons are worth $20 each when due. Also the purchaser receives the $1,000 face value 12 periods hence. The diagram is:

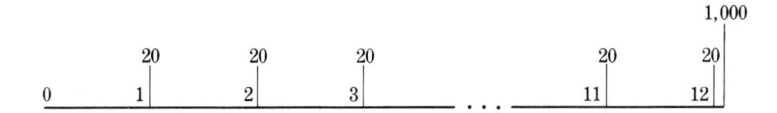

```
                                                    1,000
           20      20      20              20      20
  0        1       2       3      . . .    11      12
```

The purchaser should pay the present value of these amounts at 8% per year, or 4% per period. By Eqs. (2.2#5) and (2.1#9)

$P = 20 F_{RP,4\%,12} + 1{,}000 F_{SP,4\%,12}$

$= 20(9.3851) + 1{,}000(0.62460) = \$812.30$ purchase price

The bond sells at a discount because the coupon rate is less than the yield rate. If the coupon rate is greater than the yield rate, the bond will sell at a premium.

2.3 Double interest rates—Hoskold's formula

It is possible to consider two different rates of return in the same problem. One example of this type arises in connection with a natural resource that is exhausted after a time. The purchaser can set up a sinking fund, which bears interest at a low rate, to which he makes uniform end-of-year annual payments. At the end of

20 MATHEMATICS OF COST COMPARISONS

n years when the resource is exhausted, the sinking fund restores the purchase price. The yearly income after the sinking-fund payment can then be regarded as a return on an original investment which remains at its purchase price, inasmuch as the sinking fund will restore the investment.

Let P be the initial investment and R'' the payment to the sinking fund with rate of return i''. The sinking fund must amount to P at the end of n years. The sinking-fund payment is obtained from Eq. (2.2#15) with P substituted for S

$$R'' = P \frac{i''}{(1 + i'')^n - 1}$$

The remainder of the yearly income can be regarded as return on the original investment at some rate i', considering the original investment constant at P. This is

$$R' = Pi'$$

The total yearly income is the sum of the two

$$R = R'' + R' = P \frac{i''}{(1 + i'')^n - 1} + Pi' \qquad (2.3\#1)$$

which can be written

$$P = R \frac{(1 + i'')^n - 1}{i'[(1 + i'')^n - 1] + i''} \qquad (2.3\#2)$$

Equations (2.3#1) and (2.3#2) are equivalent and are known as *Hoskold's formula*. Here i' is the stipulated rate and i'' the sinking-fund rate. The sinking-fund rate is generally substantially less than the stipulated rate. If $i'' = i' = i$, then

$$P = R \frac{(i + i)^n - 1}{i(1 + i)^n}$$

which is Eq. (2.2#4). For the usual case with $i' > i''$ the rate of return as given by Eq. (2.2#4) will be greater than the stipulated rate. In Hoskold's formula the stipulated rate is on a constant investment, whereas the use of Eq. (2.2#4) uses only one rate of return and takes into consideration that the investment is changing with time.

Example 2.3E1 An investment of $1 million in mineral rights will produce a net of $191,700 at the end of each year for 10 years, after which the mineral rights are depleted. If the sinking-fund rate is 4% per year, find the stipulated rate using Hoskold's formula. Also find the rate of return using a single-rate-of-return model.

From Table 2.2T1, item 6,

$$\frac{i''}{(1 + i'') - 1} = F_{SR} = F_{SP}F_{PR}$$

Hoskold's formula expressed by Eq. (2.3#1) becomes

$$R = PF_{SP,4\%,10}F_{PR,4\%,10} + Pi'$$
$$191{,}700 = 1{,}000{,}000(0.67556)(0.12329) + 1{,}000{,}000i'$$
$$i = 0.108$$

or 10.8% per year, stipulated rate. The rate of return by Eq. (2.2#4) is

$$1{,}000{,}000 = 191{,}700 F_{RP,i,10}$$
$$F_{RP,i,10} = 5.216$$

Scanning Appendix 1, Table 1, shows

$$F_{RP,14\%,10} = 5.216$$
$$i = 14\% \text{ per year}$$

by single-rate-of-return model.

COST COMPARISONS

2.4 Comparisons with equal duration

The preceding sections contain all the tools required to make a cost comparison between two machines or alternate investments having equal service lives or durations. The word machine is used in a general sense. Two machines generally have cost patterns differing on a time basis, but the costs can be reduced to some common instant and the comparison made on that basis. Any instant can be chosen for the comparison, but the present instant is usually preferred. Hence the comparison is made on the basis of present worths for equal durations, which constitutes a fair comparison. The difference between the machines can have any degree of complexity, but the following example will suffice to illustrate the method.

In this and subsequent sections a uniform expense may be referred to as a uniform end-of-year cost. Actually the expense may be spread over the year and is merely expressed as an equivalent end-of-year cost. With this understanding, the expense will exist for the year even if the machine is abandoned at the end of the year.

Example 2.4E1 Two machines, each with service life of 5 years, have the following cost comparison. If money is worth 10% per year, which machine is more economical?

	A	B
First cost, $	25,000	15,000
Uniform end-of-year maintenance, $ per year	2,000	4,000
Overhaul, end of third year, $		3,500
Salvage value, $	3,000	
Benefit from quality control as a uniform end-of-year amount, $ per year		500

Construct the cost diagrams for each machine using descending lines for costs and ascending lines for receipts or benefits:

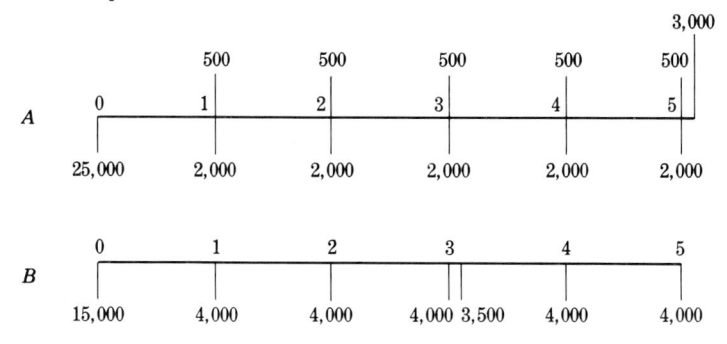

```
                              500    500    500    500    500  3,000
           0     1      2      3      4      5
    A      |─────|──────|──────|──────|──────|
        25,000  2,000  2,000  2,000  2,000  2,000

           0     1      2      3      4      5
    B      |─────|──────|──────|──────|──────|
        15,000  4,000  4,000  4,000 3,500 4,000  4,000
```

The present worth of the costs for the diagrams on a 5-year basis

$$P_{A_5} = 25{,}000 + (2{,}000 - 500)F_{RP,10\%,5} - 3{,}000F_{SP,10\%,5}$$
$$= 25{,}000 + 1{,}500(3.7908) - 3{,}000(0.62092)$$
$$= \$28{,}823$$
$$P_{B_5} = 15{,}000 + 4{,}000F_{RP,10\%,5} + 3{,}500F_{SP,10\%,3}$$
$$= 15{,}000 + 4{,}000(3.7908) + 3{,}500(0.75131)$$
$$= \$32{,}793$$

Machine A is more economical. The cost of machine A at $28,823 must be qualified by the information that the cost is the present worth for 5 years ahead with money worth 10% per year.

2.5 Comparison with unequal durations—common denominator of service lives

If two machines have different service lives, a fair comparison can be made only on the basis of equal durations. It would not be equitable to compare the present worth of the cost of 2 years of service for machine A with the present worth of the cost of 3 years of service for machine B. One method of making the comparison is to compare them on the basis of a common denominator of their service lives, here 6 years. The procedure is merely a mathematical convenience without implying that either machine will be repeated.

Example 2.5E1

First solution. Two machines have the following cost comparison. If money is worth 10% per year, which machine is more economical?

	A	B
First cost, $	18,000	25,000
Uniform end-of-year maintenance cost, $ per year	4,000	3,000
Salvage value, $	500	1,500
Service life, years	2	3

2.5   EQUIVALENCE AND COST COMPARISONS

Take 6 years as a common denominator of the service lives. The cost diagrams are:

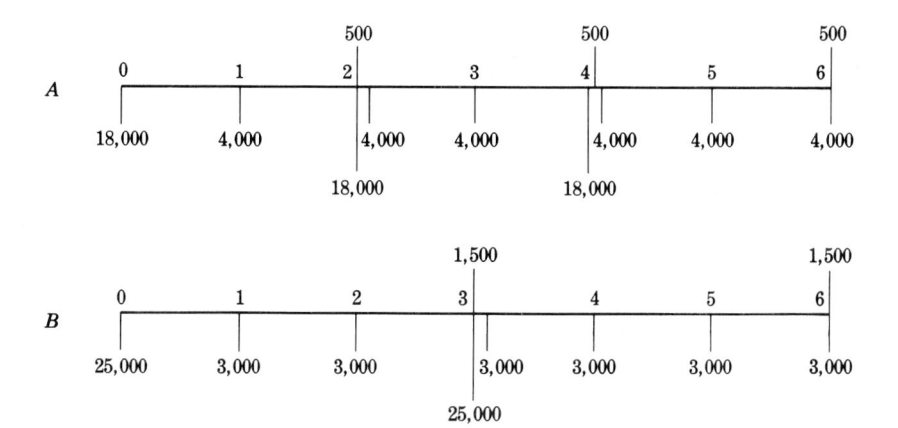

A:
```
    0       1      2|500   3      4|500   5      6|500
    |       |       |      |       |      |       |
 18,000   4,000   4,000  4,000   4,000  4,000   4,000
                 18,000          18,000
```

B:
```
    0       1      2      3|1,500  4      5      6|1,500
    |       |      |       |       |      |       |
 25,000   3,000  3,000   3,000   3,000  3,000   3,000
                         25,000
```

The example is now analogous to Example 2.4E1. Denoting by P_{A_6} and P_{B_6} the present worth of the costs for 6 years, the cost diagrams condense to

$$P_{A_6} = \$61{,}555$$
$$P_{B_6} = \$54{,}875$$

Machine B is the more economical. Ratio of costs is

$$\frac{A}{B} = \frac{61{,}555}{54{,}875} = 1.1217$$

This procedure is correct but can become very tedious if the lowest common denominator of the service lives forces a large number of replacements to be considered; e.g., the comparison of 8- and 13-year lives. The procedure, however, can be simplified by finding first the present worth of the costs of each machine for its actual service life and then repeating the present worths so obtained to fill out the common denominator of the service lives.

Second solution. The cost diagrams of each machine are first reduced to a single present worth of the costs:

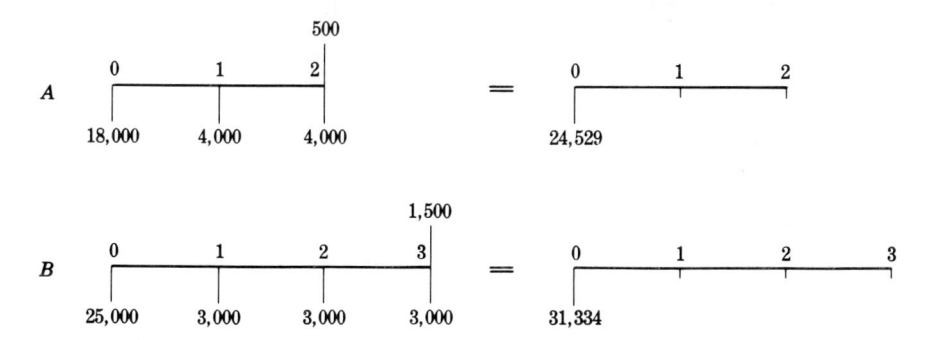

A:
```
   0     1     2|500              0     1     2
   |     |     |          =       |     |     |
 18,000 4,000 4,000              24,529
```

B:
```
   0     1     2     3|1,500         0    1    2    3
   |     |     |     |          =    |    |    |    |
 25,000 3,000 3,000 3,000           31,334
```

24 MATHEMATICS OF COST COMPARISONS

The simplified diagrams are now repeated to obtain 6 years duration. Note that the present worth of machine A is 24,529 as of its *time of installation*.

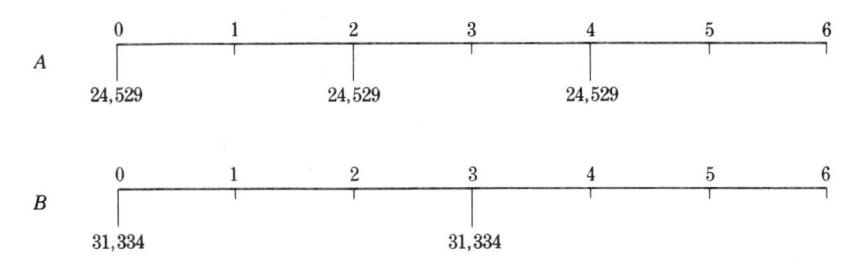

A: timeline 0 to 6, with 24,529 at years 0, 2, 4

B: timeline 0 to 6, with 31,334 at years 0, 3

The present worth of each of the above diagrams at 10% per year is

$P_{A_6} = \$61{,}555$

$P_{B_6} = \$54{,}875$

which checks the first solution and shows that the simplification is valid.

The solution just given can be simplified even further by developing a procedure that will permit converting a present worth of n_1 years to an equivalent present worth of n_2 years.

Suppose machine A with life n_1 years has present worth P_{n_1} and machine B with life n_2 years has present worth P_{n_2}. Let the machines be equal economically, with n_1 and n_2 different. A comparison made on the basis of $n_1 n_2$ years will give equal overall present worths.

Timeline left: P_{n_1} at 0, n_1, $(n_2-1)n_1$, $n_1 n_2$ = Timeline right: P_{n_2} at 0, n_2, $(n_1-1)n_2$, $n_1 n_2$

The overall present worth of the system on the left is

$$P_{n_1 n_2} = P_{n_1}\left[1 + \frac{1}{(1+i)^{n_1}} + \frac{1}{(1+i)^{2n_1}} + \cdots + \frac{1}{(1+i)^{(n_2-1)n_1}}\right]$$

The terms within the brackets are a geometrical series of n_2 terms with first term 1 and ratio $1/(1+i)^{n_1}$. Using Eq. (2.2#2), the sum of the series is

$$\frac{1 - \left[\frac{1}{(1+i)^{n_1}}\right]^{n_2}}{1 - \frac{1}{(1+i)^{n_1}}} = \frac{\frac{(1+i)^{n_1 n_2}-1}{(1+i)^{n_1 n_2}}}{\frac{(1+i)^{n_1}-1}{(1+i)^{n_1}}}$$

$$= \frac{iF_{RP,i,n_1 n_2}}{iF_{RP,i,n_1}} = \frac{F_{PR,i,n_1}}{F_{PR,i,n_1 n_2}}$$

the last step made possible by the reciprocal relationship between F_{RP} and F_{PR}

given by Eq. (2.2#10). Hence the previous relationship for $P_{n_1 n_2}$ is

$$P_{n_1 n_2} = P_{n_1} \frac{F_{PR,i,n_1}}{F_{PR,i,n_1 n_2}} \qquad (2.5\#1)$$

The overall present worth of the system on the right of the cost diagram is

$$P_{n_1 n_2} = P_{n_2} \left[1 + \frac{1}{(1+i)^{n_2}} + \frac{1}{(1+i)^{2n_2}} + \cdots + \frac{1}{(1+i)^{(n_1-1)n_2}} \right]$$

The terms within the brackets are a geometrical series of n_1 terms with first term 1 and ratio $1/(1+i)^{n_2}$. Proceeding as for the previous case, the result is

$$P_{n_1 n_2} = P_{n_2} \frac{F_{PR,i,n_2}}{F_{PR,i,n_1 n_2}} \qquad (2.5\#2)$$

a result that can be obtained also by interchanging n_1 and n_2 in Eq. (2.5 #1).
    Putting $P_{n_1 n_2}$ from Eqs. (2.5 #1) and (2.5 #2) equal gives

$$P_{n_2} = P_{n_1} \frac{F_{PR,i,n_1}}{F_{PR,i,n_2}} \qquad (2.5\#3)$$

Present-worth basis n_2 years duration = (present-worth basis n_1 years duration)

$$\times \frac{F_{PR} \text{ factor for } n_1}{F_{PR} \text{ factor for } n_2}$$

where F_{PR} is the capital-recovery factor.
    Equation (2.5#3) is an important relationship because it permits the conversion of a present worth for any duration to the equivalent present worth for any other duration.

Third solution. The example can be solved by the use of Eq. (2.5#3). From the second solution

P_A 2-year duration = \$24,529
P_B 3-year duration = \$31,334

Convert the present worth of machine B to an equivalent present worth for 2 years duration using Eq. (2.5#3)

$$P_{B_2} = P_{B_3} \frac{F_{PR,10\%,3}}{F_{PR,10\%,2}} = 31,334 \frac{0.40211}{0.57619} = \$21,867$$

Machine B is the more economical. Ratio of costs is

$$\frac{A}{B} = \frac{24,529}{21,867} = 1.1217$$

2.6 Cost comparison by unacost

The development of relationship (2.5#3) simplifies the comparison of machines or systems having different service lives. The question arises whether there are preferred durations for making the comparison or whether the duration for the

26   MATHEMATICS OF COST COMPARISONS   2.6

comparison should be left to the choice of the analyst to suit the problem. It should be clearly understood that the duration chosen for the comparison does not influence the comparison between the machines. Two machines that are economically equal will remain economically equal regardless of the duration chosen for the comparison. In practice there are two preferred durations for making the comparison. One preference, the 1-year duration as the standard for comparison, is discussed in this section. The other preference, an infinite duration as the standard for comparison, is discussed in the following section. The two methods are equivalent.

Refer to Eq. (2.5#3) and let $n_2 = 1$, thus choosing 1 year for the standard duration, and let $n_1 = n$, the life of an arbitrary machine. Equation (2.5#3) becomes

$$P_1 = P_n \frac{F_{PR,i,n}}{F_{PR,i,1}} \tag{2.6#1}$$

By Eq. (2.2#9)

$$F_{PR,i,1} = \frac{i(1+i)}{(1+i)-1} = 1+i$$

so that Eq. (2.6#1) becomes

$$P_1 = \frac{P_n}{1+i} F_{PR,i,n} \tag{2.6#2}$$

This relationship is correct as it stands and gives the equivalent cost as a present worth for a 1-year duration. The method used in practice, however, employs a 1-year duration but considers the end of the year as a vantage point, rather than the beginning of the year. Write Eq. (2.6#2) as

$$P_1(1+i) = P_n F_{PR,i,n} \tag{2.6#3}$$

but from Eq. (2.2#7)

$$R = P_1 \frac{i(1+i)}{(1+i)-1} = P_1(1+i)$$

and placing this value of $P_1(1+i)$ in Eq. (2.6#3) gives

$$R = P_n F_{PR,i,n} \tag{2.6#4}$$

Unacost = (present-worth basis n years duration)(capital-recovery factor)

This relationship is actually the definition of the F_{PR} factor given earlier by Eq. (2.2#8). The development through Eq. (2.5#3) is much more general, adds insight and perspective to the problem, permits the choice of other durations such as infinity, and will emphasize that all relationships equivalent to Eq. (2.5#3) must be equivalent to each other.

The use of an equivalent R, a uniform end-of-year annual amount, previously referred to as unacost, is a satisfactory means of comparing machines having different service lives. Fundamentally, the method converts the cost of each machine to the cost of an equivalent machine of 1 year life and paid for as of the end of the year.

Most authors refer to the method simply as the annual-cost method. The term annual cost is, however, a general term and does not necessarily imply uniformity or the end of the year to all readers. The term unacost as used in this book definitely implies uniformity from year to year and the end of the year as part of the definition. Use of the term unacost avoids the circumlocutory expression *uniform end-of-year annual amount*.

Example 2.6E1 Solve Example 2.5E1 on the basis of unacost.

From the second solution

$P_{A_2} = \$24{,}529$

$P_{B_3} = \$31{,}334$

By Eq. (2.6#4)

$R = P_n F_{PR,i,n}$

$R_A = 24{,}529 F_{PR,10\%,2} = 24{,}529(0.57619) = \$14{,}133$

$R_B = 31{,}334 F_{PR,10\%,3} = 31{,}334(0.40211) = \$12{,}600$

Machine B is the more economical. The ratio of costs is

$$\frac{A}{B} = \frac{14{,}133}{12{,}600} = 1.1217$$

2.7 Cost comparison by capitalized cost

Refer to Eq. (2.5#3) and let n_2 equal infinity, now chosen for the standard duration, and let $n_1 = n$, the life of an arbitrary machine. Equation (2.5#3) becomes

$$P_\infty = P_n \frac{F_{PR,i,n}}{F_{PR,i,\infty}} \qquad (2.7\#1)$$

By Eq. (2.2#9)

$$F_{PR,i,n} = \frac{i(1+i)^n}{(1+i)^n - 1}$$

$$F_{PR,i,\infty} = \frac{i(1+i)^\infty}{(1+i)^\infty - 1} = i$$

and substitution in Eq. (2.7#1) gives

$$P_\infty = P_n \frac{[i(1+i)^n]/[(1+i)^n - 1]}{i}$$

Letting $P_\infty = K$, capitalized cost,

$$K = P_n \frac{(1+i)^n}{(1+i)^n - 1} \qquad (2.7\#2)$$

28 MATHEMATICS OF COST COMPARISONS

$$K = P_n F_{PK} \qquad (2.7\#3)$$

Capitalized cost = (present-worth basis n years duration)(capitalized-cost factor)

F_{PK}, which converts P to K, has the complete designation

$$F_{PK,i,n} = \frac{(1+i)^n}{(1+i)^n - 1} \qquad (2.7\#4)$$

and is tabulated in Appendix 1, Table 1.

The capital-recovery factor F_{PR} and the capitalized-cost factor are related very simply. By Eq. (2.2#9)

$$F_{PR,i,n} = \frac{i(1+i)^n}{(1+i)^n - 1}$$

Comparing this with Eq. (2.7#4) shows that

$$F_{PR,i,n} = iF_{PK,i,n} \qquad (2.7\#5)$$

Capital-recovery factor = (rate of return)(capitalized-cost factor)

Also, R and K are similarly related

$$R = iK \qquad (2.7\#6)$$

Unacost = (rate of return)(capitalized cost)

Further, Eq. (2.5#3), which converts a present worth of one duration to an equivalent present worth of another duration by means of the capital-recovery factor F_{PR}, can be converted to another relationship in which the capitalized-cost factor replaces the capital-recovery factor. Substitute Eq. (2.7#5) in Eq. (2.5#3)

$$P_{n_2} = P_{n_1} \frac{F_{PR,i,n_1}}{F_{PR,i,n_2}} = P_{n_1} \frac{iF_{PK,i,n_1}}{iF_{PK,i,n_2}}$$

$$P_{n_2} = P_{n_1} \frac{F_{PK,i,n_1}}{F_{PK,i,n_2}} \qquad (2.7\#7)$$

Present-worth basis n_2 years duration

$$= \text{(present-worth basis } n_1 \text{ years duration)} \frac{F_{PK} \text{ factor for } n_1}{F_{PK} \text{ factor for } n_2}$$

where F_{PK} is the capitalized-cost factor.

The capitalized-cost factor can be derived in another manner that is instructive. Capitalized cost is the present worth on an infinite-duration basis. For a machine costing P_n and lasting n years, the present worth of all the costs out to infinity is

$$K = P_n \sum_{x=0}^{\infty} \frac{1}{(1+i)^{xn}}$$

The $\sum$ summation is an infinite series with first term 1 and ratio $1/(1+i)^n$. The sum is, by Eq. (2.2#2),

$$K = P_n \frac{1 - \left[\frac{1}{(1+i)^n}\right]^\infty}{1 - \frac{1}{(1+i)^n}} = P_n \frac{(1+i)^n}{(1+i)^n - 1} = P_n F_{PK,i,n}$$

which checks Eq. (2.7#3).

Example 2.7E1 Solve Example 2.5E1 on the basis of capitalized cost.
From the second solution

$P_{A_2} = \$24{,}529$
$P_{B_3} = \$31{,}334$

By Eq. (2.7#3)

$K = P_n F_{PK}$
$K_A = 24{,}529 F_{PK,10\%,2} = 24{,}529(5.7619) = \$141{,}330$
$K_B = 31{,}334 F_{PK,10\%,3} = 31{,}334(4.0211) = \$126{,}000$

Machine B is the more economical. The ratio of costs is

$$\frac{A}{B} = \frac{141{,}330}{126{,}000} = 1.1217$$

Example 2.7E1 has now been calculated in five ways, all equivalent. The results are summarized in Table 2.7T1.

Table 2.7T1 Comparison of Solutions to Example 2.7E1

Method	Numerical value, $	Ratio of costs A/B
Present worth on 6-year basis—common denominator of service lives; Example 2.5E1, first solution	$P_{A_6} = 61{,}555$ $P_{B_6} = 54{,}875$	1.1217
Present worth on actual basis repeated to fill 6-year basis; Example 2.5E1, second solution	$P_{A_6} = 61{,}555$ $P_{B_6} = 54{,}875$	1.1217
Present worth of machine B converted to 2-year duration; Example 2.5E1, third solution	$P_{A_2} = 24{,}529$ $P_{B_2} = 21{,}867$	1.1217
Unacost, equivalent uniform end-of-year annual cost; Example 2.6E1	$R_A = 14{,}133$ $R_B = 12{,}600$	1.1217
Capitalized cost, present worth for an infinite duration; Example 2.7E1	$K_A = 141{,}330$ $K_B = 126{,}000$	1.1217

Table 2.8T1 Summary of Unacost and Capitalized-cost Relationships—No Tax

Item no.	Item	Present worth as a cost for n years duration	Unacost — Algebraic expression	Unacost — Factor expression	Capitalized cost — Algebraic expression	Capitalized cost — Factor expression
1	C_i Initial cost for n-year life	C_i	$C_i \dfrac{i(1+i)^n}{(1+i)^n - 1}$	$C_i F_{PR,i,n}$	Multiply corresponding algebraic expression for unacost by $\dfrac{1}{i}$	$C_i F_{PK,i,n}$
2	R Uniform end-of-year annual cost	$R \dfrac{(1+i)^n - 1}{i(1+i)^n}$	R	$R1$ (factor is unity)		$R \dfrac{1}{i}$
3	R_b Uniform beginning-of-year annual cost	$R_b(1+i) \dfrac{(1+i)^n - 1}{i(1+i)^n}$	$R_b(1+i)$	$R_b(1+i)$		$R_b F_{PK,i,1}$
4	C_{ex} Irregular cost at end of xth year for article lasting n years	$C_{ex} \dfrac{1}{(1+i)^x}$	$C_{ex} \dfrac{1}{(1+i)^x} \times \dfrac{i(1+i)^n}{(1+i)^n - 1}$	$C_{ex} \dfrac{1}{(1+i)^x} F_{PR,i,n}$		$C_{ex} \dfrac{1}{(1+i)^x} F_{PK,i,n}$
5	C_{bx} Irregular cost at beginning of xth year for article lasting n years	$C_{bx} \dfrac{1}{(1+i)^{x-1}}$	$C_{bx} \dfrac{1}{(1+i)^{x-1}} \times \dfrac{i(1+i)^n}{(1+i)^n - 1}$	$C_{bx} \dfrac{1}{(1+i)^{x-1}} F_{PR,i,n}$		$C_{bx} \dfrac{1}{(1+i)^{x-1}} F_{PK,i,n}$
6	C_{nd} Nondepreciable first cost, e.g., land or an article that lasts forever	$C_{nd} \dfrac{(1+i)^n - 1}{(1+i)^n}$	$C_{nd} i$	$C_{nd} i$		$C_{nd} 1$ (factor is unity)
7	C_{sal} Salvage value at end of nth year, a receipt	$-C_{\text{sal}} \dfrac{1}{(1+i)^n}$	$-C_{\text{sal}} \dfrac{i}{(1+i)^n - 1}$	$-C_{\text{sal}} \dfrac{1}{(1+i)^n} \times F_{PR,i,n}$		$-C_{\text{sal}}(F_{PK,i,n} - 1)$ or $-C_{\text{sal}} \dfrac{1}{(1+i)^n} F_{PK,i,n}$
8	Initial cost C_i and salvage value C_{sal} taken together	$(C_i - C_{\text{sal}}) + C_{\text{sal}} \times \dfrac{(1+i)^n - 1}{(1+i)^n}$	$(C_i - C_{\text{sal}}) \dfrac{i(1+i)^n}{(1+i)^n - 1} + iC_{\text{sal}}$	$(C_i - C_{\text{sal}}) \times F_{PR,i,n} + iC_{\text{sal}}$		$(C_i - C_{\text{sal}}) F_{PK,i,n} + C_{\text{sal}}$

2.8 Examples of cost comparisons

It is desirable to develop expressions for unacost and capitalized cost for various types of costs or receipts. If the present worth of the cost for a duration of n years is calculated, as from a time diagram, multiplication by the capital-recovery factor F_{PR} and the capitalized-cost factor F_{PK} will give the unacost and the capitalized cost. For example, consider a salvage value C_{sal}, a negative cost, due at the end of n years. The present worth is

$$-C_{\text{sal}} \frac{1}{(1+i)^n}$$

The equivalent unacost by Eq. (2.2#7) is

$$R = -C_{\text{sal}} \frac{1}{(1+i)^n} \frac{i(1+i)^n}{(1+i)^n - 1} = -C_{\text{sal}} \frac{i}{(1+i)^n - 1}$$

The capitalized cost by Eq. (2.7#2) is

$$K = -C_{\text{sal}} \frac{1}{(1+i)^n} \frac{(1+i)^n}{(1+i)^n - 1} = -C_{\text{sal}} \frac{1}{(1+i)^n - 1}$$

Table 2.8T1 is a summary of a number of relationships. Indeed, there is no type of cost that is not covered by the tabulation inasmuch as all costs can be included as an irregular expense at some time and thus can be accommodated by the C_{ex} and C_{bx} items, which are for irregular costs.

Unacosts can be added together. Capitalized costs can also be added together. For a system

$$R_{SYS} = R_1 + R_2 + R_3 + \cdots$$
$$K_{SYS} = K_1 + K_2 + K_3 + \cdots$$

Example 2.8E1 A new machine costs $8,000 and lasts 10 years with negligible salvage value. If money is worth 10% per year, how much can be spent now to repair an old machine to extend its life 3 years?

Unacost for new machine, by item 1, Table 2.8T1, is

$$R_{\text{new}} = C_i F_{PR, 10\%, 10} = 8{,}000(0.16275) = 1{,}302.0$$

For a repair job having the same unacost

$$R_{\text{repair}} = 1{,}302.0 = C_i F_{PR, 10\%, 3} = C_i(0.40211)$$
$$C_i = \$3{,}238$$

That is, up to $3,238 can be spent for the repair job with money worth 10% per year.

Example 2.8E2 If, in the preceding example, the old machine can be repaired for $2,500, what is the savings?

Unacost for repair job by item 1, Table 2.8T1,

$$R_{\text{repair}} = C_i F_{PR, 10\%, 3} = 2{,}500(0.40211) = \$1{,}005$$
$$R_{\text{savings}} = 1{,}302 - 1{,}005 = \$297$$

That is, $297 per year is saved as of the end of each year for 3 years.

Example 2.8E3 A floor requires resurfacing at a cost of $5,000 and will last 2 years. If money is worth 10% per year, how long must a new floor last if it costs $19,000?

The capitalized cost of resurfacing by item 1, Table 2.8T1, is

$$K = C_i F_{PK,10\%,2} = 5{,}000(5.7619) = \$28{,}810$$

Assume a service life for the new floor and by repeated trials find the life for which the capitalized cost is $28,810:

$n = 11$: $K = C_i F_{PK,10\%,11} = 19{,}000(1.5396) = 29{,}252$
$n = 12$: $K = C_i F_{PK,10\%,12} = 19{,}000(1.4676) = 27{,}884$

By interpolation $n = 11.3$ for $K = 28{,}810$. That is, the new floor must last 11.3 years or longer.

Example 2.8E4 It will cost $5,000 to line a stack and obtain a 2-year life. For $9,400 a 4-year life can be obtained. At what rate of return are the two investments equal?

Try 6% per year rate of return. Let R_2 and R_4 be unacost for 2- and 4-year linings. By item 1, Table 2.8T1,

$$R_2 = C_i F_{PR,6\%,2} = 5{,}000(0.54544) = 2{,}727.2$$
$$R_4 = C_i F_{PR,6\%,4} = 9{,}400(0.28859) = 2{,}712.7$$

For 8% per year rate of return

$$R_2 = C_i F_{PR,8\%,2} = 5{,}000(0.56077) = 2{,}803.9$$
$$R_4 = C_i F_{PR,8\%,4} = 9{,}400(0.30192) = 2{,}838.0$$

That is,

$$R_2 - R_4$$

At 6%: $+14.5$
At 8%: -34.1

and by interpolation $R_2 - R_4 = 0$ at 6.6% per year rate of return. Below 6.6% the 4-year lining is the more economical, and above 6.6% the 2-year lining is the more economical. The example illustrates that a decision may be reversed depending upon the rate of return.

Example 2.8E5 A machine was purchased for $10,000 from a manufacturer who guaranteed the machine for 10 years and also agreed to include 6% per year for the time value of money. At the end of 8 years the machine becomes worthless. How much refund should the manufacturer pay as of that time?

First solution. The unacost acceptable to the purchaser was, by item 1, Table 2.8T1,

$$R = C_i F_{PR,6\%,10} = 10{,}000(0.13587) = \$1{,}359$$

The equivalent time pattern is:

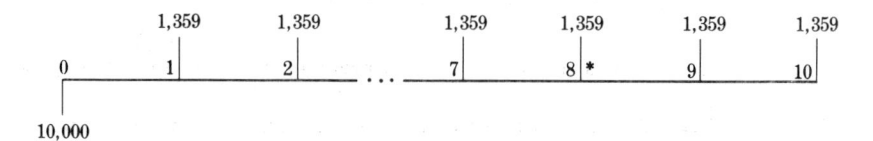

```
      1,359   1,359   1,359        1,359   1,359   1,359
        |       |       |            |       |       |
   0    1       2      ...    7      8*      9      10
   |
10,000
```

The purchaser gave $10,000 for $1,359 of service as of the end of each year. At the end of 8 years he is owed $1,359 one year away and $1,359 two years away. The immediate value of these is

$$1{,}359(1.06^{-1}) + 1{,}359(1.06^{-2}) = \$2{,}491$$

That is, $2,491 would be a fair settlement.

2.8 EQUIVALENCE AND COST COMPARISONS 33

Second solution. The purchaser is owed the value of a 2-year machine based on $10,000 for a 10-year machine. For equal unacosts by item 1, Table 2.8T1,

$$C_{i,10} F_{PR,6\%,10} = C_{i,2} F_{PR,6\%,2}$$
$$10{,}000(0.13587) = C_{i,2}(0.54544)$$
$$C_{i,2} = \$2{,}491, \text{ as before}$$

Third solution. The purchaser actually received an 8-year machine. The price for an 8-year machine by capitalized cost, item 1, Table 2.8T1, would be

$$C_{i,10} F_{PK,6\%,10} = C_{i,8} F_{PK,6\%,8}$$
$$10{,}000(2.2645) = C_{i,8}(2.6839)$$
$$C_{i,8} = \$8{,}437$$

Purchaser's overpayment 8 years ago brought up to the present is

$$(10{,}000 - 8{,}437)(1.06^8) = \$2{,}491, \text{ as before}$$

The three solutions illustrate the equivalence of various methods.

Example 2.8E6 Two machines have expenses as follows. If money is worth 10% per year, which is more economical and by how much?

	A	B
First cost, $	10,000	95,000
Uniform end-of-year annual maintenance cost, $ per year	3,000	1,000
Irregular cost beginning of third year, $	4,000	
Irregular cost beginning of fourth year, $	1,500	
Salvage value, $	0	20,000
Uniform end-of-year savings from quality control, $ per year	0	6,000
Life, years	4	10

In a more involved problem the present worths can be obtained first, after which conversion to a common-denominator basis can be made.

Present worth of 4 years of machine A is

$$P_{A_4} = 10{,}000 + 3{,}000 F_{RP,10\%,4} + 4{,}000 F_{SP,10\%,2}$$
$$+ 1{,}500 F_{SP,10\%,3}$$
$$= 10{,}000 + 3{,}000(3.1699) + 4{,}000(0.82645)$$
$$+ 1{,}500(0.75131)$$
$$= 23{,}943$$

for which the unacost is, by item 1, Table 2.8T1,

$$R_A = 23{,}943 F_{PR,10\%,4} = 23{,}943(0.31547) = \$7{,}553$$

Present worth of 10 years of machine B

$$P_{B_{10}} = 95{,}000 + (1{,}000 - 6{,}000) F_{RP,10\%,10} - 20{,}000 F_{SP,10\%,10}$$
$$= 95{,}000 - 5{,}000(6.1446) - 20{,}000(0.38554)$$
$$= 56{,}566$$

for which the unacost is

$$R_B = 56{,}566 F_{PR,10\%,10} = 56{,}566(0.16275) = \$9{,}206$$

34 MATHEMATICS OF COST COMPARISONS

Machine A is the more economical. The unacost savings is

$9{,}206 - 7{,}553 = \$1{,}653$

That is, machine A is more economical by $1,653 per year as of the end of each of the 4 years that it is in service.

2.9 Finding the best alternative

Frequently a problem arises in such a way that several alternatives are possible and the analyst must take precautions so that he arrives at the best answer, not just a better answer. The following problem illustrates the principle.

Example 2.9E1 A new tank costs $10,000 and lasts 5 years. An old tank can be repaired for $1,500 to give 1 more year of service, then for $2,000 to give 1 more year of service, then for $2,500 to give another year of service, and so forth. If money is worth 10% per year, how long should the old tank be repaired?

At zero time compare the cost of a new tank with the cost of repairing. Using capitalized cost and item 1, Table 2.8T1,

$K_{new} = C_i F_{PK,10\%,5} = 10{,}000(2.6380) = 26{,}380$
$K_{rep} = C_i F_{PK,10\%,1} = 1{,}500(11{,}000) = 16{,}500$

It is more economical to repair. Repeat the calculation 1 year later

$K_{new} = 26{,}380$, as above
$K_{rep} = 2{,}000 F_{PK,10\%,1} = 2{,}000(11{,}000) = 22{,}000$

Again it will be more economical to repair. Repeat the calculation 1 year later, at the end of the second year.

$K_{new} = 26{,}380$, as before
$K_{rep} = 2{,}500 F_{PK,10\%,1} = 2{,}500(11.000) = 27{,}500$

It will not pay to repair. As the repair cost is rising each year, it follows that the tank should be repaired for 2 years and then replaced with a new tank.

The following solution is incorrect but sometimes offered. Let $K_{r_1}, K_{r_2}, \ldots$ be the capitalized cost of repairing for $1, 2, \ldots$ years. Taking the present worths and converting to a capitalized cost by item 1, Table 2.8T1, gives

$K_{r_1} = 1{,}500 F_{PK,10\%,1} = 1{,}500(11{,}000) = 16{,}500$

$K_{r_2} = \left(1{,}500 + \dfrac{2{,}000}{1.10}\right) F_{PK,10\%,2} = 3{,}318.2(5.7619) = 19{,}119$

$K_{r_3} = \left(1{,}500 + \dfrac{2{,}000}{1.10} + \dfrac{2{,}500}{1.10^2}\right) F_{PK,10\%,3} = 5{,}384.3$

$(4.0211) = 21{,}650$

and continuing

Years repair	K, $
1	16,500
2	19,119
3	21,650
4	24,096
5	26,457

2.9   EQUIVALENCE AND COST COMPARISONS

The capitalized cost as found previously for a new tank is $26,380, and the tabulation might be interpreted to repair for 4 years because only for 5 years repairing does the capitalized cost of repairing exceed the capitalized cost of a new tank. The reasoning is incorrect, however. The capitalized cost of repairing has been taken by years as a group. The tabulation merely indicates that it is more economical to repair for 4 years than not to repair at all. The group of 4 years includes the savings of the first 2 years, which overcome the loss of the last 2 years.

The following alternative solution is correct. Compare the programs of buying a new tank every 5 years, buying a new tank every 6 years after repairing 1 year, and so forth. Take present worths and convert to capitalized costs.

$K_5 = 10,000 F_{PK,10\%,5} = 10,000(2.6380) = 26,380$

$K_6 = \left(10,000 + \dfrac{1,500}{1.10^5}\right) F_{PK,10\%,6} = 10,931(2.2961) = 25,099$

$K_7 = \left(10,000 + \dfrac{1,500}{1.10^5} + \dfrac{2,000}{1.10^6}\right) F_{PK,10\%,7} = 12,060(2.0541)$

$= 24,772$

and continuing

Total years	Years repair	K, $
5	0	26,380
6	1	25,099
7	2	24,772
8	3	25,010
9	4	26,000
10	5	26,409

The minimum occurs for repairing 2 years. Repairing for 3 or even 4 years is more economical than not repairing at all, but not the most economical.

The following variation also gives the correct analysis. Consider programs of repairing for various numbers of years and then purchasing a new tank to complete the cycle.

$K_5 = 10,000 F_{PK,10\%,5} = 10,000(2.6380) = 26,380$

$K_6 = \left(1,500 + \dfrac{10,000}{1.10}\right) F_{PK,10\%,6} = 10,591(2.2961) = 24,318$

$K_7 = \left(1,500 + \dfrac{2,000}{1.10} + \dfrac{10,000}{1.10^2}\right) F_{PK,10\%,7} = 11,583(2.0541)$

$= 23,793$

and continuing

Years repair	K, $
0	26,380
1	24,318
2	23,793
3	24,174
4	25,122
5	26,427

Again, repairing for 2 years is most economical. Repairing for 3 or 4 years is more economical than not repairing at all, but not the most economical.

2.10 Considerations in cost comparison

In a practical problem all the pertinent costs must be included, and the analyst must be on guard to avoid omissions. If alternatives have costs which are equal in all respects, such costs may be omitted because only differences affect the choice. However, equality in all respects must be strictly true. Thus, suppose the comparison is between heat-exchanger tubes lasting 2 and 5 years. The installation cost for each may be the same, but it must be included. In one case the installation cost will be incurred every 2 years, in the other every 5 years. Conversely, if the cost for cleaning the tubes is the same for each on a yearly basis, this cost can be omitted in the comparison. Of course, inclusion of equal costs is never detrimental and may prevent overlooking them in subsequent considerations.

It is not necessary that the machines or systems being compared give equal service. Benefits, or penalties, can include such considerations as extra production, better quality control, or even reduction of pollution. However, savings or losses associated with a machine should be included only if they are real. Downtime for repairs should not be penalized for lost production if the machine can attain the overall production rate even with the downtime. Frequently the downtime of a machine can be a significant consideration.

Every practical comparison contains a number of intangibles. Two machines may have different capacities although both can meet present demands. No immediate benefit can be given for the larger capacity, but it is an intangible benefit. In a comparison between air cooling and water cooling, air cooling has an intangible value because water is becoming more restricted and relatively more expensive with time. The intangibles can be an annoyance to the analyst. If they can be given a monetary value, they should be included to that extent. At least they can be enumerated so that they are there to be seen. The intangibles can easily swing the decision in a close comparison.

Sometimes such items as service life or future repair costs are not definitely known, but the comparison can be made on the basis of a range. For example, machine A can be calculated as high, best estimate, and low basis. Also, results can be presented in a form that circumvents the uncertainty. In Example 2.8E3 the service life of the second floor was not known, but the conclusion that the floor would have to last 11.3 years to be economical is a presentation that can facilitate making a decision.

It has been emphasized that two time factors are involved in making a cost comparison. They are (1) the instant at which costs are incurred and (2) the duration over which costs extend. Unacost and capitalized cost both have built-in common denominators to accommodate any duration and convert it to a standard duration. If the durations for two machines are the same, both methods are still applicable. The methods are fundamentally present-worth methods. Unacost uses a 1-year duration as an end-of-year cost, and capitalized cost uses an infinite duration with a zero-time cost. The methods do not imply respectively that an article will be used 1 year or replaced forever. The 1-year and infinite durations are chosen merely for mathematical convenience. Each method gives the correct comparison for any duration. The methods are readily converted from one to the other by the simple relationship [Eq. (2.7#6)]

$$R = iK$$

In most problems the method used drops out. Management, however, may understand a unacost figure of, say, $10,000 per year better than $100,000 capitalized cost; although both are equivalent at 10% per year rate of return.

The result of a comparison depends upon the time value of money as demonstrated by Example 2.8E4, where the decision is reversed above and below 6.6%. A discussion of what rate of return should be used is not made here.

A subsequent chapter will discuss the analysis of whole projects or ventures for which all receipts and expenses are known, or at least assigned a definite value. In the present chapter the receipts associated with a particular machine or group of machines are usually not known. Thus, in a long assembly line it is not possible to allocate the receipts of the entire operation to individual services or machines. This does not prevent the analyst, however, from using the methods of this chapter for comparing two competing machines. The rate of return used in the calculation is then merely the time value of money that the analyst places on investment for machines performing the indicated service. Generally it will not be the same as the rate of return for the venture.

The fundamental aspects of cost comparisons have been presented in this chapter. Subsequent chapters will impose additional considerations, such as taxes.

2.11 Nomenclature

A_{t_1} Amount at time 1, $
C_{bx} Irregular cost at beginning of xth year, $
C_{ex} Irregular cost at end of xth year, $
C_i Initial or first cost, $
C_{nd} Nondepreciable cost, $
C_{sal} Salvage value, $
F_{PK} Factor to convert P to K; capitalized-cost factor, dimensionless
F_{PR} Factor to convert P to R; capital-recovery factor, year^{-1}
F_{PS} Factor to convert P to S; compound-interest factor, dimensionless
F_{RP} Factor to convert R to P; unacost present-worth factor, years
F_{RS} Factor to convert R to S; equal-payment-series future-worth factor, years
F_{SP} Factor to convert S to P; single-payment present-worth factor, or present-worth factor, no units
F_{SR} Factor to convert S to R; sinking-fund factor, year^{-1}
i Rate of return, decimal/year
i' Stipulated rate of return in Hoskold's formula, decimal/year
i'' Sinking-fund rate in Hoskold's formula, decimal/year
K Capitalized cost, $
n Number as the life of an article, years
p Number of periods per year
P Present worth, $
R Uniform end-of-year annual amount; unacost, $ per year
R' Return on original investment in Hoskold's formula, $ per year

R"   Sinking-fund payment in Hoskold's formula, $ per year
R_b Uniform beginning-of-year annual amount, $ per year
S   Future worth, $
x   The *x*th year

2.12 Problems

P1. What will $15,000 amount to in 4 years at 8% per year compounded (*a*) annually, (*b*) quarterly?

P2. What sum will yield $1,850 in 5 years compounded annually at (*a*) 6% per year, (*b*) 5% per year?

P3. What is the rate of return if $10,000 in 7 years amounts to (*a*) $17,138, (*b*) $16,400?

P4. What is the effective rate of interest if interest is compounded quarterly at 8% per year?

P5. If money is worth 10% per year, find the present worth of a $10,000 receipt due in 4 years, plus a $15,000 receipt due in 6 years, plus an $8,000 debt due in 9 years, plus a $12,000 receipt due in 10 years.

P6. What is the present worth of a series of equal end-of-year payments of $1,000 for 8 years if money is worth 10% per year?

P7. A series of end-of-year payments forms a geometric series with first payment $1,000, second payment $1,210, etc. What is the present worth of these payments for 6 years if money is worth 10% per year?

P8. If $10,000 is owed, what equal yearly payments for 8 years will discharge the debt if money is worth 6% per year and payments are made (*a*) at the end of the year, (*b*) at the beginning of the year?

P9. If $20,000 is owed, and if money is worth 6% per year and equal end-of-year yearly payments of $3,000 are made, how long will be required to discharge the debt?

P10. If $30,000 is owed, and if equal payments of $5,500 at the end of each year for 8 years will discharge the debt, what is the rate of return?

P11. Given

$$F_{PR,8\%,5} = 0.25046 \qquad F_{PR,8\%,6} = 0.21636$$
$$F_{PR,10\%,5} = 0.26380 \qquad F_{PR,10\%,6} = 0.22961$$

Find $F_{PR,8.2\%,5.6}$ by double interpolation, i.e., find $F_{PR,8.2\%,5}$ and $F_{PR,8.2\%,6}$ by interpolation and then interpolate between these two values to find $F_{PR,8.2\%,5.6}$. Verify that the following procedure gives the same numerical result. Let N_j ($j = 1, 2, 3, 4$) be the four corner values that are given and *N* the required result. If A_j is the fractional horizontal distance and B_j is the fractional vertical distance from the desired value to the given values, then

$$N = \sum_{j=1}^{j=4} N_j(1 - A_j)(1 - B_j)$$

For example, in this case for $j = 1$, $N_1 = 0.25046$,

$$A_1 = \frac{8.2 - 8.0}{10.0 - 8.0} = 0.1$$

$$B_1 = \frac{5.6 - 5.0}{6.0 - 5.0} = 0.6$$

P12. If $10,000 is owed and it is agreed to pay $1,740 at the end of each year for 8 years to discharge the debt but the fourth payment is missed, what equal end-of-year payments thereafter will discharge the debt on time?

P13. A machine costs $15,000 and will have $3,000 salvage value at the end of its life in 12 years. A sinking fund is established at 6% per year to pay for the machine.
     (*a*) What is the sinking-fund payment?
     (*b*) What is the value of the sinking fund at the end of 7 years?

P14. A bond has a face value of $1,000, pays 6% per year semiannually, becomes due in 4½ years, and is bought to yield 4%. What is the purchase price?

P15. A bond has a face value of $1,000, pays 6% per year semiannually, becomes due in 3 years, and is purchased for $1,050. What is the yield rate to the purchaser?

P16. Mineral rights are bought for $2 million and will produce $500,000 for 7 years. A sinking fund bearing 4% per year is set up to repay the investment. What is (a) the stipulated rate of return and (b) the rate of return by a single-rate-of-return model?

P17. If the stipulated rate is 15% per year and the sinking-fund rate is 6% per year, how much should be paid for mineral rights which last 12 years and produce $200,000 net per year?

P18. If $5,000 is spent now to avoid $15,000 repairs 2 years from now, what rate of return is earned by repairing now?

P19. An operation can be performed manually at a cost of $12,000 per year. How much can be spent for a machine which lasts 10 years if the cost for operating the machine is $3,000 per year and money is worth 12% per year?

P20. An operation is performed manually at a cost of $10,000 per year. A machine costing $60,000 and lasting 12 years will perform the operation and eliminate the labor cost.

(a) What is the rate of return earned by the investment?

(b) If in addition the machine is worth $5,000 per year because of added production, what is the rate of return on the investment?

P21. A company can produce 1 million units per year of a product which infringes a patent. The company can pay a royalty of $0.08 per unit or invest $200,000 in equipment and incur a cost of $0.05 per unit to avoid the patent. If money is worth 12% per year, which course should the company take if only 10 years ahead is to be considered? What are the intangibles?

P22. Three machines are available for an operation. Machine A costs $100,000 and lasts 5 years; machine B costs $150,000; and machine C costs $200,000. If money is worth 20% per year, how long must machines B and C last to be economically equal to machine A?

P23. Two machines have the following costs:

	A	B
First cost, $	10,000	25,000
Salvage value, $	1,100	1,500
Uniform end-of-year expense, $ per year	3,000	2,000
Irregular expense, end first year, $	1,000	
Irregular expense, end third year, $		2,500
Benefit from quality control, as of end of each year, $ per year		600
Life of machine, years	2	5

Compare the machines on the following basis:

(a) Present worth for some common denominator of the service lives with money worth 8% per year.

(b) Present worth, basis 4 years, with money worth 8% per year.

(c) Unacost with money worth 8% per year.

(d) Capitalized cost with money worth 8% per year.

(e) The service life of B that would be economically equal to A with money worth 8% per year.

(f) The rate of return at which the two are equal.

P24. A nondepreciable asset such as land or working capital may be regarded as an article which costs C_{nd} and n years later has a salvage value C_{nd}. Use this approach to derive the relationships given as item 6 in Table 2.8T1.

P25. Derive the expression for first cost and salvage value combined as given as item 8 in Table 2.8T1.

40 MATHEMATICS OF COST COMPARISONS

P26. A machine costs $10,000 and lasts 12 years. If money is worth 10% per year, what is the loss on abandonment at the end of 8 years?

P27. Two types of pipe are available for carrying water with costs as follows:

	A	B
First cost, $	100,000	200,000
Annual end-of-year cost, $ per year	25,000	20,000
Salvage value, $	0	0
Life, years	15	20

Type A pipe must be repaired at times as part of the annual cost, but the water can become contaminated at these times. Contamination with type B pipe can be neglected. If money is worth 6% per year, how much benefit must be given to type B pipe to make it economically equal to type A pipe?

P28. A company manufactures 1 million units per year which sell at $2 less than a competitor's superior product. How much can be spent on research as of the end of this year assuming a 40% chance for success in attaining the $2 per unit extra? Money is worth 10% per year, and a period of 8 years beyond this year is to be considered.

P29. A machine which lasts 10 years can be bought for $10,000. Operating expenses for the machine form an arithmetic progression and are $20,000 for the first year as an end-of-year expense, $22,000 for the next year, and so forth. At what age should the machine be exchanged for a new one if money is worth 10% per year? Note that the arithmetic can be simplified by deducting $20,000 as being common to all the years.

P30. Two plans are available for constructing a plant which will have the same income per year at all times.

Plan A is to build a half-size plant now at a cost of $1 million and comparable operating cost of $200,000 per year for the first 4 years. At the end of the fourth year an addition costing $900,000 will be installed to double capacity. Costs thereafter are $350,000 per year.

Plan B is to build a full-scale plant now at a cost of $1.5 million with operating costs of $250,000 per year for the first 4 years, and $300,000 per year thereafter.

If money is worth 12% per year and a period of 10 years ahead is the basis for a comparison, which plan should be chosen?

P31. A company predicts and then actually realizes receipts from an operation as follows:

End of year	Predicted, $M	Actual, $M
1	1,000	1,200
2	1,300	1,400
3	1,500	1,000
4	1,700	300
5	1,200	100
6	800	0
7	400	0
8	100	0

A unit is set up at a cost that will yield 20% per year on the basis of the 8-year prediction.

(a) What was the actual rate of return?

(b) What was the loss on abandonment at the end of the fifth year based on the original 20% per year rate of return?

2.13 References

R1. Ayers, F.: "Mathematics of Finance," Schaum's Outline Series, McGraw-Hill Book Company, New York, 1963.
R2. Barish, N. H.: "Economic Analysis for Engineering and Managerial Decision Making," McGraw-Hill Book Company, New York, 1962.
R3. DeGarmo, E. P.: "Engineering Economy," 4th ed., The Macmillan Company, New York, 1967.
R4. Grant, E. L., and W. G. Ireson: "Principles of Engineering Economy," 4th ed., The Ronald Press Company, New York, 1960.
R5. Hart, W. L.: "The Mathematics of Investment," 4th ed., D. C. Heath and Company, Boston, 1958.
R6. Jelen, F. C.: Next Time Use Capitalized Costs, *Chem. Eng.*, February, 1954, pp. 199–203.
R7. Jelen, F. C.: Major Cost Analysis Methods Yield Equivalent Answers, *Chem. Eng.*, July 28, 1958, pp. 116–118.
R8. Thuessen, H. G., and W. J. Fabrycky: "Engineering Economy," 3d ed., Prentice-Hall, Inc., Englewood Cliffs, N.J., 1964.

3
Depreciation and Taxes—Equivalence After Taxes

F. C. Jelen

DEPRECIATION AND TAXES[1]

3.1 Nature of depreciation

In any economic endeavor expenditures are incurred that have various durations. For accounting and tax purposes a sharp demarcation exists between expenditures that are paid for and used up in a single accounting period and expenditures for which the duration exceeds one accounting period. A year is accepted as the period for both accounting and tax purposes; hence there is a sharp distinction between expenditures consumed within a year and expenditures which outlast 1 year. Investment in a building will last many years. It would be incorrect to charge the cost of the building entirely to operations for the first year and make no charge for the cost of the building for subsequent years. A means must be found for spreading over the years expenditures that outlast 1 year. An expenditure that decreases in value with time must be apportioned over its life. The term to describe this loss in value is *depreciation*.

Depreciation arises from two causes, wear and tear and obsolescence. A machine may wear out and eventually be unable to perform its function. A machine may show little wear and tear but become economically inefficient due to

---

[1] Certain material, examples, and problems with reference to depreciation were furnished by Dr. H. E. Schweyer, of the Department of Chemical Engineering, University of Florida.

technological advancement. The latter is called *obsolescence* and represents a loss in value just as real as wear and tear. Wear and tear and obsolescence are both recognized by tax rules as depreciation.

Depreciation is an expense. Indeed the accountant's charge for depreciation is depreciation expense. Depreciation is a fundamental aspect of accounting and cost engineering which must be considered for manufacturing costs, pricing, taxes, and cost comparisons. There is an advantage in deferring taxes to later years because of the time value of money, and consequently depreciation has become confused with the tax situation. A company may use one depreciation method for tax purposes and another method internally for costs and pricing.

Popular presentations of depreciation can lead the student to narrow interpretations. The popular conception of the existence of a depreciation fund to which payments are made so that the original investment is restored when an article is worn out is not in accord with practice. In this book depreciation is used in its mathematical sense. Depreciation arises when an expenditure outlasts 1 year, and a depreciation schedule is a means of allocating the expenditure as an expense over the years.

A depreciation schedule has two mathematical requirements, the life of the depreciable equipment and the mathematical procedure used in allocating the depreciation expense for each year of life of the equipment.

For tax purposes the allowable life of equipment is shown in Table 3.1T1 as adapted from official government publications. Variations from the table can be made only on an individual basis as established with the approval of the government. The analyst may choose any service life for internal company use.

A schedule for allocating depreciation over the years for tax purposes must meet government rules. Generally the government will accept any consistent method that gives a write-off at the end of two-thirds of the life not exceeding the write-off at that time given by the double-declining-balance method. The most common methods for tax purposes are straight-line and sum-of-digits. Several methods are discussed below.

The use of accelerated depreciation predates the tax situation. An asset, such as a machine, represents two types of cost, the initial depreciable cost and the operating cost. Operating costs tend to be low in the early years and high in the later years; hence the practice arose of using high depreciation in the early years and low depreciation in the later years to keep the sum of depreciation and operating costs more nearly constant. Accelerated depreciation, too, is more in line with the resale value of machinery at intermediate years.

3.2 Depreciation terms

Suppose an asset has an initial cost C_i, a life of n years, and a terminal, or salvage, value C_{sal}. Let D_{f_1}, D_{f_2}, ... be the fractional depreciation for each year. The total depreciation, or the *depreciable first cost* C_d is

$$C_d = C_i - C_{\text{sal}} \tag{3.2\#1}$$

Table 3.1T1 Estimated Life of Equipment*

	Life, years
Group one: general business assets	
1. Office furniture, fixtures, machines, equipment	10
2. Transportation	
a. Aircraft	6
b. Automobile	3
c. Buses	9
d. General-purpose trucks	4–6
e. Railroad cars (except for railroad companies)	15
f. Tractor units	4
g. Trailers	6
h. Water-transportation equipment	18
3. Land and site improvements (not otherwise covered)	20
4. Buildings (apartments, banks, factories, hotels, stores, warehouses)	40–60
Group two: nonmanufacturing activities (excluding transportation, communications, and public utilities)	
1. Agriculture	
a. Machinery and equipment	10
b. Animals	3–10
c. Trees and vines	Variable
d. Buildings	25
2. Contract construction	
a. General	5
b. Marine	12
3. Fishing	Variable
4. Logging and sawmilling	6–10
5. Mining (excluding petroleum refining and smelting and refining of minerals)	10
6. Recreation and amusement	10
7. Services to general public	10
8. Wholesale and retail trade	10
Group three: manufacturing	
1. Aerospace industry	8
2. Apparel and textile products	9
3. Cement (excluding concrete products)	20
4. Chemicals and allied products	11
5. Electrical equipment	
a. Electrical equipment in general	12
b. Electronic equipment	8
6. Fabricated metal products	12
7. Food products, except grains, sugar, and vegetable-oil products	12
8. Glass products	14
9. Grain and grain-mill products	17
10. Knitwear and knit products	9
11. Leather products	11
12. Lumber, wood products, and furniture	10
13. Machinery unless otherwise listed	12
14. Metalworking machinery	12

15. Motor vehicles and parts	12
16. Paper and allied products	
a. Pulp and paper	16
b. Paper conversion	12
17. Petroleum and natural gas	
a. Contract drilling and field service	6
b. Company exploration, drilling, and production	14
c. Petroleum refining	16
d. Marketing	16
18. Plastic products	11
19. Primary metals	
a. Ferrous metals	18
b. Nonferrous metals	14
20. Printing and publishing	11
21. Scientific instruments, optical and clock manufacturing	12
22. Railroad-transportation equipment	12
23. Rubber products	14
24. Ship- and boatbuilding	12
25. Stone and clay products	15
26. Sugar products	18
27. Textile-mill products	12–14
28. Tobacco products	15
29. Vegetable-oil products	18
30. Other manufacturing in general	12
Group four: transportation, communication, and public utilities	
1. Air transport	6
2. Central steam production and distribution	28
3. Electric utilities	
a. Hydraulic	50
b. Nuclear	20
c. Steam	28
d. Transmission and distribution	30
4. Gas utilities	
a. Distribution	35
b. Manufacture	30
c. Natural-gas production	14
d. Trunk pipelines and storage	22
5. Motor transport (freight)	8
6. Motor transport (passengers)	8
7. Pipeline transportation	22
8. Radio and television broadcasting	6
9. Railroads	
a. Machinery and equipment	14
b. Structures and similar improvements	30
c. Grading and other right-of-way improvements	Variable
d. Wharves and docks	20
e. Power plant and equipment	See item 3
10. Telephone and telegraph communications	Variable
11. Water transportation	20
12. Water utilities	50

* Abridged from Depreciation—Guidelines and Rules, *Treas. Dept., Int. Rev. Serv. Pub.* 456, July, 1962. The original publication should be consulted for exact accounting details.

46 MATHEMATICS OF COST COMPARISONS

The depreciation for any arbitrary year, the mth year, is

$$D_m = D_{f,m} C_d \qquad (3.2\#2)$$

The *book value* of the asset at the end of m years B_m is the original value less the accumulated depreciation expense to that time

$$B_m = C_i - C_d \sum_{m=1}^{m=m} D_{f,m} \qquad (3.2\#3)$$

Book value = initial cost − accumulated depreciation

Subtracting and adding C_d to Eq. (3.2#3) gives

$$B_m = C_i - C_d + C_d - C_d \sum_{1}^{m} D_{f,m}$$

$$= C_{\mathrm{sal}} + C_d\left(1 - \sum_{1}^{m} D_{f,m}\right) \qquad (3.2\#4)$$

Book value = salvage value + future depreciation

The book value may bear no relation to the resale value.

When the time value of money is a factor, it becomes necessary to consider the present worth of the yearly depreciation.

3.3 Straight-line depreciation (SL)

Allocation of the depreciable cost is uniform for all years in this method

$$D_{f_1} = D_{f_2} = \cdots = D_{f,n}$$

or

$$D_f = \frac{1}{n} \qquad (3.3\#1)$$

Depreciation for the mth year is

$$D_m = \frac{C_d}{n} \qquad (3.3\#2)$$

Accumulated depreciation for m years is

$$\sum D_m = C_d \frac{m}{n} \qquad (3.3\#3)$$

Book value at the end of m years is

$$B_m = C_i - C_d \frac{m}{n} \qquad (3.3\#4)$$

also

$$B_m = C_d\left(1 - \frac{m}{n}\right) + C_{\mathrm{sal}} \qquad (3.3\#5)$$

Depreciation remaining for future years is

$$C_d \sum_{m}^{n} D_{f,m} = C_d \sum_{m=m}^{m=n} \frac{1}{n} = C_d(n-m)\frac{1}{n} = C_d\left(1 - \frac{m}{n}\right) \qquad (3.3\#6)$$

The present worth of $1 of depreciation is

$$F_{SLP,i,n} = \frac{1}{n}\left[\frac{1}{1+i} + \frac{1}{(1+i)^2} + \cdots + \frac{1}{(1+i)^n}\right]$$

where the symbol $F_{SLP,i,n}$ converts straight-line depreciation to a present worth. The terms within the brackets are a geometrical series and are summed by Eq. (2.2#3).

$$F_{SLP,i,n} = \frac{1}{n}\frac{(1+i)^n - 1}{i(1+i)^n} = \frac{1}{n}F_{RP,i,n} \qquad (3.3\#7)$$

$F_{SLP,i,n}$ is the straight-line present-worth factor and is tabulated in Appendix 1, Table 1.

3.4 Sinking-fund depreciation (SF)

This method gives a yearly depreciation schedule which increases systematically with time and hence is opposite to accelerated depreciation. Suppose an annual deposit R_S is made to a sinking fund to restore the depreciable value at the end of n years. Then by item 6, Table 2.2T1,

$$R_S = C_d \frac{i}{(1+i)^n - 1} = C_d F_{SP,i,n} F_{PR,i,n} \qquad (3.4\#1)$$

The depreciation for any year is the sinking-fund increase for that year, which is the deposit for the year plus interest earned by the fund for the year.

The relationships for sinking-fund depreciation are given in Table 3.10T1. The method is employed by some governmental agencies and public utilities but is not widely used in industrial operations. It has at times been referred to as theoretical depreciation because if the sinking fund bears the same interest rate as that used in an economy study, the book value at any time will be the theoretical value of an asset having the same remaining life and salvage value. This aspect should not be overemphasized, but it is of interest.

Example 3.4E1 An asset costs $20,000, lasts 10 years, and has $1,000 salvage value. If money is worth 8% per year, find the book value at the end of 7 years using sinking-fund depreciation. Compare this to the equivalent cost of an asset having a 3-year life and $1,000 salvage value with money worth 8% per year.
The sinking-fund payment by Eq. (3.4#1) is

$R_S = (20{,}000 - 1{,}000)F_{SP,8\%,10}F_{PR,8\%,10}$
$\quad = 19{,}000(0.46319)(0.14903) = 1{,}311.6$

The amount in the sinking fund at the end of 7 years by item 5, Table 2.2T1, is

$S = RF_{RP,8\%,7}F_{PS,8\%,7} = 1{,}311.6(5.2064)(1.7138) = 11{,}703$

The book value at the end of 7 years, by Eq. (3.2#3), is

$B_7 = 20{,}000 - 11{,}703 = \$8{,}297$

This is what a 3-year machine with \$1,000 salvage value is worth. Use unacost item 8, Table 2.8T1,

$$R_{10} = (20{,}000 - 1{,}000)F_{PR,8\%,10} + 0.08(1{,}000)$$
$$= 19{,}000(0.14903) + 80 = \$2{,}911.50$$
$$R_3 = (8{,}297 - 1{,}000)F_{PR,8\%,3} + 0.08(1{,}000)$$
$$= 7{,}297(0.38803) + 80 = \$2{,}911.50$$

3.5 Declining-balance depreciation (DB)

In this accelerated depreciation method the yearly depreciation is a fixed percentage or fixed fraction of the book value at the beginning of the year. Let F_{DB} be the fixed fraction, then

$$D_1 = C_i F_{DB}$$
$$B_1 = C_i - C_i F_{DB} = C_i(1 - F_{DB})$$
$$D_2 = C_i(1 - F_{DB})F_{DB}$$
$$B_2 = B_1 - D_2 = C_i(1 - F_{DB}) - C_i(1 - F_{DB})F_{DB} = C_i(1 - F_{DB})^2$$

For the mth year the relationships are

$$D_m = C_i(1 - F_{DB})^{m-1}F_{DB} \tag{3.5\#1}$$
$$B_m = C_i(1 - F_{DB})^m \tag{3.5\#2}$$

At the end of n years

$$B_n = C_{\text{sal}} = C_i(1 - F_{DB})^n$$
$$F_{DB} = 1 - \sqrt[n]{\frac{C_{\text{sal}}}{C_i}} \tag{3.5\#3}$$

Salvage value must be known or estimated to utilize this method.

The relationships for declining-balance depreciation are given in Table 3.10T1.

3.6 Double-declining-balance depreciation (DDB)

This is an accelerated depreciation method of the same type as the declining-balance method, but the factor F_{DDB} is obtained by placing it equal to twice the straight-line method decimal depreciation. If an article lasts n years, straight-line fractional depreciation is $1/n$; double this is $2/n$, which is the value used for F_{DDB}. That is,

$$F_{DDB} = \frac{2}{n} \tag{3.6\#1}$$

The book value after n years is, by analogy with Eq. (3.5#2),

$$B_n = C_i(1 - F_{DDB})^n = C_i\left(1 - \frac{2}{n}\right)^n \qquad (3.6\#2)$$

which bears no relation to the salvage value. Tax laws prohibit the book value to be less than the salvage value, but a switch to straight-line depreciation in the later years is permissible to bring the book value down to salvage value.

The relationships for double-declining-balance depreciation are given in Table 3.10T1.

3.7 Sum-of-digits depreciation (SD)

This is an accelerated depreciation method having fractional depreciation for which the numerator is the years of life remaining as of the beginning of the year and the denominator is the sum of the digits for the total life. For example, for a 10-year life $1 + 2 + 3 + \cdots + 10 = 55$. The fractional depreciation for the first year is 10/55, for the second year 9/55, and so forth. For the mth year in a total life of n years, the factor is

$$F_{SD} = \frac{n - m + 1}{0.5n(n + 1)} \qquad (3.7\#1)$$

The present worth of $1 of depreciation is

$$F_{SDP,i,n} = \sum_{m=1}^{m=n} \frac{n - m + 1}{0.5n(n + 1)} \frac{1}{(1 + i)^m} = \frac{n - F_{RP,i,n}}{0.5n(n + 1)i} \qquad (3.7\#2)$$

$F_{SDP,i,n}$ converts sum-of-digits depreciation to a present worth and is the sum-of-digits present-worth factor. It is tabulated in Appendix 1, Table 1.

The relationships for sum-of-digits depreciation are given in Table 3.10T1.

3.8 Units-of-production depreciation (UP)

The methods discussed previously allocate depreciation on a time basis without regard to use. The units-of-production method allocates depreciation on a use basis without regard to time. If M is the total units produced and M_m that for the mth year, the fractional depreciation for the mth year is

$$F_{UP,m} = \frac{Mm}{M} \qquad (3.8\#1)$$

The relationships for units-of-production depreciation are given in Table 3.10T1.

3.9 Taxes and depreciation

The federal profits tax is based on the income after all costs have been deducted. A depreciation cost, accordingly, is of considerable interest to the Treasury Department because it affects the profit tax. Thus the modified life of equipment

Table 3.9T1 Federal Profits Tax Summary (1969)

	Percent
Normal tax up to $25,000 profit	22
Surtax on profits above $25,000	26
Combined total where applicable	48
Capital gains tax	25
Tax credit on tangible investment	7
Extra surtax added to all other taxes	10% of tax

has been established, as shown in Table 3.1T1. The regulations are subject to revision at any time, and the most recent information available should be obtained from the Treasury Department in making final computations.

A summary of corporation income taxes is shown in Table 3.9T1. In determining the influence of depreciation upon the profits tax it should be recognized that all depreciation costs reduce the tax base and are a tax savings or credit in any year amounting to tD, where t is the decimal tax rate and D is the dollars depreciation for the year. The capital gains tax replaces the normal tax and surtax but applies only to income derived from the disposal of assets held more than six months, with some exceptions. For example, salvage value in the excess of the predicted salvage value may have to be taken as regular income and not as a capital gain.

The tax situation is quite involved. Some corrections can be noted, as in Table 3.9T1. For example, up to a 7% deduction of the cost, depending upon the life, an 8-year life or more qualifies for the maximum 7%, may be taken as an investment credit, and can be used as a tax reduction in the year the asset is purchased. Generally, the credit applies to machinery and equipment. In years after 1965 this allowance need not be used to reduce the basis for computing depreciation. In addition, subject to certain limitations including a life of 6 years or more, an additional first-year deduction of 20% or $2,000 may be allowed; however, subsequent depreciation must be reduced by this amount.

The declining-balance and sum-of-digits methods are generally limited to acquisitions after 1953 with a life of at least 3 years. There are other details of profits tax accounting such as carryback of losses in a given year for credit and refund on a previous year's taxes, but these fine points will not be discussed here.

Under existing law straight-line, sinking-fund, declining-balance, double-declining-balance, and sum-of-digits methods of depreciation are all acceptable. Generally the government will accept any consistent method that gives a write-off at the end of two-thirds of the life not exceeding the write-off at that time given by the double-declining-balance method.

A switch to straight-line depreciation can be made generally if acceptable to the government but in some cases at the company's option. This is particularly true for the double-declining-balance method so as to get the terminal value equal

Table 3.10T1 Relationships for Depreciation, n-year Life*

Item no.	Method	Annual depreciation for mth year	Accumulated depreciation for m years	Present worth of m years of depreciation
1	Straight line (SL)	$\dfrac{C_i - C_{\text{sal}}}{n}$	$(C_i - C_{\text{sal}})\dfrac{m}{n}$	$\dfrac{C_i - C_{\text{sal}}}{n} F_{RP,i,m}$
2	Sinking fund (SF)	$(C_i - C_{\text{sal}}) F_{SP,i,n} F_{PR,i,n} F_{PS,i,m-1}$	$(C_i - C_{\text{sal}}) \dfrac{F_{PS,i,m} - 1}{F_{PS,i,n} - 1}$	$(C_i - C_{\text{sal}}) \dfrac{m}{1+i} F_{SP,i,n} F_{PR,i,n}$
3	Declining balance (DB)	$C_i \left(\sqrt[n]{\dfrac{C_{\text{sal}}}{C_i}}\right)^{m-1} \left(1 - \sqrt[n]{\dfrac{C_{\text{sal}}}{C_i}}\right)$ or $C_i(1 - F_{DB})^{m-1} F_{DB}$	$C_i\left[1 - \left(\sqrt[n]{\dfrac{C_{\text{sal}}}{C_i}}\right)^m\right]$ or $C_i[1 - (1 - F_{DB})^m]$	$C_i\left(1 - \sqrt[n]{\dfrac{C_{\text{sal}}}{C_i}}\right) \dfrac{1 - \left(\dfrac{\sqrt[n]{C_{\text{sal}}/C_i}}{1+i}\right)^m}{1 + i - \sqrt[n]{\dfrac{C_{\text{sal}}}{C_i}}}$
4	Double declining balance (DDB)	$C_i\left(1 - \dfrac{2}{n}\right)^{m-1} \dfrac{2}{n}$	$C_i\left[1 - \left(1 - \dfrac{2}{n}\right)^m\right]$	$\dfrac{2C_i}{n} \dfrac{1 - \left(\dfrac{1 - 2/n}{1+i}\right)^m}{i + 2/n}$
5	Sum of digits (SD)	$(C_i - C_{\text{sal}}) \dfrac{n - m + 1}{0.5n(n+1)}$	$(C_i - C_{\text{sal}}) \dfrac{m}{n(n+1)} (2n + 1 - m)$	$\dfrac{2(C_i - C_{\text{sal}})}{n(n+1)i}$ $\times [n - F_{RP,i,m} - (n-m)F_{SP,i,m}]$
6	Units of production (UP)	$(C_i - C_{\text{sal}}) \dfrac{M_m}{M}$	$(C_i - C_{\text{sal}}) \dfrac{\sum_1^m M_m}{M}$	$\dfrac{C_i - C_{\text{sal}}}{M} \sum_1^m \dfrac{M_m}{(1+i)^m}$

* Book value at end of mth year = C_i less accumulated depreciation for m years. Depreciation remaining for $n - m$ future years = book value at end of mth year less C_{sal}. For double-declining-balance depreciation, terminal value is not related to salvage value, but total write-off should be to salvage value.

52 MATHEMATICS OF COST COMPARISONS   3.10

to the salvage value. On the other hand, the book value must never fall below the salvage value as this would mean taking excessive depreciation.

The switch point for best policy occurs very close to the midlife of the asset if no salvage value is involved. With salvage value, the optimum for switching to straight line occurs beyond the midlife and depends on the ratio of salvage value to initial cost. In certain situations, the double-declining-balance-with-switch method has only a minor advantage over other methods.

Although the double-declining-balance method requires a factor $= 2/n$, it is possible and permissible to select any smaller factor, such as $1.5/n$.

It is permissible to depreciate individual properties by combining two or more assets into an account as well as by treating each as a separate account. These multiple-assets accounts are treated as a group for depreciation purposes referred to as *group depreciation*. This topic is discussed in the *Cost Engineers' Notebook* [3.16R11]. Group depreciation poses some problems for economic evaluation; these problems can be resolved by noting that for an item in a group the life for tax purposes is that of the group but the life for the economic comparison can be something else. Group depreciation is used widely for such items as pumps, motors, and the like, which would be an unnecessary burden if depreciated on an individual basis. Assets may be combined in numerous ways; e.g., same useful life, type of asset, function of asset, dates of acquisition, cost, location.

3.10 Comparison of methods

Table 3.10T1 is a summary of the relationships for depreciation for methods discussed in earlier sections. It now becomes possible to consider the relative benefits of different depreciation procedures. Table 3.10T2 shows the yearly depreciation for an asset by five different methods.

Table 3.10T2 Comparison of Depreciation Methods*

End of year	Yearly depreciation, $				
	Straight line	Sinking fund 10% per year	Declining balance	Double declining balance	Sum of digits
1	200.0	163.8	419.1	440.0	333.3
2	200.0	180.2	259.4	264.0	267.7
3	200.0	198.2	160.6	158.4	200.0
4	200.0	218.0	99.4	95.0	133.3
5	200.0	239.8	61.5	42.6†	66.7
	Present worth of 5 years of depreciation at 10% per year rate of return				
0	758.2	744.5	822.2	828.6	806.1

* Original cost = $1,100, salvage value = $100, and life = 5 years.
† Brought down to $100 salvage value.

In general, methods with accelerated depreciation show a higher present worth for the allowable depreciation costs, which is desirable because the owner has the use of capital for a longer time. However, the best method depends on the salvage value and the life of the asset.

The double-declining method yields the highest present worth for short-lived assets, whereas the sum-of-digits method is better for longer-lived assets. Since in declining balance a switch to straight line may be made to terminate with the proper salvage value, one source [3.16R11] has suggested the following:

For 1.5 declining balance switch to straight line at one-third-life
For double-declining balance switch to straight line at one-half-life

Other authors have indicated that double-declining methods with and without switch are similar, with sum-of-digits method being better for lives greater than 5 years. Others have indicated that the sum-of-digits method is most generally useful.

3.11 Special considerations

As mentioned previously, accelerated depreciation has become confused with the tax situation. The importance of accelerated depreciation in contributing to profitability lies in the greater present worth of larger depreciation allotments in the early years of an economic venture. In practice many companies use one depreciation method for tax purposes and another for internal use to maintain a better perspective for true costs and pricing. Sometimes a liability account is set up to be drawn against later when delayed taxes can become a burden.

The student should understand depreciation in its true perspective and recognize its fundamental nature although it is intermingled with taxes and even profitability. Because depreciation is an expense, the manner of allocation over the years has an effect on the profit for individual years. Cash flow, which by definition is the sum of depreciation plus profit, is discussed in a following chapter.

A depreciable asset may not be in service for the time set up for the depreciation program. If a machine becomes inoperable before it has been completely depreciated, there are provisions in the accounting procedure to allow for the unrecovered capital, such as loss on disposal. Conversely, if equipment is useful for longer periods than anticipated, it is not possible to charge additional depreciation for tax purposes. For pricing, however, some kind of cost for wear and tear might very well be included.

If on retirement or abandonment a machine has depreciation available for future years, immediate disposal may give a present-worth value which can be considered in an economic comparison, as illustrated in the following example.

Example 3.11E1 A machine has $300,000 book value, no salvage value, and 3 years of life remaining and is being depreciated by the straight-line method. If abandoned, it can be taken as an immediate loss on disposal. If the tax rate is 51% and money is worth 10% per year, find the present worth of the tax benefits by abandonment now.

Depreciation is $100,000 per year, and the savings due to tax benefit is tD, or $51,000 per year. If machine is retained, present worth of these tax savings is

$$P_{\text{ret}} = 51{,}000\left(\frac{1}{1.10} + \frac{1}{1.10^2} + \frac{1}{1.10^3}\right) = \$126{,}830$$

If disposed of now, the present worth of the tax benefit is

$P_{\text{aban}} = 300{,}000(0.51) = \$153{,}000$

The gain in present worth by abandoning now is

$153{,}000 - 126{,}830 = \$26{,}170$

3.12 Depletion

Depletion is a term used to describe the write-off of certain exhaustible natural resources such as mineral resources and oil and gas reservoirs. Depletion applies to production units withdrawn from the property, whereas depreciation is usually taken on a time basis. Although depletion is related to depreciation, there are important differences, in particular the tax situation. For tax purposes total depletion may exceed the original cost of the property, whereas depreciation is limited to original cost less estimated salvage value. The depletion allowance is supposed to be an incentive to encourage exploration for new resources as existing resources are used up.

Depletion is a complicated subject and requires special consideration because of the income tax treatment. The following discussion is summarized from the *Cost Engineers' Notebook* [3.16R11].

The effect of depletion is to increase cash flow by a factor $1 - t$ times the depletion allowance, where t is the tax rate expressed as a decimal. However, depletion applies only to exhaustible natural deposits, such as mineral property, oil and gas wells, or standing timber. There are two calculation methods, cost depletion and percentage depletion. The taxpayer can choose the method which gives him the higher depletion allowance in any year but must not deduct less than that allowable under cost depletion.

Under cost depletion, the annual expense allowance is the number of units sold during the year times the adjusted-basis original cost of property minus accumulated depreciation divided by the number of recoverable units in the property. When original cost and accumulated depletion are equal, no further cost depletion is allowed.

Under percentage depletion, the annual allowance is a fixed percentage of the gross income derived from the property during the year. The depletion allowance cannot exceed 50% of taxable income computed without depletion allowance. However, percentage depletion is not limited to original cost less salvage as is ordinarily true with depreciation of assets.

Table 3.12T1 illustrates the depletion applicable to oil and gas wells. The depletion is 27.5% of the annual gross income as limited by the 50% of taxable income criterion. The full 27.5% allowance applies whenever taxable income is at least 55% of gross income. In this case, gross income is $1,000. If expenses are $400 (case *A*), taxable income is $600 and depletion is the full 27.5% of gross income ($275). In case *B*, depletion is limited to 50% of taxable income.

Table 3.12T1 Percentage Depletion for Oil and Gas Wells

Item	Case A	Case B
Gross income	1,000	1,000
Expenses (excluding depletion)	400	700
Calculated taxable income	600	300
Percentage depletion	275	150
Actual taxable income	325	150
Tax at 48% rate	156	72
Net income	169	78
Add back depletion	275	150
Cash income	444	228

Depletion allowed is only 15% of gross income. If certain expenses can be shifted between accounting periods, cash flow can be increased by 24% of the expense. For example, if $50 expense in case B can be shifted to case A, overall cash flow for the two periods is increased $12.

When depletable property is being leased, the lessee excludes royalties paid to the lessor from his gross income for calculating depletion deductions. The lessor's gross income is the sum of any royalties received, excluding rentals not connected with the units produced. Advance royalties and bonuses received in expectation of future production are included in the gross income for depletion. When the lease is terminated, if there has been no production, no depletion is allowed. Therefore, any advance depletion taken must be included as fully taxable income in the year the lease is terminated. The effect of this on the lessor is to delay his taxes from the time the advance depletion was taken to the lease termination date. A way of avoiding the tax entirely would be to sell all financial interest in the property prior to termination of the lease. Of course, the market value when the property is sold will presumably take this into account.

Any rental payments paid by the lessee in order to defer development of a particular property constitute fully taxable income to the lessor. The lessee may elect either to deduct these rental payments as an expense each year or to capitalize them. If the property produces, these costs can be allocated to expense at that time. The lessee would maximize the present value of his tax credits by expensing these rental payments as they are paid and not setting them up as a capital item.

COST COMPARISON AFTER TAXES

3.13 Present worth after taxes

In Chap. 2 cost comparisons were made on a no-tax basis. In practice taxes enter, and the remainder of this chapter will develop the comparison of alternatives on an after-tax basis.

56   MATHEMATICS OF COST COMPARISONS 3.13

One effect introduced by the corporation tax is a reduction of the rate of return. If i is the rate of return before taxes, t the tax rate, and r the rate of return after taxes, all expressed as decimals, then

$$r = i(1 - t) \tag{3.13\#1}$$

If an investment compounds at a rate i before taxes, it will compound at a rate r after taxes.

Under existing rules corporation taxes are paid partly in the current year and partly in the succeeding year. It will be adequate to consider the tax paid in one sum at the end of the year.

Consider now an article that lasts n years with initial cost C_i, salvage value C_{sal}, and depreciable cost C_d, where

$$C_d = C_i - C_{\text{sal}} \tag{3.13\#2}$$

There is no tax consideration at the time the article is purchased. At the end of the first year depreciation amounting to $D_{f_1} C_d$, where D_{f_1} is the fractional depreciation, becomes available as an expense recognized for tax purposes. The taxable base is reduced $D_{f_1} C_d$ and a savings or reduction in taxes amounting to $D_{f_1} C_d t$ is realized. The time-cost diagram is:

```
       D_{f,1} C_d(t)  D_{f,2} C_d(t)  D_{f,3} C_d(t)    D_{f,(n-1)} C_d(t)  D_{f,n} C_d(t)
   0        1              2              3      ...       n-1                n
   |
   C_d
```

The present worth is

$$P = C_d - C_d t \left[\frac{D_{f_1}}{1+r} + \frac{D_{f_2}}{(1+r)^2} + \cdots + \frac{D_{f_n}}{(1+r)^n} \right] \tag{3.13\#3}$$

The sum of the terms within the brackets is the present worth of $1 of depreciation and depends upon the depreciation method selected. Whatever the method used, the equation can be written

$$P = C_d - C_d t \psi = C_d(1 - t\psi) \tag{3.13\#4}$$

where

$$\psi = \sum_1^n \frac{D_{f_m}}{(1+r)^m} \tag{3.13\#5}$$

The ψ factor depends upon r, n, and the method chosen for depreciation. It represents the present worth of $1 of depreciation and can be calculated for any values of r and n for any depreciation method. In particular for sum-of-digits and straight-line depreciation

$$\psi_{SD,r,n} = F_{SDP,r,n}$$

$$\psi_{SL,r,n} = F_{SLP,r,n}$$

3.13 DEPRECIATION AND TAXES—EQUIVALENCE AFTER TAXES

F_{SDP} converts sum-of-digits depreciation to a present worth and F_{SLP} converts straight-line depreciation to a present worth. Both factors are tabulated in Appendix 1, Table 1.

Sum-of-digits depreciation will be used for the remainder of this section with the understanding that any other method can be used. Equation (3.13#1) becomes

$$P = C_d(1 - tF_{SDP,r,n}) \qquad (3.13\#6)$$

It should be noted that for all depreciation methods

$$\psi_{1_r} = \frac{1}{1+r} = F_{SDP,r,1} \qquad (3.13\#7)$$

$$\psi_{\infty_r} = 0 \quad = F_{SDP,r,\infty} \qquad (3.13\#8)$$

Equation (3.13#6) can be converted to a unacost or capitalized cost by Eq. (2.2#8) or (2.7#3), respectively, giving

$$R = C_d F_{PR,r,n}(1 - tF_{SDP,r,n'}) \qquad (3.13\#9)$$

$$K = C_d F_{PK,r,n}(1 - tF_{SDP,r,n'}) \qquad (3.13\#10)$$

where n' is used to designate that the life for tax purposes can be different from n, the life for an economic study.

It now is possible to duplicate Table 2.8T1 on an after-tax basis utilizing the method just described for first determining present worth. Table 3.13T1 has been prepared in this manner.

For item 2 in the table, R is a uniform end-of-year cost occurring simultaneously with the tax instant. The cost after taxes is $R(1 - t)$ as of the end of each year for n years. The present worth by Eq. (2.2#4) with r substituted for i is

$$P = R(1 - t)\frac{(1+r)^n - 1}{r(1+r)^n} \qquad (3.13\#11)$$

For item 3, R_b, a uniform beginning-of-year cost, the tax credit $R_b t$ occurs at the end of the year. Combining the two as of the end of the year gives

$$R_b(1 + r) - R_b t = R_b\left(1 - \frac{t}{1+r}\right)(1 + r) \qquad (3.13\#12)$$

which can be converted to a present worth by Eq. (2.2#4) with r substituted for i.

For item 4, C_{ex}, an irregular cost occurring at the end of the xth year for an article lasting n years, the cost occurs simultaneously with the tax instant. The present worth is

$$P = C_{ex}(1 - t)\frac{1}{(1+r)^x} \qquad (3.13\#13)$$

For item 5, C_{bx}, an irregular cost occurring at the beginning of the xth year, the tax credit $C_{bx}t$ when brought forward to the beginning of the year becomes

Table 3.13T1 Summary of Unacost and Capitalized-cost Relationships with Tax

Item no.	Item	Present worth as a cost for n-year duration	Unacost — Algebraic expression
1	C_d Fully depreciable part of an initial cost for n-year life, n' years for tax purposes; $C_d = C_i - C_{sal}$	$C_d(1 - t\psi_{r_{n'}})$	$C_d(1 - t\psi_{r_{n'}}) \times \dfrac{r(1+r)^n}{(1+r)^n - 1}$
2	R Uniform end-of-year annual cost, depreciated fully at instant incurred	$R(1-t) \dfrac{(1+r)^n - 1}{r(1+r)}$	$R(1-t)$
3	R_b Uniform beginning-of-year annual cost, fully depreciated at end of year	$R_b\left(1 - \dfrac{t}{1+r}\right)(1+r) \times \dfrac{(1+r)^n - 1}{r(1+r)^n}$	$R_b\left(1 - \dfrac{t}{1+r}\right)(1+r)$
4	C_{ex} Irregular cost at end of xth year for article lasting n years, fully depreciated at instant incurred	$C_{ex} \dfrac{1-t}{(1+r)^x}$ or $\dfrac{C_{ex}}{(1+r)^x} \times [1 - t(1+r)\psi_{r_1}]$	$C_{ex} \dfrac{1-t}{(1+r)^x} \times \dfrac{r(1+r)^n}{(1+r)^n - 1}$
5	C_{bx} Irregular cost at beginning of xth year for article lasting n years, fully depreciated at end of year x	$C_{bx}\left(1 - \dfrac{t}{1+r}\right) \times \dfrac{1}{(1+r)^{x-1}}$ or $\dfrac{C_{bx}}{(1+r)^{x-1}}(1 - t\psi_{r_1})$	$C_{bx}\left(1 - \dfrac{t}{1+r}\right) \times \dfrac{1}{(1+r)^{x-1}} \times \dfrac{r(1+r)^n}{(1+r)^n - 1}$
6	C_{nd} Nondepreciable first cost such as land or an article that lasts forever	$C_{nd} \dfrac{(1+r)^n - 1}{(1+r)^n}$	$C_{nd} r$
7	C_{sal} Salvage value at end of nth year; treated as a nondepreciable first cost, an expense	$C_{sal} \dfrac{(1+r)^n - 1}{(1+r)^n}$	$C_{sal} r$

Unacost		Capitalized cost
Factor expression for sum-of-digits depreciation	*Algebraic expression*	*Factor expression for sum-of-digits depreciation*
$C_d(1 - tF_{SDP,r,n'})F_{PR,r,n}$	Multiply corresponding algebraic expression for unacost by $\dfrac{1}{r}$	$C_d(1 - tF_{SDP,r,n'})F_{PK,r,n}$
$R(1 - t)$		$R(1 - t)\dfrac{1}{r}$
$R_b(1 - tF_{SDP,r,1})(1 + r)$		$R_b(1 - tF_{SDP,r,1})F_{PK,r,1}$
$C_{ex}\dfrac{1}{(1+r)^x}$ $\times [1 - t(1+r)F_{SDP,r,1}]F_{PR,r,n}$		$C_{ex}\dfrac{1}{(1+r)^x}$ $\times [1 - t(1+r)F_{SDP,r,1}]F_{PK,r,n}$
$C_{bx}\dfrac{1 - tF_{SDP,r,1}}{(1+r)^{x-1}}F_{PR,r,n}$		$C_{bx}\dfrac{1 - tF_{SDP,r,1}}{(1+r)^{x-1}}F_{PK,r,n}$
$C_{nd}\,r$		C_{nd}
$C_{\text{sal}}\,r$		C_{sal}

$C_{bx}t/(1+r)$. The cost as of the beginning of the year is then reduced to a present worth at zero time, giving

$$P = \left(C_{bx} - \frac{C_{bx}t}{1+r}\right)\frac{1}{(1+r)^{x-1}} = C_{bx}\left(1 - \frac{t}{1+r}\right)\frac{1}{(1+r)^{x-1}} \qquad (3.13\#14)$$

If C_{ex} and C_{bx} cannot be written off in 1 year for tax purposes, substitute $F_{SDP,r,n'}$ for $F_{SDP,r,1}$ in items 3 and 4 of Table 3.13T1.

For item 6, C_{nd}, a nondepreciable expense such as land or working capital, an amount C_{nd} is invested now and fully recovered at the end of n years with no tax consideration. The present worth is

$$P = C_{nd} - \frac{C_{nd}}{(1+r)^n} = C_{nd}\frac{(1+r)^n - 1}{(1+r)^n} \qquad (3.13\#15)$$

Item 7 in Table 3.13T1 for salvage value C_{sal} is correct in showing the item as positive, an expense, and not a receipt. Salvage value is analogous to a nondepreciable expense, item 6. A sum is invested, and although it is fully recovered, the expense arises from the loss of interest. When there is no tax, it is possible to consider the pair C_i and C_{sal}, for which C_{sal} is a receipt. When taxes exist, the pair that must be chosen is C_d and C_{sal}, for which C_{sal} is a nondepreciable expense. The treatment of salvage value with taxes is analogous to item 8, Table 2.8T1, where C_i and C_{sal} are taken together in the form $C_i - C_{sal}$, which is C_d, the depreciable first cost. There C_{sal} appears as an expense. When taxes are a consideration, there is no choice. The initial cost must be segregated to the depreciable first cost C_d and the nondepreciable first cost C_{sal}. With this combination salvage value appears as an expense, with or without taxes.

The student should be able to make cost comparisons on an after-tax basis with the same facility as a no-tax basis developed in Chap. 2 and illustrated in Sec. 2.8 with several examples. Problems can be solved by two general methods. Each item can be reduced to a unacost or capitalized cost and the items added. On the other hand, each item can be reduced to a present worth and present worths of the same duration added and converted to unacost or capitalized cost to obtain a common denominator for different service lives.

Example 3.13E1 Two machines have the following cost comparison. If money is worth 10% per year, the tax rate is 50%, and sum-of-digits depreciation is used, which machine is more economical?

	A	B
First cost, $	18,000	24,000
Uniform end-of-year expense, $ per year	1,000	0
Salvage value, $	500	0
Service life, years	2	3
Life for tax purposes, years	5	5

3.14   **DEPRECIATION AND TAXES—EQUIVALENCE AFTER TAXES**   **61**

Refer to Table 3.13T1 and use the unacost expressions for items 1, 2, 7 in order. Unacost for machine A is

$$C_d(1 - tF_{SDP,10\%,5})F_{PR,10\%,2}$$
$$= (18,000 - 500)[1 - 0.50(0.80614)](0.57619) = \$6,018$$
$$R(1 - t) = 1,000(1 - 0.50) = 500$$
$$C_{sal}r = 500(0.10) = 50$$
$$R_A = \$6,568$$

Unacost for machine B by item 1, Table 3.13T1, is

$$C_d(1 - tF_{SDP,10\%,5})F_{PR,10\%,3} = 24,000[1 - 0.50(0.80614)](0.40211) = R_B = \$5,760$$

Machine B is the more economical.

Example 3.13E2   Repeat Example 2.8E6 using a 50% tax and sum-of-digits depreciation. The irregular expenses can be written off fully for tax purposes in the year incurred. Machine A can be written off in 4 years for tax purpose and machine B in 10 years.

The capitalized cost of machine A by Table 3.13T1 items 1, 2, 5, 5, 7 in order is

$$C_d(1 - tF_{SDP,10\%,4})F_{PK,10\%,4} = (10,000 - 0)[1 - 0.50(0.83013)](3.1547) = 18,453$$
$$R(1 - t)\frac{1}{r} = 3,000(1 - 0.50)\frac{1}{0.10} = 15,000$$
$$(C_{b_3})\frac{1 - 0.5(1/1.10)}{1.10^2} F_{PK,10\%,4} = 4,000\frac{0.54545}{1.21}3.1547 = 5,688$$
$$C_{b_4}\frac{1 - 0.5(1/1.10)}{1.10^3} F_{PK,10\%,4} = 1,500\frac{0.54545}{1.331}3.1547 = 1,939$$
$$C_{sal} = 0$$
$$K_A = \$41,080$$

The capitalized cost of machine B by Table 3.13T1, items 1, 2, and 7 in order, is

$$C_d(1 - tF_{SDP,10\%,10})F_{PK,10\%,10} = (95,000 - 20,000)[1 - 0.5(0.70099)](1.6275) = 79,280$$
$$R(1 - t)\frac{1}{r} = (1,000 - 6,000)(1 - 0.50)\frac{1}{0.10} = -25,000$$
$$C_{sal} = 20,000$$
$$K_B = \$74,280$$

Machine A is more economical. The savings per year for A over B by Eq. (2.7#5) is
$$r(K_B - K_A) = 0.10(74,280 - 41,080) = \$3,320 \text{ per year}$$

3.14   Nomenclature

B	Book value, $
C_{bx}	Irregular cost at beginning of xth year, $
C_d	Depreciable cost, $
C_{ex}	Irregular cost at end of xth year, $
C_i	Initial or first cost, $
C_{nd}	Nondepreciable cost, $
C_{sal}	Salvage value, $
D	Depreciation, $
DB	Declining-balance method of depreciation
DDB	Double-declining-balance method of depreciation
D_f	Fractional depreciation, decimal

62 MATHEMATICS OF COST COMPARISONS 3.15

F_{DB} Factor for declining-balance depreciation, decimal
F_{DDB} Factor for double-declining-balance depreciation, decimal
F_{PK} Factor to convert P to K; capitalized-cost factor, no units
F_{PR} Factor to convert P to R; capital-recovery factor, year^{-1}
F_{PS} Factor to convert P to S; compound-interest factor, no units
F_{RP} Factor to convert R to P; unacost present-worth factor, years
F_{SD} Factor for sum-of-digits depreciation, decimal
F_{SDP} Present worth of $1 for sum-of-digits depreciation, decimal
F_{SLP} Present worth of $1 for straight-line depreciation, decimal
F_{SP} Factor to convert S to P; present-worth factor, decimal
F_{UP} Factor for units-of-production depreciation, decimal
i Rate of return, generally before taxes, decimal/year
K Capitalized cost, $
m A number, generally the mth year
M Units of production
n A number, generally the service life of an item, years
n' Service life for tax purposes, years
P Present worth, $
r Rate of return, generally after taxes, decimal/year
R Uniform end-of-year annual amount; unacost, $ per year
R_b Uniform beginning-of-year annual amount, $ per year
R_s Sinking-fund deposit, $ per year
S Future worth, $
SD   Sum-of-digits method of depreciation
SF   Sinking-fund method of depreciation
SL   Straight-line method of depreciation
t Tax rate, decimal
UP   Units-of-production method of depreciation
ψ Psi, present worth of $1 of depreciation, decimal

3.15 Problems

P1. A furniture manufacturer buys special new manufacturing equipment for $1.8 million that has an estimated salvage value of $0.3 million. Find (a) the life for tax purposes from tables and (b) the book value at 6 years for sinking-fund depreciation at 8% per year and for double-declining-balance depreciation. Compare your calculations with results indicated by Table 3.10T1.

P2. A paper-box manufacturer uses cutting dies that cost $45,000 with a salvage value of $5,000. The dies are expected to produce 32 million boxes before being replaced. If the projected production schedule for 4 consecutive years is 2, 8, 16, and 6 million boxes, compare the annual depreciation by double-declining-balance and units of production depreciation.

P3. Two alternative presses A and B both show a 13.3% of original value for depreciation in the fourth year using sum-of-digits depreciation. However, A has a long life and B a short life. What is the total life of each neglecting any salvage value?

P4. Compare the present worth for the depreciation using straight-line, double-declining-balance with switch at the end of the fourth year, and sum-of-digits depreciation for an asset valued at $14,000 at zero time with $2,000 salvage value after 6 years and with money worth 12% per year.

P5. The gross income for a gas-well property is $1.2 million for 1 year, and the profits tax is 48%. What is the annual net cash flow if the annual expenses for the operation including depletion are (a) $0.7 million, (b) $0.5 million?

P6. Repeat Example 2.8E1. Use sum-of-digits depreciation, money worth 10% per year after a 52% tax, and a 10-year life for tax purposes for new machine. Maintenance expense, for tax purposes, is a repair job.

P7. In Prob. 3.15P6 what is the savings if the old machine can be repaired for $2,500?

P8. Repeat Example 2.8E3. Use sum-of-digits depreciation, money worth 10% per year after a 52% tax, resurfacing job written off in 1 year for tax purposes, and new floor written off in the years of its life.

P9. Repeat Example 2.8E4. Tax rate is 52%, relining job can be written off in 1 year for tax purposes, 4-year stack in 4 years, and depreciation method is sum of digits.

P10. Repeat Example 2.8E6. Money is worth 10% per year after a 48% tax rate using straight-line depreciation. Machine A will be written off in 8 years for tax purposes, machine B in 10 years. The irregular expenses are maintenance expenses that are written off in 1 year. Treat the savings from quality control as regular income.

P11. Repeat Prob. 2.12P14. Now the bond is bought to yield 4% per year after a 20% tax.

P12. Repeat Prob. 2.12P22. Money is worth 20% per year after a 48% tax, depreciation method is sum of digits, and life for tax purposes is 10 years for all machines.

3.16 References

R1. Anonymous: *MAPI Capital Goods Review*, nos. 27 and 28, 1956.
R2. Grant, Eugene L., and P. T. Norton, Jr.: "Depreciation," rev. ed., The Ronald Press Company, New York, 1955.
R3. Internal Revenue Service: Depreciation, Investment Credit, Amortization, Depletion, *Document* 5050, December, 1963.
R4. Jelen, F. C.: Consider Income Tax in Cost Analyses, *Chem. Eng.*, September, 1957, pp. 271–275.
R5. *J. Taxation*.
R6. Lyon, James T.: "Depreciation and Taxes," Tax Management, Inc., Washington, 1962.
R7. Meig, J. L.: "Depreciation and Replacement Policy," Quadrangle Books, Inc., Chicago, 1961.
R8. Tax Institute Inc.: "Depreciation and Taxes: A symposium," Princeton, N.J., 1959.
R9. *Taxes*.
R10. Terborgh, George: The Choice of Accelerated Depreciation Methods for Age—Heterogeneous Accounts, *MAPI-CTA Study*, 1964.
R11. Thorne, H. C., R. O. Carlson, and L. D. Thomas: How Taxes Affect Economic Evaluation, *Cost Engineers' Notebook*, D-7.8, 1965; see also *Hydrocarbon Process.*, November, 1964, pp. 225–232.

4
Continuous Interest and Discounting

W. B. Hirschmann and J. R. Brauweiler

4.1 Logic for continuous interest

Interest can be compounded periodically, e.g., annually, semiannually, or even daily, or it can be compounded continuously. Annual discounting is appropriate for handling mortgages, bonds, and similar financial transactions, which require payments or receipts at discrete times. In most businesses, however, transactions occur throughout the year; and these circumstances suggest a continuous flow of money, for which continuous compounding and discounting is more realistic than annual compounding and discounting.

This chapter develops formulas for discounting and compounding cash flows on a continuous basis. It also illustrates how continuous discounting readily and simply copes with the variety of cash flows that might result from an investment over its life.

4.2 Continuous interest as an operator

If i is the nominal interest rate expressed as a decimal and compounding occurs p times per year, then

$$\left(1 + \frac{i}{p}\right)^p$$

Table 4.2T1 Comparison of Compounding Factors

Period	Relationship	For $i = 0.06$	Factor for $i = 0.06$
Annually	$(1+i)^1$	1.06^1	1.06000
Semiannually	$\left(1+\dfrac{i}{2}\right)^2$	1.03^2	1.06090
Quarterly	$\left(1+\dfrac{i}{4}\right)^4$	1.015^4	1.0613635
Monthly	$\left(1+\dfrac{i}{12}\right)^{12}$	1.005^{12}	1.0616778
Daily	$\left(1+\dfrac{i}{365}\right)^{365}$	1.00016^{365}	1.0618305
Continuously	e^i	$e^{0.06}$	1.0618365

is the value of 1 at the end of 1 year, as developed in Sec. 2.1. Table 4.2T1 shows the effect of increasing the number of compounding periods in 1 year. Note that there is little difference between the factors for monthly and continuous compounding.

By Eq. (2.1#4)

$$S = P\left(1+\frac{i}{p}\right)^{np}$$

where S is the future amount of a present amount P after n years with nominal decimal interest rate per year i compounded p times per year. In the limit with p equal to infinity for continuous compounding

$$1+\frac{i}{p} = e^i$$

$$S = Pe^{in} \qquad (4.2\#1)$$

where e is the naperian constant 2.71828 . . . . Also solving for P in terms of S,

$$P = Se^{-in} \qquad (4.2\#2)$$

Thus the factor e^{in} is an operator that moves \$1 n years with the calendar at a nominal decimal rate per year i. Similarly, the factor e^{-in} is an operator that moves \$1 n years against the calendar at a nominal decimal rate per year i.

Generally there is no confusion between periodic and continuous interest inasmuch as the two are never used together. However, in this book a bar over a letter will be used when necessary to emphasize that continuous interest or continuous flow is intended. Thus in keeping with the terminology of Chap. 2,

$$F_{PS,\bar{i},n} = e^{+in} \qquad (4.2\#3)$$

$$F_{SP,\bar{i},n} = e^{-in} \qquad (4.2\#4)$$

66 MATHEMATICS OF COST COMPARISONS   4.2

The factor $F_{PS,\bar{\imath},n}$ converts a single amount P to a future amount S, with continuous interest at nominal decimal rate i per year, n years with the calendar. The factor is tabulated in Appendix 2, Table 1. Similarly, the factor $F_{SP,\bar{\imath},n}$ converts S to P, is a present-worth factor for continuous compounding, and is tabulated in Appendix 2, Table 2.

A useful characteristic of continuous compounding and discounting factors is evident from the tabulations. Note that in Appendix 2, Tables 1 and 2, i and n appear as a product in. Because of this circumstance, a continuous-discount function has the same value for each combination of interest rate and time period which has the same product. Consequently, continuous discounting requires only one table of factors, based on the product in, while annual discounting requires many tables, one for each interest rate.

This mathematical characteristic also permits continuous factors to be placed on a discounted cash-flow slide rule so that present-worth and other calculations can be made even more simply because of not having to refer to tables of factors.[1] The tables for continuous discounting are much more compact than those for periodic discounting. In addition, the continuous form combines readily with several functions describing common cash-flow patterns so that the summation (integral) of the present worth is easily found from one or two tabulated factors. This convenience is shown by the simple formulas and procedures developed in this chapter.

It should be noted that in this chapter i is a decimal annual rate. The discounting or compounding interval determines what the effective annual rate will be. The relationship between effective interest rate and nominal interest rate was given by Eq. (2.1#5) and for continuous compounding becomes

$$\text{Effective interest rate} = e^i - 1 \qquad (4.2\#5)$$

The converse relationship is

$$i_{\text{nom}} = 2.303 \log(1 + i_{\text{eff}}) \qquad (4.2\#6)$$

In Eq. (4.2#6) the reference is to common logarithms. Equations (4.2#5) and (4.2#6) permit conversions from nominal to effective rates and vice versa. They can be useful because at times a problem arises in terms of annual interest but discount factor tables may be available only for continuous interest, or the converse.

Figure 4.2F1 shows a comparison of equivalent annual and continuous rates. Thus by the figure

  5% annual = 4.9% continuous
 10% annual = 9.5% continuous
 20% annual = 18.2% continuous
 30% annual = 26.2% continuous

---
[1] Available from the Graphic Calculator Co., Barrington, Ill.

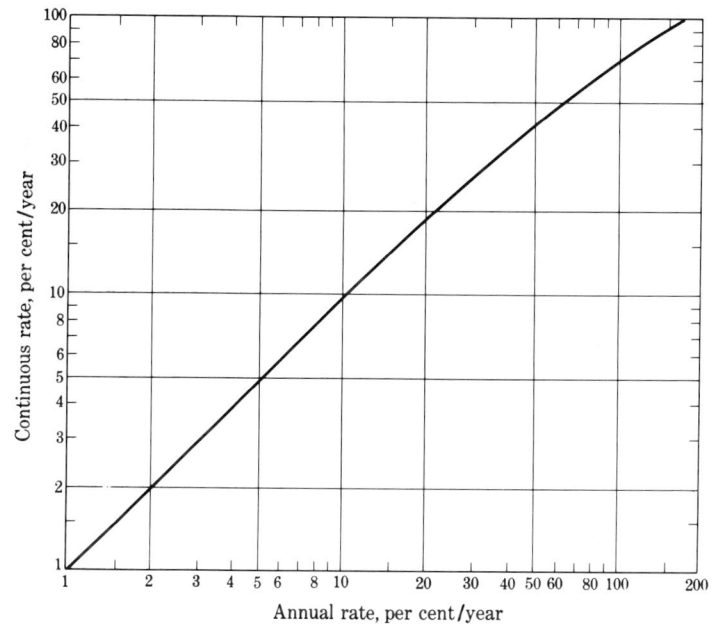

Fig. 4.2F1 Equivalent annual and continuous rates.

Tables 1 and 2 of Appendix 2 can be extended because of the properties of exponentials. Thus, from Appendix 2, Table 1, knowing further that $e^{0.003} = 1.0030$,

$$e^{10.613} = e^5 e^5 e^{0.61} e^{0.003}$$
$$= 148.41(148.41)(1.8404)(1.0030) = 40{,}666$$

Example 4.2E1 If the discount rate is 10% per year, what is the present worth of $2,500 to be received as a single payment 20 years hence?
By Eq. (4.2#2) and Appendix 2, Table 2,

$$P = Se^{-in} = 2{,}500e^{-(0.10)(20)} = 2{,}500(0.1353) = \$338.25$$

Example 4.2E2 If $5 is received now, what will it amount to in 20 years at 30% per year interest?
By Eq. (4.2#1) and Appendix 2, Table 1,

$$S = Pe^{in} = 5e^{(0.30)(20)} = 5(400.4) = \$2{,}002$$

4.3 Uniform flow

In the previous section, compounding and discounting were performed on a single amount. In this section the operations will be performed on a continuous flow. Suppose that an amount flows at the rate $\bar{R}$ per year for n years. Consider a small interval of time dX starting X years from now, as in Fig. 4.3F1. The flow during this interval is given by rate multiplied by time and is $\bar{R}\,dX$. The present worth for this small element of time from Eq. (4.2#2) is

$$P_{,\text{elem}} = \bar{R}\,dX\,e^{-iX}$$

68   MATHEMATICS OF COST COMPARISONS   4.3

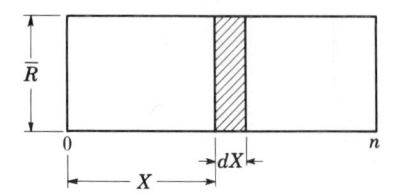

Fig. 4.3F1 Discounting a uniform flow.

and for all the elements

$$P = \bar{R}\int_0^n e^{-iX}\,dX = \bar{R}\left[\frac{e^{-iX}}{-i}\right]_0^n = \bar{R}\,\frac{1 - e^{-in}}{i} \tag{4.3\#1}$$

If the relationship above is multiplied and divided by n, it becomes

$$P = n\bar{R}\left[\frac{1 - e^{-in}}{in}\right] \tag{4.3\#2}$$

The value $n\bar{R}$ is the *total flow* for the period. The factor within the brackets now appears as a function of in only and can be tabulated compactly. In the terminology of this book

$$F_{\bar{R}P,\bar{\imath},n} = \frac{1 - e^{-in}}{in} \tag{4.3\#3}$$

and

$$F_{P\bar{R},\bar{\imath},n} = \frac{in}{1 - e^{-in}} \tag{4.3\#4}$$

The factor $F_{\bar{R}P,\bar{\imath},n}$, which converts $n\bar{R}$ to P, is tabulated in Appendix 2, Table 3, as the evaluation of $(1 - e^{-x})/x$, where $x = in$.

Example 4.3E1 A mine is expected to yield a cash income after taxes of $20,000 per year continuously for each of the next 15 years. If the minimum acceptable rate of return on investment is 12% per year, find the maximum amount that can be economically justified for buying the mine.

By Eq. (4.3#2) and Appendix 2, Table 3,

$$P = (n\bar{R})F_{\bar{R}P,0.12,15} = 15(20{,}000)(0.4637) = \$139{,}110$$

Example 4.3E2 If $1 per day is invested as received at 8% per year interest, what will the sum be in 15 years?

First find the present worth of the uniform flow of $365 per year by Eq. (4.3#2) and Appendix 2, Table 3,

$$P = 15(365)F_{\bar{R}P,0.08,15} = 15(365)(0.5823) = 3{,}188$$

Next convert to a future worth by Eq. (4.2#1) and Appendix 2, Table 1,

$$S = 3{,}188 e^{(0.08)(15)} = 3{,}188(3.3201) = \$10{,}584$$

Example 4.3E3 The parents of a baby plan to save enough to send it through college. How much must they invest monthly in 4% per year continuous-interest bonds to accumulate the $12,000 they figure will be needed 17 years hence?

Present worth of the $12,000 needed is by Eq. (4.2#2) and Appendix 2, Table 2,

$$P = 12{,}000e^{-(0.04)(17)} = 12{,}000(0.5066) = 6{,}079.20$$

which in turn can be converted to a yearly uniform flow by Eq. (4.3#2) and Appendix 2, Table 3,

$$6{,}079.20 = 17\bar{R}F_{\bar{R}P,0.04,17} = 17\bar{R}(0.7256)$$
$$\bar{R} = \$492.83 \text{ per year}$$

or

$$\frac{492.83}{12} = \$41.07 \text{ per month}$$

4.4 Flow changing at an exponential rate

It is appropriate at this point to highlight an aspect that is often unrecognized or overlooked: the most important, and perhaps the most difficult part, of an economic analysis is making a realistic estimate of what the future cash flows will prove to be. At times, this step seems elementary, but the simplicity can be deceptive. Consider a homeowner who has a 25-year 5% mortgage requiring payments every month. This seems like a straightforward cash flow: money loaned in a lump sum and repaid regularly. But what about the initial fee for writing the mortgage? What happens if the homeowner loses his job and income or dies? What about the refinance charges if he sells his home and moves to a different one?

Changes such as these are more likely to happen than not with the cash flows of any investment. Recognizing that such changes occur is more appropriate than assuming that there will be no change; but projecting them realistically is a challenge.

During initial scoping studies, it can be convenient to assume level performance—to ignore change or assume there will be none—in order to simplify the analysis. It is important to recognize, though, that this assumption is being made and to interpret the results accordingly. In real life or for a definitive analysis, such an assumption can rarely be made with safety; it may not only be misleading but disastrous.

This chapter will not dwell on methods or techniques of projecting cash flows. As a point of departure, though, it is convenient to recognize that changes which seem erratic over the short term often move in regular trends over the long term. Wage rates seem to increase continuously, and competition continually erodes profit margins. Such trends can be readily discounted or compounded by the continuous method.

If an initial flow R_0 dollars per year, increases continuously at a rate g per year expressed as a decimal, the rate of flow at any time X by analogy with Eq. (4.2#1) is

$$R_x = R_0 e^{gx}$$

Consider a small interval of time dX starting X years from now, as in Fig. 4.4F1. The flow for this interval is $R_0 e^{gX} dX$. The present worth for this small element of

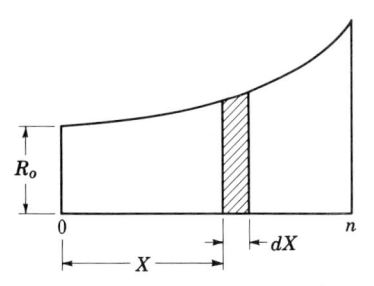

Fig. 4.4F1 Discounting a flow changing at an exponential rate.

flow from Eq. (4.2#2) is
$$P_{\text{elem}} = R_0 e^{gX} \, dX \, e^{-iX} = R_0 e^{(g-i)X} \, dX$$
and for all the elements
$$P = R_0 \int_0^n e^{(g-i)X} \, dX = R_0 \frac{e^{(g-i)n} - 1}{g - i}$$
$$= nR_0 \frac{1 - e^{-(i-g)n}}{(i-g)n} = (nR_0) F_{\bar{R}P, i-g, n} \tag{4.4#1}$$

Thus, the present worth is easily calculated from a knowledge of the initial flow rate and from the factors tabulated in Appendix 2, Table 3.

Equation (4.4#1) holds if g is negative, i.e., the flow is decreasing at a rate g per year, provided of course that g is introduced as a negative number.

Example 4.4E1 Repeat Example 4.3E1 but with a forecast that inflation will raise prices 3% per year continuously.
By Eq. (4.4#1) and Appendix 2, Table 3,
$$P = nR_0 F_{\bar{R}P, 0.12-0.03, 15} = 15(20{,}000)(0.5487) = \$164{,}610$$

Example 4.4E2 Repeat 4.3E1 with the condition that the mine will become gradually depleted so that its net income declines at the rate of 5% per year.
Here $i = 0.12$ and $g = -0.05$. Thus $i - g = 0.12 - (-0.05) = 0.17$. By Eq. (4.4#1)
$$P = 15(20{,}000) F_{\bar{R}P, 0.17, 15} = 15(20{,}000)(0.3615) = \$108{,}450$$

Example 4.4E3 Repeat 4.3E1 subject to both an inflation rate of 3% per year and a depletion rate of 5% per year.
Here $i - g = 0.12 - 0.03 - (-0.05) = 0.14$, and Eq. (4.4#1) becomes
$$P = 15(20{,}000) F_{\bar{R}P, 0.14, 15} = 15(20{,}000)(0.4179) = \$125{,}370$$

4.5 Flow declining in a straight line to zero

Consider Fig. 4.5F1, in which an initial flow, R_0 dollars per year, declines to zero by a straight-line relationship in n years. At time X the flow is R_x, and by similar triangles
$$\frac{R_x}{n - X} = \frac{R_0}{n}$$

4.5   CONTINUOUS INTEREST AND DISCOUNTING   71

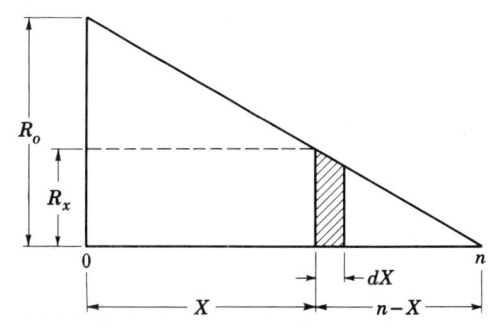

Fig. 4.5F1   Discounting a flow declining in a straight line to zero.

or

$$R_x = R_0\left(1 - \frac{X}{n}\right) \tag{4.5\#1}$$

In a small interval of time dX starting X years from now, the flow for the interval is

$$R_x\, dX = R_0\left(1 - \frac{X}{n}\right) dX$$

and the present worth for this small element of flow is, from Eq. (4.2#2),

$$P_{\text{elem}} = R_0\left(1 - \frac{X}{n}\right) dX\, e^{-iX}$$

For all the elements

$$P = R_0 \int_0^n \left(1 - \frac{X}{n}\right) e^{-iX}\, dX = R_0 \int_0^n e^{-iX}\, dX - \frac{R_0}{n} \int_0^n X e^{-iX}\, dX \tag{4.5\#2}$$

The first integral on the right has already been evaluated and is

$$R_0 \frac{1 - e^{-in}}{i}$$

Tables of integrals show

$$\int X e^{-aX}\, dX = -\frac{e^{-aX}}{a^2}(aX + 1)$$

so that the second integral on the right of Eq. (4.5#2) is

$$-\frac{R_0}{n}\left[-\frac{e^{-iX}}{i^2}(iX + 1)\right]_0^n = \frac{R_0}{i}\left(e^{-in} + \frac{e^{-in}}{in} - \frac{1}{in}\right)$$

The combined integrals on the right of Eq. (4.5#2) become

$$P = \frac{R_0}{i}\left(1 - e^{-in} + e^{-in} + \frac{e^{-in}}{in} - \frac{1}{in}\right) = \frac{R_0}{i}\left(1 - \frac{1 - e^{-in}}{in}\right)$$

MATHEMATICS OF COST COMPARISONS

The latter can be written

$$P = \frac{nR_0}{2}\frac{2}{in}\left(1 - \frac{1-e^{-in}}{in}\right) \qquad (4.5\#3)$$

The total flow Q is the area of Fig. 4.5F1 and is $nR_0/2$. Finally, Eq. (4.5#3) becomes

$$P = Q\left[\frac{2}{in}\left(1 - \frac{1-e^{-in}}{in}\right)\right] \qquad (4.5\#4)$$

A table of discount factors for such a flow is the evaluation of the bracketed terms on the right, i.e.,

$$\frac{2}{x}\left(1 - \frac{1-e^{-x}}{x}\right) \quad \text{with} \quad x = in$$

and is tabulated in Appendix 2, Table 4. This type of flow approximates sum-of-digits (SD) depreciation and in symbols is

$$F_{SDP,i,n} = \frac{2}{in}\left(1 - \frac{1-e^{-in}}{in}\right) \qquad (4.5\#5)$$

Appendix 2, Table 4, is commonly referred to as the *years-digits table*.

Example 4.5E1 A machine costs \$150,000 and can be depreciated over 20 years by sum-of-digits method of depreciation. Find the present worth of the depreciation, before taxes, if the discount rate is 16% per year.

By Eqs. (4.5#4) and (4.5#5) and Appendix 2, Table 4,

$$P = QF_{SDP,\bar{i},n} = 150{,}000 F_{SDP,0.16,20} = 150{,}000(0.4376)$$
$$= \$65{,}640$$

Internal Revenue Service regulations effectively require depreciation charges to begin at the middle of a calendar year. Consequently, if a plant begins operation just before the end of a calendar year, discounting of the actual depreciation cash flow is more closely approximated by substituting $n - \frac{1}{2}$ for n in the above function and $n + \frac{1}{2}$ if the plant goes on-stream just after the beginning of a year.

Example 4.5E2 Find the present worth of the machine in Example 4.5E1 if it is expected to begin operation in December.
The previous calculation becomes

$$P = 150{,}000 F_{SDP,0.16,20-0.5} = 150{,}000 F_{SDP,3.12} = 150{,}000(0.4446) = \$66{,}690$$

4.6 Discounting with improving performance—learning

Experience shows that practice makes perfect—that a thing can always be done better, not only the second time, but each succeeding time by trying. This experience is often reflected in a progressive increase in output or performance of a plant through increased skill of workers, advances in technology, resourcefulness of management, bottleneck removal, and a general striving to do things better. Such expected improvement can be reflected by achievement or learning as developed more fully in Chap. 9. For the presentation here assume that the learning factor for a plant unit is manifested as an increase in profit margin M. Assume an exponential relationship such that

$$M_T = M_0(2 - e^{-kT}) \qquad (4.6\#1)$$

where M_T = profit margin at time T

M_0 = initial profit margin

k = empirical constant

The present worth at i interest rate on such flow over T years is

$$\begin{aligned}P &= \int_0^T M_0(2 - e^{-kT})e^{-iT}\, dT \\ &= 2M_0 T \frac{1 - e^{-iT}}{iT} - M_0 T \frac{1 - e^{-(i+k)T}}{(i+k)T} \\ &= 2(M_0 T)F_{\bar{R}P,i,n} - (M_0 T)F_{\bar{R}P,\overline{i+k},n} \qquad (4.6\#2)\end{aligned}$$

Equation (4.6#2) can be combined with a flow changing at an exponential rate. Suppose the selling price of each production unit changes such that the profit margin changes continuously at a rate g per year, then corresponding to Eq. (4.6#1) the relationship is

$$M_T = M_0 e^{gT}(2 - e^{-kT}) \qquad (4.6\#3)$$

which by an analogous procedure leads to

$$P = 2(M_0 T)F_{\bar{R}P,\overline{i-g},n} - (M_0 T)F_{\bar{R}P,\overline{i+k-g},n} \qquad (4.6\#4)$$

In practice g is usually negative and in such cases must be introduced as a negative number.

Example 4.6E1 A plant is expected to have an initial profit margin of $100,000 per year. Find the present worth at 8% per year discount rate of this margin for 20 years of operation if:

(a) Profit margin and plant performance stay level.
(b) Performance traces an achievement curve such that

$$M_T = M_0(2 - e^{-0.10T})$$

(c) Performance traces the same curve, but margin shrinks 3% per year.

The following factors are available from Appendix 2, Table 3.

$$F_{\bar{R}P,0.08,20} = 0.4988$$
$$F_{\bar{R}P,0.08+0.10,20} = 0.2702$$
$$F_{\bar{R}P,0.08+0.03,20} = 0.4042$$
$$F_{\bar{R}P,0.08+0.10+0.03,20} = 0.2345$$

Part (a) is given by Eq. (4.3#2)

$$P = 100{,}000(20)(0.4988) = \$997{,}600$$

Part (b) is given by Eq. (4.6#2)

$$P = 2(100{,}000)(20)(0.4988) - 100{,}000(20)(0.2702) = \$1{,}454{,}800$$

Part (c) is given by Eq. (4.6#4)

$$P = 2(100{,}000)(20)(0.4042) - 100{,}000(20)(0.2345) = \$1{,}147{,}800$$

4.7 Unaflow—capital-recovery factor

In Sec. 4.3 a uniform flow was converted to a present worth or present value. The inverse of that procedure, the conversion of a present value to a uniform flow, will be considered in this section. Solving Eq. (4.3#2) for $\bar{R}$ gives

$$\bar{R} = \frac{P}{n} \frac{1}{(1 - e^{-in})/in} \qquad (4.7\#1)$$

which by Eq. (4.3#3) becomes

$$\bar{R} = \frac{P}{n} \frac{1}{F_{\bar{R}P,\bar{i},n}} \qquad (4.7\#2)$$

Equations (4.7#1) and (4.7#2) are important. They permit transforming a present value P having n years duration to a uniform flow. $\bar{R}$ will be referred to as *unaflow* and is analogous to unacost in periodic compounding. $\bar{R}$ could also be called the continuous capital-recovery amount.

Unaflow is important because like unacost it can be made the basis for comparing articles or systems having different service lives. It reduces all service lives to a common denominator, equivalent uniform flow.

Example 4.7E1 A firm has the option of getting a patent license by a single payment of $50,000 or royalty payments of $5,000 per year for the 17-year life of the patent. If the payments can be expensed in either case, and if the firm earns 15% per year before taxes, which is the more attractive choice?

Unaflow for royalty payments is $5,000 per year, as given. Unaflow for purchase of patent by Eq. (4.7#2) and Appendix 2, Table 3, is

$$\bar{R} = \frac{50{,}000}{17} \frac{1}{F_{\bar{R}P,0.15,17}} = \frac{50{,}000}{17} \frac{1}{0.3615} = \$8{,}136$$

The annual royalties of $5,000 per year are thus cheaper for this firm. The ratio of costs, purchase to lease, is $8{,}136/5{,}000 = 1.6272$.

The calculation assumes that in both cases the tax depreciation will be taken at a uniform rate and will cancel out as affecting both alternatives equally.

Example 4.7E2 A $15,000 mortgage is to be repaid over 20 years at 6% per year interest. Find the monthly payments.

By Eq. (4.7#2) and Appendix 2, Table 3, unaflow is

$$R = \frac{15{,}000}{20}\frac{1}{F_{\bar{R}P,0.06,20}} = \frac{15{,}000}{20}\frac{1}{0.5823} = \$1{,}288$$

That is, the flow must be $1,288 per year, or

$$\frac{\$1{,}288}{12} = \$107.33 \text{ per month}$$

4.8 Capitalized cost

Capitalized cost, like unaflow, can be used to compare articles or systems having different service lives. It reduces all service lives to a common denominator, i.e., present value on the basis, for mathematical purposes, of service forever.

Consider an article that has an initial cost C and lasts n years. The present worth of supplying service forever is

$$P_\infty = Ce^{-i0} + Ce^{-in} + Ce^{-2in} + Ce^{-3in} + \cdots$$

which is an infinite geometrical series with first term C and ratio e^{-in}. The sum is given by Eq. (2.2#2), and letting $P_\infty = K$,

$$K = \left[\frac{1 - (e^{-in})^\infty}{1 - e^{-in}}\right]C = \frac{1}{1 - e^{-in}}C \qquad (4.8\#1)$$

The bracketed term on the right converts a present worth of n years duration to a capitalized cost; i.e.,

$$K = P_n \frac{1}{1 - e^{-in}} \qquad (4.8\#2)$$

or

$$K = P_n \frac{e^{in}}{e^{in} - 1} \qquad (4.8\#3)$$

where the symbol P_n emphasizes that P is a present worth representing n years duration.

Equations (4.8#2) and (4.8#3) are important because they are the basis for using the capitalized-cost concept with continuous interest. Equation (4.8#3) is the more convenient form if Tables for e^{in} are available, as in the book, Appendix 2, Table 1. The reader is referred to Chap. 2 for a more complete discussion of capitalized cost.

A relationship between capitalized cost K and unaflow $\bar{R}$ is easily derived. The present worth of a unaflow $\bar{R}$ for n years is, by Eq. (4.3#2),

$$P_n = n\bar{R}\frac{1 - e^{in}}{in}$$

and the capitalized cost of this present worth becomes, by Eq. (4.8#2),

$$K = n\bar{R}\,\frac{1-e^{-in}}{in}\,\frac{1}{1-e^{-in}} = \frac{\bar{R}}{i}$$

that is,

$$\bar{R} = iK \qquad (4.8\#4)$$

Equation (4.8#4) for continuous interest and unaflow is analogous to the corresponding relationship $R = iK$, Eq. (2.7#6), for periodic interest and unacost.

Example 4.8E1 Repeat Example 4.7E1 on the basis of capitalized cost. Capitalized cost of the royalty payments, by Eq. (4.8#4), is

$$K = \frac{\bar{R}}{i} = \frac{5{,}000}{0.15} = 33{,}333$$

Capitalized cost of purchase is given by Eq. (4.8#3), which, using Appendix 2, Table 1, becomes

$$K = 50{,}000\,\frac{e^{(0.15)(17)}}{e^{(0.15)(17)}-1} = 50{,}000\,\frac{12.807}{12.807-1} = 54{,}235$$

It is cheaper to pay the royalties. The ratio of costs, purchase to lease, is $54{,}235/33{,}333 = 1.6271$. This checks the calculation by unaflow in Example 4.7E1.

Example 4.8E2 In a given exposure, a paint job lasts 4 years and costs \$0.20 per square foot. A supplier offers a new coating which is claimed to last 20 years but costs \$0.60 per square foot. Is it economically attractive to change to the coating which lasts five times as long and costs only three times as much, if money is worth 10%? Neglect taxes.

Capitalized costs can be calculated from Eq. (4.8#3) and Appendix 2, Table 3, and are for the 4- and 20-year jobs, respectively,

$$K_4 = \$0.20\,\frac{e^{(0.10)(4)}}{e^{(0.10)(4)}-1} = 0.20\,\frac{1.4918}{0.4918} = 0.6067$$

$$K_{20} = \$0.60\,\frac{e^{(0.10)(20)}}{e^{(0.10)(20)}-1} = 0.60\,\frac{7.3891}{6.3891} = 0.6939$$

The 4-year coating is the more economical. The savings as flow per year per square foot can be obtained from Eq. (4.8#4) and is

$$\bar{R} = i(K_{20} - K_4) = 0.10(0.6939 - 0.6067) = 0.00872$$

That is, use of the 4-year coating saves \$0.00872 per year per square foot in comparison with the 20-year coating.

4.9 Income tax

The reader is referred to Chap. 3 for a detailed development of the effect of income tax using periodic interest. This section is concerned with the inclusion of income tax with continuous interest. Basically nothing new is involved. Suppose an item has a depreciable first cost C_d, that it lasts n years and can be written off in n years for tax purposes, that discounting will be on a continuous basis at a decimal rate r per year after taxes, and that the decimal tax rate is t. Then Eq. (3.13#4) can be written

$$P_n = C_d(1 - t\psi) \qquad (4.9\#1)$$

where P_n is the present value for n years and ψ is the present value of \$1 of depreciation discounted continuously at rate r. The value of ψ depends upon the method of depreciation used and can be calculated for any method. For this chapter only two methods are considered, straight line and sum of digits.

Straight-line depreciation (SL) is treated as a uniform flow, i.e., as uniform continuous depreciation. For a total flow of unity, recalling that ψ is a present worth, Eq. (4.3#2) gives, with n' the life for tax purposes,

$$\psi_{SL} = \frac{1 - e^{-in'}}{in'} = F_{\bar{R}P,\bar{\imath},n'} \qquad (4.9\#2)$$

and Appendix 2, Table 3, can be used.

Sum-of-digits depreciation (SD) is approximated by a flow declining in a straight line to zero as developed in Sec. 4.5. For a total flow of unity, Eq. (4.5#5) becomes

$$\psi_{SD} = F_{SDP,\bar{\imath},n'} = \frac{2}{in'}\left(1 - \frac{1 - e^{-in'}}{in'}\right) \qquad (4.9\#3)$$

where the right side is tabulated in Appendix 2, Table 4.

If an expenditure or receipt becomes eligible for tax credit at once, such as a maintenance expense, then for such items having no capitalization, for income tax purposes

$$\psi = 1 \qquad (4.9\#4)$$

regardless of the depreciation method.

With these considerations it becomes possible to use continuous interest on an after-tax basis with the same ease as for computations with periodic interest. All items of expenditure and receipt are considered on an after-tax basis with proper regard to the timing of tax credits.

Example 4.9E1 A \$1,000 investment has an expected life of 20 years and is to be depreciated over a 15-year life at a 52% tax rate using sum-of-digits depreciation; money is worth 10% per year after taxes. Find (a) the present worth of the capital charges after taxes and (b) unaflow.

By Eqs. (4.9#1) and (4.9#3), and Appendix 2, Table 4,

$P = 1,000(1 - 0.52F_{SDP,0.10,15}) = 1,000[1 - 0.52(0.6428)]$

$P = \$678.60 \qquad$ ans. (a) $\qquad\qquad (4.9\#5)$

If $\bar{R}$ is the unaflow before taxes, then $\psi = 1$ for this item by Eq. (4.9#4), and the unaflow after taxes is

$$\bar{R}(1 - 0.52) = 0.48\bar{R} \qquad (4.9\#6)$$

Equations (4.9#5) and (4.9#6) are both on an after-tax basis and must be equivalent. Using Eq. (4.7#2) with $0.48\bar{R}$ in place of R, and Appendix 2, Table 3,

$$0.48\bar{R} = \frac{678.60}{20}\frac{1}{F_{\bar{R}P,0.10,20}} = \frac{678.60}{20}\frac{1}{0.4323}$$

$\bar{R} = \$163.51$ per year before taxes $\qquad$ ans. (b)

4.10 Equivalence

One of the major purposes of a firm is to show a profit, which it does by committing its funds to ventures which promise to do so. There are always alternatives for

Table 4.10T1 Summary of Relationships for Continuous Interest

Item no.	Item	Description	Algebraic relationship	Factor relationship
1	P to S	Moves a fixed sum P to another instant of time n years with calendar	$S = Pe^{in}$	$S = PF_{PS,\bar{i},n}$ (App. 2, Table 1)
2	S to P	Moves a fixed sum S to another instant of time n years against calendar	$P = Se^{-in}$	$P = SF_{SP,\bar{i},n}$ (App. 2, Table 2)
3	$\bar{R}$ to P	Converts a unaflow $\bar{R}$ for n years to present worth at start of flow	$P = n\bar{R}\dfrac{1 - e^{-in}}{in}$	$P = n\bar{R}F_{RP,\bar{i},n}$ (App. 2, Table 3)
4	$\bar{R}$ for 1 year to P	Present worth of 1 year of unaflow starting X years hence	$P = \bar{R}e^{-i}X\dfrac{1 - e^{i}}{i}$	$P = \bar{R}\,F_{SP,\bar{i},X}F_{RP,\bar{i},1}$
5	P of flow changing at an exponential rate for n years	Present worth of $R_x = R_0\,e^{\pm gX}$ for n years	$P = nR_0\dfrac{1 - e^{-(i\mp g)n}}{i \mp g}$	$P = nR_0\,F_{RP,(\overline{i\mp g}),n}$
6	P of flow declining in straight line to zero	Flow goes from R_0 at zero time to 0 in n years; total flow Q is $nR_0/2$	$P = Q\left[\dfrac{2}{in}\left(1 - \dfrac{1 - e^{-in}}{in}\right)\right]$	$P = QF_{SDP,\bar{i},n}$ (App. 2, Table 4)
7	P to $\bar{R}$	Converts a present worth to a unaflow of n years	$\bar{R} = \dfrac{P}{n}\dfrac{1}{(1 - e^{-in})/in}$	$R = \dfrac{P}{n}\dfrac{1}{F_{RP,\bar{i},n}}$

8	$\bar{R}$ to S	Converts a unaflow for n years to a future amount, n years hence	$S = n\bar{R}e^{in}\dfrac{1-e^{-in}}{in}$	$S = n\bar{R}F_{PS,i,n}F_{RP,i,n}$
9	S to $\bar{R}$	Converts a future sum S, n years from now, to a unaflow; sinking-fund payment	$\bar{R} = \dfrac{Se^{-in}}{n}\dfrac{1}{(1-e^{-in})/in}$	$\bar{R} = \dfrac{S}{n}F_{PS,i,n}\dfrac{1}{F_{RP,i,n}}$
10	P to K	Converts a present worth representing n years to a capitalized cost	$K = P\dfrac{e^{in}}{e^{in}-1}$	
11	K to $\bar{R}$	Converts a capitalized cost to a unaflow	$\bar{R} = iK$	
12	Before to after tax	Converts before-tax amount to after-tax amount, at tax rate t	After tax = $(1-t\psi)$ before tax	
13	ψ	Present value of \$1 of depreciation, n' years life for tax purpose	$\psi_{SL} = \dfrac{1-e^{-in'}}{in'}$ $\psi_{SD} = \dfrac{2}{in'}\left(1-\dfrac{1-e^{-in'}}{in'}\right)$ $\psi = 1$ for instantaneous tax benefit $\psi = 0$ for no depreciation, i.e., land	$\psi_{SL} = F_{RP,\bar{i},n'}$ (App. 2, Table 3) $\psi_{SD} = F_{SDP,\bar{i},n'}$ (App. 2, Table 4)

making these investments and expenditures. The function of economic analysis is to help in making better choices between alternatives by placing dollar values on quality, quantity, time, and other characteristics of these alternatives. This quantifying needs to be done in a consistent way so that the dollar values are measured by the same yardstick, i.e., expressed on an equivalent basis. Doing so highlights the better alternative, the one with the lowest economic cost or highest economic value.

Discounting and compounding at the same interest rate places the same dollar value on time. However, since the alternatives may have different lives, e.g., low-cost short-life carbon steel vs. high-cost long-life alloy steel, it is also necessary to compare them over the same time interval. Present worth compares equivalent values now; unaflow, the equivalent continuous annual cost, compares the values on a per-year basis; and capitalized cost compares them on a forever basis as a common denominator for all service lives. Comparisons can also be made on the basis of rate of return, discounted cash flow, as developed in the following chapter.

The method to be used for comparing alternatives or ventures and the choice between periodic and continuous interest is left to the analyst. There is no universal or intrinsic answer, and the choice varies with circumstances. Some analysts are more familiar with one approach and therefore prefer it. Some problems are so expressed that one solution is easier or more meaningful by one of the methods. The technique which is felt best by the analyst for getting the solution, however, is not necessarily the one best for presenting the solution to the client. Although an economic specialist may prefer one method or even be equally comfortable with all four, the client is often a manager, who is a generalist by necessity. Since he does not have time to be a specialist in every field, results must be presented in terms familiar to him—simple enough to be grasped on the run. Experience shows that if a solution is presented in unfamiliar or seemingly unrealistic terms, it will not be understood; if not understood, it will not be believed; and if not believed, it will not be accepted.

This chapter has discussed the essence of continuous discounting and compounding, showed how to develop relationships for handling commonly encountered cash flows, including those which may change over time, and illustrated the ease of applying them by simple examples. Most real problems are more complex, not so much in computation, but in defining what the cash flows will prove to be. Often, 95% of the total time in solving a problem is required on such a determination for allocating costs and incomes, determining the applicable tax and other government regulations, and projecting sales, costs, and so on. This circumstance does not mean that economic analysis of cash flows is insignificant, because even with the right cash flows, a wrong analysis or interpretation can lead to the wrong choice of alternatives. Instead, the observation is intended to put the various parts of problem solving into meaningful perspective for understanding and coping better with real situations when they arise.

A summary of the various relationships using continuous interest is given in Table 4.10T1.

4.11 Nomenclature

C_d	Depreciable first cost, $
e	Naperian constant 2.71828 $\cdots$
$F_{P\bar{R},\bar{i},n}$	Factor to convert P to $\bar{R}$ with continuous compounding; reciprocal of $F_{\bar{R}P,\bar{i},n}$, year^{-1}
$F_{PS,\bar{i},n}$	Factor to convert P to S with continuous compounding, e^{in}, Appendix 2, Table 1, dimensionless
$F_{\bar{R}P,\bar{i},n}$	Factor to convert $\bar{R}$ to P with continuous discounting; Appendix 2, Table 3, years
$F_{SP,\bar{i},n}$	Factor to convert S to P with continuous discounting, e^{-in}, Appendix 2, Table 2, decimal, dimensionless
$F_{SDP,\bar{i},n}$	Factor to convert a unit total flow declining to zero at a constant rate over n years starting with the reference point and with continuous discounting, decimal, dimensionless, approximates ψ_{SD}
g	Constant in exponential-rate flow change, decimal
i	Nominal interest rate, decimal/year
k	Empirical exponent in learning-curve relationship, decimal, dimensionless
K	Capitalized cost, $
M	Profit margin, $
n	Time, years
n'	Time for tax depreciation, years
p	Periods per year
P	Present worth, $
P_n	Present worth for n years duration, $
Q	Total flow, $
r	Nominal rate of return after taxes, decimal/year
$\bar{R}$	Uniform flow, unaflow, $ per year
R_0	Initial flow rate, $ per year
R_x	Flow rate at time X, $ per year
S	Future worth, $
SL	Straight-line depreciation
SD	Sum-of-digits depreciation
t	Income tax rate, decimal
T	Time, years
ψ	Factor associated with present worth of tax benefits arising from depreciation, dimensionless
ψ_{SL}	The ψ factor for straight-line depreciation
ψ_{SD}	The ψ factor for sum-of-digits depreciation

4.12 Problems

P1. Develop a relationship for discounting a flow increasing in a straight line from zero at zero time to $\bar{R}_n$ at time n.

P2. Develop a relationship for discounting a flow increasing in a straight line from $\bar{R}_1$ at zero time to $\bar{R}_2$ at time n.

P3. Develop a relationship for discounting a series of periodic cash flows of k payments, Y each, at intervals of n years, the first one beginning n years hence.

P4. A firm has a contributory savings plan whereby each employee can set aside 5% of his gross salary. The firm will match this amount, invest the sums in its capital stock, and reinvest all dividends in capital stock. If an employee's salary is consistently $12,000 per year, how much will he accumulate after 20 years if the company's net earnings average 8% per year and the stock consistently sells at book value?

P5. What is the average rate of growth of the employee's $600 per year portion of the contribution?

P6. Suppose the employee finds an alternative proposition which promises to double his money every 5 years. Will he be better off to participate in the savings plan or forego the company's contribution and invest his contribution in the alternative?

P7. If the parents in Example 4.3E3 continue their monthly savings during the 4 years their child attends college, e.g., for 21 instead of 17 years, how much must their monthly savings be to permit $3,000 per year to be withdrawn uniformly over the 4 years from the seventeenth to the twenty-first birthday?

P8. A new machine costs $8,000 and lasts 10 years, using sum-of-digits depreciation and a 10-year life for tax purposes. If money is worth 10% per year after a 52% tax, how much can be spent to repair an old machine to extend its life 3 years? The repair job can be written off at once for tax purposes. Compare with Prob. 3.15P6.

P9. Repeat Example 2.8E6 using continuous discounting. Money is worth 10% per year after a 48% tax rate. Use straight-line depreciation. Machine A will be written off in 8 years for tax purposes, machine B in 10 years. Maintenance costs and savings from quality control are uniform flows in years in which they occur. The salvage value is anticipated and cannot be depreciated for tax purposes.

	A	B
First cost, $	10,000	95,000
Maintenance, $ per year	3,000	1,000
Extra maintenance, year 3, $	4,000	
Extra maintenance, year 4, $	1,500	
Savings from quality control, $ per year		6,000
Salvage value		20,000
Life, years	4	10

P10. A company completed a plant 10 years ago. It was expected to be serviceable for 25 years, but technical advances and accumulated know-how suggest that obsolesence may have progressed faster than expected, so that it may be profitable to displace it now. Assume for simplicity that (1) a new plant would have the same capacity as the old and would produce the same array of products with the same initial revenue for both, so that the advantage of the new is reflected only in its lower operating costs; (2) these savings in operating costs are $180,000 per year; and (3) depreciation on the old plant is $35,000 per year on a straight-line basis, and present salvage value is zero, (4) the tax rate is 50% per year.

If the investment required for the new plant is $1 million and both its useful life and life for tax purposes are 15 years with sum-of-digits depreciation, what is the rate of return to be earned by investment in a new plant?

4.13 References

R1. Hirschmann, W. B.: Profit from the Learning Curve, *Harvard Business Rev.*, January–February, 1964, pp. 125–139.

R2. Hirschmann, W. B., and J. R. Brauweiler: Investment Analysis: Coping with Change, *Harvard Business Rev.*, May–June, 1965, pp. 62–72.

R3. Hirschmann, W. B., and J. R. Brauweiler: Continuous Discounting for Realistic Investment Analysis, *Chem. Eng.*, July 19, 1965, pp. 210–214.

R4. Hirschmann, W. B., and J. R. Brauweiler: Realistic Investment Analysis, II, *Chem. Eng.*, August 16, 1965, pp. 132–136.

5
Profitability

H. C. Thorne and R. O. Carlson

5.1 Profit

Profitability is the primary goal of a private enterprise. If profitability is not maintained, growth and even survival is not possible over the long run. Evaluation of profitability is therefore a main function of corporate management. Profitability techniques, while primarily employed in profit-seeking enterprises, are also useful to governmental bodies, nonprofit institutions, and individuals. The logic of using funds efficiently is universal.

An enterprise can be visualized as a collection of investment projects, each with a finite economic life. Profit on each investment can be stated as income generated minus expenses incurred. A profit is realized if total money returns exceed total costs over the life of the project. Costs incurred by a project include the initial investment, all subsequent costs of operation and maintenance including taxes, and any costs terminating the project. Returns include sales and other income and salvage value when terminated.

A profitability forecast of a proposed venture requires the combination of a number of estimates made by many people. The expected profitability and subsequent decision whether to undertake the project will depend primarily on these estimates. Therefore, the relative importance of each estimate and the validity of underlying assumptions must be ascertained when measuring venture profitability.

5.2 Investment evaluation

This chapter is concerned chiefly with the capital-expenditures component of a corporation's financial system. An investment evaluation usually is concerned with a single venture throughout its life, usually a number of years. The problem of time can become of crucial importance. A decision to undertake a venture involves long-term commitments of capital and other resources. The time value of money, developed in earlier chapters, is a fundamental component of investment evaluation.

Among factors to be judged in an investment evaluation are the uncertainties in the economic estimate, the possibility of operating failure, the prospect of premature obsolescense, the sensitivity of the project to such factors as demand and pricing, competition, and a host of even more intangible items. With proper application of judgment, making an investment decision is a matter of weighing the profits anticipated in the evaluation against a minimum profitability standard based on at least the corporation's cost of obtaining investment capital. The determination of a company's cost of capital or minimum acceptable standard is an important and complex problem. In brief, cost of capital can be viewed as an average of debt and equity costs, weighed in proportion to the fraction of each, in a company's capital structure. Where required in calculations in this text, the minimum acceptable returns will be assumed to be a known quantity. For further information consult [5.18R7].

5.3 Four economic guideposts

The following are four economic guideposts to consider in making an economic evaluation.

Alternatives. The importance of this item cannot be overstated. Failure to consider an important alternative can lead to a serious error in judgment. For example, plant modernization may be very attractive compared with continued current operation, but both may be unattractive compared to shutting down the plant.

Incremental return. It is possible to have two projects and prefer the one with the larger investment and lower return. For example, suppose two mutually exclusive alternatives A and B are compared with the following results:

Alternative	Investment, $M	Profitability, %
A	1,000	18
B	2,000	16
Increment ($B - A$)	1,000	14

The important question is the return on the additional investment in B, here 14%. If the rating of 14% on this additional investment is above the minimum acceptable standard, project B would be preferable to A.

Sunk costs. Money which has already been spent and cannot be recovered represents a sunk cost and should not be included in the usual evaluation.

Profit goal. The object is to maximize profit above the cost of capital invested. The goal is not to maximize profit itself, because if this were so, any investment, no matter how great the cost and how low the return, would be undertaken provided that it earned some profit. Neither is the goal to maximize return on investment. If it were, only that single opportunity which has the highest rate of return would be undertaken.

There are many methods in use for judging profitability, and many variants of each method. Six popular methods [5.17R11] are discussed below.

5.4 Payout time

Payout time is the time required to get back the initial investment.

Example 5.4E1 Project A has expenses and receipts after taxes but before depreciation (cash flow) as follows

Time, years	Cash flow, $
0	−1,000
0–1	475
1–2	400
2–3	330
3–4	270
4–5	200

Find the payout time without interest.

The following tabulation shows that the initial investment amounting to $1,000 will be returned between 2 and 3 years, or more exactly 2.38 years by interpolation.

Time, end year	Cumulative cash flow, $
0	−1,000
1	−525
2	−125
3	+205

5.5 Payout time with interest

The method allows for a return on the investment, and is subject to many variations. The variation considered below applies an interest charge only on the fixed

86 MATHEMATICS OF COST COMPARISONS 5.6

investment remaining. Another variant is to apply an interest charge on any working capital involved as well as fixed capital.

It should be noted that payout time without interest, as in the preceding section, is much more commonly used than payout time with interest.

Example 5.5E1 Repeat Example 5.4E1 and find the payout time with interest on the remaining investment at 10% per year.

The following tabulation shows that the payout time is between 2 and 3 years, or more exactly 2.95 years by interpolation.

(1) End year	(2) Investment for year	(3) Charge on investment for year 10% of (2)	(4) Cash flow	(5) Cash flow after investment charge (4) − (3)	(6) Cumulative net cash flow
0			−1,000		−1,000
1	1,000	100	475	375	−625
2	625	62.5	400	337.5	−287.5
3	287.5	28.75	330	301.25	+13.75

The investment for each year is the investment for the previous year less the cash flow after investment charge for the previous year.

5.6 Return on original investment

Return on original investment is the percentage relationship of the average annual profit (sometimes average annual cash flow) to the original investment, including nondepreciable items such as working capital.

Example 5.6E1 Repeat Example 5.4E1 and find the rate of return on original investment assuming straight-line depreciation over a 5-year life.

The average profit is obtained from the following tabulation:

Year	Cash flow	Depreciation	Profit
1	475	200	275
2	400	200	200
3	330	200	130
4	270	200	70
5	200	200	0
			Av 135

For an original investment of 1,000 and no working capital

$$\frac{\text{Average yearly profit during earning life}}{\text{Original fixed investment} + \text{working capital}} \, 100 = \frac{135}{1,000} \, 100 = 13.5\% \text{ per year}$$

5.7 Return on average investment

The return on average investment is similar to the return on original investment except that the divisor is the average outstanding investment. There are different ways of determining the average outstanding investment, depending on the depreciation schedule used.

Example 5.7E1 Repeat Example 5.4E1 and find the rate of return on average investment using straight-line depreciation.

Average investment is found from the following tabulation:

Year	Investment, $
1	1,000
2	1,000 − 200 = 800
3	800 − 200 = 600
4	600 − 200 = 400
5	400 − 200 = 200
	Av = 600

$$\frac{135}{600}(100) = 22.5\% \text{ per year}$$

5.8 Discounted cash flow (DCF)

The discounted-cash-flow method is also known as the interest-rate-of-return method, profitability index, internal rate of return, and the investor's method. It includes all cash flows over the entire life of the project and adjusts them to one point fixed in time, usually the time of original investment or start-up time, using compound-interest procedure. A trial-and-error calculation is required to determine the compound-interest rate at which the sum of all the time-adjusted cash outflows equals the sum of all the time-adjusted inflows.

Other variations of the discounted-cash-flow method include the Machinery and Applied Products Institute (MAPI) system [5.17R7] and capitalized costs [5.17R3].

Example 5.8E1 Repeat Example 5.4E1 and find the interest rate of return by the DCF method.

The DCF relationship, using zero time as the basis for comparison and assuming receipts as of the end of the year, is

$$P = \frac{-1{,}000}{(1+r)^0} + \frac{475}{(1+r)^1} + \frac{400}{(1+r)^2} + \frac{330}{(1+r)^3} + \frac{270}{(1+r)^4} + \frac{200}{(1+r)^5}$$

Values for $1/(1+r)^n = F_{SP,i,n}$ are given in Appendix 1, Table 1. By trial

$r = 0.20 \quad P = +75.16$

$r = 0.25 \quad P = -18.91$

and by interpolation for $P = 0$

$r = 23.9\%$ per year

88   MATHEMATICS OF COST COMPARISONS

The DCF rate of return on an investment is a constant annual percent return on that part of the investment outstanding each year over its life. The investment base declines over time as returns accumulate to pay interest and retire principal. Therefore, the dollar amount of return on investment varies over time.

There is some confusion in the literature between DCF rate of return earned by an investment and the average rate of return earned by a company on all its funds. The rate of return by DCF is independent of the average rate of return earned by the company. Average rate of return for the entire company is always measured against "no business," which is not always true of DCF return on a single investment. Even when measured against no business, DCF return vs. book return on an investment differs because the principal is repaid differently over time through annual depreciation allocations.

5.9 Venture worth

The venture-worth method, sometimes called the incremental present-worth method, is a variation of the DCF method. However, it avoids a trial-and-error computation by discounting at a fixed rate, usually the minimum acceptable return on capital. The present worth is then expressed as the present worth of inflow less the present worth of outflow.

The venture worth is accordingly a single amount referred to zero time and represents a premium or deficiency over some fixed rate of return. Venture worth depends upon the project life, and strictly speaking the venture worths of two projects should not be compared if they have different service lives. The venture worths should first be adjusted to some common life, say 1 year or infinity.

Example 5.9E1 Repeat Example 5.4E1 and find the venture worth based on a minimum acceptable return of 10% per year.

Assuming receipts as of the end of the year, the venture worth is

$$\frac{-1{,}000}{1.10^0} + \frac{475}{1.10^1} + \frac{400}{1.10^2} + \frac{330}{1.10^3} + \frac{270}{1.10^4} + \frac{200}{1.10^5} = 318.92$$

5.10 Three projects compared

Project A, the subject of the previous sections, features a declining income. Table 5.10T1 repeats project A along with project B having a steady income and project C having an increasing income. All projects have an initial investment amounting to $-\$1{,}000$, last 5 years, and employ straight-line depreciation. Table 5.10T1 summarizes calculations for income taken as discrete amounts at the end of the year and interest compounded discretely at the end of the year. Profitability of four common methods, return on original investment, payout time without interest, rate of return for the discounted cash flow, and venture worth, are compared for the three income patterns.

In this example, each of the two undiscounted methods gives different rankings, and neither selects project B. The undiscounted methods do have their

Table 5.10T1 Effect of Economic Yardsticks on Project Ranking*

Time, end of year	Project A, declining income Cash flow	Profit after taxes	Project B, steady income Cash flow	Profit after taxes	Project C, increasing income Cash flow	Profit after taxes
0	−1,000		−1,000		−1,000	
1	475	275	355	155	200	0
2	400	200	355	155	300	100
3	330	130	355	155	400	200
4	270	70	355	155	450	250
5	200	0	355	155	490	290
		Av = 135		Av = 155		Av = 168

		Rank		Rank		Rank
Return on original investment	13.5	3	15.5	2	16.8	1
Payout time, years	2.38	1	2.82	2	3.22	3
Discounted cash flow	23.9%	1	22.8%	2	20.8%	3
Present worth at 10%	319	3	346	1	342	2

* Depreciation in all cases is $200 per year.

place, if used with caution. Payout, in particular, is often reported along with a DCF result; but where very high returns and short payouts are desired, payout time can often be used satisfactorily as the only criterion [5.17R1].

No single criterion can be used as an absolute measure for judging profitability, and analysis in depth on a year-to-year basis might be desirable [5.17R4]. For example, payout time can be kept low by skimping on original investment and shifting some of the burden to excessive start-up costs. Indeed, payout time can be made zero by merely becoming a broker and selling the products of others! There is a growing preference for rate of return by discounted cash flow as the most suitable index of profitability, but many other factors should be considered in a proper profitability study because no single index number alone can show all relevant factors.

To calculate the compound-interest rate for the DCF method only two principal steps are required: (1) write down all the cash flows after taxes and (2) discount them and find the answer by trial and error. Forms printed with the discount factors will facilitate the calculation and allow clerks to perform the work. A computer can be used advantageously. Infrequently, multiple or no root solutions occur; methods of handling the problem exist [5.17R6] but lie beyond the scope of this chapter.

Example 5.10E1 A venture requires $1 million investment now and will have receipts of $600,000, $700,000, and $340,000 at the end of the first, second, and third years, respectively. Consider these receipts as the difference between income less expense for the year,

90 MATHEMATICS OF COST COMPARISONS

Table 5.10T2 Cash Flow for Example 5.10E1

	Time 0	End year 1	End year 2	End year 3	Cumulative
1. Total receipts		600,000	700,000	340,000	
2. Depreciation					
$\quad \dfrac{3}{1+2+3} 1{,}000{,}000$		500,000			
$\quad \dfrac{2}{1+2+3} 1{,}000{,}000$			333,333		
$\quad \dfrac{1}{1+2+3} 1{,}000{,}000$				166,667	
3. Taxable income		100,000	366,667	173,333	
4. Tax at 55%		55,000	201,667	95,333	
5. Profit after tax		45,000	165,000	78,000	288,000
6. Cash flow, item 5 + item 2	−1,000,000	545,000	498,333	244,667	288,000
DCF rate of return, discrete compounding					
$\quad$ Present worth at 14%	−1,000,000	478,069	383,450	165,143	+26,662
$\quad$ Present worth at 16%	−1,000,000	469,828	370,341	156,748	−3,083
For 0 present worth $r = 15.8\%$ by interpolation					

referred to the end of the year as a single amount but before depreciation and taxes. The combined federal and state profit tax is 55%, and the sum-of-digits method of depreciation is used. Find the rate of return earned by this venture by discounted cash flow.

Find the taxes on the receipts, net receipts after taxes, and cash flow on a year-by-year basis as in Table 5.10T2.

5.11 Continuous interest

The use of continuous interest in profitability studies is becoming more common. The reader is referred to Chap. 4 for the development and use of continuous interest. Recalculation of projects *A*, *B*, and *C* of Table 5.10T1 on the basis of continuous interest gives the following result:

	A		B		C	
		Rank		Rank		Rank
Discounted cash flow	21.5%	1	20.5%	2	18.9%	3
Present worth at 10%	304	3	328	1	322	2

The rank for both discounted cash flow and present worth at 10% with continuous compounding is the same in this case as the rank with discrete compounding (compare Table 5.10T1). Generally, discrete and continuous compounding give the same order of rank, and continuous compounding will yield somewhat lower present worths and DCF rates of return for a given set of cash flows. In addition, the continuous-compounding assumption greatly reduces the number of factors required, by using e^{-x} functions, where only the product of discount rate and time is a determinant of present worth. With discrete compounding, discount rate and time must be handled separately.

To facilitate the computation with continuous interest, the more commonly used discount or present-worth factors are tabulated in Appendix 2. Table 1 covers cash effects occurring at a point in time before time zero, the present. Table 2 covers cash effects occurring at a point in time after time zero. Table 3 covers a cash flow occurring uniformly over time. The table lists factors which discount $1 cash flow to its present worth at the start of the flow. Table 4 covers a cash flow declining to zero at a uniform rate discounted to a present worth at the start of the flow. Tax credit generated by sum-of-digits depreciation is an approximation of such a cash flow. Factors for most other special growth and decline patterns can be developed from these.

Example 5.11E1 An investment gives the following data:
Initial investment $122,000 spent uniformly from $-\frac{1}{2}$ to 0 years, all capitalized

Annual savings $200,000 uniform
10-year project life
49% income tax
7% investment credit
20-year sum-of-digits depreciation

Find the rate of return by DCF. Use $M.

Try 60% for the first rate. The investment, -122, is treated as a uniform cash flow at 60% for 0.5 year, or $in = 0.30$. The present worth at the beginning of its time, $\frac{1}{2}$ year ago, is taken from Appendix 2, Table 3, and the factor is 0.8639. This now must be moved with the calendar $\frac{1}{2}$ year at 60%, to get to zero time, the factor for which (by Appendix 2, Table 1, with $in = 0.30$) is 1.350. The combined factor is

$$0.8639(1.350) = 1.17$$

The investment credit amounts to $0.07(122) = 9$ and is taken as a savings in tax reduction at zero time.

Tax credit from depreciation is $0.49(122) = 60$, which for sum-of-digits depreciation declines to zero at a uniform rate and requires Appendix 2, Table 4, discount factor, here 0.1528 for $in = 0.60(20) = 12$.

Savings are treated as a uniform cash flow amounting to $200(10) = 2,000$ before taxes or $2,000(0.51) = 1,020$ after taxes. The discount factor is obtained from Appendix 2, Table 3, and for $in = 0.60(10) = 6$ is 0.1663.

A tabulation of the calculations for 60, 70, and 80% follows.

	Cash flow after taxes	60% rate		70% rate		80% rate	
		Factor	Present worth	Factor	Present worth	Factor	Present worth
Investment	-122	1.17	-143	1.20	-146	1.23	-150
Investment credit	9	1.00	9	1.00	9	1.00	9
Depreciation	60	0.153	9	0.133	8	0.117	7
Savings	1,020	0.166	169	0.143	146	0.125	127
Net			$+44$		$+17$		-7

The rate of return by graphical interpolation is 77%.

Table 5.12T1 Time, Cost, and Revenue Elements of a Typical Project

1. Costs incurred before construction
2. Fixed capital
3. Start-up costs
4. Working capital
5. Subsequent investment
6. Sales price and volume trends
7. Annual expenses
8. Tax effects
9. Salvage value

5.12 Some considerations in profitability studies

A checklist of the major cost and revenue elements of a typical project is shown in Table 5.12T1 with the items arranged roughly by time of occurrence. Most of these items require no discussion here.

Costs before construction include such items as research and development, market studies, economic and engineering evaluations and can cover several years. Fixed investment costs likewise occur, at least in part, in negative time, i.e., before start-up.

Start-up costs may be minor or considerable. They also can be charged off to expense or capitalized, but tax rules must be considered. Working capital represents investment items like cash and inventory, which are of such a nature that generally they can always be recovered in full. The usual assumption is that working capital is proportional to sales level.

Sales price and volume trends are predicted values and not nearly so precise as engineering investment estimate or annual expenses, but they are usually the most important in the profitability study. Income taxes are an expense item, but they can be complicated, as many special situations exist. Terminal items such as salvage value, working capital, and land, which can be recovered, should be included, also any relevant tax effects at termination. The salvage value of equipment, however, is usually small and being far in the future will have a low present-worth factor; hence it frequently can be ignored.

Table 5.12T2 Project Types for Profitability Studies

1. Abandonment
2. Process modification and cost reduction
3. Replacement and displacement
4. Expansion
5. New process, product, or market
6. Purchased know-how against internal development
7. Joint venture
8. Lease vs. buy
9. Make vs. buy

Table 5.12T3 Some Important Characteristics of Projects

1. Sunk costs
2. Differing lives
3. Cost sharing
4. Cost savings
5. Quality improvement
6. New business
7. Special financing
8. Risk and uncertainties

Table 5.12T2 lists the common project types subject to profitability studies. The mathematical treatment is the same for all. In most projects a comparison of alternatives and, say, rates of return by DCF is made. The comparisons can be of various types, e.g., in the case of abandonment, of doing nothing vs. shutting down; but the principles do not vary. The difficult task is to arrive at numerical values for all the pertinent cost items involved and not to overlook any applicable costs or benefits.

Table 5.12T3 lists some underlying characteristics on which the nine project types depend. The list is merely suggestive but will help avoid omissions. Sunk costs generally can be ignored, but the tax situation associated with them should not be omitted. For differing lives, such criteria as unacost, capitalized cost, and rate of return by DCF make fair comparisons, but criteria based on straight present worth can be misleading unless the difference in service lives has been compensated. Cost-sharing projects can introduce difficult decisions about how such costs are to be allocated.

Problems in abandonment and lease vs. buy are particularly troublesome, not because of any mathematical difficulty but because it is so difficult to assign a numerical basis for all the considerations involved. The following example of a lease-or-buy decision illustrates one situation.

Example 5.12E1 The laboratory must decide whether to buy or lease a highly specialized instrument which is undergoing considerable technological advancement.

A new instrument can be bought for $50,000. It has a technological life of 4 years and can be disposed of for $2,000 to be taken as regular income. It is fully depreciable in 4 years using sum-of-digits depreciation for tax purposes. Maintenance cost, at the end of each year, is expected to be $6,000 per year. If the instrument is owned, it can be modified and used in connection with other instruments, and this fact is given a value of $8,000 per year, as of the end of the year.

A rented instrument costs $15,000 per year, payable at the beginning of the year with free servicing. Rental is on an annual basis, renewable each year at the lessee's option. Renting gives the advantage of deferring buying a year at a time in a period of high technological advancement, and this is judged to be worth $20,000 on a present basis for a 4-year period.

If money is worth 10% per year after a 52% tax, should the instrument be bought or rented?

Unacost, the equivalent uniform end-of-year cost, for a purchased-instrument basis (Table 3.13T1, items 1, 4, and 2 in order, and Appendix 1, Table 1) is

$$C_d(1 - tF_{SDP,10\%,4})F_{PR,10\%,4} = 50,000[1 - 0.52(0.83013)]0.31547 = \$8,964$$

94   MATHEMATICS OF COST COMPARISONS   5.12

Disposal income, negative cost =

$$-C_{ex}\frac{1-t}{(1.10)^4} F_{PR,10\%,4} = -2,000\frac{1-0.52}{1.4641}0.31547 = -207$$

$$R(1-t) = (6,000 - 8,000)(1-0.52) = -960$$
$$R = \overline{\$7,797}$$

Unacost for a rented instrument (by Table 3.13T1, items 3 and 1 in order, and Appendix 1, Table 1) is

$$R_b\left(1 - \frac{t}{1+r}\right)(1+r) = 15,000\left(1 - \frac{0.52}{1.10}\right)1.10 = \$8,700$$

Delay value treated as a first cost lasting 4 years with instant tax benefit is

$$-20,000(1-t)F_{PR,10\%,4} = -20,000(1-0.52)(0.31547) = -3,028$$
$$R = \overline{\$5,672}$$

In this example it will be more economical to rent. Note that the credit given to the rented article for its value in deferring a purchase until later is the determining factor in the analysis. It is difficult to assign this value. When renting on a longer-term basis without annual renewal options, the financing effects of the rental contract must be recognized as equivalent to financing with debt. In most of these cases, purchase is more economical than renting. See Vancil [5.19R16] for further information.

In predicting the future it is not safe to conclude that it will be a simple extrapolation of the past. In a dynamic economy, the only certainty is change. As shown by Twaddle and Malloy [5.17R10], many of the cash-flow patterns associated with change can be expressed mathematically in forms easily handled by continuous discounting. Thus, when a cash flow begins at level C_0 dollars per year and changes continuously at a rate of $\pm g$ decimal per year, for example, discounting is straightforward (see Sec. 4.4).

$$\text{Present worth} = \int_0^T C_0 e^{\pm gT} e^{-iT}\, dT$$

$$= \frac{C_0}{\pm g - i}(e^{(\pm g - i)T} - 1) \qquad (5.12\#1)$$

where T is time in years.

However, some cash flows, particularly those involving market projections, are not directly integrable after being multiplied by the discount factor e^{-iT}. Such cash flows can be discounted by a simple gaussian integration technique [5.17R5]:

$$\int_{T_1}^{T_2} C_t e^{-iT}\, dT = (T_2 - T_1)\sum_{n=1}^{n} K_n(C_t e^{-iT})_n \qquad (5.12\#2)$$

where the symbol C_t emphasizes that C depends upon T. The expression gives the integral as a simple weighted average of the discounted cash flow at n particular times in the interval of integration. An n-point gaussian integration is exact, provided the function $C_t e^{iT}$ can be expressed exactly by a polynomial of degree $2n - 1$. The kinds of discounted cash-flow-vs.-time curves met in economic evaluations are usually simple enough for a four-point integration to be adequate, for which

$$K_1 = K_4 = 0.174$$
$$K_2 = K_3 = 0.326$$

and the four discounted cash flows are measured at times

$$T_0 + 0.07(T_2 - T_1)$$
$$T_0 + 0.33(T_2 - T_1)$$
$$T_0 + 0.67(T_2 - T_1)$$
$$T_0 + 0.93(T_2 - T_1)$$

The gaussian method applies to smooth curves. When the cash flow has a break, each branch should be integrated separately.

5.13 Classification system for economic appraising

Several economic evaluations are normally required during the development of a project. They arise when a decision for a different order of magnitude of capital and effort is required, when significant new data become available, or when new alternatives are conceived.

The American Association of Cost Engineers has prepared a classification system dividing these studies into four classes: (1) final, (2) intermediate, (3) preliminary, and (4) screening, depending on the amount of information available [5.17R2].

5.14 Special topics

Some additional aspects of profitability studies merit emphasis. One is the decision to invest now or later. Investing now against a few alternatives of investing at later years can be studied and compared. The analyst should always consider the possibility of delaying. A course of action may be right in the long run but might be even more opportune if started at a later date. On the other hand, delay may be fatal, but only a study of timing will reveal this circumstance and call attention to the urgency for action now.

Since technology and other factors are constantly changing, decisions made or deferred in the past should be reviewed frequently. Profitability studies never stand still.

The displacement problem, discussed in the following chapter, involves rejecting an existing machine or operation because it is no longer economical and displacing it with a new machine or operation. Profitability studies in this field are very important inasmuch as the policy of displacing machines and not waiting for them to wear out can be a critical factor in a company's success, yet the profitability study must be authoritative and convincing, or otherwise the natural tendency to wait will prevail.

Sometimes lack of time or limited data restrict the usefulness of a profitability study. In these cases, a range of estimates—perhaps simply using optimistic, best guess, and pessimistic values—is of considerable value in uncovering the critical uncertainties and recognizing the relative riskiness associated with various proposals.

Reporting results of investment evaluations has some particular problems since the reports are often aimed at a business-trained management but are usually written by technical people in a rather specialized field. Every such report is based on a number of quite complex assumptions, each of which should be stated. Reports should indicate, also, the sensitivity of the profitability to alterations in the key forecasts.

At the project decision stage, the appropriation request form is used to present management with a summary of the information it requires. The form also serves as a checklist to assure that all aspects have been considered. The major types of information given on one such form [5.17R8] are:

1. Description of the project
2. Timing
3. Amount of each type of expenditure required
4. Total appropriation
5. Key assumptions used
6. Overall profitability of the project

Another section of the form gives (7) the approximate profit or loss, rate of return, and cumulative cash position of the project for the key years over its life. Another section answers (8) whether the project is consistent with long-range plans and whether funds for the venture have been included in the budget. Any other pertinent items (9) are covered in a remarks section at the bottom of the form.

Computers are beginning to have an impact in profitability studies and in the capital expenditure system [5.17R9]. Many of these applications now are in performing calculations that were previously made by hand. However, there are several areas where computers can be used as a more sophisticated decision-aiding tool, although progress has been slow. Computers are very useful in screening a large number of alternatives at an early stage to determine the most favorable ones. Computer runs can show how projected rate of return varies with change in the major variables, such as selling price, and sensitivity to other variables. Many of the studies in which computers assist use common data of investment, income, and expense, and it becomes apparent that a complete system of programs can be developed from a single source deck of punched cards. Finally the computer permits the ideas of probability and uncertainty to replace single-valued estimates so that a range of values can be investigated with little extra effort.

5.15 Nomenclature

C_d	Depreciable cost, $
C_{ex}	Irregular cost at end of xth year, $
C_0	Initial level of cash flow in Eq. (5.12#1), $ per year
C_t	Variable cash flow in Eq. (5.12#2), $ per year
e	Naperian constant 2.71828 $\cdots$
$F_{PR,r,n}$	Factor to convert P to R; capital-recovery factor, year^{-1}
$F_{SDP,r,n}$	Present worth of $1 for sum-of-digits depreciation, decimal
$F_{SP,i,n}$	Factor to convert S to P; present-worth factor, decimal
g	Constant in Eq. (5.12#1), decimal
i	Rate of return, decimal/year
K_n	Constant for integer values of n in Eq. (5.12#2), decimal
n	A number, generally years
P	Present worth, $
r	Rate of return, after taxes, decimal/year
R	Unacost, equivalent uniform end-of-year annual cost, $ per year
R_b	Uniform beginning of year annual amount, $ per year
S	Future worth, $
t	Tax rate, decimal
T	Time, years

5.16 Problems

P1. Calculate results for project A, B, and C of Table 5.10T1, assuming incomes occur uniformly over each year, rather than at the end of each year, and continuous compounding of interest.

P2. A project requires an initial investment of $100,000 and yields cash income of $20,000 per year for a 10-year period.

    (*a*) Calculate the average book rate of return by year and for the overall project assuming straight-line depreciation. *Note:* Average investment is the average of the opening and closing investment for each time period.

    (*b*) Calculate the DCF rate of return. Use continuous interest.

    (*c*) Using trial and error, modify the book depreciation schedule to yield a constant book rate of return over the life of the project. *Note:* Total depreciation is still $100,000.

    (*d*) How do you interpret the results?

P3. Rank in terms of increasing cost of capital the following industries: petroleum industry, public utility, and textile industry. Explain your reasoning.

P4. An investment of $20,000 made 2 years from now with an 8-year depreciation life will permit before-tax savings of $10,000 per year for 4 years. What is the present value of the investment today at 12% per year? Use sum-of-digits depreciation. Assume salvage value after 4 years operation is the undepreciated balance. Use periodic interest and a 50% tax rate.

P5. A new facility costs $100,000, of which $40,000 is land and $60,000 construction, and has a 20-year economic life. Sales volume is estimated at $450,000 per year in the third and subsequent years, with an annual cash return after taxes (including depreciation) of $9,000 per year and associated working capital of $15,000. In the first and second years, volume is estimated at one-third and two-thirds of capacity, respectively. Assume working capital and annual cash return are proportional to volume and assume the depreciable facilities have no salvage value after 20 years. What is the present value at 0, 4, and 6% using periodic interest?

P6. Repeat Prob. 5.16P5 and find the DCF rate of return.

P7. The Jones Co. is considering the replacement of a group of 5-year-old machine tools with some improved units which recently became available. They are concerned with the high operating cost of the existing units but also expect to replace the entire process in 5 years, when they plan to install a system now in the final stages of development in their research department. From the attached information determine whether or not the equipment should be replaced now. Summarize your findings in a short letter to the chief engineer. Assume that the cost of capital is 9% and the income tax rate is 50%. Use continuous interest and straight-line depreciation.

	Old machines	New machines
Number of machines	6	5
Cost of each machine, $	4,200	7,800
Depreciated value at present each (tax books), $	2,100	
Trade-in value on new machines, $	1,500	
Market value of new machine in 5 years, $		3,000
Variable costs of operation, annual, $	24,000	17,000

In your letter mention some conditions under which these alternatives are equivalent, e.g., estimated future trade-in value and variable operating costs.

P8. The investment for a proposed new project is:

Fixed capital:	
Depreciable portion	$250,000
Expensed portion	175,000
	425,000
Working capital	130,000
Total	$555,000

The depreciable and expensed portions are spent uniformly from -1 to 0; working capital is spent instantaneously at time zero. Assume that a 7% investment credit is allowed on the entire depreciable portion of the investment taken at zero time. Project life is 20 years, and annual before-tax variable margin is $400,000. The tax rate is 48%. Maintenance, real estate, and personal property taxes total 2.5% of the total fixed investment. Use continuous interest and 20-year sum-of-digits depreciation.

    What is the DCF rate of return?

P9. Develop a profit and loss statement for a 15% DCF return per year, 15-year project at a 48% tax rate using continuous interest and assuming that:

1. A $1,477,000 investment is applied uniformly over $1\frac{3}{4}$ years with 7% investment credit on the full amount at the end of construction.
2. Working capital is $270,000 at capacity and is proportional to sales.
3. Start-up expense is $120,000 (spread over 3 months following the investment period) and is not capitalized.
4. Annual net sales are $1,520,000 at capacity.
5. Operating expense (ex depreciation) is $167,000 fixed and $723,000 variable.
6. Sales buildup is 40 to 60 to 80 to 100% (fourth year on).
7. Depreciation is 15 year sum of digits.

Arrange the profit and loss statement horizontally by years with vertical columns from left to right reading: net sales, operating expense (subtitled all other costs, depreciation), federal income tax, net profit, cash return, capital investment (subtitled fixed, working), cash proceeds (subtitled by years, cumulative). State any other assumptions required.

P10. An economic study will use continuous interest and a 48% tax rate. A summary is:

Plant capacity, million lb/year	10
Fixed capital, $M	3,000
Working capital, $M	696
Start-up expense, $M	480
	4,176
Variable costs, $M	1,300
Fixed costs, $M (not including depreciation)	900
	2,200
Sales buildup (annual sales level)	20, 40, 60, 80, and 100% in fifth year on
Sales price, constant, $ per pound	0.30
Construction time, years	1.5
Start-up time, months	3
Economic life, years	15
Depreciable life (straight-line method), years	15

What is the DCF rate of return?

P11. You are chief engineer of Krock Mfg. Co., a firm which makes a variety of waxes and polishes. Last week a fire completely destroyed the weeble-wax blender and management faces the decision whether to replace this unit or stop manufacturing the product.

Weeble wax was once a high-volume high-profit product but is now on the way out. The new plastic weeble (which does not need waxing) is gradually replacing the old wooden type, with the result that sales are shrinking each year and will soon disappear entirely. Krock's marketing research people project weeble-wax sales for the next 6 years as follows:

Year	M tons
1	1,100
2	800
3	550
4	350
5	200
6	0

The fire insurance company has already paid Krock $125,000, the book value of the blender that was destroyed.

A new blender will cost $500,000 installed. Although this machine normally has a 10-year life, this one will have no further use after 5 years, when it will be scrapped. Salvage value will be about the same as the cost of dismantling.

Estimated working capital requirements, including inventories, are $0.16 per annual ton sales. Sale of the product nets $2 per ton at the plant. Variable costs amount to $1.30 per ton; and fixed costs, other than depreciation, to $200,000 per year. The company pays a combined federal-state tax rate of 55%. During the past 5 years, Krock's return on total invested capital has ranged from 8 to 12%. The cost of capital is 10%.

In an hour, Krock's executive committee will meet to decide whether to replace the blender or discontinue the manufacture of weeble wax. The decision will depend largely on your opinion.

(a) What is the yearly and average book rate of return that this operation will earn?

(b) What is the discounted rate of return? Use continuous interest and sum-of-digit depreciation.

(c) What is the effect of $0.10 per ton price reduction?

(d) How is the discounted return affected if sales have been overestimated by 20,000 tons per year?

(e) What is your recommendation?

5.17 References mentioned in text

R1. Bates, A. G.: These Two Tools Simplify Evaluations, *Hydrocarbon Process. Petrol. Refiner*, March, 1966, p. 181.

R2. Classification System for Economic Appraisals, *Cost Engineers' Notebook*, D-3, pp. 1–3, 1963.

R3. Jelen, F. C.: Remember All Three in Cost Analysis, *Chem. Eng.*, Jan. 27, 1958, pp. 123–128.

R4. Jelen, F. C.: Analyze Ventures This Way, *Hydrocarbon Process. Petrol. Refiner*, March, 1964, pp. 125–128.

R5. Mickley, H. S., T. K. Sherwood, and C. E. Reed. "Applied Mathematics in Chemical Engineering." 2d ed., p. 37, McGraw-Hill Book Company, New York, 1957.

R6. Reul, R. I.: Algorithms vs. Concepts, *AACE Bull.*, vol. 7, pp. 46–49, June, 1965.

R7. Terborgh, G.: "Business Investment Management," MAPI, Washington, 1967.

R8. Thorne, H. C., and W. E. Miller: Know How to Request Money, *Hydrocarbon Process.*, January, 1966, p. 172.

R9. Thorne, H. C., and D. C. Wise: Computers in Economic Evaluation, *Chem. Eng.*, April 29, 1963, p. 1929.

R10. Twaddle, W. W., and J. B. Malloy: Evaluating and Sizing New Chemical Plants in a Dynamic Economy, *AACE Bull.*, vol. 8, p. 135, September, 1966.

R11. Weaver, J. B.: Profitability Measures, *Chem. Eng. News*, Sept. 25, 1961, p. 94.

5.18 References—books

R1. Bierman, S., and S. Smidt: "The Capital Budgeting Decision," 2d ed., The Macmillan Company, New York, 1966.

R2. Edge, C. G.: "A Practical Manual on the Appraisal of Capital Expenditure," rev. ed., The Ryerson Press, Toronto, 1964.

R3. Grant, E. L., and W. G. Ireson: "Principles of Engineering Economy," 4th ed., The Ronald Press Company, New York, 1964.

R4. Grayson, C., and J. Jackson: "Decisions under Uncertainty: Drilling Decisions by Oil and Gas Operators," Harvard Graduate School of Business Administration, Boston, 1960.

R5. Hackney, J. W.: ' Control and Management of Capital Projects," John Wiley & Sons, Inc., New York, 1965.

R6. Schweyer, H. E.: "Analytic Models for Managerial and Engineering Economics," Reinhold Publishing Corporation, New York, 1964.

R7. Solomon, E.: "The Theory of Financial Management," Columbia University Press, New York, 1964.

5.19 References—additional articles

R1. Amey, L. R.: Investment Problems, *Chem. Engr.*, (Britain) March, 1965.

R2. Canada, J. R.: Capital Budgeting: Its Nature, Present Practice, and Needs for the Future, *J. Ind. Eng.*, March–April, 1964.

R3. Cardello, R. A., J. W. Kellett, and G. G. Lukk: Determining the Proper Size of Manufacturing Projects," *Eng. Economist*, Fall, 1963.

R4. Cheslow, R. T., and A. G. Bates: Long Range Economic Price, *Chem. Eng.*, Nov. 22, 1965, pp. 161–164.

R5. Green, P. E.: Risk Attitudes and Chemical Investment Decisions, *Chem. Eng. Progr.*, January, 1963, pp. 35–40.

R6. *Harvard Business Rev.*, Capital Investment Decisions, reprints of 1961–1964 series of articles.

R7. Hawkins, H. M., and O. E. Martin: How to Evaluate Projects, *Chem. Eng. Progr.*, December, 1964, pp. 58–63.

R8. Hertz, D. B.: Risk Analysis in Capital Investments, *Harvard Business Rev.*, January–February, 1964, pp. 95–106.

R9. Hirschmann, W. B., and J. R. Brauweiler: Investment Analysis: Coping with Change, *Harvard Business Rev.*, May–June, 1965, pp. 62–72.

R10. Hirschmann, W. B., and J. R. Brauweiler: Continuous Discounting for Realistic Investment Analysis, *Chem. Eng.*, July 19, 1965, p. 214; Aug. 16, 1965, pp. 132–136.

R11. McLean, J. G.: How to Evaluate New Capital Expenditures, *Harvard Business Rev.*, November–December, 1958, pp. 59–69.

R12. Reul, R. I.: Profitability Index for Investments, *Harvard Business Rev.*, July–August, 1957, pp. 116–132.

R13. Stokes, C. A.: Economic Evaluation, Organization and Coordination, *Chem. Eng. Progr.*, May, 1959, pp. 60–67.

R14. Thorne, H. C.: Post Installation Appraisals: What American Oil Looks For, *Hydrocarbon Process Petrol. Refiner*, March, 1965, pp. 109–111.

R15. Thorne, H. C., R. O. Carlson, and L. D. Thomas: How Taxes Affect Economic Evaluation, *Hydrocarbon Process. Petrol. Refiner*, November, 1964, pp. 225–232.

R16. Vancil, Richard F.: Lease or Borrow: New Method of Analysis, *Harvard Business Rev.*, September–October, 1961, p. 122.

6
Technological Advancement—Inflation

F. C. Jelen

DISPLACEMENT

6.1 Displacement vs. replacement

Replacement will be used to refer to a situation in which an asset is worn out or cannot physically perform its intended use and must have another article substituted for it soon, if not now. *Displacement* will be used to refer to a situation in which an asset can perform its function at least to some degree but can be substituted for by another asset for an overall economic gain. One distinguishing difference is that a decision regarding displacement can be ignored or delayed, perhaps for years.

A pure replacement problem, i.e., one based solely on the inability of an existing machine to function, can be analyzed by the methods of Chaps. 2 and 3 for periodic interest and Chap. 4 for continuous interest. The analyst should always regard replacement problems with a broad perspective, for the time when one asset must be replaced may introduce an opportunity for the displacement of other assets.

The possibility of displacement arises from two causes, loss of efficiency and technological advancement. A machine becomes more expensive to operate as it becomes less efficient for such reasons as high maintenance expense or loss of quality control. Even when a new machine is no technological improvement over the old machine, it may be economical to purchase the new machine. The second cause arises from technological advancement and the introduction of improved, more economical machines, such as machines using less labor or giving improved products. The existing machine may have suffered no loss in efficiency but has become obsolescent. In a practical case both loss of efficiency of the old machine and technological advancement of the new machine are present together.

In some respects the displacement problem is more important than the replacement problem. Since the latter problem must be faced, it automatically gets action. The displacement problem is omnipresent but must be sought out and made apparent. It requires a promotional effort to obtain action, for delay may not be fatal, yet recognition of the displacement problem is a key factor in industrial leadership. Companies which merely confront replacement problems as they occur generally lag behind, but those having an active displacement policy move forward.

6.2 One year more of existent

Let an existing machine be called the *existent* and the new machine the *displacer*. A decision to purchase the displacer depends upon a comparison of the cost of keeping the existent in operation against that of having the displacer in operation. The comparison can be made on the basis of unacost or capitalized cost, and, as for all cost comparisons, only differences need be considered. Costs that are equal in all respects for the two machines can be omitted because they have no effect on the decision.

In general, operating costs and other disadvantages of the existent grow progressively more unfavorable with time, and only 1 year ahead for the existent need be considered because it will make its best showing in the coming year. Exceptions to this rule will be discussed later.

The cost of keeping the existent in service 1 year more is readily calculated. Suppose the existing machine can be sold now for $C_{sal,0}$, the present realizable salvage value, and next year for $C_{sal,1}$, the realizable salvage value at the end of 1 year. The present realizable salvage value may not be the same as the book value and indeed may be considerably less. The difference between the book value and salvage value is known as the *sunk cost*. The sunk cost has no influence on the decision except for the tax situation. A sunk cost is revealed but not created by displacement. It represents an inadequate depreciation expense in previous years and cannot be corrected by any policy of future years. The decision insofar as the existent is concerned for 1 year more is sell the machine now for its realizable salvage value $C_{sal,0}$ or keep the machine and incur an operating cost C_{e_1} as of the end of the year and recover salvage value at that time, $C_{sal,1}$. These amounts must, of course, be used with the tax situation included.

For the tax situation let B_0 be the book value now and B_1 that 1 year from now. Suppose that the machine is sold now and that the tax credit is available immediately. The loss on disposal is $B_0 - C_{sal,0}$ and the savings in taxes $t(B_0 - C_{sal,0})$. If the machine is not sold now, the receipts that are avoided must be regarded as an expense, which on an after-tax basis is

$$C_{sal,0} + t(B_0 - C_{sal,0}) \tag{6.2\#1}$$

At the end of the year depreciation amounting to D_1 can be taken, $C_{sal,1}$ is received as salvage value, and the loss on disposal is $B_1 - C_{sal,1}$. Altogether the after-tax receipt is

$$tD_1 + C_{sal,1} + t(B_1 - C_{sal,1})$$

Noting that $B_1 = B_0 - D_1$, the last relationship reduces to

$$C_{sal,1} + t(B_0 - C_{sal,1}) \tag{6.2\#2}$$

Let C_{e_1} be the operating cost for the coming year as of the end of the year subject to a tax credit as of the end of the year. Then the after-tax cost is

$$C_{e_1}(1 - t) \tag{6.2\#3}$$

Combine Eq. (6.2#1), referring to the beginning of the year, with Eqs. (6.2#2) and (6.2#3), referring to the end of the year. The cost diagram and the present worth, basis 1 year, are:

$$P_1 = C_{sal,0} + t(B_0 - C_{sal,0}) - \frac{C_{sal,1} + t(B_0 - C_{sal,1}) - C_{e_1}(1-t)}{1+r} \tag{6.2\#4}$$

This can be converted to a unacost by Eq. (2.6#4) with $F_{PR,r,1} = 1 + r$

$$R = P_1(1 + r)$$

and to a capitalized cost by Eq. (2.7#3) with $F_{PK,r,1} = (1+r)/r$

$$K = P_1 \frac{1+r}{r}$$

Unacost or capitalized cost for the displacer can be obtained in the conventional manner, as by Table 3.10T1, and a comparison with the existent will show which is the more economical.

6.2 TECHNOLOGICAL ADVANCEMENT—INFLATION

Example 6.2E1 Four years ago a machine cost $23,000. It has been depreciated on a 10-year life with $1,000 terminal salvage value using sum-of-digits depreciation. If sold now, it will bring $2,000 with immediate tax credit for any loss on disposal. If sold at the end of the year, it will bring $1,500 with immediate tax credit for any loss on disposal. Operating costs for next year are $3,800 as of the end of the year with immediate tax credit.

A new machine will cost $50,000 with a 12-year life and $3,000 terminal salvage value. Depreciate for a 10-year life for tax purposes using sum-of-digits depreciation. The operating cost will be $3,000 as of the end of each year with $6,000 per year savings due to better quality control, both subject to immediate tax credit.

If money is worth 10% per year after a 50% tax rate, should the displacer be purchased?

By item 5, Table 3.10T1, the book value now of the existent is

$$B_0 = 23{,}000 - (23{,}000 - 1{,}000)\frac{4}{10(10+1)}(20 + 1 - 4) = \$9{,}400$$

The loss on disposal at zero time is

$$B_0 - C_{sal,0} = 9{,}400 - 2{,}000 = \$7{,}400$$

and the tax credit is

$$t(7{,}400) = 0.5(7{,}400) = \$3{,}700$$

The depreciation plus loss on disposal at end of year is

$$B_0 - C_{sal,1} = 9{,}400 - 1{,}500 = \$7{,}900$$

and the tax credit is

$$t(7{,}900) = 0.5(7{,}900) = \$3{,}950$$

The after-tax cost of end-of-year expense is

$$C_{e_1}(1 - t) = 3{,}800(1 - 0.5) = \$1{,}900$$

The cost diagram is

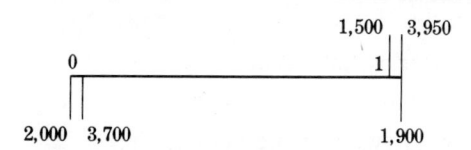

The present worth at 10% per year is

$$P_1 = 2{,}000 + 3{,}700 - \frac{1{,}500 + 3{,}950 - 1{,}900}{1.10} = \$2{,}473$$

and unacost for 1 year more of the existent is

$$R = 2{,}473(1.10) = \$2{,}720$$

Unacost for the displacer, by Table 3.13T1 items 1, 2, and 7, is

$$C_d(1 - tF_{SDP,10\%,10})F_{PR,10\%,12} = (50{,}000 - 3{,}000)[1 - 0.50(0.70099)](0.14676) = 4{,}480$$
$$R(1 - t) = (3{,}000 - 6{,}000)(1 - 0.50) = -1{,}500$$
$$C_{sal}r = 3{,}000(0.10) = 300$$
$$R \text{ displacer} = \$3{,}280$$

It will be more economical to retain the existent: unacost $2,473 against $3,280.

6.3 More than one year of existent

It was assumed in the preceding section that 1 year would be the most favorable period for the existent. The treatment of the existent for more than 1 year ahead will now be analyzed, followed by some examples.

Refer to Example 6.2E1. In addition let the salvage value at the end of the second year be $900 and the operating cost for the second year as of the end of the year C_{e_2} be $1,400. The tax timing is the same as before. Now find the unacost for the existent based on retention for 2 years.

At zero time the expense incurred by retaining the machine is the same as before, and on an after-tax basis is

$$C_{sal,0} + t(B_0 - C_{sal,1}) = 2{,}000 + 3{,}700 = 5{,}700$$

The end-of-first-year expense is $3,800, as before. Depreciation for the year by item 6, Table 3.10T1, is

$$\tfrac{6}{55}(23{,}000 - 1{,}000) = 2{,}400$$

The expense for end of first year after taxes is

$$3{,}800(1-t) - 2{,}400t = 1{,}900 - 1{,}200 = 700$$

The end-of-second-year expense is 1,400. Depreciation for the second year is

$$\tfrac{5}{55}(23{,}000 - 1{,}000) = 2{,}000$$

The book value at the end of the second year is

$$B_2 = B_0 - D_1 - D_2 = 9{,}400 - 2{,}400 - 2{,}000 = 5{,}000$$

where D_1 and D_2 are first- and second-year depreciation. The loss on disposal at the end of the second year is

$$B_2 - C_{sal,2} = 5{,}000 - 900 = 4{,}100$$

The expense for the end of second year after 0.50 decimal tax rate is

$$1{,}400(1-t) - 2{,}000t - 900 - 4{,}100(1-t) = -3{,}250$$

The cost diagram on an after-tax basis by symbols and numbers is:

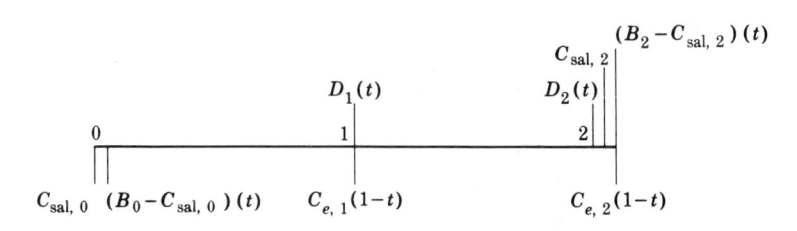

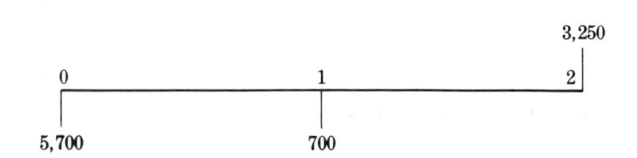

The present worth is

$$P_2 = 5{,}700 + \frac{700}{1.10} - \frac{3{,}250}{1.10^2} = \$3{,}650$$

and the unacost is

$$R = P_2 F_{PR,10\%,2} = 3{,}650(0.57619) = \$2{,}103$$

This is less than the unacost based on 1 year more, $2,720, because there is a sharp drop in operating expenses for the second year. Normally with operating costs advancing, the unacost for 1 year more will be the minimum.

The example demonstrates how more than 1 year is treated with taxes included. The tax timing must be considered whether 1 or more years ahead is investigated, but the analyst should be able to compute the unacost or capitalized cost for any tax timing and duration that the existent is continued.

Cases where multiyear service for the existent are more favorable than that for just 1 more year of service are usually evident from inspection. In practice they arise principally from two causes: (1) net realizable salvage value may decline sharply for the first year, and (2) benefits of an overhaul may extend more than 1 year. Examples of each type follow (on a no-tax basis to simplify the presentation).

Example 6.3EI An improperly designed pump has an excessive power cost. Salvage value now is $1,000, declining to $250 next year and to $100 the following year. Operating cost for 1 year more is $700 and $800 for the following year as of the end of each year. A displacer costing $3,800 will last 5 years with negligible salvage value. The operating expense will be uniform at $400 per year as of the end of the year. If money is worth 8% per year, should replacement be made now?

Capitalized cost of the existent, basis 1 year more of service, by Table 2.8T1 items 8 and 4, is

$$(1{,}000 - 250)F_{PK,8\%,1} + 250 = 750(13.500) + 250 = 10{,}375$$

$$700 \frac{1}{1.08} F_{PK,8\%,1} = \frac{700}{1.08} 13.50 = 8{,}750$$

$$K_1 = \overline{19{,}125}$$

Capitalized cost of the existent, basis 2 years of service, by Table 2.8T1 items 8, 4, 4, is

$$(1{,}000 - 100)F_{PK,8\%,2} + 100 = 900(7.0096) + 100 = 6{,}409$$

$$700 \frac{1}{1.08} F_{PK,8\%,2} = \frac{700}{1.08} 7.0096 = 4{,}543$$

$$800 \frac{1}{1.08^2} F_{PK,8\%,2} = \frac{800}{1.1664} 7.0096 = 4{,}808$$

$$K_2 = \overline{15{,}760}$$

Capitalized cost of the displacer by Table 2.8T1, item 8 and 2, is

$$(3{,}800 - 0)F_{PK,8\%,5} + 0 = 3{,}800(3.1307) = 11{,}897$$

$$400 \frac{1}{0.08} = 5{,}000$$

$$\text{Displacer } K = \overline{16{,}897}$$

108   MATHEMATICS OF COST COMPARISONS   6.4

Based on only 1 more year of service the existent is more expensive than the displacer, $K_1 = \$19,125$ against $\$16,897$; but it would be incorrect to replace now. If the existent is kept for 2 years, and despite its rise in operating cost during the second year, it will be more economical that the displacer, $K_2 = \$15,760$ against $\$16,897$.

Example 6.3E2 A tank with negligible salvage value now or later can be repaired for $3,000 to extend its life 1 year, after which $1,000 per year at the beginning of each year will extend the life 2 more years. A new tank costs $14,500, lasts 10 years with negligible salvage value, and has no annual expense. If money is worth 8% per year should a new tank be purchased now?

Use capitalized cost and Table 2.8T1. The cost of existent, 1 year of service, is

$$3,000 F_{PK,8\%,1} = 3,000(13.500) = K_1 = 40,500$$

The cost of existent, 2 years of service, is

$$3,000 F_{PK,8\%,2} = 3,000(7.0096) = 21,029$$

$$1,000 \frac{1}{1.08} F_{PK,8\%,2} = \frac{1,000}{1.08} 7.0096 = 6,490$$

$$K_2 = \overline{27,519}$$

The cost of existent, 3 years of service, is

$$3,000 F_{PK,8\%,3} = 3,000(4.8504) = 14,551$$

$$1,000 \frac{1}{1.08} F_{PK,8\%,3} = \frac{1,000}{1.08} 4.8504 = 4,491$$

$$1,000 \frac{1}{1.08^2} F_{PK,8\%,3} = \frac{1,000}{1.1664} 4.8504 = 4,148$$

$$K_3 = \overline{23,190}$$

The cost of the displacer, 10 years of service, is

$$14,500 F_{PK,8\%,10} = 14,500(1.8629) = 27,012$$

Based on 1 or 2 years more of service the existent compares unfavorably with the displacer, but it is more economical based on a 3-year period.

6.4 Uniform-gradient series

In many practical problems the operating expenses of a machine vary from year to year. If the variation from year to year is systematic, the present worth of the expenses for a number of years can be computed by an algebraic relationship. A particularly important case arises when the annual cost increases by G as of the end of each year with first-year end-of-year cost zero. The costs as of the end of the year form the sequence for n years

$$0, G, 2G, 3G, \ldots, (n-1)G$$

The series is known as a *uniform-gradient series*, and G is the uniform gradient. The present worth of this series for n years is

$$P = G\left[\frac{0}{1+i} + \frac{1}{(1+i)^2} + \frac{2}{(1+i)^3} + \cdots + \frac{n-1}{(1+i)^n}\right] \quad (6.4\#1)$$

The series is classified as a recurring series of the second order, which can be summed algebraically by special techniques developed in Chap. 14. The series for $G = 1$ is referred to as the *uniform-gradient-series present-worth factor* with symbol $F_{GP,i,n}$. Mathematically, the sum is

$$F_{GP,i,n} = \frac{1}{i}\left[\frac{(1+i)^n - 1}{i(1+i)^n} - \frac{n}{(1+i)^n}\right] \quad (6.4\#2)$$

or

$$F_{GP,i,n} = \frac{F_{RP,i,n} - nF_{SP,i,n}}{i} \quad (6.4\#3)$$

The $F_{GP,i,n}$ factor is tabulated in Appendix 1, Table 1.

Usually the gradient occurs along with a uniform annual cost, but the two are easily segregated, as shown in the following example.

Example 6.4E1 A series of costs at the end of each year increases uniformly by $100 per year and is $1,000 for the first year. If money is worth 8% per year, what is the present worth of 12 years of costs?

The present worth is

$$P = \frac{1,000}{1.08} + \frac{1,100}{1.08^2} + \frac{1,200}{1.08^3} + \cdots + \frac{2,100}{1.08^{12}}$$

which can be broken down into two series

$$P = 1,000\left(\frac{1}{1.08} + \frac{1}{1.08^2} + \cdots + \frac{1}{1.08^{12}}\right) + 100\left(\frac{0}{1.08} + \frac{1}{1.08^2} + \frac{2}{1.08^3} + \cdots + \frac{11}{1.08^{12}}\right)$$

or in sigma notation

$$P = 1,000 \sum_{1}^{12}\left(\frac{1}{1.08}\right)^n + 100 \sum_{1}^{12} \frac{x-1}{1.08^x}$$

The two sigma series on the right are respectively the present worths of a uniform annual series, Eq. (2.2#3), and a uniform-gradient series, Eq. (6.4#3). The combined present worths are

$$P = 1,000 F_{RP,8\%,12} + 100 F_{GP,8\%,12}$$
$$= 1,000(7.5361) + 100(34.634) = \$11,000$$

6.5 Best policy with a uniform-gradient cost

A practical and instructive case is an item or machine that incurs an operating inefficiency at a constant rate. Consider the simplified situation for an automobile which costs $4,000 when new and has a salvage value at the end of each year amounting to 75% of the salvage value at the beginning of the year, i.e.,

$$C_{sal} = 4,000(0.75^n)$$

where n is any year, and the yearly operating expenses of the automobile increase by $100 per year. The fixed expenses common to all the years need not be considered. The variable expenses are

$$C_{en} = (n-1)(100)$$

110 MATHEMATICS OF COST COMPARISONS 6.5

Table 6.5T1 Optimum Policy Starting with New Automobile

(1) Years retained n	(2) Present worth of first cost, $	(3) Salvage value C_{sal}, $	(4) $F_{SP,6\%,n}$	(5) Present worth of C_{sal}, $ (3) × (4)	(6) $100 F_{GP,6\%,n}$ $	(7) Total present worth, $ (2) − (5) + (6)	(8) $F_{PR,6\%,n}$	(9) Unacost, $ per year (7) × (8)
1	4,000	3,000	0.94340	2,830	0	1,170	1.0600	1,240
2	4,000	2,250	0.89000	2,002	89	2,087	0.54544	1,138
3	4,000	1,688	0.83962	1,417	257	2,840	0.37411	1,062
4	4,000	1,266	0.79209	1,003	495	3,492	0.28859	1,008
5	4,000	949	0.74726	709	793	4,084	0.23740	970
6	4,000	712	0.70496	502	1,146	4,644	0.20336	944
7	4,000	534	0.66506	355	1,545	5,190	0.17914	930
8	4,000	400	0.62741	251	1,984	5,733	0.16104	923.2
9	4,000	300	0.59190	178	2,458	6,280	0.14702	923.3
10	4,000	225	0.55839	126	2,960	6,834	0.13587	929
11	4,000	169	0.52679	89	3,487	7,398	0.12679	938

where C_{en} is an expense at the end of year n. Consider money worth 6% per year with no tax.

If an automobile is kept n years, the present worth of all the costs is

$$P_n = 4{,}000 - \frac{C_{sal}}{1.06^n} + 100\left(\frac{0}{1.06} + \frac{1}{1.06^2} + \frac{2}{1.06^3} + \cdots + \frac{n-1}{1.06^n}\right)$$

Substituting the value for C_{sal}, and $F_{GP,6\%,n}$ for the series in parentheses, this is

$$P_n = 4{,}000 - \frac{4{,}000(0.75^n)}{1.06^n} + 100 F_{GP,6\%,n}$$

Finally converting to a unacost by Eq. (2.2#8),

$$R = P_n F_{PR} = F_{PR,6\%,n}\left[4{,}000 - \frac{4{,}000(0.75^n)}{1.06^n} + 100 F_{GP,6\%,n}\right]$$

After obtaining values in Appendix 1, Table 1, for $1/1.06^n = F_{PS,6\%,n}$ and for $F_{GP,6\%,n}$, the last relationship is readily computed. A tabulation of the calculations is given in Table 6.5T1. Minimum unacost occurs at 8 years; i.e., when starting out with a new automobile, the optimum time to trade is at the end of 8 years for the schedule of costs as given.

The same conclusion is reached using the incremental method of Sec. 6.2. The used automobile makes its best showing on the basis of 1 year ahead. Consider the situation at the end of the seventh year. Salvage value then is $534, dropping 1 year later to $400. Operating costs for the coming year are $700 as of the end of the year. The equivalent cost as of the end of the year for just 1 more year of service is

$$534(1.06) - 400 + 700 = \$866$$

Inasmuch as only 1 year is involved, $866, being an end-of-year amount, is also a unacost. By Table 6.5T1 unacost for keeping a car 7 years is $930 per year. That is, trading at the end of 7 years amounts to a $930 unacost, whereas keeping the automobile another year amounts to a unacost of $866. The automobile should be kept another year.

Repeat the calculations at the end of the eighth year. Unacost for 1 year more is

$$400(1.06) - 300 + 800 = \$924$$

whereas from Table 6.5T1 unacost for operating just 8 years is $923.2. The ninth year will not pay, and the automobile should be traded at the end of 8 years, confirming the conclusion from Table 6.5T1.

The preceding analysis was made assuming that a new automobile was purchased at the start. Consider now the situation in which a 2-year-old car is bought, subject to all the previous conditions. The yearly costs will form the series

200, 300, 400, 500, ...

112 MATHEMATICS OF COST COMPARISONS

Table 6.5T2 Optimum Policy Starting with 2-year-old Automobile

(1) Years retained n	(2) Present worth of first cost, $	(3) Salvage value C_{sal}, $	(4) $F_{SP,6\%,n}$	(5) Present worth of C_{sal} (3) × (4)	(6) Constant annual expense, $	(7) $F_{RP,6\%,n}$	(8) Present worth of constant annual expense (6) × (7), $	(9) $100 F_{GP,6\%,n}$ $	(10) Total present worth, $ (2) − (5) + (8) + (9)	(11) $F_{PR,6\%,n}$	(12) Unacost $ per year (10) × (11)
1	2,250	1,688	0.94340	1,592	200	0.94340	189	0	847	1.0600	898
2	2,250	1,266	0.89000	1,127	200	1.8334	367	89	1,579	0.54544	861
3	2,250	949	0.83962	797	200	2.6730	535	257	2,245	0.37411	832
4	2,250	712	0.79209	564	200	3.4651	693	495	2,874	0.28859	829
5	2,250	534	0.74726	399	200	4.2124	842	793	3,486	0.23740	828
6	2,250	400	0.70496	282	200	4.9173	983	1,146	4,097	0.20336	833
7	2,250	300	0.66506	200	200	5.5824	1,116	1,545	4,711	0.17914	844

Table 6.5T3 Optimum Policy for Automobile

Age of automobile when purchased, year	Optimum years retained	Age when traded, years	Unacost, $ per year
0	8	8	923
1	7	8	866
2	5	7	828
3	3	6	804
4	1	5	792
5	1	6	794
6	1	7	822

which can be broken down to a constant amount of 200 and the series

0, 100, 200, 300, . . .

A tabulation similar to Table 6.5T1 can be made. The first cost is $2,250, and the constant $200 per year operating cost must be included. The tabulation is given in Table 6.5T2.

Optimum policy when starting out with a 2-year-old automobile is to trade 5 years later when the automobile is 7 years old. This is not the same conclusion that was reached when starting with a new automobile, which should be traded when it is 8 years old. Also minimum unacost starting with a 2-year-old automobile is $827.6, whereas starting with a new automobile minimum unacost is $932.2. Proceeding in this manner for all alternatives gives Table 6.5T3.

For the figures given, the overall optimum or minimum is $792 per year obtained by starting out with a 4-year-old automobile and keeping it 1 year. It has been assumed that a used automobile can be purchased for the same amount as its trade-in value. A different set of figures will lead to a different result, but the example is illustrative. If the yearly expenses and salvage value are not systematic, it will be necessary to calculate the present worths by discounting each year individually without the benefit of a systematic relationship; but the principles remain the same.

In practice not everybody can start out with a 4-year-old automobile and follow the optimum policy. In an industrial problem, however, it is not always necessary to start at the beginning of the line. Suppose that a process can use a rough ore, semirefined ore, or refined ore, all of which can be made available in any quantity at different prices. All subsequent processers can choose refined ore if that is the most economical choice.

6.6 Delay value of existent

An existent can be displaced by a new machine merely because it acquires operating inefficiency with time that has nothing to do with technological advancement. The problem is illustrated by the optimum policy for an automobile in the preceding section. On the other hand, an existent can suffer no operating inefficiency with time and yet be displaced because of technological advancement of a machine now available. Usually both factors apply. The analyst compares the existent for what it is now to the new machine for what it likewise is now.

Future technological advancement cannot be purchased ahead of time. However, the existence of future technological advancement cannot be ignored. Indeed, its value should be included as a reduction in the unacost or capitalized cost of the existent. By keeping the existent it becomes possible eventually to obtain a later model of the new machine which presumably will have even more technological advancement. Technological advancement works in two ways. The technological advancement which has been made works against the existent, but the possibility of future technological advancement works for the existent. This latter factor has generally been overlooked. For new types of assets undergoing a rapid technological advancement the delaying value of the existent may be significant. An exact mathematical evaluation is not possible because the result depends upon the model and an estimation of future technological advancement. An approximation to the value is given in [6.16R5]. The advantage in waiting 1 year for an improved model when expressed as a capitalized cost is

$$K = \frac{C_i}{i}\left(\begin{array}{c}\text{decimal technological}\\ \text{advancement rate}\end{array}\right)(1 - nF_{PR,i,n}F_{SP,i,n}) \qquad (6.6\#1)$$

where C_i is the cost of the displacer now available and n its service life. Here i is the rate of return, and the technological-advancement rate is such that multiplication by the first cost is a measure of next year's technological advancement in dollars. The corresponding relationship for unacost is obtained by multiplying Eq. (6.6#1) by i. Equation (6.6#1) has been derived on the basis of no tax.

Example 6.6E1 A new machine costs $100,000 now, and the technological-advancement rate is 12% per year. How much is the delay value of the existent worth if the new machine lasts 10 years and money is worth 8% per year?
 By Eq. (6.6#1)

$$R = iK = \frac{iC_i}{i}0.12(1 - 10F_{PR,8\%,10}F_{SP,8\%,10})$$

$$R = 100,000(0.12)[1 - 10(0.14903)(0.46319)] = \$3,716$$

The immediate delay value of the existent is $3,716, and this amount should be subtracted from the unacost of the existent.

6.7 A mathematical model for technological advancement

Consider the situation for which technological advancement alone makes displacement possible; i.e., the existing machine suffers no loss of efficiency with time. The mathematical model for the machine will be based on two assumptions:

1 Each year a new model will become available costing $1 - p$ of the cost of the model of the preceding year, where p is the technological-advancement rate

expressed as a decimal. If the cost of a new machine is C_i now, 1 year from now it will be $C_i(1-p)$, 2 years from now $C_i(1-p)^2$, and so forth.

2 Some of the operating costs of the machine will likewise incorporate technological advancement. Let R_p denote the yearly end-of-year operating expense for this year's model that is subject to technological-advancement. Next year's model will have a comparable expense $R_p(1-p)$, the following model $R_p(1-p)^2$, and so forth. Uniform yearly expenses that are not affected by technological advancement do not vary from model to model and need not be considered. When a machine is bought, the yearly expense R_p remains constant until a new machine is purchased n years later, which will drop the yearly expense to $R_p(1-p)^n$.

These two assumptions permit evaluation of the expression for the economic life of a machine for various technological advancement rates. If a machine is bought now and replaced every n years, the pertinent capitalized cost of the machine is the present worth after taxes taken to infinity for (1) the first costs occurring every n years and (2) the yearly operating cost occurring every year and changing every n years. This is

$$K = C_i(1 - t\psi_{r_n}) + C_i(1 - t\psi_{r_n})\frac{(1-p)^n}{1+r)^n}$$
$$+ C_i(1 - t\psi_{r_n})\frac{(1-p)^{2n}}{(1+r)^{2n}} + \cdots$$
$$+ \sum_1^n \frac{R_p(1-t)}{(1+r)^x} + \sum_{n+1}^{2n} \frac{R_p(1-t)(1-p)^n}{(1+r)^x}$$
$$+ \sum_{2n+1}^{3n} \frac{R_p(1-t)(1-p)^{2n}}{(1+r)^x} + \cdots \qquad (6.7\#1)$$

Although Eq. (6.7#1) appears formidable, it reduces to

$$\frac{K}{C_i} = \frac{(1+r)^n(1 - t\psi_{r_n})\dfrac{R_p}{C_i}\dfrac{(1-t)[(1+r)^n - 1]}{r}}{r - (1-p)^n} \qquad (6.7\#2)$$

where $r =$ decimal rate of return after taxes
$t =$ decimal tax rate
$\psi =$ factor associated with depreciation (see Sec. 3.13)

Multiplication of Eq. (6.7#2) by r will give an equivalent expression for unacost. Values for $(1-p)^n$ are given in Appendix 1, Table 4, as

$$F_{PS,-p,n} = (1-p)^n \qquad (6.7\#3)$$

where $F_{PS,-p,n}$ is the compound-interest factor for negative rate.

The optimum economic life for a machine subject to the conditions of Eq. (6.7#3) can be determined by finding the value of n which makes K/C_i a minimum for specified values of the other parameters, r, t, R_p/C_i, p, and depreciation method. Figure 6.7F1 obtained by machine computation gives the optimum

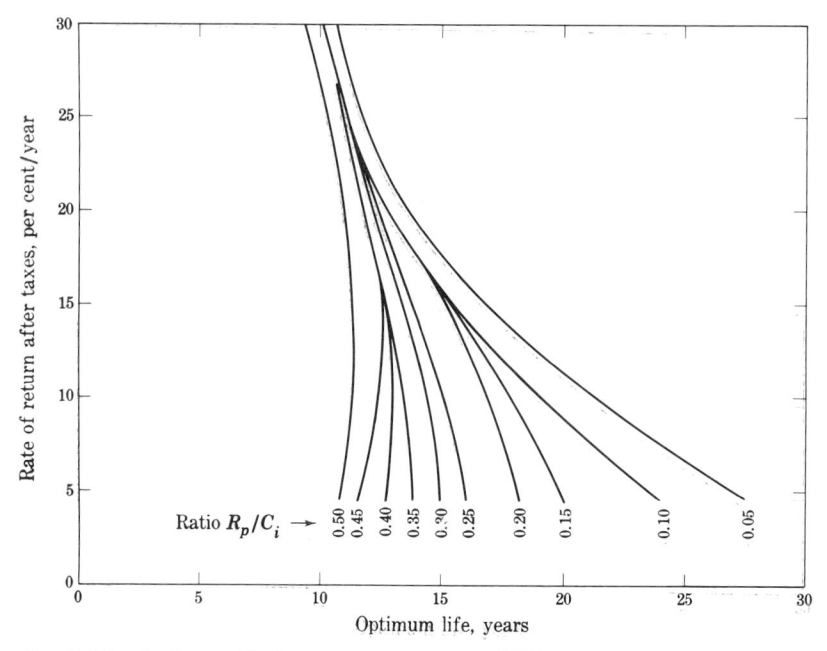

Fig. 6.7F1 Optimum life for improvement rate of 3% per year and 50% tax rate.

service life for a technological-advancement rate of 3% per year, a realistic figure, and income tax rate of 50% using sum-of-digits depreciation. From the figure, for a 10% per year rate of return after taxes and a ratio for $R_p/C_i = 0.20$, the optimum economic life is 17 years.

6.8 The MAPI model

The Machinery and Applied Products Institute (MAPI) has spent considerable effort in promoting the comparison of existing machines with current machines as a guide for modernization. The system has undergone several revisions and is offered principally in worksheet form with accompanying charts.

The MAPI model is actually based on a new machine that acquires an operating inefficiency at a uniform rate. Applications of the system are given in [6.16R9], which contains a brief development of the underlying relationships in an appendix.

Tables 6.8T1 and 6.8T2 and Fig. 6.8F1 illustrate an application using standard worksheets and charts. Table 6.8T1 is merely a checklist for computing the savings to be obtained by installing the new machine. The comparison is usually made on the basis of 1 year ahead, as in the illustration, but can be for more than 1 year ahead. The new machine will have an operating advantage of $17,020 next year, item 25.

Table 6.8T2 requires some explanation. The $2,100 of item 26 in this case is 7% of $29,800 and is the tax investment credit. In item 27, $4,000 is the disposal

MAPI CHART No. 1A

(ONE-YEAR COMPARISON PERIOD AND SUM-OF-DIGITS TAX DEPRECIATION)

INSTRUCTIONS:

1. Locate service life (in years) on the horizontal axis.
2. Ascend vertical line to point representing salvage ratio (estimate location when ratio falls between the curves).
3. Read point opposite on vertical scale. This is the percentage of retention value to net cost at the end of the year.
4. Enter in Line 29 (Column E) of MAPI form.

Copyright 1967, Machinery and Allied Products Institute

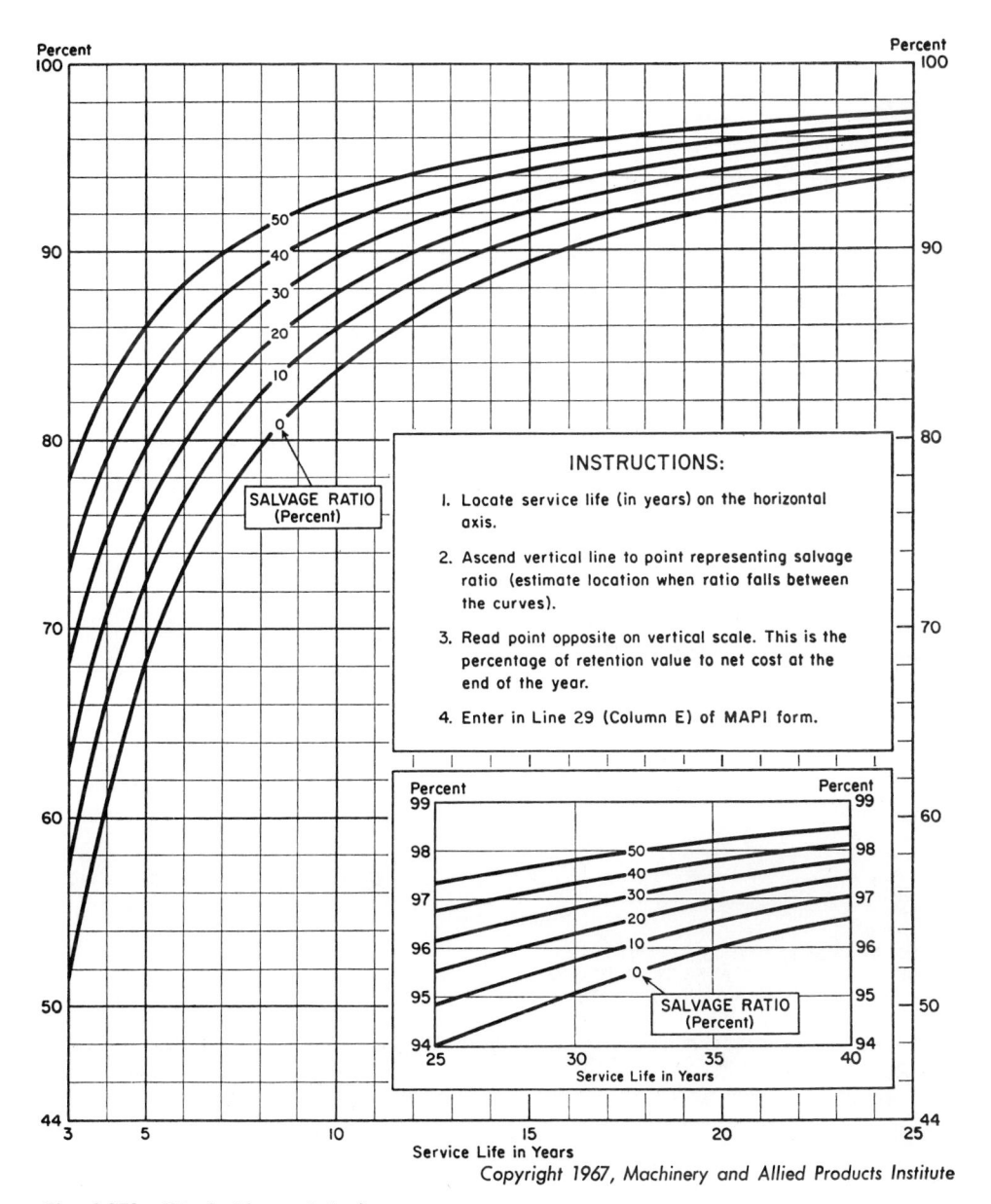

Fig. 6.8F1 (*Used with permission.*)

Table 6.8T1   MAPI Summary Form*

PROJECT NO. _____   SHEET 1

MAPI SUMMARY FORM
(AVERAGING SHORTCUT)

PROJECT ____Box Machine and Stitcher_____
ALTERNATIVE ____Continuing as is_____
COMPARISON PERIOD (YEARS)   (P) _____1_____
ASSUMED OPERATING RATE OF PROJECT (HOURS PER YEAR)   _____1,200_____

I. OPERATING ADVANTAGE
(NEXT-YEAR FOR A 1-YEAR COMPARISON PERIOD,* ANNUAL AVERAGES FOR LONGER PERIODS)

A. EFFECT OF PROJECT ON REVENUE

		INCREASE	DECREASE	
1	FROM CHANGE IN QUALITY OF PRODUCTS	$	$	1
2	FROM CHANGE IN VOLUME OF OUTPUT			2
3	TOTAL	$ X	$ Y	3

B. EFFECT ON OPERATING COSTS

4	DIRECT LABOR	$ 900	$	4
5	INDIRECT LABOR	150		5
6	FRINGE BENEFITS	190		6
7	MAINTENANCE	200		7
8	TOOLING	80		8
9	MATERIALS AND SUPPLIES		16,800	9
10	INSPECTION			10
11	ASSEMBLY			11
12	SCRAP AND REWORK			12
13	DOWN TIME			13
14	POWER	40		14
15	FLOOR SPACE		1,000	15
16	PROPERTY TAXES AND INSURANCE	320		16
17	SUBCONTRACTING			17
18	INVENTORY		1,100	18
19	SAFETY			19
20	FLEXIBILITY			20
21	OTHER			21
22	TOTAL	$ 1,880 Y	$ 18,900 X	22

C. COMBINED EFFECT

23	NET INCREASE IN REVENUE (3X−3Y)	$	23
24	NET DECREASE IN OPERATING COSTS (22X−22Y)	$ 17,020	24
25	ANNUAL OPERATING ADVANTAGE (23+24)	$ 17,020	25

* Next year means the first year of project operation. For projects with a significant break-in period, use performance after break-in.

Copyright 1967, Machinery and Allied Products Institute

*Used with permission.

Table 6.8T2   MAPI Worksheet*

SHEET 2

II. INVESTMENT AND RETURN

A. INITIAL INVESTMENT

26	INSTALLED COST OF PROJECT	$ 29,800			
	MINUS INITIAL TAX BENEFIT OF	$ 2,100	(Net Cost)	$ 27,700	26
27	INVESTMENT IN ALTERNATIVE				
	CAPITAL ADDITIONS MINUS INITIAL TAX BENEFIT	$			
	PLUS: DISPOSAL VALUE OF ASSETS RETIRED BY PROJECT *	$ 4,000		$ 4,000	27
28	INITIAL NET INVESTMENT (26−27)			$ 23,700	28

B. TERMINAL INVESTMENT

29 RETENTION VALUE OF PROJECT AT END OF COMPARISON PERIOD
(ESTIMATE FOR ASSETS, IF ANY, THAT CANNOT BE DEPRECIATED OR EXPENSED. FOR OTHERS, ESTIMATE OR USE MAPI CHARTS.)

Item or Group	Installed Cost, Minus Initial Tax Benefit (Net Cost) A	Service Life (Years) B	Disposal Value, End of Life (Percent of Net Cost) C	MAPI Chart Number D	Chart Percentage E	Retention Value $\left(\frac{A \times E}{100}\right)$ F
Box Machine and Stitcher	$ 27,700	13	10	1A	89.4	$ 24,760

	ESTIMATED FROM CHARTS (TOTAL OF COL. F)	$	
	PLUS: OTHERWISE ESTIMATED	$	$ 24,760	29
30	DISPOSAL VALUE OF ALTERNATIVE AT END OF PERIOD *		$ 4,000	30
31	TERMINAL NET INVESTMENT (29−30)		$ 20,760	31

C. RETURN

32	AVERAGE NET CAPITAL CONSUMPTION $\left(\frac{28-31}{P}\right)$	$ 2,940	32
33	AVERAGE NET INVESTMENT $\left(\frac{28+31}{2}\right)$	$ 22,230	33
34	BEFORE-TAX RETURN $\left(\frac{25-32}{33} \times 100\right)$	% 63.3	34
35	INCREASE IN DEPRECIATION AND INTEREST DEDUCTIONS	$ 4,190	35
36	TAXABLE OPERATING ADVANTAGE (25−35)	$ 12,830	36
37	INCREASE IN INCOME TAX (36×TAX RATE)	$ 6,415	37
38	AFTER-TAX OPERATING ADVANTAGE (25−37)	$ 10,605	38
39	AVAILABLE FOR RETURN ON INVESTMENT (38−32)	$ 7,665	39
40	AFTER-TAX RETURN $\left(\frac{39}{33} \times 100\right)$	% 34.5	40

* After terminal tax adjustments.

Copyright 1967, Machinery and Allied Products Institute

*Used with permission.

value now of the existing machine. In item 29, the service life of the new machine, here 13 years, must be supplied by the analyst. This in turn will fix the gradient under which operating costs for the new machine increase. The analyst should understand that the selection of the service life enters in a complicated manner and that it is connected with an operating inferiority rate and not true obsolescence. The disposal value of the new machine will be 10%, which will have to be considered also in item 35. For item 29, MAPI chart 1A is reproduced as Fig. 6.8F1. Using the chart for 13 years at 10% salvage value gives 89.4%, which multiplied by 27,700 is 24,760, the value of the new asset 1 year hence. Item 30 need not be identical to item 27, but here the disposal value is 4,000 now or 1 year later. Item 32, the average net capital consumption, is a key item which represents the cost of the machine, here reduced to its first-year cost. Item 35 is the increase in depreciation arising from purchasing the new machine plus the interest on 23,700 at this company's 30% borrowed capital ratio and 5% per year debt interest rate. Item 40 gives the single criterion 34.5%, the after-tax return on average investment for the first year of the new machine.

Charts are available for sum-of-digits, double-declining balance, straight-line depreciation or for expensing fully in 1 year, also for 1-year comparison or for multiyear comparison, making eight charts in all. The charts have several fixed parameters built-in: 0.50 tax rate, 0.25 ratio of borrowed to total capital, 0.03 decimal interest rate on borrowed capital, 0.10 decimal rate of return on company capital, and equality of tax life and service life. If other values of the parameters are required, algebraic relationships must be used, but they are complicated.

6.9 Group displacement

Some assets exist in multiples and fail on an individual basis, light bulbs being a classical example. Such assets can be replaced at a high cost per unit replacement or displaced as a group at a low cost per unit. There is an optimum policy for minimum cost obtained by replacing on an individual basis for a certain time and then displacing the entire group.[1]

Suppose that 1,000 light bulbs have the distribution of service lives given in Table 6.9T1. Let 1,000 light bulbs be installed, assume that bulbs are replaced

Table 6.9T1 Distribution of Service Lives for 1,000 Light Bulbs

Period week no.	Failures during week	Probability of failure during week
1	150	0.15
2	200	0.20
3	300	0.30
4	250	0.25
5	100	0.10

[1] The illustration to be presented can be deferred until after the chapter on probability and uncertainty.

6.9 TECHNOLOGICAL ADVANCEMENT—INFLATION 121

Table 6.9T2 Replacement of Light Bulbs

(1) Period	(2)	(3)	(4)	(5)	(6)	(7)	(13)	(14)	(15)
1	1,000								
2	150R	150							
3	200R	22R	222						
4	300R	30R	33R	363					
5	250R	45R	44R	54R	393				
6	100R	38R	67R	73R	59R	337			
7		15R	56R	109R	79R	51R			
8			22R	91R	118R	67R			
9				36R	98R	101R			
10					39R	84R			
11						34R			
12							339		
13							51R	340	
14							68R	51R	339
15							102R	68R	51R
16							85R	102R	68R
17							34R	85R	102R
18								34R	85R
19									34R

at the beginning of each week and that installation on an individual basis is $1 per bulb and on a group basis is $0.45 per bulb. At zero time 1,000 bulbs are installed at a cost of $450.

The number of bulbs that must be installed at the beginning of each week on a replacement basis is given by Table 6.9T2. An R following a number indicates replacement required. Thus column 2 shows that in accordance with the probabilities of Table 6.9T1, 150 replacements will be required at the beginning of period 2, and 200 at period 3, and so forth. Column 3 of Table 6.9T2 shows that in accordance with the probabilities of Table 6.9T1, the 150 bulbs installed at the beginning of period 2 will require 22 replacements at the beginning of period 3, and 30 at period 4, and so forth. Continuing, column 4 shows that 222 replacements will be required at the beginning of period 3 with replacements as indicated.

Table 6.9T2 shows that the replacements per period overshoot, oscillate, and stabilize at 339. The number can be obtained independently. The average life of the bulbs is

$$\frac{1(150) + 2(200) + 3(300) + 4(250) + 5(100)}{150 + 200 + 300 + 250 + 100} = 2.95 \text{ weeks/bulb}$$

The reciprocal is the bulbs per week for 1 bulb installed. For 1,000 bulbs installed

$$\frac{1,000}{2.95} = 339 \text{ bulbs/week}$$

122 MATHEMATICS OF COST COMPARISONS

Table 6.9T3 Optimum Displacement Schedule for Light Bulbs

| | Bulbs installed | | $ | | |
Period	As a group	As replacements	this period	Cumulative $	$ per period average
1	1,000		450	450	450
2		150	150	600	300
3		222	222	822	274
4		363	363	1,185	296
5		393	393	1,578	316
6		337	337	1,915	319
Indefinitely		339	339		339

Table 6.9T3 shows how the minimum-cost program is determined. The final column is the cumulative dollars divided by the cumulative periods and is the dollars per period. Minimum cost is obtained by displacing the bulbs as a group every third period with intermediate replacements of 150 and 222 bulbs. If no group displacement is made, the cost is $339 per period, as determined from the equilibrium replacement value of Table 6.9T2.

INFLATION

6.10 Cost comparisons under inflation

Inflation is a factor in cost comparisons, and this section will develop relationships for the inclusion of inflation along with rate of return and taxes. The presentation is on the basis of capitalized cost, but in the next section it will be expanded to comparisons based on an end-of-year amount.

When inflation is a factor, prices change every year. Let the inflation rate be d per year expressed as a decimal. A cost A now will become a cost $A(1 + d)$ one year from now, $A(1 + d)^2$ two years from now, and so forth. Hence there is a relationship for prices under inflation analogous to Eq. (2.1#12) so that

$$A_{t_2} = A_{t_1}(1 + d)^n$$

$ cost time 2 = ($ cost time 1)(compound-inflation factor) (6.10#1)

where n positive = moving with calendar

n negative = moving against calendar

In this section all costs are in terms of the existing dollar. The actual cost in future dollars is that given by Eq. (6.10#1).

Suppose that an item has a depreciable first cost C_d now and lasts n years. Let D_{f_x} be the decimal depreciation for the xth year. Depreciation is based on original cost and is not influenced by inflation, at least under existing law. Let t be the decimal tax rate. Capitalized cost is the present worth of the first cost plus an infinite number of replacements, all taken at their actual cost, with proper consideration of the tax benefits arising from the depreciation expense. This is

$$K = \left[C_d - tC_d \sum_{x=1}^{x=n} \frac{D_{f_x}}{(1+r)^x}\right] + \left[\frac{C_d(1+d)^n - tC_d(1+d)^n \sum_{x=1}^{x=n} \frac{D_{f_x}}{(1+r)^x}}{(1+r)^n}\right]$$

$$+ \frac{C_d(1+d)^{2n} - tC_d(1+d)^{2n} \sum_{x=1}^{x=n} \frac{D_{f_x}}{(1+r)^x}}{(1+r)^{2n}} + \cdots \quad (6.10\#2)$$

where K is capitalized cost, the expression in the first brackets is the present worth of the original purchase and its tax credits, that in the second brackets is the present worth of the first replacement at a cost $C_d(1+d)^n$ after n years and its tax credits, and so forth. Introduce the ψ factor by its definition, Eq. (3.13#5),

$$\psi_{r_n} = \sum_{x=1}^{x=n} \frac{D_{f_x}}{(1+r)^x}$$

and Eq. (6.10#2) becomes

$$K = C_d(1 - t\psi_{r_n}) + C_d(1 - t\psi_{r_n})\frac{(1+d)^n}{(1+r)^n}$$

$$+ C_d(1 - t\psi_{r_n})\frac{(1+d)^{2n}}{(1+r)^{2n}} + \cdots \quad (6.10\#3)$$

Equation (6.9#3) is an infinite geometric series with first term $C_d(1 - t\psi_{r_n})$ and ratio $(1+d)^n/(1+r)^n$. It can be summed by Eq. (2.2#2). If $1+d$ is less than $1+r$,

$$K = C_d(1 - t\psi_{r_{n'}})\frac{(1+r)^n}{(1+r)^n - (1+d)^n} \quad (6.10\#4)$$

for which any depreciation method is applicable, and n' is introduced to emphasize that the life for tax purposes need not be the same as n, the life for the economic study. Noting that $(1+r)^n = F_{PS,r,n}$ and that $(1+d)^n = F_{PS,d,n}$, Eq. (6.10#4) can be written for sum-of-digits depreciation

$$K = C_d(1 - tF_{SDP,r,n'})\frac{F_{PS,r,n}}{F_{PS,r,n} - F_{PS,d,n}} \quad (6.10\#5)$$

Relationships for capitalized cost of other items with inflation and taxes included can be derived in a similar manner. Table 6.10T1 is a summary of these relationships. In using these relationships all costs must be entered in terms of their present dollar cost. The relationships will correct for the expected change in cost with inflation when costs are actually incurred. It may be possible to treat the increase in salvage value over the expected value as subject to the capital gain tax. If so, the capital gain tax instead of the income tax rate should be used for t in item 7.

Table 6.10T1 Capitalized-cost Relationships with Inflation, $r > d$*

Item no.	Item		Algebraic relationship for capitalized cost	Factor relationship for capitalized cost $K_{r>d}$, sum-of-digits depreciation
1	C_d	Depreciable first cost†	$C_d(1 - t\psi_{rn}) \dfrac{(1+r)^n}{(1+r)^n - (1+d)^n}$	$C_d(1 - tF_{SDP,r,n}) \dfrac{F_{PS,r,n}}{F_{PS,r,n} - F_{PS,d,n}}$
2	R	Uniform end-of-year burden†	$R(1-t) \dfrac{1+d}{r-d}$	$R(1-t) \dfrac{1+d}{r-d}$
3	R_b	Uniform beginning-of-year burden†	$R_b(1 - t\psi_{r,1}) \dfrac{1+r}{r-d}$	$R_b(1 - tF_{SDP,r,1}) \dfrac{1+r}{r-d}$
4	C_{ex}	Irregular cost at end of xth year†	$C_{ex}(1-t)(1+d)^x \dfrac{(1+r)^{n-x}}{(1+r)^n - (1+d)^n}$	$C_{ex}(1-t) F_{PS,d,x} \dfrac{F_{SP,r,n-x}}{F_{SP,r,n} - F_{SP,d,n}}$
5	C_{bx}	Irregular cost at beginning of xth year†	$C_{bx}(1 - t\psi_{r,1})(1+d)^{x-1} \dfrac{(1+r)^{n-x+1}}{(1+r)^n - (1+d)^n}$	$C_{bx}(1 - tF_{SDP,r,1}) F_{PS,d,x-1} \dfrac{F_{PS,r,n-x+1}}{F_{PS,r,n} - F_{PS,d,n}}$
6	C_{nd}	Nondepreciable first cost†	$C_{nd} \, 1$	C_{nd}
7	C_{sal}	Salvage value†,‡	$C_{sal}\left[1 + t \dfrac{(1+d)^n - 1}{(1+r)^n - (1+d)^n}\right]$	$C_{sal}\left(1 + t \dfrac{F_{PS,d,n} - 1}{F_{PS,r,n} - F_{PS,d,n}}\right)$

* For $d > r$, $K_{d>r} = -K_{r>d}$. For unaburden, $R_D = (r-d)K_{r>d}$ for $r > d$ or $d > r$. For $d = r$ see Sec. 6.12.
† All costs in terms of present dollar.
‡ If excess salvage value due to inflation can be taken as capital gain, use such tax for t in item 7.

Example 6.10E1 A new tank costs $10,000 in today's dollars, lasts 3 years, and belongs to a group depreciated in 5 years by sum-of-digits depreciation. If money is worth 10% per year after a 52% tax and the inflation rate is 4% per year, how much can be spent for repairing the tank as of the end of each year so as to obtain a 5-year life?

Capitalized cost of a new tank by item 1, Table 6.10T1, is

$$K_{new} = 10,000(1 - 0.52F_{SDP,10\%,5}) \frac{F_{PS,10\%,3}}{F_{PS,10\%,3} - F_{PS,4\%,3}}$$

$$= 10,000[1 - 0.52(0.80614)] \frac{1.3310}{1.3310 - 1.1249} = 37,509$$

The capitalized cost of the tank with repairs is given by items 1 and 2 of Table 6.10T1, and for equal economy is

$$37,509 = 10,000(1 - 0.52F_{SDP,10\%,5}) \frac{F_{PS,10\%,5}}{F_{PS,10\%,5} - F_{PS,4\%,5}}$$

$$+ R(1 - 0.52) \frac{1 + 0.04}{0.10 - 0.04}$$

$$37,509 = 10,000[1 - 0.52(0.80614)] \frac{1.6105}{1.6105 - 1.2050}$$

$$+ R(0.48) \frac{1.04}{0.06}$$

$R = \$1,736$ present dollars per year

That is, $1,736, in terms of the present dollar, can be spent as of the end of each year to extend the life to 5 years. Note that the actual cost as of the end of the first year is 1,736(1.04), as of the end of the second year 1,736(1.04^2), and so forth.

6.11 Unaburden

The preceding example leads to the result that a uniform end-of-year cost in terms of the present dollar is a cost increasing by the factor $1 + d$ each year when inflation is a factor. With inflation an end-of-year criterion is not a uniform cost in actual dollars but a uniform burden, called *unaburden*. In terms of actual dollars unaburden increases by the factor $1 + d$ each year, and will be denoted by R_D. Another useful notation is to follow a unaburden with an arrow to emphasize that it increases by $1 + d$ each year.

Although unacost and capitalized cost are related by the simple relationship $R = rK$, the relationship between unaburden and capitalized cost with inflation is

$$R_D = (r - d)K_{r>d} \qquad r > d \qquad (6.11\#1)$$

Unaburden = (decimal rate of return less decimal inflation rate)

(capitalized cost with inflation, $r > d$)

With this simple relationship Table 6.10T1 can be used on the basis of unaburden.

6.12 High inflation rates

If the inflation rate is higher than the rate of return, the summation of Eq. (6.10#3) becomes infinite. Nevertheless the relationships given in Table 6.10T1 are still useful because reversing the sign of the relationships, which become negative when

126 MATHEMATICS OF COST COMPARISONS

the inflation rate is higher than the rate of return, restores them to a positive value, called the *extended capitalized cost*, that is used just like a capitalized cost. The validity of this procedure is justified in [6.16R7]; i.e.,

$$K_{d>r} = -K_{r>d} \tag{6.12\#1}$$

The expression for unaburden is still given by Eq. (6.11#1) but can also be expressed as an equivalent relationship

$$R_D = (d - r)K_{d>r} \qquad d > r \tag{6.12\#2}$$

If $d = r$, unaburden must be used. The relationships may assume indeterminate forms such as 0/0, but evaluation by the calculus leads to

$$R_D = \frac{C_d}{n}(1 - t\psi_{r_n'})(1 + r) \tag{6.12\#3}$$

$$R_D = R(1 - t)(1 + r) \tag{6.12\#4}$$

$$R_D = R_b(1 - t\psi_{r_1})(1 + r) \tag{6.12\#5}$$

$$R_D = \frac{C_{ex}}{n}(1 - t)(1 + r) \tag{6.12\#6}$$

$$R_D = \frac{C_{bx}}{n}(1 - t\psi_{r_1})(1 + r) \tag{6.12\#7}$$

$$R_D = C_{nd}(0) = 0 \tag{6.12\#8}$$

$$R_D = C_{sal}\frac{t}{n}\frac{(1 + r)^n - 1}{(1 + r)^n}(1 + r) \tag{6.12\#9}$$

Example 6.12E1 A machine lasts 2 years with negligible salvage value, can be written off in 1 year for tax purposes, and can be purchased now for $20,000. How much can be spent for a new machine which lasts 10 years, with negligible salvage value, and can be written off in 10 years for tax purposes using sum-of-digits depreciation, when money is worth 10% per year after a 52% tax, if the inflation rate is (a) 4% per year, (b) 10% per year, (c) 12% per year?

(a) For 4% per year inflation use item 1, Table 6.10T1, based on unaburden. For the 2-year machine

$$R_D = (r - d)C_d(1 - tF_{SDP,10\%,1})\frac{F_{PS,10\%,2}}{F_{PS,10\%,2} - F_{PS,4\%,2}}$$

$$= (0.10 - 0.04)(10{,}000)[1 - 0.52(0.90909)]\frac{1.2100}{1.2100 - 1.0816}$$

$$= 5{,}963$$

For the same unaburden for the 10-year machine

$$5{,}963 = (r - d)C_d(1 - tF_{SDP,10\%,10})\frac{F_{PS,10\%,10}}{F_{PS,10\%,10} - F_{PS,4\%,10}}$$

$$= (0.10 - 0.04)C_d[1 - 0.52(0.70099)]\frac{2.5937}{2.5937 - 1.4802}$$

$$C_d = \$67{,}130$$

(b) For 10% per year inflation use Eq. (6.12#3) with sum-of-digits depreciation. For the 2-year machine

$$R_D = \frac{C_d}{n}(1 - 0.52 F_{SDP,10\%,1})(1 + r)$$

$$= \frac{20{,}000}{2}[1 - 0.52(0.90909)](1 + 0.10)$$

$$= 5{,}800$$

For the same unaburden for the 10-year machine

$$5{,}800 = \frac{C_d}{n}(1 - 0.52 F_{SDP,10\%,10})(1 + 0.10)$$

$$= \frac{C_d}{10}[1 - 0.52(0.70099)(1.10)]$$

$$C_d = \$82{,}970$$

(c) For 12% per year inflation rate use item 1, Table 6.10T1, and unaburden. For the 2-year machine

$$R_D = (r - d)C_d(1 - tF_{SDP,10\%,1})\frac{F_{PS,10\%,2}}{F_{PS,10\%,2} - F_{PS,12\%,2}}$$

$$= (0.10 - 0.12)(20{,}000)[1 - 0.52(0.70099)]\frac{1.2100}{1.2100 - 1.2544}$$

$$= 5{,}748$$

For the same unaburden for the 10-year machine

$$5{,}748 = (r - d)C_d(1 - tF_{SDP,10\%,10})\frac{F_{PS,10\%,10}}{F_{PS,10\%,10} - F_{PS,12\%,10}}$$

$$= (0.10 - 0.12)C_d[1 - 0.52(0.70099)]\frac{2.5937}{2.5937 - 3.1058}$$

$$C_d = \$89{,}290$$

6.13 Inflation and technological advancement

Inflation and displacement have not been adequately considered in practice as factors in engineering economy and cost comparisons. Inflation has become permanent and ironically has been favored by advancing technology. Originally money was in the form of something tangible such as gold; but this gave way to paper money, which at first was issued merely for convenience and was only a certificate for gold. Eventually paper money gave way to checks, yet it is technological developments in business equipment that has made possible the extensive use of checks. The credit card and modern high-speed electronic data-processing equipment are in turn displacing the check. It appears that in the near future all transactions will be on tape. The individual will no longer receive a paycheck but instead a credit to his account in the form of information on a tape submitted to the banking system by his employer. In turn the individual will make purchases by means of a master credit card. Payment will be by automatic time installments against his account. Most business transactions will become merely a series of bits on a tape. The existence of money as a tangible and real thing will cease. It is not possible to prophesy exactly how this will affect government control of taxes and social measures and the attitude of the population to values; but it will certainly make inflation difficult to control. The insatiable demand for higher wages and governmental programs will then be merely a matter of computer programming with nothing to limit the decimal point.

Deflation can be treated by the mathematical methods of this chapter by giving d, the decay rate of the dollar, an appropriate negative value. However, deflation may be of historical interest only.

In engineering economy and cost comparisons inflation always enters with regard to future inflation. Thus an estimate or prediction is necessary. Nevertheless inflation does have an effect upon decisions and should not be ignored simply because it cannot be predicted exactly. Cost indexes are available which give some clue to inflation, but they give only the excess of inflation over technological advancement. Indeed it is not possible with present techniques to separate the inflation rate and technological-advancement rate completely. The inflation rate has certainly been the greater of the two and has been higher than is generally realized.

Inflation in the long run affects costs proportionally. Technological advancement, however, is highly specific and moreover tends to come in spurts as breakthroughs are made. The two differ in one other respect. Inflation enters a decision only with regard to future inflation and adds extra advantage generally to the longer-lived article. Technological advancement, on the other hand, enters with regard to existing technology. The existence of future technological advancement adds extra advantage generally to the shorter-lived article. One manifestation of this is the delay value of the existent, discussed in Sec. 6.6.

In theory inflation and technological advancement are independent factors. In practice they are intermingled. The interaction includes also the rate of return because the latter tends to rise with inflation. The topics discussed in this chapter will become increasingly important in the future.

6.14 Nomenclature

A_{t_1}	Amount at time 1, $
B	Book value, $
C_{bx}	Irregular cost at beginning of year x, $
C_d	Depreciable first cost, $
C_{ex}	Irregular cost at end of year x, $
C_i	Initial cost, $
C_{nd}	Nondepreciable cost, $
C_{sal}	Salvage value, $
d	Inflation rate, decimal/year
D	Depreciation, $
D_f	Fractional depreciation, decimal
F_{GP}	Factor to convert G to P; uniform-gradient-series present-worth factor, years
F_{PK}	Capitalized-cost factor, dimensionless
F_{PR}	Capital-recovery factor, year^{-1}
F_{PS}	Compound-interest factor, dimensionless

$F_{PS,-p,n}$ Compound-interest factor for negative compounding–used with technological advancement, dimensionless
F_{RP} Unacost present-worth factor, years
F_{SDP} Present worth of $1 for sum-of-digits depreciation, decimal
F_{SP} Present-worth factor, decimal
G Uniform-gradient amount, $ per year
i Rate of return before taxes, decimal/year
K Capitalized cost, $
$K_{r>d}$ Capitalized cost with $r > d$, $
$K_{d>r}$ Capitalized cost with $d > r$, $
n A number such as number of years
n' Number of years life for tax purpose
p Technological-advancement rate, decimal/year
P Present worth, $
r Rate of return after taxes, decimal/year
R Unacost, uniform end-of-year annual amount, $ per year
R_b Uniform beginning-of-year annual amount, $ per year
R_D Unaburden, uniform end-of-year burden with inflation, $ per year
R_p Yearly operating expense subject to improvement by technological advancement, $ per year
t Tax rate, decimal
ψ Present worth of $1 of depreciation, decimal

6.15 Problems

P1. The book value of a machine is $4,000 with 4 years life remaining at straight-line depreciation. Assume that the book value and salvage value are identical at all times. Operating cost for the machine is $10,000 per year as of the end of the year. A new machine costs $30,000 and has an 8-year life and an operating cost of $4,000 per year as of the end of the year. Neglect salvage value and taxes. If money is worth 10% per year, does it pay to install the new machine?

P2. What is the actual rate of return realized with the new machine in the preceding problem?

P3. Repeat Prob. 6.15P1 on the basis of a 48% tax rate and sum-of-digits depreciation for the new machine. Rate of return is 10% after taxes. Tax benefits can be taken at instant costs occur.

P4. Assume that 5 years ago a machine cost $35,000 and has been depreciated on a 10-year life with straight-line depreciation and $1,000 salvage value. If sold now, it will bring $6,000. The machine is part of a group, and depreciation continues at all times just as if it were in service. If sold at the end of the year, it will bring $5,000.

A new machine costs $75,000 with a 10-year life, $4,000 salvage value, and an annual end-of-year savings of $12,000. Use sum-of-digits depreciation. If money is worth 12% per year after a 52% tax, should the new machine be bought?

P5. A machine costs $20,000 and lasts 6 years with $1,000 salvage value at all times. Past records give the following data, where costs are as of the beginning of the year and include operating and repair costs:

Year	Cost, $
1	3,000
2	3,500
3	8,000
4	15,000
5	5,000
6	15,000

If money is worth 10% per year and there is no tax, how long should the machine be kept?

P6. If money is worth 12% per year find unacost and capitalized cost for the following after tax expenses:

End of year	Expense, $ per year
1	1,000
2	1,200
3	1,400
4	1,600
...	....
20	4,800

P7. In what respect is sum-of-digits depreciation related to a uniform-gradient series?

P8. It has been stated that the costs for a new machine can be compared with that of the existing machine and that future technological advancement can be treated as a delaying value of the existing machine. Comment.

P9. What is the optimum service life for a machine costing $100,000 and incurring a $40,000 per year operating rate subject to technological advancement if the technological-advancement rate is 3% per year, the rate of return is 12% per year after a 50% tax, and sum-of-digits depreciation is used?

P10. Use Eq. (6.7#2) and find the optimum value for n, the economic life under the following conditions: technological-advancement rate 6% per year, 20% annual expense subject to technological advancement, 15% per year rate of return after a 50% tax, and sum-of-digits depreciation.

P11. A new machine costs $10,000 with a salvage value of $1,000 and lasts 13 years for the analysis and tax purposes. Sum-of-digits depreciation will be used with a 50% tax rate. The existing machine has a salvage value of $500 decreasing to $400 next year. If the new machine has an annual operating advantage of $3,000 per year, find the MAPI after-tax return.

P12. Repeat Prob. 6.15P11 on the basis of unacost.

P13. If 1,000 light bulbs fail statistically according to the following pattern:

Period	Failures
1	50
2	100
3	250
4	500
5	75
6	25

and replacements are made at the beginning of each period if necessary, make a tabulation to find the steady-state number of replacements for an installation of 1,000 bulbs and check this against the calculated value.

P14. In Prob. 6.15P13, replacement costs $1 per bulb but $0.50 per bulb as a group of 1,000. Find the program for minimum cost.

P15. An article costs $10,000 and lasts 1 year. How much can be spent for an article that lasts 3 years if money is worth 8% per year with an inflation rate of 4% per year? Neglect taxes.

P16. In Prob. 6.15P15 what inflation rate would justify spending $33,000 for the 3-year article?

P17. A machine costs $10,000 and lasts 2 years. Money is worth 8% per year after a 48% tax and sum-of-digits depreciation. If the inflation rate is 4% per year and a machine can be depreciated in its service life, how much can be spent for a machine that lasts 5 years?

P18. A factory floor can be resurfaced for $10,000 and lasts 1 year. Money is worth 8% per year after a 52% tax with sum-of-digits depreciation and a tax life equal to the service life. The inflation rate is 4% per year. How long must a special resurfacing job last if it costs $36,000?

P19. Use the data of Prob. 2.12P23. Money is worth 10% per year after a 48% tax and sum-of-digits depreciation and with tax life equal to service life. The inflation rate is 4% per year. All costs are in terms of the present dollar. Which machine is cheaper and by how much?

P20. Derive the relationship for item 2, Table 6.10T1.
P21. Derive the relationship for item 4, Table 6.10T1.
P22. Derive the relationship for item 6, Table 6.10T1.
P23. Derive the relationship for item 7, Table 6.10T1.

6.16 References

R1. DeGarmo, E. Paul: "Engineering Economy," 4th ed., The Macmillan Company, New York, 1967.
R2. Fabrycky, W. J., and P. E. Torgersen: "Operations Economy," Prentice-Hall, Inc., Englewood Cliffs, N.J., 1966.
R3. Ghare, P. M., and P. E. Torgersen: The Effect of Inflation and Increased Productivity on Machine Replacement, *J. Indus. Eng.*, July–August, 1964, pp. 201–207.
R4. Grant, Eugene L., and W. G. Ireson: "Principles of Engineering Economy," 4th ed., The Ronald Press Company, New York, 1960.
R5. Jelen, F. C.: Replacement Problems by Capitalized Costs, *Chem. Eng.*, August, 1955, pp. 181–188.
R6. Jelen, F. C.: Consider Inflation in Comparative Cost Analyses, *Chem. Eng.*, May, 1956, pp. 164–169.
R7. Jelen, F. C.: Watch Your Cost Analyses, *Chem. Eng.*, June, 1950, pp. 247–252.
R8. Jelen, F. C.: Remember All Three in Cost Analyses, *Chem. Eng.*, Jan. 27, 1958, pp. 123–128.
R9. Terborgh, George: "Business Investment Management," MAPI, Washington, D.C., 1967.
R10. Thuesen, H. G., and P. E. Torgersen: The Effect of Inflation on Replacement, *J. Indus. Eng.*, July–August, 1960, pp. 336–337.

part two
Optimization

7
Break-even and Minimum-cost Analysis[1]

M. Ariet and H. E. Schweyer

7.1 Types of costs

A company in whole or in part, such as one assembly line or one profit center, can be resolved into a number of cash flows. The cash flows depend upon how the project is operated, e.g., the percentage of capacity in use, and the cash flows determine the profit. This chapter will consider several fundamental techniques associated with a cash-flow model.

Figure 7.1F1 illustrates the general cash-flow model which describes the flow of cash into an operation and how it is paid out. There are two main flows of cash. The first is income from sales and services and any other sources connected with the project. The second is expense and is the total of the variable and fixed costs. Profit is the difference between income and expense. Any accumulation or depletion of inventory or capitalization within the project itself must be allowed for. In other words, the cash-flow model states that the profits or earnings of a

---

[1] Certain material in this chapter is similar to the material in H. E. Schweyer, "Analytic Models for Managerial and Engineering Economics," Reinhold Book Corporation, a subsidiary of Chapman-Reinhold, Inc., New York, 1964, and is used with permission.

136 OPTIMIZATION

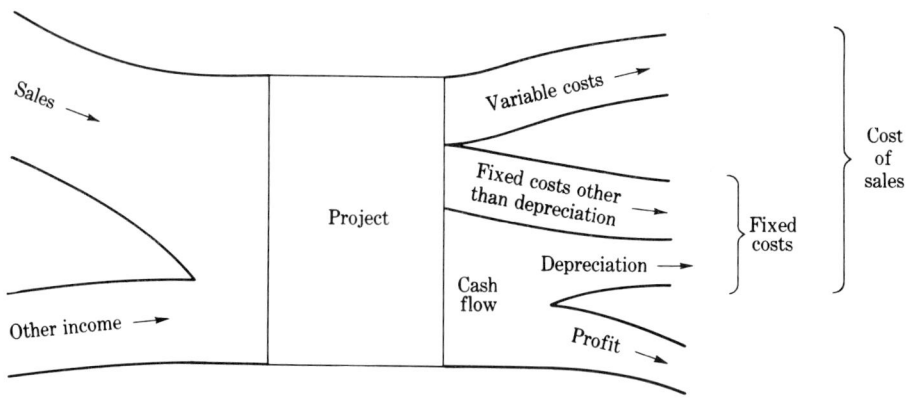

Fig. 7.1F1 Cash flow for a project.

project are determined by the difference between what the customer pays for the product and service and what it costs the project to manufacture, store, and sell the product and service, including allowance for consumption of capital (depreciation).

For the purpose of this chapter, all costs are considered to fall into two categories: *variable costs*, which depend upon production, and *fixed costs*, which remain relatively constant. For the ideal case where the variable costs change linearly with production and the fixed costs are constant, Fig. 7.1F2 applies.

Let V be the variable cost *per unit of production*, C_F the fixed cost per year, and C_T the total annual cost; then for an annual production of N units

$$C_T = NV + C_F \qquad (7.1\#1)$$

It is important to note that although V may be called a variable cost *per unit of production*, the variable cost itself is NV. In Fig. 7.1F2 C_T is a straight line because V is assumed to be independent of N and C_F is constant. Other situations are

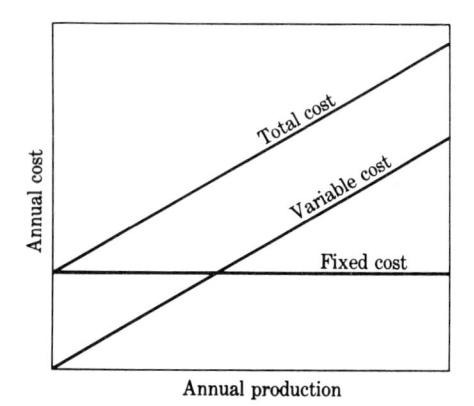

Fig. 7.1F2 Diagram of relations between costs and production.

7.1 BREAK-EVEN AND MINIMUM-COST ANALYSIS

Table 7.1T1 Detail Cost Schedule for Annual Cost of Sales in One Plant

Annual cost of sales

Annual variable costs, 60 to 70%	Annual fixed costs, 40 to 30%

A. Raw materials used in making the product, makeup solvent, or catalyst, etc.
B. Direct labor (operators and helpers): add 25% for social security, pensions, vacations, etc.
C. Process services (steam, power, water, refrigeration)
D. Maintenance (labor and materials), about 4 to 6% of fixed plant investment
E. Miscellaneous supplies and others at about 0.5% of fixed plant investment
F. Direct supervision (foremen), about 10% of direct labor
G. Laboratory charges (process control)
H. Royalty (charges for using some other company's process)
I. Packaging and storage charges
J. Credit for by-products
K. Spoilage and other losses (items I and K can be estimated at 5% of total raw materials plus labor plus services)
	A. Indirect plant cost, or plant burden, 15%
	  1. Investment costs, 5%
	    a. Depreciation, 10% of fixed plant investment
	    b. Taxes, 2% of fixed plant investment
	    c. Insurance, 1% of fixed plant investment
	    d. Financial costs (interest on inventories plant equipment, total capital where allowed)
	    e. Other assessments, penalties, etc., for certain items of inventory
	  2. Overhead, 10%
	    a. Technical (engineering)
	    b. Nontechnical (office force, plant protection, etc.)
	    c. Supplies (those not chargable to direct costs)
	    d. Rent (included where equipment, buildings, land, or a service is rented)
	    e. Others
	B. Management expense, 5%
	  1. Executives
	  2. Legal
	  3. Research (technical research and market research)
	C. Selling expense or distribution expense, 10 to 20%
	  1. Cost of selling
	  2. Delivery and warehouse costs
	  3. Technical service, 3 to 5%

considered below in which the variable cost per unit of production V depends upon N, and then the variable cost and total cost become curved.

A breakdown of annual costs into variable and fixed costs is shown in Table 7.1T1. The numbers illustrate the percentage of cost of sales on a yearly basis at 100% capacity and vary in different industries.

Fixed costs include expenditures which are independent of production rate. Three general categories are listed in the table: (1) indirect plant costs including depreciation, (2) management expense, and (3) selling expense. Details of the classification depend upon the accounting procedure.

The variable cost per unit of production is generally essentially constant. The variable cost itself is considered to be zero at no production and in the ideal case varies linearly with production, assumptions that are satisfactory in most applications. However, some variable costs per unit of production depend upon production, such as power, which is sold on a declining rate scale, or labor costs, which may increase per unit of production at high production rates because of use of inefficient labor or overtime.

7.2 Economic-production charts

The economic-production chart is a geometric chart which utilizes cost and price data and reduces them to a simple visual model. The economic-production, or break-even, chart was proposed by Rautenstrausch [7.11R5] and can be utilized in either graphical or analytical form to evaluate an economic operation. The charts make visible the interrelationship of fixed costs, variable costs, sales revenue, and profits. The cost engineer can evaluate the overall economy of the operation from the charts and determine the relative effects of changes in the components.

The mathematical relationships take a very simple form if the following assumptions are made for the purpose of this section:

1. V is constant; hence the variable costs NV are linearly dependent on production.
2. Fixed costs are independent of production.
3. There are no financial costs.
4. There is no income other than that from operations.
5. All units are sold at the same price per unit.
6. All units produced are sold.

If S is the net sales realization *per unit* and Z_g the gross profit, then using the expression for C_T obtained from Eq. (7.1#1),

$$Z_g = NS - C_T = NS - (NV + C_F) \qquad (7.2\#1)$$

If Z_t is net profit, i.e., profit after taxes, and the decimal tax rate is t,

$$Z_t = Z_g(1 - t) \qquad (7.2\#2)$$

The various relationships all plot as straight lines against N, units of production, and are shown in Fig. 7.2F1. The point at which the sales line crosses the total-cost line is called the break-even point and is the point below which operation results in a loss and above which it yields a profit.

The break-even point can be found mathematically by setting $Z_g = 0$ in Eq. (7.2#1)

$$N \text{ break-even} = \frac{C_F}{S - V} \qquad (7.2\#3)$$

This point is not a function of the tax rate since no profit is obtained at this production level.

The quantitative effects of various selling prices can be visualized from the chart by sketching a separate net-sales line for each different unit sales price, and

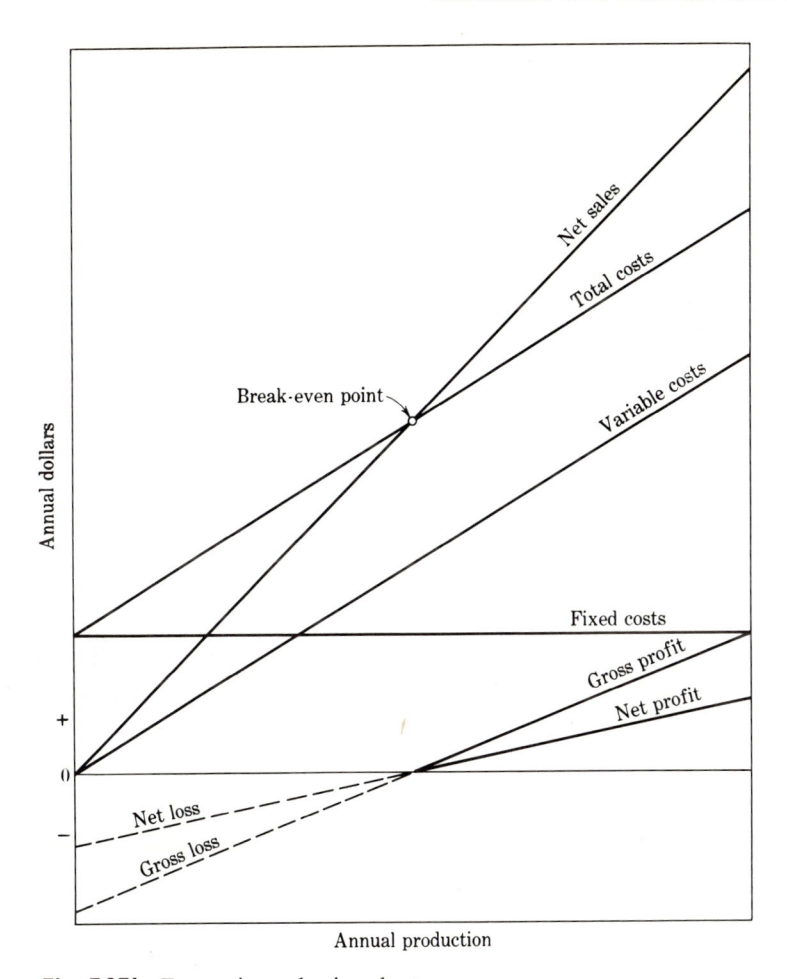

Fig. 7.2F1 Economic-production chart.

the procedure can be used for other variables. The charts can be utilized for any period of time and for any combination of products provided the pertinent costs are prorated.

7.3 Economic-production chart above 100% capacity

Usually a project operates at its maximum efficiency when producing at 100% capacity. However, even if the variable cost per unit V increases at operations above 100% capacity, the total profit probably will continue to increase. These points are illustrated in Fig. 7.3F1. If the two parts of the plot are considered as two steps, all the previous relations apply for each step, the proper terms being included for operations above 100% capacity, here denoted by primes. For

140   OPTIMIZATION

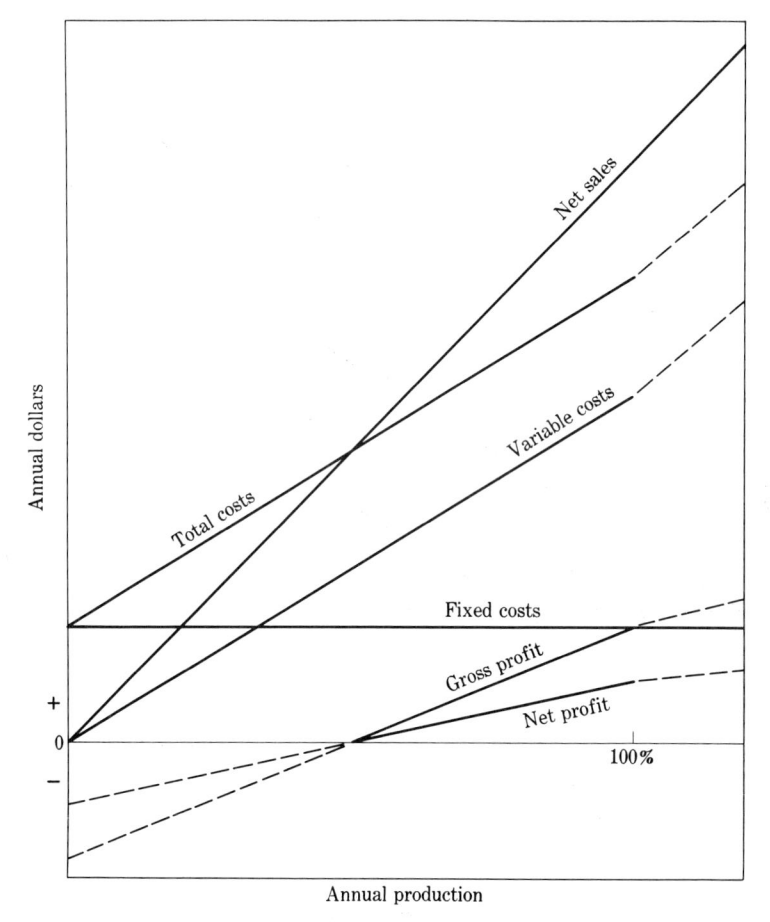

Fig. 7.3FI Economic-production chart for operations above 100% capacity.

example, gross profit can be written
$$Z_g = (N + N')S - (NV + N'V' + C_F) \qquad (7.3\#1)$$
where N' and V' are the number of production units above 100% capacity and the associated variable cost per unit and N and V are the corresponding values at 100% capacity.

Example 7.3E1 A project can produce 12,000 units per year at 100% capacity. Fixed costs are $10,000 per year. The variable cost per unit is $3 up to 100% capacity and $3.30 above 100% capacity. All units are sold at a net selling price of $5. The tax rate is 52%. Find the break-even point and the profit per year after taxes at 80 and 120% of production capacity.

The break-even point is given by Eq. (7.2#3)
$$N = \frac{C_F}{S - V} = \frac{10,000}{5 - 3} = 5,000 \text{ units per year}$$

The gross profit at 80% of capacity is given by Eq. (7.2#1)
$Z_g = 0.80(12,000)(5) - [0.80(12,000)(3) + 10,000] = \$9,200$ per year
which after a 52% tax is
$Z_t = 9,200(1 - 0.52) = \$4,416$ per year

The gross profit at 120% capacity is given by Eq. (7.3#1)
$Z_g = 1.20(12,000)(5) - [12,000(3) + 0.2(12,000)(3.30) + 10,000] = \$18,080$ per year
which after a 52% tax is
$Z_t = 18,080(1 - 0.52) = \$8,678$ per year

7.4 Economic-production chart for dumping

The principles discussed in connection with Fig. 7.3F1 apply to the practice of *dumping*, which occurs when a manufacturer sells N units of his production at one sales price, S per unit, but because demand is not sufficient to take all the production, he sells N'' units at a lower price, S'' per unit. He obtains greater sales and keeps the plant operating at higher output. The diagram is similar to Fig. 7.3F1 and shows a break in the sales line, gross profit, and net profit at N. The gross profit is given by

$$Z_g = NS + N''S'' - [(N + N'')V + C_F] \qquad (7.4\#1)$$

Example 7.4E1 For the data given in Example 7.3E1, the manufacturer finds that he can sell only 80% of rated capacity at \$5 per unit. How much should he charge for additional units if he brings production up to 100% capacity and increases profits after taxes by an additional \$1,000?

The net profit after taxes at 80% production was \$4,416. The gross profit at 100% production will be

$$\frac{4,416 + 1,000}{1 - 0.52} = 11,283$$

He will sell $0.80(12,000) = 9,600$ units at \$5 and $0.20(12,000) = 2,400$ units at S''. By Eq. (7.4#1)

$11,283 = 9,600(5) + 2,400S'' - [(9,600 + 2,400)(3) + 10,000]$ $S'' = \$3.87$ per unit

7.5 Nonlinear economic-production charts

In practice it is necessary at times to consider the analysis of economic-production charts in which some entries vary with production in a nonlinear manner. The following example has been given by Schweyer [7.11R6].

Example 7.5E1 A study of a plant operation having annual fixed costs C_F constant at \$100,000 per year indicates that the curves on the economic-production charts may be expressed in terms of production units, tons, as follows:

Average net sales: $S = 76 - 0.0036N$ \$ per ton (7.5#1)
Average variable cost per unit: $V = N^2 \times 10^{-7} - 0.0012N + 21.6$ \$ per ton
  (7.5#2)

Make an economic analysis of the operation using 1 year as a basis.

The variable cost is (N) $(V$ average) and is

$$NV = N^3 \times 10^{-7} - 0.0012N^2 + 21.6N \quad \$ \quad (7.5\#3)$$

The unit incremental variable cost is the increase in variable cost for one unit and is $(\Delta NV - NV)/N$ or in the limit

$$\frac{d(NV)}{dN} = 3N^2 \times 10^{-7} - 0.0024N + 21.6 \quad \$ \text{ per ton} \quad (7.5\#4)$$

The fixed cost is \$100,000 per year. The total cost is $NV + C_F$ or

$$C_T = N^3 \times 10^{-7} - 0.0012N^2 + 21.6N + 100,000 \quad \$ \quad (7.5\#5)$$

The unit incremental total cost is

$$\frac{dC_T}{dN} = 3N^2 \times 10^{-7} - 0.0024N + 21.6 \quad \$ \text{ per ton} \quad (7.5\#6)$$

The average unit cost is C_T/N or

$$N^2 \times 10^{-7} - 0.0012N + 21.6 + \frac{100,000}{N} \quad \$ \quad (7.5\#7)$$

The unit incremental average cost is

$$\frac{dC_T/N}{dN} = 2N \times 10^{-7} - 0.0012 - \frac{100,000}{N^2} \quad \$ \text{ per ton} \quad (7.5\#8)$$

Average net sales is given by Eq. (7.5#1). Sales revenue is (N) $(S$ average)

$$NS = 76N - 0.0036N^2 \quad \$ \quad (7.5\#9)$$

Unit incremental sales revenue is

$$\frac{d(NS)}{dN} = 76 - 0.0072N \quad \$ \text{ per ton} \quad (7.5\#10)$$

Gross profit is $Z_g = NS - NV - C_F$ or

$$Z_g = 76N - 0.0036N^2 - N^3 \times 10^{-7} + 0.0012N^2 - 21.6N - 100,000$$
$$= -N^3 \times 10^{-7} - 0.0024N^2 + 54.4N - 100,000 \quad \$ \quad (7.5\#11)$$

Unit incremental gross profit is

$$\frac{dZ_g}{dN} = -3N^2 \times 10^{-7} - 0.0048N + 54.4 \quad \$ \text{ per ton} \quad (7.5\#12)$$

Average unit gross profit is Z_g/N or

$$\frac{Z_g}{N} = -N^2 \times 10^{-7} - 0.0024N + 54.4 - \frac{100,000}{N} \quad \$ \text{ per ton} \quad (7.5\#13)$$

Unit incremental average gross profit is

$$\frac{d(Z_g/N)}{dN} = -2N \times 10^{-7} - 0.0024 + \frac{100,000}{N^2} \quad \$ \text{ per ton}^2 \quad (7.5\#14)$$

The reader will do well to understand the meaning of these expressions and the differences between them. Several are tabulated in Table 7.5T1 and plotted in Fig. 7.5F1.

Many significant points can be obtained from the charts or the relationships. For break-even the profit Z_g is zero, or by Eq. (7.5#11)

$$0 = -N^3 \times 10^{-7} - 0.0024N^2 + 54.4N - 100,000$$

The equation has three roots, which are $N = +2,030$, $N = +12,750$, and $N = -38,780$.

7.5 BREAK-EVEN AND MINIMUM-COST ANALYSIS 143

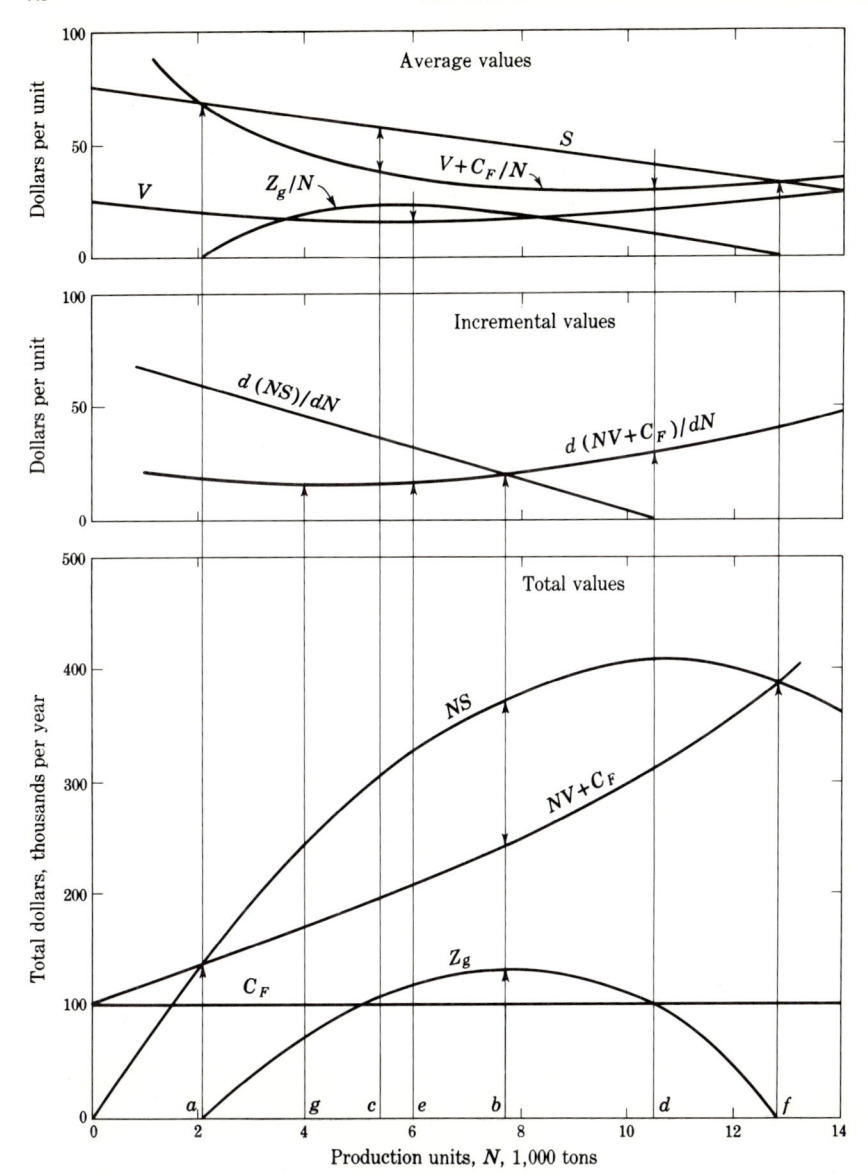

Fig. 7.5F1 Economic-production chart for Example 7.5E1.

The point corresponding to $N = 2,030$ tons/year is the break-even point, or the lowest production rate that will not result in a loss.

The point corresponding to $N = 12,750$ tons/year is known as a *profit limit point*. A production level *above* this point will result in a loss. The third point, $N = -38,780$ has no physical meaning.

A study of Table 7.5T1 will reveal several other interesting points. A summary is:

Point a: break-even point at $N = 2,030$ tons/year
Point b: maximum annual profit at $N = 7,690$ tons/year

144 OPTIMIZATION

Table 7.5T1 Tabulation for Example 7.5E1, Basis 1 Year

(1) Line no.	(2) Tons N	(3) Average net sales per unit, $ per ton S Eq. (7.5#1)	(4) Total sales, $ NS Eq. (7.5#9)	(5) Unit incremental net sales $ per ton $\dfrac{d(NS)}{dN}$ Eq. (7.5#10)	(6) Average unit variable costs, $ per ton V Eq. (7.5#2)	(7) Average unit cost, $ per ton $\dfrac{C_T}{N}$ Eq. (7.5#7)	(8) Total cost, $ C_T Eq. (7.5#5)	(9) Unit incremental total cost, $ per ton $\dfrac{dC_T}{dN}$ Eq. (7.5#6)	(10) Unit gross profit, $ per ton $\dfrac{Z_g}{N}$ Eq. (7.5#13)	(11) Gross profit, $ Z_g Eq. (7.5#11)	(12) Point in Fig. 7.5F1
1	0	76.0	0	76.0	21.6	∞	100,000	21.6	−∞	−100,000	
2	500	74.2	37,100	72.4	21.0	223.5	110,500	20.5	−146.8	−73,400	
3	1,000	72.4	72,400	68.8	20.5	120.5	120,500	19.5	−48.1	−48,100	
4	2,000	68.8	137,680	61.6	19.6	69.6	139,200	18.1	−0.80	−1,600	
5	2,030	68.8*	139,600*	61.4	19.6	68.8*	139,600*	18.0	0*	0*	a
6	4,000	61.6	246,400	46.2	18.4	43.4	173,600	16.8*	18.2	72,800	g
7	5,400	56.6	306,000	37.2	18.0	36.5	197,000	17.3	20.1	109,000	c
8	6,000	54.4	326,400	32.8	18.0*	34.7	208,000	18.0*	19.7	118,400	e
9	7,690	48.3	371,000	20.6*	18.2	31.3	240,500	20.6*	17.0	130,500*	b
10	8,000	47.2	377,600	18.4	18.4	30.9	247,200	21.6	16.3	130,400	
11	10,000	40.0	400,000	4.0	19.6	29.6	296,000	27.6	10.4	104,000	
12	10,500	38.2	402,000	0.0	20.1	29.6*	311,000	29.6	8.5	91,000	d
13	12,000	32.8	393,600	−10.4	21.6	29.9	359,000	36.0	2.9	34,800	
14	12,750	30.1*	384,000*	−16.2	22.6	30.1	384,000*	40.0	0*	0*	f
15	14,000	25.6	358,000	−24.8	24.4	31.8	442,000	46.8	−6.2	−86,800	

* Significant items for comparison.

Point c: maximum unit profit at $N = 5{,}400$ tons/year
Point d: minimum unit cost at $N = 10{,}500$ tons/year
Point e: minimum average variable cost at $N = 6{,}000$ tons/year
Point f: profit limit point at $N = 12{,}750$ tons/year
Point g: minimum incremental total cost at $N = 4{,}000$ tons/year

There is another important point, the *shut-down point*, below which it is more economical to shut down than to operate. Inspection of column 11 of Table 7.5T1 shows that the loss at shutdown is 100,000 and even low operating levels have a smaller loss. In this example it will not pay to shut down, but in practice there is a cease-operation point, below which it pays to shut down.

The maxima and minima can mean different things and should not be confused. Thus maximum profit, point b, does not correspond to maximum unit profit, point c.

However, there is one similarity that should be noted. Unit incremental net sales revenue and unit incremental total costs are equal at maximum profit, and the equality is not accidental. By (Eq. 7.2#1)

$$Z_g = NS - C_T$$

For maximum Z_g

$$\frac{dZ_g}{dN} = 0 = \frac{d(NS)}{dN} - \frac{dC_T}{dN}$$

or

$$\frac{d(NS)}{dN} = \frac{dC_T}{dN} \quad \text{at } Z_{g,\max}$$

Unit incremental net sales = unit incremental total cost

The incremental expressions are also known as marginal expressions; thus the marginal cost is the additional cost resulting from producing one more unit at a certain production level.

The unit incremental, or marginal, cost is an important criterion in analyzing production charts, and can be used to allocate production between competing production facilities.

7.6 One-product multiple-machine example

Up to this point the minimum-cost analyses were concerned only with the level at which a facility making one product should be operated. Letting the term *machine* signify a process or plant or any single producing unit, consider now two or more machines being used for making the same product with different cost relationships. The problem is to select the level at which each machine should operate so that overall production costs will be a minimum. The following example has been modified from one originally presented by Schweyer [7.11R7].

Example 7.6E1 Total annual costs for three machines A, B, and C producing N_A, N_B, and N_C annual units are

$$C_{T_A} = N_A V_A + C_{F_A} = 0.06 N_A^{1.1} + 1{,}200 \tag{7.6#1}$$

$$C_{T_B} = N_B V_B + C_{F_B} = 0.02 N_B^{1.3} + 1{,}000 \tag{7.6#2}$$

$$C_{T_C} = N_C V_C + C_{F_C} = 0.002 N_C^{1.6} + 600 \tag{7.6#3}$$

If 400 annual production units are made, how should production be alloted to the three machines?

146 OPTIMIZATION

The total cost for all three machines is obtained by adding Eqs. (7.6#1) (7.6#2), and (7.6#3).

$$C_T = 0.06N_A^{1.1} + 0.02N_B^{1.3} + 0.002N_C^{1.6} + 2{,}800 \tag{7.6#4}$$

If $N = 400$ is total production from all three plants, then

$$400 = N_A + N_B + N_C \tag{7.6#5}$$

The problem now is to minimize Eq. (7.6#4) subject to the restraint, Eq. (7.6#5). Using the method of Lagrange multipliers as developed in Chap. 12, the Lagrange expression for the problem at hand is

$$LE = 0.06N_A^{1.1} + 0.02N_B^{1.3} + 0.002N_C^{1.6} + 2{,}800 + \lambda(N_A + N_B + N_C - 400)$$

The partial derivatives are set equal to zero for a minimum.

$$\frac{\partial LE}{\partial N_A} = 0.066N_A^{0.1} + \lambda = 0 \tag{7.6#6}$$

$$\frac{\partial LE}{\partial N_B} = 0.026N_B^{0.3} + \lambda = 0 \tag{7.6#7}$$

$$\frac{\partial LE}{\partial N_C} = 0.0032N_C^{0.6} + \lambda = 0 \tag{7.6#8}$$

$$\frac{\partial LE}{\partial \lambda} = N_A + N_B + N_C - 400 = 0 \tag{7.6#9}$$

These equations show that

$$0.066N_A^{0.1} = 0.026N_B^{0.3} = 0.0032N_C^{0.6} \tag{7.6#10}$$

Comparing with the partial derivatives of Eqs. (7.6#1) to (7.6#3) gives

$$\frac{\partial C_{T_A}}{\partial N_A} = \frac{\partial C_{T_B}}{\partial N_B} = \frac{\partial C_{T_C}}{\partial N_C} \tag{7.6#11}$$

These results indicate that minimum total costs in a one-product multiple-machine program are achieved when the incremental, or marginal, costs are the same for all machines. Figure 7.6F1 illustrates the variation of the incremental costs with production. Optimum

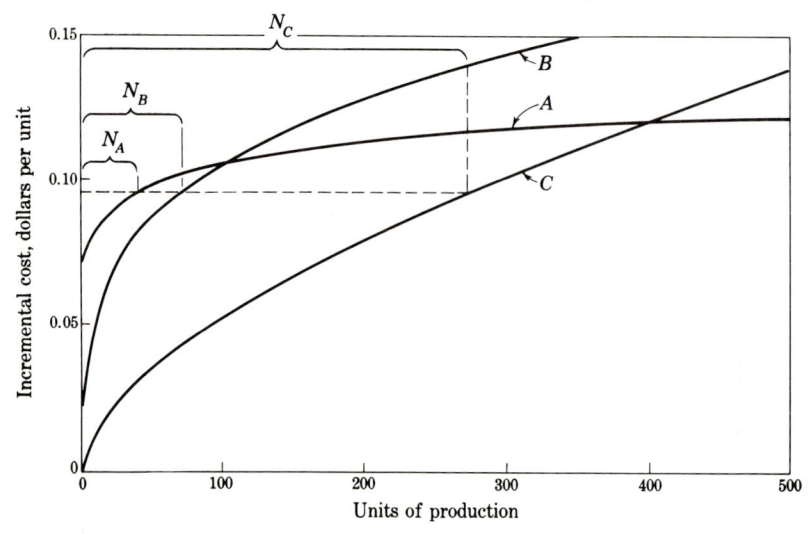

Fig. 7.6F1 Incremental costs for Example 7.6E1.

7.7   BREAK-EVEN AND MINIMUM-COST ANALYSIS   147

operation is obtained by drawing a horizontal line (equal incremental costs) and reading the value of the abscissa at the intersection of the horizontal line and each of the incremental-cost curves. The horizontal line is adjusted in position until the sum of the abscissas corresponds to the total production desired.

An analytic solution can be made by trial and error by assuming, say, N_C and calculating N_A and N_B from Eq. (7.6#10) and repeating until here $N_A + N_B + N_C = 400$. This leads to $N_A = 39$, $N_B = 75$, and $N_C = 285$, which checks the indicated graphical solution.

The treatment given in this section will give the correct answer if the incremental curves shown in Fig. 7.6F1 are regular; i.e., among other things they are continuous and single-valued. In practice the curves do resemble those of Fig. 7.6F1, and the method is generally applicable.

7.7 Multiple-products one-machine example

The analysis to this point implies that production involves one product. A more elaborate problem occurs when there are two or more activities, i.e., a mixture of products, which compete for production time on a machine. When there are multiple activities and all the relationships vary in a linear, or first-order, manner, linear programming as developed in Chap. 13 may be used. For cases where one or more relationships are nonlinear an analysis can be made on the principles of economic-production charts. The following is modified from one given by Schweyer [17.11R7].

Example 7.7E1 A machine can make product A at 1,000 per hour or product B at 2,000 per hour. The available total production time is 2,400 hr/year. Annual fixed costs are $80,000. Other data are:

Product	Average variable cost per unit, $ per unit	Average net sales per unit, $ per unit
A	$6N_A \times 10^{-8} + 0.2$	0.50
B	0.15	0.20

where N_A is the yearly production units of product A. Find the allocation of products which gives the maximum gross profit per year.

The total annual cost is

$$C_T = NV + C_F = 6N_A^2 \times 10^{-8} + 0.2N_A + 0.15N_B + 80,000 \qquad (7.7\#1)$$

where N_B is annual production of product B. Total revenue S_T is

$$S_T = 0.5N_A + 0.2N_B \qquad (7.7\#2)$$

and gross profit Z_g is the difference between Eqs. (7.7#2) and (7.7#1)

$$Z_g = 0.3N_A + 0.05N_B - 6N_A^2 \times 10^{-8} - 80,000 \qquad (7.7\#3)$$

The profit Z_g is to be maximized subject to the following restraint equation, which limits total hours for products A and B to 2,400 per year:

$$\frac{N_A}{1,000} + \frac{N_B}{2,000} = 2,400 \qquad (7.7\#4)$$

or

$$2N_A + N_B - 4,800,000 = 0 \qquad (7.7\#5)$$

148 OPTIMIZATION

The Lagrange expression is

$$LE = 0.3N_A + 0.05N_B - 6N_A^2 \times 10^{-8} - 80{,}000 + \lambda(2N_A + N_B - 4{,}800{,}000) \quad (7.7\#6)$$

The partial derivatives are set equal to zero for a maximum

$$\frac{\partial LE}{\partial N_A} = 0.3 - 12 \times 10^{-8}N_A + 2\lambda = 0 \quad (7.7\#7)$$

$$\frac{\partial LE}{\partial N_B} = 0.05 + \lambda = 0 \quad (7.7\#8)$$

$$\frac{\partial LE}{\partial \lambda} = 2N_A + N_B - 4{,}800{,}000 = 0 \quad (7.7\#9)$$

whence $N_A = 1{,}667{,}000$ units per year and $N_B = 1{,}467{,}000$ units per year.

The example can also be solved using the incremental approach. Equations (7.7#1) for total costs and (7.7#2) for total revenue as written involve N_A and N_B, but N_B can be eliminated by Eq. (7.7#5), giving equations for C_T and S_T as a function of N_A only. The derivatives of these equations must be equal at the maximum profit as shown in the previous section. Setting

$$\frac{dC_T}{dN_A} = \frac{dS_T}{dN_A}$$

will lead to the value of N_A.

The example can be solved analytically by trial and error by assuming, say, N_A, obtaining N_B from Eq. (7.7#5), and calculating and tabulating the total profit Z_g from Eq. (7.7#3). Repeating for various values of N_A will establish the maximum profit.

7.8 Critique in use of break-even and minimum-cost analysis

The basis for break-even and minimum-cost analyses is the functional equation

$$Z_g = NS - (NV + C_F)$$

It provides for mathematical manipulation when the individual relationships for S, V, and C_F are known.

Utilization of the functional equation for maximum profit is a good introduction to optimization. Other criteria for profitability have been developed in Chap. 5. One of the most serious limitations of the simple economic evaluations presented in this chapter is lack of consideration for the time value of money. Thus all of the cash flows of Fig. 7.1F1 represent an instantaneous condition.

Another simplifying assumption involves the projection of sales prices at different production levels. In practice probabilities must be utilized to predict the future values of the variables. A general comment on mathematical models seems appropriate at this point.

Mathematical models are an abstraction of a real system. In reality, the systems are much more complex than any mathematical model which could be built. Therefore, it is the task of the analyst to select the significant aspects of the real system and ignore those aspects which make a negligible contribution at the level of accuracy desired.

The analyst must always compromise between constructing the most accurate model and yet keeping it simple enough to have a manageable solution. The

7.9 Nomenclature

C_F Fixed cost, $
C_T Total cost, $
LE   Lagrange expression
N Number of units of production
N' Number of units of production above 100% capacity
N'' Number of units of production dumped
S Net realizable sales value per unit sold, $ per unit
S'' Net realizable sales value per unit dumped, $ per unit
S_T Total realizable sales value
t Tax rate, decimal
V Variable cost per unit of production, $ per unit
V' Variable cost per unit of production above 100% capacity, $ per unit
Z_g Gross profit before tax, $
Z_t Net profit after tax, $
λ Lagrange multiplier

7.10 Problems

P1. A large boiler plant now recovers 10,000 lb of fly ash per day which is disposed of by dumping in the ocean at a cost of $0.90 per ton. A plant costing $88,200 with a life of 20 years must be built to recover an additional 10,000 lb of the ash per day because of air pollution.

(a) Neglecting interest and taxes, what selling price per ton would be required for the ash to just break even if the added direct costs for additional ash collections were $0.80 per ton and a market could be developed?

(b) At what sales price would the new investment pay out in 5 years? Define the payout time used.

P2. The annual fixed costs for a plant operating at 80% capacity are $55,000, and the direct costs are $120,000 for an annual net sales of $200,000. What is the break-even point?

P3. A company with fixed costs of $200,000 and a break-even point of 60% for $400,000 net sales will show what profit before taxes at 100% capacity? If the profits tax is 38%, what is the total capitalized value, or market value, if prospective purchasers desire an 18% return after taxes based on full-capacity operations? Does the depreciation charge affect the capitalized value?

P4. A meat-waste processing plant is designed for operations of 10 tons/day at 100% capacity where the average variable costs are $0.12 per pound. At 75% capacity, the average variable costs are $0.14 per pound. The fixed costs are $260 per operating day.

(a) Compute the unit costs for both 75 and 100% capacity operations.

(b) What are the unit incremental costs in going from the lower to the higher production rate?

(c) What is the change in unit costs per unit change in production?

(d) Compute the unit costs for 100% capacity from the result in part (c) and the unit cost at 75% capacity.

P5. If the ratio of direct costs to sales dollars is 0.4 and the fixed costs are $250,000 annually for a product selling at $0.20 per pound, what is the unit cost of the product when annual net sales are (a) $500,000, and (b) at a maximum capacity of 4 million pounds?

P6. For net sales of a company amounting to $600,000 annually, when the fixed costs are $350,000 and the direct costs are 35% of the net sales dollars:
  (a) What is the gross profit?
  (b) What is the break-even point in terms of sales dollars?
  (c) What sales are required for a profit of $80,000?

P7. Economic analysis of a plant operation has shown the following empirical relations, where V is a variable cost per unit and S is net sales realization per unit with N being units of production.

  Average sales price: $S = A - BN^2$ $ per pound
  Average variable cost: $V = CN^3 + DN^2$ $ per pound

If C_F is the total constant annual fixed costs and A, B, C, and D above are constants, develop equations to evaluate N for the following in terms of A, B, C, and D:
  (a) The break-even point.
  (b) The critical production rate for maximum profit.
  (c) The maximum profit per pound.
  (d) The minimum unit cost if at a different N from that in (c).
  (e) The marginal unit cost or unit incremental cost.
  (f) Prove for the condition of part (d) that the value of marginal cost is the same as the unit cost for the equations of this problem.

P8. A demand function for price S per unit and quantity Q per period is

  $S = 100 - 0.10Q$ cents

and a total cost function C_T for the same period is

  $C_T = 50Q + 30,000$ cents

Determine (a) the marginal revenue, (b) the marginal cost, and (c) the point of maximum profit.

P9. A one-product–two-mix operation is being considered with a limit of $100,000 per time period. Labor A costs $2,000 per unit period and feedstock B costs $1,000 per unit for the period. Total production depends on the mix of A and B and has been found empirically to be

  $Q = 5AB$

  (a) What are the amounts to be spent for labor and materials, and what is the optimum production?
  (b) Show how the Lagrange multiplier solves the problem.

7.11 References

R1. Barish, N. H.: "Economic Analysis for Engineering and Managerial Decision Making," McGraw-Hill Book Company, New York, 1962.
R2. Bauman, H. C.: "Fundamentals of Cost Engineering in the Chemical Industry," Reinhold Book Corporation, New York, 1964.
R3. Levin, R. I., and C. A. Kirkpatrick: "Quantitative Approaches to Management," McGraw-Hill Book Company, New York, 1965.
R4. Morris, W. T.: "Engineering Economy: The Analysis of Manufacturing Decisions," Richard D. Irwin, Inc., Homewood, Ill., 1960.
R5. Rautenstrausch, W.: "Economics of Business Enterprise," John Wiley & Sons, Inc., New York, 1939.
R6. Schweyer, H. E.: "Process Engineering Economics," McGraw-Hill Book Company, New York, 1955.
R7. Schweyer, H. E.: "Analytic Models for Managerial and Engineering Economics," Reinhold Book Corporation, New York, 1964.
R8. Taylor, G. A.: "Managerial and Engineering Economy," D. Van Nostrand Co., Inc., New York, 1964.
R9. Thuesen, H. G., and W. J. Fabrycky: "Engineering Economy," 3d ed., Prentice-Hall, Inc., Englewood Cliffs, N.J., 1964.

8
Probability—Uncertainty—Simulation

A. M. Ali

DISCRETE FREQUENCY DISTRIBUTIONS

8.1 Distribution functions

Many practical problems involve uncertainty and are probabilistic as opposed to deterministic. As a simple example consider the checkout desk at a store. If customers arrive every 3 min on the average and are serviced every 2 min on the average, some customers will have to wait, as the figures given are only averages. The analysis of such problems depends on the distribution that makes up the average and is part of the mathematics of probability and statistics. The purpose of this chapter is to review those aspects which are essential for an understanding of some following chapters.

Consider the case of throwing dice and noting the total shown. Table 8.1T1 and Fig. 8.1F1 give data computed for one, two, and three dice, and the probabilities $P(X)$ for the occurrence of various sums.

The three distributions shown are examples of a *discrete distribution*, for only integer values can appear; i.e., the sums are not a continuous variable. The probabilities in Table 8.1T1 are easily calculated. Thus in the case of two dice

Table 8.1T1 Frequency Distribution with Dice

Sum of dice X	One die — Number of ways for appearance	One die — Probability $P(X)$ of X	Two dice — Number of ways for appearance	Two dice — Probability $P(X)$ of X	Cumulative probability $\Sigma P(X)$ of X for Sec. 8.3	Three dice — Number of ways for appearance	Three dice — Probability $P(X)$ of X
1	1	0.1667					
2	1	0.1667	1	0.0278	0.0278		
3	1	0.1667	2	0.0556	0.0833	1	0.0046
4	1	0.1667	3	0.0833	0.1667	3	0.0139
5	1	0.1667	4	0.1111	0.2778	6	0.0278
6	1	0.1667	5	0.1389	0.4167	10	0.0463
7			6	0.1667	0.5833	15	0.0694
8	6		5	0.1389	0.7222	21	0.0972
9			4	0.1111	0.8333	25	0.1157
10			3	0.0833	0.9167	27	0.1250
11			2	0.0556	0.9722	27	0.1250
12			1	0.0278	1.0000	25	0.1157
13						21	0.0972
14			36			15	0.0694
15						10	0.0463
16						6	0.0278
17						3	0.0139
18						1	0.0046
						216	

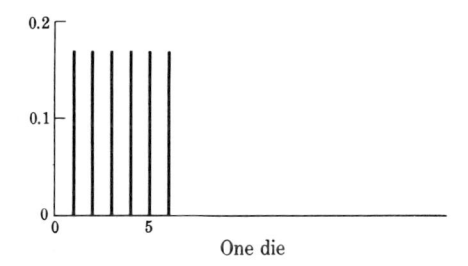

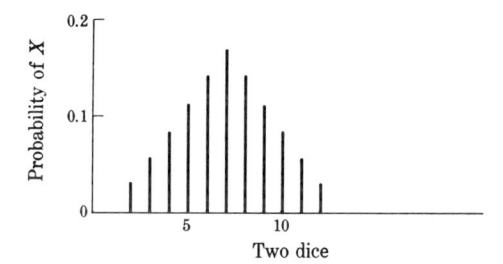

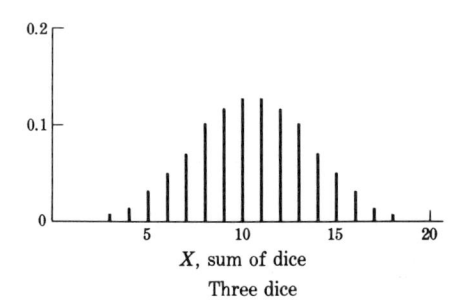

Fig. 8.1F1 Distributions of sums with dice.

there are 36 equally likely ways the dice can turn up and the sum 6 can be obtained in five ways, 1—5, 2—4, 3—3, 4—2, and 5—1. The probability for the sum 6 is $5/36 = 0.1389$.

The distributions shown are symmetrical, but in practice distributions may be nonsymmetrical, or skewed.

8.2 Properties of discrete-distribution functions

An inspection of Fig. 8.1F1 shows differences, and it is desirable to develop parameters which show these differences. Only two are considered here, the mean and the variance.

The *mean* is the arithmetic mean of the distribution or a number of samples taken from it. If X_i is the value of the ith in a total of N equally likely events,

154 OPTIMIZATION

the mean μ is

$$\mu = \frac{\sum_{i=1}^{i=N} X_i}{N} \tag{8.2\#1}$$

or in terms of the probabilities

$$\mu = \sum XP(X) \tag{8.2\#2}$$

where X is the value of the event and $P(X)$ the probability. The summation is over all values of X.

Suppose one die is thrown; then by Eq. (8.2#1) the average is

$$\mu = \frac{1+2+3+4+5+6}{6} = 3.5$$

The mean value 3.5 is unrealizable in a single throw, but what is meant is that in a large number of throws the mean will be 3.5 per throw. For two dice the mean is

$$\mu = \frac{1(2) + 2(3) + 3(4) + \cdots + 3(10) + 2(11) + 1(12)}{36} = 7.0$$

a result which can also be obtained from Eq. (8.2#1)

$$\mu = 2(0.0278) + 3(0.0556) + \cdots + 11(0.0556) + 12(0.0278) = 7$$

For three dice the mean is 10.5.

A very important concept in connection with probability is the *expectation*, which is identical with the average of the occurrences but is used in a very broad sense. The expectation of X is

$$E(X) = \sum X(PX) \tag{8.2\#3}$$

Expected value of X = sum of (value of X)(probability of X occurring)

Example 8.2E1 One die is thrown, and the player receives twice the face value if odd and one-half the face value if even. Find his expectation.

By Eq. (8.2#3)

$$E(X) = 2(1)(\tfrac{1}{6}) + \tfrac{1}{2}(2)(\tfrac{1}{6}) + 2(3)(\tfrac{1}{6}) + \tfrac{1}{2}(4)(\tfrac{1}{6}) + 2(5)(\tfrac{1}{6}) + \tfrac{1}{2}(6)(\tfrac{1}{6}) = 4$$

The second difference between distributions is shown by the *variance*, which is a measure of how much the distribution varies from the average. A small variance means that the distribution is peaked, a large variance that it is spread out. Two distributions may have the same average but differ drastically in the variance, or the way they are spread out. The variance σ^2 is defined as

$$\sigma^2 = \frac{\sum_{1}^{N}(X_i - \mu)^2}{N} \tag{8.2\#4}$$

and σ itself is known as the *standard deviation*. If the variance is calculated from a small number of samples or observations, it is better to substitute $N - 1$ for N in the denominator of Eq. (8.2#4).

Example 8.2E2 The life of a tool in hours before breakage is given by the following data obtained for 50 tools. Tabulate the frequency distribution of the tool life and find the average tool life and its variance.

28.1	31.6	29.9	31.4	31.6
29.9	33.7	30.4	33.9	31.5
30.9	26.5	33.6	31.7	36.4
32.6	30.9	29.3	33.7	32.8
27.7	30.5	30.8	34.4	33.5
29.1	37.8	30.4	33.3	30.5
30.5	32.0	26.5	29.6	31.4
29.6	29.3	29.8	34.4	34.4
30.4	31.0	29.8	38.8	38.9
27.7	26.7	31.6	28.3	26.5

The data are grouped and condensed in Table 8.2T1. The average value is given by Eq. (8.2#1).

Table 8.2T1 Tabulation for Example 8.2E2

Tool life, hr	Midpoint X	Number of tools with this life	Probability $P(X)$ of X
26.0–26.9	26.45	4	0.08
27.0–27.9	27.45	2	0.04
28.0–28.9	28.45	2	0.04
29.0–29.9	29.45	9	0.18
30.0–30.9	30.45	9	0.18
31.0–31.9	31.45	8	0.16
32.0–32.9	32.45	3	0.06
33.0–33.9	33.45	6	0.12
34.0–34.9	34.45	3	0.06
35.0–35.9	35.45	0	0.00
36.0–36.9	36.45	1	0.02
37.0–37.9	37.45	1	0.02
38.0–38.9	38.45	2	0.04
		50	

$$\mu = \frac{4(26.45) + 2(27.45) + \cdots + 1(37.45) + 2(38.45)}{50} = 31.21 \text{ hr}$$

and the variance by Eq. (8.2#4)

$$\sigma^2 = \frac{4(26.45 - 31.21)^2 + 2(27.45 - 31.21)^2 + \cdots + 2(38.45 - 31.21)^2}{50}$$

$$\sigma^2 = 8.10$$

8.3 Cumulative-distribution function

A frequency distribution function can be shown as a plot of cumulative values known as a *cumulative-distribution function*. The plots are useful in certain

156   OPTIMIZATION   8.4

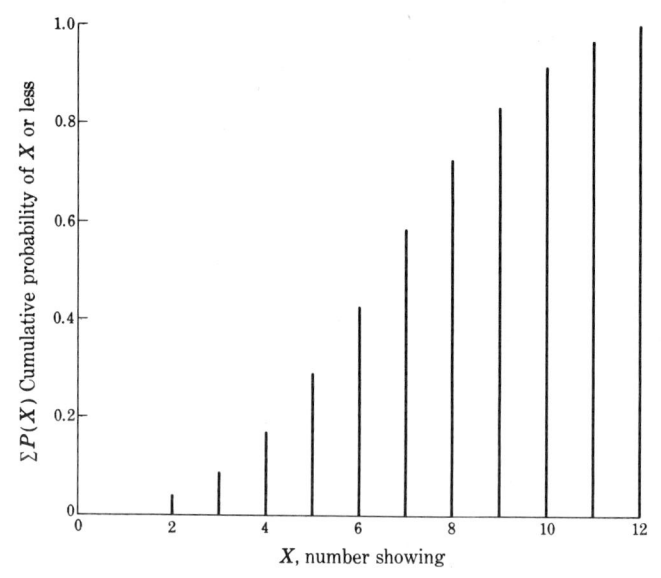

Fig. 8.3F1 Cumulative probability with two dice.

applications. Figure 8.3F1 is a plot of cumulative probability of the value X or less for two dice with data obtained from Table 8.1T1.

It is emphasized that any frequency function may be changed to a probability function by changing the area under the function equal to unity. The cumulative-probability distribution function is, accordingly, unity when taken in the limit.

Cumulative functions may be used to find the probability for a random variable X lying between two limits A and B. Thus if $A < B$, the probability is

$$P(A < X \leq B) = \sum_{i=A+1}^{B} P(X_i) = \sum_{i=0}^{B} P(X_i) - \sum_{i=0}^{A} P(X_i) \qquad (8.3\#1)$$

Example 8.3E1 Find the probability of throwing a 4, 5, 6, or 7 with two dice.
Here the range from above is 3 to 7 inclusive. By Eq. (8.3#1) and Fig. 8.3F1

$$P(3 < X \leq 7) = \sum_{0}^{7} P(X) - \sum_{0}^{3} P(X) = 0.583 - 0.083 = 0.500$$

The same result can be obtained, of course, by adding $P(4)$, $P(5)$, $P(6)$, and $P(7)$.

8.4 Binomial distribution

The binomial distribution applies to events that can take on only two values, such as the head or tail for a tossed coin, or accept or reject for an object. The relationship is

$$P(X) = \frac{N!}{X!\,(N-X)!} p^X (1-p)^{N-X} \qquad (8.4\#1)$$

where $P(X)$ is the probability of *exactly* X occurrences in N trials and p is the probability for success in one trial. In the case of an unbiased coin p and $1 - p$ are both 0.5, but in most problems p will not be 0.5. The distribution is symmetrical if and only if $p = 0.5$.

The mean and variance of a binomial distribution are respectively

$$\mu = Np \tag{8.4\#2}$$
$$\sigma^2 = Np(1-p) \tag{8.4\#3}$$

The binomial distribution assumes that the trials are independent. For sampling from a small population without replacement, the binomial distribution should be replaced by the hypergeometric distribution [8.16R4], which is

$$P(X) = \frac{\binom{H}{X}\binom{M-H}{W-X}}{\binom{M}{W}} \tag{8.4\#4}$$

where

$$\binom{H}{X} = \frac{H!}{X!\,(H-X)!}$$

$P(X)$ is the probability of obtaining exactly X objects having a certain property by withdrawing W objects without replacement from a population containing M objects H of which possess the property.

A generalization of the binomial distribution leads to the multinomial distribution. Instead of having two results A and not A with probabilities p and $1-p$, there are now k results possible each with probability $P_1, P_2, \ldots, P_k$. The probability of getting exactly $X_1, X_2, \ldots X_k$ occurrence of $A_1, A_2, \ldots, A_k$ is

$$P(X_1, X_2, \ldots, X_k) = \frac{N!}{X_1!, \ldots, X_k!} P_1{}^{X_1}, \ldots, P_k{}^{X_k} \quad \text{with } N = \sum_1^k X_i \tag{8.4\#5}$$

8.5 Poisson distribution

The Poisson distribution is of great importance and is

$$P(X) = \frac{e^{-\mu}\mu^X}{X!} \tag{8.5\#1}$$

where $P(X)$ = probability of exactly X occurrences

e = naperian constant $2.71828 \cdots$

μ = expected or average number of occurrences

The distribution is applicable only when the events occur completely at random and the number that occurs is small compared to the potential number that could occur.

The mean and variance of the Poisson function are both μ. Tables are available for the Poisson function and the accumulated Poisson function.

Example 8.5E1 At 3:00 P.M. telephone calls arrive at the company switchboard at the rate of 120 per hour. Find the probability that exactly 0, 1, and 2 calls arrive between 3:00 and 3:01.

Take 1 min as the period of time. Then

$$\mu = \frac{120}{60} = 2 \text{ calls/min expected}$$

By Eq. (8.5#1)

$$P(0) = \frac{e^{-2}2^0}{0!} = 0.1353$$

$$P(1) = \frac{e^{-2}2^1}{1!} = 0.2707$$

$$P(2) = \frac{e^{-2}2^2}{2!} = 0.2707$$

CONTINUOUS FREQUENCY DISTRIBUTIONS

8.6 Continuous distributions

Continuous distributions arise in practice particularly with measurement as opposed to counting. Although continuous distributions can be reduced to discrete distributions by grouping, much as in Example 8.2E2, frequently there are advantages in using the continuous property. Essentially this amounts to substituting the integral sign for the summation sign. With this understanding, all the principles that apply for discrete distributions are easily transferred to continuous distributions.

One distinction that must be clearly understood is the use of probability density in place of probability. If a function is continuous, the chance for an event to have exactly the value 3.00 ··· is zero. There are an infinity of possible results, and the chance for exactly 3 is $1/\infty = 0$. However, it is possible to consider a probability density in the neighborhood of 3, with units of probability per unit interval, which when multiplied by an interval length gives the probability for occurrence within the interval.

The symbol $P_d(X)$ will be used for the probability density at the point X, with the understanding that it must be multiplied by some interval of X to convert it to a probability. Generally $P_d(X)$ depends on X and is a function of X.

$$P_d(X) = F(X) \qquad (8.6\#1)$$

By analogy with discrete functions, the mean or expected value is

$$\mu = E(X) = \frac{\int X P_d(X)\,dX}{\int P_d(X)\,dX} \qquad (8.6\#2)$$

and the variance is

$$\sigma^2 = \frac{\int (X - \mu)^2 P_d(X)\, dX}{\int P_d(X)\, dX} \qquad (8.6\#3)$$

All continuous distribution functions used in this chapter are so expressed that the area under the probability-density function is unity and the cumulative probability, as for discrete functions, is unity in the limit. That is,

$$\int_{-\infty}^{+\infty} P_d(X)\, dX = 1 \qquad (8.6\#4)$$

8.7 Cumulative-distribution function

The cumulative-distribution function for a continuous distribution is obtained by integration and is

$$P_c(A) = \int_{-\infty}^{A} P_d(X)\, dX \qquad (8.7\#1)$$

where $P_c(A)$ is the cumulative probability of X having the value A or less. The cumulative probability for some distribution functions has been tabulated in the literature.

The probability that X will lie between A and B, where $A < B$, is

$$P_c(A \leq X \leq B) = \int_A^B P_d(X)\, dX = \int_{-\infty}^{B} P_d(X)\, dX - \int_{-\infty}^{A} P_d(X)\, dX$$

$$P_c(A \leq X \leq B) = P_c(B) - P_c(A) \qquad (8.7\#2)$$

The cumulative-distribution function is the integral of the probability-density function, hence the derivative of the cumulative-distribution function is the probability-density function at the point.

8.8 Rectangular or uniform distribution

Suppose a distribution is uniform over the range 0 to a. Then the probability density is

$$P_d(X) = \begin{cases} \dfrac{1}{a} & 0 \leq X \leq a \\ 0 & \text{elsewhere} \end{cases} \qquad (8.8\#1)$$

The condition for Eq. (8.6#4) is met

$$\int_{-\infty}^{+\infty} P_d(X)\, dX = \int_0^a \frac{1}{a}\, dX = 1$$

The cumulative probability for X or less is, by Eq. (8.7#1),

$$P_c(X) = \int_0^X \frac{1}{a}\, dX = \frac{X}{a} \qquad 0 \leq X \leq a \qquad (8.8\#2)$$

160 OPTIMIZATION

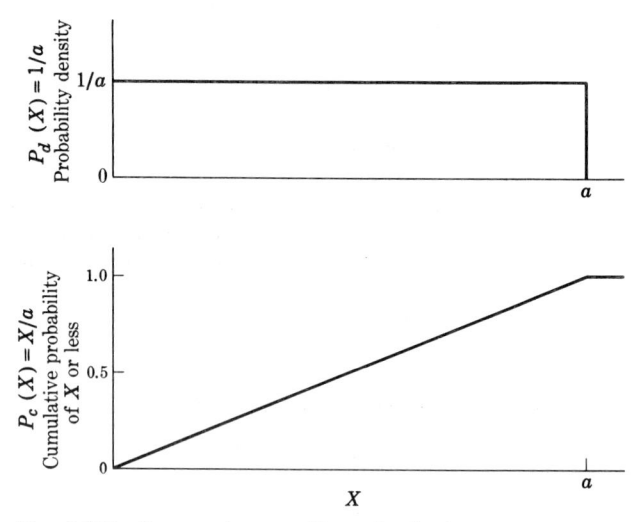

Fig. 8.8F1 Rectangular or uniform distribution.

A plot for the probability-density and the cumulative-probability functions is given in Fig. 8.8F1.

Example 8.8E1 A continuous-distribution function is uniform in the range of zero to 5. Find the average value and the variance.

Here $a = 5$, and by Eq. (8.8#1)

$$P_d(X) = 0.20 \quad 0 \leq X \leq 5 \tag{8.8\#3}$$

Substitution in Eq. (8.6#2) gives the mean value

$$\mu = \frac{\int_0^5 X(0.20)\, dX}{\int_0^5 0.20\, dX} = \frac{0.20(25/2 - 0)}{0.20(5 - 0)} = 2.5$$

which is obvious. The variance by Eq. (8.6#3) is

$$\sigma^2 = \frac{\int_0^5 (X - 2.5)^2 0.20\, dX}{\int_0^5 0.20\, dX} = 0.20 \left(\int_0^5 X^2\, dX - 5 \int_0^5 X\, dX + 6.25 \int_0^5 dX \right)$$

$$\sigma^2 = 0.20[125/3 - 5(25/2) + 31.25] = 2.083$$

8.9 Exponential distribution

The probability-density function for the distribution is

$$P_d(X) = \begin{cases} ae^{-aX} & X \geq 0 \\ 0 & X < 0 \end{cases} \tag{8.9\#1}$$

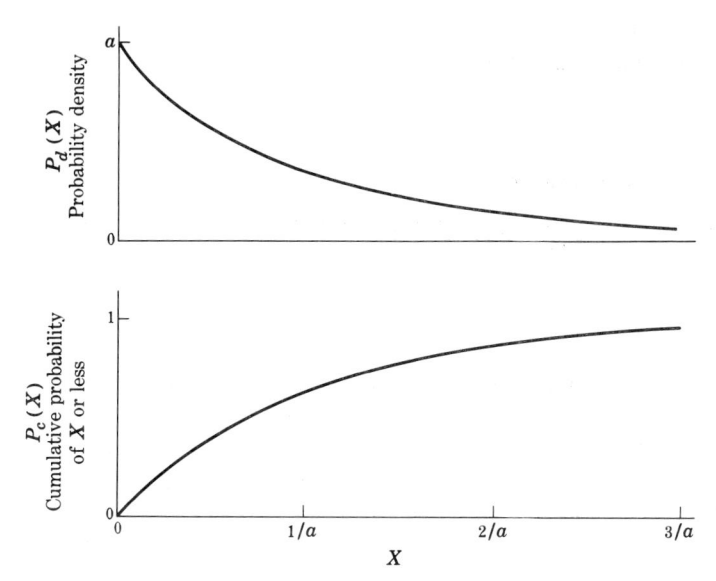

Fig. 8.9F1 Exponential distribution.

The condition for Eq. (8.6#4) is met

$$\int_0^\infty a e^{-aX}\, dX = -\frac{a}{a}|e^{-aX}|_0^\infty = 1$$

The cumulative probability for X or less is, by Eq. (8.7#1),

$$P_c(X) = \int_0^X a e^{-aX}\, dX = 1 - e^{-aX} \tag{8.9#2}$$

The mean of the exponential density distribution is $1/a$, and the variance $1/a^2$. The probability-density function and the cumulative probability of X or less are shown in Fig. 8.9F1.

There is a connection between the Poisson distribution and the exponential distribution. For example, in queuing problems if the arrival rate, in arrivals per unit time period, follows a Poisson distribution with λ average arrivals per period, then by Eq. (8.5#1)

$$P(X) = \frac{e^{-\lambda}(\lambda)^X}{X!}$$

It can be shown that the time between arrivals has an exponential distribution with probability density

$$P_d(T_a) = \lambda e^{-\lambda T}$$

where T_a is the time between arrivals measured in periods T. The cumulative probability becomes the time between arrivals of T_a or less and is

$$P_c(T_a) = 1 - e^{-\lambda \bar{T}}$$

8.10 Normal distribution in standard form

The normal distribution written in standard form using Z for the independent variable has the probability-density function

$$P_d(Z) = \frac{1}{\sqrt{2\pi}} e^{-Z^2/2} \qquad (8.10\#1)$$

The area under the curve is unity; the curve is centered on $Z = 0$, is symmetrical, has a mean equal to zero and a variance equal to unity in the standard form.

The cumulative probability of Z or less is given in Appendix 3, Table 1. The probability-density and cumulative functions are shown in Fig. 8.10F1.

The normal distribution was originally derived from theoretical considerations and has been amply verified by experimental data. It is now recognized

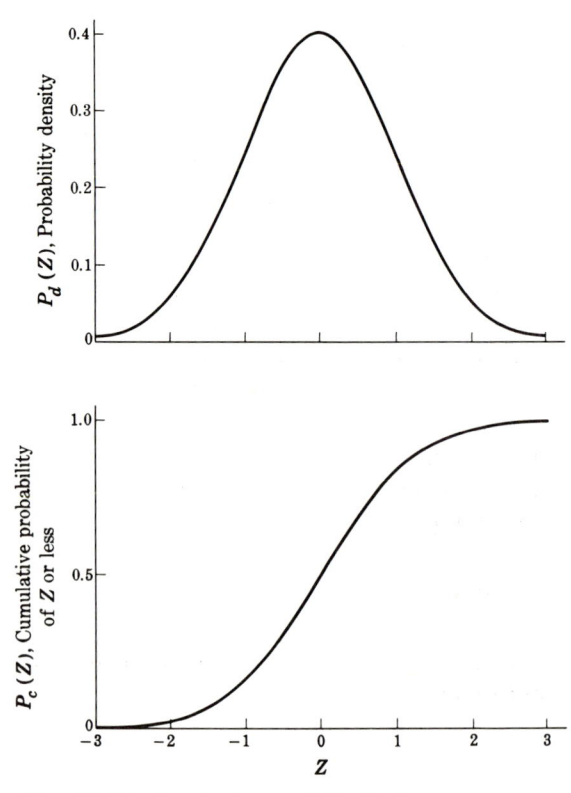

Fig. 8.10F1 Standard normal distribution.

that its usefulness is derived from the fact that even when the values in a population are not normally distributed if large groups of samples are drawn from the population, the averages of the groups will be normally distributed. For the same reason, if an experimental measurement is subject to a large number of independent causes for variation, the observations will be normally distributed.

8.11 Normal distribution with arbitrary parameters

Usually a normal distribution has a mean value that is not equal to zero; nor will the variance be unity. The probability density generally will be

$$P_d(X) = \frac{1}{\sigma\sqrt{2\pi}} e^{-(X-\mu)^2/2\sigma^2} \qquad (8.11\#1)$$

where μ is the mean and σ^2 is the variance.

If a transformation is made with

$$Z = \frac{X - \mu}{\sigma} \qquad (8.11\#2)$$

the normal curve is transformed to a standard normal curve with mean value zero and variance equal to unity. The technique, accordingly, is to transform actual conditions to the standard normal distribution using Eq. (8.11#2), work out the problem in the standard domain, and revert the answer to the actual domain by Eq. (8.11#2).

Example 8.11E1 Measurements on a production-control test give a mean value of 85 with a variance of 17.4. Find the probability for obtaining a value from 80 to 88. Also find the value which will be exceeded only 10% of the time.

Transformation to the standard domain by Eq. (8.11#2) gives

$$Z = \begin{cases} \dfrac{80 - 85}{\sqrt{17.4}} = -1.20 & \text{for } X = 80 \\ \dfrac{88 - 85}{\sqrt{17.4}} = +0.72 & \text{for } X = 88 \end{cases}$$

From Appendix 3, Table 1,

$Z = -1.20 \qquad P_c(Z) = 0.1151$
$Z = +0.72 \qquad P_c(Z) = 0.7642$
$P_c(80 \le X \le 88) = P_c(-1.20 \le Z \le 0.72)$
By (Eq. 8.7#2)
$P_c(-1.20 \le Z \le 0.72) = 0.7642 - 0.1151 = 0.6491$

The probability is 0.649 that Z will lie between -1.20 and $+0.72$, which is the same probability that X will lie between 80 and 88.

For the second part of the example note that if X is exceeded 10% of the time, 90% of the time the value will be X or less. By Appendix 3, Table 1,

For $P_c(Z) = 0.900$: $Z = +1.28$

By Eq. (8.11#2)

$$1.28 = \frac{X - 85}{\sqrt{17.4}}$$

$X = 90.34 =$ value of X which will be exceeded 10% of the time

SPECIAL TOPICS

8.12 Monte Carlo method—simulation

Problems with uncertainty can be quite complicated, and a solution by direct analytical means may become exceedingly difficult if not impossible. The most general and basic method is to resort to simulation. The number of calculations can become large, but the modern computer has eased this consideration. The application known as the Monte Carlo method generates the uncertainty within the problem in conformance with the probabilities involved. A large number of calculations are made to establish averages, distribution within the averages, and any other data sought.

It is necessary first to understand the use of random numbers in the Monte Carlo method. Random numbers are numbers generated so as to be as free as possible from any pattern or bias. Such numbers can be generated by mechanical or electrical means or as needed within a computer by appropriate procedures. Elaborate tables of random numbers are available. Appendix 3, Table 2, gives 1,000 random numbers, which happen to be the first 1,000 decimal places of the number π. Random numbers are used by reading them out horizontally, vertically, diagonally, at random, or by any method which itself is not biased or prejudiced. A large tabulation is preferable inasmuch as a short tabulation cannot have all the randomness of a large one.

Any distribution, whether empirical or theoretical, discrete or continuous, can be simulated with random numbers. It is necessary to convert the distribution to a cumulative probability of X or less and then make an assignment of random numbers.

Example 8.12E1 Show how the Poisson distribution for a mean value 2 can be simulated from a table of random numbers.

From Eq. (8.5#1)

$$P(X) = \frac{e^{-2} 2^X}{X!}$$

A tabulation is given in Table 8.12T1. If three random numbers are chosen with 000

Table 8.12T1 Assignment of Random Numbers for Poisson Distribution with Mean = 2

X	$P(X)$	$\Sigma P(X)$	Numbers assigned, inclusive
0	0.1353	0.135	001–135
1	0.2707	0.406	136–406
2	0.2707	0.677	407–677
3	0.1804	0.857	678–857
4	0.0902	0.947	858–947
5	0.0361	0.983	948–983
6	0.0120	0.995	984–995
7	0.0034	0.999	996–999
8	0.0009	1.000	000–000
9	0.0002		

Random no.	X	Random no.	X	Random no.	X
141	1	265	1	897	4
582	2	749	3	592	2
821	3	086	0	328	1
481	2	745	3	841	3
442	2	109	0	665	2
456	2	566	2	346	1
724	3	700	3	063	0

representing 1,000, then 135 of these numbers can be assigned to $P(0)$, 271 to $P(1)$, etc., to simulate the frequency of the occurrence of these events. The assignment of numbers is easily and systematically made from the cumulative probabilities, as shown in the last column of the tabulation.

The distribution can now be simulated by generating random numbers and converting them to X. Thus using the first three numbers of each group of five taken from Appendix 3, Table 2, X is generated as in the tabulation at the top of the page.

The average X is 1.90, which is reasonably close to the true value 2.0 considering the small number of trials.

The following example can be evaluated without Monte Carlo simulation but illustrates the method.

Example 8.12E2 Assemblies A and B become one product C. A and B each contain defects on a statistical basis as follows:

Defects	No. of times occurring in A	No. of times occurring in B
0	5	2
1	5	3
2	15	5
3	30	10
4	20	20
5	10	40
6	5	10
7	5	5
8	3	3
9	2	2
	100	100

The number of defects in C is the product of the defects in A and B. Using the Monte Carlo method, find the expected number of defects in C.

Table 8.12T2 shows the assignment of random numbers to simulate the defects in A and B. Random numbers are now taken in groups of four, say the first four numbers in column 1 of Appendix 3, Table 2. The first two numbers are for the simulation of defects in A, the second two numbers for the defects in B. The calculation is given in Table 8.12T3. The last column is the cumulative average defects in C obtained by dividing the cumulative defects by the cumulative number of trials. The average after 20 trials is 13.3, whereas the correct value is 16.7. Agreement will improve with the number of trials.

166 OPTIMIZATION

Table 8.12T2 Assignment of Random Numbers in Example 8.12E2

	A			B		
Defects	P(X)	Σ P(X)	Random numbers	P(X)	Σ P(X)	Random numbers
0	0.05	0.05	01–05	0.02	0.02	01–02
1	0.05	0.10	06–10	0.03	0.05	03–05
2	0.15	0.25	11–25	0.05	0.10	06–10
3	0.30	0.55	26–55	0.10	0.20	11–20
4	0.20	0.75	56–55	0.20	0.40	21–40
5	0.10	0.85	76–85	0.40	0.80	41–80
6	0.05	0.90	86–90	0.10	0.90	81–90
7	0.05	0.95	91–95	0.05	0.95	91–95
8	0.03	0.98	96–98	0.03	0.98	96–98
9	0.02	1.00	99–00	0.02	1.00	99–00

8.13 Least squares

Frequently the problem arises of fitting data or observations to an equation. The only application considered here is the case for fitting data to a straight line. The problem is related to probability and the normal distribution applied to the propagation of errors. Not all the data can be made to fall on a straight line. The amount by which each datum fails to fall on the straight is referred to as the *error*. According to the theory of probability, the best straight line is that for which the variance of the data from the straight line is a minimum. An equivalent statement is the sum of squares of the errors about the line shall be a minimum, hence the name least squares.

Let X_i be a value of the independent variable for which Y_i is a known observation. The equation of a straight line is

$$Y = sX + b \qquad (8.13\#1)$$

The error for Y_i, its vertical distance from the straight line, is

$$\text{Error} = Y_i - Y = Y_i - (sX_i + b)$$

Table 8.12T3 Calculation of Average Defects in C for Example 8.12E2

(1) Trial no.	(2) Random number	(3) Defects in A	(4) Defects in B	(5) Defects in C (3) × (4)	(6) Cumulative defects in C	(7) Average defects in C
1	14 15	2	3	6	6	6.0
2	58 20	4	3	12	18	9.0
3	82 14	5	3	15	33	11.0
...	.....	.	.	...	...	....
19	59 82	4	6	24	256	13.5
20	18 57	2	5	10	266	13.3

For the sum of the squares of the error to be a minimum it is necessary to minimize the expression

$$\sum \text{error}^2 = \sum (Y - sX - b)^2$$

where the *i* designation has been dropped, it being understood that the summation is for all the observed points. For a minimum (see Chap. 12)

$$\frac{\partial \sum}{\partial s} = 2 \sum (Y - sX - b)(-X) = 0$$

$$\frac{\partial \sum}{\partial b} = 2 \sum (Y - sX - b)(-1) = 0$$

The two relationships are

$$\sum XY = s \sum X^2 + b \sum X$$
$$\sum Y = s \sum X + \sum b = s \sum X + Nb$$

where N is the number of observations.

The last two equations are known as the *normal equations*. Solved together, they give

$$s = \frac{N \sum XY - \sum X \sum Y}{N \sum X^2 - (\sum X)^2} \qquad (8.13\#2)$$

$$b = \frac{\sum X^2 \sum Y - \sum X \sum XY}{N \sum X^2 - (\sum X)^2} \qquad (8.13\#3)$$

The last two equations give the value of s and b for the best straight line. The calculations are easily made by tabulation.

An alternative calculation for b is based on summing Eq. (8.13#1) for the N pairs of X, Y data, giving

$$b = \frac{\sum Y}{N} - s \frac{\sum X}{N} \qquad (8.13\#4)$$

If the relationship is in the form

$$Y' = K(X')^s$$

there results by taking logarithms

$$\log Y' = s \log X' + \log K$$

By substituting Y for $\log Y'$, X for $\log X'$, and b for $\log K$ the equation reduces to a straight line and can be treated by the method of this section.

A calculation by the method of least squares is given in the succeeding chapter in Example 9.7E1.

8.14 Nomenclature

- a Constant
- A One of k kinds of events in the multinomial distribution
- b Constant in the equation for a straight line
- e Naperian constant $2.71828\cdots$
- $E(X)$ Expected value of X
- H Number of objects in population with desired property; used in hypergeometric distribution
- k Number of kinds of events in the multinomial distribution
- K Constant
- M Number of objects in the population
- N Number of trials or data
- p Probability for success in a single trial in the binomial distribution
- $P(X)$ Probability for event with value X
- $P_c(X)$ Cumulative probability of X or less
- $P_d(X)$ Probability density at X, probability per unit interval
- s Slope of straight line
- T Time in periods
- T_a Time between arrivals, periods
- W Number of objects withdrawn from population in hypergeometric distribution
- X Value of an event
- Z Independent variable in standard normal distribution measured from mean value
- λ Average arrivals per period
- μ Mean or average value
- σ Standard deviation
- σ^2 Variance

8.15 Problems

P1. Two products are drawn from a box containing nine products, three of which are defective. Find the probability that of the two drawn products (*a*) both are defective, (*b*) one is defective, and (*c*) both are good.

P2. A box contains 30 cans of paint, 5 of which are defective. The policy is to withdraw 3 cans at random from the box and reject the box if one or more of the samples drawn is defective. Find the probability of rejecting the box.

P3. The probability of producing a good unit of product at a certain work center is 90%. If the work center makes an order of 10 units, find the probability that the order will have (*a*) two units defective, (*b*) five units defective, and (*c*) no units defective.

P4. Show that the mean value of the Poisson distribution, Eq. (8.5#1), is μ.

P5. Tabulate and draw the normal density function with mean value unity and variance equal to 4. Use a standard normal table for the calculations.

P6. Tabulate and draw the cumulative distribution function of Prob. 8.15P5.

P7. Given

$$F(X) = \begin{cases} \frac{1}{4}e^{-X/4} & X \geq 0 \\ 0 & X < 0 \end{cases}$$

    (*a*) Find the mean and variance of the function.
    (*b*) Find the cumulative distribution function.

P8. A product can be manufactured with three independent processes A, B, and C. Process A follows a normal distribution with a mean time of 1 hr and a variance of 0.25 hr. Process B follows an exponential distribution with a mean time of 2 hr. Process C has a constant time of 4 hr. By using the Monte Carlo method find the average time required for producing five units if the sequence of processes is ABC.

P9. The following table shows the observed values of two variables X and Y

X	6	5	8	8	7	6	10	4	9	7
Y	8	7	7	10	5	8	10	6	8	6

(*a*) Construct a scatter diagram.
(*b*) Find a straight-line relationship between Y and X using the method of least squares.

8.16 References

R1. Adams, J. K.: "Basic Statistical Concepts," McGraw-Hill Book Company, New York, 1956.
R2. Alder, H. L., and E. B. Roessler: "Introduction to Probability and Statistics," W. H. Freeman and Company, San Francisco, 1964.
R3. Beyer, W. H.: "CRC Handbook of Tables for Probability and Statistics," The Chemical Rubber Co., Cleveland, Ohio, 1967.
R4. Brownlee, K. A.: "Statistical Theory and Methodology in Science and Engineering," John Wiley & Sons, Inc., New York, 1960.
R5. Burford, R. L.: "Introduction to Finite Probability," Charles E. Merrill Books, Inc., Columbus, Ohio, 1967.
R6. Hoel, P. G.: "Introduction to Mathematical Statistics," John Wiley & Sons, Inc., New York, 1962.
R7. Lindgren, B. W., and G. W. McElrath: "Introduction to Probability and Statistics," The Macmillan Company, New York, 1959.
R8. Mood, A. M., and F. A. Graybill: "Introduction to the Theory of Statistics," 2d ed., McGraw-Hill Book Company, New York, 1963.
R9. Ostle, B.: "Statistics in Research," The Iowa State University Press, Ames, 1963.

9
The Learning Curve

H. J. Behrens

9.1 Practice improves performance

It is a fundamental human characteristic that a person engaged in a repetitive task will improve his performance. This distinguishing quality is one manifestation of optimization, a human trait, to be discussed in Chap. 12. In a broad sense this quest for improvement is the basis of technological advancement which passes endlessly from generation to generation.

The improved performance of workers on a repetitive operation, such as the manufacture of aircraft or automobiles, is due to many causes. The workers learn to use the tools more effectively, less supervision is needed, work is allotted more expediently, there are fewer rejects, the routine is disturbed less—all these are contributing causes. Not only does the worker improve, but management in turn becomes more efficient. Engineers create new tools and the worker, who may have reached perfection with one tool, receives a new tool and a new cycle of improving performance starts.

In a large-scale repetitive project the improvement goes on smoothly and continuously. The phenomenon is real and has a specific application in cost analysis, cost estimating, or profitability studies related to examination of future costs and confidence level in an analysis.

The importance of improved performance in manufacture was developed as

9.2 The learning curve and learning-curve function

Figure 9.2F1 shows the effort required, expressed as direct man-hours per pound, plotted against the cumulative plane number for the Century series aircraft from government World War II production data released as part of the Aeronautical Material Planning Report (AMPR) data. The curve is the composite data for eight types of fighter planes, with several series in some types, produced by four manufacturers.

The curve is typical and shows a progressive improvement in productivity, but at a diminishing rate. This suggests an exponential relationship between productivity and cumulative production. Figure 9.2F2 is a plot of the data on log-log graph paper, where the data plot as a straight line. This suggests a relationship of the form

$$E_N = KN^s \tag{9.2\#1}$$

where E_N = effort per unit of production, such as man-hours, required to produce Nth unit
K = constant, numerically theoretical effort required to produce first unit
s = slope constant

The *slope constant s* is negative because the effort per unit decreases with production.

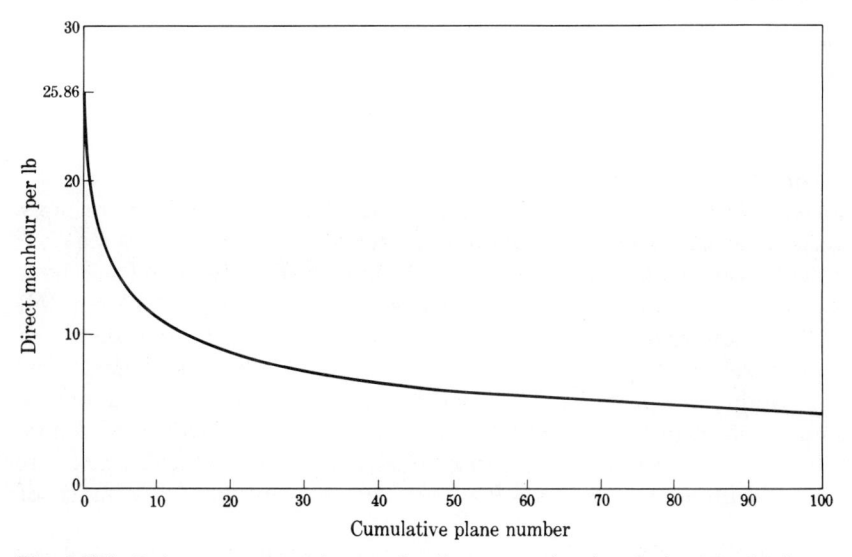

Fig. 9.2F1 Industry average unit curve for Century service aircraft. (*AMPR data.*)

172 OPTIMIZATION

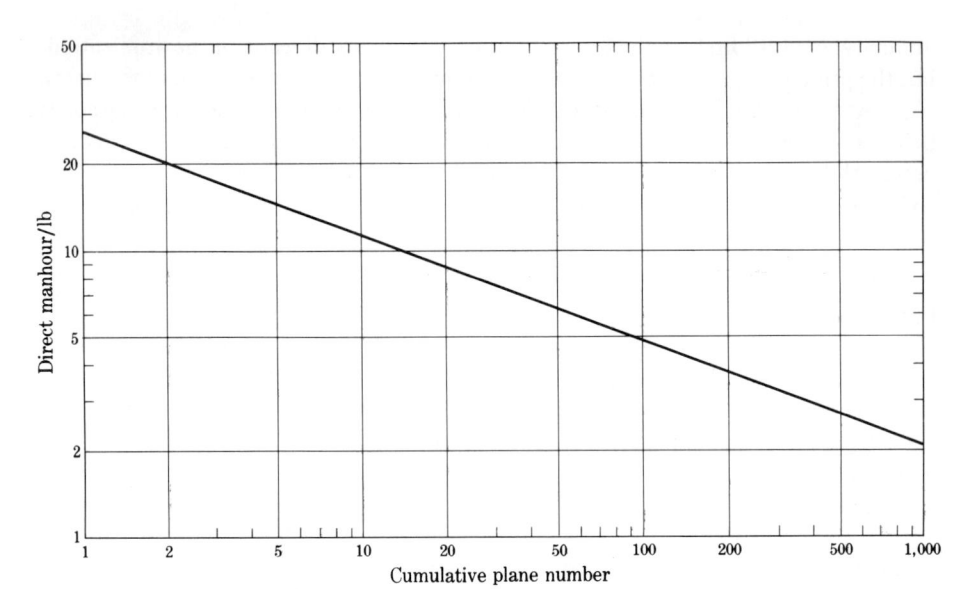

Fig. 9.2F2 Log-log plot of industry average unit curve for Century series aircraft. (*AMPR data.*)

The effort per unit E_N can be expressed in any convenient units. The effort can be converted to dollars and eventually will be in many cases. Nevertheless, the use of dollars directly in the learning-curve function should be undertaken with care because the dollar is subject to considerable inflation and use of the dollar may mask the true reduction of effort per unit with production.

Relationship (9.2#1) will plot as a straight line on log-log graph paper. Taking logarithms of both sides,

$$\log E_N = s \log N + \log K$$

which in terms of $Y = \log E_N$, $X = \log N$, and $b = \log K$ has the form

$$Y = sX + b$$

the equation of a straight line.

A *learning curve*, sometimes called a manufacturing progress curve or simply progress curve, is merely a representation of the decrease in effort per unit required for a repetitive manufacturing operation. Figures 9.2F1 and 9.2F2 are both learning cuvres. Equation (9.2#1) is a *learning-curve function*. Not all data will fit the simple relationship of Eq. (9.2#1), and some effort has been made to use more refined relationships in specific cases. Nevertheless, Eq. (9.2#1) has surprising validity for manufacturing operations and is the only relationship considered in this chapter. Moreover, a log-log plot for the relationship will be used exclusively for the obvious advantage of producing a straight-line plot. A log-log representation has the advantage also of compacting a wide range of variables.

Although Eq. (9.2#1) will be referred to as the learning-curve function and

Fig. 9.2F2 as the learning curve, strict usage would perhaps require that they be referred to respectively as the exponential learning-curve function and exponential learning curve.

9.3 Properties of the learning-curve function

Equation (9.2#1) embodies many important properties. It implies a constant fractional or percentage reduction in effort for doubled (or tripled, etc.) production. For example, for any fixed value for s Eq. (9.2#1) gives

$$E_1 = K(1^s)$$
$$E_2 = K(2^s)$$
$$\frac{E_2}{E_1} = \frac{K(2^s)}{K(1^s)} = 2^s$$

also

$$E_2 = K(2^s)$$
$$E_4 = K(4^s)$$
$$\frac{E_4}{E_2} = \frac{K(4^s)}{K(2^s)} = 2^s$$

Similarly $E_8/E_4 = 2^s$, and so forth. Every time production is doubled, the effort per unit required is a constant 2^s of what it was. Inasmuch as s is negative, the effort per unit required decreases with production.

It is common practice to express the learning-curve function in terms of the gain for double production. Thus a 90% learning-curve function requires only 90% of the effort per unit every time production is doubled.

Let L_D be the decimal ratio of effort, per production unit, required for doubled production. Then by Eq. (9.2#1)

$$L_D = \frac{E_{2N}}{E_N} = \frac{K(2N)^s}{K(N)^s} = 2^s$$

Taking logarithms,

$$\log L_D = s \log 2 \qquad (9.3\#1)$$

or

$$s = \frac{\log L_D}{\log 2} \qquad (9.3\#2)$$

Equation (9.3#2) establishes a relationship between s, the slope constant, and L_D, the *decimal learning ratio*. Table 9.3T1 gives some corresponding values. Because of the occurrence of negative logarithms it is sometimes more convenient to use L_P, the *percentage learning ratio*, which by definition is $100 L_D$. If $L_P/100$ is substituted for L_D in Eq. (9.3#2), it becomes

$$s = \frac{\log(L_P/100)}{\log 2} = \frac{\log L_P - 2}{\log 2}$$

Table 9.3T1 Conversion of Decimal Learning Ratio to Slope Constant

Decimal ratio of effort per unit for doubled production L_D	Slope constant s
1.00	0
0.95	-0.0740
0.90	-0.1520
0.85	-0.2345
0.80	-0.3219
0.75	-0.4150
0.70	-0.5146
0.65	-0.6215
0.60	-0.7370
0.55	-0.8625
0.50	-1.0000

which in terms of minus s, a positive number, is

$$-s = \frac{2 - \log L_P}{\log 2} \qquad (9.3\#3)$$

Example 9.3E1 If 846.2 man-hr is required for the third production unit and 783.0 for the fifth unit, find the percentage learning ratio and the man-hours required for the second, fourth, tenth, and twentieth units.

By Eq. (9.2#1),

$E_3 = 846.2 = K(3^s)$
$E_5 = 783.0 = K(5^s)$

By division

$$\frac{846.2}{783.0} = 1.0807 = \left(\frac{3}{5}\right)^s = 0.6^s$$

$\log 1.0807 = 0.03371 = s \log 0.6 = s(9.77815 - 10) = s(-0.22185)$

$$s = \frac{0.03371}{-0.22185} = -0.1520$$

By Eq. (9.3#3)

$$-(-0.1520) = \frac{2 - \log L_P}{0.30103}$$

$\log L_P = 1.95424$
$L_P = 90.0\% = $ percentage learning ratio

Using the data for $N = 3$ and $S = -0.1520$ in Eq. (9.2#1),

$846.2 = K(3^{-0.1520})$
$\log 846.2 = \log K - 0.1520 \log 3$
$2.9278 = \log K - 0.07252$
$\log K = 3.0000$
$K = 1,000$

so that the learning-curve function is

$$E_N = 1{,}000 N^{-0.1520}$$

The effort required for any unit can now be calculated directly. Thus for the twentieth unit

$$E_{20} = 1{,}000(20^{-0.1520})$$
$$\log E_{20} = \log 1{,}000 - 0.1520 \log 20$$
$$= 3.0000 - 0.1520(1.30103) = 2.80224$$
$$E_{20} = 634.2$$

A tabulation for other units is

E_1	1,000.0
E_2	900.0
E_4	810.0
E_5	783.0
E_{10}	704.7
E_{20}	634.2

Note that

$$\frac{E_2}{E_1} = \frac{E_4}{E_2} = \frac{E_{10}}{E_5} = \frac{E_{20}}{E_{10}} = 0.900$$

Example 9.3E2 Every time production is tripled the unit man-hours required is reduced by 20%. Find the percentage learning ratio.

It will require 80%, or 0.80, for the ratio of effort per unit for tripled production. By Eq. (9.2#1),

$$\frac{E_{3N}}{E_N} = 0.80 = \frac{K(3N^s)}{K(N^s)} = 3^s$$

$$s = \frac{\log 0.80}{\log 3} = \frac{9.90309 - 10}{0.47712} = \frac{-0.09691}{0.47712} = -0.20311$$

By (Eq. 9.3#3) for doubled production

$$-(-0.20311) = \frac{2 - \log L_P}{\log 2}$$

$$\log L_P = 1.93886$$
$$L_P = 86.86\% = \text{percentage learning ratio}$$

Another important property of the learning-curve function is that when plotted on log-log graph paper, the slope of the line is numerically equal to s, the slope constant.

Example 9.3E3 If 423 man-hr is required for the third production unit and 372 for the seventh, find the slope constant by graphical means.

The points are plotted in Fig. 9.3F1. The slope of the line from measurements, before reproduction, is

$$\text{Slope} = \frac{\Delta Y}{\Delta X} = \frac{-11.4 \text{ mm}}{75.0 \text{ mm}} = -0.152 \text{ slope constant}$$

The modulus of the vertical and horizontal log scales must be the same when using the method, as in the example.

176 OPTIMIZATION 9.4

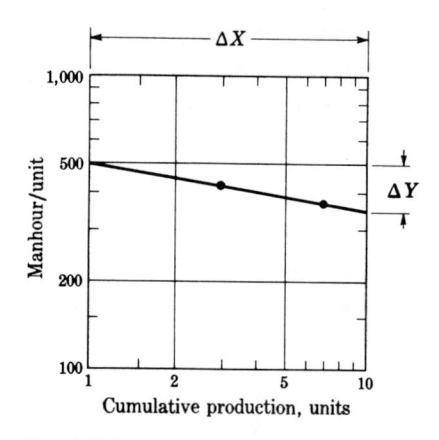

Fig. 9.3F1 Plot for Example 9.3E3

9.4 Cumulative values

Equation (9.2#1) gives instantaneous values of effort per unit, thus the man-hours for the Nth unit.

For the total effort for N units from 1 through N, the *cumulative effort* required E_T is

$$E_T = E_1 + E_2 + \cdots + E_N = \sum_{N=1}^{N=N} E_N \qquad (9.4\#1)$$

An exact summation can be made by summing term by term, which can be tedious; from tables, if available; or by approximation relationships.

An approximation is obtained by treating Eq. (9.2#1) as a continuous function instead of a discrete function and integrating with a suitable change of limits.

$$E_T \cong K \int_{0.5}^{N+0.5} N^s \, dN = K \left[\frac{N^{s+1}}{s+1} \right]_{0.5}^{N+0.5}$$

$$\cong \frac{K}{s+1} [(N+0.5)^{s+1} - 0.5^{s+1}] \qquad (9.4\#2)$$

The approximation improves as N increases. If N is very large compared to 0.5, Eq. (9.4#2) reduces to

$$E_T = \frac{K}{s+1} N^{s+1} \qquad (9.4\#3)$$

The cumulative average unit effort required is the cumulative effort required for the first N units divided by the cumulative number of units N, that is,

$$\frac{E_T}{N} = \frac{\sum_{N=1}^{N=N} E_N}{N}$$

which from Eqs. (9.4#2) and (9.4#3) respectively can be approximated by

$$\frac{E_T}{N} \cong \frac{K}{N(s+1)} [(N+0.5)^{s+1} - 0.5^{s+1}] \qquad (9.4\#4)$$

$$\frac{E_T}{N} \cong \frac{K}{s+1} N^s \qquad (9.4\#5)$$

Example 9.4E1 If 846.2 man-hr is required for the third production unit and 783.0 for the fifth, find the total man-hours required for the fifteenth through twentieth units and the average man-hour for the six units.

From the solution to Example 9.3E1, the slope constant s is -0.1520, and $K = 1,000$. The man-hours required for the first 14 units from Eq. (9.4#2) with $s + 1 = -0.1520 + 1 = 0.8480$ is

$$E_{T,14} = \frac{1,000}{0.8480} [(14+0.5)^{0.8480} - 0.5^{0.8480}]$$

$$= \frac{1,000}{0.8480} (9.6570 - 0.5556) = 10,733 \text{ man-hr}$$

For the first 20 units, by the same equation

$$E_{T,20} = \frac{1,000}{0.8480} [(20+0.5)^{0.8480} - 0.5^{0.8480}]$$

$$= \frac{1,000}{0.8480} (12.953 - 0.556) = 14,619 \text{ man-hr}$$

Net man-hours for fifteenth to twentieth units is

$$E_{T,20} - E_{T,14} = 14,619 - 10,733 = 3,886 \text{ man-hr}$$

The average for the group of six is

$$\frac{3,886}{6} = 647.7 \text{ man-hr/unit}$$

The exact answer is 648.0. The approximation equation gives a close answer in this example because N is reasonably large, and moreover the effect of the early units is wiped out.

9.5 Learning curve and economic evaluation

The learning curve should be considered in making economic evaluations for the future and can be used along the way as a criterion for judging the achievement actually realized. The time value of money becomes an ingredient of the analysis when looking into the future.

Example 9.5E1 A company has just received an order for four sophisticated space gadgets. The purchaser will take delivery of one unit starting 1 year hence, and one unit at the end of each of the succeeding 3 years. He will pay for each unit immediately upon receipt and will not take delivery ahead of time. The seller, however, can make the units ahead of time, if he prefers, and store them at no cost for later delivery.

The only pertinent cost in making these units is labor at $10 per hour. All units made in the *same* year are subject to an 80% learning ratio for the hours required, and the first unit requires 100,000 hr of labor. Learning occurs only within a year and is not carried over from one year to another.

Consider the labor costs to be paid as of the end of the year. If money is worth 16% per year after a 52% tax, decide which of the following two plans is more economical:

(a) Build four units the first year.
(b) Build one unit each of the 4 years.

Revenue and its timing is the same for either plan and need not be considered. The object is to choose the plan with the lower present worth of cost after taxes. For an 80% learning ratio $s = -0.3219$ from Table 9.3T1. The first unit costs $10(100,000) = \$1,000,000$. The cost of units made in same year with learning is

First: $1,000,000(1^{-0.3219}) = 1,000,000$
Second: $1,000,000(2^{-0.3219}) = 800,000$
Third: $1,000,000(3^{-0.3219}) = 702,104$
Fourth: $1,000,000(4^{-0.3219}) = 640,000$
Total $= \overline{3,142,104}$

Present worth of cost after taxes for all units made in first year is

$$PW = (1 - 0.52)\frac{3,142,000}{1.16} = \$1,300,200$$

Present worth of cost after taxes for the four units made in successive years is

$$PW = (1 - 0.52)\left(\frac{1,000,000}{1.16} + \frac{1,000,000}{1.16^2} + \frac{1,000,000}{1.16^3} + \frac{1,000,000}{1.16^4}\right) = \$1,343,100$$

It will pay to make the four units the first year. The gain from the learning curve offsets the advantage in deferring the labor costs by the alternate plan. Making four the first year, however, is not necessarily the best possible plan, as there are other combinations such as three the first year and one the last year.

9.6 The learning-curve function from single-unit data

For a given set of data Eq. (9.2#1) is established by determining the best values for K and s. If the data are all in the form giving the effort required for single, individual units of production, the data can be plotted on log-log graph paper and the best line drawn by eye. Having established the best line, any two points on the line can be used to determine, graphically or analytically, the slope of the line (the slope constant) and K, which is numerically the intercept on the ordinate $N = 1$. The graphical method is rapid but depends upon judgment, and can become inaccurate if the points are badly scattered.

The most accurate method for determining the best straight line is application of the method of least squares described in the previous chapter.

9.7 The learning-curve function from grouped data

In practice the effort required to produce single, individual units may not be known but instead only the average effort to produce a group, or lot, of units. Data for such a circumstance are given in Table 9.7T1. A total of 35 units has been made, but the precise man-hours required for any single unit is not known. Before the man-hours can be plotted, it is necessary to take each group and convert it to a point. This point within a group is some unit number, not necessarily an integer, to which the average man-hour can be associated. It is a balance or

9.7 THE LEARNING CURVE

Table 9.7T1 Man-hours for Consecutive Lots

Lot no.	Quantity in lot	Man-hours for lot	Average man-hours per unit for lot
1	3	621.76	207.24
2	4	357.72	89.43
3	8	428.72	53.43
4	10	449.80	44.98
5	10	368.10	36.81

focus point and a single value to be paired with the average effort per unit for the group. It is loosely referred to as the *lot midpoint,* but *lot equivalent point* is perhaps more descriptive.

Several methods are available for determining the lot equivalent point. The *lot-midpoint method* uses the arithmetical mean of the first and last unit numbers in the lot. For example, for a lot of 6 units, the equivalent point is at $(1 + 6)/2 = 3.5$, or 3.5 units from the last unit of the preceding lot.

The *rule-of-thumb lot-midpoint method* places the lot equivalent point by means of the following rules:

First lot Less than 10, take half of last unit number.
  10 or more, take one-third of last unit number.
Subsequent lots Take one-half of number of units in lot.

For the data in Table 9.7T1:

  Lot 1: $3/2 = 1.5$ lot equivalent point
  Lot 2: $4/2 = 2$

or 2 units from unit 3, the last unit in the preceding lot. Thus $3 + 2 = 5$, or unit 5.

  Lot 3: $8/2 = 4$

or 4 units from 7, last unit in preceding lot, thus $7 + 4$, or unit 11. The complete tabulation is given in Table 9.7T2.

Table 9.7T2 Data of Table 9.7T1 after Adjustment by Rule-of-thumb Method

Lot no.	Quantity in lot	Assigned to unit	Average man-hours per unit for lot
1	3	1.5	207.24
2	4	5	89.43
3	8	11	53.43
4	10	20	44.98
5	10	30	36.81

Table 9.7T3 Geometric Means for Lot Sizes

No. in lot	Geometric mean	No. in lot	Geometric mean
1	1.0000	9	4.1472
2	1.4142	10	4.5287
3	1.8171	15	6.4235
4	2.2134	20	8.3044
5	2.6052	25	10.177
6	2.9938	30	12.045
7	3.3800	40	15.768
8	3.7644	50	19.483

The *geometric-mean lot-midpoint method* uses the geometric mean to determine the equivalent point of each lot. For a lot of five the geometrical mean is

$$\sqrt[5]{1(2)(3)(4)(5)} = 2.6052$$

which is added to the last unit number of the preceding group. Some geometric means are given in Table 9.7T3.

The *true lot-midpoint method* is the most accurate method for determining the lot equivalent point but the most difficult to execute. It involves two separate steps. In the first step an approximate method is used for the data to establish an approximate value for s, the slope constant. The approximate value is then used in the second step to find the true equivalent point for the lots. The data so generated are then used with the method of least squares to establish a revised but accurate value of s.

As an example consider the second lot in Table 9.7T1. It will be shown below that an approximate value for s for the data in Table 9.7T1 is $s = -0.57616$. The second lot contains the fourth, fifth, sixth, and seventh units, and for $K = 1$, Eq. (9.2#1) gives

$$E_4 = 1(4^{-0.57616}) = 0.44990$$
$$E_5 = 1(5^{-0.57616}) = 0.39562$$
$$E_6 = 1(6^{-0.57616}) = 0.35617$$
$$E_7 = 1(7^{-0.57616}) = 0.32590$$
$$\text{Total} = 1.52759$$

$$\text{Av} = \frac{1.52759}{4} = 0.38190$$

The individual unit which will have an effort of 0.38190 with $K = 1$ and $s = -0.57616$, as before, is

$$0.38190 = 1N^{-0.57616}$$

$$N = 5.3159 = \text{true lot equivalent point}$$

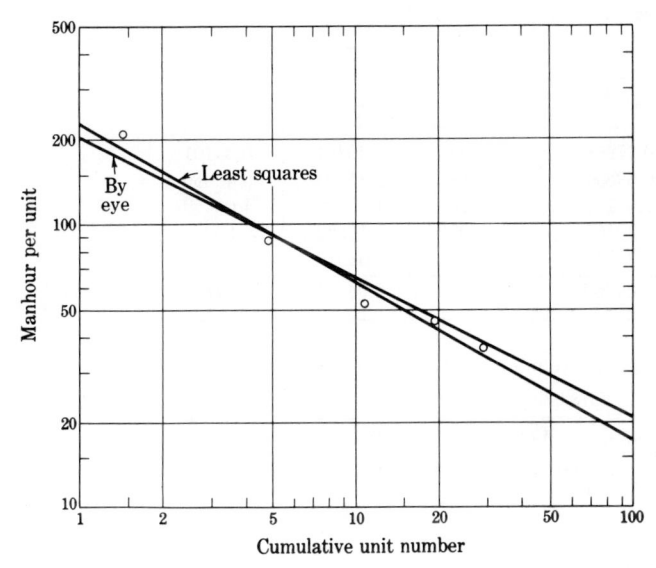

Fig. 9.7F1 Plot of data and learning curves for Example 9.7E1.

Thus for the second lot, 89.43 man-hr average per unit is assigned to unit number 5.3159. Other lots are treated similarly. The points so obtained can be subject to a least-squares calculation to determine the best values of s and K.

If tables of cumulative values are available for values of s reasonably close to the approximate value, the numerical work for the true lot-midpoint method can be simplified.

Example 9.7E1 Using the data in Table 9.7T1 and the rule-of-thumb lot-midpoint method, determine the learning-curve function that represents the data.

Application of the rule-of-thumb lot-midpoint method to the group data leads to the five points given by the last two columns of Table 9.7T2. The points are plotted in Fig. 9.7F1.

A line put through the points by eye is shown. Using the extreme points on the line, the slope as determined by measurement, before reproduction, is $\Delta Y/\Delta X = -73.6/148.5 = -0.496$.

The percentage learning ratio corresponding to the slope can be obtained from Eq. (9.3#3)

$$-(-0.496) = \frac{2 - \log L_P}{\log 2}$$

$$\log L_P = 1.8507$$

$$L_P = 70.91\% = \text{percentage learning ratio}$$

and the value for K is the intercept on the axis $N = 1$ and is about 204. Thus the line drawn by eye gives 70.91% learning ratio and the learning-curve function

$$E_N = 204 N^{-0.496}$$

The data can also be subjected to a least-squares analysis, described in the previous

182　OPTIMIZATION

Table 9.7T4. Least-squares Calculation for Ex. 9.7E1

N assigned	Effort E_N, man-hr	X log N	Y log E	XY	X^2
1.5	207.24	0.17609	2.31647	0.40791	0.03101
5	89.43	0.69897	1.95148	1.36403	0.48856
11	53.39	1.04139	1.72746	1.79896	1.08449
20	44.98	1.30103	1.65302	2.15063	1.69268
30	36.81	1.47712	1.56597	2.31313	2.18188
		4.69460	9.21440	8.03466	5.47862

chapter and exhibited for the five points in Table 9.7T4.

$$s = \frac{5 \Sigma XY - \Sigma X \Sigma Y}{5 \Sigma X^2 - (\Sigma X)^2} = \frac{5(8.03466) - 4.69460(9.21440)}{5(5.47862) - 4.69460^2} = -0.57616$$

$$\log K = \frac{\Sigma Y}{5} - s\frac{\Sigma X}{5} = \frac{9.21440}{5} + 0.57616 \frac{4.69460}{5} = 2.38385$$

$$K = 242.02$$

The learning-curve function resulting from the least-squares computation is

$$E_N = 242.02 N^{-0.57616}$$

and the slope constant of -0.57616 corresponds to 67.075% learning ratio. The straight line represented by the relationship above is plotted in Fig. 9.7F1.

Although the slope constant, -0.57616, is not exact because the rule-of-thumb lot-midpoint method was followed, the true lot-midpoint method can now be used, as indicated previously, to establish an even better representation for the learning-curve function.

9.8 Development of learning-curve tables

Tables can be readily constructed for use with the learning-curve function. The decimal or percentage learning ratio is a parameter and the unit number a variable. The three most important items to tabulate are:

E_N = effort for the Nth unit taking unity as the effort for the first unit

$E_T = \sum_{1}^{N} E_N$ = cumulative effort for units 1 through N

$\dfrac{E_T}{N} = \dfrac{\sum_{1}^{N} E_N}{N}$ = cumulative average unit effort for units 1 through N

Tables can be programmed easily and printed out by a computer for any value of L_D, the decimal learning ratio. An abbreviated tabulation for $L_D = 0.90, 0.80$, and 0.70 is given in Appendix 4, Table 1.

Some conveniences simplify the preparation of a table by manual calculation. Thus instead of calculating E_N, for $K = 1$, by the relationship

$$E_N = N^s$$

where s is negative, it is easier to calculate E_N from the relationship

$$E_N = \frac{N^{s+1}}{N}$$

where $s + 1$ is positive.

9.9 Nomenclature

E_N Effort required to produce the Nth unit, e.g., man-hr/unit
E_T Cumulative effort to produce units 1 through N, e.g., man-hr
E_T/N Cumulative average unit effort, e.g., man-hr/unit
K Constant in Eq. (9.2#1): theoretical effort required for first unit, e.g., man-hr
L_D Decimal learning ratio, dimensionless
L_P Percentage learning ratio, dimensionless
N Cumulative number of units produced, dimensionless
s Slope constant, decimal, dimensionless
ΣE_N Same as E_T
$\dfrac{\Sigma E_N}{N}$ Same as E_T/N

9.10 Problems

P1. Find the first unit value when the unit value of unit 100 is 30 hr with an 80% learning ratio.
P2. Find the value for unit 300 when the value for unit 3 is 1,000 hr with a 70% learning ratio.
P3. Find the unit average hours for units 21 to 40 when unit 1 is 250 hr with a learning ratio of (a) 90% and (b) 83%.
P4. Units 1 through 200 have accumulated 45,000 hr. Find the unit time for unit 100 with a learning ratio of (a) 70% and (b) 75%.
P5. Using the rule-of-thumb lot-midpoint method, the geometric-mean lot-midpoint method, and the true lot-midpoint method for an 80% learning ratio, find the lot midpoints or lot equivalent points for:

Lot 1, units 1 through 14
Lot 2, units 15 through 40
Lot 3, units 41 through 80
Lot 4, units 81 through 100

P6. Additional information for the Prob. 9.10P5 is:

Lot 1, 15,000 hr total time
Lot 2, 20,000 hr total time
Lot 3, 25,000 hr total time
Lot 4, 10,000 hr total time

Continuing the problem, develop the slope constant by plotting on log-log graph paper. Using the method of least squares for the rule-of-thumb lot-midpoint method, establish the learning-curve function.
P7. Analyze the answers to the Prob. 9.10P6. What can be said about the slope of the curve?
P8. A company has produced machine parts as a subcontractor for a large military order for a

number of years, during which production was consistent with an 89% learning ratio. A commercial subcontract for making similar machine parts, but with a rigid schedule, is under consideration. Should you use the same percentage learning ratio for a schedule that is twice as fast as the military schedule? How would you develop the learning curve anticipated for this contract?

9.11 References

R1. Behrens, H. J.: Improvement Curve, Real or Imaginary?, *AACE Bull.*, vol. 8, p. 75, June, 1966.

R2. Fabrycky, W. J., and P. E. Torgersen: "Operations Economy," Prentice-Hall, Inc., Englewood Cliffs, N.J., 1966.

R3. Hirschmann, W. B.: Profit from the Learning Curve, *Harvard Business Rev.*, January–February, 1964, pp. 125–139.

R4. Jordan, R.: "How to Use the Learning Curve," Material Management Institute, Boston, 1965.

R5. Kottler, J. L.: The Learning Curve: A Case History in Its Application, *J. Ind. Eng.*, vol. 15, pp. 176–180, July–August, 1964.

R6. Noah, L. W., and R. W. Smith: *U.S. Air Force Project Rand Res. Mem.* MR-2786-Pr., January, 1962.

R7. Paterson, S. F.: Predicting Learning Time, *Production*, July, 1963.

10
Inventory Problems

A. M. Ali

DETERMINISTIC MODELS

10.1 Definitions

Inventory problems offer excellent opportunities for optimization. Inventories are maintained at a cost to gain advantages having monetary value, and there is an economic balance leading to some optimum policy. Inventory is simply a stock of physical assets having value, which can be material, money, or labor. Material inventory can be raw material, tools and accessories used in production, unfinished or in-process inventory, and finished products. Figure 10.1F1 illustrates the classes of inventory with regard to the manufacture of steel.

Inventory of materials may also be classified as centralized inventory, for which there is only one store of inventory for a material, or decentralized inventory, for which more than one store for a specific type of inventory exists within an organization.

Money may also be stored, and every organization requires some cash on hand to transact its business. Finally labor may be stored so that it will be available when needed. As an example consider a repair crew for the oil pumps in an oil field, where the size of the crew is balanced against the cost of delay in getting pumps repaired.

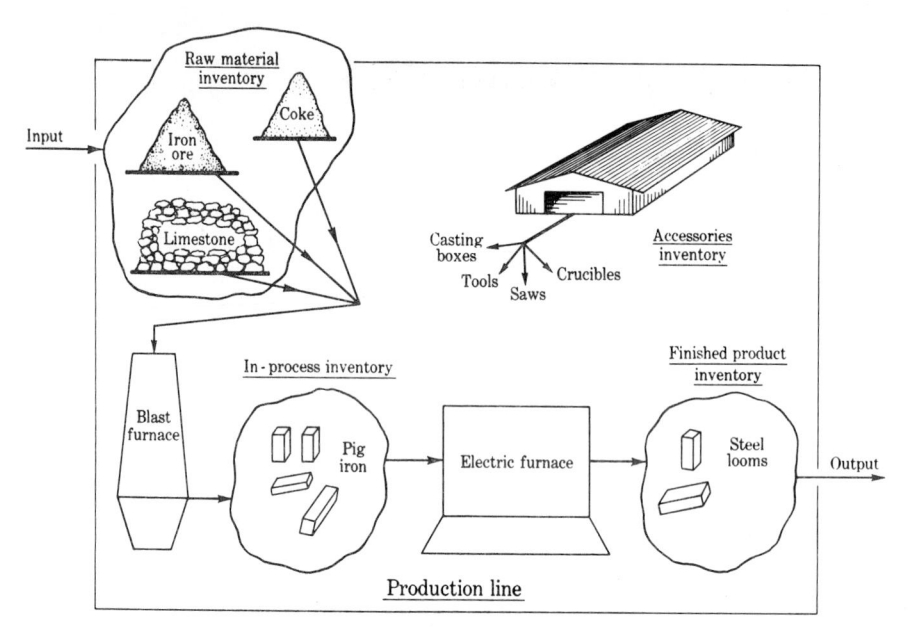

Fig. 10.1F1 Classification of materials inventory in manufacture of steel.

10.2 General inventory model

A model can be described as an abstraction of a real system and four types are recognized: physical, physical analog, schematic, and mathematical. Mathematical models employ the language and symbols of mathematics and may be deterministic models, for which all information and values are treated as being definite, or probabilistic, for which uncertainty in some of the values is recognized and considered.

The general inventory system is shown in Fig. 10.2F1. Ordinates represent the number of units available in the stock against time represented on the axis of abscissas.

Consider the quantity Q units to be received at the beginning of the period T_1.

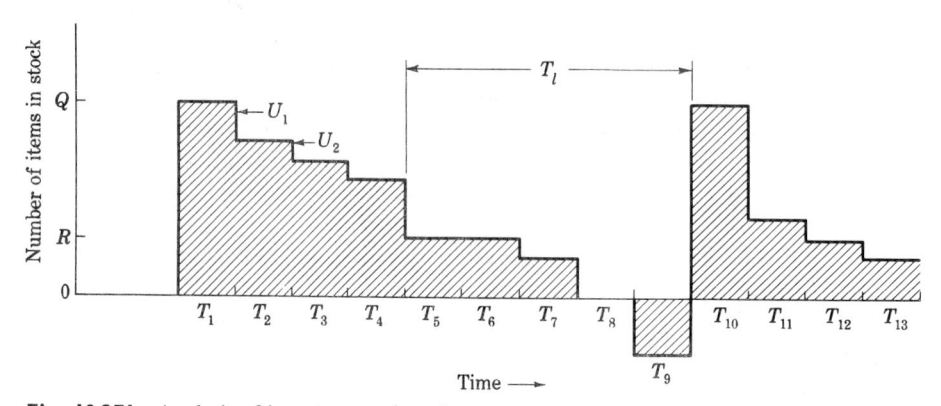

Fig. 10.2F1 Analysis of inventory against time.

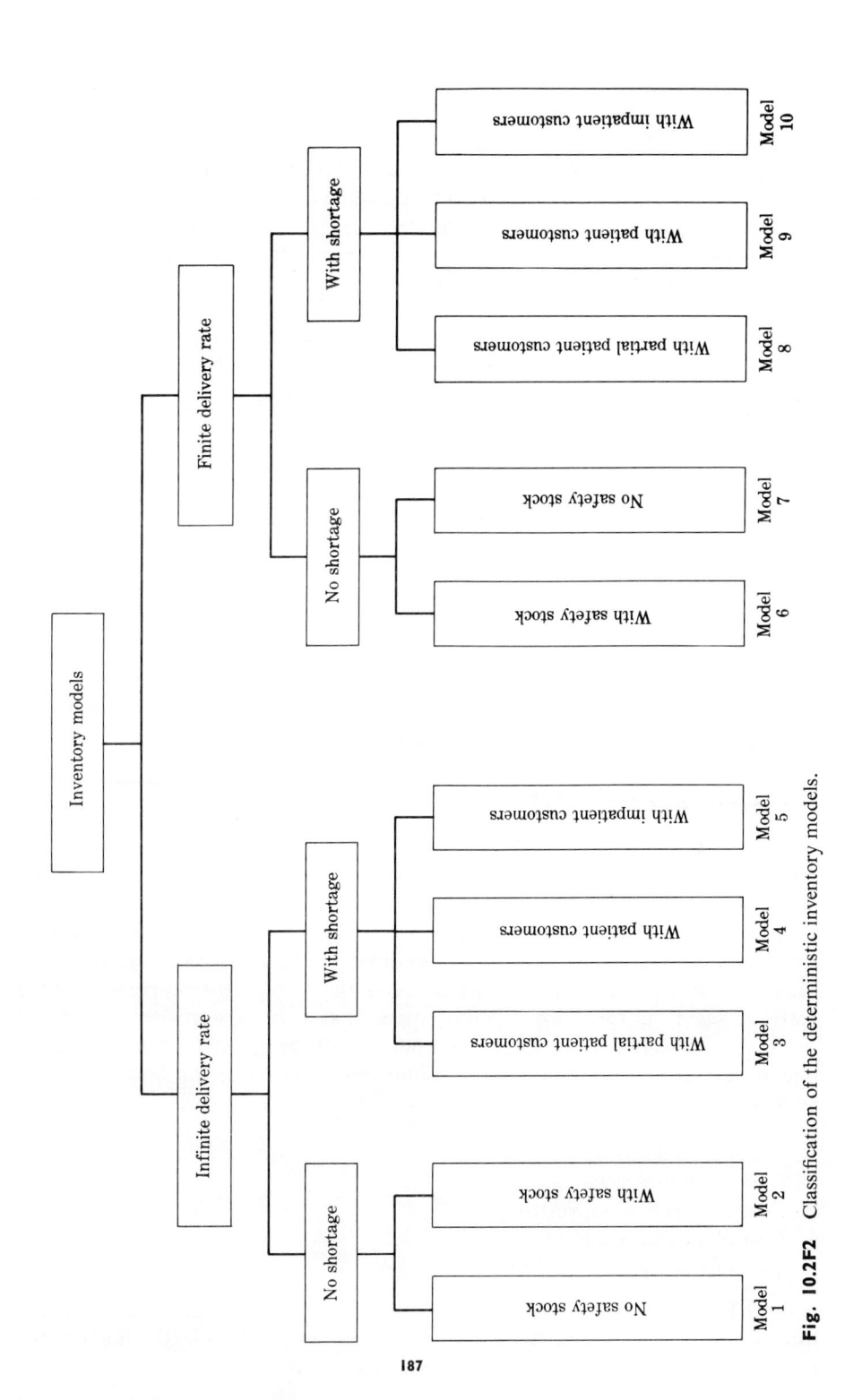

Fig. 10.2F2 Classification of the deterministic inventory models.

The use during this period U_1 is subtracted from the stock to give a lower stock for the second period. U_2 is the use during the second period, and so forth. At the end of the fourth period T_4 the level of inventory reaches the reorder level R, and so an order equal to Q units is instigated at that time. The order is eventually received at the beginning of the tenth period. The procurement time, or lead time T_l, is the time required in periods to receive an order after it is placed. During the procurement time the level of stock may reach zero. If the level goes to zero and further demand arises, there are shortages, which are shown as areas below the zero ordinate line.

The discussion above has developed the analysis of inventory against time in general terms for comprehension of the inventory system. This understanding is necessary to determine the reorder level, the procurement quantity, and the procurement source with regard to the relevant costs and the properties of demand and procurement time. The object, of course, is to minimize the total cost of the system.

It is important to note that what is desired is minimum cost per period, not per cycle. Also the analyst must clearly understand that some costs are connected with the cycle, such as the cost of placing and receiving an order, whereas other costs are connected with a period, such as storage costs. Confusion between a period and cycle is the most common source of error for a beginner.

The deterministic inventory models treated are classified in Fig. 10.2F2. The models are classified with respect to delivery rate, infinite or finite; shortage, with or without; safety stock, with or without; and if with shortage, consideration of whether customers are patient or impatient.

10.3 Model I of Fig. 10.2F2

The model assumes that the delivery rate is infinite; i.e., all units are delivered simultaneously when delivery is eventually made. Also it assumes that no shortage is allowed and that no safety stock is provided. The parameters in the model—demand, storage cost, and the cost of placing and receiving an order—are known in advance and do not vary with time. Under these assumptions the total variable cost per period C_t is a function of the storage cost per period and the cost of placing and receiving an order expressed as a period cost.

Costs of storage are incurred as a function of the quantity on hand and the time duration. The cost per unit per unit time consists of the following components, among others:

1 Cost of warehousing space
2 Cost of obsolescence risk
3 Cost of interest on invested capital
4 Cost of insurance and taxes
5 Cost of warehouse overhead

It depends also upon the utilization Z of storage area for a given item. If the storage area is reserved for this and only this item, then Z has the fractional value 1.0 inasmuch as the storage charge will be based on maximum storage. If the

10.3 INVENTORY PROBLEMS

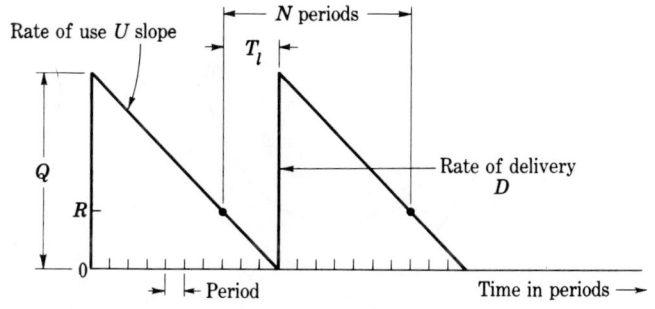

Fig. 10.3F1 Diagram for model 1.

storage charge is based on average area used for storage, then Z has the fractional value 0.5 for purposes of this chapter.

The schematic diagram for model 1 is illustrated in Fig. 10.3F1. It shows that the cycle is the number of time periods N from one point to the successive similar point on the diagram. The rate of use in units per period is constant for all time periods. The lead time T_l is the time between the order time and delivery of the order.

The total variable cost per period C_t equals the sum of the storage cost per period and the cost of placing and receiving an order per period C_{o_p}

$$C_t = ZMC_h + C_{o_p} \qquad (10.3\#1)$$

where M = maximum inventory = Q
Z = utilization fraction for allocating warehouse space
ZM = average inventory for costing purposes
C_h = storage or holding cost *per unit per period*
C_o = cost of placing and receiving order

Also

$$C_{o_p} = \frac{C_o}{N} = \frac{C_o}{Q/U} = \frac{C_o U}{Q} \qquad \text{and} \qquad M = Q$$

so that Eq. (10.3#1) becomes

$$C_t = ZQC_h + \frac{C_o U}{Q} \qquad (10.3\#2)$$

The graphical presentation of Eq. (10.3#2) is shown in Fig. 10.3F2. Equation (10.3#2) shows that the storage cost is directly proportional to lot size and the order placing and receiving cost is inversely proportional to the lot size.

The minimum value for C_t can be obtained by differentiating Eq. (10.3#2) with respect to Q and equating with zero

$$\frac{dC_t}{dQ} = ZC_h - \frac{C_o U}{Q^2} = 0$$

from which the optimum Q is

$$Q_{\text{opt}} = \sqrt{\frac{C_o U}{ZC_h}} \qquad (10.3\#3)$$

190 OPTIMIZATION

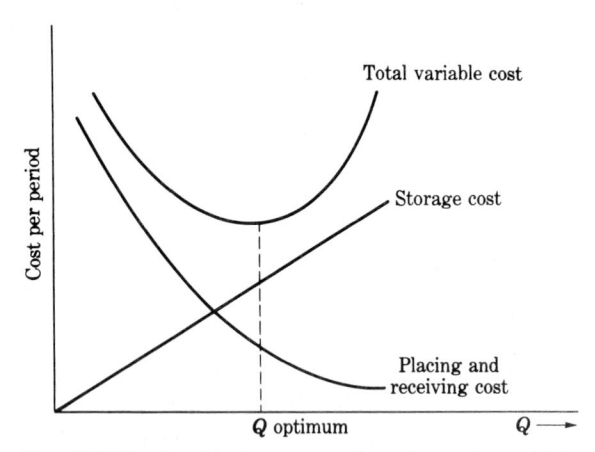

Fig. 10.3F2 Graphical representation of costs in model 1.

The lead time T_l multiplied by the rate of use per period U gives the reorder level R

$$R = T_l U \qquad (10.3\#4)$$

By placing Q_{opt} from Eq. (10.3#3) in Eq. (10.3#2),

$$C_{t,\text{opt}} = ZC_h \sqrt{\frac{C_o U}{ZC_h}} + \frac{C_o U}{\sqrt{C_o U/ZC_h}} = 2\sqrt{ZC_h C_o U} \qquad (10.3\#5)$$

Example 10.3E1 The demand for a unit is 100 per day. Cost of placing and receiving an order is $50 with infinite delivery rate. Storage cost is $10 per unit per year based on the actual inventory at any time. Find the optimum order size, minimum cost, and reorder level for 8-day delivery time. No shortages are allowed.

The storage charge is based on actual inventory. The average inventory for one cycle will be the average ordinate for one cycle from Fig. 10.3F1. More generally it is the area represented by the inventory-time plot divided by time. Choose one cycle. Then the average inventory is

$$\frac{0.5QN}{N} = 0.5Q$$

Thus for this case the average inventory is half the maximum, or $Z = 0.5$. Storage charge per unit per day is

$$^{10}\!/_{365} = 0.0274$$

and by Eq. (10.3#3)

$$Q_{\text{opt}} = \sqrt{\frac{50(100)}{0.5(0.0274)}} = 604$$

In practice 600 units would be a satisfactory procurement level. The minimum cost by Eq. (10.3#2) is

$$C_t = 0.5(600)(0.0274) + \frac{50(100)}{600} = \$16.55 \text{ per day, variable cost}$$

The reorder level by Eq. (10.3#4) is

$$R = 8(100) = 800$$

However, inventory never exceeds 600. If orders are placed 8 days before the end of a cycle, they will be placed 2 days before the end of a previous cycle when the inventory is 200 units.

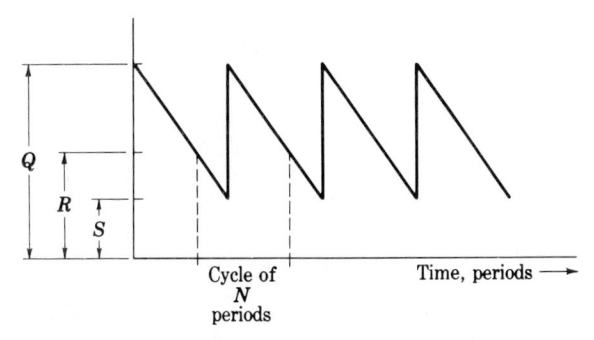

Fig. 10.4F1 Diagram for model 2 with safety stock.

10.4 Model 2 of Fig. 10.2F2

In some situations the decision maker wants to be sure that a shortage of an item will not occur. He adds more items to the store, called *safety stock*. This is shown in Fig. 10.4F1, where safety stock is denoted as S. The model has the same assumptions as model 1 and in addition includes the safety stock. The total variable cost per period C_t is the sum of the storage cost per period for the regular stock, the storage cost per period for the safety stock, and the cost of placing and receiving an order per period. By analogy with Eq. (10.3#1),

$$C_t = ZMC_h + SC_h + C_{op} \qquad (10.4\#1)$$

and by analogy with Eq. (10.3#2)

$$C_t = ZQC_h + SC_h + \frac{C_oU}{Q} \qquad (10.4\#2)$$

The safety-stock storage cost per period is independent of the lot size.

Optimum lot size Q_{opt} and minimum cost per period C_t can be obtained by steps analogous to those used in model 1. The results are

$$Q_{opt} = \sqrt{\frac{C_oU}{ZC_h}} \qquad (10.4\#3)$$

$$C_{t,min} = 2\sqrt{ZC_hC_oU} + SC_h \qquad (10.4\#4)$$

The reorder level in this case is

$$R = S + T_lU \qquad (10.4\#5)$$

With S equal to zero the three relationships reduce to those for model 1.

10.5 Model 3 of Fig. 10.2F2

The model includes a shortage cost and a reneging cost. A shortage cost is the penalty incurred for being unable to meet the demand at the time of demand for patient customers. The reneging cost is the loss of profit and good will of the impatient customers. Patient customers wait until the store is able to satisfy their demand, although a penalty and loss is involved. Impatient customers are treated as representing an additional loss in dollars per unit of unsatisfied demand

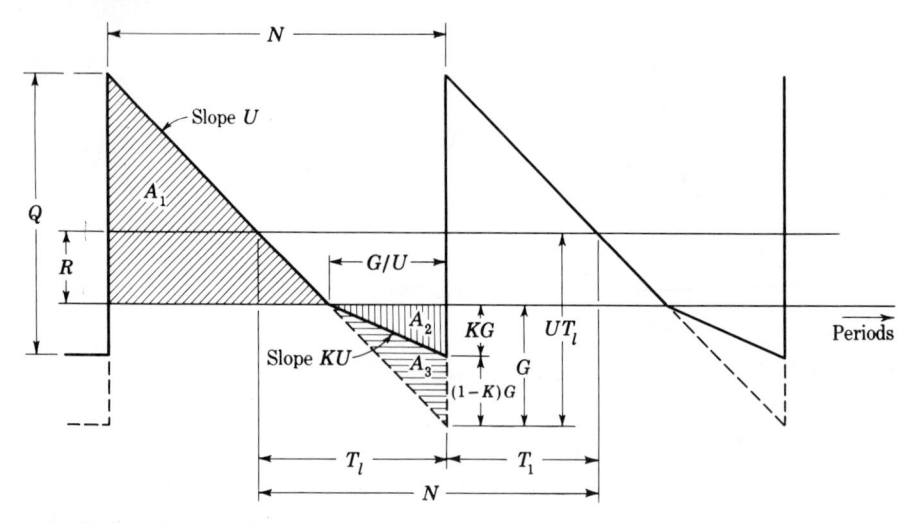

Fig. 10.5F1 Diagram for model 3 with partial patient customers.

over that experienced for patient customers. Impatient customers may be lost permanently in practice, but in the model they are assumed to be replaced by other impatient customers. In this manner, the fraction of patient customers remains constant and each cycle repeats the previous cycle.

The costs associated with the model are the cost of placing and receiving an order, the cost of storage, the cost of shortage, and the cost of reneging.

The costs of storage, shortage, and reneging depend on the average of units per period. The delivery rate of procurement is infinite, and the rate of use constant.

The total variable cost per period is

$$C_t = \begin{array}{c}\text{order}\\\text{cost per}\\\text{period}\end{array} + \begin{array}{c}\text{storage}\\\text{cost per}\\\text{period}\end{array} + \begin{array}{c}\text{shortage}\\\text{cost per}\\\text{period}\end{array} + \begin{array}{c}\text{reneging}\\\text{cost per}\\\text{period}\end{array} \qquad (10.5\#1)$$

The cost per period for any component cost is the component cost per cycle divided by N, the number of periods per cycle (see Fig. 10.5F1)

$$N = T_l + T_1$$

but from the slope of the inventory line, which is U,

$$T_1 = \frac{Q - R - KG}{U}$$

$$N = T_l + \frac{Q - R - KG}{U}$$

where K is the fraction of patient customers and G is the terminal shortage in units. But by the slope of the inventory line

$$G = UT_l - R$$

Substitute this value of G in the previous relationship for N

$$N = T_l + \frac{Q - [R + (UT_l - R)K]}{U} = \frac{(1 - K)(UT_l - R) + Q}{U} \quad (10.5\#2)$$

The area A_1 shown in Fig. 10.5F1 represents the number of unit periods of stock on hand per cycle and is

$$A_1 = [Q - K(UT_l - R)]\frac{Q - K(UT_l - R)}{2U}$$

$$A_1 = \frac{[Q - K(UT_l - R)]^2}{2U}$$

The area A_2 represents the number of unit periods per cycle due to shortage and is

$$A_2 = \frac{KG}{2}\frac{G}{U} = \frac{K}{2U}G^2 = \frac{K}{2U}(UT_l - R)^2$$

The area A_3 represents the number of unit periods per cycle due to reneging and is

$$A_3 = (1 - K)G\frac{G}{2U}\frac{(1 - K)(UT_l - R)^2}{2U}$$

If C_o is the order cost per cycle, then C_{o_p}, the order cost per period, is

$$C_{o_p} = \frac{C_o}{N}$$

If C_h is the storage cost per unit per period, then A_1C_h/N is the storage cost per period. Similarly A_2C_s/N and A_3C_r/N are the shortage and reneging costs per period, respectively. Substituting the values for A_1, A_2, A_3, and N, and using Eq. (10.5#1), the final result is

$$C_t = \frac{C_o U}{(1 - K)(UT_l - R) + Q} + \frac{C_h[Q - K(UT_l - R)]^2}{2[(1 - K)(UT_l - R) + Q]}$$
$$+ \frac{C_s K(UT_l - R)^2}{2[(1 - K)(UT_l - R) + Q]} + \frac{C_r(1 - K)(UT_l - R)^2}{2[(1 - K)(UT_l - R) + Q]} \quad (10.5\#3)$$

The total variable cost per period C_t is thus a function of the reorder level R and the lot size Q as independent variables in terms of the other parameters.

10.6 Model 4 of Fig. 10.2F2

The model is a special case of model 3 but with all customers patient. Thus K is unity and Eq. (10.5#3) becomes

$$C_t = \frac{C_o U}{Q} + \frac{C_h[Q - (UT_l - R)]^2}{2Q} + \frac{C_s(UT_l - R)^2}{2Q} \quad (10.6\#1)$$

The model is presented schematically in Fig. 10.6F1. The area A_3 under the zero-quantity line is caused entirely by shortages because no reneging occurs.

Equation (10.6#1) can be minimized by the methods developed in Chap. 12, but first let

$$T' = UT_l - R$$

194 OPTIMIZATION

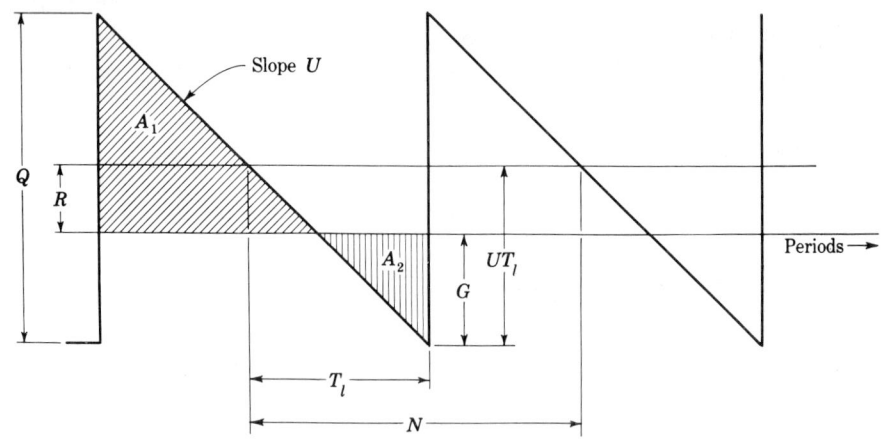

Fig. 10.6F1 Diagram for model 4 with patient customers.

Then Eq. (10.6#1) becomes

$$C_t = \frac{C_o U}{Q} + \frac{C_h(Q-T')^2}{2Q} + \frac{C_s(T')^2}{2Q}$$

or

$$C_t = \frac{C_o U}{Q} + \frac{C_h Q}{2} - C_h T' + \frac{(C_h + C_s)(T')^2}{2Q} \qquad (10.6\#2)$$

For minimum C_t (see Chap. 12)

$$\frac{\partial C_t}{\partial T'} = -C_h + \frac{(C_h + C_s)T'}{Q} = 0 \qquad (10.6\#3)$$

$$\frac{\partial C_t}{\partial Q} = -\frac{C_o U}{Q^2} + \frac{C_h}{2} - \frac{(C_h + C_s)(T')^2}{2Q^2} = 0 \qquad (10.6\#4)$$

Eliminate T' from the last two relationships. The result is

$$Q_{\text{opt}} = \sqrt{\frac{2C_o U(C_h + C_s)}{C_h C_s}} \qquad (10.6\#5)$$

Substitute Eq. (10.6#5) in Eq. (10.6#3) remembering that $T' = UT_l - R$. The result is

$$R_{\text{opt}} = UT_l - \sqrt{\frac{2C_o U C_h}{C_s(C_h + C_s)}} \qquad (10.6\#6)$$

Finally substituting in Eq. (10.6#1) leads to

$$C_{t,\text{opt}} = \sqrt{\frac{2C_o C_h C_s U}{C_h + C_s}} \qquad (10.6\#7)$$

This can be compared with Eq. (10.3#5), in which no shortage was allowed. Place $C_s = \infty$ in Eq. (10.6#7) to eliminate shortage. Equation (10.6#7) then becomes

$$C_{t,\text{opt}} = \sqrt{2C_o C_h U}$$

which agrees with Eq. (10.3#5) for $Z = 0.5$.

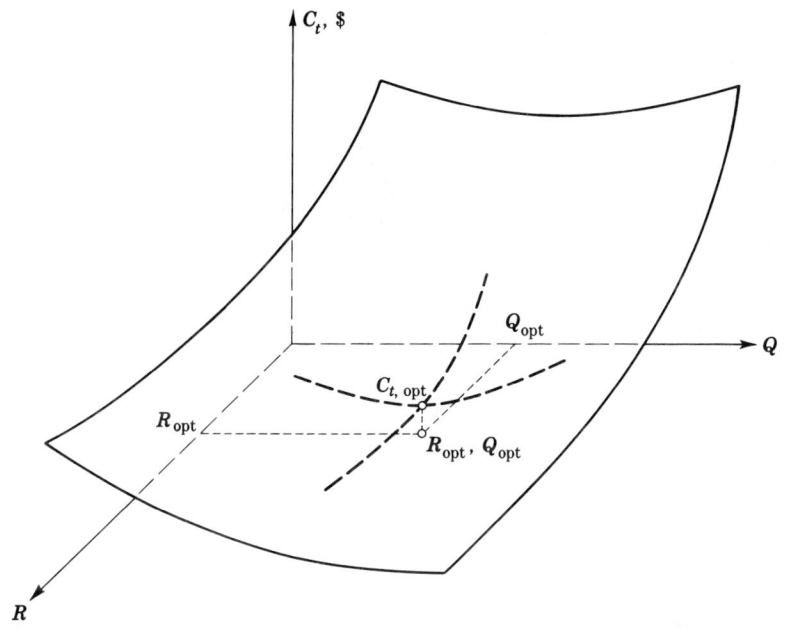

Fig. 10.6F2 Total variable-cost surface for model 4 with patient customers.

Figure 10.6F2 shows the variable surface and the location of R_{opt}, Q_{opt}, and $C_{t,\text{opt}}$ on the surface.

10.7 Model 5 of Fig. 10.2F2

The model is a special case of model 3 but with all customers impatient. Thus K is zero, and Eq. (10.5#3) becomes

$$C_t = \frac{C_o U}{UT_l - R + Q} + \frac{C_h Q^2}{2(UT_l - R + Q)} + \frac{C_r(UT_l - R)^2}{2(UT_l - R + Q)} \quad (10.7\#1)$$

The expression can be treated analytically as in the previous section or optimized on a computer.

10.8 Model 6 of Fig. 10.2F2

The model assumes that the rate of delivery of stock has a constant finite rate and not an infinite rate as in the previous models. A finite rate is associated with manufacture. The model has a safety stock and no shortages. The schematic diagram is given in Fig. 10.8F1.

The number of periods N in a cycle is the quantity delivered per cycle divided by the rate of use per cycle

$$N = \frac{Q}{U}$$

196 OPTIMIZATION 10.8

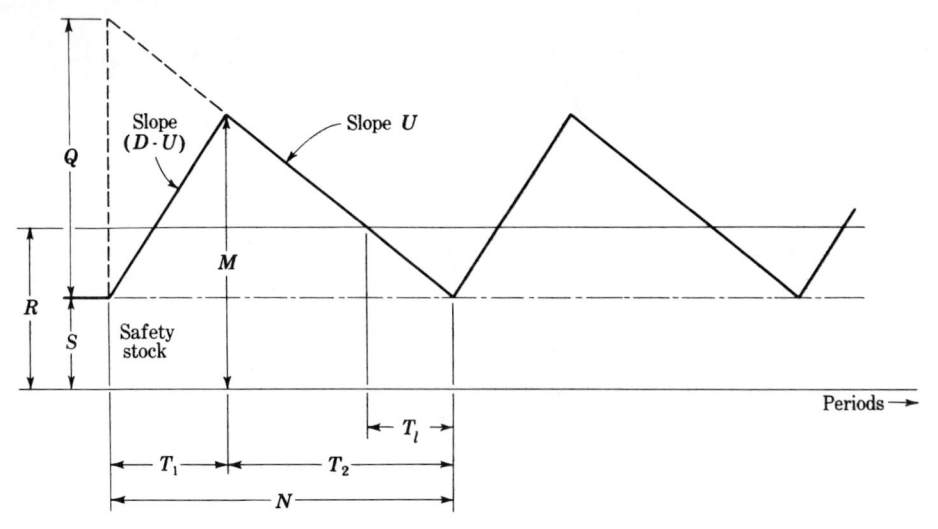

Fig. 10.8F1 Diagram for model 6 with finite delivery rate.

The total variable cost per period C_t is the sum of storage cost per period and the cost of placing an order per period. This will be the same as Eq. (10.3#1)

$$C_t = ZMC_h + C_{o_p} \tag{10.8#1}$$

The maximum stock can be determined from Fig. 10.8F1, where D is the replenishment rate

$$M - S = T_1(D - U) = \frac{Q}{D}(D - U)$$

$$M = \frac{Q(D - U)}{D} + S$$

Storage cost per period is ZMC_h or

$$C_h \left[\frac{ZQ}{D}(D - U) + S \right]$$

and ordering cost per period is C_o/N or C_oU/Q. Equation (10.8#1) becomes

$$C_t = C_h \left[\frac{ZQ}{D}(D - U) + S \right] + \frac{C_oU}{Q} \tag{10.8#2}$$

For a minimum

$$\frac{dC_t}{dQ} = ZC_h \frac{D - U}{D} - \frac{C_oU}{Q^2} = 0 \tag{10.8#3}$$

$$Q_{\text{opt}} = \sqrt{\frac{C_oUD}{ZC_h(D - U)}} \tag{10.8#4}$$

The reorder quantity is

$$R = T_l U$$

Equation (10.8#2) leads to the expression

$$C_{t,\text{opt}} = 2\sqrt{ZC_hC_oU\left(1 - \frac{U}{D}\right)} + C_hS \qquad (10.8\#5)$$

10.9 Model 7 of Fig. 10.2F2

The model is the same as model 6, but no safety stock is provided. With safety stock S zero the relationships for model 6 become

$$Q_{\text{opt}} = \sqrt{\frac{C_oUD}{ZC_h(D-U)}} \qquad (10.9\#1)$$

$$C_{t,\text{opt}} = 2\sqrt{ZC_hC_oU\left(1 - \frac{U}{D}\right)} \qquad (10.9\#2)$$

Example 10.9E1 A unit is used at the rate of 100 per day and can be manufactured at the rate of 600 per day. It costs $2,000 to set up the manufacturing process and $0.1 per day per unit in inventory based on the actual inventory at any time. No shortages are allowed. Find the minimum cost and the optimum number of units per manufacturing run.

Inventory is charged against average inventory, which is one-half maximum inventory. Thus $Z = 0.5$. From Eq. (10.9#2)

$$C_{t,\text{opt}} = 2\sqrt{0.5(0.1)(2,000)(100)(1 - 100/600)} = \$182.6 \text{ per day}$$

From Eq. (10.9#1)

$$Q_{\text{opt}} = \sqrt{\frac{2,000(100)(600)}{0.5(0.1)(600-100)}} = 2,190 \text{ units}$$

10.10 Model 8 of Fig. 10.2F2

The assumptions for this model are finite delivery rate equal to D units per period, use rate of U units per period, shortage is allowed, and impatient and patient customers, the patient customers being a fraction K of the whole. The model assumes further that storage costs, shortage costs, and reneging costs are determined by the average applicable to each category.

Figure 10.10F1 gives the schematic model. No derivation is given here, but the total variable cost per period C_t is composed of the ordering cost per period, the storage cost per period, the shortage cost per period, and the reneging cost per period as follows:

$$C_t = \frac{C_oU}{(1-K)(T_iU-R)+Q} + \frac{C_h[Q(1-U/D)+K(R-UT_i)]^2}{2(1-U/D)[(1-K)(T_iU-R)+Q]}$$
$$+ \frac{C_sK(T_iU-R)^2[D+(1-K)U]}{2(D-U)[(1-K)(T_iU-R)+Q]} + \frac{C_r(1-K)(T_iU-R)^2}{2[(1-K)(T_iU-R)+Q]}$$
$$(10.10\#1)$$

198 OPTIMIZATION

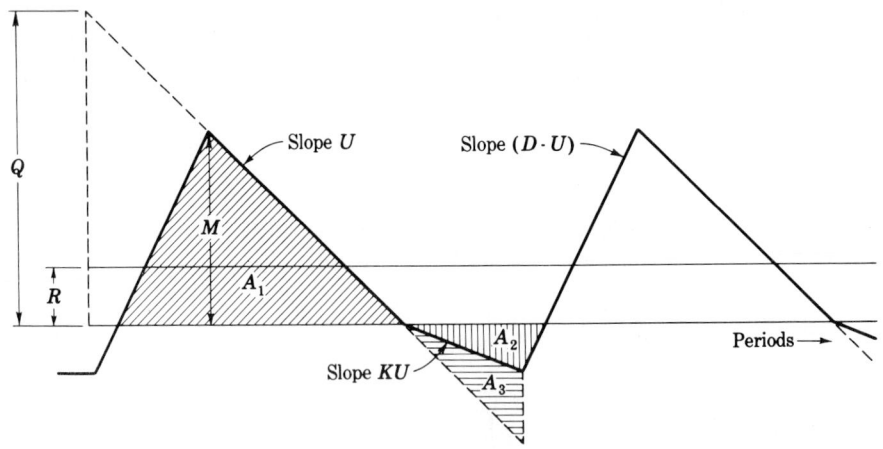

Fig. 10.10F1 Diagram for model 8 with finite delivery rate and partial patient customers.

The total variable cost is a function of two variables, the reorder level R and the lot size Q. T_l, the lead time, is not an independent variable. Minimum C_t can be found by a computer program.

10.11 Model 9 of Fig. 10.2F2

The model is a special case of model 8 but with no impatient customers; that is, $K = 1$. Equation (10.10#1) becomes

$$C_t = \frac{C_o U}{Q} + \frac{C_h[Q(1 - U/D) + (R - UT_l)]^2}{2Q(1 - U/D)} + \frac{C_s(T_l U - R)^2}{2(1 - U/D)Q} \quad (10.11\#1)$$

The relationship can be treated by the procedure of Sec. 10.6. The results are

$$Q_{\text{opt}} = \sqrt{\frac{2C_o U(C_h + C_s)}{C_h C_s(1 - U/D)}} \quad (10.11\#2)$$

$$R_{\text{opt}} = UT_l - \sqrt{\frac{2C_h C_o U(1 - U/D)}{C_s(C_h + C_s)}} \quad (10.11\#3)$$

$$C_{t,\text{opt}} = \sqrt{\frac{2C_o C_h C_s(1 - U/D)}{(C_s + C_h)}} \quad (10.11\#4)$$

10.12 Model 10 of Fig. 10.2F2

The model is a special case of model 8 but with all impatient customers; that is, $K = 0$. Equation (10.10#1) becomes

$$C_t = \frac{C_o U}{(T_l U - R) + Q} + \frac{C_h[Q(1 - U/D)]^2}{2(1 - U/D)[(T_l U - R) + Q]} + \frac{C_r(T_l U - R)^2}{2[(T_l U - R) + Q]} \quad (10.12\#1)$$

The independent variables are the reorder level R and the lot size Q. Equation (10.12#1) can be run on a computer to obtain the optimum R and Q and the minimum C_t.

10.13 General analytical method

An arbitrary situation may not conform to any of the models described. The analyst can then set up a model for the particular case. The principles follow those used in the previous sections. An expression for C_t, the variable cost per period, is developed and optimized. In this section the model permits an analytical solution to be obtained. If an analytical solution cannot be obtained or is too complicated, a tabular or computer solution is always possible, as developed in the next section.

Example 10.13E1 An item is used at a uniform rate of 10 units per day. No shortage is allowed, and delivery is at an infinite rate. It costs $10 to process an order. Inventory charge is $0.02 per day for each item actually in inventory plus $3 per year per unit based on the maximum number of units in inventory.

If Q is the quantity ordered, the maximum inventory is Q and the average inventory is $0.5Q$, inasmuch as demand is uniform. Then on a period basis, remembering that $NU = Q$,

$$\frac{C_o}{N} = \frac{C_o}{Q} U$$

and letting C_t be the cost per day

$$C_t = \frac{C_o U}{Q} + \tfrac{1}{2} Q C_h + \frac{3.00}{365} Q$$

$$= \frac{10(10)}{Q} + \tfrac{1}{2} Q (0.02) + 0.00822$$

$$= \frac{100}{Q} + 0.01822 Q$$

For minimum

$$\frac{dC_t}{dQ} = \frac{-100}{Q^2} + 0.01822 = 0$$

$Q_{\text{opt}} = 74.1$ units per order

10.14 Graphical or tabular method

In many cases the problem is too complicated to yield an analytical solution. A graphical or tabular solution can usually be obtained, however. The following example will illustrate this case.

Example 10.14E1 A manufacturing concern has a fixed weekly cyclic demand as follows:

Mon	Tue	Wed	Thur	Fri	Sat	Sun
9	17	2	0	19	9	14

Table 10.14T1 Example 10.14E1 with 8 Initial Stock

Day	On hand start of day	Demand	Inventory end of day	Shortage cost, $	Inventory cost, $
Mon	8	9	−1	4	0
Tue	−1 + 10 = 9	17	−8	32	0
Wed	−8 + 10 = 2	2	0	0	0
Thur	0 + 10 = 10	0	10	0	40
Fri	10 + 10 = 20	19	1	0	1
Sat	1 + 10 = 11	9	2	0	2
Sun	2 + 10 = 12	14	−2	8	0
Mon	−2 + 10 = 8			44 +	43 = $87

Policy is to maintain constant daily production 7 days a week. Shortage cost is $4 per unit per day, and storage cost depends upon Q, the quantity carried, as follows:

Cost per unit for 1 day, $	Q
1	$1 \leq Q \leq 3$
4	$4 \leq Q \leq 20$
10	$Q > 20$

the charges being based on the end-of-day situation.

Let the manufacturing rate be the average of the total sales, which is

$$\frac{9 + 17 + 2 + 0 + 19 + 9 + 14}{7} = 10 \text{ units/day}$$

Assume various initial starting stocks for Monday and by tabulation find the weekly cost. Tables 10.14T1, 10.14T2, and 10.14T3 are for starting stocks of eight, nine, and ten units, respectively. Minimum cost is obtained with a starting stock of nine at $82 per week.

Table 10.14T2 Example 10.14E1 with 9 Initial Stock

Day	On hand start of day	Demand	Inventory end of day	Shortage cost, $	Inventory cost, $
Mon	9	9	0	0	0
Tue	0 + 10 = 10	17	−7	28	0
Wed	−7 + 10 = 3	2	1	0	1
Thur	1 + 10 = 11	0	11	0	44
Fri	11 + 10 = 21	19	2	0	2
Sat	2 + 10 = 12	9	3	0	3
Sun	3 + 10 = 13	14	−1	4	0
Mon	−1 + 10 = 9			32 +	50 = $82

Table 10.14T3   Example 10.14E1 with 10 Initial Stock

Day	On hand start of day	Demand	Inventory end of day	Shortage cost, $	Inventory cost, $
Mon	10	9	1	0	1
Tue	1 + 10 = 11	17	−6	24	0
Wed	−6 + 10 = 4	2	2	0	2
Thur	2 + 10 = 12	0	12	0	48
Fri	12 + 10 = 22	19	3	0	3
Sat	3 + 10 = 13	9	4	0	16
Sun	4 + 10 = 14	14	0	0	0
Mon	0 + 10 = 10			24 + 70 = $94

In Example 10.14E1 the cycle time was known. In other problems the optimum cycle time may have to be determined, and the variety of problems is endless.

PROBABILISTIC MODELS

10.15 Optimum stock by incremental analysis

When uncertainty is involved in any of the factors, the problem can become complicated. This section and the two following illustrate a few examples to acquaint the analyst with some methods.

Example 10.15E1   The cumulative probability for the sales of a certain item in season is:

Cumulative sales	Cumulative probability of this many sales or less	Cumulative probability of this many sales or more
0	0.00	1.00
1,000	0.03	0.97
2,000	0.09	0.91
3,000	0.18	0.82
4,000	0.29	0.71
5,000	0.44	0.56
6,000	0.60	0.40
7,000	0.80	0.20
8,000	0.94	0.06
9,000	0.98	0.02
10,000	1.00	0.00

An item costs $3, sells for $4 in season, and is disposed of for $1 if not sold in season. There is no storage charge. Determine the optimum number to stock at the start of the season.

The number to stock is such that the last item stocked has an expectation equal to its cost. If another were stocked, its expectation would be less than the cost.

Recall that

Expectation = Σ (value)(probability)

202 OPTIMIZATION

and let $P(X)$ be the probability of selling the last unit and $1 - P(X)$ be the probability of not selling the last unit. If bought, the last unit costs $3 and it brings either $4 or $1. The mathematical relationship for break-even is

$$3.00 = 4.00P(X) + 1.00[1 - P(X)]$$
$$P(X) = 0.67$$

The probability of selling the last unit must be 0.67 and of not selling it $1 - 0.67$, or 0.33. By interpolation in the tabulation, or from a plot, a stock of 4,300 meets the requirements. If a stock of 4,300 is ordered, the probability of selling the last unit is the probability of selling 4,300 or more, that is, 0.67. The analyst must be wary of incorrect reasoning and can assist himself by recognizing the two complementary cumulative probabilities as was done in the tabulation of data for the example.

10.16 Optimum inventory based on expectation

The expectation of a variable can be used in many ways to reduce a problem to a tabular or graphical solution. The following example is an illustration.

Example 10.16E1 The average demand for an item is 4 per week and follows a Poisson distribution. Find the number of units to be stocked at the beginning of each week so that the number of customers turned away on the average will not exceed 10% of demand.

For a Poisson distribution with an average demand of 4, the probability of a demand for exactly X, by Eq. (8.5#1), is

$$P(X) = \frac{4^X e^{-4}}{X!}$$

and by calculation or from tables

$P(0) = 0.0183$	$P(1) = 0.0732$	$P(2) = 0.1464$
$P(3) = 0.1950$	$P(4) = 0.1950$	$P(5) = 0.1560$
$P(6) = 0.1040$	$P(7) = 0.0594$	$P(8) = 0.0296$
$P(9) = 0.0132$	$P(10) = 0.0053$	$P(11) = 0.0019$
$P(12) = 0.0006$	$P(13) = 0.0002$	$P(14) = 0.0001$
$P(15) = 0.0000$		

Let the starting stock be 6. Sales will be lost only when the demand is 7 or greater. Table 10.16T1 shows how the expected lost sales are computed using the underlying relationship

Expected lost sales = Σ (lost sales) (probability)

Table 10.16T1 Example 10.16E1 with 6 Initial Stock

Demand X	$P(X)$	Lost sales $(X - 6)$	$(X - 6)P(X)$
7	0.0594	1	0.0594
8	0.0296	2	0.0592
9	0.0132	3	0.0396
10	0.0053	4	0.0212
11	0.0019	5	0.0095
12	0.0006	6	0.0036
13	0.0002	7	0.0014
14	0.0001	8	0.0008
15	0.0000	9	0.0000
			$\Sigma = 0.195$ expected lost sales per week

If the initial stock is 6, the expected lost sales is 0.195, and the average demand is 4.0. Lost sales as a fraction of demand is

$$\frac{0.195}{4} = 0.05$$

Inasmuch as the ratio may be 0.10, a stock of 6 is more than adequate.

If the calculation is repeated on the basis of a starting stock of 5, the expected lost sales is found to be 0.409, which as a fraction of demand is $0.409/4 = 0.102$. The conditions of the example can be very nearly met by stocking 5 units.

10.17 Monte Carlo simulation in inventory

Monte Carlo simulation can be used very effectively to solve probabilistic inventory problems. In this method variables subject to uncertainty are generated by the use of random numbers in such a way that real frequences of distribution are obeyed on the average by the generated values. A number of cycles are simulated to establish the most probable values. Machine computation makes the method very versatile. Not only can average and expected values be predicted, but frequency distributions are easily established.

The method will be illustrated in a simple form in this section with an inventory problem in which the lead time and demand each follow known probabilistic distributions. The Monte Carlo method itself was described in Chap. 8.

Example 10.17E1 The mean demand for an article U_m is 4.7 units per day. The distribution of this demand is as follows, with the last column representing the assignment of random rectangular variates.

Demand	$P(U)$	Cumulative relative frequency	Random numbers assigned
2	0.05	0.05	01–05
3	0.15	0.20	06–20
4	0.20	0.40	21–40
5	0.30	0.70	41–70
6	0.20	0.90	71–90
7	0.10	1.00	91–00

The mean lead time T_{t_m} is 4 days. The distribution of this time is as follows, with the last column representing the assignment of random rectangular variates.

Lead time T_t	$P(T_t)$	Cumulative relative frequency	Random numbers assigned
3	0.25	0.25	01–25
4	0.50	0.75	26–75
5	0.25	1.00	76–00

204 OPTIMIZATION

Table 10.17T1 Monte Carlo Method for Example 10.17E1 with $Q = 30$, $R = 20$

Cycle	Period cumulative	Random no.	Demand	Random no.	Lead time	Stock end of day	Shortage cost, $	Inventory cost, $	Lot order cost, $	Cumulative cost, $	Average cost per period, $
	0			79	5	20					
1	1	13	3			17	0	17	0	17	17
	2	28	4			13	0	13	0	30	15
	3	77	6			7	0	7	0	37	12
	4	60	5			2	0	2	0	39	10
	5	29	4			−2	4	0	0	43	9
	6	16	3	68	4	$30 - 2 - 3 = 25$	0	25	15	83	14
	7	70	5			20	0	20	0	103	15
2	8	09	3			17	0	17	0	120	15
	9	24	4			13	0	13	0	133	14
	10	16	3			10	0	10	0	143	14
	11	19	3			7	0	7	0	150	14
	12	14	3	45	4	$30 + 7 - 3 = 34$	0	34	15	199	17
	13	29	4			30	0	30	0	229	18
	14	49	5			25	0	25	0	254	18
	15	08	3			22	0	22	0	276	18
	16	80	6			17	0	17	0	293	18

It costs $15 to place an order, inventory cost is $1 per unit per day, and shortage cost is $2 per unit per day. Assume that orders are placed and arrive at the end of a day and that charges are based on the end-of-day inventory but before arrival of a new lot.

Find the optimum lot size and reorder level.

Make a Monte Carlo simulation assuming a lot size Q of 30 and a reorder level R of 20. Start the first cycle with 20 units on hand. This is arbitrary, but the effect will be washed out when a great number of cycles is considered.

The tabulation is made in Table 10.17T1. All random numbers were selected in a unbiased fashion from a table of random rectangular variates. A cycle is assumed to start the day following the placing of a new order, and a new order is placed whenever inventory falls to 20 or less at the end of a day.

At zero time the random number 79 indicates a lead time of 5 days for the order placed at that time. During the first period the demand is 3, and the inventory drops to 17 at the end of the first day. This continues, but between the end of the fifth day and the start of the sixth day, a new lot of 30 arrives and is available for the sixth day. At the end of the sixth day inventory is 25, being the 30 received less the 2 short the previous day less the 3 used during the sixth day. This day is also charged with the lot order cost. The cumulative cost divided by the cumulative days or periods is the average cost per day for $Q = 30$ and $R = 20$. If enough cycles are taken, the simulation will be exceedingly good. Other combinations are tried to find the optimum Q and R.

The method can be used to get averages and distributions of the various variables. Thus by the proper tabulation it is possible to determine the average shortage and distribution of shortage per cycle.

10.18 Nomenclature

C_h Storage or holding cost per unit per period, $/(unit)(period)
C_o Cost of placing and receiving an order, $
C_{o_p} Cost of placing and receiving an order per period, $ per period
C_r Reneging cost per unit per period, $/(unit)(period)
C_s Shortage cost per unit per period, $/(unit)(period)
C_t Total variable cost per period, $ per period
C_u Purchase price per unit, $ per unit
D Delivery or replenishment rate per period, units/period
e Naperian constant, $2.71828\cdots$
K Fraction of patient customers, decimal
M Maximum number of units in stock, units
N Number of periods per cycle, dimensionless
$P(X)$ Probability of X occurring, decimal
Q Lot size, units
R Reorder level, units
S Safety stock, units
T Time, periods
T_l Procurement or lead time, periods
U Demand or use rate, units/period
W Lead-time demand or demand during lead time, units
Z Factor connected with utilization of warehouse space and inventory storage cost, decimal; generally $Z = 0.5$ for charge made on average inventory, and $Z = 1.0$ for charge based on maximum inventory

10.19 Problems

P1. The rate of use of an item is 20 units per year. The cost of placing and receiving an order is $40. The cost of storing one unit 1 year is $0.16, and it depends on the average stock. Find (a) the economic lot size, (b) the minimum total variable cost, and (c) the reorder level if the lead time is 3 months.

P2. Repeat Prob. 10.19P1 with a safety stock of four units.

P3. A store has to satisfy a daily demand of 10 units of a product. The holding cost is $0.10 per unit per day. The cost of expediting due to shortage is $0.05 per unit per day, and the lost profit due to unsatisfied demand is $0.50 per unit per day. The cost of procuring one order is $20, and it takes 3 days for delivery. If the minimum number of units per order is 50 and the maximum is 200 with increments of five units, and if the replenishment rate is infinite:

    (a) Find the minimum total variable cost quantity if the reorder level is one unit and 50% of the demand represents unsatisfied customers in case of shortage.

    (b) Solve part (a) with 0% unsatisfied demand in case of shortage.

    (c) Solve part (a) with 100% unsatisfied demand in case of shortage.

P4. Repeat Prob. 10.19P3 with a finite replenishment rate of 20 units per period.

P5. A manufacturer has the following fixed weekly cyclic demand:

Mon	Tue	Wed	Thur	Fri	Sat	Sun
900	1,500	200	200	1,900	800	1,500

Policy is to maintain constant daily production 5 days a week. Storage cost is $1 per unit per day, and shortage cost is $2 per unit per day. Charges are based on the end-of-day situation. Find the minimum cost starting stock if the daily production is 1,400 units.

10.20 References

R1. Abramovitz, I.: "Production Management," The Ronald Press Company, New York, 1967.

R2. Arrow, K. J., S. Karlin, and H. Scarf: "Studies in the Mathematical Theory of Inventory and Production," Stanford University Press, Stanford, Calif., 1958.

R3. Buchan, J., and E. Koenigsberg: "Scientific Inventory Management," Prentice-Hall, Inc., Englewood Cliffs, N.J., 1963.

R4. Churchman, C. W., R. L. Ackoff, and E. L. Arnoff: "Introduction to Operations Research," John Wiley & Sons, Inc., New York, 1962.

R5. Fabrycky, W. J., and P. E. Torgersen: "Operations Economy," Prentice-Hall, Inc., Englewood Cliffs, N.J., 1966.

R6. Fabrycky, W. J., and J. Banks: "Procurement and Inventory Systems," Reinhold Publishing Corporation, New York, 1967.

R7. Hausmann, F.: "Operations Research in Production and Inventory Control," John Wiley & Sons, Inc., New York, 1962.

R8. Hoffman, R. A.: "Inventories," The Ronald Press Company, New York, 1962.

R9. Starr, M., and D. Miller: "Inventory Control: Theory and Practice," Prentice-Hall, Inc., Englewood Cliffs, N.J., 1962.

R10. Whitin, T. M.: "The Theory of Inventory Management," 2d ed., Princeton University Press, Princeton, N.J., 1953.

11
Queuing Problems

A. M. Ali

11.1 Prevalence

A queue is a waiting line, but queuing is a term now widely used in a broad sense covering a wide variety of problems, usually for economic balance and optimization, involving waiting and delay in serving people or servicing machines and equipment. Queuing covers too all facets of the problem such as the optimum number of long-distance lines required between two cities or the optimum number of repairmen and their equipment required to keep an assembly line in operation.

Modern society with its crowded population and interdependent functions has focused considerable attention on queuing problems. There is now strong competition between service industries to gain and retain the customer, and all companies must consider internal queuing for the economic balance of manufacturing and operational efficiency.

11.2 Description of queuing system

A queuing system is illustrated in Fig. 11.2F1. The term *machine* will be used in a general way for the object to be serviced. The main elements in the system are the input source and the service system. The latter is characterized by queue discipline and service facility.

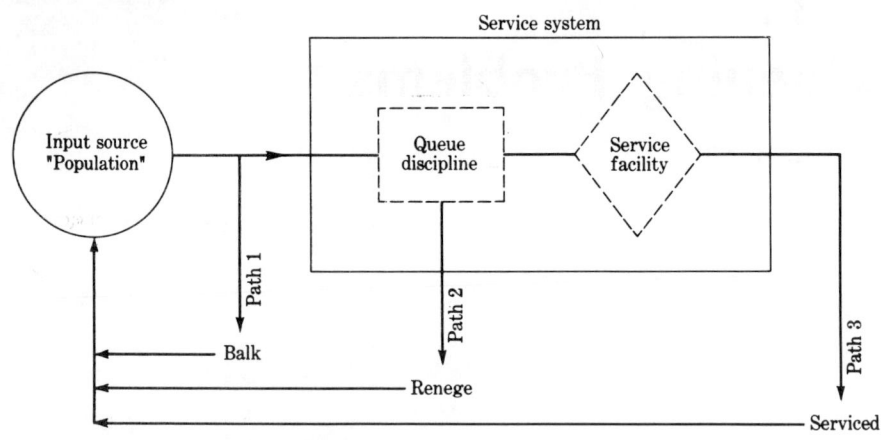

Fig. 11.2F1 Chart of queuing system.

A machine needing servicing can follow three possible paths:

1. Return to population without servicing, called *balking*, path 1
2. Join the queue but return to population without servicing, called *reneging*, path 2
3. Return to population after being serviced, path 3

To solve queuing problems, six sets of estimates or forecasts are required either from past data or policy. They are:

1. Arrivals-frequency function
2. Waiting costs
3. Service-time frequency functions
4. Cost of providing and maintaining service facility
5. Priority rules
6. Relation of demand to service facility

Alternate courses of action that may require economic evaluation are:

1. Changing the number of service stations
2. Reorganizing service stations to change servicing time
3. Changing queue discipline
4. Changing service policy

Three steps are considered in the analysis of a queuing problem:

1. Determination of the properties, specifications, or assumptions, of the system
2. Formulation of a mathematical model for the system
3. An analysis and evaluation of the system for an optimal solution

11.3 Classification of queuing systems

A queuing system can be classified with respect to input source, queue, and service facility.

The input source, or population, is classified as *infinite* or *finite*, which is chiefly the relative size between the population and the number in the queue and being serviced. If the characteristics of the input source (Fig. 11.2F1) are changed by the number of withdrawals, the population is considered finite and the problem solved with recognition of the changes in the population.

The queue itself can be classified as *infinite* if it is allowed to grow to any size or *finite* if characterized by a maximum permissible size. Queues can be classified further as *single* or *multiple*. A one-chair barber shop is a good example of a single queue. The multiple-queue case is exemplified by a work center having two input queues from different operations.

Service facilities have two basic characteristics, phase and channel. A *channel* is composed of a complete set of work centers. A channel may comprise a number of work centers in series, called *phases*. Figure 11.3F1 illustrates the relationship.

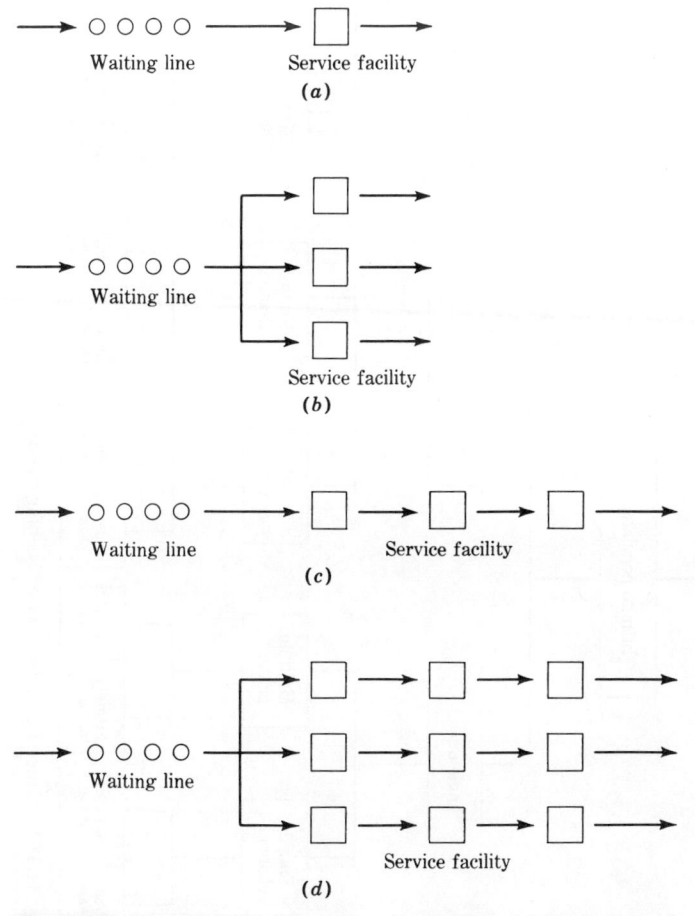

Fig. 11.3F1 Four basic structures of service facility. (*a*) Single channel, single phase; (*b*) multiple channel, single phase; (*c*) single channel, multiple phase; (*d*) multiple channel, multiple phase.

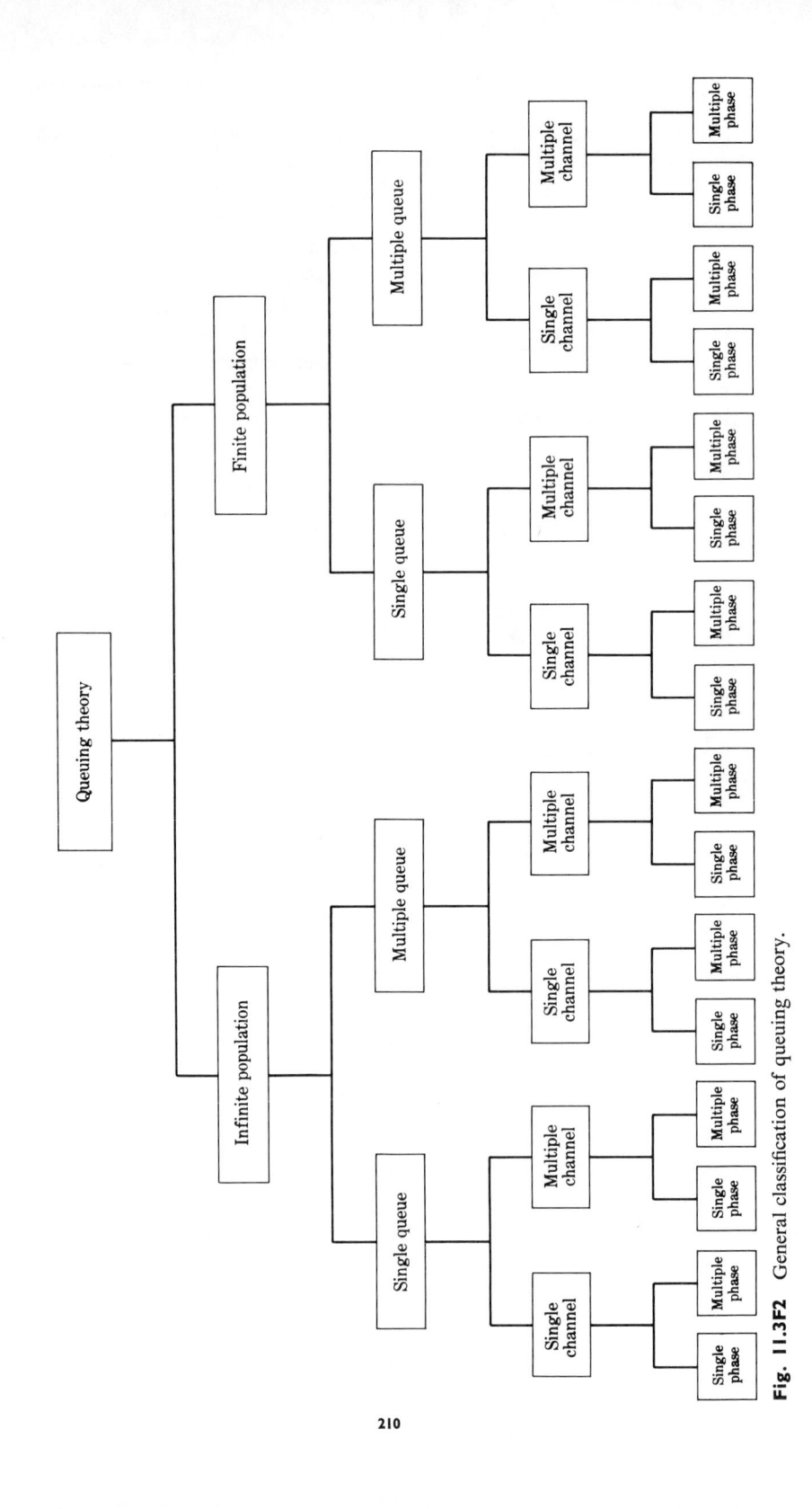

Fig. 11.3F2 General classification of queuing theory.

Table 11.4T1. Characteristics of Queuing Models

Item	\multicolumn{7}{c}{Model number}
	1	2	3	4	5	6	7
Source input	Infinite	Infinite	Infinite	Infinite	Infinite	Infinite	Finite
Queue	Single	Single	Single	Single	Single	Single	Single
Queue limitations	Infinite	Infinite	Infinite	Infinite	Infinite	Infinite	Infinite
Service facility, channels	Single	Multiple	Single	Single	Single	Single	Multiple
Phases	Single	Single	Single	Single	Single	Single	Single
Arrival distribution	Constant	Constant	Poisson	Arbitrary	Poisson	Poisson	Poisson
Service distribution	Constant	Constant	Poisson	Arbitrary	Arbitrary	Constant	Poisson
Service discipline, first in first out	✓	✓	✓	✓	✓	✓	✓

212   OPTIMIZATION   11.5

The service facility can be further classified according to the service-time distribution, such as constant, Poisson, and so forth, and according to the service discipline, i.e., the means for selection of customers or machines from the queue for service. There are many ways for selection such as first in first out, priority rating, etc.

Figure 11.3F2 shows the general classification of queuing-theory models. Individual cases require in addition specific treatment for such considerations as arrival-time distribution, attitude of customers, service-time distribution, and the service discipline.

11.4 Solution of queuing problems

Two methods are available for solving queuing problems, the mathematical approach and simulation. In the mathematical approach, the actual arrival- and service-time distributions are approximated by any of the well-known mathematical distribution functions. Relevant costs are introduced and the system optimized for minimum total variable cost.

In the simulation method, a Monte Carlo approach is made, much as in the probabilistic inventory problem of Sec. 10.17. A computer can give considerable output beyond the optimization result, such as average facility idle time or average waiting time in the queue.

This chapter considers a variety of queuing problems with characteristics summarized in Table 11.4T1. In addition two examples are given with solution by general methods. The nomenclature must be used strictly as defined. The chief items are:

T = time, periods
T_a = time, periods between two consecutive arrivals
T_s = time, periods to service one unit
C_t = total variable cost per period
C_w = waiting cost per unit per period
C_f = cost of servicing one unit
L = number of channels
λ = average arrival rate, or average arrivals per period
μ = average servicing rate, or average number of service completions per period
χ = load factor, or ratio of arrival rate to potential service completion rate, λ/μ
N_e = expected number of units in the system during period
$P(0)$ = probability of zero units in system at time T
$P(N)$ = probability of N units in system at time T

11.5 Model I of Table 11.4T1

The model is single channel, single phase, single queue, and has infinite population. Specific considerations included are constant arrival-time distribution and constant service-time distribution. It is assumed that T_a, the time between arrivals, is greater than T_s, the servicing time. The waiting time, or lost time, here will be equal numerically to T_s, the servicing time only, because no queue forms. The number of units entering the service system per period is $1/T_a$, and each requires T_s servicing time. The cost for waiting per period is accordingly

$$C_w \frac{1}{T_a} T_s \tag{11.5\#1}$$

In addition there is the cost of servicing per period. If C_f is the cost for servicing one unit and $1/T_s$ units are serviced per period, the servicing cost per period is

$$C_f \frac{1}{T_s} \tag{11.5\#2}$$

The total variable cost per period C_t is the sum of the two and is

$$C_t = C_w \frac{T_s}{T_a} + \frac{C_f}{T_s} \tag{11.5\#3}$$

Minimum cost per period treating T_s, the servicing time, as the independent variable is obtained by differentiation of Eq. (11.5#3)

$$\frac{dC_t}{dT_s} = 0 = \frac{C_w}{T_a} - \frac{C_f}{T_s^2}$$

$$T_{s,\text{opt}} = \sqrt{\frac{C_f T_a}{C_w}} \tag{11.5\#4}$$

Substitution of Eq. (11.5#4) in Eq. (11.5#3) leads to

$$C_{t,\text{opt}} = 2\sqrt{\frac{C_f C_w}{T_a}} \tag{11.5\#5}$$

Example 11.5E1 For Model 1 of Table 11.4T1 the arrival rate is constant at three units per hour. The cost of providing and maintaining a service facility is $25 per hour for servicing four units per hour and is proportional to capacity. If a unit waits 1 day, it represents a cost of $2,400. Find the optimum time to service one unit and the minimum variable cost per unit.

Take 1 hr as one period

$C_f = 25/4 = \$6.25$ per unit

$T_a = 1/3$ hr between arrivals

$C_w = \dfrac{2{,}400}{24} = \$100$ per hr-unit

By Eq. (11.5#4)

$$T_{s,\text{opt}} = \sqrt{\frac{6.25(1/3)}{100}} = 0.1443 \text{ hr} = \text{optimum servicing time}$$

The total variable cost per period is by Eq. (11.5#5)

$$C_{t,\text{opt}} = 2\sqrt{\frac{6.25(100)}{\frac{1}{3}}} = \$86.60$$

but three units enter the system per period. The total variable cost per period per unit is $\frac{86.60}{3} = \$28.87$ per unit

11.6 Model 2 of Table 11.4T1

This is the same as the previous model except that there are L channels or service facilities. The total variable cost per period is

$$C_t = C_w \frac{T_s}{T_a} + \frac{C_f L}{T_s} \tag{11.6#1}$$

and calculations analogous to that of the previous section lead to

$$T_{s,\text{opt}} = \sqrt{\frac{C_f T_a L}{C_w}} \quad T_s \leq LT_a \tag{11.6#2}$$

$$C_{t,\text{opt}} = 2\sqrt{\frac{C_f C_w L}{T_a}} \tag{11.6#3}$$

11.7 Model 3 of Table 11.4T1

The model is developed on the assumption that the number of arrivals per period follows a Poisson distribution with λ average arrivals per period and that the number of units serviced per period follows a Poisson distribution with μ average completions per period. To prevent explosive conditions, μ must be greater than λ.

Under these conditions and for one servicing station, it can be shown that

$$P(0) = 1 - \frac{\lambda}{\mu} \tag{11.7#1}$$

$$P(N) = \left(1 - \frac{\lambda}{\mu}\right)\left(\frac{\lambda}{\mu}\right)^N \tag{11.7#2}$$

$$N_e = \frac{\lambda}{\mu - \lambda} \tag{11.7#3}$$

where N_e is the expected number of units in the system during a period.

The expected total variable cost per period is the sum of the expected waiting cost per period and the expected service cost per period, or

$$C_t = C_w N_e + C_f \mu \tag{11.7#4}$$

$$C_t = C_w \frac{\lambda}{\mu - \lambda} + C_f \mu \tag{11.7#5}$$

For minimum C_t

$$\frac{\partial C_t}{\partial \mu} = 0 = -C_w \lambda (\mu - \lambda)^{-2} + C_f$$

whence

$$\mu = \lambda + \sqrt{\frac{\lambda C_w}{C_f}} \qquad (11.7\#6)$$

which gives the optimum value of μ in terms of λ, C_w, and C_f.

In Eq. (11.7#6) the best value of μ depends upon λ, but there is some value of λ, say λ', which gives a value of μ, say μ', which is best of all. For this value of λ, Eq. (11.7#6) is

$$\mu' = \lambda' + \sqrt{\frac{\lambda' C_w}{C_f}} \qquad (11.7\#7)$$

Substitution of Eq. (11.7#7) in Eq. (11.7#5) gives

$$C_t = \frac{C_w \lambda'}{\lambda' + \sqrt{\left(\frac{\lambda' C_w}{C_f}\right)} - \lambda'} + C_f\left(\lambda' + \sqrt{\frac{\lambda' C_w}{C_f}}\right) \qquad (11.7\#8)$$

which reduces to

$$C_t = \lambda' C_f + 2\sqrt{\lambda' C_f C_w} \qquad (11.7\#9)$$

The lowest cost per period can be found by differentiating Eq. (11.7#9), which gives

$$\frac{\partial C_t}{\partial \lambda'} = 0 = C_f + 2\sqrt{C_f C_w}\, \frac{1}{2}\frac{1}{\sqrt{\lambda'}}$$

or

$$\lambda'_{\text{opt}} = \frac{C_w}{C_f} \qquad (11.7\#10)$$

Substituting Eq. (11.7#10) in Eq. (11.7#7) gives

$$\mu'_{\text{opt}} = \frac{C_w}{C_f} + \sqrt{\frac{(C_w/C_f)C_w}{C_f}} = 2\frac{C_w}{C_f} \qquad (11.7\#11)$$

Substitution of Eqs. (11.7#10) and (11.7#11) in Eq. (11.7#5) gives

$$C_t = C_w \frac{C_w/C_f}{2C_w/C_f - C_w/C_f} + C_f\left(2\frac{C_w}{C_f}\right) = 3C_w \qquad (11.7\#12)$$

The distinction between Eq. (11.7#6) and the pair of equations (11.7#10) and (11.7#11) should be noted. In the latter pair λ'_{opt} and μ'_{opt} are specific values of the independent variables λ' and μ' at which the lowest cost of the system occurs.

Example 11.7E1 Cost of waiting per unit per period is $4, and the servicing cost per unit is $2. If arrivals and servicing rates follow Poisson distributions, find the lowest cost policy.

By Eqs. (11.7#10) and (11.7#11)

$$\lambda'_{opt} = \frac{C_w}{C_f} = \frac{4}{2} = 2 \text{ units/period}$$

$$\mu'_{opt} = 2\frac{C_w}{C_f} = 2\frac{4}{2} = 4 \text{ units/period}$$

The lowest expected total variable cost per period by Eq. (11.7#12) is

$$C_t = 3C_w = 3(4) = \$12 \text{ per period}$$

11.8 Model 4 of Table 11.4T1

In a more general case of the preceding section, the arrivals and service distributions may not be Poisson distributions but somewhat arbitrary. As before, let

λ = expected number of arrivals per period
μ = expected number of service completions per period

To avoid explosive conditions, $\lambda/\mu < 1$.

The total variable cost per period is given by Eq. (11.7#4)

$$C_t = C_w N_e + C_f \mu$$

where N_e is the expected number of units in the system for one period. No derivation is given here, but it can be shown that N_e can be expressed approximately as

$$N_e = \frac{E(r^2) - \lambda/\mu}{2(1 - \lambda/\mu)} + \frac{\lambda}{\mu} \quad (11.8\#1)$$

so that as an approximation

$$C_t = C_w \left[\frac{E(r^2) - \lambda/\mu}{2(1 - \lambda/\mu)} + \frac{\lambda}{\mu} \right] + C_f \mu \quad (11.8\#2)$$

where r is the number of arrivals per period and $E(r^2)$ is averaging r^2 over time. If something is known about the distributions, then $E(r^2)$ can be found and Eq. (11.8#2) optimized. Two special cases of model 4 will be considered. Model 5 has Poisson distributed arrivals and arbitrary servicing time, and model 6 has Poisson distributed arrivals and constant serving time.

11.9 Model 5 of Table 11.4T1

In this model the arrivals have a Poisson distribution with λ average arrivals per period, and the servicing time follows an arbitrary distribution with μ mean or average completions per period and variance σ^2. In the treatment that follows, λ^2 and σ^2 must have reciprocal dimensions. Thus if λ is expressed as units per period, σ^2 must be obtained as a variance in (periods per unit)^2.

No proof is given here, but it can be shown that for model 5 an approximation is

$$E(r^2) = \frac{\lambda}{\mu} + \lambda^2\sigma^2 + \frac{\lambda^2}{\mu^2} \qquad (11.9\#1)$$

and substitution of Eq. (11.9#1) in Eq. (11.8#2) gives

$$\begin{aligned}C_t &= C_w\left[\frac{\lambda/\mu + \lambda^2\sigma^2 + \lambda^2/\mu^2 - \lambda/\mu}{2(1-\lambda/\mu)} + \frac{\lambda}{\mu}\right] + C_f\mu \\ &= C_w\left[\frac{\lambda^2\sigma^2 + \lambda^2/\mu^2}{2(1-\lambda/\mu)} + \frac{\lambda}{\mu}\right] + C_f\mu \qquad (11.9\#2)\end{aligned}$$

Equation (11.9#2) is an equation in three variables, λ, μ, σ. For a fixed value of λ it can be optimized as a two-variable equation by the methods given in Chap. 12. A more systematic method has been developed by Ali [11.16R1]. Define χ as the load factor, where

$$\chi = \frac{\lambda}{\mu} \qquad (11.9\#3)$$

By introducing χ, Eq. (11.9#2) can be transformed to the expression

$$C_t = C_w\left[\frac{\chi^2 + \lambda^2\sigma^2}{2(1-\chi)} + \chi\right] + C_f\frac{\lambda}{\chi} \qquad (11.9\#4)$$

When λ, C_w, and C_f are given, the procedure for calculating the optimum servicing rate μ_{opt} and minimum total variable cost per period $C_{t,\text{opt}}$ is:

Step 1. Calculate

$$R = \frac{C_w}{C_f}$$

$$q = \lambda^2\sigma^2 + 2\left(1 - \frac{\lambda}{R}\right)$$

$$v = \frac{4\lambda}{R}$$

$$F = -\frac{\lambda}{R}(\lambda^2\sigma^2 + 1)$$

$$H = -\frac{1}{9}\left[\left(\frac{\lambda}{R} - 1\right) - \frac{\lambda^2\sigma^2}{2}\right]^2$$

$$G = \frac{2}{27}\left[\left(\frac{\lambda}{R} - 1\right) - \frac{\lambda^2\sigma^2}{2}\right]^3 + F$$

Step 2. Calculate c, where

$$c = \left(\frac{-G + \sqrt{G^2 + 4H^3}}{2}\right)^{1/3} + \left(\frac{-G - \sqrt{G^2 + 4H^3}}{2}\right)^{1/3} - \frac{F}{3}$$

Step 3. Calculate a and b, where

$$a = \sqrt{2c + 1 - q}$$

$$b = -\frac{2c + v}{2a}$$

Step 4. Calculate the load factor from

$$\chi_{1,2} = \frac{(1 + a) \pm \sqrt{(1 + a)^2 - 4(c - b)}}{2}$$

$$\chi_{3,4} = \frac{(1 - a) \pm \sqrt{(1 - a^2) - 4(c + b)}}{2}$$

Step 5. The positive value of χ from step 4 which is less than unity is χ_{opt}. If there is more than one positive χ less than unity, substitute these values of χ in Eq. (11.9#4). That χ which gives the minimum value of C_t should be chosen as χ_{opt}.

Step 6. Calculate μ_{opt}

$$\mu_{opt} = \frac{\lambda}{\chi_{opt}}$$

and $C_{t,opt}$ by Eq. (11.9#4).

Example 11.9E1 For a system corresponding to model 5, the average number of arrivals per hour is 0.2 with a Poisson distribution. The cost of waiting per unit per hour is $2, and the cost of servicing one unit is $4. The variance of servicing time is 9 hr². Find the optimum servicing rate and the expected minimum total variable cost per period.

From the data

$\lambda = 0.2$ unit/hr

$C_w = 2.00$ $/(unit)(hr)

$C_f = 4.00$ $ per unit

$\sigma = 3$ hr

Step 1:

$R = 2/4 = 0.5$

$q = 0.2^2(3^2) + 2\left(1 - \dfrac{0.2}{0.5}\right) = 1.56$

$v = \dfrac{4(0.2)}{0.5} = 1.6$

$F = -\dfrac{0.2}{0.5}[0.2^2(3^2) + 1] = -0.544$

$H = -\dfrac{1}{9}\left[\left(\dfrac{0.2}{0.5} - 1\right) - \dfrac{0.2^2(3^2)}{2}\right]^2 = -0.0676$

$G = \dfrac{2}{27}\left[\left(\dfrac{0.2}{0.5} - 1\right) - \dfrac{0.2^2(3^2)}{2}\right]^3 - 0.544 = -0.5792$

Step 2:
$$c = \left[\frac{0.5792 + \sqrt{(-0.5792^2) + 4(-0.0676^3)}}{2}\right]^{1/3}$$
$$+ \left[\frac{0.5792 - \sqrt{(-0.5792^2) + 4(-0.0676^3)}}{2}\right]^{1/3} - \frac{0.554}{3} = 1.0966$$

Step 3:
$$a = \sqrt{2(1.0966) + 1 - 1.56} = \sqrt{1.6332} = 1.278$$
$$b = -\frac{2(1.0966) + 1.6}{2(1.278)} = -1.4840$$

Step 4:
$$\chi_{1,2} = \frac{2.278 \pm \sqrt{2.278^2 - 4(1.0966 + 1.4840)}}{2} \quad \text{imaginary}$$
$$\chi_{3,4} = \frac{-0.278 \pm \sqrt{(-0.278^2) - 4(1.0966 - 1.4840)}}{2}$$
$$\chi_3 = +0.4988 \qquad \chi_4 = -0.7768$$

Step 5:
$$\chi_{\text{opt}} = 0.4988$$
$$\mu_{\text{opt}} = \frac{\lambda}{\chi} = \frac{0.2}{0.4988} = 0.4010 \text{ unit/period}$$

Step 6:
$$C_{t,\text{opt}} = 2\left[\frac{0.4988^2 + 0.2^2(3^2)}{2(1 - 0.4988)} + 0.4988\right] + 4\frac{0.2}{0.4988}$$
$$= \$2.7099 \text{ per hour}$$

11.10 Model 6 Table 11·4T1

The model is a special case of model 4 and has Poisson distributed arrivals and constant service time. Service-time distribution may be assumed constant in situations where automatic mechanical means are provided as service stations. With constant service time, there is no variance, hence $\sigma^2 = 0$; and the model can be regarded as a special case of model 5 with $\sigma^2 = 0$. Under these conditions Eq. (11.9#4) becomes

$$C_t = C_w\left[\frac{\chi^2}{2(1-\chi)} + \chi\right] + C_f\frac{\lambda}{\chi} \qquad (11.10\#1)$$

The model can be optimized by the procedure of the previous section placing $\sigma^2 = 0$.

11.11 Finite queuing—Model 7 of Table 11.4T1

The previous models were developed for populations or input sources that are infinite or very large in comparison to the number of units in the queue and being serviced. If this condition is not met, the situation becomes one in finite queuing. Analytical solutions for finite queuing problems can become quite complicated, and only one case, model 7, is considered here. The classification is finite source input, single queue with no limit on length, multiple channel, single phase, Poisson distribution for the arrival rate, and Poisson distribution for the servicing rate. Nomenclature is that used before with additions:

M = number of units in population
N = number of units in service system, queue plus service stations, at time T
S = number of service stations in system
C_q = cost for one unit in queue for one period
C_e = cost for one idle station per unit time

As before, λ is the expected number of units calling for service per unit time. Also, μ is now the expected number of units serviced *per service station* per unit time. The load factor χ is again λ/μ. To avoid explosive conditions $\chi < S$.

The total variable cost is the sum of the cost for idle service stations and the cost for waiting in the queue. Cost for servicing stations while actually performing service and cost for lost time by units while being serviced are not part of the variable cost inasmuch as the costs are not dependent on S, the number of stations. The total variable cost per period C_t is

$$C_t = C_e \sum_{N=0}^{N=S}(S-N)P(N) + C_q \sum_{N=S+1}^{N=M}(N-S)P(N) \qquad (11.11\#1)$$

where

$$P(N) = \frac{M!}{N!(M-N)!}\chi^N P(0) \qquad 1 \le N \le S \qquad (11.11\#2)$$

$$P(N) = \frac{M!}{S!S^{N-S}(N-M)!}\chi^N P(0) \qquad S < N \le M \qquad (11.11\#3)$$

with

$$\sum_{N=0}^{N=M} P(N) = 1 \qquad (11.11\#4)$$

The analytical optimization of Eq. (11.11#1) relative to S is too complicated. Solution by tabulation will indicate the optimum number of service stations to provide. Tables for finite queuing problems are available [11.16R16]. The distribution $P(N)$ in Eq. (11.11#1) can be calculated from Eqs. (11.11#2) and (11.11#3) or from the following relationships instead:

$$\theta_N = \begin{cases} \dfrac{M-N+1}{N}\chi\theta_{N-1} & 1 \le N \le S \qquad (11.11\#5) \\[2ex] \dfrac{M-N+1}{S}\chi\theta_{N-1} & S < N \le M \qquad (11.11\#6) \end{cases}$$

By definition

$$\theta_N = \frac{P(N)}{P(0)}$$

therefore

$$\theta_0 = \frac{P(0)}{P(0)} = 1 \qquad (11.11\#7)$$

Table 11.11T1 Finite Queuing Calculations for Example 11.11E1*

(1) S No. of crews	(2) N No. of pumps in queue and being serviced	(3) θ_N Eqs. (11.11#5) and (11.11#6) $\theta_0 = 1$	(4) $P(N) = \dfrac{\theta_N}{\sum_0^M \theta_N}$ Eq. (11.11#9) Probability of N pumps in queue or being serviced	(5) $(S-N)P(N)$ Expectation of idle crews	(6) $(N-S)P(N)$ Expectation of pumps in queue
4	0	1.00	0.146	0.584	
	1	2.00	0.292	0.876	
	2	1.90	0.277	0.554	
	3	1.14	0.165	0.165	
	4	0.49	0.071	0.000	
				$\overline{2.179}$	
	5	0.20	0.029	$\sum_0^S (S-N)P(N)$	0.029
	6	0.08	0.016		0.032
	7	0.03	0.003		0.009
	8	0.01	0.001		0.004
		$\overline{6.85}$			$\overline{0.074}$
		$\sum_0^M \theta_N$			$\sum_{S+1}^N (N-S)P(N)$
5	0	1.00	0.148	0.740	
	1	2.00	0.296	1.184	
	2	1.90	0.281	0.843	
	3	1.14	0.168	0.336	
	4	0.49	0.071	0.071	
	5	0.157	0.022	0.000	
				$\overline{3.174}$	
	6	0.04	0.006		0.006
	7	0.008	0.001		0.002
		$\overline{6.735}$			$\overline{0.008}$
6	0	1.000	0.148	0.888	
	1	2.000	0.297	1.485	
	2	1.900	0.282	1.128	
	3	1.140	0.169	0.507	
	4	0.490	0.072	0.144	
	5	0.157	0.023	0.023	
	6	0.04	0.006	0.000	
				$\overline{4.175}$	
	7	0.009	0.001		0.001
		$\overline{6.736}$			$\overline{0.001}$

* $M = 20$, $\mu = 2$, $\lambda = 0.2$, $\chi = 0.1$.

Table 11.11T2 Cost Analysis for Example 11.11E1*

No. of crews	(1) $\sum_{N=0}^{N=S} (S-N)P(N)$ Expected idle time, crew-periods	(2) $\sum_{N=S+1}^{N=M} (N-S)P(N)$ Expected queue, crew-periods	(3) $C_e \sum (S-N)P(N)$ Expected idle per cost, $ per period	(4) $C_q \sum (N-S)P(N)$ Expected queue cost, $ per period	(5) (3) + (4) Expected total variable cost, $ per period
4	2.197	0.074	2,197	1,110	3,307
5	3.174	0.008	3,174	120	3,294
6	4.175	0.001	4,175	15	4,190

* C_e = $1,000 per month per idle crew; C_q = $15,000 per month per broken pump.

also

$$P(N) = \frac{\theta_N}{1 + \sum_{N=1}^{N=M} \theta_N} \qquad (11.11\#8)$$

$$P(N) = \frac{\theta_N}{\sum_{N=0}^{N=M} \theta_N} \qquad (11.11\#9)$$

Example 11.11E1 An oil company has 20 pumps working in an oil field. Calls for service follow a Poisson distribution with mean 0.2 pump per month. A crew consists of two men, each of whom receives $500 per month. Servicing time follows a Poisson distribution with mean 2 pumps per month. Money lost due to breakdown of a pump is $15,000 per month. Find the optimum number of crews to be provided.

The tabulation for the finite queuing factors is given in Table 11.11T1. Here $M = 20$, $\mu = 2$, $\lambda = 0.2$, and $\chi = 0.2/2 = 0.1$. Calculations for four, five, and six crews are shown with 1 month taken as a period. It is not necessary to make the tabulations through $N = 20$ in the table since, for example, in the case of four crews, the terms in the summation for $N = 9$ and above have approached zero and do not contribute to the totals.

Table 11.11T2 shows a tabulation of the cost calculations with $C_e = 500(2) = \$1,000$ and $C_q = \$15,000$, and is made from Eq. (11.11#1). The minimum variable cost per period is attained with five crews at $3,294 per month.

11.12 General method with certainty

In many cases an analytical solution is difficult or perhaps impossible. Such cases must be reduced to a tabulation and may require considerable ingenuity to reduce the problem to a representation on paper. The following example is straightforward but would be quite complicated if a reduction to mathematical equations were attempted.

Example 11.12E1 Five units of a product must be processed at three different stations, A, B, C. The processes are independent. Process time in days at each station is

  A   5 days
  B   7 days
  C   9 days

11.12 QUEUING PROBLEMS

The five products must have the same operating sequence. Handling time and cost between stations is negligible.

Stations are all started at zero time and are shut individually when the fifth unit has gone through the station. Idle time for product is counted whenever a product arrives at a station and must wait for entry. Idle time for a station is counted whenever a station is waiting for work.

Find the most economical sequence of work centers for the following conditions, where C_w is the waiting cost in dollars per part per day and C_e is the cost of idle time in dollars per station per day.

	C_w	C_e
(a)	10	30
(b)	20	20
(c)	30	10

Table 11.12T1 Time-analysis Tabulation for Example 11.12E1

Sequence	Part no.	Station 1 In	Station 1 Out	Station 2 In	Station 2 Out	Station 2 Part waiting	Station 2 Station idle	Station 3 In	Station 3 Out	Station 3 Part waiting	Station 3 Station idle
ABC	1	0	5	5	12	0	5	12	21	0	12
	2	5	10	12	19	2	0	21	30	2	0
	3	10	15	19	26	4	0	30	39	4	0
	4	15	20	26	33	6	0	39	48	6	0
	5	20	25	33	40	8	0	48	57	8	0
ACB	1	0	5	5	14	0	5	14	21	0	14
	2	5	10	14	23	4	0	23	30	0	2
	3	10	15	23	32	8	0	32	39	0	2
	4	15	20	32	41	12	0	41	48	0	2
	5	20	25	41	50	16	0	50	57	0	2
BAC	1	0	7	7	12	0	7	12	21	0	12
	2	7	14	14	19	0	2	21	30	2	0
	3	14	21	21	26	0	2	30	39	4	0
	4	21	28	28	33	0	2	39	48	6	0
	5	28	35	35	40	0	2	48	57	8	0
BCA	1	0	7	7	16	0	7	16	21	0	16
	2	7	14	16	25	2	0	25	30	0	4
	3	14	21	25	34	4	0	34	39	0	4
	4	21	28	34	43	6	0	43	48	0	4
	5	28	35	43	52	8	0	52	57	0	4
CAB	1	0	9	9	14	0	9	14	21	0	14
	2	9	18	18	23	0	4	23	30	0	2
	3	18	27	27	32	0	4	32	39	0	2
	4	27	36	36	41	0	4	41	48	0	2
	5	36	45	45	50	0	4	50	57	0	2
CBA	1	0	9	9	16	0	9	16	21	0	16
	2	9	18	18	25	0	2	25	30	0	4
	3	18	27	27	34	0	2	34	39	0	4
	4	27	36	36	43	0	2	43	48	0	4
	5	36	45	15	52	0	2	52	57	0	4

Table 11.12T2 Cost Tabulation for Example 11.12E1

Sequence	Total product waiting, product-days	Cost of waiting, $ (a)	(b)	(c)	Total station idle, station-days	Cost of idle stations, $ (a)	(b)	(c)	Total variable cost per period, $ (a)	(b)	(c)
ABC	40	400	800	1,200	17	510	340	170	910	1,140	1,370
ACB	40	400	800	1,200	27	810	540	270	1,210	1,340	1,470
BAC	20	200	400	600	27	810	540	270	1,010	940	870
BCA	20	200	400	600	39	1,170	780	390	1,370	1,180	990
CAB	0	0	0	0	47	1,410	940	470	1,410	940	470
CBA	0	0	0	0	49	1,470	980	490	1,470	980	490

Table 11.12T1 shows the waiting time of products and the idle time of machines for all possible sequence of work centers. The total time required to produce five parts is 57 days for all the sequences; but the waiting and idle times vary, and in summary are:

Sequence	Part waiting	Station idle
ABC	40	17
ACB	40	27
BAC	20	27
BCA	20	39
CAB	0	47
CBA	0	49

Table 11.12T2 is the calculation for costs based on the relationship

$$C_t = C_w \begin{pmatrix} \text{total waiting time} \\ \text{for product} \end{pmatrix} + C_e \begin{pmatrix} \text{total idle time} \\ \text{for stations} \end{pmatrix}$$

Minimum cost for (a) is $910 per period for sequence ABC, for (b) $940 per period for BAC or CAB, and for (c) $470 per period for CAB.

11.13 General method with uncertainty

The analysis of queuing problems with uncertainty in arrivals or servicing time can become exceedingly complicated. The most general method is to subject the data to a Monte Carlo computation, which is essentially a simulation process. The distributions are simulated by the use of random numbers, and a large number of periods are taken to get a good average. The Monte Carlo method was discussed in Chap. 8, and an inventory example based on a Monte Carlo analysis was given in Chap. 10. The following example was run on a computer, but the method should be clear.

11.13 QUEUING PROBLEMS

Example 11.13E1 A product must be processed in three stations A, B, C. The order can be selected but once selected cannot be changed. Servicing time at each station follows a normal distribution as follows:

	Mean value, days	Standard deviation, days
A	5	1
B	8	2
C	4	1

Waiting cost is \$0.01 per unit per day, and the cost for an idle station is \$10 per day. Find the best sequence for processing the units.

The simulation will involve 600 units, which is large enough to establish average data. Time in each station can be generated from the use of random numbers in connection with the mean and standard deviations for the stations. Table 11.13T1 shows some of these data for the sequences BCA and BAC. Table 11.13T2 shows total values for 600 units

Table 11.13T1 Sample of Computer-output Operation-time Analysis for Example 11.13E1

Sequence	Part no.	Station 1 In	Station 1 Out	Station 2 In	Station 2 Out	Station 3 In	Station 3 Out
BCA	1	0.00	9.23	9.23	14.20	14.20	20.90
	2	9.23	15.54	15.54	18.37	20.90	25.57
	3	15.54	21.34	21.34	25.51	25.57	30.42
	4	21.34	31.59	31.59	35.94	35.94	42.88
	5	31.50	41.14	41.14	44.22	44.22	52.03
	...	...	...	...	...	...	...
	596	4,810.14	4,817.38	4,817.38	4,823.40	4,823.40	4,827.75
	597	4,817.38	4,824.11	4,824.11	4,827.75	4,827.75	4,833.56
	598	4,824.11	4,830.66	4,830.66	4,834.46	4,834.46	4,842.99
	599	4,830.66	4,835.71	4,835.71	4,840.81	4,842.99	4,848.65
	600	4,835.71	4,849.76	4,849.76	4,855.97	4,855.97	4,858.56
BAC	1	0.00	8.71	8.71	13.67	13.67	17.08
	2	8.71	17.24	17.24	21.80	21.80	23.86
	3	17.24	26.52	26.52	31.91	31.91	35.51
	4	26.52	35.75	35.75	41.70	41.70	45.70
	5	35.75	43.78	43.78	49.06	49.06	51.24
	...	...	...	...	...	...	...
	596	4,734.78	4,744.85	4,744.85	4,750.58	4,750.58	4,753.07
	597	4,744.85	4,753.31	4,753.31	4,757.91	4,757.91	4,761.07
	598	4,753.31	4,761.06	4,761.06	4,765.47	4,765.47	4,768.63
	599	4,761.06	4,768.33	4,768.33	4,773.26	4,773.26	4,777.79
	600	4,768.33	4,774.64	4,774.64	4,780.35	4,780.35	4,786.34

226 OPTIMIZATION

Table 11.13T2 Waiting and Idle Time for 600 Units in Exercise 11.13E1

Sequence	Total waiting time of units, unit-days	Station idle time, station-days			
		Station 1	Station 2	Station 3	Total
ABC	515,430	0	5.6	2,333.6	2,339.2
ACB	545,330	0	644.51	6.87	674.38
BCA	100.2	0	2,411.8	1,864.5	4,276.3
BAC	73.2	0	1,770	2,402.2	4,172.2
CAB	70,629	0	3.90	9.15	13.05
CBA	739,870	0	4.6625	1,853	1,857.6

processed for all work sequences possible. Table 11.13T3 gives the cost analysis based on 600 units. Sequence *CAB* gives the minimum cost.

11.14 Nomenclature

- a Intermediate term for evaluation of Eq. (11.9#2)
- b Intermediate term for evaluation of Eq. (11.9#2)
- c Intermediate term for evaluation of Eq. (11.9#2)
- C_e Cost for one idle service facility per period, \$/(facility)(period)
- C_f Cost for servicing one unit, \$ per unit
- C_q Cost for one unit in the queue for one period, \$/(unit)(period)
- C_t Total variable cost per period, \$ per period
- C_w Cost for one unit waiting one period, \$/(unit)(period)
- $E(r^2)$ Average of r^2 with respect to time where r is the number of arrivals per period
- F Intermediate term for evaluation of Eq. (11.9#2)
- G Intermediate term for evaluation of Eq. (11.9#2)
- H Intermediate term for evaluation of Eq. (11.9#2)
- L Number of channels in service facility, dimensionless
- M Number of units in the population, dimensionless
- N Number of units in the service system, queue plus service facilities, at time T, dimensionless
- N_e Expected value of N, dimensionless
- $P(0)$ Probability of zero units in the service system at time T, dimensionless
- $P(N)$ Probability of N units in the system at time T, dimensionless
- q Intermediate term for evaluation of Eq. (11.9#2)

Table 11.13T3 Cost Tabulation for Example 11.13E1

Sequence	Queuing cost		Idle-station cost		Total cost, \$ 600 units
	Unit-days	Cost, \$	Station-days	Cost, \$	
ABC	515,430	5,154.30	2,339.2	23,392	28,546
ACB	545,330	5,453.30	274.38	6,743.8	12,197
BCA	100.2	1.00	4,276.3	42,763	42,764
BAC	73.2	0.73	4,172.2	41,722	41,723
CAB	70,629	706.29	13.05	130.5	837
CBA	739,870	7,398.70	1,857,6	18,576	25,975

R	Intermediate term for evaluation of Eq. (11.9#2)
S	Number of service stations in system, dimensionless
T	Time, period
T_a	Time between two consecutive arrivals, periods/unit
T_s	Time in periods to service one unit, periods/unit
v	Intermediate term for evaluation of Eq. (11.9#2)
θ_N	Theta of N; factor connected with probabilities $P(N)$ in finite queuing, dimensionless
λ	Average or expected arrival rate, units/period
λ'	Specific values of λ in Eq. (11.7#6), units/period
μ	Average or expected servicing rate, units/period
μ'	Optimum values of μ in Eq. (11.7#6), units/period
σ^2	Variance of a service distribution, periods^2
χ	Load factor, or ratio of arrival rate to potential service rate, λ/μ, dimensionless

11.15 Problems

P1. A gasoline station receives a car every 10 min. The cost of waiting in the station is $0.10 per car per minute and the cost of servicing a car is $0.16. If the station has one pump, for a variable service time:
   (a) Plot the service cost as a function of the service time in minutes.
   (b) Plot the waiting cost as a function of the service time in minutes.
   (c) Plot the total variable cost as a function of the service time in minutes.
   (d) Find the service time for the lowest cost per car.

P2. If in Prob. 11.15P1, the station has two, three, or four pumps, find the lowest cost situation.

P3. The arrival rate for an automatic car-wash station obeys a Poisson distribution with a mean of 5 cars per hour. The rate of service follows a Poisson distribution with a mean of 10 cars per hour.
   (a) Develop the probability distribution of N cars in the station.
   (b) Find the expected number of cars in the station at any time.
   (c) Find the probability for two or more cars in the station.

P4. If the service rate in Prob. 11.15P3 is varied, the waiting cost per car per hour is $0.10, and the cost of servicing one car is $0.30, find (a) the lowest cost service rate and (b) the lowest operating cost per hour.

P5. The arrival rate in a queuing system obeys a Poisson distribution with a mean of 0.5 unit per hour. The cost of waiting is $2 per unit per hour, and the cost of servicing one unit is $4. If the service-time variance is 2 hr^2, find (a) the service rate that gives minimum total variable cost and (b) the minimum expected total cost.

P6. In Prob. 11.15P5, the service-time variance is set equal to zero by automating the service station. Find the service rate that gives minimum expected total variable cost.

P7. A company has 30 automatic machines in a production area. Calls for service follow a Poisson distribution with a mean of 0.3 machine per month. A repair crew can service machines according to a Poisson distribution with a mean of 3 machines per month. Loss due to breakdown is $20,000 per machine per month. A crew costs $1,000 per month. Find the optimum number of repair crews.

P8. Ten units of product X are to be processed on machines A, B, C, and D. Machine A must be used first, but the other machines can be selected in any order. The process times in days are

A	B	C	D
3	2	7	5

The waiting costs are $10 per unit per day and $15 per machine per day.

The same sequence of operations must be used for all the units. A machine must finish one unit before starting another. Handling time between machines is negligible.

Find the optimum sequence of operations.

11.16 References

R1. Ali, A. M.: "Sensitivity Analysis of Queuing Models," unpublished Ph.D. dissertation, Oklahoma State University, Stillwater, 1968.
R2. Barish, N. H.: "Economic Analysis for Engineering and Managerial Decision Making," McGraw-Hill Book Company, New York, 1962.
R3. Bhatia, A., and A. Gary: Basic Structure of Queuing Problems, *J. Ind. Eng.*, vol. 14, pp. 13–17, January–February, 1963.
R4. Bowman, E. H., and R. B. Fetter: "Analysis for Production and Operations Management," Richard D. Irwin, Inc., Homewood, Ill., 1967.
R5. Buffa, E. S.: "Modern Production Management," John Wiley & Sons, Inc., New York, 1965.
R6. Churchman, C. W., R. L. Ackoff, and E. L. Arnoff: "Introduction to Operations Research," John Wiley & Sons, Inc., New York, 1957.
R7. Fabrycky, W. J., and P. E. Torgersen: "Operations Economy: Industrial Applications of Operations Research," Prentice-Hall, Inc., Englewood Cliffs, N.J., 1966.
R8. Flagle, C. D., and others: "Operations Research and System Engineering," The Johns Hopkins Press, Baltimore, 1960.
R9. Goetz, B. E.: "Quantitative Methods: A Survey and Guide for Managers," McGraw-Hill Book Company, New York, 1965.
R10. Goode, H. H., and R. E. Machol: "System Engineering," McGraw-Hill Book Company, New York, 1957.
R11. Hillier, F. S.: Application of Waiting Line Theory to Industrial Problems, *J. Ind. Eng.*, vol. 15, pp. 3–8, January–February, 1964.
R12. Hillier, F. S.: Cost Models for the Application of Priority Waiting Line Theory to Industrial Problems, *J. Ind. Eng.*, vol. 16, pp. 178–185, May–June, 1965.
R13. Kaufmann, A.: "Methods and Models of Operations Research," Prentice-Hall, Inc., Englewood Cliffs, N.J., 1963.
R14. Miller, D. W., and M. K. Starr: "Executive Decisions and Operations Research," Prentice-Hall, Inc., Englewood Cliffs, N.J., 1960.
R15. McMillan, C., and R. F. Gonzalez: "System Analysis: A Computer Approach to Decision Models," Richard D. Irwin, Inc., Homewood, Ill., 1965.
R16. Peck, L. G., and R. N. Hazelwood: "Finite Queuing Tables," John Wiley & Sons, Inc., New York, 1958.
R17. Prabhu, N. V.: "Queues and Inventories," John Wiley & Sons, Inc., New York, 1965.
R18. Saaty, T. L.: "Elements of Queueing Theory," McGraw-Hill Book Company, New York, 1961.
R19. Shelton, J. R.: Solution Methods for Waiting Line Problems, *J. Ind. Eng.*, vol. 11, pp. 293–303, July–August, 1960.
R20. Takacs, L.: "Introduction to the Theory of Queues," Oxford University Press, New York, 1962.

12
Optimization

M. S. Peters and F. C. Jelen

ONE VARIABLE

12.1 Optimization—a human trait

Optimization, or the urge for efficiency, has a basic psychological origin. The human mind can confront a task or problem and recognize more than one course of action, followed by a second phase, the selection of what is considered the best action. The second phase is the decision step. The two steps taken together, recognition of alternatives and decision, constitute optimization. Optimization can be qualitative (judged by human preference) or quantitative (detected by exact mathematical means). Optimization permeates society and technology to a far greater degree than is realized. The musical composer struggling for just the right combination of notes, the mathematician seeking an expression for a mathematical or physical principle, and the designer of a bridge are all involved in optimization as each sees it. In a more prosaic sense the golfer striving for a minimum score, the student hoping for a high IQ rating, and the newspaper headline screeching the greatest airplane fatality of all time likewise are manifestations of the allurement of optimization and extreme values. Optimization is as old as antiquity, and even the ancients suspected that a circle has the greatest ratio of area to perimeter.

230 OPTIMIZATION

As engineering becomes more advanced and the business and industrial world more competitive, the methods for optimizing become more exact and the rewards increasingly greater. Detailed consideration of optimization now pervades all successful human endeavor. There are basically three categories of optimization. The first is preferential, as exemplified by the musical composer struggling for just the right combination of notes, a category subject to preference and taste only. The second category is mathematical or physical, such as the demonstration that a sphere contains the maximum volume for a given surface, a fact not subject to human preference or fancy. The third category is economic optimization, which is a combination of the two other categories but with the human preference elements introduced in a quantitative way. Economic optimization or engineering optimization, which is the subject of this chapter, has to consider human values, but they must be expressible in quantitative form. Thus the designer of a bridge is concerned with more than an engineering design for maximum strength-to-weight basis. He must consider a myriad of quantitative factors such as the cost of on-site welding relative to the cost of prefabricated sections, extra construction costs for the safety of the workers, overdesign now to meet future demand, and so forth.

12.2 Nature of optimization

Optimization in a general sense involves the determination of a highest or lowest value over some range. Which is desired is a matter of statement. Thus a problem can be maximized for profit or minimized for loss. Optimization will be used as a general term for either case. To the mathematician maximum and

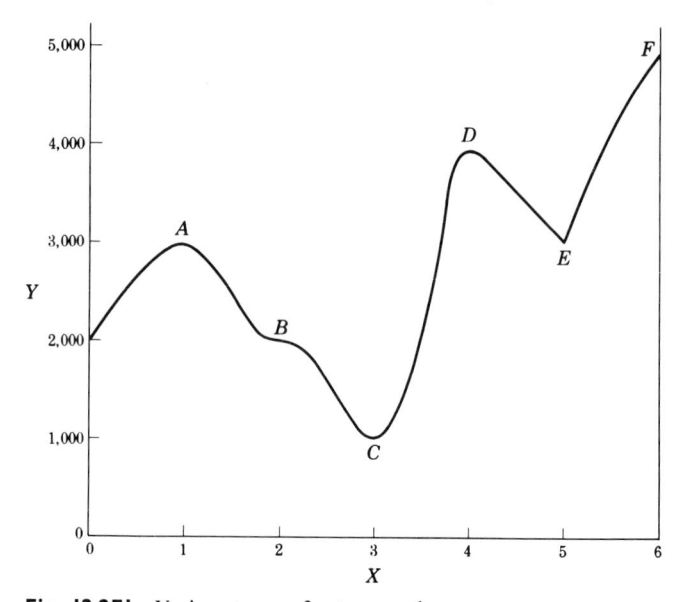

Fig. 12.2F1 Various types of extreme values.

minimum values have special qualities, and it is assumed that the analyst is familiar with these from his study of the calculus. There may be more than one mathematical maximum or mathematical minimum in a region, and the highest and lowest values in the region may or may not correspond to mathematical maximum and minimum values. Mathematical optima occur in the case of one independent variable when the slope of the curve is horizontal or zero. This is a necessary condition but not sufficient, as the point may be an inflection point. Certain other conditions must be met; e.g., the function must be continuous at the point in question. Figure 12.2F1 is a review of the circumstances. Points A and D are mathematical maxima, but the highest value is point F, which is not a mathematical maximum. Point C is a mathematical minimum and also the lowest value. Point B meets the condition that the slope is zero and the curve is horizontal, but B is neither a mathematical maximum nor a mathematical minimum and is instead a point of inflection. Point E is not a mathematical minimum because the slope or first derivative is not continuous at point E. Maximum and minimum points which are not highest and lowest values are referred to as *local optimum points*. Thus point A is a local maximum. Although the highest and lowest values in a region may not correspond to mathematical optima, a study of mathematical optima is fundamental to a study of optimization.

In working optimization problems the analyst must formulate the problem in such a way that he optimizes for the proper goal. This is quite elementary but frequently a source of error because the result depends upon the goal sought. Having obtained a result, the analyst should establish the following three considerations:

1 Is the answer feasible or realizable?
2 Is the answer optimal?
3 How sensitive is the optimum value to the parameters and how responsive to a variation of the independent variables from their optimum values?

12.3 Optimization methods

A great number of methods have been introduced to determine optimum procedure or policy. This chapter is fundamental and considers three powerful general methods:

1 Analytical
2 Graphical or tabular
3 Incremental

A large part of this book is devoted to optimization, and other chapters describe specialized methods. The search or calculation for a highest or lowest value in a region can become exceedingly complicated in practice, and the analyst must be capable of originality in setting up solutions. Problems involving manufacturing or processing operations are referred to as economic balance. Usually cost data are involved, e.g., operation for maximum profit, but not necessarily so, e.g., operation for maximum output with cost disregarded. The problem may involve a single unit, such as a welding machine, or a combination of units, such as an assembly line. For multiunit systems optimization is on an overall basis, and it does not follow that optimization of each unit on an individual basis will result in overall optimization.

In practice many data will be empirical and economic in origin, so that the optimization will be based on parameters which are not rigorously fixed or exact numbers. Also the more variables and parameters that are involved, the flatter the optimum conditions become, generally. Nevertheless optimization as a goal is an essential ingredient of successful operation even though there are some uncertainties.

Problems reducible to one independent variable will be discussed first, followed by an extension to more than one variable. The literature is replete with special problems leading to mathematical relationships which require only that the analyst substitute numerical values. In doing so he assumes all the limitations, assumed values, and other fixed data in the model. Problems are so varied that the analyst must be prepared to derive his own relationships.

12.4 Analytical method for optimization

Let the problem be to optimize Y, which is a function of the single independent variable X. That is,

$$Y = F(X) \qquad (12.4\#1)$$

Generally an optimum value of Y will be a mathematical maximum or minimum. For this condition, as given by the calculus,

$$\frac{dY}{dX} = \frac{dF(X)}{dX} = 0 \qquad (12.4\#2)$$

If the problem can be formulated so that Y can be expressed in terms of X, the analytical method can be used. Equation (12.4#1) may represent an exact physical or mathematical relationship, an empirical relationship, or a combination. The means of establishing the relationship is not important, only its existence being necessary.

If Y is not a continuous function of X, it can be treated as a series of regions in which it is continuous. Differentiation at a point having a discontinuity is not permissible inasmuch as the value of Eq. (12.4#2), the derivative at the point, depends upon from which side of the point $\Delta Y/\Delta X$ is taken. At times, too, X can assume only integral values, e.g., the number of stories in an office building. Only continuous functions can be differentiated rigorously. Discrete variables should be treated by the calculus of finite differences or subjected to a tabular analysis. In many cases a function of discrete variables can be differentiated just as if it were a continuous function, but solutions so obtained should be investigated carefully.

If Eq. (12.4#1) can be set up, it is differentiated to satisfy Eq. (12.4#2) leading to a value or X that is, perhaps, optimum. The value of X so obtained can be substituted in Eq. (12.4#1) to give an optimum X, Y. The differentiation of Eq. (12.4#1) may be difficult, and the resulting Eq. (12.4#2) may be so complicated that solution by trial and error may be required, but such considerations merely make the solution more tedious.

The solution to Eq. (12.4#2) will give, perhaps, several values of X, say $X_1, X_2, \ldots, X_n$. Each value of X, say X_1, can be tested analytically to determine whether it represents a maximum, minimum, or a point of inflection, which is neither. For maximum and minimum, if

$$\left.\frac{dY}{dX}\right|_{X=X_1} = 0 \quad \text{and} \quad \left.\frac{d^2Y}{dX^2}\right|_{X=X_1} = +$$

then
$\quad Y$ at $X = X_1$ is a minimum

If

$$\left.\frac{dY}{dX}\right|_{X=X_1} = 0 \quad \text{and} \quad \left.\frac{d^2Y}{dX^2}\right|_{X=X_1} = -$$

then
$\quad Y$ at $X = X_1$ is a maximum

The sign of the second derivative indicates whether the point is a maximum or minimum. The second derivative may be zero at the point, however, in which case the test is inconclusive. Further testing is necessary, which requires formulating higher-order derivatives. Find the lowest-order derivative that becomes nonzero for $X = X_1$. If this is an odd derivative, then X_1 is an inflection point. If this is an even derivative and positive in value for $X = X_1$, then X_1 is a minimum point, but if it is negative in value, X_1 is a maximum point.

In practice it is rarely necessary to test beyond the second derivative. Another test is to calculate Y in the neighborhood of $X = X_1$ and from the tabulation or plot observe the behavior of Y at X_1.

12.5 Graphical method for optimization

If
$$Y = F(X) \qquad (12.5\#1)$$

then a tabulation and plot of Y against X over the feasible range of X will yield all the information for the optimization of Y. Figure 12.2F1 shows such a graph.

A plot or tabulation has the advantage that it distinguishes between mathematical maxima and minima, inflection points, and highest and lowest values. Also it discloses how responsive the optimum value is to a variation in the independent variable. The graphical method is widely applicable, and the data and information can be in analytical, tabular, or graphical form.

For one trial in one independent variable the analytical method has little advantage over the graphical or tabular method, although the analytical method will give the mathematical optima without a search procedure. Even so, the

234 OPTIMIZATION 12.7

analytical method should be supplemented with some graphical or tabular data in a thorough analysis. The advantage of having an analytical expression for the optimum condition is very real, however, and permits a representation of the problem as mathematical relationships that are particularly valuable for theoretical studies or as expressions in compact, directly usable form.

12.6 Incremental method for optimization

The incremental method is instinctive and basic. In essence it amounts to operating at one value of the independent variable, changing the variable not too greatly, and determining by calculation or observation whether the change is advantageous. Referring to Fig. 12.2F1, operation at $X = 3.5$ gives $Y = 2,000$, and incrementing to $X = 3.6$ gives $Y = 2,500$, an improvement. In this fashion small increments will lead to the local optimum D. Some precautions to be observed are evident from Fig. 12.2F1. It may be necessary to enter at several values of X to avoid determining a local optimum only.

The incremental method is suitable for trial by experiment, including uncertainty in individual observations. With uncertainty, trials are repeated to establish probable values by means of statistical analysis. The incremental method is applicable to analytical or tabular data and can be used for continuous or discrete variables. It is analysis about a point.

12.7 A cyclic process

An example in optimization will be developed in detail to illustrate the principles. It is typical of a variety of problems in which at some point in a process it becomes economical to pay a penalty and start over again.

Example 12.7E1 In drilling wells in a certain type of terrain, an oil company finds that the depth it can drill before changing drill bits is given by the relationship
$$Q_c = 300 T_d^{0.5}$$
Where
Q_c = cumulative feet
T_d = drilling time, days

Drilling costs are \$4,250 per day. It requires 18 hr, or 0.75 day, to install a new drill bit at a total cost of \$10,500.

(a) Find the optimum cycle time for minimum monthly cost at a drilling rate of 2,000 ft/month.

(b) Find the optimum cycle time for minimum monthly cost at a drilling rate of 4,750 ft/month.

(c) Find the optimum cycle time for maximum drilling depth per month without regard to cost.

(d) Find the optimum cycle time for maximum profit if each foot drilled has a return value to the company of \$60 per foot.

Part (a). Basis 2,000 ft/month. Let N = cycles/month. Then
$NQ_c = 2,000$

$$N = \frac{2,000}{Q_c} = \frac{2,000}{300 T_d^{0.5}} = \frac{6.667}{T_d^{0.5}} \tag{12.7#1}$$

12.7 OPTIMIZATION

Set up an expression for cost in dollars per month for N cycles/month

$$\text{\$/month} = N\underbrace{\frac{\text{cycles}}{\text{month}} T_d \frac{\text{days}}{\text{cycle}} 4{,}250 \frac{\$}{\text{day}}}_{\text{drilling expense}} + \underbrace{10{,}500 \frac{\$}{\text{cycle}} N \frac{\text{cycles}}{\text{month}}}_{\text{bit expense}} \qquad (12.7\#2)$$

Eliminate N by Eq. (12.7#1)

$$\text{\$/month} = 28{,}333 T_d^{0.5} + 70{,}000 T_d^{-0.5} \qquad (12.7\#3)$$

Differentiate and set equal to zero

$$\frac{d(\$/\text{month})}{dT_d} = 0 = 0.5(28{,}333) T_d^{-0.5} - 0.5(70{,}000) T_d^{-1.5}$$

$T_d = 2.471$ days drilling each cycle

Check for feasibility

$$N = \frac{6.667}{T_d^{0.5}} = \frac{6.667}{2.471^{0.5}} = 4.241 \text{ cycles/month}$$

Total days/cycle = $\underbrace{2.471}_{\text{drilling}} + \underbrace{0.75}_{\text{changing}} = 3.221$

$3.221 \dfrac{\text{days}}{\text{cycle}} 4.241 \dfrac{\text{cycles}}{\text{month}} = 13.66$ days/month

which is feasible inasmuch as $13.66 < 30$.

$$\frac{\$}{\text{ft}} = \frac{\$/\text{month}}{\text{ft/month}} = \frac{4{,}250 N T_d + 10{,}500 N}{2{,}000}$$

and for $N = 4.241$ and $T_d = 2.471$, $ per foot = 44.53. Check for optimum by second derivative. Differentiate Eq. (12.7#3)

$$\frac{d^2(\$/\text{month})}{dT_d^2} = -0.25(28{,}333) T_d^{-1.5} + 0.75(70{,}000) T_d^{-2.5}$$

which is positive for $T_d = 2.471$, hence a minimum cost.

Graphical solution. Return to Eq. (12.7#3). A tabulation for various values of T_d is given in Table 12.7T1, which shows a minimum cost of $89,069 per month or $44.53 per

Table 12.7T1 Example 12.7E1, Part (a)*

(1)	(2)	(3)	(4)	(5)	(6)
				$ per month	$ per foot
T_d, days	$T_d^{0.5}$	$28{,}333 T_d^{0.5}$	$700{,}000 T_d^{-0.5}$	(3) + (4)	(5) ÷ 2,000
1.00	1.000	28,333	70,000	98,333	49.17
1.50	1.225	34,708	57,143	91,851	45.93
2.00	1.414	40,063	49,505	89,568	44.78
2.25	1.500	42,500	46,667	89,167	44.58
2.471	1.572	44,534	44,535	89,069	44.53
2.75	1.659	47,004	42,194	89,198	44.60
3.00	1.732	49,073	40,416	89,489	44.74
4.00	2.000	56,666	35,000	91,666	45.83

* $ per month = $28{,}333 T_d^{0.5} + 70{,}000 T_d^{-0.5}$.

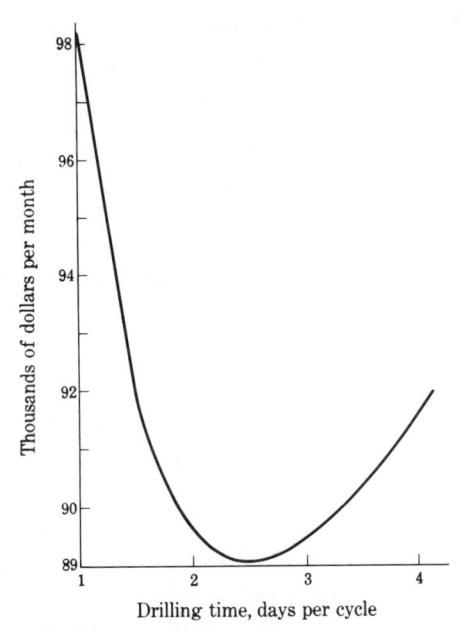

Fig. 12.7F1 Optimum drilling time per cycle for 2,000 ft/month.

foot at $T_d = 2.471$ drilling days/cycle. A plot of Table 12.7T1 is given in Fig. 12.7F1, which confirms that $T_d = 2.471$ is both a mathematical minimum and a lowest value, thus here the optimum.

Part (b). Basis 4,750 ft/month.

$NQ_c = 4,750$

$$N = \frac{4,570}{300T_d^{0.5}} = 15.833 T_d^{-0.5} \qquad (12.7\#4)$$

$/month = NT_d(4,250) + 10,500N$

Eliminate N by Eq. (12.7#4)

$/month = 67,290 T_d^{0.5} + 166,250 T_d^{-0.5}$

$$\frac{d(\$/month)}{dT_d} = 0 = 33,645 T_d^{-0.5} - 83,125 T_d^{-1.5}$$

$T_d = 2.471$ days drilling each cycle

Check for feasibility

$N = 15.833 T_d^{-0.5} = 15,833(2.471^{-0.5}) = 10.07$ cycles/month

Total days/cycle $= 2.471 + 0.75 = 3.221$

$3.221 \dfrac{\text{days}}{\text{cycle}} \; 10.07 \dfrac{\text{cycles}}{\text{month}} = 32.44$ days/month

12.7   OPTIMIZATION

which is not feasible as 32.44 > 30. Collecting results

$$N = 15.833 T_d^{-0.5} \quad \text{cycles/month necessary}$$

$$\frac{30}{T_d + 0.75} \quad \text{cycles/month available}$$

and setting these equal gives

$$15.833 T_d^{-0.5} = \frac{30}{T_d + 0.75}$$

or

$$T_d - 1.895 T_d^{0.5} + 0.75 = 0$$

which is a quadratic equation in $T_d^{0.5}$. Solve this by the quadratic formula giving $T_d^{0.5}$ and then square to get T_d

$$T_d = 0.317 \quad \text{or} \quad 1.775 \text{ days}$$

The tabulation in Table 12.7T2 shows that the feasible range for T_d is 0.317 to 1.775 days and that the optimum time for minimum cost is $T_d = 1.775$ days.

Comparing parts (a) and (b), it should be understood that 2.471 days drilling per cycle is optimum if production can be met. If not, it becomes necessary to change the drill bit more often. That $T_d = 1.775$ days in part (b) should be evident without the tabulation, as the closer the value is to 2.471, the less the cost per foot drilled. Figure 12.7F1 gives the same conclusions. For T_d in the range 0.317 to 1.775, the minimum cost per foot drilled is at $T_d = 1.775$. The mathematical minimum at $T_d = 2.471$ is outside the range and is not feasible.

Part (c). Maximized feet per month drilled. Set up an expression for feet per month drilled.

$$\text{Ft/month} = \frac{30 \text{ days/month}}{(T_d + 0.75) \text{days/cycle}} \; 300 T_d^{0.5} \; \frac{\text{ft}}{\text{cycle}} = 9{,}000 \; \frac{T_d^{0.5}}{T_d + 0.75}$$

Table 12.7T2   Example 12.7E1, Part (b)

(1)	(2)	(3)	(4)	(5)	(6)	(7)
T_d, days	$15.833 T_d^{-0.5}$ cycles/month necessary	$\dfrac{30}{T_d + 0.75}$, cycles/month available	$300 T_d^{0.5}$, ft/cycle	$4{,}250 T_d$ + 10,500, $ per cycle	$ per foot (5) ÷ (4)	$ per month (6) × 4,750
0.250	31.67	30.00				
0.317	28.12	28.12	168.9	11,847	70.14	333,160
0.600	20.43	22.22	232.5	13,050	56.13	266,620
1.000	15.83	17.14	300.0	14,750	49.16	233,510
1.250	14.16	15.00	335.4	15,813	47.15	223,960
1.500	12.92	13.33	367.5	16,875	45.92	218,120
1.775	11.89	11.89	339.6	18,044	45.16	214,510
2.000	11.20	10.91				

238 OPTIMIZATION

For maximum

$$\frac{d(\text{ft/month})}{dT_d} = 0 = 9{,}000 \frac{(T_d + 0.75)(0.5)T_d^{-0.5} - T_d}{(T_d + 0.75)^2}$$

$T_d = 0.75$ drilling day/cycle

$T_{tot} = 0.75 + 0.75 = 1.50$ days/cycle

Ft/cycle $= 300 T_d^{0.5} = 300(0.75^{0.5}) = 260$

\$/cycle $= 4{,}250 T_d + 10{,}500 = 4{,}250(0.75) + 10{,}500 = 13{,}688$

$$\$/\text{ft} = \frac{13{,}688 \ \$/\text{cycle}}{260 \ \text{ft/cycle}} = 52.65$$

$$\$/\text{month} = 13{,}688 \ \frac{\$}{\text{cycle}} \ \frac{30}{0.75 + 0.75} \ \frac{\text{days/month}}{\text{days/cycle}} = 273{,}760$$

Part (d). Maximum profit per month. Set up an expression for profit with

Profit = income − expenses

$$\frac{\text{Profit \$}}{\text{Cycle}} = \underbrace{300 T_d^{0.5} \ \frac{\text{ft}}{\text{cycle}} \ 60 \ \frac{\$}{\text{ft}}}_{\text{income}} - \underbrace{T_d \ \frac{\text{days}}{\text{cycle}} \ 4{,}250 \ \frac{\$}{\text{day}}}_{\text{drilling}} - \underbrace{10{,}500 \ \frac{\$}{\text{cycle}}}_{\text{bits}}$$

$$\frac{\text{Profit \$}}{\text{Cycle}} = -4{,}250 T_d + 18{,}000 T_d^{0.5} - 10{,}500$$

$$\frac{\text{Profit \$}}{\text{Month}} = \frac{\text{profit \$}}{\text{cycle}} \ \frac{\text{cycles}}{\text{month}}$$

$$\frac{\text{Profit \$}}{\text{Month}} = (-4{,}250 T_d + 18{,}000 T_d^{0.5} - 10{,}500) \frac{30}{T_d + 0.75}$$

For maximum

$$\frac{d(\$/\text{month})}{dT_d} = 0$$

$$= 30 \ \frac{(T_d + 0.75)(-4{,}250 + 9{,}000 T_d^{-0.5}) - (-4{,}250 + 18{,}000 T_d^{0.5} - 10{,}500)}{(T_d + 0.75)^2}$$

which is

$-9{,}000 T_d^{0.5} + 6{,}750 T_d^{-0.5} + 7{,}313 = 0$

By trial and error or by the quadratic formula

$T_d = 1.86$ days drilling/cycle

$$\text{Ft/month} = 9{,}000 \ \frac{T_d^{0.5}}{T_d + 0.75} = 9{,}000 \ \frac{1.86^{0.5}}{1.86 + 0.75} = 4{,}703$$

Income (\$/month) $= 60(4{,}703) = 282{,}180$

Expenses (\$/month) $= [4{,}250(1.86) + 10{,}500] \ \frac{\$}{\text{cycle}} \ \frac{30}{1.86 + 0.75} \ \frac{\text{cycles}}{\text{month}} = 211{,}550$

Profit (\$/month) $= 282{,}180 - 211{,}550 = 70{,}630$

Expenses (\$/ft drilled) $= \dfrac{211{,}550 \ \$/\text{month}}{4{,}703 \ \text{ft/month}} = 44.98$

A summary of the results for this example is given in Table 12.7T3. The optimum policy is different for each of the four conditions specified.

12.8

Table 12.7T3 Summary of Example 12.7E1

Condition optimized	T_d optimum drilling, days/cycle	Ft/month	Cost, $ per foot	Cost, $ per month	Profit, $ per month
Drilling expense at 2,000 ft/month	2.471	2,000	44.53	89,069	30,931
Drilling expense at 4,750 ft/month	1.775	4,750	45.16	214,510	70,490
Feet drilled per month	0.750	5,198	52.65	273,760	37,640
Profit per month at $60 per foot drilled	1.86	4,703	44.98	211,550	70,630

It is instructive to find the maximum profit by the *incremental method*. The expression for the profit in dollars per month can be written

$$\text{Profit (\$/month)} = 18{,}000 T_d^{0.5} \frac{30}{T_d + 0.75} - (4{,}250 T_d^{0.5} + 10{,}500) \frac{30}{T_d + 0.75}$$

A summary of the calculation is given in Table 12.7T4. Starting at $T_d = 1.4$, the profit increases with each increment of T_d; that is, $\Delta \text{profit}/\Delta T_d$ is positive until at $T_d = 1.86$ there is no further profit as T_d is increased; thus $\Delta \text{profit}/\Delta T_d$ is zero. As T_d is incremented beyond 1.86, the incremental profit is negative, a loss.

12.8 An example involving rate of return

The time value of money can be included. Thus if the time period is made 1 year and the end of the year is taken as the vantage point, all costs and receipts can be reduced to unacosts and the analysis made on that basis. The following example is instructive because rate of return is used as a criterion.

Example 12.8E1 An office building can be built 5, 10, 15, or 20 stories high. Investment and revenue representing receipts less expenses as a uniform end-of-year amount are:

	Stories			
	5	10	15	20
Investment, $	5,000,000	7,500,000	11,000,000	15,000,000
Revenue, $ per year	662,500	1,450,000	1,782,000	2,209,000

The figures are before a 48% tax rate. The life of the building is 25 years for both economic and tax purposes. Sum-of-digits depreciation with no salvage value will be used. Each dollar invested in the building must earn 10% per year or more after taxes. Find the maximum number of stories that should be constructed under these circumstances.

If C_d represents the fully depreciable first cost, the unacost by item 1, Table 3.13T1, is

$$R = C_d(1 - 0.48 F_{SDP,r,25}) F_{PR,r,25}$$

Using numerical values from Appendix 1, Table 1, and designating

$$(1 - 0.48 F_{SDP,r,25}) F_{PR,r,25}$$

Table 12.7T4 Example 12.7EI, Part (d) by Incremental Method*

(1) T_d, days	(2) ΔT_d	(3) Income, $ per month	(4) Δ income, $ per month	(5) Expenses, $ per month	(6) Δ expenses, $ per month	(7) Δ profit, $ per month (4) − (6)	(8) $\dfrac{\Delta\ profit}{\Delta T_d}$ (7) ÷ (2)	(9) Profit, $ per month
1.40		297,170		229,530				67,640
1.60	0.20	290,660	−6,510	220,850	−8,680	2,170	10,850	69,810
1.80	0.20	284,110	−6,550	213,530	−7,320	770	3,850	70,580
1.86	0.06	282,150	−1,960	211,550	−1,980	20	333	70,600
1.90	0.04	280,890	−1,260	210,290	−1,260	0	0	70,600
2.00	0.10	277,700	−3,190	207,270	−3,020	−170	−1,700	70,430
2.20	0.20	271,490	−6,210	201,850	−5,420	−790	−3,950	69,640

* Income ($ per month) $= 18{,}000 T_d^{0.5} \dfrac{30}{T_d + 0.75}$

Expense ($ per month) $= (4{,}250 T_d + 10{,}500) \dfrac{30}{T_d + 0.75}$

by Y, a tabulation is:

r, %	Y	r, %	Y
4	0.0418	12	0.1006
6	0.0547	14	0.1177
8	0.0689	16	0.1354
10	0.0843	20	0.1722

If R_v represents the end-of-year revenue, the unacost by item 2, Table 3.13T1, is
$$R = R_v(1 - t) = 0.52R_v$$
For the 5-story building with expenses and receipts equal on the basis of unacost
$$C_d Y = 0.52 R_v$$
$$5{,}000{,}000\, Y = 0.52$$
$$Y = 0.0689$$
and from the tabulation
$$r = 8\%$$
and so a 5-story building cannot be considered. For a 10-story building
$$7{,}500{,}000\, Y = 0.52(1{,}450{,}000)$$
$$Y = 0.1006$$
$$r = 12\%$$
and so a 10-story building will pay. For a 15-story building
$$11{,}000{,}000\, Y = 0.52(1{,}782{,}000)$$
$$Y = 0.0843$$
$$r = 10\%$$
but this is overall and includes the rate of return on the first 10 stories. Based on the incremental upper 5 stories,
$$(11{,}000{,}000 - 7{,}500{,}000)\, Y = 0.52(1{,}782{,}000 - 1{,}450{,}000)$$
$$Y = 0.493$$
$$r = 5.2\% \text{ approx. by interpolation}$$

Hence a 15-story building is not justified because the investment in the upper 5 stories does not earn 10% per year. The calculation is extended to a 20-story building and the results given in Table 12.8T1. The only investment justified is the 10-story building if the investment, including the last dollar invested, is to earn 10% per year or more after taxes.

12.9 A two-step example with recycle

The example developed in this section pertains to a two-step process. The requirement is not to optimize each step on an individual basis but to optimize the two steps together on an overall basis. In addition, the example includes feedback of material to an earlier step, a feature quite common in the process industries. In this example there is an economic balance between the two steps, the reactor and the separator. If the reactor is made large, the conversion is high and the separation costs low; but there is an optimum size reactor which results in lowest overall cost.

242   OPTIMIZATION

Table 12.8T1 Summary of Example 12.8E1

| | All stories ||| Incremental stories |||
Stories	Initial investment, $	Yearly revenue, $	Rate of return, %	Initial investment, $	Yearly revenue, $	Rate of return, %
5	5,000,000	662,500	8			
				2,500,000	787,500	19.1
10	7,500,000	1,450,000	12			
				3,500,000	332,000	5.2
15	11,000,000	1,782,000	10			
				4,000,000	427,000	6.1
20	15,000,000	2,209,000	9			

Example 12.9E1 The following homogeneous reaction

$$2A + B = D \quad \text{lb mole basis}$$

is carried out continuously in a liquid-phase reactor in which the conversion depends upon the residence time according to the relationship

$$r = 0.25T^{0.33} \quad 0.5 < T < 10 \qquad (12.9\#1)$$

where

r = mole D formed per mole B fed
T = residence time in reactor, hr

Fresh feed and recycle are fed to the reactor always in the proportion of $2A$ to $1B$. The density of the feed liquor is 0.60 lb mole/cu ft.

Operation will be 4,000 hr/year to produce 3 lb mole of D per on-stream hour. Reactors cost $2,500 per cubic foot of contained liquid and have a 4-year life with no salvage value for economic and tax purposes. Use sum-of-digits depreciation and a 10% per year rate of return after a 48% tax. The output from the reactor is run to a separator and is treated at a cost of $1.66 per lb mole of unreacted A and B. The unreacted A and B are recycled back to the reactor.

Find the size reactor in cubic feet that will give the minimum overall cost per year.

First construct the flowsheet basis 1 hr and start with a basis of $2A$ and $1B$ to the reactor. If T is the residence time in the reactor, then by Eq. (12.9#1), materials out of the reactor are

$0.25T^{0.33}$ = lb moles D or lb moles reacted B per hour
$2 - 2(0.25)T^{0.33}$ = lb moles unreacted A per hour
$1 - 0.25T^{0.33}$ = lb moles unreacted B per hour

Fresh feed which must be added to maintain $2A + 1B$ feed to the reactor is

$0.50T^{0.33}$ = lb moles A per hour
$0.25T^{0.33}$ = lb moles B per hour

and the flowsheet is given in Fig. 12.9F1.

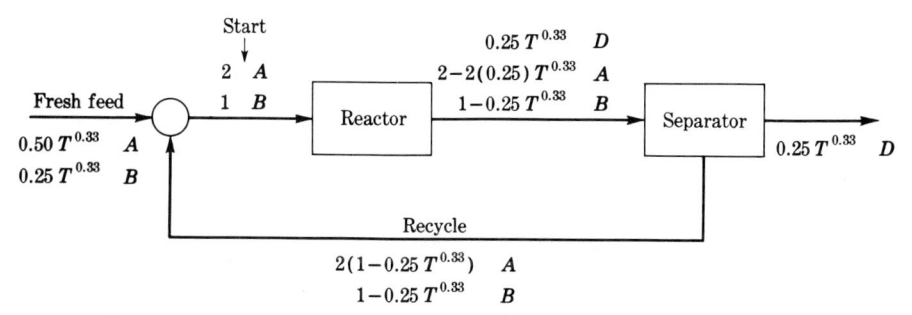

Fig. 12.9F1 Flow rates, pound moles per hour, basis $2A + 1B$ to reactor per hour.

If every flow is multiplied by $3/0.25T^{0.33}$, the pound moles per hour of D produced becomes 3, the desired rate. Figure 12.9F2 so prepared becomes the flowsheet for the process. The volume of feed to the reactors in cubic feet per hour is

$$\left(\frac{6}{0.25T^{0.33}} + \frac{3}{0.25T^{0.33}}\right)\frac{\text{lb moles}}{\text{hr}} \frac{1}{0.60 \text{ lb mole/cu ft}} = \frac{60}{T^{0.33}} \frac{\text{cu ft}}{\text{hr}}$$

The volume V of the reactor in cubic feet and the residence time are related by

$$T = \frac{V(\text{cu ft})}{\text{feed}(\text{cu ft/hr})}$$

so that by the last two relationships

$$V = \frac{60}{T^{0.33}} \frac{\text{cu ft}}{\text{hr}} T\frac{\text{hr}}{1} = 60T^{0.67} \quad \text{cu ft}$$

The cost of reactor basis unacost and item 1, Table 3.13T1, is

$$R = C_d[1 - tF_{SDP,10\%,4}]F_{PR,10\%,4}$$
$$= 2{,}500(60T^{0.67})[1 - 0.48(0.83013)]0.31547$$
$$= 28{,}465T^{0.67} \quad \text{\$ per year}$$

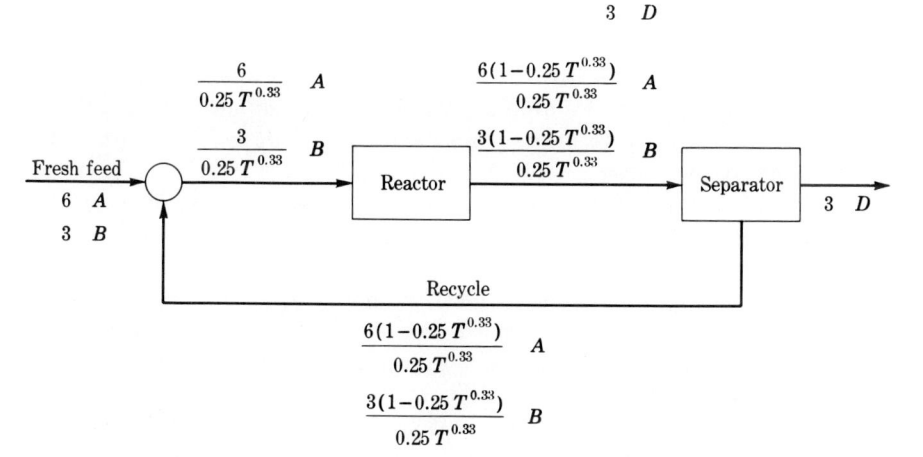

Fig. 12.9F2 Flow rates, pound moles per hour, basis 3 lb mole/hr for product D.

The amount of recycle per hour is

$$\frac{6(1 - 0.25T^{0.33})}{0.25T^{0.33}} + \frac{3(1 - 0.25T^{0.33})}{0.25T^{0.33}} = 36T^{-0.33} - 9 \quad \text{lb mole/hr}$$

Cost of separation, basis unacost and item 2, Table 3.13T2, and assuming end-of-year cost, is

$$R(1 - t) = (36T^{-0.33} - 9) \frac{\text{lb moles}}{\text{hr}} 4{,}000 \frac{\text{hr}}{\text{year}} 1.66 \frac{\$}{\text{lb mole}} (1 - 0.48)$$

$$= 124{,}300T^{-0.33} - 31{,}075 \quad \$ \text{ per year}$$

Total cost after taxes in dollars per year is

$$\$/\text{year} = 28{,}465T^{0.67} + 124{,}300T^{-0.33} - 31{,}075 \qquad (12.9\#2)$$

For minimum

$$\frac{d(\$/\text{year})}{dT} = 0 = 28{,}465(0.67)T^{-0.33} + 124{,}300(-0.33)T^{-1.33}$$

$$= 1 - 2.151T^{-1}$$

$$T = 2.151 \text{ hr} = \text{optimum retention time}$$

$$V = 60T^{0.67} = 60(2.151^{0.67}) = 100 \text{ cu ft} = \text{optimum reactor volume}$$

A plot of Eq. (12.9#2) will verify that a minimum value for dollars per year is actually obtained at $T = 2.151$ hr.

Although this process involves two steps, it can be resolved in terms of a single variable. Equation (12.9#2), of course, can be superseded by a relationship in terms of V as the independent variable. The example illustrates that problems in economic balance demand a good model and care in setting up the expression for the condition to be optimized. In particular the analyst must guard against errors in units and dimensions.

12.10 Variocyclic processes

Many processes are cyclic in nature or can be treated as such for convenience. In Example 12.7E1 concerned with drilling an oil well, the underlying physical relationship was

$$Q_c = 300T_d^{0.5}$$

where Q_c was cumulative feet drilled for a period of T_d days after installing a new drill bit. It was inherent in the problem that each cycle duplicated the others. In some cases, however, there are cycles within cycles. Repetitions within the cycle will be referred to as *rounds*. A cycle comprises a number of rounds. The rounds within a cycle show differences, but a cycle repeats the previous cycle. Such cycles are referred to as *variocyclic* processes to denote the variation of the rounds with a cycle.

Catalytic processes offer some excellent examples of a variocyclic process. Frequently a catalyst can be rejuvenated but becomes less efficient with each rejuvenation until finally it is discarded and the cycle is repeated with new catalyst. Figure 12.10F1 is a graph of the situation which shows a series of rounds to complete one cycle. There is a progressive degradation from round to round.

In practice the situation can be very complicated, for more than one variable is usually involved. The temperature of the catalyst can have a pronounced effect

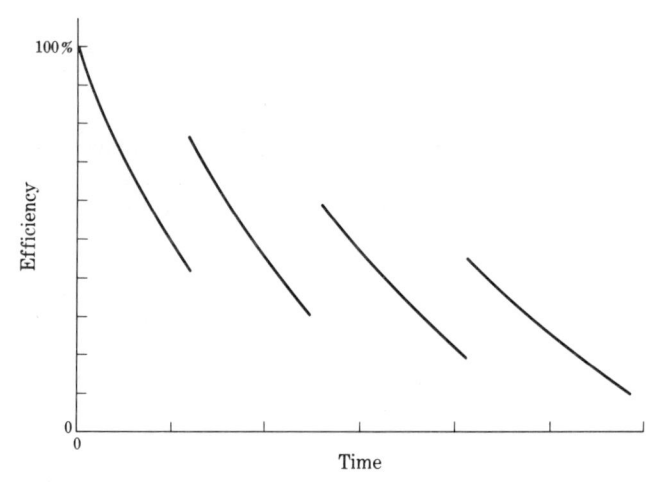

Fig. 12.10F1 Efficiency in a variocyclic process.

so that the optimization for time-temperature relationship for all the rounds can become exceedingly intricate. The problem is discussed here in only an elementary and simplified way. In variocyclic processes it is important that the analyst understand the significance and use of such terms as instantaneous rate, instantaneous efficiency, cumulative throughput, cumulative efficiency, average rate, and average efficiency. An average depends upon how the average is computed; e.g., an average with respect to time can be different from an average based on input.

If there is some systematic relationship between the rounds, an analytic solution is generally possible. Frequently tabular solutions are convenient, and they may be necessary if the data are in tabular form or if the variables are discrete. Dynamic programming can be used successfully in many cases.

Example 12.10E1 An absorbent clay is used to clarify a liquor. The clay costs $50 per ton and $25 for each activation including the first round. One ton of clay will treat 10,000 lb of liquor in the first round but diminishing to 85% of the previous round for subsequent rounds. How many rounds should the clay be used?

The calculation is shown in Table 12.10T1. If the clay is used for four rounds, a minimum cost of $0.00471 per pound treated is obtained.

Table 12.10T1 Optimum Use of Clay

Round	Treated, lb	Cumulative amount treated, lb	Catalyst cost, $	Activation cost, $	Total cost, $	Cumulative cost, $	Cumulative average, $ per pound
1	10,000	10,000	50	25	75	75	0.00750
2	8,500	18,500		25	25	100	0.00541
3	7,225	25,725		25	25	125	0.00486
4	6,141	31,866		25	25	150	0.00471
5	5,220	37,086		25	25	175	0.00472
6	4,436	41,523		25	25	200	0.00481

MULTIVARIABLE OPTIMIZATION

12.11 Analytical method

The same principles and methods that are useful for one independent variable apply to more than one independent variable but become much more complicated as the number of variables increases. Consider first the analytical method for some criterion W, a function of X and Y, which is to be optimized

$$W = F(X, Y) \tag{12.11#1}$$

For a mathematical optimum, two conditions must be met

$$\frac{\partial W}{\partial X} = 0 \tag{12.11#2}$$

$$\frac{\partial W}{\partial Y} = 0 \tag{12.11#3}$$

Generally each of these relationships involves X and Y; but there will be two equations with two unknowns, and sets of X, Y can be obtained. Each set is a possible optimum for W as given by Eq. (12.11#1).

An analytical test is available to establish whether a maximum or minimum exists. A maximum for W exists if the three following conditions are satisfied for the X, Y pair considered:

$$\frac{\partial^2 W}{\partial X^2} \text{ negative} \qquad \frac{\partial^2 W}{\partial Y^2} \text{ negative} \qquad \frac{\partial^2 W}{\partial X^2} \frac{\partial^2 W}{\partial Y^2} > \left(\frac{\partial^2 W}{\partial X \partial Y}\right)^2$$

Similarly there will be a minimum if

$$\frac{\partial^2 W}{\partial X^2} \text{ positive} \qquad \frac{\partial^2 W}{\partial Y^2} \text{ positive} \qquad \frac{\partial^2 W}{\partial X^2} \frac{\partial^2 W}{\partial Y^2} > \left(\frac{\partial^2 W}{\partial X \partial Y}\right)^2$$

In either case if

$$\frac{\partial^2 W}{\partial X^2} \frac{\partial^2 W}{\partial Y^2} < \left(\frac{\partial^2 W}{\partial X \partial Y}\right)^2$$

W is neither maximum nor minimum but a saddle point. If the last relationship is an identity, the nature of the point is inconclusive and further testing of higher-order derivatives is necessary.

If W is a function of three variables, X, Y, and Z

$$W = F(X, Y, Z)$$

the three following conditions are necessary, but not sufficient, for mathematical optima

$$\frac{\partial W}{\partial X} = 0 \qquad \frac{\partial W}{\partial Y} = 0 \qquad \frac{\partial W}{\partial Z} = 0$$

In general these will each contain X, Y, and Z, but the three equations in three unknowns can be solved for sets of X, Y, Z. The extension to four or more variables is obvious.

12.12 Graphical Method

A graphical method in the form of a three-dimensional space model can be used for two independent variables. For

$$W = F(X, Y) \qquad (12.12\#1)$$

X and Y can be measured in a horizontal plane and W measured by the perpendicular distance from the XY plane. In a complicated case the space model will appear like a mountain range. Inasmuch as space is limited to three dimensions, it is not possible to treat higher-order systems by this method.

There are techniques for simplifying multivariable systems which are explained here for the two-variable system of Eq. (12.12#1). Let Y be given a series of successive fixed values and replace the single relationship by a series of relationships

$$W_1 = F(X, Y_1)$$
$$W_2 = F(X, Y_2)$$
$$\dots\dots\dots\dots$$
$$W_N = F(X, Y_N)$$

which reduces the two-variable problem to a series of one-variable problems. If the range taken for Y is wide enough, it becomes possible to find the optimum W from a series of tabulations, augmented with a plot if desirable.

Such a plot is shown in Fig. 12.14F1, where a cost in dollars per year is plotted for two variables S and P. P is given successive fixed values, and the optimization for each is shown as a series of dotted curves. Connecting these incidental minima leads to the true minimum at $S = 1{,}049$, $P = 300$.

Another method involves calculating W for various points X, Y using only a two-dimensional plot and connecting points corresponding to equal values of W by contour curves. Such a plot resembles a typographical map. Details are given in Chap. 14.

12.13 Incremental method

The incremental method involves changing the independent variables singly or in groups. As the number of variables increases, considerable precaution must be exercised to avoid false conclusions. An increase in X alone may lower the value of W, the function to be optimized, yet the optimum may lie in the direction of increasing X and Y simultaneously. Chap. 14 should be consulted for details.

The incremental method with multivariables is suitable for trial by experiment including uncertainty as mentioned in Sec. 12.6 for one variable. For further study see Chap. 14.

12.14 A two-variable optimization example

Example 12.14E1 An electronic manufacturer prepares a plastic in a special batch reactor-mixer. The time required to process a mixture varies directly as the square root of the capacity of the mixer and inversely as the square of the power to the stirrer. Quantitatively

$$T = 1,000 \frac{S^{0.5}}{P^2} \qquad (12.14\#1)$$

Where T = total time required, hr/batch
S = capacity of reactor-mixer, lb
P = power to stirrer, kw

Cost for the reactor-mixer reduced to a yearly basis is

Cost of mixer ($ per year) = $316.2S^{0.5}$

Electricity costs $0.01 per kilowatt hour, and there is an overhead or indirect cost expressible in terms of the power requirement as follows:

Overhead ($ per year) = $34.3P$

The full year is available, and 10^7 lb/year must be processed. Time for loading and unloading the reactor-mixer is negligible. Find the optimum size and optimum stirrer power.

Set up an expression for cost basis 1-year operation.
Let N = number of batches per year.

$$S \frac{\text{lb}}{\text{batch}} \, N \frac{\text{batches}}{\text{year}} = 10^7 \frac{\text{lb}}{\text{year}}$$

$$N = \frac{10^7}{S} \qquad (12.14\#2)$$

$$\text{\$/year} = \underbrace{316.2S^{0.5}}_{\text{capitol}} + \underbrace{T \frac{\text{hr}}{\text{batch}} N \frac{\text{batches}}{\text{year}} P \frac{\text{kwhr}}{\text{hr}} 0.01 \frac{\$}{\text{kwhr}}}_{\text{electricity}} + \underbrace{34.3P}_{\text{overhead}}$$

Replace T by Eq. (12.14#1) and N by Eq. (12.14#2)

$$\text{\$/year} = 316.2S^{0.5} + \frac{1,000S^{0.5}}{P^2} \frac{10^7}{S} P(0.01) + 34.3P$$

$$= 316.2S^{0.5} + 10^8 P^{-1} S^{-0.5} + 34.3P \qquad (12.14\#3)$$

For minimum cost set partial derivatives of above expressions equal to zero

$$\frac{\partial(\text{\$/year})}{\partial S} = 0 = 0.5(316.2)S^{-0.5} - 10^8 P^{-1}(-0.5)S^{-1.5}$$

$$316.2PS = 10^8 \qquad (12.14\#4)$$

$$\frac{(\partial(\text{\$/year})}{\partial P} = 0 = -10^8 P^{-2} S^{-0.5} + 34.3$$

$$34.3 S^{0.5} P^2 = 10^8 \qquad (12.14\#5)$$

Solving Eqs. (12.14#4) and (12.14#5) simultaneously gives

$S = 1,049$ lb = capacity

$P = 300$ kw = power to stirrer

Check for feasibility.

$$T = 1,000 \frac{S^{0.5}}{P^2} = 1,000 \frac{1,049^{0.5}}{300^2} = 0.360 \text{ hr/batch}$$

Table 12.14T1. Yearly Cost for Example 12.14E1

S, lb	P, kw	Cost, $ per year	Δ cost, $ per year
1,049	300	30,823	
1,049	315	30,848	+25
1,049	285	30,851	+28
997	300	30,834	+11
997	315	30,843	+20
997	285	30,872	+49
1,101	300	30,828	+5
1,101	315	30,864	+41
1,101	285	30,842	+19

Using all the hours in a year, 8,760,

$$1{,}049 \,\frac{\text{lb}}{\text{batch}} \,\frac{8760 \text{ hr/year}}{0.360 \text{ hr/batch}} = 2.55 \times 10^7 \text{ lb/year possible}$$

so that 10^7 lb/year is feasible.

A check is given in Table 12.14T1, where increments of $\pm 5\%$ in S or P, or both simultaneously, are considered and the yearly cost is calculated from Eq. (12.14#3). Regardless of how S and P are varied, the cost increases over that for $S = 1{,}049$, $P = 300$. The cost is not very sensitive to S and P, however, and a 5% variation in each simultaneously adds only $49 per year to $30,823 per year. It will be noted further that the cost is more responsive to a change in P than a change in S, making the comparison on the same percentage change in each.

The example can be solved as a one-variable problem by placing successive fixed values for P in Eq. (12.14#3) and plotting the resulting curves. Figure 12.14F1 is such a plot confirming an overall minimum at $S = 1{,}049$ and $P = 300$.

12.15 Lagrange multipliers

A powerful method for finding mathematical optima in multivariable problems involving supplementary conditions that must be observed, called *restraints*, was introduced by the French mathematician Lagrange (1736–1813). Consider

$$W_1 = F_1(X,Y,Z) \qquad (12.15\#1)$$

subject to the two conditional relationships, or restraints,

$$F_2(X,Y,Z) = 0 \qquad (12.15\#2)$$
$$F_3(X,Y,Z) = 0 \qquad (12.15\#3)$$

In an ideal situation the last two relationships can be used to eliminate, say, Y and Z from Eq. (12.15#1) leaving a relationship for W in terms of X only. This may not be possible, however, in an actual case. Lagrange's method is applicable to the general case and may make an analytical solution possible.

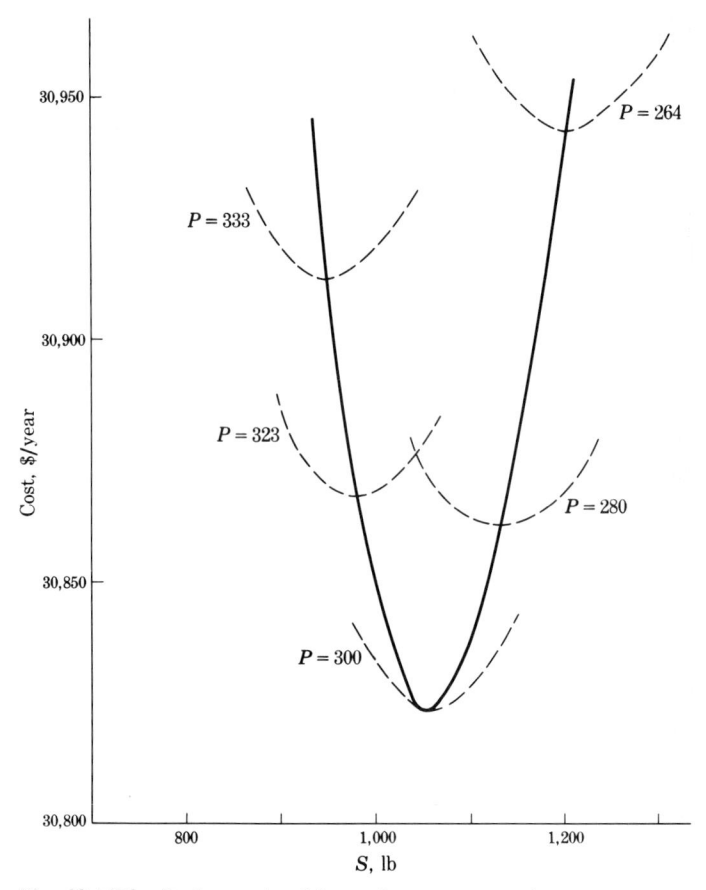

Fig. 12.14F1 Optimum size S for various power to stirrer P.

The method in application requires forming a new function, called the Lagrange expression, made up by linear addition of the original relationship and each restraint relationship multiplied by a Lagrange multiplier. There are as many multipliers as there are restraints. The Lagrange expression for the problem at hand is

$$\text{LE} = F_1(X,Y,Z) + \lambda_1 F_2(X,Y,Z) + \lambda_2 F_3(X,Y,Z) \tag{12.15\#4}$$

and the optima for Eq. (12.15#1) are the optima of the Lagrange expression. Equation (12.15#4) includes the three original variables X, Y, Z and the two Lagrange multipliers, λ_1 and λ_2. Five relationships must be satisfied to find the optima for the Lagrange expression in this case

$$\frac{\partial \text{LE}}{\partial X} = 0 \quad \frac{\partial \text{LE}}{\partial Y} = 0 \quad \frac{\partial \text{LE}}{\partial Z} = 0 \quad \frac{\partial \text{LE}}{\partial \lambda_1} = 0 \quad \frac{\partial \text{LE}}{\partial \lambda_2} = 0$$

whereas only three are necessary to find the optima for Eq. (12.15#1)

$$\frac{\partial W_1}{\partial X} = 0 \quad \frac{\partial W_1}{\partial Y} = 0 \quad \frac{\partial W_1}{\partial Z} = 0$$

Nevertheless the Lagrange expression with its five relationships has the constraints built in and may be much easier to solve than Eq. (12.15#1) subject to the restraint equations (12.15#2) and (12.15#3).

For an example return to Example 12.7E1 part (a), which has already been optimized. The requirement is to minimize

$$\text{\$ per month} = NT_d(4{,}250) + 10{,}500N \qquad (12.15\#5)$$

subject to the condition or restraint

$$N = 6.667 T_d^{-0.5} \qquad (12.15\#6)$$

Write the restraint frunction as

$$N - 6.667 T_d^{-0.5} = 0$$

The Lagrange expression becomes

$$\text{LE} = NT_d(4{,}250) + 10{,}500N + \lambda(N - 6.667 T_d^{-0.5}) = 0$$

Set the three partial derivatives equal to zero

$$\frac{\partial \text{LE}}{\partial N} = 0 = 4{,}250 T_d + 10{,}500 + \lambda = 0$$

$$\frac{\partial \text{LE}}{\partial T_d} = 0 = 4{,}250 N - \lambda(6.667)(-0.5) T_d^{-1.5} = 0$$

$$\frac{\partial \text{LE}}{\partial \lambda} = N - 6.667 T_d^{-0.5} = 0$$

Solving the three equations for N, T_d, and λ gives

$$N = 4.241 \text{ cycles/month}$$
$$T_d = 2.471 \text{ hr drilling/cycle}$$
$$\lambda = -21{,}000$$

The values for N and T_d check those previously found.

In this example the use of Lagrange multipliers was not as direct as using Eq. (12.15#6) in Eq. (12.15#5) to reduce the latter to an equation in one independent variable. Nevertheless the use of Lagrange multipliers can lead to a solution that otherwise would not be obtained. On the other hand, the use of Lagrange multipliers does not always produce expressions that are solvable by analytical means.

12.16 Sensitivity and response analysis

In a detailed analysis it is desirable to know the optimum and also how sensitive the optimum is to changes in various parameters that make up the problem. For example, suppose Y is expressed by the relationship

$$Y = AX + \frac{B}{X} \qquad (12.16\#1)$$

252 OPTIMIZATION

where X is the independent variable and A and B are parameters. In a given problem A and B may be constant, but they may be subject to change in practice. For example, A and B may be estimates and it becomes desirable to know how much Y_{opt} is changed by changes in the estimates of A and B. What is desired mathematically is

$$\frac{\partial T_{opt}}{\partial A} \quad \text{and} \quad \frac{\partial Y_{opt}}{\partial B}$$

The determination of such values is called *sensitivity analysis*.

An analytical solution is easily obtained for the relationship Eq. (12.16#1). For Y_{opt}

$$\frac{dY}{dX} = 0 = A - \frac{B}{X^2} \quad \text{and} \quad X_{opt} = A^{-0.5}B^{0.5}$$

which substituted in Eq. (12.16#1) gives

$$Y_{opt} = 2A^{0.5}B^{0.5}$$

and leads directly to the relationships

$$\frac{\partial Y_{opt}}{\partial A} = A^{-0.5}B^{0.5} \quad \frac{\partial Y_{opt}}{\partial B} = A^{0.5}B^{-0.5}$$

For the specific case for $A = 10$, $B = 40$

$$\frac{\partial Y_{opt}}{\partial A} = \sqrt{\frac{40}{10}} = 2$$

The value can be obtained in another way which is particularly useful if the analytical method is too involved or even not available. The procedure is to start with Eq. (12.16#1) or graphical or tabular data and for $A = 10$ and $B = 40$ find Y optimum. This is found to be

$$Y_{opt} = 40 \quad A = 10$$
$$B = 40$$

Next repeat the calculation for, say, $A = 10.1$, $B = 40$. Y_{opt} is found to be

$$Y_{opt} = 40.1995 \quad A = 10.1$$
$$B = 40$$

From the last two relationships

$$\frac{\Delta Y_{opt}}{\Delta A} = \frac{40.1995 - 40.000}{10.1 - 10} = 1.995$$

Thus a sensitivity analysis can be made even if analytical expressions are unwieldy or unavailable. A sensitivity analysis is also made in the same manner if there is more than one independent variable.

The sensitivity analysis as such cannot be applied to the independent variable. Thus for the case under study

$$\frac{\partial Y_{\text{opt}}}{\partial X} = 0$$

That is, Y_{opt} is determined by A and B and not X. However, it is possible to evaluate the change in Y as a consequence of not operating at the optimum X. This is

$$\frac{Y - Y_{\text{opt}}}{X - X_{\text{opt}}} = \frac{\Delta Y}{\Delta X}$$

and X can be taken as, say, a 1% change. The procedure can be called a *response analysis* to avoid confusion with a true sensitivity analysis. The reader should refer to Table 12.14T1, which was essentially a response analysis for a reactor-mixer having independent variables S and P.

12.17 Simplification of multivariable problems

Optimization in the fields of economic balance can become exceedingly complicated because the problems can be intricately involved with physical, engineering, and cost considerations. This chapter was concerned with general methods, but the analyst must acquire the facility of representing engineering systems in terms of real models, either mathematical or empirical.

As the number of variables mounts, the complexity and scope of the problem increases disproportionately; hence every effort should be made to reduce the number of variables. This can be done by taking fixed values for some variables, particularly if practical considerations will limit the range. If a single value is too restricted, the study might be limited to a few values. Complicated expressions can sometimes be replaced with simpler expressions which might be satisfactory. Thus a linear expression might replace a quadratic expression for which the curvature is small in the feasible range.

As the number of variables and parameters increases and the number of constraints and practical limitations grows larger, the optimum has a propensity to grow flatter with less likelihood that the realizable optimum will be a mathematical optimum. The tendency towards flatness is real in practical large-scale problems. This does not signify that a problem can be slighted but does portend that some optimization should be considered in deciding upon how much detail a particular problem merits.

Finally, optimization is a continuous study, and old problems take on a fresh challenge as technology, economics, and society change.

12.18 Nomenclature

A Parameter as in Eq. (12.16#1)
B Parameter as in Eq. (12.16#1)
C_d Depreciable cost, $

254 OPTIMIZATION

F_{SDP} Present worth of $1 for sum-of-digits depreciation, decimal
F_{PR} Factor to convert a present worth to a unacost, year^{-1}
LE Lagrange expression
N Cycles/month in Example 12.7E1; batches/year in Example 12.14E1
P Power to stirrer in Example 12.14E1, kw
Q_c Cumulative feet drilled from start of cycle in Example 12.7E1
r Rate of return after taxes, decimal/year
r Conversion rate, moles D formed per mole B, in Example 12.9E1; depends on residence time
R Unacost, uniform end-of-year amount, $ per year
R_v Revenue, end-of-year, in Example 12.8E1, $ per year
S Capacity of reactor-mixer in Example 12.14E1, lb
t Tax rate, decimal
T Residence time in reactor in Example 12.9E1, hr
T Total time required per batch in Example 12.14E1, hr
T_d Drilling time from start of cycle in Example 12.7E1, days
V Volume of reactor in Example 12.9E1, cu ft
W Dependent variable
Y Independent variable, generally
Y $(1 - 0.48F_{SDP,r,25})F_{PR,r,25}$ in Example 12.8E1
λ Lagrange multiplier

12.19 Problems

P1. A causeway is to be built over a long swamp. If X is the distance between piers, for the range $40 \leq X \leq 200$ the following cost data apply:

$$2X^2 = \text{\$ per pier}$$
$$2{,}000X^{-1/2} = \text{\$ per foot, span between piers}$$

Find the optimum distance between piers for minimum cost.

P2. The cost to produce electric energy in a unit rated at 20,000 kw is defined by the relationship

$$Y = 12 + 0.2X + 0.27X^2$$

where Y = cost, per hour

X = load generated, Mw

Income from sale of electricity expressed in dollars per hour is

$$16X - 0.2X^2$$

Find the generated load that gives the maximum profit.

P3. The fixed cost for a steam line per foot of pipe is

$$3X + 6 \quad \text{\$ per year}$$

and cost for loss of heat from the pipe per foot of pipe is

$$\frac{21}{X} \quad \text{\$ per year}$$

where X is the thickness of insulation in inches. Find the optimum thickness of insulation.

P4. A commercial location makes a study to predict added gross income in dollars per year for investment in additional parking space. The survey predicts:

Invested in parking lot, $M	Added to gross income, $M per year	Invested in parking lot, $M	Added to gross income, $M per year
18	48	153	153
36	69	189	165
54	90	225	174
75	111	270	183
99	126	315	192
126	141		

Added net income can be taken as 33.3% of added gross income. Use the incremental method and find how much should be invested in additional parking-lot space if the return on investment is 17% or more.

P5. A heat-treating furnace must process 1 million machine parts per year. The furnace can process only one batch per 8-hr shift for one shift per day for a maximum of 250 days per year. Cost of furnaces is

$$25X^{0.7} \quad \text{\$ per year}$$

where X is the number of machine parts processed per batch. Operating costs for the furnace is $200 per shift.

Find the optimum size furnace to be installed.

P6. Repeat Prob. 12.19P5, now letting furnacing time be dependent on the furnace size and be given by

$$0.04X^{0.5} \quad \text{hr}$$

The operating cost is $104 fixed cost per batch and $12 per hour for labor. A shift can run over 8 hr, but only 1 shift per day for 250 days per year maximum is allowed.

P7. In certain operations it is necessary to provide one spare unit to ensure continuity of operations at full capacity when one machine is being overhauled. If the cost of machines varies as the 0.8 power of capacity, find the optimum number of units, including the spare, that should be provided.

P8. A pressure vessel is to be made from a cylinder of diameter X ft capped with a hemisphere at each end. Cost for the cylindrical section is

$$300X^{1.2} \quad \text{\$ per foot of length}$$

and cost for one hemispherical end is

$$80X^{2.4} \quad \text{\$}$$

The vessel is to hold 10,000 gal, 1,377 cu ft.

Find the optimum dimensions and cost.

P9. A chemical is produced by a batch process. Chemicals X and Y are used to make Z with the following relationship for the pounds Z produced and the pounds of X and Y supplied:

$$Z = 1.5(1.1XZ + 1.3YZ - XY)^{0.5}$$

X costs $0.09 per pound, Y $0.04 per pound, and Z sells for $0.80 per pound. One-half of the selling price for Z is due to costs other than raw materials. Only Z is recovered from the process. Find the maximum profit obtainable per pound of Z.

P10. Suppose that 86,000 lb of water per day for 300 days per year is to be evaporated from a salt solution. One pound of steam will evaporate $0.7N$ lb water, where N is the number of effects.

256   OPTIMIZATION   12.19

Steam costs $0.50 per 1,000 lb. Cost of the first effect is $15,000, and each additional effect costs $12,000, to be written off over a 10-year period. Repairs, taxes, and insurance cost 10% of the first cost per year. Other costs may be neglected as they are independent of the number of effects.

If the charge for the use of capital is 13.8% per year based on initial investment, find the optimum number of effects.

P11. An evaporator shows the following variation of U, the overall heat-transfer coefficient in Btu/(hr)(sq ft)(°F), with time T in hours measured from starting time with clean tubes:

$$\frac{1}{U^2} = 0.21(10^{-6})T + 2.6(10^{-6})$$

A cleanout costs $66 and requires 16 hr downtime. The allocable operating cost is $3 per hour; 50 tons a day for 250 days of the year is to be evaporated from 3,000-sq-ft area. The latent heat of evaporation is 1,000 Btu/lb, and the driving force is 50°F temperature difference.

Find the optimum time for operation before recleaning.

P12. Jewels, along with recycled jewels, are polished in a special machine for the space project. The retention time in the polisher is inversely proportional to the number of jewels fed per hour and is 1 hr when 1,000 per hour are fed.

The fraction of acceptable jewels produced is $1 - e^{-0.5T}$, where T is the retention time in hours. The acceptable and reject jewels are separated in a separator. Rejected jewels are returned by way of the recycle stream to the polisher, where they perform like raw jewels.

It costs $1,000 per hour to operate the polisher. Cost of operating the separator is proportional to the number of rejects fed per hour and is $2 per hour for one reject per hour. Acceptable jewels sell for $10 each above the cost of raw jewels.

Find (a) the maximum profit per hour and (b) the number of acceptable jewels produced per hour under maximum profit per hour conditions.

P13. A catalytic process uses a catalyst which must be regenerated periodically because of reduction in conversion efficiency. The cost data are

One regeneration = $800

Feed = $2.50 per pound

Operation = $300 per day

Value of product = $14 per pound

Overhead = $100,000 per year

The feed rate is maintained constant at 150 lb/day.

The efficiency of the catalyst expressed as pounds of product to pounds of feed is

0.87 average $0 \leq T = 1$

$\dfrac{0.87}{T^{0.52}}$ instantaneous $T > 1$

where T is the time in days from the last regeneration.

Assuming that no other costs are involved, find the maximum annual profit that can be obtained.

P14. Show how you would obtain the average efficiency in a variocyclic process such as from the graph of Fig. 12.10F1. Does it matter if the input to the equipment is not constant?

P15. An evaporator scales and tests show that the steam condensed in the heating tubes varies with time according to the relationship

$S = A(10 - 0.10T)$ $T < 1,000$

where S = condensation rate, lb/hr

A = heating area, sq ft

T = evaporating time, hr, since last clean-out

The evaporation will evaporate 0.9 lb of water per pound of steam condensed. Cost of evaporators is $38.75 per square foot written off over a 10-year life. Allocable labor cost is $3 per hour of operation. Each cleaning costs $500; 10 million pounds of water is to be evaporated per year, and operating time is not to exceed 6,000 hr/year.

(a) Find the optimum evaporating time per cycle before recleaning the tubes.

(b) Find the optimum heating area to be installed.

P16. Maximize the product XY subject to the restraint that X and Y lie on a circle of radius 5; that is, $X^2 + Y^2 = 5^2$.

(a) Use ordinary methods of the calculus.

(b) Use the Lagrange multiplier method.

P17. From the Lagrange expression find the values of X, Y, and Z that minimize the function $X + 2Y^2 + Z^2$ subject to the constraint that $X + Y + Z = 1$.

P18. For the expression

$$Y = AX^2 - ABX + \frac{BC}{X^2}$$

verify that for $A = B = C = 2$, Y has a minimum value at $X = 1.54$. Find which parameter, A, B, or C, has the greatest effect on the minimum value of Y for the conditions given.

12.20 References

R1. Boas, A. H.: How to Use Lagrange Multipliers, *Chem. Eng.*, Jan. 7, 1963, pp. 95–98.

R2. Fan, L. T.: "The Continuous Maximum Principle," John Wiley & Sons, Inc., New York, 1966.

R3. Gessner, A. W.: Incremental Return Gives Economic Optimization, *Chem. Eng.*, May 25, 1964, p. 150.

R4. Himsworth, F. R.: Empirical Methods of Optimisation, *Trans. Inst. Chem. Engrs. (London).*, vol. 40, p. 345, 1962.

R5. Iscol, L.: How to Solve Optimization Problems, *Chem. Eng.*, Feb. 19, 1962, pp. 107–116.

R6. Kermode, R. I., Geometric Programming: A Simple, Efficient Optimization Technique, *Chem. Eng.*, Dec. 18, 1967, pp. 97–100.

R7. Lapidus, L. E., E. Shapiro, S. Shapiro, and R. E. Stillman: Optimization of Process Performance, *AIChE J*, vol. 7, p. 288, February, 1961.

R8. Lavi, A., and T. P. Vogl, (eds.): Recent Advances in Optimization Techniques," John Wiley & Sons, Inc., New York, 1966.

R9. Neuwirth, S. I., and L. M. Naphtali: New Statistical Method Rapidly Determines Optimum Conditions, *Chem. Eng.*, June, 1957, p. 238.

R10. Peters, M. S., and K. D. Timmerhaus: "Plant Design and Economics for Chemical Engineers," 2d ed., McGraw-Hill Book Company, New York, 1968.

R11. Schweyer, H. E.: "Process Engineering Economics," McGraw-Hill Book Company, New York, 1955.

R12. Taborek, J. J.: Optimization in Process Equipment Design, *Chem. Eng. Progr.*, vol. 56, p. 37, August, 1960.

R13. Tao, L. C.: Process Optimization, *Chem. Eng.*, April 26, 1965, pp. 143–148.

R14. Trombetta, M. L.: Optimum Design of Chemical Processes: Variational Methods, *Chem. Eng. Progr. Symp. Ser.*, vol. 61, no. 55, p. 42, 1965.

R15. Wilde, D. J., and C. S. Beightler: "Foundations of Optimization," Prentice-Hall, Inc., Englewood Cliffs, N.J., 1967.

13
Linear and Dynamic Programming

A. H. Boas

LINEAR PROGRAMMING (LP)

13.1 Optimization of an objective function

Linear programming is a mathematical tool for finding the optimum solution to a certain class of problems. The word *linear* implies that the relations involved will be linear, while the term *programming*, in the context used here, means *planning* of activities. The concern will be with planning of activities of problems in an optimal manner for which the mathematical relations involved are linear.

In any type of optimization problem, linear or nonlinear, the problem can be represented as indicated in Fig. 13.1F1. The black box constitutes the mathematical model, i.e., relations that describe some physical situation. The input to the black box is composed of two quantities, fixed and variable. The fixed quantities are those which are inherent in the problem; the formulator has no control over these. On the other hand, the variable inputs are the unknowns in the problem; the values of these variables determine the optimum solution to the problem. Hence, the interest is in the values of the variables that will give the optimum value to a term called the *objective function*, which is the output from the black box.

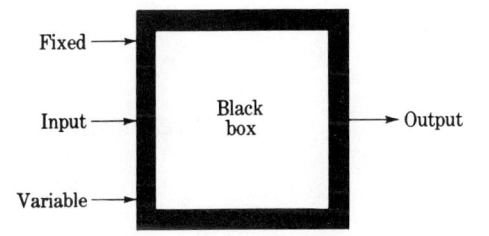

Fig. 13.1F1 A mathematical model.

Example 13.1E Given a set of values of X_i and Y_i. Assume that the relationship to be curve-fitted takes the form

$$Y = AX^B + C \ln X \tag{13.1\#1}$$

It is required to find the best values of A, B, and C by least squares. What are the fixed and variable inputs? What form does the objective function take?

A set of X_i and the corresponding Y_i is given:

i	X_i	Y_i
1	X_1	Y_1
2	X_2	Y_2
...	...	...
n	X_n	Y_n

According to the criterion of least squares, the following equation is defined:

$$F = \sum_{i=1}^{n} (Y_{i,\text{calc}} - Y_{i,\text{obs}})^2 \tag{13.1\#2}$$

$Y_{i,\text{calc}}$ = calculated value of Y by Eq. (13.1#1)

where

$Y_{i,\text{obs}}$ = observed value of Y, for corresponding X

Now

$$Y_{i,\text{calc}} = A(X_i)^B + C \ln X_i \tag{13.1\#3}$$

therefore

$$F = \sum_{i=1}^{n} [A(X_i)^B + C \ln X_i - Y_{i,\text{obs}}]^2 \tag{13.1\#4}$$

The fixed input would be the values of X_i and Y_i which are given. The variable input would be the values of A, B, and C. The objective function is given by F in Eq. (13.1#4). The problem is therefore to find a set of values of A, B, and C that minimizes the value of the objective function F. This example was purposely chosen to illustrate the fact that Fig. 13.1F1 applies to nonlinear as well as linear problems.

13.2 Development of linear-programming equations

Define each of the variable inputs by X_j and assume that there are n of them. These variables are also called *activity levels*. In LP problems a restriction that is imposed on these variables is that they be nonnegative; i.e.,

$$X_i \geq 0 \qquad (13.2\#1)$$

The objective function, the output from the black box, will be called Z and defined as

$$Z = C_1 X_2 + C_2 X_2 + \cdots + C_n X_n \qquad (13.2\#2)$$

where the C_j values, $j = 1, 2, \ldots, n$, are unit costs. Associated with each variable X_j is a cost coefficient C_j, which may be zero, positive, or negative. Some examples of C_j values are:

X_j	C_j	$C_j X_j$
lb/hr	$/lb	$/hr
Btu/hr	$/Btu	$/hr
man-hr/hr	$/man-hr	$/hr

In each case, the product of X_j and C_j represents a cost in dollars per hour. These may be added together to represent the total cost, in dollars per hour, and could therefore represent a meaningful objective function. Mathematically, the objective function may be represented as

$$Z = \sum_{j=1}^{n} C_j X_j \qquad (13.2\#3)$$

Note that this equation is linear, as required in LP models.

The mathematical model itself may be represented as

$$A_{11}X_1 + A_{12}X_2 + \cdots + A_{1j}X_j + \cdots + A_{1n}X_n = B_1 \qquad (13.2\#4)$$

$$A_{21}X_1 + A_{22}X_2 + \cdots + A_{2j}X_j + \cdots + A_{2n}X_n = B_2 \qquad (13.2\#5)$$

$$\cdots\cdots\cdots\cdots\cdots\cdots\cdots\cdots\cdots\cdots\cdots\cdots\cdots\cdots\cdots$$

$$A_{i1}X_1 + A_{i2}X_2 + \cdots + A_{ij}X_j + \cdots + A_{in}X_n = B_i \qquad (13.2\#6)$$

$$\cdots\cdots\cdots\cdots\cdots\cdots\cdots\cdots\cdots\cdots\cdots\cdots\cdots\cdots\cdots$$

$$A_{m1}X_1 + A_{m2}X_2 + \cdots + A_{mj}X_j + \cdots + A_{mn}X_n = B_m \qquad (13.2\#7)$$

Each equation in a LP model takes this form. An equation in LP is called a *row* or *constraint*. The B_i values are right-hand sides. Let us look at these equations more closely. It will be noted that in Eq. (13.2#4) each constant multiplier A_{ij} has a value of $i = 1$. This indicates that we are dealing with the first row, or equation, of the model. Any variable in Eq. (13.2#4), X_j, has a coefficient A_{1j} associated with it. For example, X_3 has the constant A_{13}, X_{46} the constant $A_{1,46}$ etc.

In the general row i, each coefficient has i as its first subscript. The general value X_j in the general row i has the general multiplier A_{ij}, which may be zero,

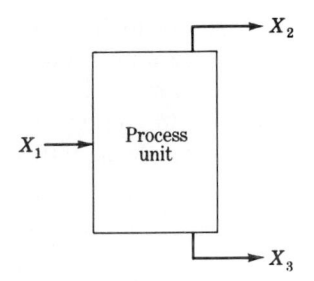

Fig. 13.2F1 A process unit.

positive, or negative. Equations (13.2#4) to (13.2#7) can be expressed mathematically

$$\sum_{j=1}^{n} A_{ij}X_j = B_i \qquad i = 1, 2, \ldots, m \tag{13.2#8}$$

Consider now some examples of constraint equations. A process unit in a chemical plant is shown in Fig. 13.2F1, where X_1, X_2, and X_3 are all in pounds per hour. There is no accumulation or origination within the unit, and a material balance around the unit gives

$$X_1 = X_2 + X_3 \tag{13.2#9}$$

In order to transform this equation into standard LP form, all the variables are transposed to the left side of the equation,

$$X_1 - X_2 - X_3 = 0 \tag{13.2#10}$$

Assume that this is the first equation of the model. Comparing Eq. (13.2#10) with Eq. (13.2#4), it is seen that

$$n = 3: \quad A_{11} = 1 \quad A_{12} = -1 \quad A_{13} = -1 \quad B_1 = 0$$

Let H_1, H_2, and H_3 be unit enthalpies in Btu per pound for streams 1, 2, and 3, respectively. No external heat is involved, and a heat balance around the same process unit gives

$$H_1 X_1 = H_2 X_2 + H_3 X_3$$

or in standard LP form

$$H_1 X_1 - H_2 X_2 - H_3 X_3 = 0$$

Assume that this is the second equation of the LP model. Then

$$n = 3: \quad A_{21} = H_1 \quad A_{22} = -H_2 \quad A_{23} = -H_3 \quad B_2 = 0$$

13.3 Slack variables

Referring to Fig. 13.2F1, suppose that the process unit can handle a maximum of 100 lb/hr of stream 1. Mathematically,

$$X_1 \leq 100 \tag{13.3#1}$$

It is necessary to express this fact within the LP model. Any solution to the problem which violates this capacity limit is not a valid solution because the process unit cannot physically handle such a quantity of stream 1. Equation (13.3#1) is not in the form of a linear equation, and it becomes necessary to convert the inequality equation to an equality relationship. This is done through the introduction of a *slack variable*. Express Eq. (13.3#1) as

$$X_1 + X_4 = 100 \qquad (13.3\#2)$$

The variable X_4, the slack variable, is treated like any other variable with the restriction of nonnegativity imposed on it. When X_4 assumes its minimum value of 0, then X_1 is equal to 100 and the unit is running at full capacity. The slack is equal to zero. For any other value of $X_4 \leq 100$ this indicates the slack, or unused capacity. For example, $X_4 = 35$, $X_1 = 65$ indicates that the feed rate to the unit is 65 lb/hr and the unused capacity is 35 lb/hr.

Referring to Fig. 13.2F1 again, suppose the following inequality appears

$$X_2 \geq 10 \qquad (13.3\#3)$$

This equation states that X_2 must equal *at least* 10 lb/hr. In a manner similar to the foregoing illustration, a *negative* slack variable X_5 is introduced, so that Eq. (13.3#3) becomes

$$X_2 - X_5 = 10 \qquad (13.3\#4)$$

The slack variable X_5 must meet the nonnegativity restriction, of course. Thus, a method is available of converting inequalities to equalities and satisfying the form of the standard LP constraint equations.

13.4 Quality constraints

Another type of constraint encountered in LP work is the *quality* constraint. Normally, some type of specification or quality of product must be met. As an example, let us consider the blending of gasoline components to meet a certain octane number. The assumption of linear blending will be made so that the following relation holds:

$$Q = \frac{X_1 Q_1 + X_2 Q_2 + X_3 Q_3}{X_1 + X_2 + X_3} \qquad (13.4\#1)$$

where X_i = quantity of blending stock i, bbl
Q_i = quality of ith blending stock, octane numbers/bbl

Equation (13.4#1) then represents the octane number of a three-component mixture. In general

$$Q = \frac{\sum X_i Q_i}{\sum X_i} \qquad (13.4\#2)$$

Example 13.4E1 Three components with respective octane numbers 108, 93, and 100 are to be linearly blended such that the final octane number of the mixture is at least 98. Express this condition as a standard equation in an LP model.

The final octane number of the mixture can be obtained from Eq. (13.4#1), and it must be a minimum of 98. That is

$$\frac{108X_1 + 93X_2 + 100X_3}{X_1 + X_2 + X_3} \geq 98$$

or

$$108X_1 + 93X_2 + 100X_3 \geq 98X_1 + 98X_2 + 98X_3$$

or

$$10X_1 - 5X_2 + 2X_3 \geq 0$$

Introducing the slack variable X_4, the required relationship is

$$10X_1 - 5X_2 + 2X_3 - X_4 = 0$$

which is in standard LP form and can be used as one of the equations in the model to represent the quality constraint on octane blending.

13.5 Method of solution

Refer back to Fig. 13.1F1 and identify the various inputs and outputs to a standard LP problem. The fixed inputs would be all the constants in the problem, A_{ij}, B_i, and C_j; the variables would be the X_j values. The model within the black box would be all the constraint equations, given by Eq. (13.2#8). The output from the black box is represented by the objective function, Eq. (13.2#3). Figure 13.5F1 is a representation of the standard LP problem.

The formulation of the problem, the variables, the constraint equations, and the objective function have all been discussed. The problem of finding the optimal solution remains. Examine the constraint Eqs. (13.2#8). Where the number of variables n is equal to the number of equations m, one can solve this set of independent linear equations. One unique solution will be obtained. There is no problem in optimization here because there is only one solution. The values obtained for the variables from the constraint equations are substituted in the equation for the objective function, and the solution is obtained immediately.

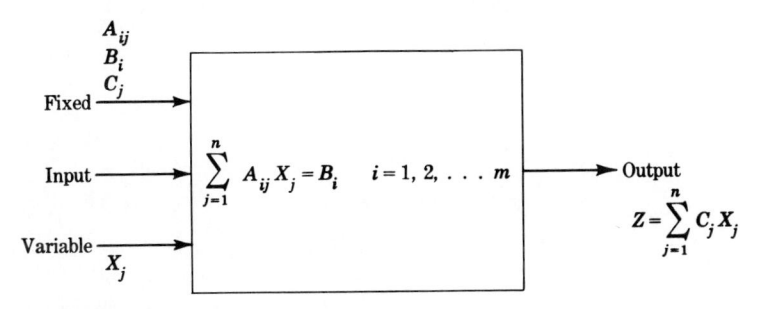

Fig. 13.5F1 Linear-programming model.

264 OPTIMIZATION 13.5

It is when there are more variables than equations, that is $n > m$, that a problem arises. Now, there is not one unique solution but an infinite number of solutions. From all these solutions, it is desired to find that one which optimizes the objective function.

The method used is to set $n - m$ variables equal to zero, i.e., the excess number of variables. Then there will be m variables left and m equations to solve. For example, if $n = 23$ variables and $m = 10$ equations, set $23 - 10$, or 13, variables equal to zero and solve the 10 equations for the 10 unknowns. The object is to determine which variables to set equal to zero. By examining every possible way of selecting $n - m$ variables from n variables, setting these equal to zero, and solving for the m remaining variables, it can be shown that the optimum solution lies among these many solutions [13.14R3].

The $n - m$ variables set equal to zero are called *nonbasic variables*; the remaining m variables are known as *basic variables*, and the collection of them is called a *basis*. The solution of the equations involving the basic variables is termed a *basic solution*. If the values of the basic variables are nonnegative and do not violate any of the constraint equations, the solution is called a *basic feasible solution*. The optimal solution is to be found among the basic feasible solutions. Therefore, once a basic feasible solution is obtained, the object is to find a more optimal solution. This process is continued until a point is reached at which no further improvement is possible.

Example 13.5E1 A production facility manufactures two products, A and B. Each product must pass through a bank of type 1 machines and a bank of type 2 machines serially, as shown in Fig. 13.5F2. Each bank consists of many machines of its particular type. Product A requires 2 hr on type 1 machines and 1 hr on a type 2 machine, while product B requires 1 hr on type 1 and 4 hr on type 2 machines. The total time available per week on machines of type 1 is 6,000 hr, while the time available for type 2 machines is 10,000 hr. The net profit is \$5 per unit of product B and \$3.5 per unit of product A. Find the optimal solution, the production schedule which will maximize profit per week.

First, present all the data in tabular form.

Machine type	Time required, hr — Product A	Time required, hr — Product B	Maximum hr/week
1	2	1	6,000
2	1	4	10,000
Profit, $ per unit	3.5	5.0	

The first task is to represent all the data in the form of standard LP equations. Let X_1 be the quantity of product A produced per week, and X_2 correspondingly will be the quantity of product B produced per week. For each unit of product A, $2X_1$ hr will be required on type 1 machines; similarly, X_2 hours will be required on type 1 machines for product B. The total time required on type 1 machines is $2X_1 + X_2$, and the maximum

13.5 LINEAR AND DYNAMIC PROGRAMMING

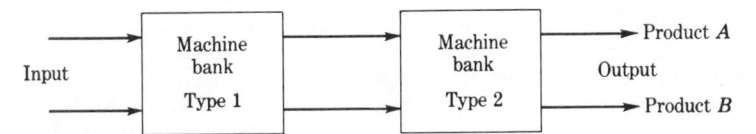

[Diagram: Input → Machine bank Type 1 → Machine bank Type 2 → Output → Product A, Product B]

Fig. 13.5F2 Model for Example 13.5E1.

weekly time is 6,000 hr; hence

$$2X_1 + X_2 \leq 6{,}000 \tag{13.5\#1}$$

which becomes upon introduction of slack variable X_3

$$2X_1 + X_2 + X_3 = 6{,}000 \tag{13.5\#2}$$

Similarly, for type 2 machine with slack variable X_4

$$X_1 + 4X_2 + X_4 = 10{,}000 \tag{13.5\#3}$$

Equations (13.5#2) and (13.5#3) are the constraint equations of the LP model. The variables are X_1, X_2, X_3, and X_4. It remains to define the objective function and solve the problem. Based on the unit profit figures, the objective function is

$$Z = 3.5X_1 + 5X_2 \tag{13.5\#4}$$

At this point it might be instructive to see a geometric interpretation of the problem. Equation (13.5#1) is plotted in Fig. 13.5F3 as line BD. Any point (X_1, X_2) that lies above this line violates the constraint on maximum available time on machine type 1. The

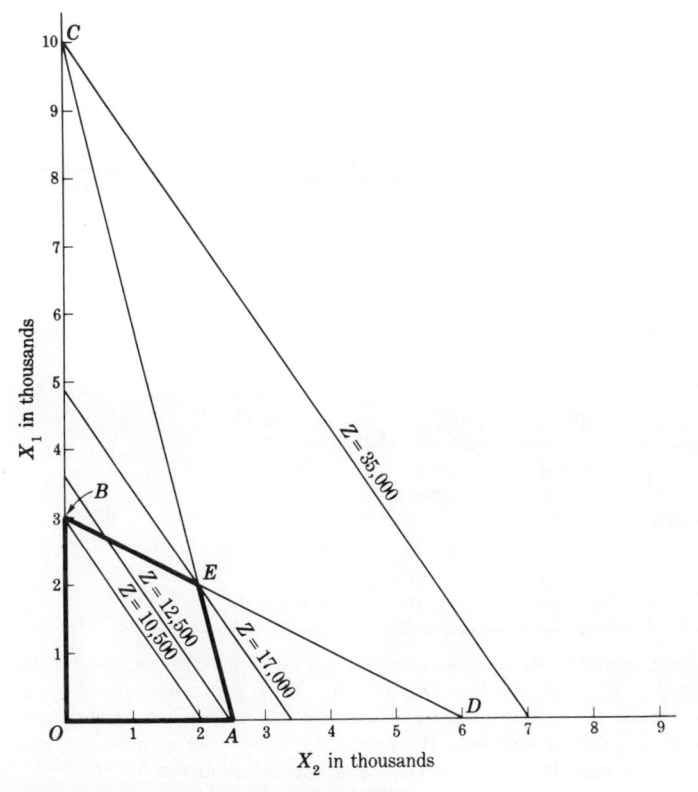

[Graph showing X_1 in thousands vs X_2 in thousands, with points O, A, B, C, D, E marked and lines $Z = 10{,}500$, $Z = 12{,}500$, $Z = 17{,}000$, $Z = 35{,}000$]

Fig. 13.5F3 Graph for Example 13.5E1.

solution must, therefore, lie in the region OBD. However, there is another restriction on the solution. Equation (13.5#3) is plotted as line AC. A feasible solution that does not violate the maximum available time on machine 2 must lie in area OCA. Therefore, in order to satisfy both constraints of the problem, the solution must lie in area $OBEA$. Thanks to the nonnegativity restriction on the variables, it was necessary to consider only the first quadrant. The problem, therefore, is to seek a point (X_1, X_2) that lies within the region $OBEA$ and maximizes the profit function. Equation (13.5#4) represents the profit function and can be plotted on Fig. 13.5F3 for various values of Z. Four of these lines have been plotted for illustrative purposes. Any point along the line $Z = 10,500$ indicates a profit of $10,500. There are an infinite number of these points along the line. However, the line for $Z = 12,500$ is a line of higher profit and thus indicates a more favorable direction. The line for $Z = 17,000$ has only one point within the feasible region, the intersection of the two constraint lines. Any line to the right of this line, like $Z = 35,000$, contains points that yield higher profits, but the constraints of the problem are violated and hence these solutions are not feasible. By inspection, therefore, the optimal solution is

$X_1 = 2,000$ units/week product A
$X_2 = 2,000$ units/week product B
$X_3 = 0$
$X_4 = 0$
$Z = \$17,000$ per week net profit

In describing the method of solution, it was stated that the excess number of variables should be set equal to zero and the remaining variables solved for. If every possible way of doing this is investigated, one should be able to find the optimal solution. Let us now illustrate this. Equations (13.5#2) and (13.5#3) indicate that there are four variables and two equations. Two of these four variables must be set equal to zero and the other two solved for. For example, setting X_1 and X_2 equal to zero and solving for X_3 and X_4, one obtains $X_3 = 6,000$ and $X_4 = 10,000$. How many ways are there to set two variables equal from a total of four? This is the well-known problem for the number of combinations of P things taken Q at a time, which is

$$\frac{P!}{Q!(P-Q)!} \tag{13.5#5}$$

which for $P = 4$ and $Q = 2$ gives

$$\frac{4!}{2!(4-2)!} = \frac{4(3)(2)(1)}{2(1)(2)(1)} = 6 \text{ combinations}$$

Tabulating all six solutions:

X_1	X_2	X_3	X_4	Z	Fig. 13.5F3
0	0	6,000	10,000	0	0
0	6,000	0	−14,000	NF	
0	2,500	3,500	0	12,500	A
3,000	0	0	7,000	10,500	B
10,000	0	−14,000	0	NF	
2,000	2,000	0	0	17,000	E

where NF indicates a solution that is nonfeasible. It will be noted that the four feasible solutions correspond to O, A, B, and E of Fig. 13.5F3. These points are called *extreme points* or *vertices*. In all LP problems these extreme points correspond to basic feasible solutions. In examining the six solutions, the nonfeasible ones were eliminated immediately; of the remaining basic feasible solutions, the optimal solution was found.

13.6 Algebraic method

The technique used will follow four steps:

1. Select the basic variables.
2. Solve the constraint equations and the objective function for the basic variables in terms of the nonbasic variables.
3. Inspect the objective function equation. Decide which variable will leave the basis and which will enter in order to improve the value of the objective function.
4. Continue until no further improvement is possible.

Example 13.6E1 Repeat Example 13.5E1 using the algebraic technique.

Step 1. Select the slack variables X_3 and X_4 as basic variables. This is done initially to give a feasible solution.

Step 2. Solve the constraint Eqs. (13.5#2) and (13.5#3) in terms of the nonbasic variables X_1 and X_2.

$$X_3 = 6{,}000 - 2X_1 - X_2 \qquad (13.6\#1)$$

$$X_4 = 10{,}000 - X_1 - 4X_2 \qquad (13.6\#2)$$

The objective function was given by Eq. (13.5#4)

$$Z = 3.5X_1 + 5X_2 \qquad (13.6\#3)$$

For $X_1 = X_2 = 0$, the initial solution from the above is

$$X_1 = 0 \qquad X_2 = 0 \qquad X_3 = 6{,}000 \qquad X_4 = 10{,}000 \qquad Z = 0$$

This basic feasible solution corresponds to point O in Fig. 13.5F3.

Step 3. By inspecting Eq. (13.6#3) it is noted that it is better to introduce X_2 than X_1 since X_2 has the larger coefficient and will improve the objective function more than X_1. How much X_2 should be introduced? Obviously, as much as possible. Equation (13.6#2) indicates that when X_2 exceeds 2,500, X_4 becomes negative. Therefore, the most that X_2 can be is 2,500. The variable X_2 enters the *basis*; it becomes a *basic variable*, and X_4 leaves the basis and becomes a *nonbasic* variable. When one variable enters the basis, another must leave to make room for it. The variable that is driven to zero is the one that leaves the basis. Now repeat steps 1, 2, and 3 for the next iteration.

Solving the constraint equations and the objective-function equation for X_2 and X_3 in terms of X_1 and X_4 gives from Eqs. (13.6#2) and (13.6#3), respectively,

$$X_2 = 2{,}500 - \tfrac{1}{4}X_1 - \tfrac{1}{4}X_4 \qquad (13.6\#4)$$

$$X_3 = 6{,}000 - 2X_1 - (2{,}500 - \tfrac{1}{4}X_1 - \tfrac{1}{4}X_4) = 3{,}500 - \tfrac{7}{4}X_1 + \tfrac{1}{4}X_4 \qquad (13.6\#5)$$

and

$$Z = 3.5X_1 + 5(2{,}500 - \tfrac{1}{4}X_1 - \tfrac{1}{4}X_4) = 12{,}500 + \tfrac{9}{4}X_1 - \tfrac{5}{4}X_4 \qquad (13.6\#6)$$

For $X_1 = 0$ and $X_4 = 0$, the solution is

$$X_1 = 0 \qquad X_2 = 2{,}500 \qquad X_3 = 3{,}500 \qquad X_4 = 0 \qquad Z = 12{,}500$$

This basic feasible solution corresponds to point A in Fig. 13.5F3. The improvement in the objective function has been from 0 to 12,500. Upon examination of Eq. (13.6#6) it is seen that X_1 should be introduced since it has a positive coefficient. Inspection of

Eqs. (13.6#4) and (13.6#5) shows that Eq. (13.6#5) limits the value of X_1 to 2,000, at which point X_3 goes to zero. Therefore, X_1 enters the basis and X_3 leaves. Repeating the technique of solving for the basic variables in terms of the nonbasic variables,

$$X_1 = 2{,}000 - \tfrac{4}{7}X_3 + \tfrac{1}{7}X_4 \qquad (13.6\#7)$$

$$X_2 = 2{,}000 + \tfrac{1}{7}X_3 - \tfrac{2}{7}X_4 \qquad (13.6\#8)$$

$$Z = 17{,}000 - \tfrac{9}{7}X_3 - \tfrac{13}{14}X_4 \qquad (13.6\#9)$$

For $X_3 = 0$ and $X_4 = 0$ the solution is

$$X_1 = 2{,}000 \qquad X_2 = 2{,}000 \qquad X_3 = 0 \qquad X_4 = 0 \qquad Z = 17{,}000$$

This basic solution corresponds to point E in Fig. 13.5F3. It is the optimal solution because both coefficients of the nonbasic variables in Eq. (13.6#9) are negative; introducing any of these nonbasic variables would only lower the value of Z and lead to a less optimal solution.

13.7 Simplex method

The method of solution most widely used is the simplex method developed by Dantzig [13.14R2]. It will be seen that this method facilitates the actual calculations of the algebraic method just described. The development will make many references to the equations just derived in the algebraic method.

The first step requires a representation of the problem in matrix form. Start by listing the variables X_1, X_2, X_3, and X_4 with the respective cost coefficients directly above. Note that the slack variables X_3 and X_4 have zero cost coefficients because they do not appear in the objective function. The original Eqs. (13.5#2) and (13.5#3) are now entered with the right-hand sides given under B_i.

$i \quad \backslash \quad j$	3.5 X_1	5 X_2	0 X_3	0 X_4	B_i
	2	1	1	0	6,000
	1	4	0	1	10,000

At this point, the basic variables must be selected. Following the first iteration of the algebraic method, X_3 and X_4 will be chosen and entered on the left, with the cost coefficients alongside, as shown in Table 13.7T1. The rest of the manipulation is the solution of the constraint equations and the objective function for the basic variables in terms of the nonbasic variables. The following calculations are required:

$$Z_j = \sum_{i=1}^{m} C_i A_{ij} \qquad (13.7\#1)$$

$$\Delta_j = Z_j - C_j \qquad (13.7\#2)$$

where C_i refers to the cost coefficient of the ith basic variable. In the first iteration, X_3 and X_4 have been chosen as basic variables. Therefore, $C_1 = C_2 = 0$ since these are the values of the cost coefficients for X_3 and X_4 in the objective function. For the first basic variable X_3 use the first line of the matrix for $i = 1$ and read

$$A_{11} = 2 \quad A_{12} = 1 \quad A_{13} = 1 \quad A_{14} = 0$$

For the second basic variable X_4 use the second line of the matrix for $i = 2$ and read

$$A_{21} = 1 \quad A_{22} = 4 \quad A_{23} = 0 \quad A_{24} = 1$$

Therefore

$$Z_1 = C_1 A_{11} + C_2 A_{21} = 0(2) + 0(1) = 0$$
$$Z_2 = C_1 A_{12} + C_2 A_{22} = 0(1) + 0(4) = 0$$
$$Z_3 = C_1 A_{13} + C_2 A_{23} = 0(1) + 0(0) = 0$$
$$Z_4 = C_1 A_{14} + C_2 A_{24} = 0(0) + 0(1) = 0$$

The Δj values can now be calculated.

$$\Delta_1 = Z_1 - C_1 = 0 - 3.5 = -3.5$$
$$\Delta_2 = Z_2 - C_2 = 0 - 5.0 = -5.0$$
$$\Delta_3 = Z_3 - C_3 = 0 - 0 = 0$$
$$\Delta_4 = Z_4 - C_4 = 0 - 0 = 0$$

Note that the Δj values are the coefficients of the nonbasic variables with the sign reversed.

These values are entered in the appropriate spaces, giving the first tableau in Table 13.7T1. The value of Z, the objective function, is also listed in the lower right-hand corner. It is obtained from the relationship

$$Z = \sum_{i=1}^{m} C_i B_i \qquad (13.7\#3)$$

The bottom row is examined for the most negative coefficient. This is seen to be under column X_2, which indicates that it is desirable to introduce this variable into the basis. Each right-hand side is divided by the element in the X_2 column to determine which is limiting. It is that calculation which gives the smallest

Table 13.7T1 First Tableau of Simplex Method

		3.5 X_1	5 X_2	0 X_3	0 X_4	B_i	Corresponding equation
X_3	0	2	1	1	0	6,000	(13.5#2)
X_4	0	1	4	0	1	10,000	(13.5#3)
Z_j		0	0	0	0	0	
Δ_j		−3.5	−5	0	0		

Table 13.7T2 Second Tableau of Simplex Method

		3.5 X_1	5 X_2	0 X_3	0 X_4	B_i	Corresponding equation
X_3	0	$-7/4$	0	-1	$1/4$	$-3,500$	(13.6#5)
X_2	5	$1/4$	1	0	$1/4$	2,500	(13.6#4)
Z_j		$5/4$	5	0	$5/4$	12,500	
Δ_j		$-9/4$	0	0	$5/4$		

positive number. For this example,

$$\frac{6{,}000}{1} = 6{,}000$$

$$\frac{10{,}000}{4} = 2{,}500$$

The second row controls since X_4 cannot be larger than 2,500 (lest X_4 become a negative number). Hence, X_2 enters the basis and X_4 leaves. Element $A_{22} = 4$ is called the *pivot element*. The variable that enters the basis is on the *pivot column*, and the variable leaving lies on the *pivot row*. Their intersection is the pivot element.

Some matrix manipulations are required here:

1. The pivot element is made equal to unity. This requires dividing every element in the pivot row by the value of the pivot element. In Table 13.7T1 this requires dividing each element in row 2 by the number 4.
2. All other elements in the pivot column must be made equal to zero by the proper manipulation. In Table 13.7T1 this requires multiplying row 1 by the number -1 and adding to row 2.

The Z_j and Δ_j calculations are then carried out with the results given in Table 13.7T2, the second tableau. Note the equations corresponding to the algebraic method.

The final iteration is carried out in the same way, with the final and third tableau given in Table 13.7T3. The bottom row has no negative coefficients, and hence no further improvement is possible.

Table 13.7T3 Third Tableau of Simplex Method

		3.5 X_1	5 X_2	0 X_3	0 X_4	B_i	Corresponding equation
X_1	3.5	1	0	$4/7$	$-1/7$	2,000	(13.6#7)
X_2	5	0	1	$-1/7$	$2/7$	2,000	(13.6#8)
Z_j		3.5	5	$9/7$	$13/14$	17,000	
Δ_j		0	0	$9/7$	$13/14$		

13.8 Applications

One of the first applications of LP was concerned with a diet problem. Generally, the problem is formulated as follows. Certain foods are available, say type 1 and type 2. Each food has its own nutritional value expressed as units of protein per unit of food, units of vitamins per unit of food, units of carbohydrates per unit of food, etc. Usually, a minimum-cost diet is sought that will meet certain requirements. The previous development of the simplex method was based on maximization. However, it can be applied to a minimization problem by changing the signs of all cost coefficients from positive to negative and treating the problem as one in maximization. The maximization of the negative function is the same as the minimization of the function itself. Suppose the following data apply to the diet problem:

Food type	Units vitamin Unit food	Units protein Unit food	Units carbohydrate Unit food	Cost of food
1	A_{11}	A_{21}	A_{31}	C_1
2	A_{12}	A_{22}	A_{32}	C_2
Minimum required	B_1	B_2	B_3	

Let X_1 be the units of type 1 food and X_2 the units of type 2 food. To satisfy the vitamin, protein, and carbohydrate requirements, respectively,

$$A_{11}X_1 + A_{12}X_2 \geq B_1$$
$$A_{21}X_1 + A_{22}X_2 \geq B_2$$
$$A_{31}X_1 + A_{32}X_2 \geq B_3$$

The objective function is to minimize

$$Z = C_1 X_1 + C_2 X_2$$

Another type of problem is the *transportation problem*, diagrammed in Fig. 13.8F1. Each supplier has production $A_1, A_2, \ldots, A_m$. The demand at each warehouse is $B_1, B_2, \ldots, B_n$. The cost of transporting material from supplier i to warehouse j is C_{ij}. Determine the quantities to ship from each supplier to each warehouse to minimize total transportation cost.

Let X_{ij} be the quantity transported from supplier i to warehouse j. The total amount shipped from supplier 1 is A_1, its production

$$\sum_{j=1}^{n} X_{1j} = A_1$$

or for all the suppliers individually

$$\sum_{i=1}^{n} X_{ij} = A_i \qquad i = 1, 2, \ldots, m \qquad (13.8\#1)$$

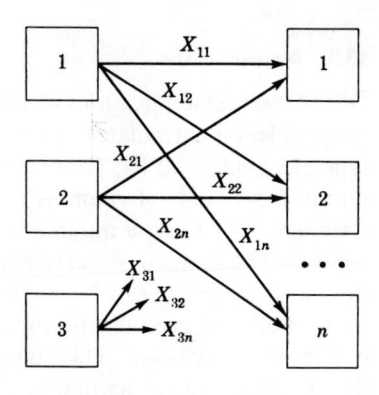

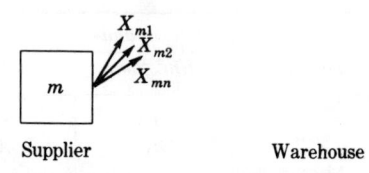

Fig. 13.8F1 Transportation model.

Similarly receipts for all the warehouses individually

$$\sum_{i=1}^{m} X_{ij} = B_j \quad j = 1, 2, \ldots, n \tag{13.8#2}$$

Equations (13.8#1) and (13.8#2) represent the constraint equations. The total cost must be summed from all suppliers to all warehouses. The transportation cost Z becomes

$$Z = \sum_{i=1}^{m} \sum_{j=1}^{n} C_{ij} X_{ij} \tag{13.8#3}$$

The problem is to minimize Z subject to the constraints of Eqs. (13.8#1) and (13.8#2) with the further condition

$$X_{ij} \geq 0 \quad \text{for all } i, j \tag{13.8#4}$$

The special structure of this problem has been studied and is a special type of LP problem [13.14R3]. Due to the special structure, it is possible to modify the simplex method and take advantage of this structure.

DYNAMIC PROGRAMMING (DP)

13.9 An allocation example

Dynamic programming is an optimization technique that is especially applicable to the solution of multistage problems. *Programming* is used in the same context

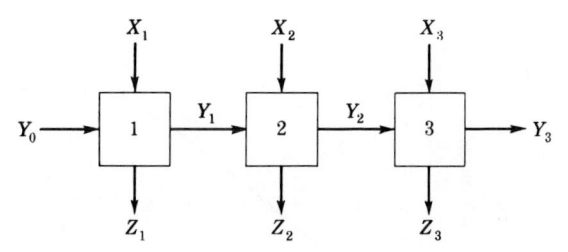

Fig. 13.9F1 Model for multistage problem.

as in linear programming, i.e., the planning of activities. Bellman introduced the concept of dynamic programming through the principle of optimality. "An optimal policy has the property that whatever the initial state and initial decision are, the remaining decisions must constitute an optimal policy with regard to the state resulting from the first decision."[1]

Consider the following optimization problem consisting of three black boxes shown in Fig. 13.9F1. The output Y_3 from black box 3 is related to the input Y_2 and the *decision variable* X_3. The profit function Z_3 from black box 3 is also related to Y_2 and X_3. Once Y_2 is known, the optimization problem is to find the best value of X_3. The path taken to arrive at point Y_2 is no longer important. The object is to do the best possible from this point to Y_3. If the procedure is repeated for all possible values of Y_2, then the optimal values of X_3 corresponding to every possible value of Y_2 become known.

Now consider black box 2. Assume that Y_1 is known and the best value of X_2 must be chosen. By selecting a value of X_2, Y_2 can be calculated from the model for black box 2, also the profit function Z_2. Once Y_2 is calculated, X_3 has already been determined as well as Z_3 from the study made on black box 3. It will be assumed that the profit functions are additive so that the total profit function at this point is $Z_2 + Z_3$. Various values of X_2 are tried for an assumed value of Y_1 until that value is found which optimizes the objective function $Z_2 + Z_3$. We therefore have found the best values of X_2 and X_3 for a given Y_1. This process is repeated for all possible values of Y_1. We are now in a position to specify the optimal policy for any Y_1. The quantities Y_1 and Y_2 are called *state variables*, being the outputs from one stage and the inputs to another stage. Then, for any state variables we have determined the best decision variables. The process is continued until Y_0 is reached. This is the input variable, and it is assumed that this quantity is known. The optimal policy can actually be determined for any input. The technique of dynamic programming can best be illustrated by examples.

Example 13.9E1 A decision must be made with respect to the allocation of a fixed sum of money, $4 million. Three types of research and development are shown graphically in

---

[1] Richard E. Bellman, "Dynamic Programming," p. 83, Princeton University Press, Princeton, N.J., 1957.

274 OPTIMIZATION

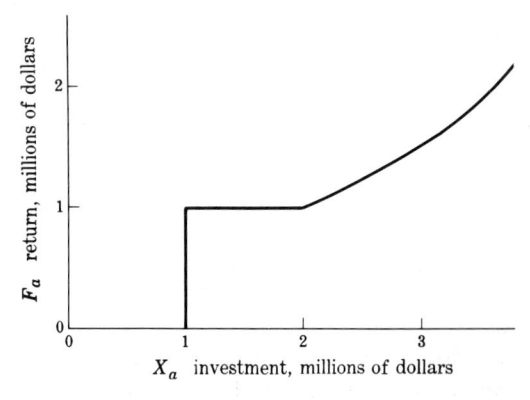

Fig. 13.9F2 Project A.

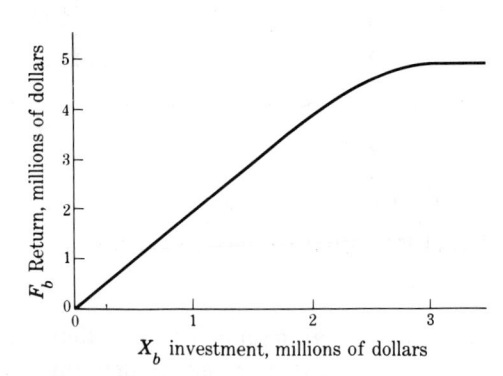

Fig. 13.9F3 Project B.

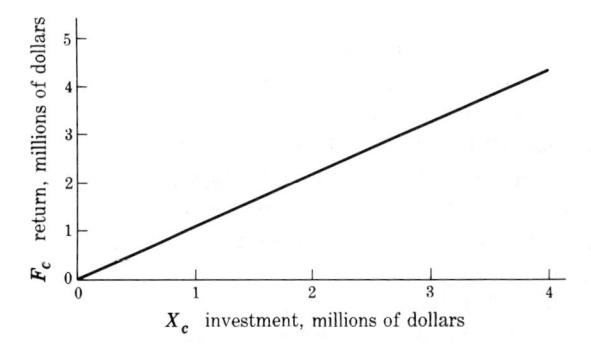

Fig. 13.9F4 Project C.

Figs. 13.9F2, 13.9F3, and 13.9F4, respectively, and by tabulation in Table 13.9T1. In project A returns do not materialize until appreciable money is invested, in project B the law of diminishing returns applies, and in project C the return is linear with respect to the investment.

If $4 million is available for the three projects, what is the optimal way to allocate these funds assuming integral million dollars investments in each project?

Table 13.9T1 Investments for Example 13.9E1

Project A		Project B		Project C	
Investment X_a, $MM	Return F_a, $MM	Investment X_b, $MM	Return F_b, $MM	Investment X_c, $MM	Return F_c, $MM
0	0	0	0	0	0
1.0	1.0	1.0	2.0	1.0	1.05
2.0	1.0	2.0	4.0	2.0	2.10
3.0	1.5	3.0	5.0	3.0	3.15
4.0	2.5	4.0	5.0	4.0	4.20

Table 13.9T2 Investment in Projects B and C Only

Total investment $MM	Invest Project B $MM	Return F_b, from B $MM	Invest project C, $MM	Return F_c, from C, $MM	Return from B and C, $MM
4	4.0	5.0	0.0	0.0	5.0
	3.0	5.0	1.0	1.05	6.05
	2.0	4.0	2.0	2.10	6.10
	1.0	2.0	3.0	3.15	6.15
	0.0	0.0	4.0	4.20	4.20
3	3.0	5.0	0.0	0.0	5.0
	2.0	4.0	1.0	1.05	5.05
	1.0	2.0	2.0	2.10	4.10
	0.0	0.0	3.0	3.15	3.15
2	2.0	4.0	0.0	0.0	4.0
	1.0	2.0	1.0	1.05	3.05
	0.0	0.0	2.0	2.10	2.10
1	1.0	2.0	0.0	0.0	2.0
	0.0	0.0	1.0	1.05	1.05

Consider projects B and C only. Table 13.9T2 gives all possible combinations for investing $4 million and less among the two projects. A summary of the optimal conditions for projects B and C together is given in Table 13.9T3. The table was prepared from the optimum conditions found in Table 13.9T2. Thus if $3 million is the total investment available for projects A and B, the maximum profit, $5.05 million, is obtained by investing $2.0 million in project A and $1 million in project C. It should be noted that the 14 calculations of Table 13.9T2 can now be replaced by the 5 calculations of Table 13.9T3.

Projects A, B, and C can now be considered together, but this requires consideration only of project A in conjunction with the optimum policies for projects B and C together. A tabulation is given in Table 13.9T4. In the tabulation the investment in projects A, B, and C all together is $4 million inasmuch as there are no other projects to invest in.

Table 13.9T3 Optimum Profit Projects B and C Only

Total investment in B and C, $MM	Invest in project B, $MM	Invest in Project C, $MM	Optimal profit from $B + C$, $MM
0	0	0	0
1.0	1.0	0	2.0
2.0	2.0	0	4.0
3.0	2.0	1.0	5.05
4.0	1.0	3.0	6.15

Table 13.9T4 $4 Million Investment in Projects A, B, and C

Total investment $MM	Invest project A $MM	Return from A, F_a, $MM	Invest B + C, $MM	Optimal return B + C, $MM	Return from A + B + C, $MM
4	0.0	0.0	4.0	6.15	6.15
	1.0	1.0	3.0	5.05	6.05
	2.0	1.0	2.0	4.0	5.0
	3.0	1.5	1.0	2.0	3.5
	4.0	2.5	0.0	0.0	2.5

The optimal policy is to invest $0 million in project A, and $4 million in projects B and C together, which in turn should be $1 million in project B and $3 million in project C for a maximum total profit of $6.15 million.

13.10 A transportation example

Example 13.10E1 A salesman must travel from city A to city B. The territory is divided into three districts, and he is required to visit at least one city in each district. Travel costs between cities are indicated in Fig. 13.10F1. The object is to meet the objective of visiting at least one city in each district at the minimum total travel cost. Use the technique of dynamic programming to solve this problem.

The solution is given in Tables 13.10T1 to 13.10T6 obtained as follows. Consider destination city B. There are three routes from district 1 to city B; J–B, K–B, L–B. Having arrived in district 1, therefore, there is no decision to be made. Only one route is available from any city in district 1 to city B as given in Table 13.10T1.

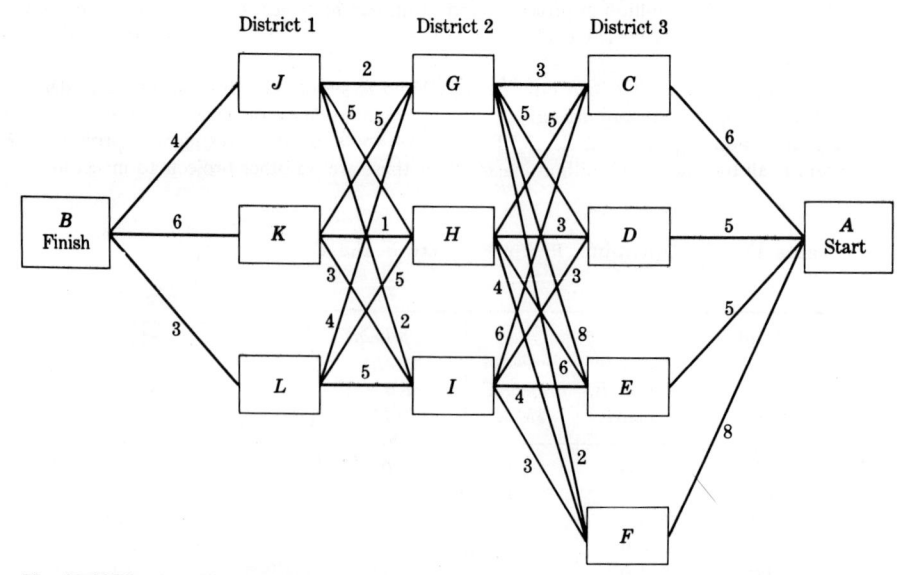

Fig. 13.10F1 Travel costs between cities.

13.10   LINEAR AND DYNAMIC PROGRAMMING

Table 13.10T1 District 1 to City B

Route	Cost
J–B	4
K–B	6
L–B	3

Table 13.10T2 District 2 to City B

Route	Cost
G–J–B	2 + 4 = 6
G–K–B	5 + 6 = 11
G–L–B	4 + 3 = 7
H–J–B	5 + 4 = 9
H–K–B	1 + 6 = 7
H–L–B	5 + 3 = 8
I–J–B	2 + 4 = 6
I–K–B	3 + 6 = 9
I–L–B	5 + 3 = 8

Table 13.10T3 Optimal Routes District 2 to City B

Route	Cost
G–J–B	6
H–K–B	7
I–J–B	6

Table 13.10T4 District 3 to City B

Route	Cost
C–(G–J–B)	3 + 6 = 9
C–(H–K–B)	5 + 7 = 12
C–(I–J–B)	6 + 6 = 12
D–(G–J–B)	5 + 6 = 11
D–(H–K–B)	3 + 7 = 10
D–(I–J–B)	3 + 6 = 9
E–(G–J–B)	8 + 6 = 14
E–(H–K–B)	6 + 7 = 13
E–(I–J–B)	4 + 6 = 10
F–(G–J–B)	2 + 6 = 8
F–(H–K–B)	4 + 7 = 11
F–(I–J–B)	3 + 6 = 9

Table 13.10T5 Optimal Routes District 3 to City B

Route	Cost
C–G–J–B	9
D–I–J–B	9
E–I–J–B	10
F–G–J–B	8

Table 13.10T6 City A to B

Route	Cost
A–(C–G–J–B)	6 + 9 = 15
A–(D–I–J–B)	5 + 9 = 14
A–(E–I–J–B)	5 + 10 = 15
A–(F–G–J–B)	8 + 8 = 16

Now go back one stage, one district, and examine the situation from district 2 to city *B*. All the combinations are given in Table 13.10T2, and the optimal routes in Table 13.10T3. Thus if the salesman is in city *H* his best route is *H–K–B* and he need not consider other routes originating from *H*.

Next go back another stage to district 3. All the *pertinent* combinations are given in Table 13.10T4 prepared from Table 13.10T3 and the costs from district 3 to district 2. Table 13.10T5 gives the optimal routes from district 3 to city *B*.

Finally, Table 13.10T6 gives all the pertinent combinations from city *A* to city *B*. The optimal path is route *A–D–I–J–B* at a cost of 14.

There may of course be ties so that more than one optimal path can exist. The problem is subject to many variations. If no path exists between two cities, it can be included by placing a very high cost on the route so that it will eliminate itself but not break up the systematic formulation of the solution.

13.11 Pros and cons of dynamic programming

In the dynamic programming examples discussed it has been assumed tacitly that the manner in which a stage has been reached has no influence on the stages ahead. The existence and importance of this limitation should be appreciated. Thus in Example 13.10E1 the road ahead is not influenced by the road behind, and use of the optimality principle was very effective in reducing the number of calculations. However, the stages ahead can be influenced by the manner in which the stages behind have occurred. For example, suppose in Exercise 13.10E1 the state of fatigue of the salesman must be considered and that his fatigue contributes to the cost of travel. That is, the more tired he becomes, the more he will require extra service, and the greater the travel cost. It then becomes necessary to consider the degree of fatigue of the salesman at each city, which in turn depends upon the manner in which the previous steps were executed.

Some of the pros and cons of dynamic programming are as follows:

1 At any stage, the optimization technique to use is left up to the user. The most efficient method can therefore be used for any particular problem.
2 The problem of constraints usually hinders most optimization techniques. In dynamic programming, however, the constraints are actually helpful because they limit the range to be investigated.
3 Discontinuities in the objective function can be handled by dynamic programming because no analytical function need be used; tables and curves are quite adequate.
4 Dynamic programming greatly reduces the number of optimization problems to be examined. In general, where there are N stages and K decisions to be made at each stage, the overall optimization problem involves K^N possible solutions. For a five-stage problem with three decisions at each stage, this means 3^5, or 243, possible combinations. By dynamic programming, only 3×5, or 15, one-stage optimization problems would have to be solved. The main disadvantage of dynamic programming is the problem of dimensionality (many variables), which arises in the optimization at each stage. For example, when many decisions are to be made at one time, the single-stage optimization itself may become quite complex.

13.12 Nomenclature

A_{ij} Coefficient in restraint equation, ith row, jth column, LP
B_i Right side of the ith restraint equation, LP
C_i Unit cost associated with basic variable in ith row, LP
C_j Unit cost associated with X_j, LP
DP   Dynamic programming
F Objective function
F_a Return from project A, DP
i The ith row
j The jth column
LP   Linear programming
N The Nth stage, DP
Q Quality coefficient
X_a Investment in project A, DP
X_j Variable input, LP
X_N Decision variable associated with Nth stage, DP
Y_N Output from Nth stage, input to $(N+1)$-st stage, DP
Z Objective function
Z_j $\sum_{i=1}^{m} C_i A_{ij}$, LP
Δ_j $Z_j - C_j$

13.13 Problems

P1. Verify all terms in the first and second rows of the second and third tableaus for Example 13.7E1, Tables 13.7T2 and 13.7T3.

P2. Verify the Z_j and Δ_j values in Table 13.7T3.

P3. Set up the equations for the following diet problem given by Garvin [13.14R3]. One unit of hog's liver contains 1 unit of carbohydrates, 3 units of vitamins, and 3 units of proteins and costs 50 units. Suppose 1 unit of castor oil contains 3, 4, and 1 units of these items respectively and costs 25 units. Assume that the minimum daily requirements are 8 units of carbohydrates, 19 units of vitamins, and 7 units of proteins. Obtain the minimum-cost diet subject to the constraints of the problem.

P4. Refer to Prob. 13.13P3. Express this problem geometrically, indicating the feasible region.

P5. Solve Prob. 13.13P3 by the enumeration of all solutions.

P6. Solve Prob. 13.13P3 by the algebraic method.

P7. Verify the equations in the algebraic method of Prob. 13.13P6 by solving the problem by the simplex method.

P8. Refer to Example 13.9E1. What is the optimal policy if $3 million were available for all three projects instead of $4 million?

P9. Repeat Prob. 13.13P8 for (a) $2 million and (b) $1 million. Plot the optimal return against available funds.

P10. Repeat Example 13.10E1 but traveling from city B to city A.

P11. Describe some applications of dynamic programming to problems with which you are familiar, e.g., investment decisions, staged engineering calculations, network problems.

P12. Find the number of each of three items to include in a package so that the value of the package will be a maximum subject to the limitation that the weight must not exceed 6 lb.

Item	Weight, lb	Value, $
1	3	6
2	2	4
3	4	7

13.14 References for linear programming

R1. Charnes, A., and W. W. Cooper: "Management Models and Industrial Application of Linear Programming," John Wiley & Sons, Inc., New York, 1960.
R2. Dantzig, G. B.: The Simplex Method, *Rand Corporation Rept.* P-891, 1956.
R3. Garvin, W. W.: "Introduction to Linear Programming," McGraw-Hill Book Company, New York, 1960.
R4. Gass, S. I.: "Linear Programming: Methods and Applications," 3d ed., McGraw-Hill Book Company, New York, 1969.
R5. Hadley, G.: "Linear Programming," Addison-Wesley Publishing Company, Inc., Reading, Mass., 1962.
R6. Vajda, S.: "Readings in Linear Programming," John Wiley & Sons, Inc., New York, 1958.

13.15 References for dynamic programming

R1. Bellman, Richard E.: "Dynamic Programming," Princeton University Press, Princeton, N.J., 1957.
R2. Bellman, R., and S. Dreyfus: "Applied Dynamic Programming," Princeton University Press, Princeton, N.J., 1962.
R3. Hadley, G. "Nonlinear and Dynamic Programming," Addison-Wesley Publishing Company, Inc., Reading, Mass., 1964.
R4. Nemhauser, G. L.: "Introduction to Dynamic Programming," John Wiley & Sons, Inc., New York, 1966.

14
Special Mathematical Techniques

A. H. Boas

UNIVARIABLE SEARCH METHODS

14.1 Search techniques

Very often a problem is not detailed in specific analytical form. An objective function, such as a maximum or minimum value, may be evaluated, however, by trial of some sort. This may entail a direct laboratory measurement or experimentation, a computer run, an iterative procedure involving graphs and table look up, and so forth. Referring to Fig. 13.1F1, we see that the contents of the black box are not in analytical form but nevertheless provide the means for calculating the value of the objective function for a given set of input data. The problem is then to select the proper values of the input data to optimize a specified objective function. How are these values selected? The problem is solved by the use of search techniques.

Many search techniques have been described in the literature [14.15R1, 14.15R2, 14.15R16, 14.15R17]; all, however, are based on the same principle. A base point is given or assumed; then the next set of values for the variables is chosen and the objective function evaluated once again. Based on this result, another group of variables is chosen and the process repeated. A judicious choice of these variables can eliminate many unnecessary experiments or calculations.

282 OPTIMIZATION

After performing a certain number of experiments, there is something that can be said about the interval within which the optimum value must lie. The object is to make this interval as small as possible for a fixed number of experiments. The approach that will be taken is the most conservative: whatever can go wrong will go wrong. With this apparent disadvantage, some conclusive statements about the optimum can still be made. Each search procedure will be evaluated with this conservative approach; the result will be the maximum value for the width of the interval. Then the best procedure will be taken to mean that procedure which gives the minimum value of this maximum width; hence, the name *minimax*.

14.2 Uniform search

Let us assume that we are concerned with only one independent variable and that the experimental error of measuring (or computing) is negligible. Furthermore, the assumption of *unimodality* (one peak) will be made; the value of the dependent variable decreases (increases) as the value of the independent variable changes in either direction from the maximum (minimum). The assumption of unimodality is an important restriction and should be clearly understood.

There are several univariable search methods, and the same example will be used to illustrate each procedure. This section develops the *uniform-search method*, in which experimental or trial points are spaced equally within the allowable range.

Example 14.2E1 A function F is given by the relationship

$$F = 1.3X^2 - 4X + 3 \qquad (14.2\#1)$$

It is known that the function is unimodal and that the range of the answer lies between 0 and 5. Four experiments, or computations, are permitted. Find the minimum value of F.

It should be emphasized that the form of the function F as given by Eq. (14.2#1) may or may not be known to the analyst. If known, the solution proceeds by computation; if unknown, by experimentation. The method of analysis is the same, however, which requires only that for each value of X the corresponding value of F can be determined by some means or other.

Spacing four experimental points equidistantly within the interval leads to a choice $X = 1, 2, 3, 4$, and experiment gives

X	F
1	0.3
2	0.2
3	2.7
4	7.8

The results are plotted in Fig. 14.2F1. The minimum may lie between 1 and 2, as indicated by curve A, or between 2 and 3, as indicated by curve B. It must lie between 1 and 3. Originally the range covered five units, and after four experiments the range has been narrowed down to two units, or 40% of the original range.

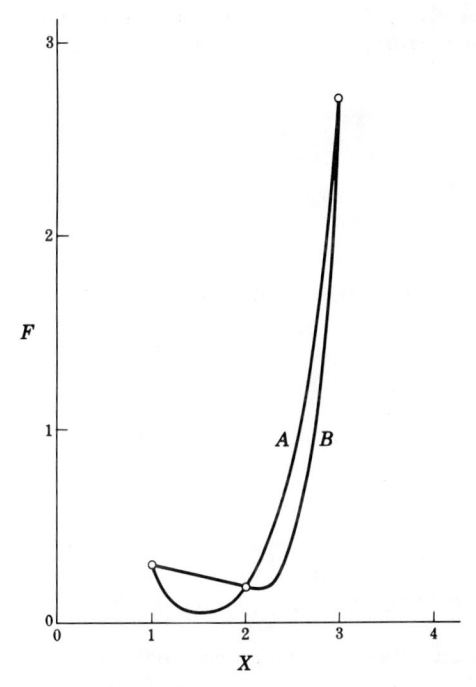

Fig. 14.2F1 Unimodal search of $F = 1.3X^2 - 4X + 3$.

The problem will now be generalized. Referring to Fig. 14.2F1, the independent variable is X, and the range extends from 0 to L. If N is the number of experiments allowed, the entire interval is divided into $N + 1$ intervals each of width $L/(N + 1)$. Since the final answer spans two of these intervals, F_r, the fraction of the original interval within which the optimum lies after performing N experiments, is given by

$$F_r = \frac{2L/(N + 1)}{L} = \frac{2}{N + 1} \qquad (14.2\#2)$$

For Example 14.2E1, $N = 4$, $F_r = \tfrac{2}{5} = 0.40$.

14.3 Uniform dichotomous search

In this procedure, experiments are performed in pairs to establish whether the function is increasing or decreasing at a point.

Example 14.3E1 Repeat Example 14.2E1 using a dichotomous search.
  Four experiments, or two pairs, are allowed. Divide the range 0 to 5 into three equal intervals, thus let

$$X = \tfrac{1}{3}(5) = 1.667 \qquad X = \tfrac{2}{3}(5) = 3.333$$

One pair of experiments is used in the neighborhood of $X = 1.667$ to establish the trend of F at that point. Similarly the second pair of experiments establishes the trend at $X = 3.333$. For the latter pair

X	F
3.30	3.96
3.36	4.24

At $X = 3.333$ the function is increasing; hence the minimum must be below that value of X. The other pair of experiments gives

X	F
1.60	−0.072
1.70	−0.043

so that the function is increasing with increasing X. The minimum must be below $X = 1.667$. The four experiments have established at the best that the minimum must lie in the range 0 to 1.667, which is one-third of the total range 0 to 5.

The procedure will now be generalized. For N experiments there will be $N/2$ pairs, and the entire interval is divided into $(N/2) + 1$ intervals, each of width $L/(N/2 + 1)$. The optimum is located over the width of one interval, $L/(N/2 + 1)$. Therefore,

$$F_r = \frac{L/(N/2 + 1)}{L} = \frac{2}{N + 2} \qquad (14.3\#1)$$

For the example $N = 4$, $F_r = 2/6 = 0.33$.

This method has reduced the original interval to 33% and is seen to be superior to a uniform search, which reduced the original interval to 40%.

14.4 Sequential dichotomous search

The two methods described require planning all the experiments in advance. A *sequential search* is one where the investigator takes advantage of the information available from the previous experiments before performing the next one.

A *sequential dichotomous search* involves running two experiments near the middle of the region under consideration. In the test problem, two experiments are run very close to $X = 2.5$ (close enough to distinguish between the two outcomes). In the neighborhood of $X = 2.5$ experiment shows that the function is increasing; therefore, the region above $X = 2.5$ is eliminated. Another pair of experiments is performed near the middle of the remaining region at $X = 1.25$. Experiment shows that the function is decreasing at $X = 1.25$; therefore, the region below $X = 1.25$ is eliminated. The remaining interval indicates that the solution lies between $X = 1.25$ and 2.50, or one-quarter of the range 0 to 5.

Generalizing this procedure, it is seen that each pair of experiments bisects the previous interval. At the end of the first pair of experiments, the remaining interval is one-half of the original interval; after the next pair, it is one-quarter of the original interval. After $N/2$ pairs of experiments, the remaining interval is $\frac{1}{2}^{N/2}$ of the original interval.

$$F_r = \frac{1}{2^{N/2}} \qquad (14.4\#1)$$

Referring again to the example, $N = 4$, $F_r = \frac{1}{2}^2 = 0.25$. The original interval has now been reduced to 25%, which is the lowest value obtained thus far.

14.5 Fibonacci search technique

A more efficient sequential technique is the *Fibonacci search*. It has been shown [14.15R12, 14.15R13] that this is the optimal routine to follow for the case of one variable and where the assumption of unimodality prevails. Although the name Fibonacci may not be very familiar, *Fibonacci numbers* are far from new. The theory of these numbers goes back to the days of Leonardo of Pisa, also known as Fibonacci. The original derivation of Fibonacci numbers was presented in "Liber Abacci," a book about the abacus written in 1202 (a second edition appeared in 1228). Table 14.5T1 gives the values of some Fibonacci numbers corresponding to an index N.

It will be noted from the table that the Nth Fibonacci number is the sum of the two previous Fibonacci numbers. For example, F_{i_8} is the sum of F_{i_6} and F_{i_7} $(34 = 13 + 21)$.

It turns out that these numbers play an important role in univariable optimization problems. The technique will be illustrated by applying it to the text example.

Table 14.5T1 Some Fibonacci Numbers

N	$F_{i,N}$	N	$F_{i,N}$
0	1	8	34
1	1	9	55
2	2	10	89
3	3	11	144
4	5	12	233
5	8	13	377
6	13	14	610
7	21	15	987

$$F_{i_{N+2}} = F_{i_N} + F_{i_{N+1}}$$
$$F_{i,0} = 1$$
$$F_{i,1} = 1$$

Example 14.5E1 Repeat Example 14.2E1 using a Fibonacci search technique.

First a pair of experiments is run equidistant from each end of the interval. The distance D_1 is determined from the expression,

$$D_1 = \frac{F_{i_{N-2}}}{F_{i_N}} L \tag{14.5\#1}$$

where F_{i_N} = Nth Fibonacci number
N = number of experiments
L = interval length

For the example, $N = 4$, $L = 5$, $F_{i_{N-2}} = F_{i_2} = 2$, $F_{i_N} = F_{i_4} = 5$. From Eq. (14.5#1)

$$D_1 = \tfrac{2}{5}(5) = 2$$

Therefore, two experiments are run two units from each end of the interval, i.e.,

$X = 0 + 2 = 2$
$X = 5 - 2 = 3$

The experiments give

X	F
2	0.200
3	2.700

The region for X greater than 3 is eliminated.

Second, the procedure is repeated for the remaining interval, changing N to $N - 1$ because one experiment less remains. Equation (14.5#1) becomes

$$D_2 = \frac{F_{i_{N-2-1}}}{F_{i_{N-1}}} L = \frac{F_{i_1}}{F_{i_3}} L = \tfrac{1}{3}(3) = 1$$

The next two experiments should be run 1 unit from each end of the remaining interval.

$X = 0 + 1 = 1$
$X = 3 - 1 = 2$

However, one of these two new experiments has already been run (at $X = 2$). Hence, only one new experiment is added, at $X = 1$. It will always turn out that one of the previous experiments is a Fibonacci experiment for the next run. Performing the new experiment gives the pair

X	F
1	0.300
2	0.200

The region for X less than 1 is eliminated.

Third, the procedure is repeated again with $L = 3 - 1 = 2$, changing N to $N - 2$. Equation (14.5#1) becomes

$$D_3 = \frac{F_{i_{N-2-2}}}{F_{i_{N-2}}} L = \frac{F_{i_0}}{F_{i_2}} L = \tfrac{1}{2}(2) = 1$$

This indicates that the last experiment should be run at

$X = 1 + 1 = 2$
$X = 3 - 1 = 2$

which experiment is run around $X = 2$ to determine in which half of the remaining region the answer lies. Choose $X = 2 \pm \varepsilon$, where ε is a small number but large enough to detect a difference in F. Taking $\varepsilon = 0.05$

X	F	
2.05	0.263	New experiment
2.00	0.200	Old experiment

The function is increasing in the neighborhood of $X = 2$; thus the minimum is below $X = 2$. The fraction of the original interval is $1/5 = 0.20$, or 20%, which is the lowest obtained. For the general case the result is

$$F_r = \frac{1}{F_{i_N}} \qquad (14.5\#2)$$

For the example $N = 4$, $F_{i_4} = 5$, $F_r = 1/5 = 0.20$.

Table 14.5T1 provides a method of determining the number of experiments to perform to obtain a certain F_r value. For example, if it is desired to narrow the original interval to at least 1%, then

$$\frac{1}{F_{i_N}} \leq 0.01$$

or

$$F_{i_N} \geq 100$$

At least 11 Fibonacci experiments would have to be performed since $F_{i,11}$ is the first Fibonacci number above 100.

14.6 Comparison of methods

Table 14.6T1 summarizes the results obtained by the various methods described. Figure 14.6F1 presents these results graphically and illustrates the advantage of the Fibonacci technique over all the others. As N gets larger, the advantage increases.

Table 14.6T1 Comparison of Methods for Univariable Search Techniques

Search technique	Interval left after N experiments / Original interval	For $N = 4$
Uniform	$\dfrac{2}{N+1}$	0.40
Uniform dichotomous	$\dfrac{2}{N+2}$	0.33
Sequential dichotomous	$\dfrac{1}{2^{N/2}}$	0.25
Fibonacci	$\dfrac{1}{F_{i,N}}$	0.20

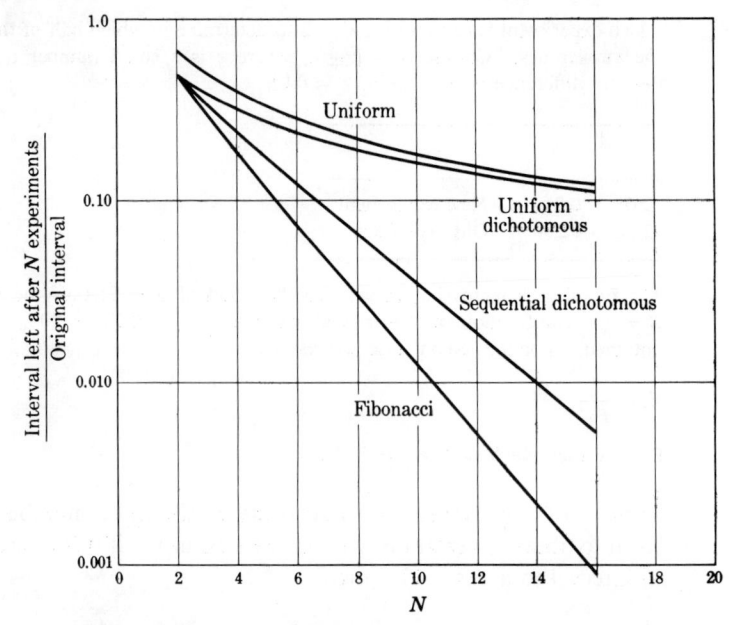

Fig. 14.6F1 Comparison of search methods.

MULTIVARIABLE FUNCTIONS

14.7 One-at-a-time method

Up to now the univariable problem has been discussed. Much more common, and much more complex, is the multivariable optimization problem. A review of some widely used methods follows.

The technique for the one-at-a-time method is the most elementary of all

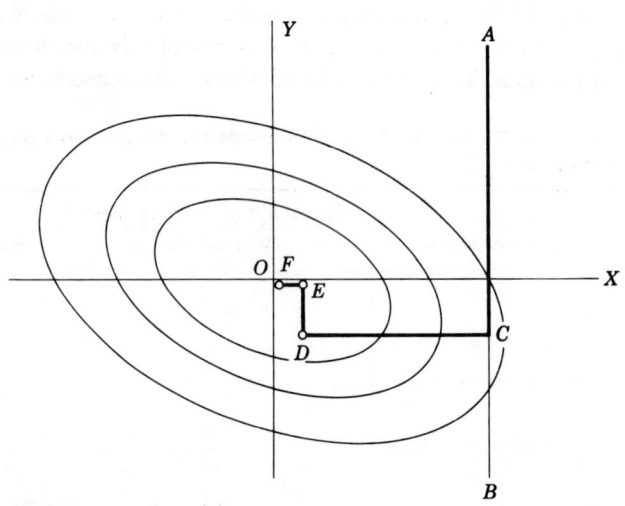

Fig. 14.7F1 One-at-a-time method.

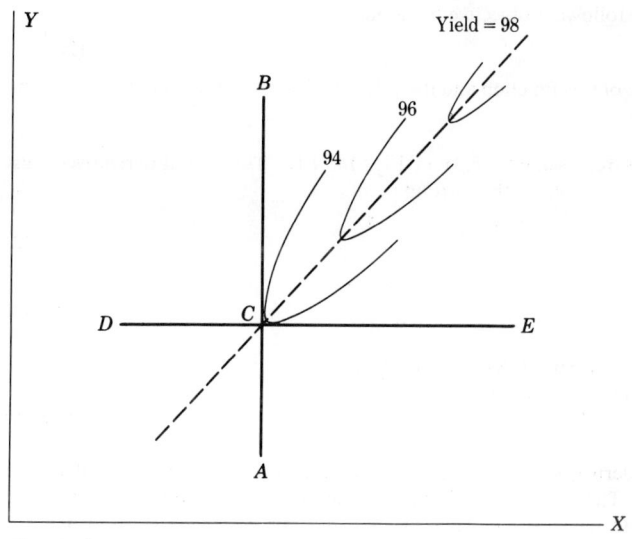

Fig. 14.7F2 One-at-a-time method can fail.

and deserves some mention. Friedman and Savage [14.15R9] described this method, which involves keeping all the variables constant except one and varying this one to obtain an improvement in the objective function. This technique works well when searches are conducted along axes parallel to the axes of the contour surfaces. If this is not the case, the search proceeds toward the optimum less efficiently. Referring to Fig. 14.7F1, an initial search is started, with a constant value of X, along the line AB. A univariable search is made along this line until the lowest value of the objective function is obtained at point C. A new search is started along line CD until point D is reached, which represents the best value along this line. The process is continued to points E, F, etc., until the optimum is approached very closely. A word of caution is in order. Referring to Fig. 14.7F2, it is noted that point C is located along line ACB; then, searching along line DCE, point C is located once again. However, this is not the optimum point. The search method has failed to explore areas of higher response that lie along the slope of the ridge. It is seen, therefore, that when the contours come to a sharp point, this method might not work.

14.8 Method of steepest ascent

The direction of the gradient is the one that gives the greatest response of the objective function per unit length of independent variable. The incremental change in each variable is taken to be proportional to its partial derivative, which determines the gradient direction. This direction is called the direction of steepest ascent for maximization (and steepest descent for minimization). This method is not new (it dates back to Cauchy) and will be illustrated by an example.

Example 14.8E1 Given the following objective function,

$$Z = X^2 + 2Y^2 + XY \qquad (14.8\#1)$$

find the minimum value of this function and the values of X and Y at the minimum, starting at $X = 2$, $Y = 2$.

The starting point is represented by M in Fig. 14.8F1. The partial derivatives must first be calculated and evaluated at the starting point.

$$\frac{\partial Z}{\partial X} = 2X + Y \qquad (14.8\#2)$$

$$\frac{\partial Z}{\partial Y} = 4Y + X \qquad (14.8\#3)$$

At the starting point, these partial derivatives become

$$\frac{\partial Z}{\partial X} = 6 \quad \text{and} \quad \frac{\partial Z}{\partial Y} = 10 \qquad (14.8\#4)$$

Because both partial derivatives are positive, the objective function varies in the same direction as X and Y. Therefore, as this is a minimization problem, both X and Y should be decreased in order to decrease the value of Z. The ratio of the decrease in X to the decrease in Y is taken to be proportional to their respective partial derivatives, that is, $6/10$. An arbitrary step size ΔY of -0.5 is chosen initially; the corresponding ΔX would then be $0.60(-0.50) = -0.30$.

Initially $X_0 = 2$; $Y_0 = 2$; $Z_0 = 16$. After the first step

$X_1 = X_0 + \Delta X = 2 - 0.30 = 1.70$

$Y_1 = Y_0 + \Delta Y = 2 - 0.50 = 1.50$

$Z_1 = 1.70^2 + 2(1.50^2) + 1.70(1.50) = 9.94$

As long as the objective function is decreasing, the procedure is continued along the same gradient line. Table 14.8T1 summarizes the results of the calculations.

Referring to Fig. 14.8F1, point P corresponds to (X_5, Y_5) and point N to (X_6, Y_6). Table 14.8T1 indicates that at point N the objective function is no longer decreasing. Point P,

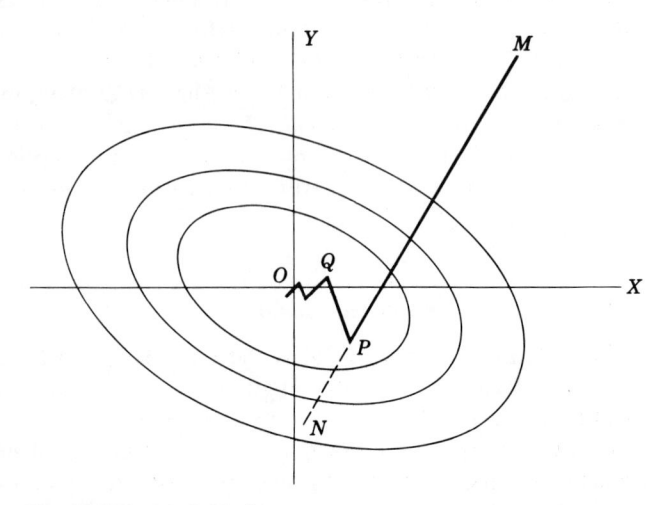

Fig. 14.8F1 Method of steepest ascent.

Table 14.8T1 Calculations along First Gradient

i	X_i	Y_i	Z_i
0	2.00	2.00	16.00
1	1.70	1.50	9.94
2	1.40	1.00	5.36
3	1.10	0.50	2.26
4	0.80	0.00	0.64
5	0.50	−0.50	0.50
6	0.20	−1.00	1.84

in fact, represents the last successful calculation. A new gradient direction is now calculated at this point and the entire procedure repeated. At point P, the gradient direction is

$$\frac{\partial Z}{\partial X} = 2X + Y = 2(0.5) - 0.5 = 0.50$$

$$\frac{\partial Z}{\partial Y} = 4Y + X = 4(-0.5) + 0.5 = -1.50$$

It is noted that $\partial Z/\partial X$ is positive but $\partial Z/\partial Y$ is negative. Therefore, in order to decrease the value of Z, X should be decreased and Y should be increased. Inasmuch as the solution should now be close at hand, the step size in Y will be arbitrarily reduced from 0.5 to 0.3. From the recently calculated partial derivatives, the ratio of $\Delta X/\Delta Y = -\frac{1}{3}$ so that $\Delta X = -0.1$.

Step 6 is calculated as follows:

$X_6 = X_5 + \Delta X = 0.50 - 0.1 = 0.40$
$Y_6 = Y_5 + \Delta Y = -0.50 + 0.3 = -0.20$
$Z_6 = 0.40^2 + 2(-0.20^2) + 0.40(-0.20) = 0.16$

Continuing along this new gradient line, the following points are obtained:

i	X_i	Y_i	Z_i
6	0.40	−0.20	0.16
7	0.30	0.10	0.14
8	0.20	0.40	0.44

Since Z_8 is greater than Z_7, it is obvious that the extrapolation has gone too far along this line. The last successful step, point Q (X_7, Y_7), is indicated on Fig. 14.8F1. The direction is changed once again, the step size increased, etc., until the optimum point is finally approached.

A few comments about the method of steepest ascent are in order at this point. Two decisions must be made as this technique is used. When should one calculate a new gradient direction (in the example chosen the policy was to go as far as one could until indications were that one had gone too far) and what step size should one use? Both these decisions greatly influence the efficiency of the method. There are no hard and fast rules to adopt. One learns by becoming familiar with the particular response surface involved and the nature of the problem. Another problem that arises in applying the method is the proper choice of scales. Surfaces with spherical contours give the fastest convergent rates; the closer the contours are to being spherical, the better the convergence. Very often, a transformation will convert the variables to the proper scales.

In practice an analytical expression such as Eq. (14.8#1) giving Z in terms of X and Y may not be available. The steepest gradient cannot, then, be established from partial derivatives such as Eqs. (14.8#2) and (14.8#3). Instead it is necessary to explore by experimentation the value of Z in various directions from M (Fig. 14.8F1) and establish the steepest gradient experimentally. Further experiments along this line proceed to point P, where the steepest gradient is again established experimentally. Continuing in this fashion will lead to point O, the optimum.

The method can be applied to problems involving more than two variables. It is difficult to portray problems in more than two variables although they are readily handled by vector analysis techniques using orthogonal unit vectors in three or more directions.

There are many other methods in the literature, e.g., direct search [14.15R11], gradient search [14.15R18], lattice method [14.15R16], contour tangent method [14.15R16], and ridge analysis [14.15R10].

14.9 Constrained optimization

So far the discussion has been limited to unconstrained optimization problems. Now, let us suppose that there are bounds or constraints imposed on the problems. These may be restrictions on the independent variables or restrictions on some calculated value which depends on the independent variables. Equality constraints can be handled by the technique of Lagrange multipliers discussed in Sec. 12.15, while the Kuhn-Tucker conditions can be used for handling inequality constraints.

Roberts and Lyvers [14.15R14] use a method which "rides the constraint." In this method, once a constraint is violated, the point is put back on the constraint line and values of the independent variables are taken so that the points lie on the constraint. The assumption made in the method is that the optimum solution lies on a constraint. Another technique from the same reference is the *hemstitching method*. In this technique, a base point is chosen that lies within the feasible region. The search is started according to the method of steepest ascent. After the next point is calculated, it is checked to see whether any of the constraints have been violated. If not, the search continues. When a constraint is violated, the gradient is calculated with respect to the constraint rather than with respect to the objective function.

A shortcoming of both these methods is that calculations are made in the infeasible region. Very often, this involves calculations of square roots of negative numbers, logarithms of negative numbers, etc., which play havoc with computer programs.

A technique which modifies the objective function introduces penalties each time a constraint is violated. An unconstrained optimization method can then be used which should keep away from the bound since it would be unattractive to get too close. Calculations are allowed in the infeasible region, however, and hence the comments above apply here as well. Furthermore, steep valleys are created at the constraints which make the optimization more difficult. If the search procedure is restricted to the feasible region only, a more efficient procedure might be expected. Two of the more popular methods in this class are due to Carroll [14.15R3] and Rosenbrock [14.15R15]. As an example Carroll introduced the created response surface technique (CRST). Violations of constraints are avoided through the use of a penalty function, the penalty becoming more severe as a constraint is approached. The reader is referred to the work of Fiacco and McCormick [14.15R4 to 14.15R8], for additional references on this subject.

SUMMATION OF SERIES

14.10 Recurring power series

Frequently it is necessary to sum a discrete power series, such as a present-worth series

$$P = \frac{A_0}{(1+i)^0} + \frac{A_1}{(1+i)^1} + \cdots + \frac{A_m}{(1+i)^m} + \cdots + \frac{A_n}{(1+i)^n} \qquad (14.10\#1)$$

The series generally is more complicated than a geometric series and it is desirable to develop a method for summing these more complicated types. The subject of series summation is involved, but one method, summation of recurring power series, depends upon algebraic methods and is easily understood upon demonstration. Moreover, the method will accommodate most series that arise in economic analysis.

If $U = 1/(1+i)$, then Eq. (14.10#1) can be written more compactly

$$\sum = A_0 + A_1 U^1 + \cdots + A_m U^m + \cdots + A_n U^n \qquad (14.10\#2)$$

Each A is a coefficient, and the series is a *recurring power series* if and only if successive coefficients are connected by a recurring relationship.

For example, consider the series

$$\sum = 1 + 3U + 7U^2 + 15U^3 + 31U^4 + \cdots \qquad (14.10\#3)$$

Every three successive coefficients in the series are related by the equation (where the constant multiplying the highest coefficient has been made equal to unity)

$$2A_m - 3A_{m+1} + 1A_{m+2} = 0 \qquad (14.10\#4)$$

Thus

$$2(1) - 3(3) + 1(7) = 0$$
$$2(3) - 3(7) + 1(15) = 0$$

294 OPTIMIZATION

Table 14.10T1 Summing a Recurring Power Series

$$\sum = A_0 + A_1 U + A_2 U^2 + \cdots + A_n U^n$$
$$-3U\sum = -3A_0 U - 3A_1 U^2 - \cdots - 3A_{n-1}U^n - 3A_n U^{n+1}$$
$$+2U^2 \sum = +2A_0 U^2 + \cdots + 2A_{n-2}U^n + 2A_{n-1}U^{n+1} + 2A_n U^{n+2}$$
$$(1 - 3U + 2U^2)\sum = A_0 + (A_1 - 3A_0)U + 0 + \cdots + 0 + (2A_{n-1} - 3A_n)U^{n+1} + 2A_n U^{n+2}$$

with $A_0 = 1 \quad A_1 = 3 \quad A_n = 2^{n+1} - 1$

$$\sum = \frac{1 + [2(2^n - 1) - 3(2^{n+1} - 1)]U^{n+1} + 2(2^{n+1} - 1)U^{n+2}}{(1 - 2U)(1 - U)}$$

$$\sum = 2\frac{1 - (2U)^{n+1}}{1 - 2U} - \frac{1 - U^{n+1}}{1 - U}$$

$$\sum = 1 + 3U + 7U^2 + \cdots + (2^{m+1} - 1)U^m + \cdots + A_n U^n$$
Scale of relation $= 2A_m - 3A_{m+1} + 1A_{m+2} = 0$

Equation (14.10#4) has the algebraic form

$$B_2 A_m + B_1 A_{m+1} + 1 A_{m+2} = 0 \tag{14.10#5}$$

where each B is constant and independent of m and the right side is zero. Equation (14.10#5) is known as the *scale of relation*, and the B multipliers are referred to as the *constants of the scale*. Equation (14.10#4) has two independent constants of the scale; hence Eq. (14.10#3) is a recurring series of the second order.

Recurring power series were first investigated by the French mathematician de Moivre (1667–1754). A recurring power series is readily summed when its scale of relation and an expression for the general coefficient are known. The general term for Eq. (14.10#3), as will be shown, is

$$(2^{m+1} - 1)U^m \tag{14.10#6}$$

The summation is accomplished by adding the original series and others derived from it in a way that will utilize the scale of relation and compel most of the terms in the addition to become zero and vanish. For example, to find the sum $\sum$ for Eq. (14.10#3) use the numbers $+1$, -3, and $+2$, taken reading from right to left in the scale of relation, form the series

$$+1\sum \; -3U\sum \; +2U^2 \sum$$

and add the series so formed. The work is shown in Table 14.10T1.

14.11 General term from generating function

In summing Eq. (14.10#3) by Table 14.10T1, an expression for the general term coefficient A_m was needed. Consider the following fraction taken from Table 14.10T1

$$\frac{A_0 + (A_1 - 3A_0)U}{1 - 3U + 2U^2} = \frac{1}{1 - 3U + 2U^2}$$
$$= 1 + 3U + 7U^2 + 15U^3 + 31U^4 + \cdots$$

The fraction is known as the *generating function*. The generating function can be used to find the general term inasmuch as it generates the series. By the method of partial fractions developed in standard textbooks of college algebra

$$\frac{1}{1 - 3U + 2U^2} = \frac{2}{1 - 2U} - \frac{1}{1 - U}$$

and

$$\frac{2}{1 - 2U} = 2 + 4U + \cdots + 2^{m+1}U^m + \cdots$$

$$-\frac{1}{1 + U} = -1 - U + \cdots \quad -1U^m + \cdots$$

The general term is $(2^{m+1} - 1)U^m$, as used previously.

14.12 Some recurring power series

The following series all have the scale of relation

$$A_m - 2A_{m+1} + A_{m+2} = 0$$

$$\Sigma = U + 2U^2 + 3U^3 + \cdots + nU^n \quad (14.12\#1)$$

$$\Sigma = U^2 + 2U^3 + 3U^4 + \cdots + (n - 1)U^n \quad (14.12\#2)$$

$$\Sigma = BU + (B + A)U^2 + (B + 2A)U^3 + \cdots + [B + (n - 1)A]U^n \quad (14.12\#3)$$

Summations, up to and including the term in U^n, are, respectively, where A or B can be negative

$$\Sigma = U\frac{1 - (n + 1)U^n + nU^{n+1}}{(1 - U)^2} \quad (14.12\#4)$$

$$\Sigma = U^2\frac{1 - nU^{n-1} + (n - 1)U^n}{(1 - U)^2} \quad (14.12\#5)$$

$$\Sigma = U\frac{B - (B - A)U - (B + A_n)U^n + (B - A + A_n)U^{n+1}}{(1 - U)^2} \quad (14.12\#6)$$

The series

$$\Sigma = GU^2 + 2GU^3 + \cdots + (n - 1)GU^n$$

is particularly important because it arises in connection with a machine for which the annual expense increases at a constant rate, G per year. The summation is given by Eq. (14.12#5), which when multiplied by G and with $1/(1 + i)$ replacing U reduces to

$$\Sigma = \frac{G}{i(1 + i)^n}\left[\frac{(1 + i)^{n-1}}{i} - n\right]$$

The uniform-gradient series was discussed in Sec. 6.4.

Another series of considerable importance is the present worth of $1 of depreciation taken with sum-of-digits method of depreciation. Sum-of-digits is algebraically $0.5n(n+1)$, and the series is

$$\Sigma = \frac{n}{0.5n(n+1)}U + \frac{n-1}{0.5n(n+1)}U^2 + \cdots + \frac{1}{0.5n(n+1)}U^n$$

The series can be summed by Eq. (14.12#6), which after multiplication by $1/[0.5n(n+1)]$ and with $B = n$, $A = -1$, and $U = 1/(1+i)$, becomes

$$\Sigma = \frac{1}{0.5n(n+1)i}\left[n - \frac{(1+i)^n - 1}{i(1+i)^n}\right] \qquad (14.12\#7)$$

or

$$\Sigma = \frac{n - F_{RP,i,n}}{0.5n(n+1)i} \qquad (14.12\#8)$$

14.13 Nomenclature

- B Constant in scale of relation Sec. 14.10
- D Distance from end of interval in Fibonacci search
- F Objective function to be optimized
- F_i Fibonacci number
- F_r Fractional ratio of interval left to original interval
- $F_{RP,i,n}$ The factor $[(1+i)^n - 1]/i(1+i)^n$; see Sec. 2.2
- G Gradient amount, or constant increase or decrease
- i Decimal rate of return in Secs. 14.10 to 14.12
- L Range of a variable
- m The mth or general term
- n The nth or last term
- N Number of experiments or calculations allowed
- P Present worth, $
- U The factor $1/(1+i)$

14.14 Problems

P1. Assume that the model is really the evaluation of the square root of 3. Assume that the solution is known to lie in the range of 0 to 5. Evaluate $\sqrt{3}$ to an interval that is 0.05 wide. Use the Fibonacci search technique. *Hint*: $|X^2 - 3|$ is a minimum if $X = \sqrt{3}$.

P2. Repeat Prob. 14.14P1 using the sequential dichotomous search method.

P3. Using the method of steepest ascent, find the minimum value of

$$Z = X^2 + 2Y^2 + XY$$

starting at the point $X = 2$, $Y = 3$. Use an initial step size on Y of 0.5.

P4. Given the objective function

$$Z = X^2 + 25Y^2$$

How can this problem be transformed into one giving spherical contours?

P5. Repeat Prob. 14.14P3 using the one-at-a-time-method.

P6. Find the scale of relation and the next term of the series

$$\Sigma = 1 + 3U + 6U^2 + 10U^3 + 15U^4 + 21U^5 + 28U^6 + \cdots$$

P7. Find the generating function for Prob. 14.14P6.
P8. Verify Eq. (14.12#5).
P9. Verify Eq. (14.12#7).

14.15 References on search methods

R1. Boas, A. H.: How Search Methods Locate Optimum in Univariable Problems, *Chem. Eng.*, Feb. 4, 1963, p. 105.
R2. Boas, A. H.: Optimizing Multivariable Functions, *Chem. Eng.*, March 4, 1963, p. 97.
R3. Carroll, C. W.: The Created Response Surface Technique for Optimizing Nonlinear Restrained Systems, *J. Operations Res. Soc. Am.*, vol. 9, pp. 169–185, March, 1961.
R4. Fiacco, A. V., and G. P. McCormick: SUMT without Parameters, *Northwestern U. Techn. Inst. Systems Res. Mem.* 121, April, 1965.
R5. Fiacco, A. V., and G. P. McCormick: Programming under Nonlinear Constraints by Unconstrained Minimization: A Primal-Dual Method, *Res. Analysis Corp. Tech. Paper* RAC-TP-96, September, 1963.
R6. Fiacco, A. V., and G. P. McCormick: Computational Algorithm for the Sequential Unconstrained Minimization Technique for Non-linear Programming, *Management Sci.*, vol. 10, no. 4, pp. 601–617, 1964.
R7. Fiacco, A. V., and G. P. McCormick: The Sequential Unconstrained Minimization Technique for Nonlinear Programming, a Primal-Dual Method, *Management Sci.*, vol. 10, no. 2, pp. 360–366, 1964.
R8. Fiacco, A. V., and G. P. McCormick: Extensions of SUMT for Non-linear Programming: Equality Constraints and Extrapolation, *Management Sci.*, vol. 12, no. 11, pp. 816–828, 1966.
R9. Friedman, M., and L. S. Savage: "Selected Techniques of Statistical Analysis," McGraw-Hill Book Company, New York, 1947.
R10. Hoerl, A. E.: Optimum Solution of Many Variables Equations, *Chem. Eng. Progr.*, vol. 55, no. 11, pp. 69–78, 1959.
R11. Hooke, R., and T. A. Jeeves: Direct Search Solution of Numerical and Statistical Problems, *J. Assoc. Computing Machinery*, vol. 8, no. 2, p. 212, 1961.
R12. Johnson, S. M.: Best Exploration for Maximum Is Fibonaccian, *U.S. Air Force Project Rand Res. Mem.* RM-1590, Nov. 18, 1955.
R13. Keifer, J.: Sequential Minimax Search for a Maximum, *Proc. Am. Math. Soc.*, vol. 4, no. 3, 1953.
R14. Roberts, S. M., and H. I. Lyvers: The Gradient Method in Process Control, *Ind. Eng. Chem.*, vol. 53, no. 11, pp. 877–882, 1961.
R15. Rosenbrock, H. H.: Automatic Method for Finding the Greatest or Least Value of a Function, *Computer J.*, vol. 3, no. 3, pp. 175–184, 1960.
R16. Wilde, D. J.: "Optimum Seeking Methods," Prentice-Hall, Inc., Englewood Cliffs, N.J., 1964.
R17. Wilde, D. J., and C. S. Beightler: "Foundations of Optimization," Prentice-Hall, Inc., Englewood Cliffs, N.J., 1967.
R18. Zellnik, H. E., N. E. Sondak, and R. S. Davis: Gradient Search Optimization, *Chem. Eng. Progr.*, vol. 58, no. 8, pp. 35–41, 1962.

14.16 References on series summation

R1. Chrystal, G.: "Algebra," pt. 2, chap. 31, Dover Publications, Inc., New York, 1961.
R2. Fine, H. B.: "College Algebra," chap. 35, Dover Publications, Inc., New York, 1961.
R3. Jelen, F. C.: Series Summation for Economic Analysis, *Hydrocarbon Proces.*, December, 1967, pp. 153–157.

part three
Cost Estimation and Control

15
Capital Investment Cost Estimation

O. T. Zimmerman

15.1 Fixed capital and working capital

The total quantity of money required to put a project in operation is known as capital investment. It is composed of two parts: (1) the fixed capital investment to provide the physical facilities and (2) the working capital investment, a sort of revolving fund to keep the facility in operation. An investment cost is a one-time cost, as opposed to operating costs, which are continuous.

Fixed capital investment is the capital required to provide *all* the facilities needed for the project regardless of how remote they might be to manufacturing operations; e.g., a rolling mill or a refrigerator in the employees' cafeteria. Fixed capital investment can be divided into various categories such as design and engineering, land purchase and improvement, manufacturing and allied buildings, equipment, utilities and services, receiving and shipping, and start-up.

Although land does involve a capital investment, some prefer to include in fixed capital only those items for which depreciation is allowed by the Internal Revenue Service [15.19R73], thus excluding land. However, if land costs are included in the total investment, it makes little difference in what subcategory they appear.

Working capital is the funds, in addition to fixed capital and start-up expenses, needed by a company to get a project started and meet subsequent obligations

[15.19R73]. For a manufacturing enterprise, working capital consists of inventories, accounts receivable, cash for wages and materials, etc., and other accounts payable.

In general, working capital is taken as the sum of the above items for a 1-month period. In manufacturing industries, working capital is about 10 to 20% of fixed capital investment, and for a rough estimate can be taken as 20% of total investment. However, in some industries, e.g., those with high sales costs and service industries, the figure can become 50% and higher.

15.2 Types of estimates

A cost estimate for a project can vary from an instant estimate, or *quickie*, to a detailed estimate prepared from complete drawings and specifications with accuracy depending on how much is known about the project and how much time and effort is spent on the preparation of the estimate.

Edmunds [15.19R24] gives six basic types of estimates for building construction used by architects and engineers:

1. Quickie
2. Original
3. Preliminary
4. Official or budget
5. Final or definitive
6. Revised

The American Association of Cost Engineers [15.19R1] has proposed five classifications of estimating types:

1. Order-of-magnitude (ratio estimate)
2. Study (factored estimate)
3. Preliminary (budget authorization estimate)
4. Definitive (project control estimate)
5. Detailed (firm estimate)

Another classification of estimate types [15.19R30] based on probable accuracy is:

1. Detailed unit cost $\pm 3\%$
2. Material takeoff $\pm 6\%$
3. Defined equipment ratio $\pm 12\%$
4. Preliminary equipment ratio $\pm 25\%$
5. Capacity-cost curve $\pm 40\%$

15.3 Cost of making estimates

The cost of making an estimate of a given accuracy can vary over a large range [15.19R9, p. 41]. The figures in Table 15.3T1 show at least that an estimate of 50% accuracy costs very little, while one of 5% accuracy can cost considerably.

Table 15.3T1 Typical Costs for Preparing Estimates*

Accuracy range, %	Project cost, $MM					
	0.5	1	5	10	15	20
	Cost of estimate, $					
−3 to +12	15,000	25,000	45,000	70,000	90,000	120,000
−5 to +15	7,000	13,000	20,000	35,000	45,000	60,000
−10 to +28	2,500	4,500	8,000	13,000	16,000	20,000
−20 to +40	900	1,700	2,800	4,500	6,300	8,000
−30 to +50	500	950	1,500	2,500	3,500	4,500
−40 to +60	300	600	1,000	1,700	2,300	3,000
−50 to +70	250	350	600	900	1,300	1,700

* Positive estimate is underestimate, minus estimate is overestimate. Figures based on [15.19R47].

15.4 Functions of capital-cost estimates

Estimates of capital costs are made for various purposes, the most important of which are:

1. Feasibility studies
2. Selection from among alternative designs
3. Selection from among alternative investments
4. Appropriation of funds
5. Presentation of bids

Before private funds are appropriated for capital expenditures, feasibility studies must show that the expected profit is sufficient to justify the risk of capital. For the allocation of public funds, such as a project to land a man on the moon, there is no simple measure of feasibility. Nevertheless, such funds are not unlimited, and some kind of feasibility study is important.

Capital-cost estimates serve many functions, such as order of magnitude for screening purposes. In general an engineering problem has no unique solution. Somehow a selection must be made based on economic studies. Again, those with money to invest have a choice of investments, and decisions can be determined only by cost studies. Appropriation requests from simple requisitions to large-scale expenditures must be based on cost estimates.

Finally, vendors or contractors must estimate bids very carefully. If the bid is too high, they may not be awarded the job, but if the bid is too low, they may be awarded the job and then take a substantial loss.

15.5 Representation of cost data

Cost estimates are prepared from the cost of similar projects or the cost of the components of the project. Many companies have extensive files of cost data derived from previous projects. Published cost information is voluminous, but the accuracy is not always known.

Cost data are usually published in the form of figures, such as Figs. 15.5F1 and 15.5F2, or tables, such as Tables 15.7T2 and 15.7T3. Costs are expressed either as total cost or as cost per unit of capacity or size. The cost of buildings is usually expressed as dollars per square foot of floor area or dollars per cubic foot, and building components in terms such as dollars per thousand (brick) and dollars per ton (structural steel). Labor rates are expressed as dollars per hour.

Generally a plot of unit cost is more compact than one for total cost, as in Fig. 15.5F1.

Unfortunately, when using published cost data it is not always clear what is included in the cost. Some equipment costs refer to purchased prices, while others are installed costs, which in turn may or may not include auxiliary equipment. A similar difficulty exists with plant cost data. Some costs are for complete new plants including land, utilities, and auxiliary facilities. Other costs are restricted to battery-limits costs. Ordinarily, all manufacturing facilities are within the battery limits, but administrative offices, storage areas, utilities, and other auxiliary facilities are outside these limits. Battery limits are defined in Sec. 18.7.

Published cost data should be used only for order-of-magnitude estimates since their accuracy is seldom known, and discrepancies of 50% are not uncommon. Some cost data are based on specific information, and are not generally applicable. Other cost data are average values, and an average is questionable when applied to a particular case.

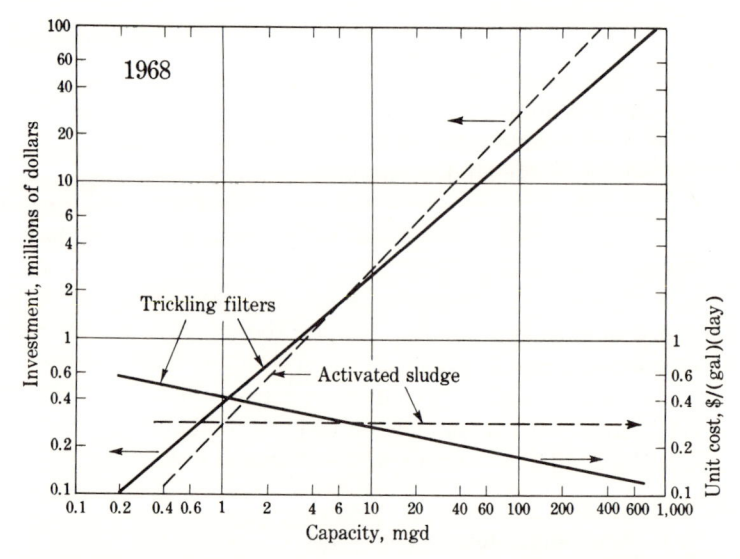

Fig. 15.5F1 Cost of sewage plants with primary and secondary (activating sludge and trickling filter) treatment. (*H. E. Klei, J. M. Tamborra, and R. T. Wood, Capital Cost of Sewage Plants, Water Wastes Eng., vol. 5, p. 61, April, 1968.*)

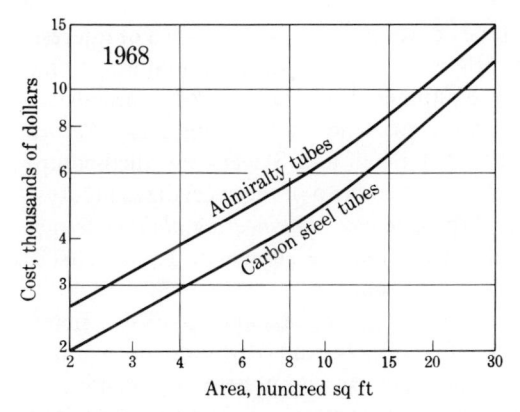

Fig. 15.5F2 Cost of floating-head removable-bundle heat exchangers with ¾-in. by 16-gauge tubes, 1 in. square pitch, for 150 psi. Add 15% for 300 psi. (*W. E. Hand, Estimating Capital Costs from Process Flow Sheets, AACE Cost Engineers' Notebook, Paper A3, January,* 1964.)

15.6 Cost indexes

The dollar depreciates and now falls in value continuously [15.19R77], as shown in Fig. 15.6F1. This means that all published cost data are out of date. A means for converting past to present costs is usually accomplished by means of a cost index which gives the relative cost of an item in terms of the cost at some particular base period.

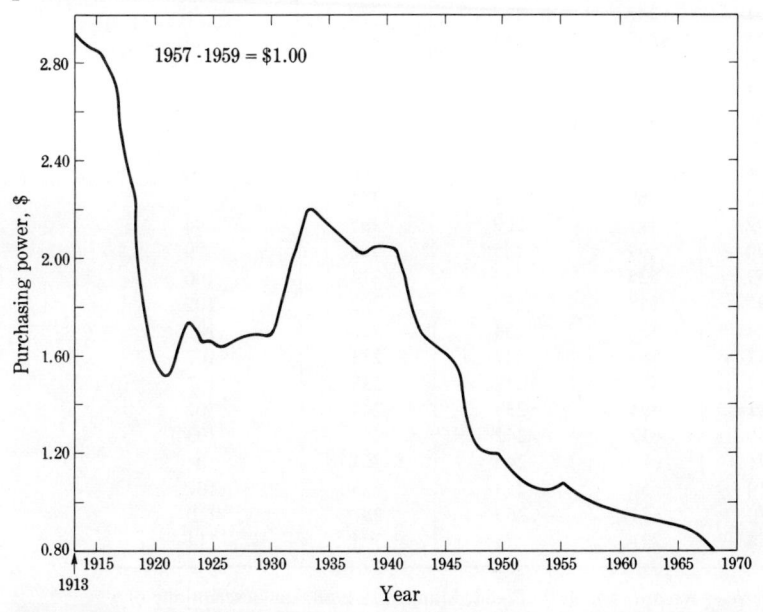

Fig. 15.6F1 Purchasing power of the consumer dollar in the United States, 1913–1968.

306 COST ESTIMATION AND CONTROL

There are many cost indexes, and they cover practically every area of interest. Some are based on national averages, others on costs in individual cities. Some cover broad areas of construction or equipment, others are very specialized. Perhaps the most frequently used indexes are the *Engineering News-Record* construction and building indexes and the Marshall and Stevens installed-equipment index shown in Table 15.6T1, which also shows two of the specialized indexes, the *Nelson refinery construction index* and the *Chemical Engineering plant construction index*. A few of the many specialized indexes are shown in Table 15.6T2. The values have been rounded off to the nearest unit.

The Bureau of Labor Statistics of the Department of Labor publishes many data on price changes of many types of products and earnings of workers in practically all industries. Some of these data are components of many cost indexes, and others are useful for the construction of highly specialized indexes.

The *Engineering News-Record* index [15.19R26] is usually based on 100 for

Table 15.6T1 Some Major Cost Indexes*

Year	Engineering News-Record Construction 1913 = 100	Engineering News-Record Building 1913 = 100	Marshall and Stevens installed-equipment 1926 = 100	Nelson refinery construction 1946 = 100	Chemical Engineering plant construction 1957–1959 = 100
1948	461	345	163	133	70
1949	477	352	161	140	71
1950	510	375	168	146	74
1951	543	401	180	157	80
1952	569	416	181	162	81
1953	600	431	183	174	85
1954	628	446	185	180	86
1955	660	469	191	184	88
1956	692	491	209	195	94
1957	724	509	225	206	99
1958	759	525	229	214	100
1959	797	548	235	222	102
1960	824	559	238	228	102
1961	847	568	237	233	102
1962	872	580	239	238	102
1963	901	594	239	244	102
1964	936	612	242	252	103
1965	971	627	245	261	104
1966	1019	650	253	273	107
1967	1070	671	263	287	110
1968	1154	721	273	304	114

* See *Engineering News-Record*, vol. 180; 77–88, March 21, 1968, for descriptions of a number of indexes.

Table 15.6T2 Some Specialized Cost Indexes

Year	Sewage-treatment plants* 1957–1959 = 100	Sewer-line construction* 1957–1959 = 100	Water-utility plants† 1913 = 100	Irrigation and hydro-electric plants‡ 1949–1951 = 100	Highway bid prices§ 1957–1959 = 100
1957	98	97	675	122	103
1958	102	100	729	130	101
1959	104	105	751	128	96
1960	105	106	769	127	94
1961	106	108	786	126	95
1962	107	110	806	128	99
1963	108	113	826	130	101
1964	109	115	853	132	102
1965	111	116	881	134	106
1966	115	120	916	137	113
1967	118	124	957	142	118
1968	123	128	998	150	122

* From Department of the Interior.
† From Weber, Fick, and Wilson.
‡ From U.S. Bureau of Reclamation.
§ From U.S. Bureau of Public Roads.

the year 1913, although indexes are also prepared on the bases of 1926 = 100 and 1949 = 100. The components of these indexes are:

Component	Construction index	Building index
Structural steel shapes, base mill price, cwt	25	25
Portland cement 20-cities average, bulk, bbl	6	6
2 × 4, S4S lumber, 20-city average, MBF	1.088	1.088
Common labor, 20-city average, hr	200	
Skilled labor, 20-city average, hr		68.38

The Marshall and Stevens equipment cost index is the average index of installed costs in 47 industries and is obtained by a complex procedure involving equipment appraisals, modifying factors, and a judgment of current economic conditions [15.19R65].

The Nelson refinery construction cost index is based on a 40% material and 60% labor distribution, as explained in [15.19R46].

308 COST ESTIMATION AND CONTROL

The *Chemical Engineering* chemical plant cost index is a complex index [15.19R3], consisting of four major components.

Component	Percent
Equipment machinery and supports	61
Erection and installation labor	22
Buildings, material, and labor	7
Engineering and supervision manpower	10
Total	100

The equipment component is made up of seven subcomponents, and the others are made up from Bureau of Labor Statistics data, the last combined with salary data from other sources.

Figure 15.6F2 shows indexes based on Bureau of Labor Statistics data [15.19R67, 15.19R68]. The labor index is the average hourly earnings, in cents per hour, in the durable goods industries, and the material index is the wholesale

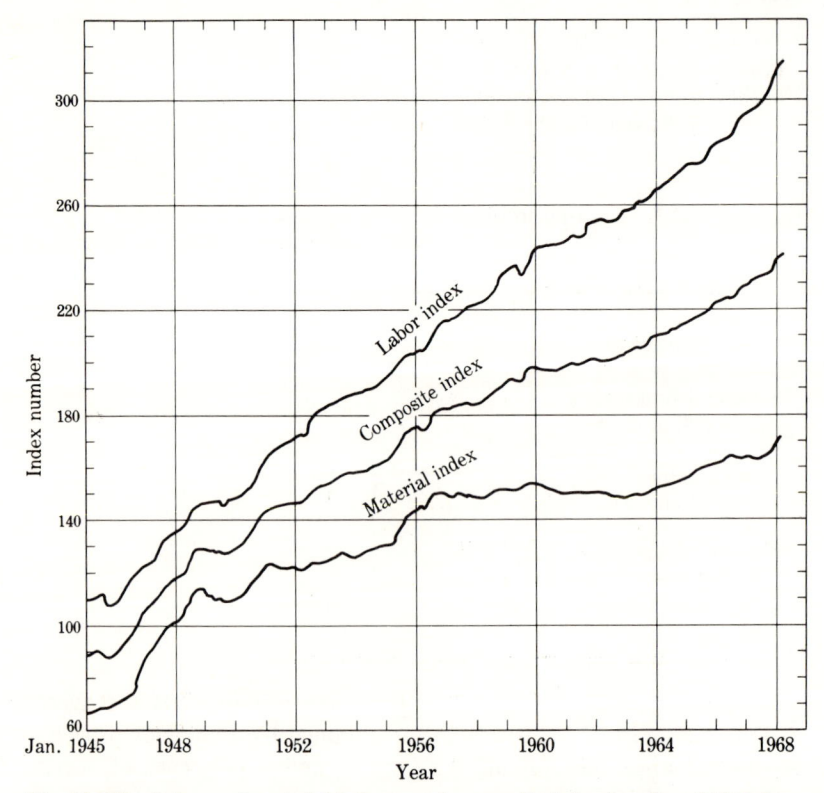

Fig. 15.6F2 Labor and material indexes and composite index based on 50% labor, 50% materials, 1945–1968.

Table 15.6T3 Comparison of Cost Indexes

Index	Ratio $\dfrac{1967 \text{ index}}{1957 \text{ index}}$
Engineering News-Record construction	1.48
Engineering News-Record building	1.32
Marshall and Stevens	1.18
Nelson refinery construction	1.39
Chemical Engineering plant construction	1.11
Sewage-treatment plants	1.20
Sewer-line construction	1.28
Water-utility plants	1.42
Irrigation and hydroelectric plants	1.16
Highway bid prices	1.15
Bureau of Labor Statistics, 50:50 material-labor	1.25

price index for the metals and metal products group, 1947 to 1949 = 100. The composite index is based on a 50:50 material-labor distribution. These indexes are published in each issue of *Cost Engineering*.

For ordinary carbon steel construction, equipment cost is about equally divided between labor and material costs, and the 50:50 composite index is satisfactory. For stainless steel a similar curve can be prepared using a 65:35 material-labor distribution.

When cost indexes are converted to the same base and plotted on the same graph for comparison, the curves are very irregular [15.19R76]. Therefore, any comparison of cost indexes is valid only for the specific time interval used. Table 15.6T3 shows a comparison for the indexes given in Table 15.6T1 and 15.6T2 for the 10-year period from 1957 to 1967.

Cost indexes have limitations on accuracy and like all statistical devices must be used with caution [15.19R15, 15.19R58, 15.19R76]. As we have just pointed out, two indexes may give results that differ considerably.

Since most indexes are based on data combined in more or less arbitrary fashion, there is no assurance that the indexes truly represent the cost of the complete article or structure. Even if the index was good when started, changes in labor productivity may make the index less useful.

A cost index, like cost data themselves, can hope only to reflect average changes, and an average often has little meaning when applied to a specific case.

Under the most favorable conditions over a 4- or 5-year period, a 10% accuracy is the most that can be expected. For periods greater than 10 years, the accuracy falls off rapidly.

Example 15.6E1 An air-conditioning system was purchased for $50,000 in 1958. Estimate its cost in 1965 using Marshall and Stevens indexes.

$$50,000 \frac{245 \text{ index } 1965}{229 \text{ index } 1958} = \$53,500, \text{ cost } 1965$$

Using the 50:50 curve of Fig. 15.6F2,

$$50{,}000 \; \frac{218 \text{ index } 1965}{187 \text{ index } 1958} = \$58{,}300, \text{ cost } 1965$$

For the 7-year period, the two indexes give results that differ by about 9%.

15.7 Cost-capacity factors

Cost estimates can be approximated for a plant or for equipment where cost data are available for similar projects but of different capacity than that desired. In general costs do not rise in strict proportion to size. The relationship can be expressed in the form

$$C_2 = C_1 \left(\frac{Q_2}{Q_1}\right)^X \qquad (15.7\#1)$$

where C_2 = desired cost of capacity Q_2
C_1 = known cost of capacity Q_1

The exponent X in Eq. (15.7#1) is known as the *cost-capacity* factor. On the average, X is about 0.6, and the relationship is referred to as the *six-tenths factor rule* [15.19R20, 15.19R74]. Q can be in any consistent units as it enters only as a ratio.

Example 15.7E1 An ethylene plant of 100,000 tons/year capacity costs $8 million. Estimate the cost of a 200,000 ton/year plant.
Using the 0.6 factor rule for Eq. (15.7#1),

$$C_2 = 8{,}000{,}000 \left(\frac{200{,}000}{100{,}000}\right)^{6.0} = \$12{,}100{,}000$$

An equation for unit cost, C/Q, analogous to Eq. (15.7#1), is easily derived by multiplying the equation by Q_1/Q_2.

$$C_2 \frac{Q_1}{Q_2} = C_1 \frac{Q_1}{Q_2}\left(\frac{Q_2}{Q_1}\right)^X = C_1 \left(\frac{Q_2}{Q_1}\right)^{-1}\left(\frac{Q_2}{Q_1}\right)^X$$

$$\frac{C_2}{Q_2} = \frac{C_1}{Q_1}\left(\frac{Q_2}{Q_1}\right)^{X-1} \qquad (15.7\#2)$$

Hence if total costs vary as the Xth power of capacity in Eq. (15.7#1), unit costs C/Q will vary as the $(X-1)$st power of the capacity ratio in Eq. (15.7#2).

A plot of total cost against capacity on log–log paper has a slope equal to X. Similarly, a plot of unit costs has a slope of $X-1$.

Although 0.6 is an average value for the cost-capacity factor, it ranges from less than 0.2 to greater than 1.0. Many cost-capacity curves are not straight lines

Table 15.7T1 Error Introduced by Use of 0.6 Factor

Ratio of Q_2/Q_1	Actual cost-capacity factor									
	0.2	0.3	0.4	0.5	0.6	0.7	0.8	0.9	1.0
	Percent error								
5:1	+89	+61	+37	+17	0	−16	−28	−39	−48
10:1	+150	+100	+59	+26	0	−21	−37	−50	−60

on log–log paper and often show sharp breaks. In such cases, two or more cost-capacity factors, each covering a certain range, give better results than an overall factor.

The 0.6 factor should be used only in the absence of other information. Table 15.7T1 gives the magnitude of the error introduced by using the 0.6 factor in place of various actual cost-capacity factors.

Tables 15.7T2 and 15.7T3 give examples of costs and typical cost-capacity factors. Many other cost-capacity factors can be found in the literature or can be calculated by plotting published data, [15.19R10 to 15.19R13, 15.19R54, 15.19R59].

15.8 Equipment installation cost ratios

In many cases a cost is estimated by multiplying one cost by a factor to get another cost. Thus, the cost of a building complete with electrical, plumbing, heating, ventilation, and air-conditioning systems might be estimated by multiplying the cost of shell by 1.6. Such factors are called *ratio cost factors* [15.19R78], which might be good to an accuracy of ±20% when applied to the known cost of key items.

A common use of ratio cost factors is the estimation of the installed cost of equipment from the purchase cost applying an *equipment installation cost ratio*. The installed cost is the sum of the f.o.b. cost, transportation cost, and costs of foundations, erection, and making connections to service facilities. Although each of these costs can be estimated separately, it is much easier to multiply the f.o.b. cost by a factor to give the installed cost.

On the average, the installed cost of equipment is about 1.5 times the purchase cost, but the installation costs of individual items can vary considerably from this 50% installation factor, as shown in Table 15.8T1.

A wide spread in installation costs arises because some installation costs include the cost of auxiliary equipment as well as the cost of installation. The installation cost for an electric motor can vary by 200%, depending on whether or not the cost of the motor control is considered part of the installation cost, for the purchase cost of controls varies from about twice that of the motor for small motors to about 40% for large motors.

Table 15.7T2 Cost of Battery-limits Plants*

Process	Capacity	Unit	Cost,† $/unit	Cost-capacity factor	Capacity range	Reference, Sec. 15.19
Acetylene	10	Tons/day	200	0.73	3.5–250	12
Aluminum (from alumina)	100 M	Metric Tons/yr	900	0.76	20 M–200 M	17
Ammonia (by steam-methane reforming)	100	Tons/day	26 M	0.72	100–3 M	14
Butadiene	10 M	Tons/yr	690	0.65	5 M–300 M	13
Butyl alcohol	100 MM	Lb/yr	0.027	0.55	8.5 MM–700 MM	13
Carbon black	1	Tons/day	15.3 M	0.53	1–150	44
Chlorine	100	Tons/day	90 M	0.62	10–800	13, 63
Ethanol, synthetic	10 MM	Gal/yr	0.36	0.60	3 MM–200 MM	11
Ethylene	100 M	Tons/yr	91	0.72	20 M–800 M	45
Hydrogen (from refinery gases)	10 MM	Cu ft/day	0.26	0.64	500 M–10 MM	18, 23
Methanol	10 MM	Gal/yr	0.36	0.83	5 MM–100 MM	12
Nitric acid (50–60%)	100	Tons/day	11.4 M	0.66	100–1 M	28
Oxygen	100	Tons/day	18 M	0.72	1–1.5 M	12, 36, 51, 69
Power plants, coal	100	Mw(elec)	200 M	0.88	100–1 M	16
Nuclear	100	Mw(elec)	270 M	0.68	100–4 M	16, 60
Styrene	10 M	Tons/yr	200	0.68	4 M–200 M	11
Sulfuric acid (100%)	100	Tons/day	6.2 M	0.67	100–1 M	6, 13, 28
Urea	250	Tons/day	13 M	0.67	100–250	28
Urea	250	Tons/day	13 M	0.20	250–500	28

* From O. T. Zimmerman and I. Lavine, *Cost Eng.*, vol. 6, pp. 16–18, July, 1961; and O. T. Zimmerman, *Cost Eng.*, vol. 12, pp. 12–19, October, 1967.
† Cost-capacity factor − 1 = cost-capacity factor for unit costs.

Table 15.7T3 Cost of Process Equipment*

Item	Capacity or size	Unit	Cost, $ per unit	Purchased P or installed I	Cost-capacity factor	Range
Centrifuges:						
Automatic batch:						
Horizontal basket, steel	30	In.	840	P	1.0	25–65 in. basket diam.
Stainless steel	30	In.	1,000	P	1.0	20–65 in. basket diam.
Vertical basket, steel	30	In.	600	P	1.0	40–50 in. basket diam.
Bottom driven, steel	30	In.	120	P	1.0	20–48 in. bowl diam.
Rubber-covered	30	In.	150	P	1.0	20–48 in. bowl diam.
Stainless steel	30	In.	180	P	1.0	20–48 in. bowl diam.
Compressors, air, centrifugal	5,000	Hp	3,800	P	1.0	100–10,000 hp
Crystallizers, batch, vacuum:						
Welded steel	6	Ft	2,400	P	0.50	4.5–11.25 ft diam.
Rubber-lined	6	Ft	3,100	P	0.64	4.5–11.25 ft diam.
304 SS-clad	6	Ft	5,600	P	0.64	4.5–11.25 ft diam.
Disintegrators, single-cage type	100	Tons/hr	90	P	0.71	30–450 tons/hr
Double-cage type	100	Tons/hr	105	P	0.56	10–300 tons/hr
Dryers (with auxiliaries):						
Direct rotary	1,000	Sq ft	56	P	0.90	300–3,000 sq ft peripheral area
Drum, atmospheric	100	Sq ft	190	P	0.60	20–400 sq ft drum surface
Vacuum	30	Sq ft	1,200	P	0.18	20–40 sq ft drum surface
	100	Sq ft	750	P	0.88	41–200 sq ft drum surface
Tunnel	500	Sq ft	140	P	0.94	150–1,000 sq ft conveying surface

Table 15.7T3 (continued)

Item	Capacity or size	Unit	Cost, $ per unit	Purchased P or installed I	Cost-capacity factor	Range
Dust collectors:						
Cloth filter, continuous, automatic	1,000	Cfm	0.94	P	0.78	100–15,000 cfm
Electrostatic precipitators, high voltage	10,000	Cfm	2.2	P	0.90	7,000–19,000 cfm
Low voltage	5,000	Cfm	1.3	P	0.90	1,000–19,000 cfm
Washers, with precleaner	5,000	Cfm	0.67	P	0.85	1,000–19,000 cfm
Without precleaner	5,000	Cfm	0.46	P	0.87	1,000–19,000 cfm
Evaporators:						
Agitated falling film (less motors and drives)						
316 SS	10	Sq ft	1,400	P	0.30	5–30 sq ft
	100	Sq ft	400	P	0.60	31–150 sq ft
Long-tube, rising-film, SS tubes	20	Sq ft	160	P	1.2	18–35 sq ft heating surface
Filters:						
Cartridge-type, cast iron or steel	1,000	Gal	0.17	P	0.41	300–2,000 gal capacity
316 SS	1,000	Gal	0.60	P	0.40	300–2,000 gal capacity
Continuous drum (complete unit) SS	30	Sq ft	740	P	0.40	3–100 sq ft filter area
Plate-and-frame, aluminum	200	Sq ft	19	P	0.65	10–600 sq ft filter area
Cast-iron	200	Sq ft	13	P	0.58	10–600 sq ft filter area
PVC-coated iron	200	Sq ft	27	P	0.61	10–600 sq ft filter area
Rubber-covered iron	200	Sq ft	36	P	0.60	30–600 sq ft filter area
Stainless steel	200	Sq ft	63	P	0.90	10–300 sq ft filter area
Wood	200	Sq ft	10	P	0.50	10–600 sq ft filter area
Heat exchangers (see Fig. 15.5F2)						
Kettles, jacketed (with accessories) lead-lined	500	Gal	245	I	0.32	500–1,000 gal
	2,000	Gal	106	I	0.50	1,100–2,200 gal
316 SS-clad	1,000	Gal	245	I	0.40	900–2,000 gal
	3,000	Gal	140	I	0.67	2,000–3,800 gal

Kneaders, stationary, upright double-arm (with accessories; less motor and starter) Monel					
Steel	200	Gal	220	P	0.60	100–750 gal
304 SS	200	Gal	130	P	0.60	100–750 gal
316 SS	200	Gal	195	P	0.60	100–750 gal
	200	Gal	210	P	0.60	100–750 gal
Motors, ac electric, 220/440 volt, 1,800 rpm						
Drip-proof	10	Hp	28	P	0.70	2–30 hp
Explosion-proof	10	Hp	37	P	0.70	2–30 hp
Open	10	Hp	22	P	0.80	2–30 hp
Totally enclosed, fan-cooled	10	Hp	34	P	0.70	2–30 hp
Pumps, canned	5	Hp	350	P	0.50	1–15 hp
Centrifugal, 316, SS end suction						
Pump only	5	Hp	220	P	0.50	1–15 hp
With motor	5	Hp	320	P	0.40	1–15 hp
Refrigeration	50	Ton	260	P	0.80	12–150 tons
Tanks, polyester-fiberglass	1,000	Gal	1.06	P	0.70	10–10,000 gal
Storage, carbon steel (with accessories; less foundations) Cone roof	10,000	Bbl	1.75	I	0.80	8,000–90,000 bbl
Expansion roof, 5-ft lift	50,000	Bbl	1.90	I	0.70	20,000–90,000 bbl
10-ft lift	50,000	Bbl	2.30	I	0.70	15,000–90,000 bbl
Hemispheroid	20,000	Bbl	2.90	I	0.60	6,000–48,000 bbl
Pontoon, floating roof	30,000	Bbl	1.85	I	0.70	4,000–90,000 bbl
Spheroid, 5 psi	20,000	Bbl	4.10	I	0.70	6,000–45,000 bbl
15 psi	20,000	Bbl	4.80	I	0.70	6,000–45,000 bbl
20 psi	20,000	Bbl	5.50	I	0.70	6,000–45,000 bbl
Storage (with accessories; including foundation) horizontal, steel						
Vertical, steel	5,000	Gal	1.25	I	0.70	2,000–22,000 gal
	5,000	Gal	0.97	I	0.40	2,000–10,000 gal
	15,000	Gal	0.58	I	0.70	11,000–22,000 gal
304 SS	2,000	Gal	2.65	I	0.40	600–4,500 gal
	10,000	Gal	1.35	I	0.60	4,600–22,000 gal

* From O. T. Zimmerman and I. Lavine, *Cost Eng.*, vol. 6, pp. 13–22, April, 1961; vol. 7, pp. 8–10, April, 1962; vol. 7, pp. 6–8, January, 1962.

Table 15.8T1 Typical Equipment Installation Factors

Item	Reference, Sec. 15.19	Installation cost, %
Belt conveyors	70	20–25
Bucket elevators	70	25–40
Centrifugals, disk or bowl	57, 62	5–6
Top suspended	57, 62	30–40
Continuous	62	10–25
Crystallizers	70	30–50
Dryers, continuous drum	41	100*
Vacuum rotary	41	150–200*
Rotary	41	50–100*
Dust collectors, wet	61	220–450*
Dry	53	10–200*
Electrostatic precipitators	64	33–100*
Electric motors plus controls	2	60
Filters	48	25–45
Gas producers	66	45–250
Instruments	72	6–300
Ion exchangers	56	30–275*
Towers	48, 49	25–50
Turbine generators	50	10–30

* Includes accessories

15.9 Plant cost ratios

Plant cost ratios are factors used to obtain plant costs from major equipment costs. Lang [15.19R40] suggested multiplying the delivered cost of equipment by the following factors to obtain total process plant costs:

3.10 for solid process plants
3.63 for solid-fluid process plants
4.74 for fluid process plants

Such factors can be used only for order-of-magnitude estimates because they make no allowance for process variations and many other variables that affect costs.

Example 15.9E1 The delivered cost of the major equipment for a fluid process plant is $1 million. Estimate the total cost of the plant.
    Using a Lang factor,
  1,000,000 × 4.74 = $4,740,000

Greater accuracy can be achieved by using factors based on the different types of equipment. Hand [15.19R32] recommends the following factors:

4 for fractionating columns, pressure vessels, pumps, and instruments
3.5 for heat exchangers
2.5 for compressors
2 for fired heaters

Table 15.9T1 Process-plant Cost Ratio from Individual Equipment*

Equipment	Factor†
Blender	2.0
Blowers and fans (including motor)	2.5
Centrifuges (process)	2.0
Compressors:	
Centrifugals, motor-driven (less motor)	2.0
Steam turbine (including turbine)	2.0
Reciprocating, steam and gas	2.3
Motor-driven (less motor)	2.3
Ejectors (vacuum units)	2.5
Furnaces (package units)	2.0
Heat exchangers	4.8
Instruments	4.1
Motors, electric	8.5
Pumps:	
Centrifugal, motor-driven (less motor)	7.0
Steam turbine (including turbine)	6.5
Positive displacement (less motor)	5.0
Reactors—factor as approximate equivalent type of equipment	
Refrigeration (package unit)	2.5
Tanks:	
Process	4.1
Storage	3.5
Fabricated and field-erected (50,000 + gal)	2.0
Towers (columns)	4.0

* W. F. Wroth, Factors in Cost Estimation, *Chem. Eng.*, vol. 67, p. 204, October, 1960.

† Multiply purchase cost by factor to obtain installed cost, including cost of site development, buildings, electrical installations, carpentry, painting, contractor's fee and rentals, foundations, structures, piping, installation, engineering, overhead, and supervision.

These factors are very close to those in the more complete list shown in Table 15.9T1.

Example 15.9E2 Estimate the battery-limits cost of a process plant having the following purchase cost of major equipment:

Blowers and fans	$ 10,000
Compressors, reciprocating	50,000
Furnaces	100,000
Heat exchangers	80,000
Instruments	50,000
Motors electric	60,000
Pumps, centrifugal, motor-driven	20,000
Tanks, process	25,000
Field-erected	90,000
Towers	200,000
Total	$685,000

Using the individual cost ratios from Table 15.9T1,

Blowers and fans	$ 10,000 × 2.5 = $ 25,000
Compressors, reciprocating	50,000 × 2.3 = 115,000
Furnaces	100,000 × 2.0 = 200,000
Heat exchangers	80,000 × 4.8 = 384,000
Instruments	50,000 × 4.1 = 205,000
Motors, electric	60,000 × 8.5 = 510,000
Pumps, centrifugal, motor-driven	20,000 × 7.0 = 140,000
Tanks, process	25,000 × 4.1 = 102,500
Field-erected	90,000 × 2.0 = 180,000
Towers	200,000 × 4.0 = 800,000
Total	$2,661,500

The cost is approximately $2,700,000. If the plant is assumed to be a solid-fluid process plant, its cost based on 3% delivery charge and 3.63 for the Lang factor is

685,000(1.03)(3.63) = $2,560,000

15.10 Plant component ratios

Another approach to plant estimation is the use of separate factors for erection of equipment, foundations, and anything the estimator wants to include. Table 15.10T1 shows the usual range of principal battery-limits components for process plants [15.19R5, 15.19R28, 15.19R29, 15.19R33, 15.19R34, 15.19R55].

Table 15.10T1 Process-plant Investment Components

Item	Percent of total plant investment
Direct process cost:	
Principal equipment items	15–40
Installation of principal equipment items	6–16
Process piping (installed)	2–25
Instruments (installed)	1–8
Electrical (installed)	1–5
Buildings, process	0.5–15
Average total process costs	53
Other direct costs:	
Utilities (installed)	3–20
General services	0.5–10
Buildings, general	4–14
Receiving, shipping, storage (installed)	2–12
Average total direct costs	78
Indirect costs:	
Engineering, overhead, etc.	8–16
Contingencies	9–22
Average indirect costs	22
Grand total cost	100

15.11 CAPITAL INVESTMENT COST ESTIMATION 319

Example 15.10E1 The principal equipment items for a fluid processing plant, highly automated, with equipment erected in the open are estimated to cost $500,000. Estimate the battery-limits plant cost.

For such a plant instrumentation costs will be high and building costs low. On the basis of Table 15.10T1 the percentage assigned to the various components, other than principal equipment items and their installation, is now assumed to be

(a) Process piping, installed	20%
Instruments, installed	6
Electrical, installed	4
Process buildings	1
General buildings	5
	36%

and for the components for which no special information is available

(b) Utilities installed	6%
General services	2
Receiving, shipping, storage, installed	5
Engineering, overhead, etc.	12
Contingencies	10
	35%

Sum of (a) and (b)

$36 + 35 = 71\%$

Equipment + installation = $100 - 71 = 29\%$
Take 40% as the equipment installation cost; then

$\dfrac{1}{1.40} 29 = 21\%$ principal equipment items

$\dfrac{500{,}000}{0.21} = \$2{,}400{,}000$ battery-limits plant cost

Table 15.10T2 shows a subdivision of costs by components for one $10 million process plant. Unless a great deal of information is available, an overall factor will probably be as good as a number of component factors, as in Tables 15.10T1 and 15.10T2.

15.11 Plant cost by analytical procedure

Today, with the emphasis on computers, there is interest in the use of equations, instead of tables and charts, for cost estimation. Hirsch and Glazier [15.19R35] developed the following equation, suitable for computer calculation:

$$I = E[A(1 + F_L + F_P + F_M) + B + C] \qquad (15.11\#1)$$

320 COST ESTIMATION AND CONTROL

Table 15.10T2 Typical Plant-cost Breakdown

Item	Percent	Cost, $M
Principal equipment	24	2,400
Installation of principal equipment (exclusive of foundations, painting, and insulation)	7	700
Foundations	1	100
Process piping (installed, exclusive of painting and insulation)	7	700
Painting and insulation of equipment, piping, and structures	2	200
Electrical (installed)	4	400
Instruments (installed)	3	300
Buildings, process	2	200
General	4	400
Receiving, shipping, and storage (installed)	5	500
Utilities (installed)	9	900
Site improvement, fences, parking lots, etc.	3	300
Land	1	100
Engineering and supervision	8	800
Construction expenses	8	800
Contractors' fees	2	200
Contingencies	10	1,000
	100	$10,000

where I = total battery-limits investment, $

A = total purchased equipment cost on an f.o.b. basis less incremental cost for corrosion-resistant alloys, $

B = installed equipment cost, $[1]

C = incremental cost of alloy materials used only for their corrosion-resisting properties, $

E = indirect cost factor representing contractors' overhead and profit, engineering, supervision, and contingencies; E is normally assumed to be 1.4

F_L = cost factor for field labor; $F_L A$ is total cost for field labor, less supervision, and excluding the labor charges in item B

F_M = cost factor for miscellaneous items; $F_M A$ includes materials cost for insulation, instruments, foundations, structural steel, buildings, wiring, painting, and the cost of freight and field supervision

F_P = cost factor for piping materials; $F_P A$ is the total cost of piping materials, including pipe, fittings, valves, hangers, and supports but excluding insulation and installation charges

---
[1] All vessels larger than 12 ft in diameter should be considered as field-erected unless specifically designated as shop-fabricated.

15.11 CAPITAL INVESTMENT COST ESTIMATION

The three factors F_L, F_P, and F_M are not simple ratios, but are defined by the equations

$$\log F_L = 0.635 - 0.154 \log A_0 - 0.992 \frac{e}{A} + 0.506 \frac{f}{A} \qquad (15.11\#2)$$

$$\log F_P = -0.266 - 0.014 \log A_0 - 0.156 \left(\frac{e}{A}\right) + 0.556 \frac{p}{A} \qquad (15.11\#3)$$

$$F_M = 0.344 + 0.033 \log A_0 + 1.194 \frac{t}{A} \qquad (15.11\#4)$$

where $A_0 = A/1,000$, $M
      e = total heat exchanger cost, less incremental cost of alloy, $
      f = total cost of field-fabricated vessels, less incremental cost of alloy, $;
          ordinarily all vessels larger than 12 ft in diameter are field-erected
      p = total pump plus driver cost less incremental cost of alloy, $
      t = total cost of tower shells less incremental cost of alloy, $

These equations are easily solved, but the effort can be reduced by a nomograph prepared by Walas [15.19R71].

Example 15.11E1 Estimate the total battery-limits investment for a process plant with estimated equipment costs shown in Table 15.11T1.

Table 15.11T1 Estimated Major Equipment Costs for Example 15.11E1

Item	Cost calculated on carbon steel basis, $M	Total calculated cost, including incremental alloy, $M	Incremental cost of alloy, $M
Towers:			
Shells, 12 ft diam. or less	$200		
Over 12 ft diam.	60	340	280
Trays and internals	400	500	100
Drums, 12 ft diam. or less	80		
Over 12 ft diam.	105		
Miscellaneous vessels:			
Shells, 12 ft diam. or less	40		
Over 12 ft diam.	350		
Total internals	55	75	20
Heat exchangers	1,200		
Pumps	140		
Pump drives	120		
Compressors	1,500		
Miscellaneous f.o.b. equipment	60		
Total f.o.b. equipment cost	$4,310		
Erected equipment costs:			
Fired heaters	360		
Tanks	11		
Total erected equipment costs	$371		

322 COST ESTIMATION AND CONTROL 15.12

From the data given, the following factors are derived:

$A = \$4,310,000$
$A_0 = \$4,310$
$B = \$371,000$
$C = \$280,000 + \$100,000 + \$20,000 = \$400,000$

$$\frac{e}{A} = \frac{\$1,200,000}{\$4,310,000} = 0.278$$

$$\frac{f}{A} = \frac{\$60,000 + \$105,000 + \$350,000}{\$4,310,000} = 0.119$$

$$\frac{p}{A} = \frac{\$140,000 + \$120,000}{\$4,310,000} = 0.060$$

$$\frac{t}{A} = \frac{\$200,000 + \$60,000}{\$4,310,000} = 0.060$$

from which Eqs. (15.11#2) to (15.11#4) give F_L, F_P, and F_M.

$$\log F_L = 0.635 - 0.154 \log A_0 - 0.992 \frac{e}{A} + 0.506 \frac{f}{A}$$

$$= 0.635 - 0.154 \log 4,310 - 0.992(0.278) + 0.506(0.119) = -0.140$$

$$F_L = 0.724$$

$$\log F_P = -0.266 - 0.014 \log A_0 - 0.156 \frac{e}{A} + 0.556 \frac{p}{A}$$

$$= -0.266 - 0.014 \log 4,310 - 0.156(0.278) + 0.556(0.060) = -0.327$$

$$F_P = 0.471$$

$$F_M = 0.344 + 0.033 \log A_0 + 1.194 \frac{t}{A}$$

$$= 0.344 + 0.033 \log 4,310 + 1.194(0.060)$$

$$= 0.536$$

Finally, from Eq. (15.11#1)

$$I = 1.4[4,310,000(1 + 0.724 + 0.471 + 0.536) + 371,000 + 400,000]$$

$$= \$17,600,000$$

or approximately $18 million.

It is interesting to note that the ratio of total investment to major equipment costs is

$$\frac{17,600,000}{4,310,000 + 371,000 + 280,000 + 100,000 + 20,000} = 3.5$$

and the ratio of total investment to f.o.b. costs of equipment is

$$\frac{17,600,000}{4,310,000 + 280,000 + 100,000 + 20,000} = 3.7$$

These factors are very close to overall plant-investment factors given previously.

In the absence of other information, multiplying the cost of major equipment items by 4 seems to be the easiest way to get a reasonable figure for total process-plant investment cost.

15.12 Building costs

An order-of-magnitude estimate for building costs can be made by multiplying the square feet of floor area or cubic feet of volume by a unit cost, as shown in

Table 15.12T1 Typical Costs of Industrial Buildings

	$ per square foot of floor area	$ per cubic foot
Single story:		
Manufacturing buildings	20	1.35
Warehouses	15	0.90
Multistory:		
Manufacturing buildings	17	1.20
Warehouses	12	0.80
Laboratories (equipped)	67	
Shops: carpenter, electrical, machine (equipped)	60	

Table 15.12T1. Large deviations from the average exist depending on construction, site, etc., with an example shown in Table 15.12T2 for a particular type of construction taken from Cherry. A more accurate method is to use unit costs for walls, floors, foundations, etc.; but these figures too can be in error for specific cases.

Table 15.12T3 shows a breakdown of costs for a particular building and gives unit costs for various components. Table 15.12T4 shows some unit material costs.

A percentage factor applied to the overall cost is often used for order-of-magnitude cost estimates for buildings in process plants, and as shown in Table 15.10T1 process buildings account for 0.5 to 15% of total process-plant cost and general buildings 4 to 14%.

An interesting method based on the *volumetric-ratio* concept was proposed by Knox [15.19R39], who found that process equipment occupies only 3.75% of the total building volume. Therefore, the volume of the equipment divided by

Table 15.12T2 Average Cost of All-concrete, Precast, Nonprocess Industrial Plant and Office Buildings*

Region	Average cost per square foot, 1967, $	
	One-story plants	Two-story offices
Northeast	9.27	23.18
Midwest	8.60	21.94
Southeast	7.50	17.80
West central	8.94	18.42
West coast	8.43	19.04
U.S. average	8.43	20.70

* From J. R. Cherry, *Civil Eng.*, vol. 38, p. 43, January, 1968.

324 COST ESTIMATION AND CONTROL   15.12

Table 15.12T3* Cost Analysis of Building for Printing Plant†

Frame	Reinforced concrete
Exterior walls	Masonry
No. of floors, excluding basement	10
No. of basement floors	1
Basement area, sq ft	21,000
Gross area supported (excluding slab on grade), sq ft	229,000
Face brick area, sq ft	40,500
Curtain walls, including glass, sq ft	30,000
Net finished area, sq ft	208,000
No. of elevators	3
Story height, typical floor, ft	12

Item	Unit	No. of units	$ per unit	Cost, $M	Cost, %
General conditions and fee	Sq ft	229,000	1.48	340	9.00
Excavation	Sq ft	21,000	6.48	136	3.60
Foundation	Sq ft	21,000	10.81	227	6.01
Concrete, formed	Sq ft	229,000	5.79	1,326	35.12
Exterior masonry	Sq ft	40,500	7.31	297	7.87
Interior masonry				83	2.20
Stone, granite, marble				44	1.17
Structural steel	Sq ft	229,000	1.32	302	8.00
Miscellaneous metal, including stairs	Floor	11	6,182	68	1.80
Carpentry				41	1.09
Waterproofing and dampproofing	Sq ft	30,000	0.20	6	0.16
Roofing and flashing	Sq ft	21,000	1.38	29	0.77
Metal doors and frames	Floor	10	9.00	9	0.24
Metal windows	Sq ft	30,000	1.13	34	0.90
Hardware	Floor	10	60	6	0.16
Glass and glazing	Sq ft	30,000	0.90	27	0.72
Curtain walls	Sq ft	30,000	0.93	28	0.74
Lath and plastic	Sq ft	208,000	0.02	5	0.13
Tile work				12	0.32
Acoustical ceiling				3	0.08
Toilet partitions				2	0.05
Elevators	Each	3	49,667	149	3.95
Plumbing				120	3.18
Heating and ventilation	Sq ft	208,000	0.85	176	4.66
Electrical	Sq ft	208,000	1.42	296	7.84
Miscellaneous trades	Sq ft	208,000	0.05	10	0.26
Total				3,776	100

* From *Eng. News-Record*, vol. 180, p. 139, June 20, 1968.
† Building in Brooklyn, N.Y.; costs as of June, 1968.

0.0375 gives the volume of the buildings, and from this the cost can be estimated by using a dollar per cubic foot factor (Knox used $0.80 per cubic foot).
    When estimating installed costs from unit costs and man-hour requirements, it is necessary to take into account overhead, costs of supervision, and other charges. For piping, insulation, earthwork, structural work, and other building

Table 15.12T4 Unit Prices of Various Building Materials*

	Unit	Atlanta, $	Kansas City, $	Philadelphia $
Asbestos-cement pipe, 6 in.	Ft	1.19	1.25	1.25
Asphalt, paving, tank-car lots	Ton		18.60	21.50
Drums	Gal	0.012		
Asphalt emulsion (tank car)	Gal	0.1288	0.10	
Asphalt felt roofing	Cwt	2.04	3.20	2.15
Asphalt roof coating	Gal	0.90	0.20	0.63
Bars, reinforcing, steel	Cwt	7.57	6.50	8.23
Beams, structural steel	Cwt	9.97	9.85	8.85
Brick, common backing	M	37.00	45.00	45.00
Straight, hard	M	48.00	62.00	55.00
Cement, Portland (paper bags)	Bbl	4.66	5.80	4.40
Concrete, ready-mix	Cu yd	12.75	14.50	15.30
Copper water tubing, $\frac{3}{8}$ in., type L	Ft	0.237	0.2575	0.2200
Crushed stone, $1\frac{1}{2}$ in.	Ton	1.95	1.90	2.20
Drain tile, clay, 6 in.	M ft	235.00	260.00	110.00
Explosives, 40% ammonia gelatin	Lb	0.30	0.32	0.32
Glass, window, s.s., 14 × 20 in.	Box	12.83	16.93	9.40
Gravel, $1\frac{1}{2}$ in.	Ton	2.50		1.65
Lime, hydrated, finish	Ton	35.50	44.00	36.00
Lumber, 1 × 6 S4S, pine	MBF	103.00	156.00	90.00
Fir	MBF	123.25	135.00	80.00
Oil, road	Gal		0.0675	
Paint, ready-mixed, aluminum	Gal	4.15	3.54	3.90
Perlite, plaster aggregate	4-cu-ft bag	1.70	1.55	1.30
Plaster, gauging	Ton	54.00	35.00	32.00
Plywood, fir, $\frac{5}{8}$ in., interior	MSF	91.00	125.00	108.65
$\frac{3}{4}$ in., exterior	MSF	185.00	205.00	183.00
Sand	Ton	3.50	1.90	1.35
Sewer pipe, clay, 8 in.	Ft	0.602	0.681	1.66
Concrete, 12 in.	Ft	1.00	1.40	1.80
Sheets, aluminum, 0.063 in.	Lb		0.398	0.341
Corrugated steel roofing, 0.032 in.	Sq	29.50	28.95	27.02
Stainless steel, 20 gauge	Cwt	55.75	73.00	49.26
Tile, structural clay, $4\frac{1}{2}$ × 12 × 12 in.	M	193.70	158.00	200.00
Vermiculite, insulation pellets	4-cu-ft bag	1.70	1.05	1.45

* Delivered prices as of mid-1968 on carload lots or large quantities. Prices are subject to quantity discounts and sales taxes.

activities Edmunds [15.19R25] recommends that direct material costs be multiplied by 1.2 to 1.4 and direct labor costs by 1.3 to 1.5. The material factor covers general overhead, administrative costs, and a reasonable profit; the labor factor covers the same plus a 5 to 10% allowance for such nonmanual personnel as field engineers, chief supervisors, draftsmen, and clerks.

326 COST ESTIMATION AND CONTROL 15.14

Example 15.12E1 Estimate the cost, exclusive of earthwork, of installing 5,000 ft of 10-in. pipe in a trench. Material cost for the pipe is $4.50 per foot, and it requires 0.45 man-hr of labor per foot at $5.30 per hour for unloading, handling, laying, and joining.

Material costs = 5,000($4.50) = $22,500
Direct labor costs = 5,000(0.45)($5.30) = $11,925
Total costs = $22,500(1.3) + ($11,925)(1.4) = $46,000 approx.

15.13 Engineering costs

Indirect costs chargeable to engineering are incurred at the home office and in the field, and have been listed and estimated by Bauman [15.19R7]. Engineering costs are often taken at 10% of the overall project cost but can vary considerably. Figure 15.13F1 shows average engineering costs for different types of projects. As can be seen from this figure, the percentage of cost due to engineering drops considerably as the size of the project increases. However, these curves merely represent averages, and individual projects may have engineering costs that differ as much as 50% from the values read from the curves.

15.14 Piping costs

Piping costs may vary from 1% of total fixed investment for manufacturing plants where operations are largely mechanical to as high as 25% in some fluid-process chemical plants. Piping costs can vary as much as 25 to 50% depending on market conditions and size of order. For the common materials of construction, the purchase price is often a minor part since installation costs may be three or four times material costs.

For order-of-magnitude and preliminary cost estimates, process piping costs are usually estimated as a percentage of fixed capital investment or of installed

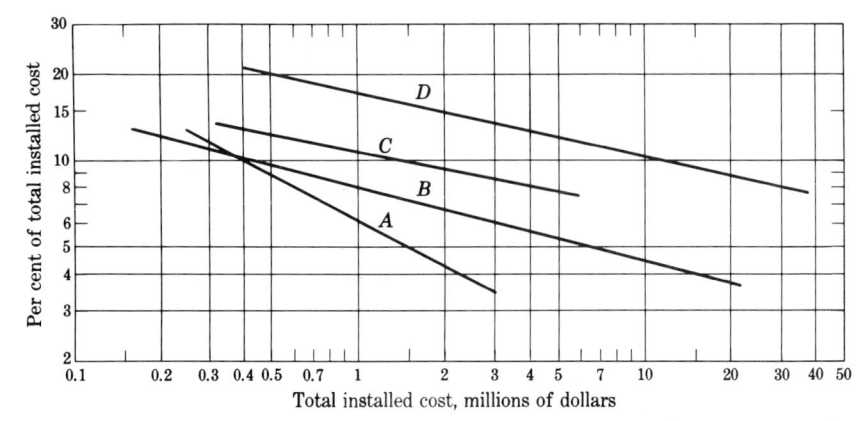

Fig. 15.13F1 Engineering costs as average percent of total installed costs. *A*, office buildings and laboratories; *B*, power plants, cement plants, kilns, and water systems; *C*, battery-limits chemical process plants; *D*, complex chemical and grass-roots chemical plants and pilot plants.

equipment costs, as shown in Table 15.10T1. Nonprocess piping, as in office buildings, is treated as part of the plumbing, heating, and air-conditioning costs.

For detailed cost estimates, the total length of all pipes and the number of fittings can be determined from drawings, prices can be obtained as from Figs. 15.14F1 to 15.14F3, and installation costs can be estimated on the basis of man-hours of labor per foot of pipe and per fitting (Table 15.14T1). The installation labor is the largest unknown in a detailed piping-cost estimate. Rates vary with location, and productivity even more. Some reasonably good information is available [15.19R4, 15.19R8, 15.19R21, 15.19R37, 15.19R42].

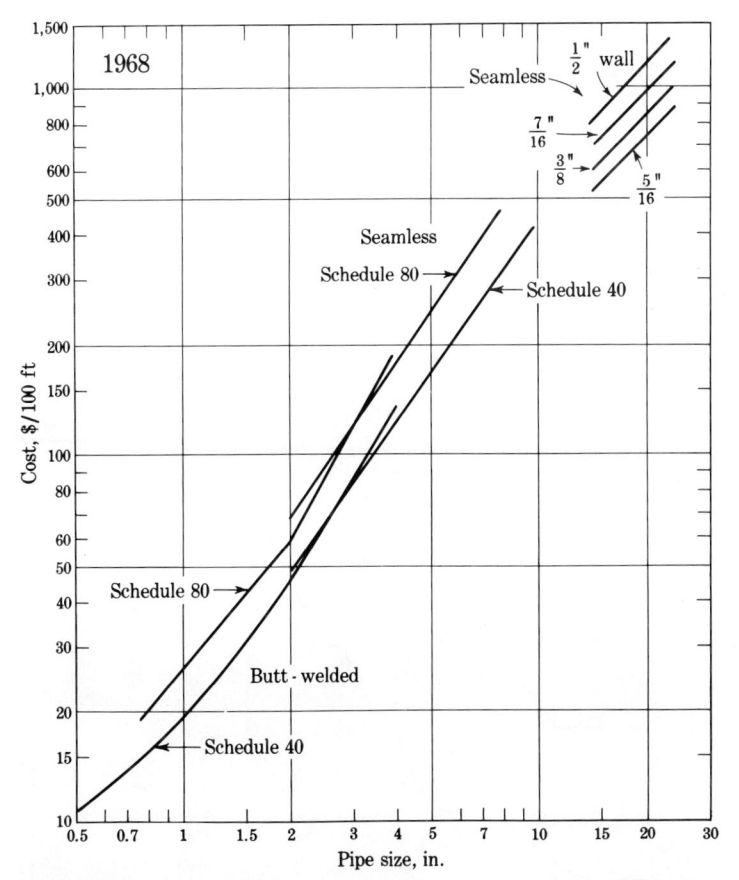

Fig. 15.14F1 Delivered cost of wrought steel pipe. Schedule 40 and 80 are nominal pipe size; large pipe is outside diameter. Curves are for black, plain-end pipe in standard lengths.
For galvanized pipe add 20%;
for threads and couplings add:
  schedule 40, black 6%, galvanized 5%;
  schedule 80, black 11%, galvanized 10%.

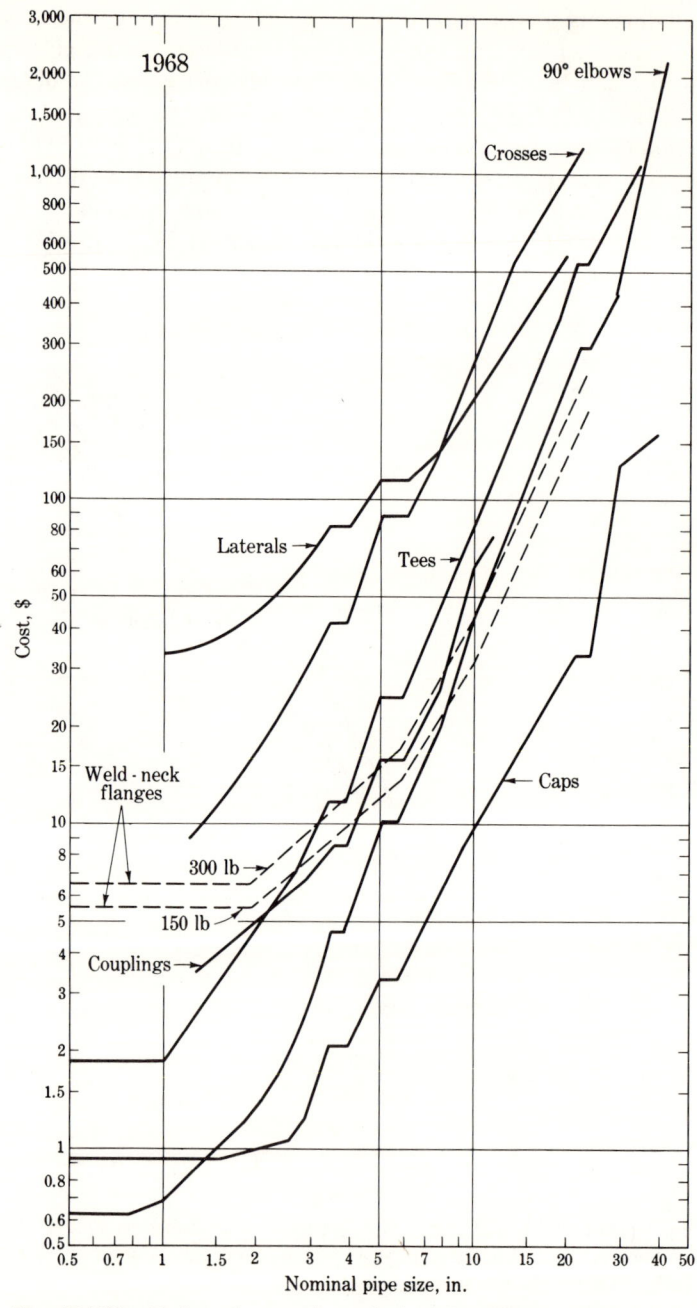

Fig. 15.14F2 Delivered cost of standard steel welding fittings. Typical prices based on large quantities.

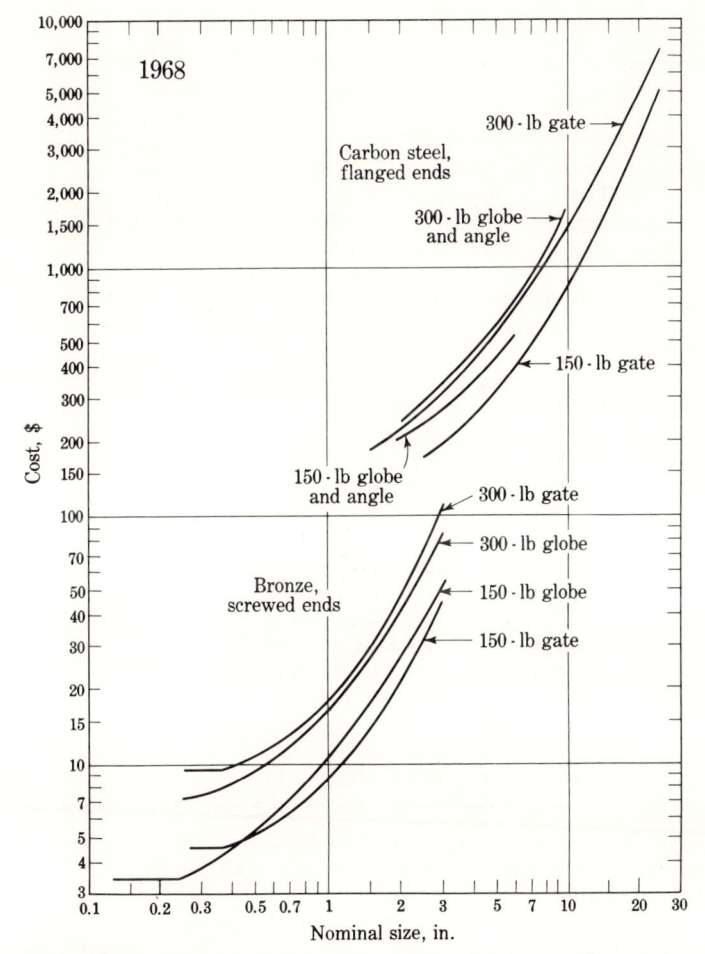

Fig. 15.14F3 Purchased cost of screwed-end bronze valves and flanged-end carbon steel valves.

An intermediate type of estimate can be made from Fig. 15.14F4, which is installed cost and includes an average number of valves and fittings.

A very satisfactory method for estimating piping labor is the *diameter-inch* method, which consists of counting the number of fittings and multiplying this number by the number of connections per fitting, the nominal pipe diameter in inches, and a labor factor to obtain the installation man-hours. For a rough estimate, a total of 1.5 man-hr/diam.-in. can be assumed for each welded joint including pipe layout, cutting, welding, threading, and erection.

A similar method recommended by Roberts [15.19R52] involves separate factors for welds, flange joints, valves, and feet of pipe, as shown in Table 15.14T1.

Of course, an amount for overhead, profit, and other indirect charges should be added to the material and direct labor charges.

330 COST ESTIMATION AND CONTROL

Table 15.14T1 Installation Labor Requirements for Carbon Steel Piping

(1)	(2)	(3)	(4)	(5)	(6)	(7)	(8)	(9)	(10)	(11)
	Butt welds per connection		Flange joint handling per flange‡		Flanged valve handling per value§		Pipe handling, per foot of pipe¶		Screwed joints per connection**	
Nominal pipe size, in.	Std. wt.*	Extra heavy†	150 lb	300 lb	150 lb	300 lb	Std wt.	Extra heavy	Malleable iron	Forged steel
3/4	0.80	0.90	0.6	0.7	0.3		0.7	0.08	0.4	0.6
1	0.95	1.1	0.7	0.8	0.4		0.08	0.09	0.5	0.8
1 1/4	1.1	1.3	0.7	0.8	0.5		0.09	0.10	0.6	1.0
1 1/2	1.2	1.4	0.8	0.9	0.6	0.7	0.10	0.11	0.8	1.4
2	1.4	1.7	0.8	1.1	0.7	0.8	0.11	0.14	1.2	2.0
2 1/2	1.8	2.1	0.8	1.4	0.8	1.0	0.14	0.16	1.5	
3	2.0	2.5	0.9	1.4	1.0	1.2	0.16	0.20		
4	2.5	3.0	1.1	1.4	1.3	1.5	0.20	0.25		
6	3.4	4.5	1.3	2.0	1.7	2.6	0.30	0.40		
8	4.0	6.2	1.3	2.5	2.5	3.8	0.40	0.50		
10	5.7	7.4	2.2	3.5	3.5	5.2	0.50	0.65		
12	6.0	8.5	2.2	4.0	4.5	7.5	0.60	0.70		
14	7.0	9.4	2.6	5.0	6.0	10.0	0.65	0.78		
16	7.9	10.5	3.5	6.0	7.0	13.0	0.70	0.85		
18	8.8	11.9	4.0	6.5	10.0	16.0	0.75	0.90		
20	9.7	13.1	4.5	7.0	12.0	20.0	0.80	1.00		
24	11.4	15.8	5.5	9.0	17.0	30.0	0.95	1.15		

* Man-hours per connection to receive, store, handle through fabrication, fit, weld, and align on pipe racks; includes standard-weight tees, elbows, reducers, and 150-lb standard weld-neck flanges. For 5% chrome, stainless steel, brass, aluminum, and Monel piping add 100%.
† Same as (2) except extra heavy fittings and 300-lb standard weld-neck flanges.
‡ Man-hours for installing gasket and bolting tight.
§ Man-hours to receive, store, erect, and align on pipe racks, ready for bolting up.
¶ Man-hour to receive, store, handle through fabrication, erect, and align on pipe racks ready for bolting or welding.
** Man-hour to receive, store, handle, cut, thread, fit, and make up service-tight; includes tees, elbows, unions, reducers, couplings, and valves.

Example 15.14E1 Estimate the installed cost of the piping system sketched in Fig. 15.14F5. Material required is

   398 ft 6-in. schedule 40 pipe
   six 6-in. standard-weight welding elbows
   six 6-in. 150-lb weld-on flanges
   two 6-in. 150 lb carbon steel gate valves

The total number of welds is

   12 (6 elbows) + 6 (flanges) + 14 (pipe) = 32

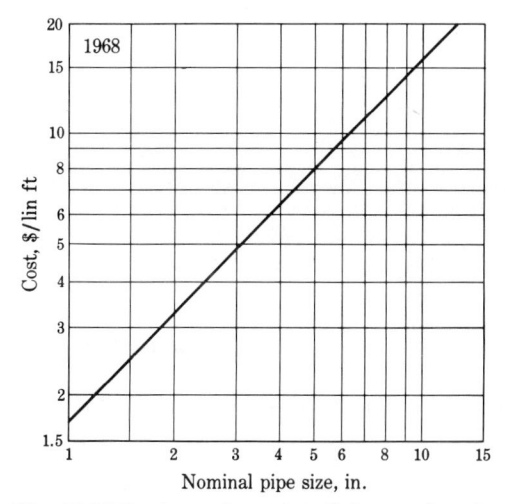

Fig. 15.14F4 Approximate installed cost of steel piping including valves and fittings.

Cost of material is:

Pipe, Fig. 15.14F1: $^{398}/_{100}(210)$ = $836
Elbows, Fig. 15.14F2: 6(10) = 60
Flanges, Fig. 15.14F2: 6(12) = 72
Valves, Fig. 15.14F3: 2(390) = 780
                                    ──────
                                    $1,748

Man-hours of erection labor from Table 15.14T1 is:

32 welds at 3.4 hr/weld   = 108.8
6 flange joints at 1.3 hr/joint   =   7.8
2 flanged valves at 1.7 hr/valve   =   3.4
398 ft of pipe at 0.30 hr/ft   = 119.4
                                     ──────
                     Total man-hr = 239.4

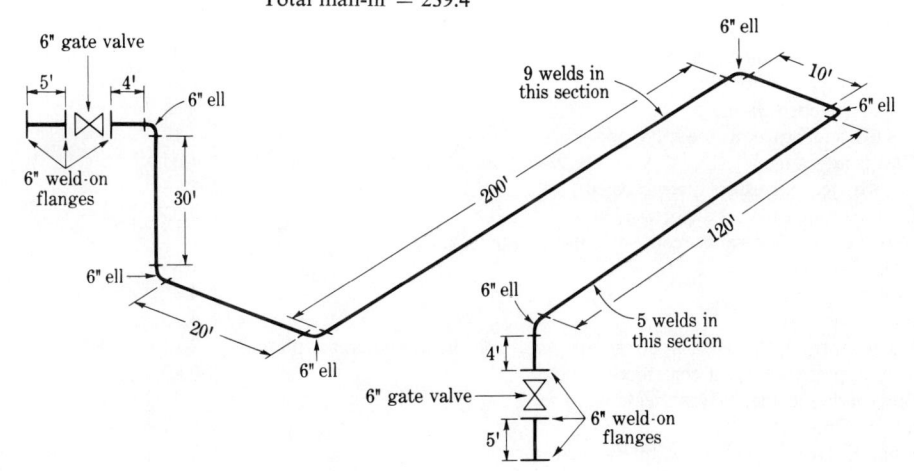

Fig. 15.14F5 Diagram of 6-in. piping for Example 15.14E1.

Assume $7 per hour as labor cost.

239.4(7) = $1,676

Total direct material and labor is

1,748 + 1,676 = $3,424

However, if allowance is made for general overhead, administrative costs, etc., the total cost becomes (compare Example 15.12E1)

1,748(1.3) + (1,676)(1.4) = $4,618

The average cost per foot is

$$\frac{4,618}{398} = \$11.60$$

which is not too far from $10 per foot read from Fig. 15.14F4.

Although carbon steel is the most common material of construction for piping systems, other metals and plastics are widely used. For preliminary estimates, data are available on the relative cost of special piping compared to carbon steel piping. Some ratios are based on material costs only; others, such as those of Mendel [15.19R43] and Table 15.14T2, are based on total installed cost including fittings and flanges, shop fabrication, and field installation.

Table 15.14T2 Relative Installed Cost of Piping

Aluminum, 3003 or 6061, welded	2.04
Aluminum bronze, welded	3.31
Brass, red, 85%, screwed	1.66
Carbon steel, seamless, black welded	1.00
Galvanized, screwed	0.76
Glass-lined, flanged	3.17
Lead-lined, flanged	2.28
Phenolic resin-coated, flanged	1.23
Polyethylene-lined, flanged	1.22
Polyvinyl chloride-lined, flanged	1.36
Rubber-lined, flanged	1.64
TFE fluorocarbon-lined, flanged	3.17
Cast iron, flanged	1.04
Chlorinated polyester, thermosealed socket	3.28
Chrome-moly, 5Cr: ½Mo, welded	2.53
Epoxy resin, glass-reinforced, solvent-cemented socket	1.16
Glass, flanged	1.84
Monel, welded	4.01
Nickel, welded	4.53
Phenol-formaldehyde resin, epoxy-armored, solvent-cemented coupling	2.12
Polypropylene, solvent-cemented socket	0.82
Polyvinyl chloride, solvent-cemented socket	0.77
Silicon iron, flanged	2.02
Stainless steel, type 304, seamless, welded	2.90
Type 316, seamless, welded	3.77

15.15 Insulation costs

Generally insulation costs are not among the major cost items. Even in process plants, insulation costs are usually of the order of 1 to 2% of plant costs, although in some plants where a large amount of piping and equipment is used at either high or low temperature, the costs of insulation can run higher. For some insulation costs in a refinery see [15.19R22].

For preliminary estimates insulation costs are usually included as part of installation costs and not treated separately. For detailed estimates, tables and charts of installed insulation costs can be prepared [15.19R9, pp. 119 to 130] from material and labor costs and man-hour requirements.

15.16 Start-up costs

After plant construction has been completed, a number of changes usually have to be made before the plant can operate at an optimum level. These changes cost money for equipment, materials, labor, and overhead and result in loss of income while the plant is not producing or is operating at only partial capacity. These funds should be part of any capital appropriation, for they are essential to the success of the venture. Also, some of these funds are normally capitalized and for accounting purposes do become part of the capital investment.

Start-up expense may be as high as 12% of the fixed capital investment although it is usually under 10%. In general, an allowance of 10% for start-up cost is satisfactory. The topic is discussed in Chap. 18.

15.17 Nomenclature

Note: Nomenclature for Chap. 15 is restricted for use within the chapter and conflicts, in part, with nomenclature used elsewhere.

- A Total cost of all battery-limit investment, Eqs. (15.11#1) to (15.11#3), $
- A_0 $A/1,000$, Eqs. (15.11#2) to (15.11#4), $M
- B Cost of all erected equipment, Eq. (15.11#1), $
- C Cost, Eqs. (15.7#1) and (15.7#2), $
- C Incremental cost of alloys used for corrosion resistance, Eq. (15.11#1), $
- e Total head-exchanger cost less incremental cost of alloy, Eqs. (15.11#2) and (15.11#3), $
- E Indirect cost factor, Eq. (15.11#1), dimensionless; normally assumed to be 1.4
- f Total cost of field-fabricated vessels, Eq. (15.11#2), $
- F_L Cost factor for field labor, Eqs. (15.11#1) and (15.11#2), dimensionless
- F_M Cost factor for miscellaneous items, Eqs. (15.11#1) and (15.11#4), dimensionless
- F_P Cost factor for piping material, Eqs. (15.11#1) and (15.11#3), dimensionless
- I Total battery-limits investment, Eq. (15.11#1), $
- p Total pump plus driver cost less incremental cost of alloy, Eq. (15.11#3), $
- Q Capacity, Eqs. (15.7#1) and (15.7#2), any convenient dimensions
- t Total cost of tower shells less incremental cost of alloys, Eq. (15.11#4), $
- X Total cost-capacity factor, Eq. (15.7#1), dimensionless
- $X - 1$ Unit cost-capacity factor, Eq. (15.7#2), dimensionless

15.18 Problems

P1. A construction project cost $600,000 in 1961. Estimate the cost in 1967.
P2. Equipment for a process plant cost $150,000 in 1961. Estimate the cost in 1967.
P3. An aluminum (from alumina) plant will cost $25 million. Estimate the cost of a unit twice as large.
P4. A horizontal steel tank of 10,000 gal capacity cost $8,500 installed in 1958. Estimate the cost for a 15,000-gal tank in 1968.
P5. The delivered cost of the major equipment for a solid-fluid process plant is $2 million. Estimate the total cost of the plant.
P6. Estimate the total battery-limits investment for a process plant with estimated equipment cost based on carbon steel as follows:

	$ M	Incremental cost of corrosion-resisting alloy, $ M
Tower shells over 12 ft diam.	200	500
Trays and internals	350	600
Drums over 12 ft diam.	150	250
Miscellaneous vessels over 12 ft diam.	400	
Heat exchangers	600	
Pumps and drivers	165	300
Miscellaneous f.o.b. equipment	135	
Erected equipment cost	225	

P7. Estimate the installed cost of an 8-in. carbon steel pipeline requiring the following material and operations with labor at $6.50 per hour:

600-ft pipe with 18 welds in pipe
8 weld-on elbows
2 gate valves
3 weld-on flanges

The line is designed for 150 psi.

P8. If the installed piping cost for lead-lined flanged pipe is $28,000, estimate the cost for the same line in welded Monel piping.

15.19 References

R1. *AACE Bull.*, vol. 1, p. 12, November, 1958.
R2. Adams, C. A.: A.C. Electric Motor Costs, *Chem. Eng.*, vol. 66, p. 164, Sept. 21, 1959.
R3. Arnold, T. H., and C. H. Chilton: New Index Shows Plant Cost Trends, *Chem. Eng.*, vol. 70, pp. 143–152, Feb. 18, 1963.
R4. Bach, N. G.: Fabrication Costs of Steel Piping, *Chem. Eng. Costs Quart.*, vol. 5, pp. 17–22, January, 1955.
R5. Bach, N. G.: More Accurate Plant Cost Estimates, *Chem. Eng.*, vol. 65, pp. 155–159, Sept. 22, 1958.
R6. Barr, J. A.: H_2SO_4 Buy or Build, *Chem. Eng.*, vol. 57, pp. 106–109, April, 1950.
R7. Bauman, H. C.: Engineering Costs, in *AACE Cost Engineers' Notebook*, paper A7, December, 1964.

R8. Bauman, H. C.: Costing Piping: The Bugaboo of Chemical Plant Estimating, *Ind. Eng. Chem.*, vol. 51, pp. 81A–83A, January, 1959.
R9. Bauman, H. C.: "Fundamentals of Cost Engineering in the Chemical Industry," Reinhold Book Corporation, New York, 1964.
R10. Berk, J. M., and J. E. Haselbarth: Cost-capacity Data, I, *Chem. Eng.*, vol. 67, pp. 172–174, Dec. 12, 1960.
R11. Berk, J. M., and J. E. Haselbarth: Cost-capacity Data, II, *Chem. Eng.*, vol. 68, pp. 161–162, Jan. 23, 1961.
R12. Berk, J. M., and J. E. Haselbarth: Cost-capacity Data, III, *Chem. Eng.*, vol. 68, pp. 174–178, Feb. 20, 1961.
R13. Berk, J. M., and J. E. Haselbarth: Cost-capacity Data, IV, *Chem. Eng.*, vol. 68, pp. 182–186, March 20, 1961.
R14. Bianco, R. E., J. M. Holmes, R. Salmon, and J. W. Ullman: Ammonia Costs and Electricity, *Chem. Eng. Progr.*, vol. 63, pp. 46–50, April, 1967.
R15. Birchard, R.: Indexes Aren't Infallible, *Cost Eng.*, vol. 3, pp. 60–62, April, 1958.
R16. Butler, W. S.: Nuclear Power in the CPI, *Chem. Eng. Progr.*, vol. 63, pp. 39–40, April, 1967.
R17. *Chemical Engineering* Costs for Building and Operating Aluminum-producing Plants, vol. 70, pp. 120–122, Sept. 2, 1963.
R18. *Chemical Engineering* Process Clears Hydrogen from Hydrocarbons, vol. 69, pp. 90–92, May 14, 1962.
R19. Cherry, J. R.: Cost of Concrete Industrial Buildings, *Civil Eng.*, vol. 38, pp. 42–45, January, 1968.
R20. Chilton, C. H.: Six-tenths Factor Applies to Complete Plant Costs, *Chem. Eng.*, vol. 57, pp. 112–114, April, 1950.
R21. Clark, W. G.: Accurate Way to Estimate Pipe Costs, *Chem. Eng.*, vol. 64, pp. 243–246, July, 1957.
R22. *Cost Engineers' Notebook*, AACE Paper A6, October, 1964.
R23. Cronan, C. S.: Small Volume Price Hydrogen at Bulk Cost, *Chem. Eng.*, vol. 66, pp. 60–62, August, 1959.
R24. Edmunds, K. B.: Cost Estimating Building Service Systems, 1, *ACHV*, vol. 62, pp. 93–94, February, 1965.
R25. Edmunds, K. B.: Cost Estimating Building Service Systems, 6, *ACHV*, vol. 62, pp. 101–102, September, 1965.
R26. *Eng. News-Record*, vol. 180, pp. 77–80, March 21, 1968.
R27. *Eng. News-Record*, Relate Building Costs Using Parameter Measurements, vol. 180, pp. 138–140, June 20, 1968.
R28. Gallagher, J. T.: Rapid Estimation of Plant Costs, *Chem. Eng.*, vol. 74, pp. 89–96, Dec. 18, 1967.
R29. Gilmore, J. F.: Short Cut Estimating of Processes, *Petrol. Refiner*, vol. 32, pp. 97–101, October, 1953.
R30. Hackney, J. W.: "Control and Management of Capital Projects," p. 94, John Wiley & Sons, Inc., New York, 1965.
R31. Hand, W. E.: Estimating Capital Costs from Process Flow Sheets, *AACE Cost Engineers' Notebook*, Paper A3, January, 1964.
R32. Hand, W. E.: From Flow Sheet to Cost Estimate, *Petrol. Refiner*, vol. 37, pp. 331–334, September, 1958.
R33. Haselbarth, J. E., and J. M. Berk: Chemical Plant Cost Breakdown, *Chem. Eng.*, vol. 67, p. 158, May 16, 1960.
R34. Haselbarth, J. E., and M. M. Harris, Jr.: Preliminary Cost Estimating, *Chem. Eng. Progr.*, vol. 60, pp. 23–25, December, 1964.
R35. Hirsch, J. H., and E. M. Glazier: Estimating Plant Investment Costs, *Chem. Eng. Progr.*, vol. 56, pp. 37–43, December, 1960.
R36. Katell, S., and J. H. Faber: What Does Tonnage Oxygen Cost, *Chem. Eng.*, vol. 66, pp. 107–110, June 29, 1959.

R37. Keating, C. J.: Accurate Way to Estimate Pipe Installation Costs, *Chem. Eng.*, vol. 69, pp. 125–128, June 15, 1962.
R38. Klei, H. E., J. M. Tamborra, and R. T. Wood: Capital Cost of Sewage Plants, *Water Wastes Eng.*, vol. 5, p. 61, April, 1968.
R39. Knox, W. G.: Estimating the Cost of Process Buildings via Volumetric Ratios, *Chem. Eng.*, vol. 75, pp. 292–294, June 17, 1968.
R40. Lang, J. H.: Simplified Approach to Preliminary Cost Estimates, *Chem. Eng.*, vol. 55, pp. 112–113, June, 1948.
R41. Lapple, W. C., W. E. Clark, and E. C. Dybdal: Drying Design and Costs, *Chem. Eng.*, vol. 62, pp. 177–200, November, 1955.
R42. Mattiza, D. S.: Cost Factors for Estimation of Piping and Electrical Work, *Cost Eng.*, vol. 3, pp. 19–21, January, 1958.
R43. Mendel, O.: Cost Comparisons for Process Piping, *Chem. Eng.*, vol. 75, pp. 255–256, June 17, 1968.
R44. Nelson, W. L.: Cost of Small Carbon-black Plant, *Oil Gas J.*, vol. 57, p. 89, July 20, 1959.
R45. Nelson, W. L.: How to Estimate the Cost of Ethylene Plants, *Oil Gas J.*, vol. 66, pp. 116–117, March 4, 1968.
R46. Nelson, W. L.: Refinery Construction Cost Indexes, *Oil Gas J.*, vol. 54, pp. 110–111, Oct. 1, 1956.
R47. Nichols, W. T.: Capital Cost Estimating, *Ind. Eng. Chem.*, vol. 43, pp. 2295–2298, October, 1951.
R48. Peters, M. S., and K. D. Timmerhaus: "Plant Design and Economics for Chemical Engineers," 2d ed., p. 109, McGraw-Hill Book Company, New York, 1968.
R49. Prater, N. H., and D. W. Antonacci: How to Estimate Fractioning Column Costs, *Petrol. Refiner*, vol. 39, pp. 119–126, July, 1960.
R50. Prater, N. H., and D. W. Antonacci: Steam Generator Turbine Costs, *Petrol. Refiner*, vol. 39, pp. 185–188, April, 1960.
R51. Roberts, I.: Economics of Tonnage Oxygen Production, *Chem. Eng. Progr.*, vol. 46, pp. 79–88, February, 1950.
R52. Roberts, O. R.: How to Estimate Piping Labor, *Petrol. Refiner*, vol. 37, pp. 147–149, March, 1958; vol. 39, pp. 207–212, March, 1960.
R53. Samfield, J.: Dust Collecting Equipment., *Cost Eng.*, vol. 2, pp. 106–109, October 1957.
R54. Schofield, B. P.: How Plant Costs Vary with Size, *Chem. Eng.*, vol. 62, p. 185, October, 1955.
R55. Schwartz, C. C.: Estimate Plant Costs Quickly, Accurately, *Oil Gas J.*, vol. 61, pp. 156–159, Nov. 11, 1963.
R56. Seamster, A. H., and R. M. Wheaton: Ion Exchange Becomes Powerful Processing Tool, *Chem. Eng.*, vol. 67, pp. 115–120, Aug. 22, 1960.
R57. Sharples, L. P.: Centrifuges, chap. 10 of "Chemical Engineering Costs," pp. 142–143, Industrial Research Service, Inc., Dover, N.-H., 1950.
R58. Shellenberger, D. J.: A Comparison of Cost Indexes, *AACE Bull.*, vol. 7, pp. 62–66, June, 1965.
R59. Sherwood, P. W.: Effect of Plant Process Size on Capital Costs, *Oil Gas J.*, vol. 48, pp. 81–83, 95, March 9, 1950.
R60. Sindt, H. A., I. Spiewak, and T. D. Anderson: Costs of Power from Nuclear Desalting Plants, *Chem. Eng. Progr.*, vol. 63, pp. 41–45, April, 1967.
R61. Smith, E. M.: Wet Dust Collection Equipment, *Cost Eng.*, vol. 3, pp. 49–54, April, 1958.
R62. Smith, L. C.: Cost and Performance of Centrifugals, *Chem. Eng.*, vol. 59, pp. 140–145, April, 1952.
R63. Sommers, H. A.: The Chlor-alkali Industry, *Chem. Eng. Progr.*, vol. 61, pp. 94–109, March, 1965.
R64. Stasny, E. P.: Choosing Your Electrostatic Precipitator, *Power*, vol. 104, pp. 61–64, January, 1960.

R65. Stevens, R. W.: Equipment Cost Indexes for Process Industries, *Chem. Eng.*, vol. 54, pp. 124–126, November, 1957.
R66. Swift, L. L.: Mechanical Gas Producers, *Chem. Eng. Cost Quart.*, vol. 2, pp. 10–14, January, 1952.
R67. U.S. Dept. of Labor, Bureau of Labor Statistics, *Monthly Rept. on the Labor Force*, Washington.
R68. U.S. Dept. of Labor, Bureau of Labor Statistics, *Wholesale Prices and Price Indexes*, Washington.
R69. Van Dyke, H., and W. J. Dougherty: Cost of Low Temperature Processing, *Chem. Eng. Progr.*, vol. 51, pp. 157–161, April, 1955.
R70. Vilbrandt, F. C., and C. E. Dryden: "Chemical Engineering Plant Design," 4th ed., p. 214, McGraw-Hill Book Company, New York, 1959.
R71. Walas, S. M.: Plant Investment Costs by the Factor Method, *Chem. Eng. Progr.*, vol. 57, pp. 68–69, June, 1961.
R72. Warren, A. S., and V. A. Pardo: Cost of Industrial Instruments, *Cost Eng.*, vol. 2, pp. 10–21, January, 1957.
R73. Weaver, J. B., and H. C. Bauman: Glossary of Cost Estimating Terms, I, *Ind. Eng. Chem.*, vol. 52, pp. 69A–72A, June, 1960.
R74. Williams, R., Jr.: Six-tenth Factor Aids in Approximating Costs, *Chem. Eng.*, vol. 54, pp. 124–125, December, 1947.
R75. Wroth, W. F.: Factors in Cost Estimation, *Chem. Eng.*, vol. 67, p. 204, October, 1960.
R76. Zimmerman, O. T.: Comparison of Cost Indexes, *Cost Eng.*, vol. 9, pp. 12–17, July, 1964.
R77. Zimmerman, O. T.: Productivity, *Cost Eng.*, vol. 9, pp. 11–15, October, 1964.
R78. Zimmerman, O. T.: Use of Ratio Cost Factors in Estimating, *Cost Eng.*, vol. 10, pp. 13–17, October, 1965.
R79. Zimmerman, O. T., and I. Lavine: Cost-capacity Factors–Equipment, *Cost Eng.*, vol. 6, pp. 13–22, April, 1961.
R80. Zimmerman, O. T., and I. Lavine: Cost-capacity Factors–Plants, *Cost Eng.*, vol. 6, pp. 16–18, July, 1961.

16
Operating-Cost Estimation[1]

J. H. Black

16.1 Definitions

Operating cost, or manufacturing cost, is the expense involved in keeping a project, operation, or piece of equipment running and producing. The terminology and the connection between the component cost items is shown in Table 16.1T1.

In this chapter the terms *operating cost* and *manufacturing cost* are used synonymously. In a broad sense this cost is at the factory level. In addition a company incurs costs above the factory level associated more with management; here it is termed *general expense*, but it is also known as *administrative, sales,* and *general expense*. The sum of operating cost, or manufacturing cost, and general expense is designated here as *total product cost*.

The present chapter is concerned with operating cost, or manufacturing cost, and not total product cost. General expense and total product cost are discussed in Chap. 18. Terminology in connection with operating cost should not be used

---

[1] Certain material in this chapter is similar to the material in J. W. Hackney, "Control and Management of Capital Projects," John Wiley & Sons, Inc., New York, 1965, and is used with permission.

Table 16.1T1 Components of Total Product Cost*

I. Operating cost or manufacturing cost
   A. Direct production costs
      1. Materials
         a. Raw materials
         b. Processing materials
         c. By-product and scrap credit
         d. Utilities
         e. Maintenance materials
         f. Operating supplies
         g. Royalties and rentals
      2. Labor
         a. Direct operating labor
         b. Operating supervision
         c. Direct maintenance labor
         d. Maintenance supervision
         e. Payroll burden on all labor charges
            (1) FICA tax
            (2) Workmen's compensation coverage
            (3) Contributions to pensions, life insurance, etc.
            (4) Vacations, holidays, sick leave, overtime premium
            (5) Company contribution of profit sharing
   B. Indirect production costs
      1. Plant overhead or burden
         a. Administration
         b. Indirect labor
            (1) Laboratory
            (2) Technical service and engineering
            (3) Shops and repair facilities
            (4) Shipping department
         c. Purchasing, receiving, and warehousing
         d. Personnel and industrial relations
         e. Inspection, safety, and fire protection
         f. Automotive and rail switching
         g. Accounting, clerical, and stenographic
         h. Plant custodial and plant protective
         i. Plant hospital and dispensary
         j. Cafeteria and clubrooms
         k. Recreational activities
         l. Local contributions and memberships
         m. Taxes on property and operating licenses
         n. Insurance—property, liability
         o. Nuisance elimination—waste disposal
      2. Depreciation
   C. Contingencies
   D. Distribution costs
      1. Containers and packages
      2. Freight
      3. Operation of terminals and warehouses
         a. Wages and salaries—plus payroll burden
         b. Operating materials and utilities
         c. Rental or depreciation

* Adapted from R. H. Perry et al., "Chemical Engineers' Handbook," 4th ed., pp. 26-27, McGraw-Hill Book Company, New York, 1963.

Table 16.1T1 (continued)

II. General expense
   A. Marketing or sales costs
      1. Direct
         a. Salesmen salaries and commissions
         b. Advertising and promotional literature
         c. Technical sales service
         d. Samples and displays
      2. Indirect
         a. Sales supervision
         b. Travel and entertainment
         c. Market research and sales analysis
         d. District office expenses
   B. Administrative expense
      1. Salaries and expenses of officers and staff
      2. General accounting, clerical, and auditing
      3. Central engineering and technical
      4. Legal and patent
         a. Within company
         b. Outside company
         c. Payment and collection of royalties
      5. Research and development
         a. Own operations
         b. Sponsored, consultant, and contract work
      6. Contributions and dues to associations
      7. Public relations
      8. Financial
         a. Debt management
         b. Maintenance of working capital
         c. Credit functions
      9. Communications and traffic management
     10. Central purchasing activities
     11. Taxes and insurance

indiscriminately, and the meaning of terms should always be made clear by good delineation and labeling of costs.

The arrangement shown in Table 16.1T1 is subject to variation depending upon accounting procedure and circumstances. Thus royalty payments may be directly proportional to throughput and treated as a direct production cost. In some cases, however, the purchase of a patent in connection with a project may be regarded as an expense in lieu of research and development and appear as part of general expense. Nevertheless, Table 16.1T1 illustrates the classification and will serve well for defining the terms and showing their relationship.

Operating costs fall into two major classifications, direct and indirect. *Direct costs* tend to be proportional to throughput, such as raw materials, and are called also *variable costs*. *Indirect costs* tend to be independent of throughput, such as local property taxes, and are called also *fixed costs*. Some costs are neither fixed nor directly proportional to output and are known as *semivariable costs.* These concepts were developed in Chap. 7 in connection with break-even and minimum-cost analysis.

16.2 Operating-cost estimation—general

Operating-cost estimates are made for a variety of reasons. Preliminary estimates perform the function of a screening procedure to minimize the expenditure of time, effort, and money on uneconomical projects and to choose the more economical route among alternatives to the same end result. The use of preliminary estimates to guide research efforts is common practice. Detailed cost estimates are made after screening estimates when the choice has been narrowed to a relatively few alternatives.

Some judgment is required in determining how far to investigate individual operating-cost items. The estimate will indicate which costs dominate and deserve more study and which costs, even if drastically misjudged, will not produce significant changes in the estimate.

It is important to calculate costs at full and reduced levels inasmuch as in practice operating costs are not a linear function of production rate. Calculations should be made and reported in such a way that they can be reviewed in the future without ambiguity.

Frequently, the operating cost to be calculated is connected with changes and additions to existing equipment and processing, and an incremental analysis can be made. Costs based on an incremental analysis should be used only in connection with the specific project for which they were intended. Even so it might be well to make an integral evaluation for the entire project. The increment might pay off, yet it may be wise to abandon the entire project.

Operating costs are commonly calculated on one of three bases, daily, unit-of-product, or annual basis. Unit-of-product cost is usually expressed as dollars per unit of end product. The annual basis has some advantages over the daily basis because (1) the effect of seasonable variations is evened out, (2) the on-stream time or equipment operating factor is considered, (3) it is more adaptable to less than full-capacity operation, (4) it provides an expeditious way of considering infrequently occurring large expenses, such as the regularly scheduled replacement of parts or equipment or the periodic turnaround costs in a refinery, and (5) the calculations are more directly usable in a profitability analysis.

It is best to use a prepared form for estimating operating costs, and it should conform as closely as possible to that used for recording and controlling costs. The form should provide ideally such supplementary information as the date, the capital investment, a cost index, identification of the product or service, plant location, plant capacity, and operating rate or operating days. The supplementary information is important because these factors affect the component costs, and hence the finished estimate.

Table 16.2T1 illustrates a prepared form and Table 16.2T2 an outline or checklist to match it.

342 COST ESTIMATION AND CONTROL

Table 16.2T1 Form for Operating-Cost Estimation

ADDED MANUFACTURING COST FOR ADDED PRODUCTION ANNUAL BASIS				Appropriation Number			Supp.
				06	41	4120	--

Title: 50 T/D Kiln for New Ores

Plant Production, principal product
Added Tons of Roast /Year   17,500   13,130   8,750
Added, in % of added capacity   100 %   75 %   50 %
Total production rate
Total rate, in % of new total capacity   ____ % Same ____ %   ____ %

Raw Material and Fuel Cost

Type	Units	Unit Cost	Usage T/Roast			
"B" Ore	Tons	$20.00	1.32	$ 461,000	$ 347,000	$231,000
NaOH Anhyd.	100 lbs.	5.00	3.00	262,000	197,000	131,000
Limestone	Tons	5.00	0.15	13,000	9,800	6,600
Natural Gas	M. c. f.	0.25	52.0	227,000	171,000	113,500

Subtotal, Raw Materials and Fuel $ 963,100 $ 724,800 $482,100

Utilities

Type	Units	Unit Cost	Usage /T			
Electricity	KWH	$0.02	50	17,500	13,100	8,800
Steam	-	-	-	-	-	-
Water	M. Gal	0.03	10	5,300	3,900	2,600

Subtotal, Utilities $ 22,800 $ 17,000 $ 11,400

Labor

	Units	Unit Cost	Usage /Year			
Operating	M.H.	$3.00	35,00	105,000	105,000	105,000
Repair	60% of 5.2% of $370,000			11,500	11,500	11,500
Supervision	20% of operating labor			21,000	21,000	21,000
Indirect Payroll Cost @	20 % H.,	20	% S.	27,400	27,400	27,400

Subtotal, Labor $ 164,900 $ 164,900 $164,900

Supplies & Miscellaneous
Operating Supplies   6% of operating labor   6,300   6,300   6,300
Repair Supplies   40% of 5.2% of #370,000   7,700   7,700   7,700
Laboratory   --   --   --
Royalties & Rentals $1.00/T   17,500   17,500   17,500
                                                 -        -   -
Contingencies, 3 % of non-Fixed costs   35,400   28,400   20,700
Subtotal, Supplies & Misc. $ 66,900 $ 59,900 $ 52,200

Fixed Costs
General Works Expense, inc. Taxes & Ins.   72,900   72,900   72,900
Depreciation 8 % of $352,000   28,100   28,100   28,100
Subtotal, Fixed Costs $ 104,000 $ 104,000 $104,000

Loading, Packing & Shipping
Materials, inc. 3 % cont. $.80/T   14,000   10,500   7,000
Labor 1900 hr. at $2.70   5,100   5,100   5,100
G.W.E. 45 % IP 20 % Sup. 20 % Cont. 3 % of labor 5,400 5,400 5,400
Subtotal, Loading, Packing & Shipping $ 24,500 $ 21,000 $ 17,500

Total Added Manufacturing Cost, inc. depreciation $1,346,000 $1,092,000 $826,000
Notes

Table 16.2T2 Manufacturing Cost Checklist*

   I. Direct production costs
      A. Raw material and fuel costs
      B. Utilities
         1. Electricity
         2. Steam
         3. Water
         4. Others
      C. Labor
         1. Operating labor
         2. Repair labor
         3. Supervision
         4. Indirect payroll cost
      D. Supplies and miscellaneous
         1. Operating supplies
         2. Repair supplies
         3. Laboratory
         4. Other
         5. Contingencies
  II. Fixed costs
      A. Factory overhead including taxes and insurance—general works expense
      B. Depreciation
 III. Distribution costs—loading, packing, and shipping
      A. Materials
      B. Labor
      C. Overhead

* (Matches Table 16.2T1)

The best source of information for use in operating-cost estimates is the data from similar or identical projects within the company. Most companies have extensive records of their operations, so that reliable estimates of operating costs for new projects can be made from the existing records if the new project is similar to installations now operated by the company. Adjustments for increased costs as a result of inflation must be made, and differences in plant site and geographical location must also be considered. Company experience, however, probably yields the most accurate information, particularly for preliminary estimates.

Literature references also provide much information concerning costs [16.18R6]. Many engineering journals and magazines publish cost information.

Methods for estimating the cost elements in the absence of specific information are discussed in the following sections. The elements of cost are presented essentially in the order shown in Table 16.2T2.

Perhaps the most serious sources of error in estimating operating costs result from overlooking elements of cost. A tabular form and checklist cannot always guide the analyst to every cost component. Detailed cost estimation requires that the cost engineer be much more the engineer than a cost accountant. Technical familiarity with the project is essential, and no analyst should undertake detailed cost estimation in fields not directly within his specialty.

Computer programs can be set up which will print out operating-cost calculations from input data on punched cards. The initial program may be expensive but sometimes can be justified, particularly if a number of variations are to be calculated. Manual calculation is generally used at present, however, because it is assembling and appraising the data that takes most of the effort, not making the calculations.

16.3 Raw materials

Raw materials may constitute one of the largest items in manufacturing cost. The operating-cost estimate should list raw materials, the units in which the material is purchased, unit cost, and use in quantities per unit of time or per unit of production. Credit should be given for by-products and scrap.

Information on the quantities of the raw materials required can come from published articles, from experiments, or from calculations to which reasonable yields or waste allowances are applied.

Prices of raw materials purchased from outside sources are available on request from the sources of supply. Quality is an important consideration when buying raw materials, such as concentration of an ore, surface finish of a metal, and so forth. Generally, unit price decreases with quantity. However, if the material is available at a low price as a by-product, it may be available in large quantities, if at all, only at a substantially higher unit price.

Prices suitable for estimating purpose can be obtained from catalogs, price lists, or from such sources as spot prices published in *Iron Age*, *Oil Paint and Drug Reporter*, and *European Chemical News* for European prices. Actual prices are negotiated and will vary from the quotations depending on quantity, quality, and such factors as the state of competition, the duration of a contract, and penalties for contract violations.

Raw materials produced captively present a special situation. If the product is now sold, the transfer price is normally the going market price, sales price, less any direct sales costs not incurred, plus freight and other transportation costs for the transfer. If the transferred material is at an intermediate stage that has no going market price, the transfer price can be taken as the going price of the nearest downstream converted product having a going price, less any direct sales cost not incurred, less standard manufacturing costs for any operations which are avoided by the transfer, plus the distribution cost necessary for the transfer.

Periodic makeup of losses, such as catalyst in a chemical process, is included as a raw material. If the initial fill of these materials has a life of more than 1 year, its cost is treated as nondepreciable capital investment or working capital. If the life is less than 1 year, the cost is included as start-up expense. In any case, the periodic makeup is an operating cost.

Fuels used by a project, such as natural gas for a heat-treating furnace, may be considered as a raw material or a utility, depending upon the accounting procedure and circumstances. Costs of fuels are discussed in the following section under utilities. In some chemical processes fuels may be used as a bona fide raw material, e.g., cracking refinery gases for the production of ethylene, and also as a fuel. The two uses may be combined as one raw material or segregated into two costs as desired.

The quantities of by-products are estimated in much the same fashion as the raw-material quantities. The prices of by-products can be estimated from market or selling prices of salable materials less purification, packaging, selling, and transportation costs. If the by-products are intermediate products for which no market exists, they may be credited at their net value to downstream or subsequent operations at a cost value equal to their value as a replacement.

Many price quotations for raw materials will be f.o.b. vendor's plant or some basing point, and freight to the plant and local handling costs must be added. Shipping rates are a complicated topic. The company's traffic department can help, or the carriers can be consulted. A valuable source of basic transportation costs is Perry [16.18R19, sec. 9].

Large-volume, long-haul (over 250 miles) rates in dollars per ton-mile are about 0.002 for pipelines, 0.0025 for barge and tankers, 0.01 for rail, and 0.03 for trucks. Short-haul rates may be two to five times higher. Small-volume rates may be two to three times higher.

16.4 Utilities

Utility prices can be obtained from company cost records for nominal utility increments. Otherwise they will have to be made by inquiry from outside sources or a study of the company-owned system if the utility is self-generated. Unit costs often decrease substantially as demand goes up. Rates for most utilities vary considerably with location. Bauman [16.18R3] gives a comprehensive study of rates. Table 16.4T1 gives typical values for common utilities.

All major contracts for electrical energy contain a demand component, an energy component, and a variable-fuel-cost component. The demand charge is based on the maximum power requirement drawn by a plant during a measurable period, usually 15 or 30 min in any 1 month. The energy charge is based on kilowatt-hours used. The ratio of average usage to demand is termed the load factor. Most electric-power rate schedules are designed to yield greater savings by preferably improving the load factor more than by increasing the load. The fuel-adjustment charge ties the cost, say, to the price of coal; but it is an escalation clause and is used even for electricity generated from water power.

Electric rates may be obtained from the utilities. The Federal Power Commission publishes and distributes at a nominal charge the published rates of all public utilities in the United States. Bauman [16.18R3] gives a summary for some loads and load factors throughout the United States.

Steam can be used at several pressure levels. High-pressure steam can be reduced to lower pressures by the use of steam turbines that are used for the production of motive power. This is an economical practice if use at various

Table 16.4T1 Rates for Industrial Utilities*

Utility	(1967) cost, $	Unit
Steam:		
500 psig	0.06–1.20	1,000 lb
100 psig	0.50–1.00	
Exhaust	0.25–0.40	
Electricity:		
Purchased	0.008–0.028	Kwhr[†]
Self-generated	0.006–0.015	
Cooling water:		
Well	0.03–0.15	1,000 gal
River or sale	0.02–0.06	
Tower	0.02–0.08	
Process water:		
City	0.10–0.35	1,000 gal
Filtered and softened	0.15–0.40	
Distilled	0.70–1.20	
Compressed air:		
Process air	0.02–0.06	1,000 cu ft (at SC)[‡]
Instrument	0.04–0.12	
Natural gas	0.35–0.95	1,000 cu ft (at SC)[‡]
Manufactured gas	0.50–1.50	1,000 cu ft (at SC)[‡]
Fuel oil	0.05–0.15	Gallon
Coal	7.00–14.00	Ton
Refrigeration (ammonia) to 34°F	0.60	Ton-day (288,000 Btu removed)

* From M. S. Peters and K. D. Timmerhaus, "Plant Design and Economics for Chemical Engineers," 2d ed., McGraw-Hill Book Company, New York, 1968.
[†] Highly dependent upon load factor and location.
[‡] For these cases, standard conditions are designated as a pressure of 29.92 in. Hg and a temperature of 60°F.

pressure levels can be kept in balance. The allocation of costs between the different pressure levels can become complicated, and the balance can be upset.

Steam is generally charged on the basis of thousand pounds used but can be charged on the basis of million Btus. Credit should be given for the heating value of condensate returned to the boiler. If the condensate is frequently contaminated by processing leaks, a penalty may be assessed.

The cost of steam depends principally upon the cost of the fuel and the capacity and pressure level of the generating units. The full cost of steam includes fuel, boiler-water treatment, operating labor, depreciation, and maintenance. A rough estimate is two to three times the cost of fuel.

Water costs vary widely depending upon the quality and quantity required. If the water can become contaminated, some provision for purification cost before disposal should be provided. Table 16.4T1 gives some representative water costs. Water rates may be obtained from the local water supplier or through the American

Water Works Association. River water on a once-through basis without treatment costs only a few cents per thousand gallons, while most industrial water falls in the range of $0.10 to $0.30 per 1,000 gal.

Cost of fuels varies with the type of fuel and the number of Btus per unit of fuel. Special preheating and firing equipment is required to burn the cheaper but heavier fuel oils. An analysis of fuel economy is sometimes necessary to select the type and quality of fuel for a particular location and situation. Choice of fuel must allow for the required storage, which can make a difference in coal vs. oil vs. gas.

The estimator must check carefully to make sure that proper provisions are made for delivery of utilities to the site. A common estimating error is the assumption that utilities are available at the site when, in fact, they may not be.

The required utilities can sometimes be estimated in the early stages of project development from available information about similar operations or estimated from a preliminary design. A factor should be applied to the estimated quantities of utilities to allow for equipment efficiencies, other losses, and contingencies. Appropriate factors for the various utilities are suggested in the literature [16.18R8]. Utility consumption does not vary directly with production rate, and variation to the 0.9 power of the capacity ratio might be a better relationship.

16.5 Operating labor

The most accurate means of establishing operating labor requirements is with a complete manning table, but shortcut methods are satisfactory for most cost estimates.

If the project is a novel one, man-hour requirements can be estimated using elemental time values as developed by Haines [16.18R11]. Wessel [16.18R28] relates labor requirements to plant capacity by the equation

$$\frac{\text{Operating man-hours}}{\text{Tons of product}} = t \frac{\text{no. of process steps}}{(\text{capacity in tons/day})^{0.76}} \qquad (16.5\#1)$$

where t is determined by the type of process as follows:

Batch operations with a maximum of labor, 23
Operations with average labor requirements, 17
Well-instrumented continuous-process operations, 10

The equation recognizes the improvement in labor productivity as plants increase in throughput, and can be used to extrapolate known man-hour requirements from one plant to another of different capacity.

It has been suggested that labor requirements vary to about the 0.2 to 0.25 power of the capacity ratio when processing-plant capacities are scaled up or down [16.18R13, 16.18R18].

The average hourly rate for labor can be obtained from company records or data in the literature like that in *Engineering News-Record*, the *Cost Engineers' Notebook* of the AACE, and from the Department of Labor publications *Monthly Report on the Labor Force* and *Survey of Current Business*.

Labor rates have been increasing, seemingly on an accelerated basis; hence care must be taken to get the current figures. Average rates should include the effect of shift and scheduled overtime premiums, but care is required to avoid the overlap with indirect payroll items which are added separately.

Supervision of labor is generally estimated as a percentage of operating labor, a typical value being 20%.

For preliminary appraisals $50 per man-shift can be used to cover labor, supervision, technical and clerical support, and labor burden.

16.6 Maintenance

Records for the company's existing plants are the only reliable source of maintenance cost. Little has been published on the subject, but, with experience, maintenance can be estimated as a function of investment. Maintenance cost as percentage of investment per year ranges from 10% for a complex plant with severe corrosive conditions to 3% for a relatively simple plant with mild, noncorrosive conditions. For example, average maintenance in the petroleum refinery is about 5% of investment per year, but for individual units ranges from about 3% for dewaxing units to about 7% for sulfuric acid alkylation units.

Generally, maintenance can be taken as 60% labor cost and 40% material cost. When a unit is operating at 75% capacity, maintenance cost will be about 85% of the maintenance cost at 100% capacity. When operating at 50% capacity, maintenance cost will be about 75% of maintenance cost at 100% capacity.

Maintenance is known to increase with the age of equipment, but the estimator must use an average figure. The procedure is equalized, in part, by the use of average value for depreciation, whereas accelerated depreciation may, in fact, be used for tax purposes. Thus the overall cost estimate is balanced because average values for maintenance and depreciation are used.

A project may create the need for additional maintenance supervisors and foremen. For major projects, maintenance manning and cost tables may be required to establish the additional maintenance supervision cost; but for small additions no additional maintenance supervision may be required.

16.7 Indirect payroll cost

Indirect payroll cost is the cost of workmen's compensation, pensions, group insurance, paid vacations and holidays, social security and unemployment taxes, contribution to profit sharing, and a growing list of other fringe benefits. It is computed as a percentage of labor and supervision cost, and generally the same rate is used for both labor and supervision. The best figures are from company's records, but accounting definition is important to avoid counting some items that may be included under general expense. A rough estimate is 20 to 30% of the labor plus supervision cost. This figure is rising and may go eventually to 50% and above, figures already reached in parts of Europe.

16.8 Operating supplies

Operating supplies include such things as lubricating oil, instrument charts, brooms, and other items normally used by the project exclusive of those included as raw, repair, or packaging materials. Company records should be used for this cost where they are available. If they are not, operating supplies may be assumed to be about 6% of operating labor. Some authorities base such costs on a percentage of investment.

16.9 Laboratory and other service costs

Depending on company practice and the type of project, operating costs may include service charges by other units of the company. Charges made by a central control laboratory are one example.

Laboratory costs can be estimated (1) on the basis of past experience; (2) on the basis of man-hours required, using ample allowance for the overhead associated with a laboratory technician's pay, thus $10 to $20 per hour; (3) as a percentage of operating labor cost, in the range of 3 to 10%, but for complex situations as high as 20%; and (4) from the literature [16.18R6, 16.18R11].

16.10 Royalties and rentals

Royalties and licensing costs are generally an operating expense. If the charge is proportional to production, it can be treated as a direct cost. A single-sum payment will become part of the project's capital investment. A tax specialist may be required to handle specific situations.

Royalty payments may range between 1 and 5% of the product's sales price, but the agreement may involve so many combinations that such an approximation should be used only when no data are available.

Certain royalty payments and patent purchase costs may be treated by the accountants under general expense as they can be regarded as a replacement for research and development expense.

The cost of rentals can be obtained through the purchasing department. Payments for rentals, along with taxes and insurance on the items, are a current expense, and should not be overlooked in estimating operating expense.

16.11 Contingencies

An allowance for contingencies should be made for both the direct and indirect costs. Contingencies for the direct costs can be applied as a percentage of the direct cost, in the range of 1 to 5%.

16.12 Indirect costs

The items making up factory overhead can be segregated into two groups, one chiefly dependent on investment and the other chiefly dependent on labor. Some figures for new plants [16.18R10] are:

	Investment factor, % per year	Labor factor, % per year
Heavy chemical plants—large capacity	1.5	45
Power plants	1.8	75
Electrochemical plants	2.5	45
Cement plants	3.0	50
Heavy chemical plants—small capacity	4.0	45

The investment is multiplied by the investment factor to give a cost. The annual labor cost including operation, repair, supervision, loading, packaging, and shipping is multiplied by the labor factor to give a second cost. The sum of the two is factory overhead.

In Table 16.2T2, the factory overhead is detailed as including taxes and insurance. General works expense, as used in Table 16.2T1, is a synonym for factory overhead but should not be confused with general expense.

Depreciation is generally taken on the basis of straight-line depreciation over the useful life of the project, although accelerated depreciation may be used for tax purposes. The useful life as used for the cost estimation is not necessarily the life required for tax purposes. The depreciation charge does not include any return on investment.

A separate contingency charge may not be necessary for the indirect costs. A contingency cost is included in the investment cost. If the factory overhead is based chiefly on the investment, a contingency allowance is automatically included.

16.13 Distribution costs

Loading, packing, and shipping costs are best estimated from other similar company operations, modified to the situations under study. Most companies have cost-control systems and standard costs which provide such information. Published data are available in Perry [16.18R19, Sec. 8] and Aries [16.18R2].

The cost of containers can be obtained from suppliers or from Perry [16.18R19]. Returnable containers take a variety of forms from small drums to tank cars and barges, and their cost includes repair, cleaning, testing, refurbishing, and either depreciation or rental.

Transportation costs were discussed briefly in Sec. 16.3. Railroad-car rental rates can be obtained from the railroads or the leasing companies. When railroad cars are owned or leased by the company, the railroads credit the company with about $0.3 per car-mile traveled by the unit.

Distribution charges are segregated from other manufacturing costs to show the effect of various containers and method of shipment. The cost without distribution costs is bulk cost, or manufacturing cost before (packaging and) distribution.

16.14 Avoidance of nuisances

An increasingly important item of consideration is the cost for the reduction of nuisances of all sorts. Common nuisances are the pollution of air and water, but any nuisance, such as odor or noise, must be considered. Even if the nuisance is confined to company property, it must not be overlooked. For example, a moderately high noise level may appear to be only a harmless nuisance, but it may become a costly liability from lawsuits instigated by employees for alleged impairment of health caused by the noise.

Waste disposal is one form of nuisance. There are no readily available data on the cost of waste disposal and elimination of other nuisances, and each case must be calculated individually.

Nuisance control is an item that may no longer be overlooked.

16.15 An example

Table 16.2T1 is an example of the incremental manufacturing cost for increasing production capacity by 17,500 tons/year of roasted ore at three levels of added production. A few additional comments will make the calculations self-explanatory.

Total added investment is $370,000, of which $352,000 is depreciable and $18,000 is nondepreciable working capital. Maintenance at 5.2% of total investment per year has been obtained from company records and is distributed 60% as labor and 40% as materials.

General works expense is calculated on the basis of an investment factor of 2.5% on a $352,000 investment and a labor factor of 45% of operating, repair, supervision, and loading labor, $142,600 (105,000 + 11,500 + 21,000 + 5,100).

Under loading, packing, and shipping $5,100 has been multiplied by 1.20 (20% supervision costs) to give a nonrecorded $6,120 labor plus supervision cost. This is turn has been multiplied by 88% (45 + 20 + 20 + 3) to give $5,400 for the sum of overhead, indirect payroll cost, supervision, and contingency for loading, packing, and shipping. The calculation made in this fashion includes a duplication of indirect payroll cost for the supervision but is close enough.

16.16 Shortcut methods

There would be an obvious advantage to shortcut methods of estimating operating costs. One method would involve writing an equation which contains all the cost elements discussed in the preceding sections. To make this possible, some sort of average values must be decided upon for the factors to apply to the primary cost elements of materials, utilities, labor, and investment. The urge to use such a

Table 16.16T1 Preliminary Operating-cost Estimate

A. Direct production costs
   1. Materials
      a. Raw materials—estimate from price lists
      b. By-product and scrap credit—estimate from price lists
   2. Utilities—from literature or from similar operations
   3. Labor—from literature or from similar operations
   4. Supervision—10 to 25% of labor
   5. Payroll charges—15 to 25% of labor plus supervision
   6. Maintenance—3 to 6% of investment per year
   7. Operating supplies—0.5 to 1.0% of investment per year
   8. Laboratory—20% of labor
   9. Royalties—1 to 5% of sales
  10. Contingencies—2 to 10% of direct costs

B. Indirect costs
   1. Depreciation—5 to 10% of investment per year
   2. Property taxes—2% of investment
   3. Interest—6 to 8% of investment
   4. Insurance—1% of investment
   5. Plant overhead—40 to 60% of labor or 15 to 30 percent of direct costs

C. Distribution costs
   1. Packaging—estimated from container costs
   2. Labor—from similar operations
   3. Shipping—from carriers or 1 to 3% of sales
   4. Overhead—50 to 75% of distribution labor cost

method should be discouraged because the results of such an estimate are stereotyped. The method makes no allowances for differences between situations and does not challenge the imagination of the estimator.

There have been attempts to develop shortcut methods, however. Berry [16.18R4] proposed a method of estimating conversion costs based on the number of processing steps and capacity. Care must be exercised in choosing the correct number of processing steps.

Another shortcut method for batch operations has been proposed by Horton [16.18R12]. Conversion costs are estimated for ratios from 5.6 to 1.0 for conversion cost to operating wages. To this conversion cost must be added raw-material costs, royalties, and container costs. The ratio was derived from literature information on man-hours required for various batch processes.

A preliminary or shortcut estimate can be made from a few basic data and estimating other items as a percentage of these. A suggested form, and range of values for a process industry, is given in Table 16.16T1.

16.17 Questions

Q1. What does manufacturing cost include?
Q2. What expenses in addition to manufacturing cost must be considered in computing total product cost?
Q3. Define incremental cost.

Q4. Why are incremental costs significant in project appraisal?
Q5. Why is it sometimes necessary to compute the return of the business as a whole after the proposed project is completed if the proposed project itself is profitable on an incremental basis?
Q6. Why are average figures justified for maintenance cost and depreciation expense although neither may be constant with time?
Q7. The chapter included some comment on situations where items are considered to be capital investment rather than operating cost. Why is this distinction important in figuring profitability?
Q8. Your company is already making a product at a raw-material cost of precisely $0.512 per pound out of a total operating cost of a $1.623. You are responsible for investigating a proposed new project to quadruple the present capacity. Should the price of raw materials be investigated? Why?
Q9. Why is the cost of raw materials or fuels obtained from another company division included as part of the operating cost of the project using them?
Q10. What is the procedure for computing transfer prices between one company division and another?
Q11. Name at least three project characteristics which affect operating labor.
Q12. Why do maintenance cost estimates depend on the size of the project?
Q13. The text mentions that when a unit is being operated at 50% capacity the repair costs will be about 75% of the repair cost at 100% capacity. Why not 50%?
Q14. What project characteristics make high ratios of supervision to labor necessary?
Q15. Why is it desirable to examine the original agreement documents specifying royalty and other patent right payments?
Q16. Define general works expense.
Q17. What is the difference between general works expense and administrative, sales, and general expense?
Q18. What is the difference between bulk cost and total manufacturing cost? Why are both computed?

16.18 References

R1. *AACE Cost Engineers' Notebook, Wage Rate Suppl.* Paper A5, Index 4.200, January, 1968.
R2. Aries, R. S., and R. D. Newton: "Chemical Engineering Cost Estimation," McGraw-Hill Book Company, New York, 1955.
R3. Bauman, H. C.: "Fundamentals of Cost Engineering in the Chemical Industry," Reinhold Publishing Corporation, New York, 1963.
R4. Berry, E. M.: Estimate Manufacturing Costs, *Chem. Eng.*, vol. 67, p. 123, June 27, 1960.
R5. Black, J. H.: Estimating Operating Costs for New Ventures, *AACE Bull.*, vol. 4, p. 42, June, 1962.
R6. Chilton, C. H., "Cost Engineering in the Process Industries," McGraw-Hill Book Company, New York, 1960.
R7. Couch, J. C.: Learning Curve Techniques Illustrated by Ship Production, *AACE Bull.*, June, 1964, p. 50.
R8. Dybdal, E. C.: Engineering and Economic Evaluation of Projects, *Chem. Eng. Progr.*, vol. 46, pp. 57–66, February, 1950.
R9. Hackney, J. W.: Estimate Production Costs Quickly, *Chem. Eng.*, vol. 68, pp. 179–184, April 17, 1961.
R10. Hackney, J. W.: "Control and Management of Capital Projects," John Wiley & Sons, Inc., New York, 1965.
R11. Haines, T. B.: Direct Operating Requirement for Chemical Processes, *Chem. Eng. Progr.*, November, 1957, pp. 556–562.
R12. Horton, R. L.: Manufacturing Costs for Batch Produced Chemicals, *Chem. Eng.*, vol. 72, p. 236, Oct. 11, 1965.
R13. Isard, W., and E. W. Schooler: "Location Factors in the Petrochemical Industry," Department of Commerce, Washington, 1955.

R14. Nelson, W. L.: Transportation Costs by Pipeline, *Oil Gas J.*, May 18, 1964, p. 132.
R15. Nelson, W. L.: Transportation Costs by Ocean Tankers, *Oil Gas J.*, June 22, 1964, pp. 183–184.
R16. Nelson, W. L.: Operating Costs Indexes, *Oil Gas J.*, July 1, 1968, p. 117.
R17. Nelson, W. L.: Operating Costs Abroad—Labor, *Oil Gas J.*, Aug. 3, 1964, p. 109.
R18. O'Connell, F. P.: Chart Gives Operating Labor for Various Plant Capacities, *Chem. Eng.*, vol. 69, p. 150, Feb. 19, 1962.
R19. Perry, J. H.: "Chemical Business Handbook," McGraw-Hill Book Company, New York, 1954.
R20. Perry, R. H., et al.: "Chemical Engineers' Handbook," 4th ed., McGraw-Hill Book Company, New York, 1963.
R21. Peters, M. S., and K. D. Timmerhaus: "Plant Design and Economics for Chemical Engineers," 2d ed., McGraw-Hill Book Company, New York, 1968.
R22. *Petroleum Refiner*, Optimum Overtime for Maintenance, vol. 42, p. 121, January, 1963.
R23. Sweet, E. R.: Preparation of Operating Cost Estimates, *Chem. Eng. Progr.*, vol. 52, p. 180, May, 1956.
R24. Thomas, H. R.: Transportation Costs for LP Gas, by Pipeline, Railroad and Truck, *Oil Gas J.*, May 18, 1964, p. 126.
R25. Van Noy, C. W.: "Guide for Making Cost Estimates for Chemical-type Operations," *U.S. Bur. Mines Rept. Investigation* 4534, Washington, 1949.
R26. Verseput, J. P.: How Shell Maintains Its World Wide Refineries, *Hydrocarbon Process.*, January, 1965, pp. 78–81.
R27. Walton, P. R.: Sources of Error in Operating-cost Estimates, *Chem. Eng.*, July 15, 1968, pp. 150–152.
R28. Wessell, H. E.: New Graph Correlates Operating Labor Data for Chemical Processes, *Chem. Eng.*, July, 1952, p. 209.

17
Cost Control

J. F. Lovett

CAPITAL-COST CONTROL

17.1 The nature of control

Cost engineering cannot end with analysis and prediction of capital costs. Plants and factories must be built, and it is essential that costs be controlled during their erection. Plants and factories must be operated, and it is equally important that operating costs be controlled. This chapter is divided into three sections, the first describing the components of capital-cost control, the second the components of operating-cost control, and the third one of the networking methods for planning and controlling capital costs. Cost control of capital and operating costs is a major and critical activity of cost engineering.

In the building of a plant, cost control means the regulation of expenditures to within the authorized estimated cost while providing a plant of the desired quality within the time limit specified. The plant should be capable of producing a quality product at the design capacity.

17.2 Elements of cost-control program

The elements of cost control are similar to those for controlling an engineering property, e.g., the temperature of a room. The control engineer will:

1. Have an objective, say maintain room at 72°F.
2. Have a plan, say install a thermostat.
3. Determine performance, i.e., compare thermostat reading with objective.
4. Take action and improve the performance

These four elements when applied to capital-cost control become:

1. Define the scope, the objectives to be achieved.
2. Define the estimates by developing a plan and schedule.
3. Accumulate data and compare actual performance with the estimates.
4. Take corrective action when necessary.

17.3 Scope definition

Table 17.3T1 gives the conformation and terminology of topics for capital-cost control. The first requirement of a control program is that the scope, the objectives to be achieved, be defined. The scope is classified in four parts. The first part, the design philosophy, establishes management's desiderata in designing and constructing the project. The factors are listed in Table 17.3T2. The second part, the manufacturing and process description, provides all the known technical information and specifies the assumptions and extrapolations to be used in the design. The items specified are given in Table 17.3T3. The third part, the plant-facilities description, provides all the known information on the plant site, utilities,

Table 17.3T1 Outline of Capital-cost Control

1. Define project scope
    a. Design philosophy
    b. Manufacturing and process description
    c. Plant-facilities description
    d. Mechanical description
2. Define estimations
    a. Project plan
    b. Project schedule
    c. Capital cost
3. Cost reporting
    a. Progress reporting
    b. Expenditure reporting
    c. Quality reporting
4. Corrective action
    a. Causes for need of corrective action
    b. Types of corrective action

Table 17.3T2 Factors in the Design Philosophy

1. Required plant capacity
2. Required start-up date
3. Life expectancy of the project
4. Integration requirements with other projects
5. Product quality control
6. Limitation or other financial requirements including economics of capital use and operating costs
7. Provisions for expansion
8. Specific logistic requirements, e.g., packaging, raw-material handling, maximum and minimum inventories, shipping
9. For multiproduct plants, limits to capacity requirements for each product
10. Special timing requirements, e.g., start-up sequence and related matters
11. Supplementary services to be provided
12. Operator and maintenance convenience requirements
13. Provision of spares
14. Metering and measurement for material balances, operation, and quality control
15. Environmental requirements, e.g., enclosures, pollution control, cleanliness
16. Plant appearance, landscaping, etc.

and auxiliary buildings and equipment requirements. The items specified are given in Table 17.3T4. The fourth part, the mechanical description, establishes the quality and extent of the equipment and facilities to be installed. The items specified are given in Table 17.3T5.

17.4 Project planning and scheduling

The *project plan* states in detail the plans for accomplishing the required work, including division of responsibility, and methods to be employed. It is a logical plan of action from start to finish. It considers all work phases of the project,

Table 17.3T3 Factors in Manufacturing and Process Description

1. Technology of manufacture and processing
2. Physical and technological data of raw materials, intermediates, and final products
3. Capacity and performance capability of equipment
4. Material input, output, and losses
5. Energy and heat balances
6. Equipment description and flowsheets
7. Manufacturing conditions and treatments, e.g., heating time, humidity control
8. Raw-material, intermediate, and product specifications
9. Manufacture and process-control requirements
10. Quality-control requirements
11. Waste control and disposal, antipollution problems
12. By-product problems
13. Process and aging time
14. Critical manufacture and process items
15. Safety, including personnel safety, fire, explosion, toxicity, noise abatement, etc.
16. Operating manuals including normal and emergency start-up and shutdown procedures

Table 17.3T4 Plant-facilities Description

1. Plant layout inside and outside, within and beyond battery limits, showing rough grading and general fencing plans
2. Site survey, soil investigations, test borings, and test wells
3. Plant-utilities facilities, e.g., well water, river water, city water, process water, fire water, cooling water, steam, refrigeration, boilers, electricity, gas, inert gas, compressed air, suction, storm and sanitary sewers, sumps, incinerators, condensate systems, including blueprints, line diagrams, and equipment and process specifications as necessary
4. Locker rooms and change houses
5. Maintenance and stores facilities
6. Tank farm, coal pile, and similar facilities including specifications for all equipment
7. Waste disposal and antipollution facilities, including flowsheets
8. Logistics of materials shipping and receiving, including railroad facilities, waterway facilities, and truck facilities with such details as truck turnarounds, vehicle scales, tank-car or truck cleaning facilities, car shakers and car thawers
9. River docks, river-water pumping stations
10. Grade-crossing safety considerations
11. Parking facilities
12. Mobile equipment
13. Nonmanufacturing equipment, e.g., office, safety and medical, laboratory and inspection, housekeeping, locker room, fire fighting, and telephone and intercommunication equipment

including engineering design, equipment and material purchasing, expediting and inspection, contract negotiation, construction, mechanical checkout, start-up, and any special requirement of management such as early start-up of some part of the project.

Planning can be done by many methods. Some popular ones are based on network or arrow diagrams. One of these, the critical-path method (CPM) is developed separately in the third section of this chapter to familiarize the reader with the principles of such methods.

The *project schedule* defines the timing by which the plan is to be executed, and is developed from the project plan, recognizing such factors as the time required before equipment and material quotations can be designed and requested,

Table 17.3T5. Mechanical Description

1. Equipment flowsheet
2. Equipment specifications
3. Instrument specifications
4. Piping specifications
5. Electrical specifications
6. Insulation specifications
7. Structural specifications
8. Engineering schedule
9. Procurement schedule
10. Construction schedule
11. Composite project schedule

the time to receive and evaluate quotations, delivery time, availability of engineering manpower, availability of construction labor, practical limitation of efficient use of labor, and special requirements such as early start-up of some part of the project.

The project plan and the project schedule together provide the basis for the definitive *capital-cost estimate* which defines the expenditures for construction of the project. The capital-cost estimate must present detailed, clear, easily recognizable elements of the plan and schedule.

17.5 Cost reporting

Defining the project scope and estimates must be done before a project starts. In practice variations occur, and projects rarely proceed exactly as expected. Construction projects become very fluid, and many decisions must be made on the job. Some variations may be favorable, others unfavorable. Some favorable variations can have concomitant unfavorable factors, e.g., early delivery of equipment before sheltered storage space is available.

For good control it is necessary to have current information on the pertinent matters at all times, a requirement demanding good reporting. There are three types of reports. In the first type, progress reporting, progress is reported by the responsible groups, engineering, purchasing, and construction showing what has been accomplished by the date of the report, resolved into the recognizable elements of the project plan and project schedule.

In the second type, expenditure reporting, expenditures and commitments are reported by engineering, purchasing, and construction by daily time sheets, copies of purchase orders and store requisitions, rental equipment utilization reports, and so forth. These are resolved into the recognizable elements of the capital-cost estimate.

In the third type, quality reporting, deviations from the bid evaluation forms received from purchase-order descriptions and specifications are reported by the purchasing department and shop and field inspectors.

Gathering information for these reports and digesting them requires good organization. Most of these reports will be submitted on standard forms, like that shown in Table 17.5T1. Reports cost money and, as in all accounting procedures, there is some point beyond which the gain is not worth the cost. The reports must be current, active, and faithful. Reports can be digested only by those who have some familiarity with actual conditions in the field, those who can sense the situation and recognize that reports can be accurate but misleading.

The data acquired must be compared with the estimates. These comparisons fall into five broad categories:

1 Man-hours expended vs. actual accomplishment
2 Calendar days expended vs. actual schedule
3 Estimated vs. actual equipment-cost commitments
4 Actual items of equipment and materials vs. project objectives
5 Quality of equipment and materials vs. project objectives

360   COST ESTIMATION AND CONTROL

Table 17.5T1   Sample Form for Reporting Results

		BUDGET			EXPENSE			FINAL COST FORECAST			OVER (UNDER)	PERCENT COMP.
CODE NO.	DESCRIPTION	QUANTITY	UNIT COST	AMOUNT	QUANTITY	UNIT COST	AMOUNT	QUANTITY	UNIT COST	AMOUNT		

MONTHLY COST REPORT
CONTRACT NO.
CUSTOMER
LOCATION
REPORT NO.   DATE   PAGE   OF
DIRECT LABOR
CODE - 200

Each of these can be subdivided to be more specific, e.g., engineering man-hours, craft labor man-hours, supervisory man-hours, engineering schedule, procurement schedule, construction schedule. Thus, with actual man-hours expended, work accomplished, number of items committed, costs of equipment committed, and equipment and material deliveries reported promptly, deviations from schedules and estimates are easily detected and the areas where control action is necessary become apparent.

A good method for the first three comparisons is to develop the standard S curve by plotting the cumulative estimate vs. the planned schedule, for recognizable

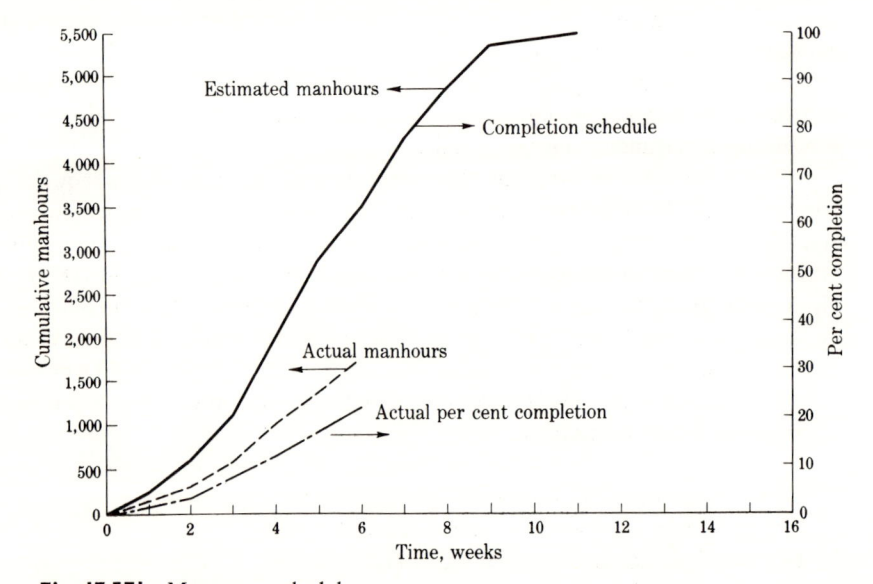

Fig. 17.5F1   Manpower schedule.

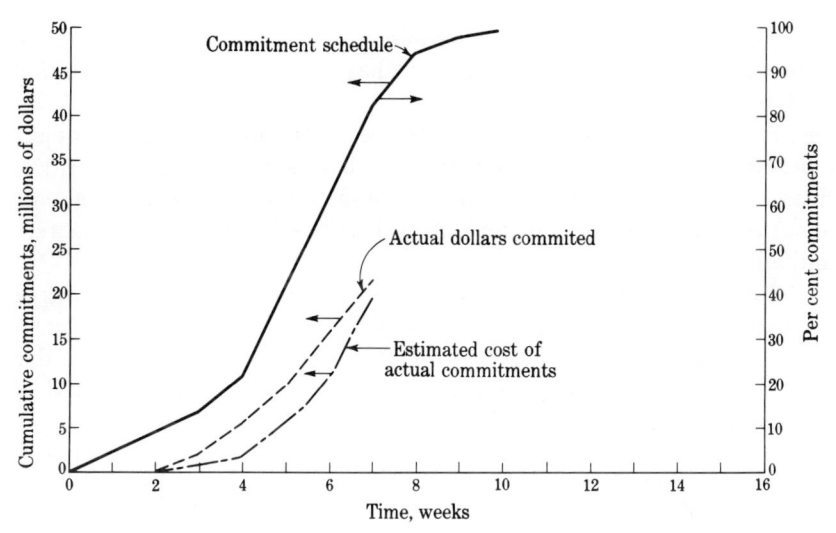

Fig. 17.5F2 Commitment schedule.

portions of the job, as a control curve and then plot actual values against actual time on the same plot. The fourth and fifth comparisons, quantity and quality, are then made by direct comparison with the project objectives.

Figure 17.5F1 is a typical example of the standard S curve showing cumulative man-hours, such as craft man-hours or engineering man-hours, to do a particular part of the project and percent completion plotted against time. Figure 17.5F1 indicates that the project requires corrective action. At the reporting period of 6 weeks, the actual man-hours expended are only half the scheduled hours. It also shows that instead of being 33% completed for the actual man-hours expended, it is only 22% completed. Only two-thirds of the scheduled work has been completed for the actual man-hours expended. In other words the plot shows that the project is 3 weeks behind schedule and overexpended by 600 man-hours.

Figure 17.5F2 is another typical S plot showing cumulative commitments (for equipment, material, and subcontracts) and percent committed plotted against time. Here, after 6 weeks, only half the scheduled commitments have been made, and the cost of commitments is 10% greater than estimated. In other words, commitments are 2 weeks behind schedule, indicating that deliveries may be delayed an equal amount with serious consequences.

Figures 17.5F1 and 17.5F2 do not show the cause for the overruns in time and money, but they do show that corrective action is required. In fact, this was apparent at the end of the third week, when action should have been taken.

17.6 Corrective action

Usually the corrective action to be taken is apparent from a detailed analysis of the causes for the project being off control limits. However, getting the correct answers can be a difficult task and may require tact and diplomacy. Thus, the helpful approach rather than the critical one will be more productive when working with people.

There are certain critical items that must be accomplished during a project before others can be started. It should be noted that the number of truly critical items on large projects is rarely more than 20% of the total. If the newer methods, such as the critical-path method, are used, the truly critical items are made apparent in a quantitative way.

The number, magnitude, and character of control problems encountered during the execution of a capital project are seemingly without end. No attempt is made here to classify them completely, if indeed it were possible, but Table 17.6T1 is a checklist of the major types of control problems and the kind of control action they require.

A corrective action must be followed through to be successful. Figure 17.6F1 shows the effect of cost control applied to the project of Fig. 17.5F1.

Table 17.6T1 Control-problem Classification and Corrective Action Required—Capital Costs

Control problem	Types of corrective action
1. Too early job start	a. Establish resulting extra cost
	b. Require that extra costs be justified
2. Lack of information	a. Make direct contact with information source
	b. Assign more personnel on temporary or pemanent basis
3. Lack of personnel	a. Hire or rent additional personnel
	b. Adjust priorities to make personnel available
	c. Subcontract
	d. Use overtime
4. Lack of equipment, tools, or material	a. Expedite deliveries
	b. Reschedule to work around shortage
	c. Authorize vendor's overtime
5. Inefficient personnel	a. Provide more detailed work definition
	b. Increase supervision
	c. Adjust priorities to make more efficient personnel available
6. Inefficient use of personnel	a. Provide more detailed work plan
	b. Increase supervision
	c. Increase or reduce crew size
7. Inefficient work methods	a. Develop alternate methods
	b. Provide more detailed work plan
	c. Provide superior supervision
8. Oversights and additions	a. Allow minimum interference with project plan or schedule
9. Escalation	a. Keep job on schedule
	b. Develop maximum labor efficiency
10. End-of-job stretch-out	a. Develop detailed checklist of cleanup work
	b. Develop detailed schedules for cleanup
	c. Reduce crew sizes promptly
	d. Eliminate maintenance or other work outside the objectives
	e. Expedite management decision to terminate construction

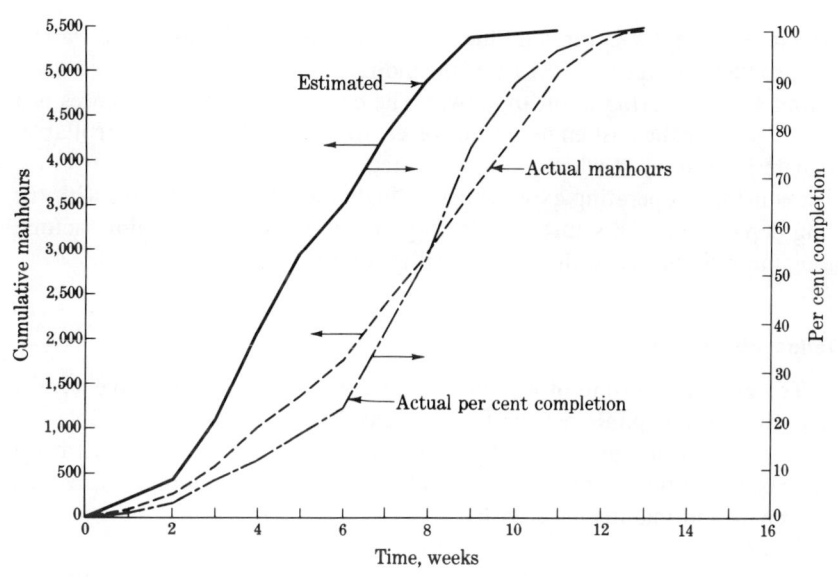

Fig. 17.6F1 Corrective action applied to Fig. 17.5F1.

Improved efficiency due to improved work methods made it possible to complete this work for the estimated man-hours and to gain 1 of the 3 weeks that it was behind schedule.

OPERATING-COST CONTROL

17.7 Operating costs are repetitive

Operating costs continue repetitively over the life of the plant and will exceed the capital cost manyfold, hence their importance. Operating-cost control means the regulation of expenditures on materials, labor, utilities, and associated costs while producing a quality product at a competitive price. Since the principles for operating and capital cost are essentially alike, the former will be discussed in less detail.

Operating-cost control requires a program that is updated periodically to meet the changing conditions for such factors as varying material price and quality, changing product quality, demand and price, increasing maintenance costs, technological obsolescence, and a myriad of other causes. It must define the objectives, provide a plan, provide a means of comparing performance with the plan, and indicate steps necessary to reduce costs.

17.8 Conjunction with cost accounting

Accounting personnel are set up to obtain information on costs. A knowledge of cost accounting, at least the principles developed in Chap. 19, will help the engineer cooperate with the accounting department.

The present chapter is limited chiefly to direct material costs, direct labor, and direct production expense. Most of the indirect cost is not subject to control, at least from an engineering point of view. The control of indirect expenses is a legitimate subject for the cost engineer, however, for items which are controllable, e.g., the material and labor which go into indirect cost.

Cost control of operating expense accordingly requires cooperation with the accounting department. Because engineering and technology are major factors, the cost engineer should have the responsibility for operating-cost control.

17.9 Define objectives

Table 17.9T1 gives an outline of operating-cost control resembling Table 17.3T1 previously given for capital-cost control. Many of the items in the table are established during the design and construction of the project; hence good operating-cost control begins at the design stage. Good plant layout will minimize operating labor and repair and maintenance costs.

Production schedules require careful review of inventory requirements, sales forecast, input material inventory, quality control, and efficient utilization of labor equipment and material. Similarly labor schedules should include scheduling of direct operating labor, maintenance labor, and indirect labor for housekeeping, packing, and shipping. The labor schedules should be reviewed frequently for efficient use of both straight time and overtime.

During the early stages of plant operation large expenditures for quality control may be required, but they should diminish with time. However, they should not be reduced below a reasonable frequency that will provide a continuing check on the operating personnel, material, and technical factors.

Table 17.9T1 Outline of Operating-cost Control

1. Define objectives
    a. Production schedules
    b. Labor-utilization schedules
    c. Input-material quality specifications
    d. Input-material utilization schedules
    e. Inventory requirements
    f. Repair and maintenance requirements
    g. Quality-control requirements
    h. Utility requirements
    i. Product-quality specifications
    j. Waste-disposal requirements
    k. Off-specification material rework
2. Define standards
    a. Standard costs
3. Cost reporting
    a. Periodic reports
    b. Special investigations
4. Corrective action

Inventory control is a critical part of plant operating costs and is discussed in Chap. 10. Some inventories are perishable, and some fluctuate in price seasonably, factors which must be recognized in sizing the inventory.

17.10 Standard costs

Standards are necessary to judge whether costs are satisfactory. These standards are used for comparison and like all standards can be somewhat arbitrary—whether boys are measured by feet or yards does not change a tall boy into a short boy. However, there is some advantage in establishing standard costs in relationship to technological and optimum considerations rather than, say, to some normal historical cost. Standard costs of this nature are sometimes referred to as industrial engineered standards. Setting standard costs is a task that requires engineering knowledge of plant operations and is one of the most important functions of an engineer in operating-cost control since it is comparison of actual costs with the standard costs which instigates action.

17.11 Cost reporting

Although it is the responsibility of the engineers to set standard costs, it is the responsibility of the accounting department to report the comparison of actual against standard costs. Standard forms are used with periodic reporting by the various departments. The object, of course, is to reduce the collection of data to a routine basis.

There are occasions, however, when additional or more detailed information is required. Cost centers can be set up on a temporary basis. Frequently the cost analysis requires considerable engineering effort, and experimental equipment will have to be installed to establish material and cost data.

17.12 Corrective action

After a plant has been designed and built, it must be operated so as to produce the desired quality of product at minimum cost with the plant as it exists. Modifications to correct operating inefficiencies, e.g., high maintenance cost, can be effected throughout the life of the plant, but they must be justified on the basis of savings in operating costs.

The plant supervisor or manager is responsible for operating-cost control and overseeing that proper scheduling and use of resources is executed. It is his responsibility to review the reports and to see that corrective action is taken where necessary.

The need for corrective action is indicated by comparison of the reported values with the standard costs. The cost engineer can be a valuable advisor in interpreting the comparison. Implementation of corrective action is the responsibility of plant supervisors, who also must follow through to see that corrective action is carried out satisfactorily.

Table 17.13T1 Control-problem Classification and Corrective Action Required—Operating Costs

Control problem	Types of corrective action
1. Low yields—material usage too high	a. Check usage directions; see that they are being followed b. Check material-weighing and metering devices c. Check material quality d. Check for leaks, spills, even theft
2. High off-specification production and high waste, reworking, and downgrading	a. Check processing procedures b. Check material quality c. Check equipment cleaning and changeover procedures d. Check control instruments
3. Low production rates	a. Check for excessive rework b. Check maintenance downtime and causes c. Check for excessive changeover and downtime d. Check processing procedures
4. High maintenance costs	a. Review preventive and routine maintenance procedures b. Check that maintenance is performed by qualified personnel c. Emphasize maintenance scheduling against waiting for emergencies d. Displace equipment requiring excessive maintenance
5. High utility costs	a. Check for proper control and eliminate leaks b. Check that utilities are shut off when not required c. Check utility metering for accuracy
6. High labor costs	a. Check for avoidable overtime b. Check production scheduling for economic labor scheduling c. Check absenteeism and lateness records for chronic offenders d. Check for excessive personnel turnover causing high overtime and training expenditures

17.13 Classification of operating-cost control problems

Control problems can vary considerably depending on the type of project and kind of equipment involved and also on material variations, sales-forecast variations, inventory requirements, etc. Although the number, magnitude, and character of the problems encountered are seemingly without end, many can be classified. Table 17.13T1 gives a checklist for some common types of control problems and the control action required.

CRITICAL-PATH METHOD (CPM)

17.14 Network diagrams

In the late 1950s the Navy with a consulting firm developed program evaluation and review technique (PERT) for scheduling the Navy's Polaris missile program. PERT was originally a method of scheduling to complete a project on time. It has since been modified to include additional factors, such as cost. About the same time Walker and Kelley developed the critical-path method (CPM) to expedite construction projects and included costs.

Both PERT and CPM are based on network or arrow diagrams. They were an immediate success, and have been followed by many modifications such as LOB, IMPACT, CRAM, LESS, COMET, PERT/COST, and many others [17.19R4]. The remainder of the chapter will be devoted to CPM, which is the most popular network method used for construction and capital costs.

17.15 A simple network

A problem taken from Sayre [17.19R7] has a network with normal completion times in days as shown in Fig. 17.15F1.

Each small circle with a number is an *event*. The terminal numbers are start and finish, and intermediate numbers correspond to completion of any intermediate task such as finishing foundations, or finishing third-story plumbing. An arrow represents an *activity*. Thus the arrow 2 → 3 is the activity to go from event 2 to event 3. No activity can be started until all the arrows, or activities, leading to its tail event have been completed. Frequently it is necessary to use dummy activities, shown by dotted lines or solid lines with zero time requirement, which utilize no time and have no cost requirement but are necessary to keep the sequence in order. The lengths of the arrows are not related to time or cost. The figure shown has five events and seven activities, none of which happen to be dummies.

The *critical path* is the path through the network between the beginning and end with the longest time, traveling along arrows only in the direction tail to head. By the methods of Chap. 13, or here by inspection, the critical path is 1–2–4–5 or a total of 12 days, as shown in Fig. 17.15F2. This is the shortest normal time in which the project can be completed. Note that event 4 can be touched in 4 days, path 1–3–4, but requires 8 days for completing, path 1–2–4.

To shorten the project's duration, one or more of the activities, 1–2, 2–4, or 4–5 will have to be expedited. Each activity has a crash time representing the

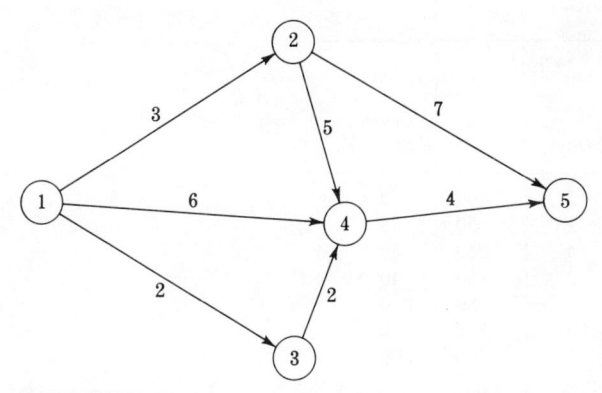

Fig. 17.15F1 Network with normal time.

368 COST ESTIMATION AND CONTROL   17.15

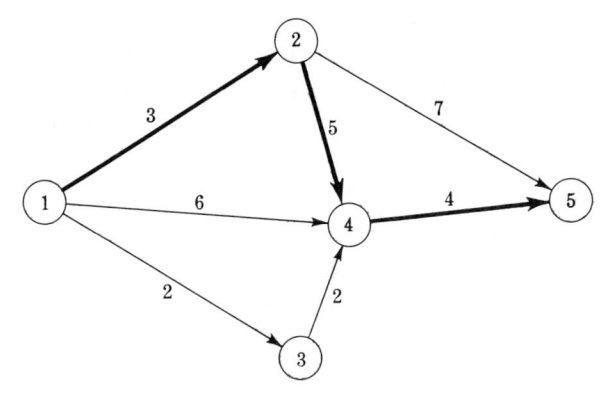

Fig. 17.15F2 Critical path with normal time.

minimum time for completion. It will be assumed that there is a straight-line, linear relationship between cost and time. Table 17.15T1 summarizes the cost data for all the activities. Thus, taking activity 1–4 as an example, the normal time is 6 days at a cost of $140, and the crash time is 4 days at $260. As a linear relationship is assumed, the crash cost rate for the activity is

$$\frac{260 - 140}{6 - 14} = \$60 \text{ per day}$$

It is now possible to develop various project durations and the cost:

12-day schedule: normal for the project, cost $610.
11-day schedule: least expensive way to gain 1 day is to reduce activity 2–4 by 1 day at a cost of $40, project cost $650.
10-day schedule: reduce activity 2–4 by another day at $40 additional, project cost $690.

Table 17.15T1 Cost for Activities

	Normal		Crash		Crash
Activity	Days	$	Days	$	$ per day
1–2	3	50	2	100	50
1–3	2	25	1	50	25
1–4	6	140	4	260	60
2–4	5	100	3	180	40
3–4	2	80	2	80	0
2–5	7	115	5	175	30
4–5	4	100	2	240	70
Totals		610		1,085	

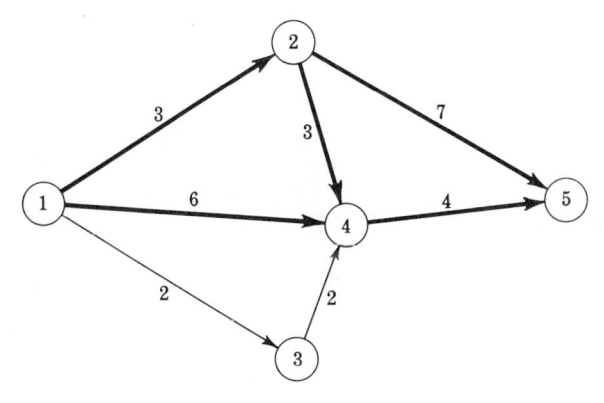

Fig. 17.15F3 Network with 10-day schedule.

For a 10-day schedule there are three critical paths, 1–2–5, 1–2–4–5, and 1–4–5. Further cuts in activity 2–4 will not help since the project's duration is also determined by other activities. The situation is shown in Fig. 17.15F3.

9-day schedule: cut activities 1–2 and 4–5 each one day at a combined extra cost of $120. However, in so doing activity 2–4 can be extended 1 day at a savings of $40. Net cost is $80 additional, project cost $770.
8-day schedule: reduce activities 2–5 and 4–5 each by 1 day at a combined cost of $100, project cost $870. The situation is shown in Fig. 17.15F4.
7-day schedule: an activity on each of the three critical paths must be expedited. The cheapest combination of reductions is 1 day for activities 1–4, 2–4, and 2–5 for an additional cost of $130, project cost $1,000.

The 7-day schedule is the minimum since no further crashing to reduce the schedule to 6 days is possible.

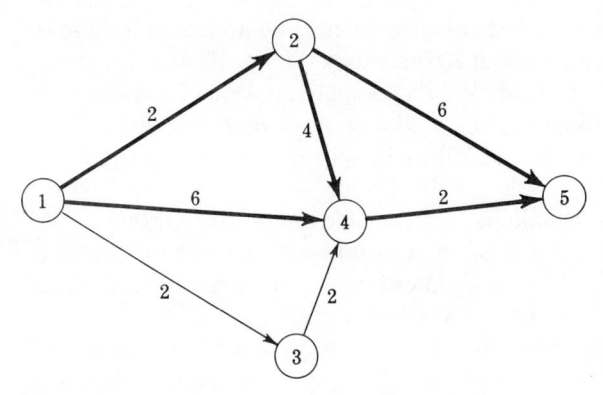

Fig. 17.15F4 Network with 8-day schedule.

Table 17.15T2 Total Cost for Project

Days	Direct cost, $	Indirect cost, $	Total cost, $
12	610	900	1,510
11	650	810	1,460
10	690	740	1,430
9	770	690	1,460
8	870	650	1,520
7	1,000	620	1,620

The costs considered so far are the direct costs. The total cost is the sum of the direct and indirect costs. As the latter decrease with time, there can be an overall cost advantage in reducing the normal time. Table 17.15T2 gives the total cost for the project. In this case the optimum schedule is 10 days, shown in Fig. 17.15F3 with three critical paths, and a cost of $1,430.

17.16 Advantages of CPM

CPM makes critical activities known at all times so that those requiring special attention will receive it. On the other hand, activities not on a critical path have some flexibility. The extra time that a noncritical activity can be delayed before it becomes critical is known as *float*. Total float is the time an activity can be delayed without affecting the completion of a project. Free float is the time an activity can be delayed without affecting the earliest starting time of *any* other activity. Float can frequently be used to advantage; thus in the preceding section in reducing the 10-day schedule to a 9-day schedule, activity 2–4 developed 1 day of float which could then be used to regain $40. Activities on a critical path have no float.

CPM is very adaptable to computer programming and can be reevaluated along the way to keep it current. CPM can also be done by a manual technique with the break-even point at perhaps about 200 activities. Large projects involving thousands of activities can only be justified on a computer. A hand computation on a simplified basis is recommended for a first trial so that the analyst gets completely familiar with the project and knows how to modify it to get the best network.

CPM, like other network techniques, is a valuable tool and can reveal all the information needed to keep a project going smoothly with respect to time and expenditure. It cannot correct deficiencies in estimates, but it can disclose them early enough for reassessment and reduce their frequency.

A project can be accomplished in more than one way, thus by more than one network diagram; hence the analyst in setting up the network should not grasp any network just because it is feasible. A better network may exist.

17.17 Problems

P1. Define the critical path for the following network for the production of an instrument.

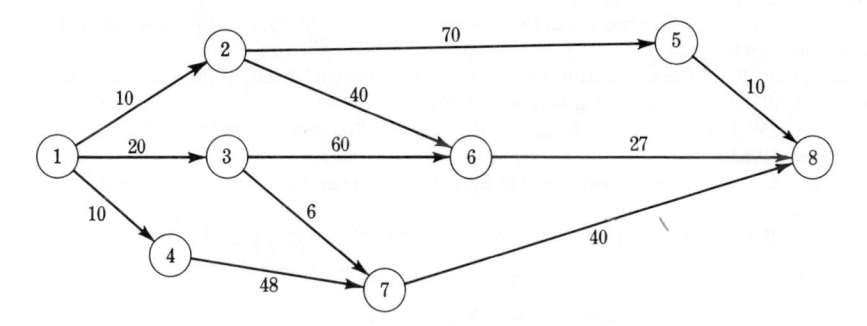

P2. Define the critical path for the following process to produce an electronic device. Find the free float and total float for each operation.

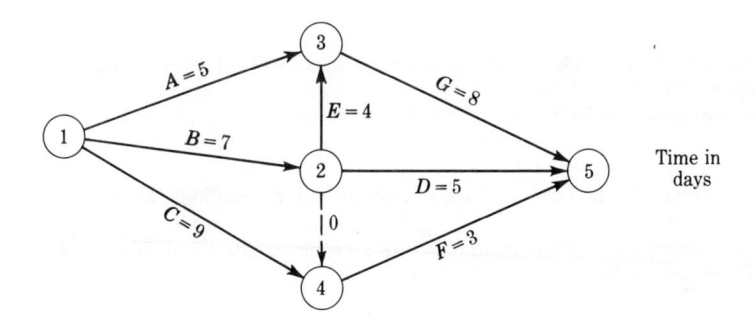

P3. The following additional information applies to Prob. 17.17P2:

		Normal		Crash	
Operation	Duration	Operation cost, $	Duration	Operation cost, $
A	5	100	4	150
B	7	200	6	300
C	9	400	8	450
D	5	150	4	200
E	4	100	3	150
F	3	300	2	350
G	8	700	7	850

(a) What is the total cost of the project?
(b) What would be the minimum additional cost required to finish the project 2 days earlier?

17.18 References on cost control

R1. Bauman, H. C.: "Fundamentals of Cost Engineering in the Chemical Industry," Reinhold Publishing Corporation, New York, 1964.
R2. Chilton, C. H.: "Cost Engineering in the Process Industries," McGraw-Hill Book Company, New York, 1960.
R3. Friedman, I. R.: "Cost Controls and Profit Improvement through Product Analysis," Prentice-Hall, Inc., Englewood Cliffs, N.J., 1966.
R4. Hackney, J. W.: "Control and Management of Capital Projects," John Wiley & Sons, Inc., New York, 1965.
R5. McNeill, W. I.: "Effective Cost Control Systems," Prentice-Hall, Inc., Englewood Cliffs, N.J., 1965.
R6. Nitchie, E. B.: Cost Control Systems, *Chem. Eng.*, October, 1957, pp. 233–248.

17.19 References on CPM and network methods

R1. Baker, B. N., and R. L. Eris: "An Introduction to PERT/CPM," Richard D. Irwin, Inc., Homewood, Ill., 1964.
R2. Bock, R. H., and W. K. Holstein: "Production Planning and Control," Charles E. Merrill Books, Inc., Columbus, Ohio, 1963.
R3. Dooley, A. R., and others: "Operations Planning and Control," John Wiley & Sons, Inc., New York, 1964.
R4. Levin, R. I., and C. A. Kirkpatrick: "Planning and Control with PERT/CPM," McGraw-Hill Book Company, New York 1966.
R5. Martino, R. L.: Problems with PERT, *Chem. Week*, vol. 95, p. 101, July 18, 1964.
R6. Moder, J. J., and C. R. Phillips: "Project Management with CPM and PERT," Reinhold Publishing Corporation, New York, 1964.
R7. Sayre, J. S., J. E. Kelley, Jr., and M. R. Walker: Critical Path Scheduling, *Factory*, July, 1960, pp. 74–78.
R8. Van Slyke, R. M.: Monte Carlo Methods and the PERT Problem, *Operations Res.*, vol. 11, pp. 839–860, September, 1963.

18
Total Cost and Profit[1]

H. C. Bauman

18.1 Elements of complete cost

The elements of the complete costs of manufacturing and selling a product have been outlined in Table 16.1T1. The purpose of this chapter is to discuss several topics in the latter part of the table, items beyond manufacturing cost.

For a business venture to be successful, it must earn a profit. It will be shown that the concept of profit is no longer a simple one and requires an examination in depth.

18.2 Estimating general and selling expense

The estimation of operating costs was covered in Chap. 16. Consider now the costs involved in selling the product.

The product is ready for market, and there must be a sales force ready to market it as effectively as possible. Marketing costs include salesmen's salaries and commissions, advertising and promotion, technical sales services, samples,

---

[1] This chapter contains in part material from the author's "Fundamentals of Cost Engineering in the Chemical Industry," Reinhold Book Corporation, a subsidiary of Chapman-Reinhold, Inc., New York, 1964, and such material is used with permission.

Table 18.2T1 Typical Breakdown of Annual Sales in the Processing Industries*

Item	Typical percentage of sales Range	Typical percentage of sales Median
1. Plant costs	50–75	62
Cost of sales	45–60	52
Material	20–35	30
Labor	10–17	14
Plant overhead	6–10	8
Depreciation	4–8	6
Distribution costs	2–5	3
2. Selling and advertising expense	14–18	15
3. Administrative expense	5–7	6
4. Research and development	1–6	3
5. Financial—interest, etc.	0.2–0.5	0.3
6. Taxes, insurance, pensions	1–4	2.5
7. Earnings before income taxes	5–25	14
8. Federal, state, and foreign income taxes	3–12	8
9. Net earnings	2–10	6

* Based on continuous operation. Processing industries include pharmaceuticals, glass, cement, gypsum, concrete, petroleum refining, chemicals, soaps, cosmetics, paper and allied products, rubber, food, and beverages.

displays, and other similar items related to sales. To these direct costs for sales are added such indirect costs as supervision, travel and entertainment, market research and sales analysis, and district office expenses. Referring to Table 18.2T1, selling and advertising expense in the large processing industries generally varies between 14 and 18% of total costs of sales. Selling and advertising expense are generally considerably higher on a percentage of total sales basis for proprietary products in the drug and cosmetic field.

Another appreciable item of total cost is administrative expense. All efficient industrial establishments concentrate on the reduction of this type of expense to a minimum to remain competitive. Administrative expense includes all such items of cost which cannot be charged directly to a specific product item and includes salaries and expenses of officers and staff, all the general accounting, clerical and auditing functions, central engineering not chargeable to a capital project, technical, legal and patent services, public-relations expense, communication and traffic management, central purchasing activities, and contributions and dues to technical and industrial associations. For most processing industries this expense runs between 5 and 7% of total sales. Modern technology and worldwide competition results in a growing tendency in the process industries to spend more money for research and development of new products. For the chemical industry as a whole, median expenditure for research and development approaches 3%

of total sales and ranges from 1 to 6%. This expense increases as technology becomes more complex and the need for optimization of manufacturing processes becomes urgent.

A very small fraction of total sales must be allocated for interest payment on debts, maintenance of working capital, and various credit functions. Generally this amounts to less than 0.5% of sales for most companies. The growing fringe benefits in all of industry have resulted in a larger percentage of total sales being allocated to pension funds and other employee benefits. In addition, provisions must be made for local property taxes and insurance. The sum of these expenses ranges from 1 to 4% of total sales with a median of about 2%.

The total of all the foregoing items represents the total actual cost of production. However, inasmuch as companies try to operate at a profit, an added item is provision for federal, state, and foreign income taxes, which amount to more than 52% of earnings on the average, and represent from 3 to 12% of total sales.

18.3 Start-up costs

Although all the elements of total cost of a product have been outlined in the preceding text, several need to be examined separately, since they do not occur predictably in all business enterprises.

A large gray area exists between the nominal end of construction of a new facility and the production of specification quality and quantity of product. Actually, it is almost impossible to determine when construction ends and start-up begins. It is equally difficult to separate construction alterations, modifications, and adjustments from initial debugging operations. Yet, there is a significant economic reason for making such a separation. Construction changes during start-up are items of capital cost, according to most accepted practice. Production start-up costs are generally charged against operations.

Total start-up expense seldom exceeds 10% of the fixed capital cost. Of this, the construction portion may be as high as 3% with a median value of 1%. Time of start-up may vary from 1 month for well-known processes to as much as 1 year for new ones. The relatively small added cost of the start-up becomes insignificant compared with the cost of lost production when long delays are experienced. Consequently, firms prepare well in advance for the start-up operations. Skilled crews of engineering supervisors who are production-oriented are assigned early in the engineering phase to consult with the project and design engineers to build into the plant features calculated to ease and reduce the time of start-up. They are stationed at the site during the latter stage of construction to start operator-training programs, make minor changes for convenience in operating, and then supervise final adjustments and the actual start-up program.

Operations start-up costs are generally expensed along with other production costs; therefore, funds must be provided in the operating estimate. Included are salaries and wages for start-up supervision and operators, raw materials and finished products that are spoiled or off grade, maintenance labor and materials, supplies, and general plant expense. Operating costs during start-up are generally high, often exceeding product market price on a per-unit basis. As plant design capacity is neared, unit costs can be better appraised to determine whether the goals set in the profitability forecasts will be achieved. Often market evaluations are optimistic, and price decreases must be overcome by more efficient operation. At this point in the start-up, changes can be made to break process bottlenecks and simplify operations.

Start-up operations are considered complete when the plant has been demonstrated at design capacity for some predetermined period of time. There is a growing tendency in the process industry to demonstrate at some capacity less than 100%. It has been found that most process plants will produce at capacities far in excess of these for which they were designed after operations have been optimized. This comes as a result of a natural tendency for engineers to design on the safe side to be sure to satisfy code and capacity requirements. By approving a demonstration run at 90% of design capacity, management recognizes the tendency to overdesign and takes a calculated risk that ultimate capacity will still be achieved and perhaps exceeded.

Analysis of past start-up difficulties reveals that seldom do the problems result from errors in technology. Intensive laboratory work and pilot operations

Table 18.3T1 List of Start-up Problems

Vessel and piping leaks
Piping interferences
Changing valve positions
Tools and other foreign material sealed into piping
Bearing troubles
Construction debris left in equipment, vessels, and piping
Defective valves
Plugged lines
Frozen water lines
Defective insulation
Lubrication failures
Incorrect installation of equipment components
Undue corrosion and contamination
Incorrect wiring
Defective equipment
Blank flanges sealed in vessels and piping
Expansion problems
Defective instruments and gages
Utility supply failures
Incorrect piping and wiring
Correction of supports and structures
Correction of lighting deficiencies
Rearrangement of controls for more efficient operation
Correction of equipment bottlenecks
Operators' errors
Off-specification raw material and spoiled catalysts

of new processes give adequate assurance that the new plant will ultimately produce the desired product. Troubles experienced during start-up are more frequently traced to the many small errors in design that seem to pass the closest scrutiny of the checkers. Since in dollars the cost of start-up averages about 1% of total cost, this cannot be interpreted as an indictment of the design engineer but gives him a batting average just short of perfection. Furthermore, only part of the errors which are encountered during start-up can be attributed to the engineer. Errors in field installation, faulty materials, and unusual weather conditions also contribute to the cost of start-up.

Table 18.3T1 lists some typical situations which must be corrected before the process plant can be considered on-stream on a continuous basis.

Careful checking at all points in the design and construction stages will tend to minimize these occurrences, but experience teaches they can never be entirely eliminated. The fact of human error must be accepted philosophically and dealt with expeditiously on the proving ground of the start-up operation.

Recognition of the inevitability of start-up problems can lead to the kind of planning which minimizes the time required to go on-stream. It is this element which far outweighs the capital cost of start-up, since production time lost in a continuous 24-hr process can never be made up. Typical start-up time for fluid process and fluid-solid process plants is 2 to 3 months. Start-ups have been known to extend a full year and longer. Construction start-up expenses for some actual plants, expressed as percent of plant installed cost, are shown in Table 18.3T2.

Table 18.3T2 Construction Start-up Expense as Percent of Plant Installed Cost

Plant type	Capital value, $MM	%
Solid	2–10	2.0
Fluid	2–10	0.7
Solid	0.5–2	0.5
Fluid–solid	> 10	0.4
Fluid–solid	> 10	1.6
Solid	2–10	2.7
Solid	2–10	0.3
Fluid	< 0.5	1.5
Solid	0.5–2	0.8
Solid	0.5–2	0.3
Fluid	2–10	1.0
Power plant	2–10	2.5
Effluent disposal	2–10	0.2
Fluid	> 10	1.8
Laboratory	< 0.5	0.7
Boiler plant	< 0.5	0.4
Fluid–solid	> 10	1.9
		Average 1.1
		Median 1.0

18.4 Contingencies

The contingency classification, as used in this book, covers uncertainty and should not be used as a catchall to cover ignorance. It is poor engineering and a poor philosophy to make second-rate estimations and then try to make them safe by using a large contingency account. For example, it is customary to include in the fixed-capital estimate some funds to cover the cost of labor, material, and overhead for design modifications due to errors. These items cannot rightfully be included in the contingency as it is known that this work will be necessary to some degree. The contingency allowance is construed to cover unpredictable items of cost not known at the time of the estimate. For instance, an allowance for water batch testing of vessels and piping is a necessity before process fluids are circulated. This cost must then be part of the construction start-up cost. However, should one of the vessels yield structurally during the test, the cost of its replacement must come out of the job contingency.

The contingency allowance is a judgment value applied to the total of known costs by experienced estimators. It will vary with the quantity and quality of information available. Traditionally contingencies in authorization requests seldom exceed 10% of estimated project costs.

18.5 Financing

The most obvious method of financing a new venture including the working capital needs is through earnings retained in the business. Most small capital additions and replacement are financed this way in well-managed companies. Indeed, profits retained in the business do not yield returns unless invested.

For large capital investments most firms go to the money market, and this is done in many ways. The money can be borrowed from commercial banks on a long- or short-term basis. Again, bonds can be issued carrying fixed interest rates and specific retirement dates. This is a form of borrowing, generally from the public to whom the bonds are offered.

The method of funding for growth frequently used by publicly owned corporations is by stocks. The method carries minimum financial penalties but increases the base of ownership in the company. There are variations of stock issues, but they reduce to two types, preferred and common stock. The preferred stockholder is guaranteed a stated dividend but cannot vote the stock, which is a privilege of the common stockholder, who shares equitably in the company's earnings, if any. One variation of the preferred stock is the convertible type, which can be converted to equitable common stock after a prestated time interval.

18.6 Plant-location studies

The cost of manufacturing, selling, and distributing a product is significantly affected by the location of the plant in which it is made. In an earlier age manufacturing facilities were located in the market area in which the product was sold.

High transportation costs may still limit the location of large bulk-product plants, such as steel mills and fertilizers, to primary market areas; but other factors have increasing weight in site determination for most other products.

The Regional Science Research Institute in Philadelphia indicates there are about 100 different factors involved in the selection of a site for an industrial plant. The most significant are listed in Table 18.6T1.

Table 18.6T1 Significant Factors in Selection of a Site for a Plant

1. Accessibility to market
2. Availability of raw materials
3. Qualified and productive labor force
4. Adequate utilities
    a. Electricity
    b. Water
    c. Steam
    d. Gas
5. Construction costs
6. Fuel availability
    a. Coal
    b. Oil
    c. Gas
7. Effluent disposal
    a. Local sewage plants
    b. Lagoons
    c. Deep wells
    d. Large bodies of diluting waters
    e. Legislation affecting cost of pollution control
8. Transportation facilities
    a. Rail
    b. Truck
    c. Water
    d. Pipeline
    e. Air
9. Legislation affecting business activities
    a. Tax concessions
    b. Restrictive ordinances
    c. Real estate values and taxation
10. Site considerations
    a. Cost of acquisition, preparing, and maintaining
    b. Accessibility
    c. Need for services such as parking, cafeteria, recreational facilities, etc.
11. Taxes
    a. Sales
    b. Business
    c. State and local
    d. Gasoline and oil
    e. Severance and depletion
12. Climate effects
    a. Absenteeism
    b. Heating
    c. Air conditioning

380   COST ESTIMATION AND CONTROL

A full treatment of factors affecting plant locations is beyond the scope of this book. The reader can find helpful information from such sources as Perry [18.11R2], local chambers of commerce, utility companies, railroads, labor union organizations for labor rates and working conditions, maps from the U.S. Geodetic Survey (Department of Interior), Department of Labor for excellent statistics on factory labor rates published in its *Statistical Abstract of the United States*, the Federal Power Commission for electric power rates, the Interstate Commerce Commission, and the Federal Communications Commission. A complete list of the publications of the government agencies can be obtained from the Superintendent of Documents, Government Printing Office, Washington.

Private organizations such as *Fortune Magazine, Engineering News-Record*, The Industrial Conference Board, the American Manufacturers Association, and McGraw-Hill, Inc., publish data useful in industrial site selection.

18.7 Offsite costs

This topic has been mentioned earlier in Chap. 15 but is frequently misunderstood. The commonly accepted definition for offsites includes all structures, equipment, and services which do not enter directly into the manufacture of a product. Within this broad category there are two major classifications, namely, utilities and service facilities, as shown in Table 18.7T1.

Chemical plant auxiliaries vary from 20 to 40% of the total installed plant cost, being in the lower range for a single-product small continuous plant and in the upper limit of the range for large multiprocess grass-roots plants.

Except for large grass-roots plant complexes it is unlikely that all auxiliary facilities will be required in all process plants, which explains the variation shown in Table 18.7T2. A grass-roots plant is defined as a complete plant erected on a

Table 18.7T1   Classification of Offsite Facilities

1. Utilities
   a. Steam
   b. Electricity
   c. Gas
   d. Water—wells, intakes, pumping stations, cooling towers, distribution
   e. Water treatment
   f. Refrigeration
   g. Plant air
   h. Sanitary- and industrial-waste disposal systems
2. Service facilities
   a. Auxiliary buildings
   b. Railroads
   c. Roads and walks
   d. Fire-protection systems
   e. Communication systems
   f. Storage facilities—exclusive of intermediate product storage
   g. Plant service vehicles, loading, and weighing devices

Table 18.7T2 Typical Variation in Percent of Total Installed Plant Cost of Auxiliary Facilities (Grass Roots and Large Additions)

Auxiliary	Range, %	Median, %
1. Auxiliary buildings	3.0–9.0	5.0
2. Steam generation	2.6–6.0	3.0
3. Refrigeration including distribution	1.0–3.0	2.0
4. Water-supply cooling and pumping	0.4–3.7	1.8
5. Finished-product storage	0.7–2.4	1.8
6. Electric main substation	0.9–2.6	1.5
7. Process waste systems	0.4–1.8	1.1
8. Raw-material storage	0.3–3.2	1.1
9. Steam distribution	0.2–2.0	1.0
10. Electric distribution	0.4–2.1	1.0
11. Air compression and distribution	0.2–3.0	1.0
12. Water distribution	0.1–2.0	0.9
13. Fire-protection system	0.3–1.0	0.7
14. Water treatment	0.2–1.1	0.6
15. Railroads	0.3–0.9	0.6
16. Roads and walks	0.2–1.2	0.6
17. Gas supply and distribution	0.2–0.4	0.3
18. Sanitary-waste disposal	0.1–0.4	0.3
19. Communications	0.1–0.3	0.2
20. Yard and fence lighting	0.1–0.3	0.2

virgin site. Investment includes all costs of site preparation, battery-limits facilities, and auxiliary facilities. Battery limits is a geographical designation referring to the coverage of a specific project. It usually means the process area of a proposed project, including all process equipment and appurtenances such as electrical, piping, and instrumentation but does not include auxiliary facilities. It can be an extension of an existing plant or a unit within a complex. A careful appraisal and application of good judgment as to the extent that auxiliary facilities are used in the plant should result in selecting from Table 18.7T2 a reasonable cost ratio applicable to a specific problem.

18.8 Forecasting

Much has been written on the subject of forecasting venture profitability. Of the many factors involved, those listed in Table 18.8T1 are the most significant. The table lists 18 factors and the probable variations of each from forecasts over an assumed 10-year plant life.

The cost of the *fixed capital investment* may be appraised within a range of -10% to $+25\%$. *Construction time* may vary from -5% to as high as 50% of the estimated time but generally can be predicted more accurately. *Start-up costs* have even a wider variation, ranging from -10% to $+100\%$, but have a negligible

Table 18.8T1 Factors Affecting Profitability Forecasts

Factor	Probable variation from forecasts over 10-year plant life, %
1. Cost of fixed capital investment	−10 to +25
2. Construction time	−5 to +50
3. Start-up costs and time	−10 to +100
4. Sales volume	−50 to +150
5. Price of product	−50 to +20
6. Depreciation method	None
7. Plant replacement and maintenance costs	−10 to +100
8. Obsolescence of process or equipment	Indeterminate
9. Income tax rate	−5 to +15
10. Inflation rates	−10 to +100
11. Interest rates	−50 to +50
12. Working capital	−20 to +50
13. Legislation affecting product	Indeterminate
14. Raw-material availability and price	−25 to +50
15. Competition	Indeterminate
16. Salvage value	−100 to +10
17. Intuition or calculated risk	Indeterminate
18. Profit	−100 to +10

effect on profitability if the gap left by delay in reaching the market with the product is not filled by a competitor.

Forecasts of *sales volume* and *price* for a new product are probably the most challenging factors. Such forecasts are not within the scope of this book, but they constitute the heart of the business process. Predictions of sales volume and prices are made from studies involving market and product research activities. Most companies now employ market research and commercial development specialists to assist production and sales managements in determining the extent of the market, potential sales, and probable price of product over the life of the production assets. Actual sales and price can vary widely from the predicted levels as indicated in the table. Perry [18.11R2, chaps. 5 and 6] list many source references for complete market and product searches. In competitive times it is unlikely that price will be higher than the forecast unless an unusual inflationary period or national crisis occurs during the life of the asset.

Another factor that is difficult to assess is that of process or equipment *obsolescence*. Processes have been known to be obsolete within a year after start-up, and in a technological era, specific pieces of equipment become obsolete years before the end of their forecasted lives.

Among factors affecting profitability, the impact of *legislature changes* must be considered. It is difficult to forecast to what degree this factor will affect profitability. For instance, government interest in health, pollution, quotas, tariff agreements, among others, are all factors in economic evaluation. In addition there is the possibility of income tax changes.

Competition from abroad is an increasingly important factor in assessing profitability. Many single products in some industries have already been affected, and the outlook is that increasing competition from abroad will tend to depress prices and profits in the United States. By and large, the individual effect of this factor on profitability is indeterminate at this time.

There is still one other consideration. After carefully weighing all known factors affecting profitability, the *go* or *no-go* decision is sometimes reached through a complex mental process which reflects the experience of the individual making the decision. Since it is impossible to characterize this process, it has been referred to as *intuition, calculated risk*, or *educated guess* in the prediction of profitability.

18.9 Profit

Like all terms in common use, profit is not easily defined. In a broad sense profit connotes success and is not a simple concept.

Consider the case of depreciation. How depreciation is scheduled over the years influences the apparent profit for the individual years. This is true for other expenses that can be allocated over the years. For example, one power company lost an entire generating station because of a landslide at the river edge. Instead of taking the entire loss in 1 year, the company preferred to allocate the loss over a number of future years. This decision affected the apparent profits for many years ahead.

A detailed analysis of all the aspects of profit is beyond the scope of this book. Companies exist to prosper and grow; but the measure of this, particularly over a short time, can be deceiving.

18.10 Questions

Q1. Why must the cost engineer be familiar with expenses beyond operation costs?
Q2. Classify the elements of general expense as controllable and noncontrollable by the cost engineer.
Q3. Discuss the major elements of general and selling expense.
Q4. What is included in start-up expense?
Q5. What policy is used to determine whether a start-up cost is charged to capitalization or expenses?
Q6. Compare a public utility to a manufacturing company concerning the policy of charging start-up costs.
Q7. Name the elements that will probably lead to high start-up costs.
Q8. When can start-up be considered completed?
Q9. Describe the difference between a contingency and a masking of ignorance.
Q10. Discuss the various methods of financing new ventures.
Q11. What is the effect of taxes on the different financing methods?
Q12. What are the principal factors involved in the selection of an industrial plant site?
Q13. Consult the literature, such as the annual plant-site report of *Chemical Week* (Oct. 5, 1968), and compare how factors vary in the United States.
Q14. Discuss why nontechnical considerations, such as opportunities in education, must be considered in choosing a plant site.
Q15. What are the two major classifications of offsite costs?

Q16. Define a grass-roots plant.
Q17. Define a battery-limits plant.
Q18. How is forecasting done?
Q19. What elements are likely to show the greatest variation from the forecast?
Q20. Describe the difference between profit and profitability.
Q21. What are some of the difficulties involved in determining profit over a short time?
Q22. In what way does depreciation affect profit?
Q23. In an inflationary period profits have been referred to as *phantom* profits. Discuss.

18.11 References

R1. Bauman, H. C.: "Fundamentals of Cost Engineering in the Chemical Industry," Reinhold Publishing Corporation, New York, 1964.
R2. Perry, J. H.: "Chemical Business Handbook," McGraw-Hill Book Co., New York, 1954.
R3. Perry, R. H., et al.: "Chemical Engineers' Handbook," 4th ed., McGraw-Hill Book Company, New York, 1963.
R4. Peters, M. S., and K. D. Timmerhaus: "Plant Design and Economics for Chemical Engineers," 2d ed., McGraw-Hill Book Company, New York, 1968.

part four
Associated Topics

19
Cost Accounting

E. H. Weinwurm

BASIC CONCEPTS

19.1 Cost accounting and the cost engineer

Accountants are responsible for cost data, but there are several reasons why the cost engineer should be conversant with the accountant and understand his language. Cost data frequently require allocation to different products and processes, and to be done fairly require considerable technical and engineering familiarity with operations. As technology advances, and in addition as manufacturing approaches more and more a processing operation, the allocation costs become a larger percentage of the whole. The accountant is not an engineer, but he needs the help of engineers in establishing the rules by which these allocations are properly made. In turn the engineer must have a knowledge of the language and methods of accounting if he is to interpret and use accounting data properly.

This chapter will present a brief survey of the concepts and practices of accounting to the extent required to provide cost engineers with the basic minimum information needed for their professional work.

19.2 Accounting definitions

Accounting is a technique of measuring economic events in terms of money. A general definition is[1]

> *Accounting is the art of recording, classifying and summarizing in a significant manner and in terms of money, transactions and events which are, in part at least, of a financial character, and interpreting the results thereof.*

Accounting uses a *double-entry* system for every transaction, always with valuation in terms of money. Just as in engineering, input = output, assuming no accumulation, so in accounting, credit = debit. The double-entry system can be interpreted as a sequence of equations; therefore, the two sides of the equation, the debits and the credits, must always balance.

The terms *debit* and *credit* are conventional and have no particular significance as such. The distinction between the terms can always be resolved by reduction to a transfer of money value between accounts with the accountant acting as an intermediate. Thus suppose a company pays John Smith, a supplier, $100 cash that is owed to him. The cash account gives (input) the accountant $100 and the accountant in turn gives (output) John Smith $100. The balanced transaction then is:

	Dr. (Debit)	Cr. (Credit)
John Smith	$100	
Cash		$100
To record cash payment		

The economic resources which represent the input consist of a variety of factors—merchandise, labor, buildings, equipment, etc.—acquired at different times with different terms and conditions. They are reduced to a common denominator by a process of *valuation*. The application creates many difficult problems. Money, the measuring standard of accounting, lacks stability, but no better standard has yet been developed.

19.3 The operating accounting system

Accounting includes three basic steps, recording, classifying, and summarizing economic data in terms of money.

Classification of accounts must be decided before recording is performed, but once accounts are classified, recording and classification of individual transactions are carried out at the same time. Classification of accounts is based on a listing called the *chart of accounts*. Its contents is determined by accounting

---
[1] P. Grady, Inventory of Generally Accepted Principles for Business Enterprises, *AICPA Accounting Res. Study* 7, p. 2, 1965.

management, and the cost engineer has to make arrangements with the accounting staff to have the type of data he is interested in included.

The introduction of modern machines has increased the number of classifications that can be accommodated. However, it is possible to classify and accumulate data outside the formal chart of accounts by statistical techniques, often more conveniently.

The activity represented by the first two steps, recording and classifying, is known as *journalizing*, or the primary accounting procedure. Journal is derived from the French word *jour*, meaning day. It is important to appreciate that this original recording represents the final classification of data within the accounting system; therefore, it is of great importance in the development of accounting data used by the cost engineer.

Errors made during the classification procedure may creep into the system as a result, and they may not be detected at all or only at the cost of considerable time and effort.

The data of each individual transaction are summarized in an *account* by transferring them from the journal in a procedure known as *posting*. An account includes all the data of a particular classification. Posting is called the secondary recording procedure.

Two basic classes of accounts must be distinguished. *Real accounts* are allowed to accumulate indefinitely and are of two types. Those which represent items owned by the organization are called *assets*, and those owed by it are called *liabilities*. In accordance with the double-entry equation,

Debits = credits

Assets = liabilities + ownership

The second classification of accounts includes those accounts known as *nominal accounts* which are set back to zero periodically. They are revenue and expense accounts which are merely subclassifications of the ownership or capital accounts. At the end of each accounting period they are consolidated with the capital accounts by a procedure known as *closing the accounts*.

The procedure of accumulating data in the accounts can be continued indefinitely. However, periodic reports of the data are summarized, usually monthly or annually, by the preparation of *statements*, requiring additional steps.

The first step is setting up a *trial balance*. Accounts contain both debits and credits, but each account is reduced to a net debit or credit, and a summary of the net positions is made. Because of the equality of debits and credits in the double-entry system, both sides of the summary listing, or trial balance, must be in balance. If not, an error exists which must be found. However, the major purpose of the trial balance is to serve as a starting point for the preparation of the financial statements, and in this context is called the beginning trial balance.

The next step is to *adjust* the trial balance. Some significant transactions, e.g., depreciation and insurance, as well as others related to specific time periods such as updating of inventories, are not passing through the journal. These data have to be computed and posted to the trial balance.

The next step is the *closing* of the nominal accounts. The real accounts remain unchanged and are carried over into the next accounting period. These accounts and the capital account represent the *opening trial balance* for the next period.

The real accounts and the capital account are presented in the *statement of financial position*, generally known as the *balance sheet*. These are the adjusted accounts at the date of closing.

The nominal accounts are shown on the *statement of profit and loss*. They are the balances after adjustment but before the accounts have been closed into the profit and loss account. The statement establishes the profit or loss for the accounting period. Profit or loss are finally combined (after dividends, etc.) with the capital account.

19.4 Types of accounting

The preceding sections have discussed what is known as historical *financial accounting* that presents a record of transactions which have been completed. It serves primarily the *stewardship function* whereby those in charge of funds explain how they have handled the funds. Another function, the *audit function*, tests the adequacy of the accounting system in performing the stewardship function. The audit function may be carried out by the organization's own staff, internal auditors, or by outside experts, public accountants.

Another type of accounting is directed to the managers of the organization and is known as *managerial accounting*. *Cost accounting*, the principal objective of this chapter, is among the most important parts of managerial accounting. Cost accounting expands the techniques of financial accounting. Its major application is in the planning and control functions of management, which have increased in importance during the last few decades from the introduction of scientific techniques to managerial decision making.

19.5 Development and objectives of cost accounting

Cost-accounting techniques have been traced back a long time. Modern cost-accounting concepts began with scientific-management movements whose father was Frederick W. Taylor. The attention was focused mainly on the measurement of physical activities but with great interest in cost reduction and thus in cost accounting. The earlier volumes of the *Transactions of the American Society of Mechanical Engineers* contain many articles on cost-accounting problems by well-known engineers. Thus cost measurement originated with engineers.

Accountants became interested in techniques of cost measurement early in the century. There was a large expansion of cost accounting in World War I and a larger expansion during World War II resulting from the need of government agencies to control the cost of military orders when there was no competition to keep prices down. Recently, the impact of management science and operations research has greatly stimulated the expansion of cost-measurement techniques and increased demand for greater detail and accuracy. Many of the modern management techniques depend on data which only cost accounting can furnish. This branch of accounting is destined to overshadow in importance even financial accounting, the traditional leader insofar as operating management is concerned.

The growing importance of managerial accounting places emphasis on looking forward, in contrast to the traditional historical approach of earlier cost-accounting practices. This agrees, of course, with the objectives of the cost engineer, who is concerned with future costs. However, future-directed costs are related to historical costs to some extent, and so an understanding of accounting techniques of computing historical costs is indispensable to the cost engineer. He should be aware, also, of the complex considerations involved in the computation of historical costs if he wishes to be proficient in cost estimation.

19.6 Definitions and classification of costs

The term *cost* has numerous meanings and definitions. The AICPA *Inventory* states[1]

> *Cost is the amount, measured in money, or cash expended or other property transferred, capital stock issued, services performed, or a liability incurred, in consideration of goods or services received. Costs can be classified as unexpired and expired. Unexpired costs (assets) are those which are applicable to the production of future revenues* ···. *Expired costs are those which are not applicable to the production of future revenues and for that reason are treated as deductions from current revenues, or are charged against retaining earnings* ···.

Dean [19.23R1] lists more than 20 cost classifications and his list is not all-inclusive. Cost data found in conventional financial statements, usually the so-called actual costs, are for the specific purposes of reporting to interested outsiders and therefore not necessarily useful for other applications. The requirement of selecting the appropriate cost type for individual objectives is important. No general rules are possible because of the wide variety of circumstances.

19.7 Historical against future-directed costs

It was mentioned earlier that the cost estimator needs future-directed predetermined data and not historical costs. Insufficient attention is often given to this important difference. In an era of great change, as presently, the easy assumption that the past will repeat itself in the future cannot be accepted with even a minimum of assurance. The cost estimator, therefore, will frequently hesitate to accept historical data without attempting to make his own adjustments of the recorded data after soliciting information from knowledgeable representatives of the organization.

[1]Ibid., p. 228.

The same approach will be even more necessary with regard to the future-directed data he wishes to use. The cost estimator cannot predict all future developments. He will depend on the sales manager for an estimate of future sales volume by individual product lines and on operating management for most of the needed production data.

COST-ACCOUNTING CYCLE

19.8 Production cycle and cost cycle

The cost accountant is not independent in selecting the system he will use but must adjust to the procedures of the manufacturing activities whose costs he wishes to compute even if this should result in a loss of efficiency for his own system. The cycle of physical operating activities comes first, and the cost-accounting cycle has to adjust itself as best as possible. Whenever there is a change in operating methods, the cost-accounting cycle must also be changed regardless of the cost accountant's own specific requirements. This important but unavoidable situation can have a significant impact upon the data arising from the cost-accounting system.

The production cycle consists of three parts, input, processing, and output. Input refers to the factors of production, materials, labor, and other facilities such as buildings, machinery, utilities, etc. The productive factors are processed in the factory. After the desired product has been completed, it is transferred as output to a storage area or sometimes shipped immediately to the customer. Measurements within the production cycle are in terms of physical units, such as units produced, labor and machine hours, kilowatthours of power, etc.

The cost-accounting cycle accompanies the production cycle and therefore consists of three parts. In accordance with the techniques of accounting, these parts are represented by individual accounts, and the measurements are performed in terms of money. Each part may consist of several accounts. Figure 19.8F1 illustrates the relationship of the two types of cycles.

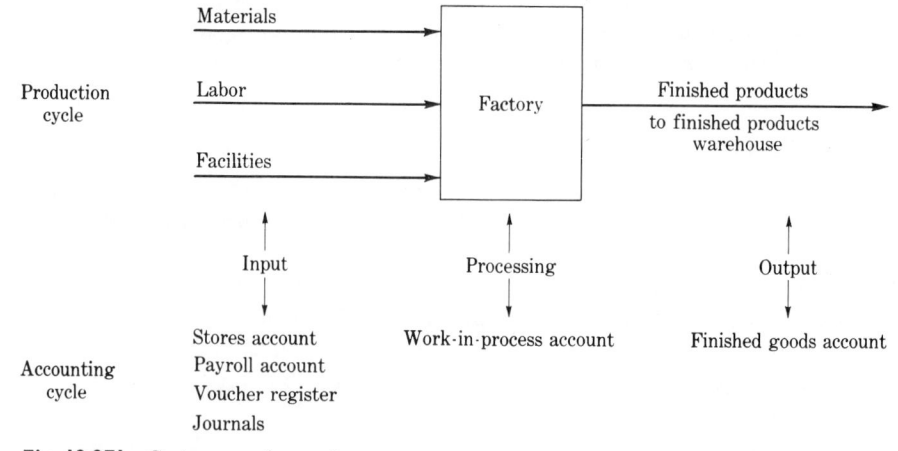

Fig. 19.8F1 Cost-accounting cycle.

The cost of manufacturing operations is accumulated through three separate accounts:

1 *Direct material*, cost of materials, assemblies and parts which are used for the completion of the project
2 *Direct labor*, wages of workers who are participating in the completion of the product
3 *Overhead* (also called burden), the cost of all other factors contributing to the completion of the product

As the production input factors are used in the factory, they are charged to a *work-in-process* account, which may be broken down into the three subaccounts listed above. When the completed product is physically removed from the factory and transferred to the finished-product stores area, its accumulated cost is transferred from the work-in-process account to the *finished-products* account. It follows that the balance in the work-in-process account represents the accumulated cost of the products being manufactured but not yet completed.

The cost of materials is the purchase price and all incidental expenses to transfer them into the purchaser's premises, such as transportation, tariff duties, insurance, etc. In most cases, purchased materials and parts are charged to a *materials-stores* account, which is credited when the materials and parts are physically transferred to the factory floor and become part of the work-in-process account.

An important problem, with a significant effect on the cost of the product, is the specific method of inventory valuation used for determining the cost charged to the work-in-process account.

Labor cost is the result of several factors. It includes the basic hourly rate and the hours worked but must be augmented by certain provisions—overtime, social security taxes, etc.—and contractual agreements—vacation pay, health, pension payments, etc.

The labor cost is the gross pay although the worker receives a smaller net, or take-home, pay because of deductions for his taxes, union dues, etc.

19.9 Direct costs against indirect costs

Direct costs are also called prime costs and are directly traceable to the product being processes, e.g., the fabric in clothing. This may be called a *one-step* procedure, work—cost.

Indirect costs are all the costs of manufacture that cannot be classified as direct costs. To do so may be either impossible or impractical. Each classification is initially accumulated in a separate account, and at the end of the accounting period allocated to the individual benefiting activities, such as cost centers or products. Therefore, this is a *two-step* procedure, work—accumulation—allocation.

To illustrate, supervisory services benefit many units of product and are allowed to accumulate in a separate account. At the end of the accounting period the cost is allocated to individual products as part of the overhead.

Modern technology tends to increase the share of indirect costs of manufacturing cost while the share of direct labor cost is declining. In fact, this is the purpose of automation, to replace direct labor cost with the indirect cost of machines. Hence an understanding of indirect costs and allocation is becoming increasingly more important.

19.10 Cost centers, unit costs

Manufacturing operations are organized by departments headed by a foreman who usually has an office with a small staff to care for the clerical work associated with production, such as materials requisitions, labor time control, and so forth.

Costs are accumulated by *cost centers*, which may or may not coincide with operating departments. Cost centers are placed at points in the production process where costs can be measured and recorded as conveniently and accurately as possible.

The advantage of having departments and cost centers cover the same activities results from the availability of the foreman's office, where cost records can be conveniently accumulated. A department may be broken down into several cost centers to obtain more detailed cost data, or several departments may be combined. The choice of cost centers is important. The cost engineers should maintain liaison with the cost accountants and those who design the cost-accumulation system. The cost engineer's requirements must be known in order to be met within the limitations of cost and practicality.

Cost data must be related to an activity factor such as volume of production. Comparison merely of total costs of different time periods is meaningless. Therefore, all cost reports should present unit cost as well as total cost. Selection of a suitable activity factor can be difficult in the frequent case of multiproduct operations when there are substantial differences in the unit cost of the various products.

19.11 Job-order costing and process costing

There are two basic types of accounting techniques for accumulating unit costs, job-order costing and process costing. The older is *job-order costing*. In this type, the production cycle and the cost cycle are of equal length, the latter being extended until the former has been completed. Job-order costs are used for specialized production jobs, e.g., electric generators manufactured to individual specifications. Costs can be computed accurately, but considerable paper work and effort are required. For mass production of repetitive units a job order can constitute a multiple number of units. Job orders can be issued for individual customers or for stock.

Process costing is used for continuous-process industries which operate 24 hrs/day, such as oil, chemical, steel, and others. Process costing accumulates average costs for a time period, most frequently a month. The production cycle continues without interruption while the cost cycle is cut for each accounting period to determine the result of operations. Process costs use averages and are less accurate than job-order costs but simpler and cheaper to operate. One specific requirement is the need to estimate inventories at the point of the cost cutoff whereby the incomplete units are evaluated in terms of completed units.

Process costing is the more widely used technique of cost accumulation. It serves the continuous-process industries, which have no alternative, but also mass-production industries, which could use either method. Measurement of efficiency is accomplished by statistical methods which implement the costing technique.

In the job-order costing method, the cost of the basic input factors, direct material and direct labor, are charged to the specific numbered job orders by posting periodically on the *job-order sheets,* one for each job order. Upon completion of the job order, overhead is *applied* on the basis of an activity factor, as explained in the next section.

Process costs are accumulated by departments (processes) for a time period, usually 1 month. In many instances materials are introduced to the process at an early stage, and in the subsequent processes only the *cost of conversion,* direct labor and overhead, has to be added. Some units may be lost, e.g., for technical reasons in chemical industries, and the cost must be absorbed by the salable units. In other instances an increase in units may occur. Costs are accumulated on process cost sheets which show input and output for both physical units and costs, also unit costs by individual processes.

Tables 19.11T1 and 19.11T2 show respectively forms used for reporting results on a job-order cost sheet and a process cost sheet.

Table 19.11T1 Job-order Cost Sheet

Job-Order Cost Sheet

Job order no._____   Customer_____
Part no._____   Work started_____
Number of units_____   Work completed_____

Week of	Material		Labor		Applied overhead	Total
	Requisition no.	Amount	Hours	Amount		
Total						

Table 19.11T2 Process Cost Sheet

	Process Cost Sheet for the Month of _____		
	Process 1	Process 2	Process 3
Quantity schedule (units)			
Input: Transferred from preceding department			
Added in department			
Total			
Output: Transferred to next department			
Work-in-process inventory			
Lost (added) units			
Total			

	Amount	Units	Amount	Units	Amount	Units
Cost schedule						
Input						
Cost transferred from preceding department						
Cost added in department						
Material						
Labor						
Overhead						
Adjustment for lost (added) units						
Total input						
Output						
Cost transferred to next department						
Work-in-process inventory						
Cost from preceding department						
Cost in department						
Material						
Labor						
Overhead						
Total inventory						
Total output						

19.12 Techniques of overhead-cost accounting

The overhead-cost classification includes all production costs which are not considered prime costs (direct material and direct labor). There is no limit to the number of overhead classifications; however, a few principal groups can be distinguished:

Indirect materials, also known as supplies, are materials such as lubricants that
    do not become a part of the finished product.

Indirect labor, the wages and salaries of employees who are not directly connected with the manufacture of a product, such as supervisors, maintenance workers, and internal transportation. Frequently fringe benefits are included in this classification.

Facilities costs, both short-term costs of the current year and long-term costs which are depreciated over a number of years. The former includes building maintenance, local real estate taxes, and others; the latter, buildings and equipment.

Service-department costs, for facilities which support production but are not part of production, e.g., accounting, laboratories, stores, cafeteria, and first aid stations.

It is difficult, if not impossible, to enumerate the many different types of costs which make up the overhead-cost classification. Indeed, overhead accounting is known as one of the most complex problems of cost accounting.

The accumulated overhead costs are allocated in two stages. First the overhead costs are allocated to the cost centers (departments), which in turn allocate the overhead to job-order costs and process costs.

Assuming a large number of cost classifications and a large number of cost centers, the number of computations can become quite extensive. In practice various shortcut techniques are used to reduce the clerical work.

The cost engineer must recognize that the cost data which finally emerge from this procedure are significantly affected by the measure used for determining the indirect cost and the method used for allocation. Therefore, he should not accept these data unless he is familiar with the techniques used in computing them.

In order to select a *basis for overhead-cost allocation* a measure must be found that reflects closely the actual benefit furnished by a cost classification. Allocation must be made on this particular basis. As an example consider building maintenance. This can be measured on the basis of square feet and allocated on the basis of floor space occupied by each cost center.

In turn, cost centers must have a measure by which allocation of the accumulated overhead is made to each job order or process. This may be, for example, labor hours, machine hours, or some material quantity for which appropriate data are available. Introduction of computers has greatly simplified the clerical and computational job but has not necessarily improved the quality of the resulting data.

The procedure for allocating overhead, or burden, up to this point has two disadvantages. It is complicated, and moreover the overhead can be allocated only at the end of the period. The overhead applicable to units made early in the month cannot be calculated until the end of the month, when the accumulated overhead becomes known. A shortcut method has evolved to overcome the disadvantages.

Two estimates are required to accomplish this. First an estimate is made for each overhead-cost classification covering specific periods, usually a year. Second, the estimate of some measure must be chosen which permits charging each job order with the appropriate share of the overhead cost. Direct labor, either in the form of dollars or hours, has been the most widely used measure to accomplish this.

Now a rate can be established by dividing the total estimated overhead cost by the estimated quantity of the selected measure, and this is called the *burden rate*. As an illustration, assume that the estimate of overhead cost for cost center A is $50,000 per year and the estimated direct labor cost is $25,000. The burden rate is 50,000/25,000, or $2, for each direct labor dollar. If the direct labor cost of job order number 750 is $2,000, the applied overhead is 2,000(2) or $4,000.

It must be kept in mind that the applied burden rate is an estimate and not necessarily the actual overhead. A difference or variance must be expected, as discussed in Sec. 19.16. Moreover, other problems arise because overhead-cost classifications react differently to volume fluctuations, as discussed in Sec. 19.13.

There are two principal advantages from the use of burden rates. The first, the savings in time and cost, has been mentioned. The second, and perhaps the more important, is the possibility of obtaining data more satisfactory for determination of operating efficiency. Use of an actual overhead cost subjects the data to fluctuations within the period such as payment of taxes, the cost of an overhaul, and so forth. An applied burden rate, on the other hand, equalizes such charges by spreading them over the year. The abrupt overhead costs are eliminated as factors influencing the determination of efficiency.

RELATED TOPICS

19.13 Cost behavior against activity volume

The importance of the volume of activity in the accumulation of cost data has already been stressed. Businessmen have been aware for a long time that profits increase faster than sales when activity is expanding, and conversely. The cause is the fact that different cost classifications react differently to changes in production volume and sales volume. Costs are broken down into fixed costs, variable costs, and semivariable costs, as developed in Chap. 7. It is one of the principal responsibilities of cost accountants to study the relationship of the various costs classifications to volume fluctuations.

A number of methods of accomplishing this task have been developed. It must be remembered that all are approximations with often a considerable margin of error. The widely used break-even chart has been developed in Chap. 7. Charts that are not elaborate incorporate a number of simplifying assumptions which limits their usefulness. From a theoretical point of view of accurate measurement, most cost classifications are semivariable. However, this circumstance can be accommodated by not limiting the charts to the simplest type.

The result of the division of costs into fixed and variable is a relationship which is considered applicable within a limited range of volume fluctuations only.

In computing burden rates the estimated overhead is divided by the estimated quantity of measure, such as estimated direct labor hours for the same period.

The overhead will to some extent depend upon volume, and the estimated labor hours much more so and in a complicated fashion. Hence, the burden rate will depend on volume; or a burden figure is correct only for a particular volume.

The distinction between fixed and variable costs refers to short-term considerations. In the long run all costs can be thought of as variable. Costs are fixed as a result of a previous management decision. The cost estimator should recognize that some fixed costs may be subject to change by new arrangements.

19.14 Normal volume

The cost analyst is interested in measuring the effect of fluctuations of efficiency; therefore, he tries to eliminate the influence of other factors, volume fluctuations in particular.

If the accountant computes the burden rate by the relationship previously expressed, the result will be that unit costs of production decline when volume increases and increase when volume declines. This makes it difficult to judge the efficiency of operations.

To avoid this result, the concept of normal volume was introduced. A specific volume figure is selected in consideration of the most important factors, such as plant capacity, market conditions, and long-range aspects. This figure is used for the computation of burden rates. The effect of an actual volume that differs from the normal volume is eliminated, but it still exists and appears as a separate classification, namely, as a volume variance, discussed in Sec. 19.16.

The problem of selecting the normal volume figure is complex and cannot be discussed here. It is the management which sets the figure, based on available information and judgment. The decision is important in connection with the analysis of variances and deserves the attention of the cost estimator, who depends on overhead-cost data supplied by the accounting system.

19.15 Direct costing and absorption costing

The system of applying overhead described so far is known as *absorption costing* because the direct, fixed, and variable costs are absorbed by the work in process and in turn become part of the inventory. If now production is greater than sales, inventory of the finished products will be increasing. Suppose volume is high enough so that the overhead applied to the work in process, which is an estimate, is greater than the actual overhead. As a consequence, inventory will be overvalued. Under such conditions the apparent profit of the organization can be increased by increasing production beyond the normal volume and adding to inventory. This contradicts a basic principle of accounting that profits should be recognized only if they result from sales to outsiders, arm-length sales.

Another system of applying overhead known as *direct costing* attempts to overcome the disadvantage but introduces some problems of its own. In direct costing the fixed part of the overhead, and only the fixed part, is not applied to the work in process but is regarded as a period cost and is entirely absorbed as an expense against income in the period. In this way the applied overhead burden includes only variable costs, and no over- or underestimation of the inventory occurs.

There are differences between absorption and direct costing. Inventory will always be held at lower value under direct costing. Over a period of time the two methods will give the same cumulative net income because fluctuations in inventory are smoothed out. Over a short period of time the two can differ depending upon volume and how much the inventory changes during the period.

Direct costing was suggested some 30 years ago but recently has been receiving added attention. It eliminates the need of determining the normal volume figure and establishes the correlation between sales volume and profits desired by businessmen. There is a difference of opinion among professional accountants about the applicability of the direct-costing technique. It underestimates the cost of the inventory because it does not include the fixed charges. The cost estimator must be alert to the use of these alternative methods, which can have a significant effect on cost and profit data.

19.16 Variance analysis

Estimated data cannot be expected to agree with actual data and lead to a difference, or *variance*. Individual companies have developed a variety of variances for use in controlling efficiencies and costs. Only the two most important basic types are discussed here.

One represents the cost variance related mainly to the fixed costs and results from the difference between normal and actual volume, as evaluated in the preceding section. The variance is known as *volume variance* and depends on the considerations which led to the selection of the normal volume. The numerical amount of the variance itself is not a measure of the efficiency.

The difference between the total variance and the volume variance is called budget variance or *controllable variance*. It relates mainly to the variable costs, and the major portion is the effect of fluctuations in efficiency, the latter being controllable in part.

Frequently only one principal variance is shown. Subvariances for material, labor, and overhead are segregated statistically in accordance with managerial demands for cost control.

19.17 Standard costs and budgets

Up to this point, most of the discussion has been concerned with the accumulation of historical costs. A very important aspect is the use of these data for future-directed costs. The true analysis of efficiency depends on the previous determination of measures or yardsticks against which the actual performance is evaluated. These future-directed and estimated costs are particularly important to the cost engineer; and since they can depend upon technological factors, he should cooperate with those who have charge of the determination of such costs.

Standard costs are determined through scientific techniques and objective quantitative measurement. In contrast, estimated costs are based on individual judgment with limited significance. Standard costs do not necessarily represent expected performance but rather desired objectives.

Materials standards developed by engineers are valued in accordance with actual or estimated purchase prices to be converted into standard costs. Labor standards, after measurement, are converted into standard costs from appropriate labor rates. Overhead-cost standards are difficult to establish and often are merely estimates based on past performance.

Standard cost variances are computed in accordance with the practices described in the preceding section. The analysis and evaluation should be a joint effort of engineers and accountants.

Budgets serve for both planning and control purposes with emphasis generally on planning. Budgets reflect mainly expected performance and have to be adjusted more frequently than standards. Budget data may be especially valuable to the cost engineer.

19.18 Joint costs

A most intricate problem of accounting arises when data are related to more than one activity or transaction and the share of each cannot be measured accurately. Then the costs cannot be allocated appropriately; some activities will be overcharged and some undercharged. An interesting case arises in connection with the costing of so-called by-products and joint products.

Several products are often derived from a single source such as crude oil. Another well-known case is the meat packing industry. The relationship in which these products are developed is often the result of technological rather than market conditions. Sometimes there is no market at all for a product that arises in connection with another which is in great demand.

A product for which there is no demand or only a limited demand is called a *by-product*. The product produced at the same time which is in great demand is the *main product*. Several main products derived from a single source are called *joint products*.

As an illustration, consider the carcass of a slaughtered animal carried through several processes. After it has been divided into several parts, a product remains which cannot be sold but for which there is some market if it is improved. This may be called the by-product. At the next stage, several marketable products become available. The point of separation is called the *split-off point*. The problem arises of how to allocate the accumulated cost at that point to the several products. The most widely used techniques are:

1. In the case of a by-product, the total cost at the split-off point is absorbed by the main product after crediting any net incidental revenue from the by-product.
2. The allocation for joint products is more difficult. The simplest method is related to quantities, e.g., number of units, weights, with the allocation

proportional to this measure. However, the measure generally used is selling price. The sales price is weighted by the number of units sold and allocation made in proportion to sales realization. Here the allocation of costs is based on selling price, which may or may not be realistic. At any rate a change in selling prices changes costs.

The current techniques are justified by their simplicity. Better methods can be expected in the future in this era of operations-research techniques and electronic computers.

The cost engineer should be aware of the pitfalls associated with cost allocation for joint costs, since the allocation can have a decisive impact on the cost data.

19.19 Relevant and differential costs

The user of cost data can choose from a large variety of alternative cost classifications. The choice is made on the basis of *relevancy*. Relevancy should not be confused with accuracy. Future-directed data are not usually so accurate as historical data computed in accordance with the strict regulations of the accounting system, but they will be relevant to the user if he can accomplish his specific objective with them.

In many decisions, the question of which data are relevant can be the most important one. For example, in comparing data of alternative projects, only those data are relevant which differ between the projects. Data which are the same for all projects are irrelevant as they have no effect on the decision to be made.

The case of differential costs is pertinent in this context. The use and significance of differential cost has been illustrated in several of the earlier quantitative chapters. It is emphasized again, however, that a differential-cost analysis should be used only for the circumstance for which the data were collected.

Differential costs are not found in existing accounting records but are determined from the additional revenues and costs related to the project being estimated. They should be evaluated with great care, since the calculation is very sensitive to variations in the figures.

19.20 Inventory valuation

This and the following section deal with problems of financial accounting which affect cost figures.

Identical items in inventory may have been acquired at different times and at different prices. In such cases a rule is required to determine the value at which units shall be transferred into work in process. The rule applies to pricing and has nothing to do with which unit is physically removed from the inventory. Physically the units are all alike, and the unit removed is generally the one that is most conveniently removed.

The most common method is called first in first out or FIFO. The cost of the oldest unit in inventory, as it is on the record, is used. Under conditions of increasing prices, such as during inflation, the lower acquisition prices are matched with the higher selling prices resulting in higher accounting profit figures and higher income taxes.

To avoid these unsatisfactory effects the so-called last in first out, or LIFO, method was introduced. The cost of the last unit added to inventory, as it is on the record, is used. Now the last additions which supposedly reflect current prices are matched with the selling prices of the same period and thus the *paper profits* resulting from the FIFO method are eliminated. The inventory, however, will reflect the prices of the earlier and cheaper additions; and, therefore, will be lower in comparison with conditions under the FIFO method.

The use of average valuation represents an effort to find a compromise between the two methods. Either a moving average can be used or new averages can be computed periodically.

The use of material or finished-goods inventory data from the accounting records requires that the user be aware of the cost differences that may result from different inventory-pricing methods.

19.21 Depreciation

Depreciation has been discussed in detail in earlier chapters. Depreciation becomes part of the fixed cost of overhead. The importance of depreciation is steadily increasing because of the growing trend toward automation. Thus labor cost is replaced by machine cost, which is reflected in a depreciation charge.

It should be noted here that the manner in which depreciation is taken does affect the current period costs. Moreover, accountants generally prefer to group items together for accounting purposes and thus a single piece of equipment loses its individuality. Again, in some processes a part of the equipment may be fully depreciated, and current costs are not realistic since they make insufficient allowance for wear and tear of equipment.

The cost estimator is not bound by the depreciation expense used by the accounting method but can set rates for his computations which he considers realistic regardless of whether they are acceptable from a tax perspective and therefore an accounting procedure.

In concluding this chapter it can be said that the introduction of more efficient equipment as well as scientific techniques will develop a new appraisal of present accounting practices. There is no doubt that closer cooperation of cost engineers, who are major users of accounting data, and those who are responsible for designing the systems should be encouraged.

19.22 Questions

Q1. Discuss the reasons why cost engineers need to be familiar with the fundamental concepts of accounting and particularly cost accounting.
Q2. Distinguish between historical and managerial accounting.
Q3. Describe the basic steps for accumulating accounting data.

Q4. Explain the techniques of adjusting and closing of the accounts and the reasons for the techniques.
Q5. Discuss the historical evolution of accounting and the contribution made by the engineering profession.
Q6. Discuss the reasons for the large number of cost definitions and list some of the most important.
Q7. Explain the reasons for the use of future-directed cost from the cost engineer's point of view.
Q8. Discuss the relationship of the production cycle and the cost cycle.
Q9. Discuss the principal accounts used in the course of the cost cycle.
Q10. Explain the distinction between direct (prime) costs and indirect (overhead) costs. Give examples.
Q11. Explain the importance of cost centers and their relationship to departments.
Q12. Discuss the importance of presenting unit costs in all cost statements.
Q13. Describe the difference between job-order costs and process costs. Give examples.
Q14. Explain the difficulties in dealing with overhead costs. Give examples for several kinds of overhead costs.
Q15. Discuss the reasons for the need of overhead allocation and the techniques used.
Q16. Explain the technique of computing burden rates and the advantages and difficulties arising from their use.
Q17. Explain the importance of the concept of activity volume for cost-accounting purposes. Give examples of variable, semivariable, and fixed costs.
Q18. Explain the advantages and disadvantages of the concept of normal volume.
Q19. Explain the benefits and shortcomings of absorption costing as compared with direct-costing techniques.
Q20. Distinguish between the principal types of variances.
Q21. Explain the techniques and benefits of standard costs and overhead budgets.
Q22. Explain the techniques used for dealing with by-product costs and joint costs. Give examples for each type of cost.
Q23. Explain the significance of the terms relevant costs and differential costs.
Q24. Discuss the relationship between cost engineers and cost accountants.

19.23 References

R1. Dean, J.: "Managerial Economics," Prentice-Hall, Inc., Englewood Cliffs, N.J., 1951.
R2. Dickey, R. I. (ed.): "Accountants' Handbook," The Ronald Press Company, New York, 1956.
R3. Gordon, M. J., and G. Shillinglaw: "Accounting: A Management Approach," 3d ed., Richard D. Irwin, Inc., Homewood, Ill., 1964.
R4. Grady, P.: Inventory of Generally Accepted Accounting Principles for Business Enterprises, *AICPA Accounting Res. Study* 7, 1965.
R5. Grant, E. L., and L. F. Bell: "Basic Accounting and Cost Accounting," 2d ed., McGraw-Hill Book Company, New York, 1963.
R6. Horngren, C. T.: "Cost Accounting: A Managerial Emphasis," Prentice-Hall, Inc., Englewood Cliffs, N.J., 1962.
R7. Nickerson, C. B.: "Managerial Cost Accounting and Analysis," 2d ed., McGraw-Hill Book Company, New York, 1962.
R8. Specthrie, S. W.: "Industrial Accounting," 2d ed., Prentice-Hall, Inc., Englewood Cliffs, N.J., 1959.
R9. Wixom, R. (ed.): "Accountants' Handbook," The Ronald Press Company, New York, 1956.

20
Social Values and Nonmathematical Aspects

J. H. Black and A. L. Horstmeyer

SOCIAL ASPECTS

20.1 Social values

There are times when companies will choose a course of action influenced by factors other than sheer mathematical profitability. Examples can be classified into the broad categories of those ventures affected by *social values* and *nonmathematical aspects*. It is worthwhile now to consider the effect that these considerations have on the engineer and his work.

For many years now, both the engineering profession and industrial concerns have been giving increasing attention to the role of the engineer and to the role of the company as good citizens. Because engineers do not live in a social vacuum, and because of the impact of the engineer's work on society, engineering curricula have been placing increasing emphasis on the study of the humanities. It is important that the engineer, if he is to be more than a mere technician, give consideration to the social implications of his work [20.23R9].

A dramatic and well-known example of this problem is provided by the dangers of large-scale contamination by the products of atomic fission. A feeling of social responsibility prompts prominent engineers and scientists to direct their efforts toward reduction and control of the contamination and toward peaceful applications of the nuclear energy developed as a wartime weapon.

Industrial concerns are also vitally interested in their role as good citizens and in their social responsibilities. The goodwill and other benefits which eventually derive from this interest probably defy profitability analysis by the methods described in previous chapters. The engineer, as an employee of these industrial concerns, is intimately involved with the activities of these concerns and with the social consequences of their activities. In general, a company's social responsibilities are manifested in community relations, employee relations, and educational activities.

20.2 Community relations

The relationship between a company or industry and the community in which it is located is of vital concern to both. The community depends upon the industry for continued prosperity and growth of the area, and the company depends upon the community to provide an attractive environment in which the employees can live and the company can operate.

One problem of this type prominent today is atmospheric and water pollution. This problem increases, of course, as both industry and population grow. Many millions of dollars are spent each year to avoid air and stream pollution, and it is difficult to picture these expenditures as anything but an added expense to industry. The indirect benefits to the companies, however, are real but difficult to measure. There have been studies which show economic justification for pollution abatement in terms of increased use of recreational facilities and increased economic activity as a result of these recreational facilities [20.23R2, 20.23R11]. These benefits, however, do not generally accrue directly to the company which installed the waste-treatment facilities.

Another area of social responsibility displayed by industry is encouraging employees to participate in political activities by giving leaves of absence to serve in legislative bodies. This is a further manifestation of the social responsibility felt by industry and engineers.

For many years, industrial concerns have provided the leaders in such community activities as urban redevelopment, the United Fund and other charity drives, and the redevelopment of slum areas. Industrial leaders have served these activities without pay for such work, and they have their company's support purely to improve the community. Many companies have been instrumental in the development of local recreational facilities, not only for the benefit of their own employees, but also for the benefit of the other residents of the particular community.

20.3 Employee relations

Industrial concerns have demonstrated their social responsibilities also in the field of employee relations. The engineer is intimately concerned with some aspects of this, e.g., plant safety, in his design work. Safety of the public must also be considered by the engineer not only in plant design but also in product design. The engineer must consider his social responsibility to the ultimate user of the company's product. Laws have been passed, such as those requiring seat belts in all new automobiles, directing the responsibility of manufacturers to safety.

Many years ago industry adopted safety programs for the protection of employees. These programs involve safety meetings, safety awards, and provision for safe working conditions. Accident-free work performance is of vital concern to the company, and careless, sloppy working conditions or habits are not tolerated. These safety programs generally extend to advice and reminders concerning safety also in the home and on the highway. The economic justification for these safety programs is again difficult to measure, but the benefits of decreased absenteeism are real.

The economic well-being of employees is another social responsibility which has been undertaken by employers. Evidence of concern on the part of industry is shown in the provisions for pensions, life insurance, hospitalization plans, savings plans, and unemployment insurance. In past generations, these items were considered the individual's problem, but employers today all provide these fringe benefits at very reduced cost to employees. Here, again, the economic benefits to the company would be difficult to justify on the basis of cold calculations.

20.4 Educational activities

Taxes are an expense of business enterprises. Part of these taxes, of course, go to the support of the local public schools. Less obvious are some of the other contributions by industry and individual engineers to public schools and to colleges and universities. These activities are further manifestation of social responsibility on the part of industry and its employees.

One traditional way of aiding education has been gifts to the schools, such as money for unrestricted uses, also gifts of equipment, scholarships, fellowships, and teaching aids. Most companies participate, in one form or another, in visits to schools to explain their activities or visits by students to industrial installations for first-hand experiences with industrial activities. Such aid to education also takes the form of summer employment opportunities for students and faculty, opportunities not only for the student to finance his education but also for him to learn.

More recently, industry has increased the opportunities for employees to continue their educations after employment. These opportunities include not only leaves of absence to return to school but also short courses or after-hours refresher courses in work-related subjects. Tuition-rebate plans are often provided by industrial concerns.

Justification for many of these activities cannot be formulated in precise mathematical expressions, but engineers must develop an awareness of the social impact of engineering work [20.23R9].

20.5 Effect of technical developments

There are other forces at work in our society which also have an effect on social and economic values. It is worthwhile to discuss the role of technical developments, the role of government, and the role of social changes in bringing about modifications in our social and economic values. These modifications and changes are very pronounced over a period of time, and every forward-looking engineer should give them consideration.

One technical development which has had an obvious effect on our civilization is the computer. One commonplace application on probably every college campus is the computerized dating service. While this may be a more efficient system of choosing escorts, it somehow seems less romantic.

Another computer application that is having an effect on our sense of values is in the field of banking as we approach a moneyless and checkless economy [20.23R12 and 20.23R13]. This topic was mentioned in Sec. 6.13.

20.6 Effect of government

The activities of governmental agencies have an effect also on our sense of values. Governments are more sensitive to political pressures than to economic pressures. A case in point is the well-publicized power failure in the northeastern part of the United States. The blackout occurred because the system was designed taking into account the cost and the low probability of a set of conditions which would cause failure. This set of conditions did occur, however, and the resulting blackout caused great inconvenience. The public utilities have been forced to install more expensive equipment to prevent the recurrence of these events. The report of this blackout stated that if there is a conflict between economic and service-reliability factors in power-system design, the need for security of service should be given heavy weighting [20.23R3].

Another example of the role of government agencies in cost considerations is afforded by the Fair Packaging and Labeling Act. This act prescribes that the labels on foods, nonprescription drugs, and cosmetics must conform to certain rules, particularly with respect to net quantity statements, the naming of ingredients, and the identification of the manufacturer or distributor [20.23R1]. Without arguing the merits of this legislation, it is obvious that meeting special requirements increases costs, not only in carrying out the requirements themselves but also in keeping track of the regulations.

The net effect of the role of government on our sense of values comes about because government does not have the same incentive as individuals or corporations to give weight to economic considerations, yet the role of government is constantly increasing.

20.7 Effect of social changes

As civilization progresses from a caveman environment to the environment in a modern city, the citizen's attention and energy are taken up less and less with providing for his own necessities and he begins to give consideration to the welfare of his neighbors. Thus, man progresses from a dog-eat-dog society eventually to a welfare society.

The effects of continued prosperity with its accompanying vast increases in population hasten the change to a welfare society. These changes bring about different sets of values, both economic and social, changes which are obvious when one contrasts our willingness today to tolerate hippies and beatniks with the necessity these nonproductive people would have felt to provide for themselves in the frontier days. In the days of the battles between the farmer and the Indian, the individual was so busy providing food for himself that he had no time for writing protest songs and poetry.

The net effect of these influences of technical developments, government, and social changes, is a decay, but not elimination, in the time value of money. This change, of course, influences and modifies our sense of values.

The cost engineer should, then, be aware of the fact that there are influences which affect his work other than cold mathematics and economics. He should recognize these social effects and nonmathematical aspects on the field of engineering.

STRATEGIC ASPECTS

20.8 Company policy

In addition to the effect of social awareness there are other considerations which can be referred to as strategic or policy decisions. Often the engineer is disappointed or dismayed that an obviously profitable venture has been rejected or worse that an apparently unprofitable venture has been chosen. This section and the three following cite instances in which the results of economic studies may not be the overriding consideration in venture decisions.

A company may be restricted by charter or by decision of the management to ventures in a narrow field. If this field is a growing and profitable one, proposals to expand into related or outside fields may not be accepted even though such proposals have attractive possibilities. The company has perhaps already committed its financial resources and efforts to expansion within its present field of interest.

The converse situation is also a possibility. For instance, a company may find itself in an obsolescent or dying industry and therefore commits itself to expansion into related or remote fields. The decision might possibly be made to enter into a marginal venture to establish that company in a new field with the hope that increased production and demand in the future will improve the project's economic performance. This type of decision is sometimes made by a company which has large cash reserves and no incentive to invest in its present field for which the long-term prospects are doubtful.

Another strategic factor which might affect investment decisions is the problem of monopolies or antitrust considerations. There is the possibility that attractive proposals could be turned down if accepting them might mean that the company would dominate the particular industry. While this domination might seem to be the logical and proper result of a competitive or free-enterprise system, it has long been decided that this is socially undesirable in view of the possible abuses. Therefore, company policy would prevent the acceptance of attractive proposals which would result in a monopoly.

20.9 Customer relations

Another reason for what appears to be arbitrary rejection of an attractive proposal is the company's relationship with its customers. A long-standing customer will not be pleased with competition from a supplier and may take his business to a more sympathetic supplier. Good customer relations, built up carefully over many years, cannot be taken lightly.

The development of good customer relations could be another reason for adoption of marginal or even uneconomic projects. If the company's best customer needs a new product to serve a particular function, the venture may be undertaken purely to boost sales of the primary product. The same argument applies both to production of new products and to completing a present line of products. For instance, with the rise in motorboat ownership over the past years and with the widespread use of power lawnmowers, the oil companies have found it to their advantage to produce a special two-cycle engine oil so that the customer, in one trip to the service station, can buy his gasoline already mixed with the required oil.

Such tie-in sales also work to the advantage of the customer by cutting down on the number of sources with which he must deal. A company may have to offer a complete line, and for this reason, it may pay to produce an unprofitable item to boost the sales of profitable ones.

20.10 Maintaining market position

Further reasons for the adoption of marginal projects, when more profitable projects are available, can be found in the necessity for a company to maintain its market position. This situation can arise in a growing field when the company has not increased its capacity commensurate with the growth of the market. If this situation is allowed to persist, the company may find itself eclipsed and therefore a decreasing force in the market. To keep from standing still in a growing industry, a company must be able to predict future demand and install facilities to be ready when increased demand appears. Because of the time required to construct new facilities, the decision to expand may have to be made at a time when market conditions show that the expansion is marginally attractive.

20.11 Raw-material position

The raw-material position of a company is also strategic. The need to dispose of a waste product might require a company to adopt a marginal or unprofitable project, even though the overall project is profitable. Many years ago, Consolidated Mining and Smelting Company of Canada [20.23R10] at Trail, B.C., installed sulfuric acid facilities because sulfur-bearing off-gases were destroying vegetation across the border in the State of Washington. The company therefore found itself in the sulfuric acid business with acid markets far removed from the point of production. Only during World War II did demand for the acid exceed the supply.

If a company plans to produce a new product and does not have a satisfactory source of raw material, perhaps because of a small availability, it might be necessary to integrate operations backward to the production of the raw material. At the market price for the raw material, the operation may not be particularly attractive but the overall project may be. In these circumstances the company may invest in a marginal project to ensure the success of another more profitable project. This same argument applies to the installation of raw-material producing facilities to provide an alternate source of supply if only a few suppliers exist.

Another example of marginal projects being accepted for raw-material reasons is afforded by the use of captive raw material for expansion into new fields in the hope that the new use will prosper and become profitable as the production increases. It may be necessary to install a facility to produce a raw material, but a small plant may be uneconomical. A larger plant may be built and an alternate use developed for the excess capacity to make the overall project economically justifiable. In these circumstances, a loss or a break-even on the alternate use may be acceptable on the basis of a projected increase in demand and production which would improve the economic outlook sometime in the future.

ETHICAL ASPECTS

20.12 Meaning of ethics

As the engineering profession continues to grow in impact and in importance, the question of ethical behavior is receiving increasing attention by the individual engineer and by the professional engineering societies. Ethics is defined by Webster [20.23R14] as "moral principles, quality, or practice; a system of moral principles." Each profession has its code or canons of ethics. These codes or canons set forth the rules for proper behavior for members of the profession. The Canons of Ethics of Engineers adopted by the Engineers' Council for Professional Development are presented in Table 20.12T1.

One might say that this code of behavior can be reduced to the golden rule—"Do unto others as you would have others do unto you." Inherent in the golden rule, of course, is the corollary that "Honesty is the best policy." These thoughts are the basis of the canons.

The canons are organized into rules governing the individual engineer's relationships with the public, with his employer or clients, and with other engineers. Adherence to these rules is important to the individual engineer's personal reputation and to the public image and dignity of the profession.

Table 20.12T1*

Canons of Ethics of Engineers

Fundamental Principles of Professional Engineering Ethics

The Engineer, to uphold and advance the honor and dignity of the engineering profession and in keeping with high standards of ethical conduct:

I. Will be honest and impartial, and will serve with devotion his employer, his clients, and the public;
II. Will strive to increase the competence and prestige of the engineering profession;
III. Will use his knowledge and skill for the advancement of human welfare.

Relations With the Public

1.1 The Engineer will have proper regard for the safety, health and welfare of the public in the performance of his professional duties.
1.2 He will endeavor to extend public knowledge and appreciation of engineering and its achievements, and will oppose any untrue, unsupported, or exaggerated statements regarding engineering.
1.3 He will be dignified and modest in explaining his work and merit, will ever uphold the honor and dignity of his profession, and will refrain from self-laudatory advertising.
1.4 He will express an opinion on an engineering subject only when it is founded on adequate knowledge and honest conviction.
1.5 He will preface any ex parte statements, criticisms, or arguments that he may issue by clearly indicating on whose behalf they are made.

Relations With Employers and Clients

2.1 The Engineer will act in professional matters as a faithful agent or trustee for each employer or client.
2.2 He will act fairly and justly toward vendors and contractors, and will not accept from vendors or contractors, any commissions or allowances, directly or indirectly.
2.3 He will inform his employer or client if he is financially interested in any vendor or contractor, or in any invention, machine, or apparatus, which is involved in a project or work of his employer or client. He will not allow such interest to affect his decisions regarding engineering services which he may be called upon to perform.
2.4 He will indicate to his employer or client the adverse consequences to be expected if his engineering judgment is over-ruled.
2.5 He will undertake only those engineering assignments for which he is qualified. He will engage or advise his employer or client to engage specialists and will cooperate with them whenever his employer's or client's interests are served best by such an arrangement.
2.6 He will not disclose information concerning the business affairs or technical processes of any present or former employer or client without his consent.
2.7 He will not accept compensation—financial or otherwise—from more than one party for the same service, or for other services pertaining to the same work, without the consent of all interested parties.
2.8 The employed engineer will engage in supplementary employment or consulting practice only with the consent of his employer.

Relations With Engineers

3.1 The Engineer will take care that credit for engineering work is given to those to whom credit is properly due.
3.2 He will provide a prospective engineering employee with complete information on working conditions and his proposed status of employment, and after employment will keep him informed of any changes in them.
3.3 He will uphold the principle of appropriate and adequate compensation for those engaged in engineering work, including those in subordinate capacities.
3.4 He will endeavor to provide opportunity for the professional development and advancement of engineers in his employ or under his supervision.
3.5 He will not injure maliciously the professional reputation, prospects, or practice of another engineer. However, if he has proof that another engineer has been unethical, illegal, or unfair in his practice, he should so advise the proper authority.
3.6 He will not compete unfairly with another engineer.
3.7 He will not invite or submit price proposals for professional services which require creative intellectual effort, on a basis that constitutes competition on price alone. Due regard should be given to all professional aspects of the engagement.
3.8 He will cooperate in advancing the engineering profession by interchanging information and experience with other engineers and students, and by contributing to public communication media, to the efforts of engineering and scientific societies and schools.

Approved by Engineers' Council for Professional Development, September 30, 1963

* Engineers' Council for Professional Development, Thirty-third Ann. Rept., p. 86, Sept. 30, 1963. (*Used with permission.*)

Several articles in recent years [20.23R4 to 20.23R7] discuss various aspects of ethical behavior and present actual and hypothetical circumstances. The canons and the literature references are worth careful study and periodic review.

20.13 Applications

As an illustration of the application of the canon of ethics, consider the following situation. A company engineer is in charge of an installation using an outside electrical contractor. The contractor, by invitation, goes to the engineer's home to see about doing some electrical work there. The engineer asks what the cost will be, and the contractor replies that he can take care of the work easily and that there will be no charge. What is the proper thing for the engineer to do? What canons might he be violating by accepting this free work?

LEGAL ASPECTS

20.14 Contracts

An engineer is not an attorney, but he will encounter legal problems of various sorts. The remainder of this chapter calls attention to some common legal aspects, but its chief purpose is to alert the engineer to the importance of this topic. There are many articles [20.24R2 to 20.24R8] and books [20.24R9, 20.24R10, 20.24R12, 20.24R13] on the legal aspects of engineering. One good source of information is the regular feature Focus: The Law in the *American Engineer* [20.24R11].

It should be realized that law implies interpretation, and interpretation changes with time. As a society matures, it tends to approach a welfare society, and interpretation tends to favor public over private rights, the consensus over the individual. For this reason an alert engineer must give some thought to future interpretations.

The most common branches of law of interest to engineers include contracts, real and personal property, patents, copyrights, sales, insurance, and administrative law. Probably more engineers are involved in contracts than any other phase of law [20.24R16].

Assume that a cost engineer will be working with several specialty design engineers who have the responsibility of preparing the bid documents on a given project. The cost engineer, whether he is part of a team preparing bid documents or one making cost estimates against bid documents, must recognize legal pitfalls in contract documents which occur in two general areas: (1) The contract itself and (2) supplementary drawings, diagrams, or plans and the description, specifications, notes, or written word. Generally the written word takes precedence over drawings and the larger-scale drawings over smaller-scale drawings.

Decisions relative to group 1 are usually outside the cost engineer's domain, but generally he has the responsibility of decisions relative to group 2.

The contractor who bids on this contract has a legal right before bid opening to request clarification, correction, or interpretation of all uncertainties, unless this is specifically ruled out. The contractor can obtain clarification by telephone, the most economical method but the poorest from a legal viewpoint. Timing is important. If the request is made too early, other questions may arise requiring more calls. Waiting too long, however, can compel making decisions at great risk just before bid time.

The legal phrase in some bid documents, that the qualifying of a bid is cause for rejections, has had many interpretations. Generally it would be well to qualify the bid at the risk of being rejected. A bid should not be priced assuming that the qualifications can be written into the contract after the bids are opened.

The time limits for performing work have many legal ramifications. Limits established in bid documents are often unrealistic with little regard for such items as availability of equipment or skilled labor, weather, and so forth. The time limits can be costly and can lead to serious legal complications, especially if clause *B* in the examples of hedge clauses in the next section appears in the same bid document.

20.15 Hedge clauses

Technology has become so complicated that it becomes difficult to prepare drawings and specifications which are completely free from misinterpretation. As a result hedge, or bludgeoning, clauses have developed at a rapid rate. These clauses do not apply to anything in particular; indeed, they are general so that they may be applied to any unforseen condition that may arise.

Some typical hedge clauses taken from actual bid documents, both government and private, are quoted.

A. Omissions from the drawings or specifications or the misdescription of details of work which are manifestly necessary to carry out the intent of the drawings and specifications, or which are customarily performed, shall not relieve the contractor from performing such omitted or misdescribed details of the work but they shall be performed as if fully and correctly set forth and described in the drawings and specifications.

B. The Contractor shall furnish sufficient forces, construction plant and equipment, and shall work such hours, including night shifts, overtime operations and Sunday and holiday work, as may be necessary to insure the prosecution of the work in accordance with the approved progress schedule. If, in the opinion of the architect, the Contractor falls behind the progress schedule, the Contractor shall take such steps as may be necessary to improve his progress and the architect may require him to increase the number of shifts, and/or overtime operations, days of work and/or the amount of construction plant, all without additional cost to the owner.

C. Titles to divisions and paragraphs in this specification are introduced merely for convenience and are not to be taken as part of the specification and are furthermore not to be taken as correct or complete segregation of several units of material and labor. No responsibility, either direct or implied, is assumed by architect or owner for omission or duplications by Contractor or his sub-contractors due to real or alleged error in arrangement of matter in this specification.

D. Examination of Documents and Site. Each bidder and subbidder shall examine carefully the site of the work, drawings, specifications, and other documents related to the work contemplated, and it will be assumed that each bidder has investigated and is satisfied as to the conditions to be encountered, as to character, quality and quantities of work to be performed and materials to be furnished, and as to the requirements of all contract documents. It is mutually agreed that the submission of a proposal shall be considered prima facie evidence that the bidder has made such examination.

E. Where on any of the drawings a portion of the work is drawn out and the remainder is indicated in outline, the parts drawn out shall also apply to all other like portions of the work.

F. The Contractor shall comply with requirements of all authorities having jurisdiction.

G. The owner reserves the right to accept or reject any alternate prices or modifications to the contract at any time during which the contract is being performed.

The hedge clauses, although general, can be enforced. In one case, the specifications omitted reference to shoring a shale bank. A request for clarification was made by the contractor, and the owner stated verbally that shoring would be unnecessary. The bank caved, breaking a retaining wall. The owner denied his verbal interpretation. The jury found for the owner stating that the contractor should have known better than the owner.

A cost engineer who is bidding against hedge clauses is required to place an extra cost against every hedge clause in a set of bid documents as these clauses may affect the cost calculation. This can become very difficult and often results in a contingency item at the end of the estimate.

Counter hedge clauses are used in the case of requests for modifications while work is in progress such as "If the above quotation is not accepted within 10 days, it will be subject to a change in price." The need for a time limit on a quotation for work in progress is extremely important; e.g., the accessibility of the work area and work can change drastically as the project progresses.

20.16 Cost engineer's obligation to employer

Legal clauses affecting penalties, brand names, delayed decisions, work by owner, patents, segregated bids, and so forth, are so dispersed throughout the bid documents that the cost engineer must become familiar with all documents to evaluate the risks involved, usually in a comparatively short time. A knowledge of the habits of the owner—asking for bids, requiring prompt approval of shop drawings, permitting substitution of materials, attitude, and so forth—can be of great value. Such information is available from past experience, competitors, and from suppliers and subcontractors.

Practically every general condition states that the word of the engineer shall be final. Many people contend the judge's or jury's word is final. Juries, composed of lay people, are unschooled in technical engineering and perhaps are influenced by anything except the facts of a case. There is a ray of hope in arbitration, but a cost engineer might recall that "an ounce of prevention is worth a pound of cure." It is the obligation of the cost engineer to be aware fully of all legal aspects and advise his employer—even to not bid the job when the bid documents have a multiplicity of hazards. Starter sheets, described in Sec. 20.18 are helpful in this respect.

20.17 To bid or not to bid

Checklists for preparing many types of estimates are available from many sources, depending on the type of work to be performed. A checklist for legal aspects is given in Table 20.17T1. The cost engineer must include sufficient contingency to cover the negative answers and advise management in writing of the pitfalls.

Table 20.17T1 Checklist for Legal Aspects

1. Do you understand the contract?
2. Is the contract workable and fair?
3. Are the plans, specifications, and other descriptions of work accurate and clear?
4. Can you make bond as required by the contract?
5. Would this job strain your bonding capacity?
6. Will you be required to be responsible for the performance and quality of more than your portion of the project?
7. Is there a possibility of unusual inspection?
8. Will you require financial assistance to perform this contract?
9. What do you know about the client's reputation?
10. Are there any unusual terms or conditions?
11. Have you checked cost of insurance requirements?
12. Are plans and specifications adequate or are there many uses of "as directed"?
13. Time penalties?
14. Inclusions to or exclusions from the contract?
15. Potential job hazards:
    a. Weather
    b. Traffic
    c. Car parking for employees
    d. Underground and overhead utilities
    e. Below surface conditions
    f. Will you be forced to use subcontractors with whom you are not familiar?

20.18 Starter sheets

Losses and legal complications can be greatly reduced by the use of starter sheets shown in Tables 20.18T1 and 20.18T2. Legal complications can be more easily avoided by refusing to prepare an estimate than attempting to obtain clarification and interpretations and ending up with a complicated and confusing document.

20.19 Patents and proprietary information

Patent law, for convenience in this discussion, includes not only patents, but trade secrets, proprietary information, copyrights, and trademarks [20.24R6].

The subject of patents is involved, and much information is available [20.24R6, 20.24R12]. The purpose of a patent is, of course, to give the inventor a monopoly on the use of the patent for a specified term of years as a reward for revealing the patentable ideas to the public. Care should be exercised, then, not to infringe on the patents of others. This may involve a patent search and royalty payments in cases where it is necessary to use the patents of others.

The problem of trade secrets and proprietary information has received considerable publicity [20.24R1, 20.24R6, 20.24R14, 20.24R17]. When an engineer, in his daily work, has developed a certain procedure, method, information,

Table 20.18T1 Estimate Start Order

```
                                          Date: _____
Contract, serial or invitation no. _____
Job name & location _____

Architect or engineer _____
Estimate due _____ at _____
              (Date)      (Time)              (Place)
Estimated total cost $_____ Est. sq ft _____ at $ _____
                                       Est. sq ft _____ at $ _____
Type of estimate Prel. ( ) Lump w/competition ( ) Guar. max. w/fee ( )
Quantity survey by _____ at ____
Sub bids by _____ at ____
Cost estimate by _____ at ____
Plans available at _____
Type of bid guarantee required _____ Percent _____
            Payable to _____
            Bids to be submitted in _____
                                   (single, duplicate etc.)
Time allowed for completion _____ Liquidated damages ___
Job being bid by _____
Bid guarantee to be secured by _____
Remarks: _____

Cost engineer's recommendations regarding preparation of bid:
_____

Copies to:                            Start order by: _____
```

Table 20.18T2 Quotation by Phone

```
Project_____Date_____
Vendor quoting_____
Address _____
Party quoting_____Phone _____
Type of work _____
Spec. sect. _____
Complete plans and specs. Yes ( ) No ( ) Installed Yes ( ) No ( )
Addenda no. _____F.O.B. Where_____
Tax included? Yes ( ) No ( ) BASE BID
_____
_____
_____
ALTERNATES_____
_____
_____
EXCEPTIONS _____
_____
_____
_____
By_____File no.
```

or device to perform his work by the most economical or expeditious manner, the courts have conceded that, when he changes employers, he may use his knowledge of this method but may not bring to his new employer any plans, charts, descriptions, or printed matter whatsoever. It is best, when leaving an employer, for the engineer to be forthright in stating just what material he would like to take with him.

20.20 Dealings with administrative bodies

Administrative law, as used here, means the law involved with administrative bodies, such as zoning boards, professional engineering registration boards, industrial accident commissions, water- and air-pollution commissions, public service commissions, and many others [20.24R8].

If an engineer carries out his work with methods which violate safety, health, or water- and air-pollution control laws, he cannot avoid responsibility by the excuse that he was obeying his employer's instructions. The Canons of Ethics of Engineers (Table 20.12T1) compel him to have proper regard for these considerations (Canon 1.1) and require him to indicate to his employer or client the adverse consequences to be expected if his engineering judgment is overruled (Canon 2.4). With the increasing interest in safety and pollution, the duty of the engineer to make his influence felt is of increasing importance.

20.21 Professional registration

Another important facet of administrative law is the registration of professional engineers by state boards. This is an important topic and one which is certain to come up in each engineer's career [20.24R13].

Some discussion of engineering as a profession is worthwhile here, to establish the importance of engineering registration. One characteristic of a profession is that it is partly closed to the public. An individual is not entitled to practice the profession unless he is qualified and is authorized by some organization with the power to certify the qualifications. Such boards are set up for many professional groups such as medicine, dentistry, law, and many other groups who deal with the public.

Registration was instituted in engineering because of the considerable attraction there seems to be to having a title containing the word engineer. Perhaps this happens because engineer means, in the public view, a capacity for getting things done and done well. There does not seem to be the same attraction in attaching "lawyer" onto titles, but one often sees such titles as "moving engineer" or "beauty engineer."

As another reason, engineers all aspire to be recognized as both professional and as an engineer. To prevent nonengineers from adopting the title engineer, engineers as a group have adopted a Code of Ethics and licensing or registration of engineers.

Some people do not believe engineering is a profession. They argue that the relation between the engineer and the public is entirely different from that of the lawyer or doctor and the public. Lawyers and doctors deal directly and personally with the public, whereas engineers normally work in large groups and do not have personal contact with the members of the public who will be ultimately affected by engineering work.

While all this is true, there are points of similarity between engineering and the learned professions. Therefore, it does not follow that engineering is not a profession. Actually, a learned profession is one in which academic learning is held to play an important part in preparation or practice [20.24R15]. Engineering is a learned profession, requiring continuing study as the other professions do. The learning in engineering is applied in such a fashion as to have a great impact on society, and engineering is a profession despite its differences from other professions, such as medicine and law.

It has long been settled that each state, under its police power which the federal government does not have, has the right to regulate any occupation or calling in order to protect the public health, safety, or welfare. Not all licensing regulations are based on police power. Some are based on the power to tax. If a licensing regulation has for its primary purpose the collection of revenue rather than protection of the public, a contract in violation of the licensing statute would be legal. But if the licensing statute is based on police power to protect the public, the practice of that occupation without a license would be illegal and would affect contracts made with other persons. Thus, if a person not licensed to practice engineering enters into a contract to perform engineering services, he cannot recover for his services because the contract is not legal. The registration of professional engineers is based on the police power to protect the public safety, health, and welfare.

While many engineers will not deal directly with the public in matters of public health, safety, or welfare, it is still wise for the engineer to become registered for two reasons. First, it is impossible to tell what the future holds. Perhaps sometime in the future the license will be needed for work in a matter involving the public welfare. Second, every engineering organization, whether part of a privately held company or not, must have at least one registered engineer. This is one position which the unlicensed engineer cannot fill.

For these reasons, the engineering profession encourages its members to become registered, not only for the benefit of the profession but also to increase the qualifications of the members of the profession and advance their own careers.

20.22 Questions

Q1. What incentives are there for companies to finance or sponsor, partially or wholly, such community projects as public parks or public zoos?

Q2. What incentives are there for a company to provide such fringe benefits as a golf course, tennis courts, or a softball diamond?

Q3. List some reasons why a company would expend time and effort on promoting highway safety among its employees.

Q4. Why is industry interested in helping support public schools, colleges, and universities? Is there any economic justification for aid to education?

Q5. Your research work discloses a very profitable project for your company. Cite possible reasons for your company's lack of interest in the venture.

Q6. An engineer finds that during a temporary lull in his employer's workload he can do some outside consulting work using his employer's facilities. He can underbid another consulting engineer because of the absence of overhead expense. Also he hints to the outside source that a competing consulting engineer has done some unreliable work. Discuss the various canons of ethics which apply.

Q7. You work for a metal-fabricating company. A small metal fabricator gets in touch with you about working for him. During an interview it becomes obvious that as part of your employment he expects you to reveal information about a novel fabricating procedure of your present employer. What is your reaction? What canons of ethics are involved?

Q8. In what places are legal pitfalls to be found in contract documents?

Q9. How do hedge clauses come into being?

Q10. Give one example of a hedge clause.

Q11. Discuss the rights of a bidder to request clarification of ambiguities in bid documents.

Q12. What is the value of a starter sheet?

Q13. When a cost engineer changes his employment, what is his right regarding a procedure or device he has developed with his former employer?

Q14. A dishwasher has professional business cards printed with the title Sanitary Engineer. Is it legal for him to use these cards? If not, what should be done about it?

Q15. The dishwasher of the previous question has been called into court to testify as a sanitary engineer. Can he testify as an expert? Is his claim for payment enforceable?

Q16. You as a contractor working for an employer, the second party, are advised by him to infringe a patent belonging to a third party, with the understanding that the second party will be responsible for all damages. Does this relieve you of responsibility?

Q17. You have worked out a special form which is published in a copyrighted professional journal. Many fellow engineers duplicate this form on office copying machines and use it in their work. Is this a violation of the copyright law? Who has the copyright? What should you have done to obtain the copyright?

Q18. Discuss the pros and cons of registration for engineers.

20.23 References on social and nonmathematical aspects

R1. *Advertising Age*, vol. 39, April 1, 1968.

R2. Bramer, H. C.: The Economic Aspects of the Water Pollution Abatement Program in the Ohio River Valley, Ph.D. dissertation, University of Pittsburgh, 1960 (microfilm on file with University Microfilms, Ann Arbor, Mich.).

R3. *Business Week*, Blackout Study Points to New FPC Powers, Dec. 11, 1965, p. 34.

R4. *Chem. Eng.*, How Useful Are Our Ethical Codes, vol. 70, Sept. 2, 1963, pp. 87–90.

R5. *Chem. Eng.*, Engineers Speak Out on Ethics, vol. 70, Dec. 9, 1963, pp. 177–184.

R6. *Chem. Eng.*, Gathering Competitive Intelligence, vol. 73, April 25, 1966, pp. 143–148.

R7. *Chem. Eng.*, A Not-so-slight Case of Industrial Espionage, vol. 73, April 25, 1966, pp. 148–150.

R8. Engineers' Council for Professional Development: *Thirty-third Ann. Rept.*, p. 86, Sept. 30, 1963.

R9. Happel, J.: "Chemical Process Economics," chap. 8, John Wiley & Sons, Inc., New York, 1958.

R10. King, R. A.: Economic Utilization of Sulfur Dioxide from Metallurgical Gases, *Ind. Eng. Chem.*, vol. 42, pp. 2241–2248, November, 1950.

R11. Kneese, A. V.: "The Economics of Regional Water Quality Management," chap. 4, The John Hopkins Press, Baltimore, 1964.

R12. Lee, N. F.: What's This Checkless Society All About?, *Financial Executive*, vol. 35, p. 18, June, 1967.

R13. Reistad, D. L.: Coming Cashless Society, *Business Horizons*, vol. 10, pp. 23–32, Fall, 1967.

R14. "Webster's New International Dictionary," 2d ed., p. 877, G. & C. Merriam Company, Springfield, Mass., 1960.

20.24 References on legal aspects

R1. Arnold, T. H., Jr.: Are You Locked into Your Job by What You Know?, *Chem. Eng.*, vol. 73, pp. 141–148, May 9, 1966.

R2. Betz, G. M.: Points of Law Affecting Plant Engineers, *Plant Eng.*, vol. 20, p. 120, January, 1966.

R3. Betz, G. M.: *Plant Eng.*, vol. 20, p. 161, April, 1966.

R4. Betz, G. M.: *Plant Eng.*, vol. 20, p. 150, August, 1966.

R5. Betz, G. M.: *Plant Eng.*, vol. 20, p. 180, October, 1966.

R6. Betz, G. M.: *Plant Eng.*, vol. 21, p. 180, May, 1967.

R7. Betz, G. M.: *Plant Eng.*, vol. 21, p. 170, September, 1967.

R8. Betz, G. M.: *Plant Eng.*, vol. 22, p. 66, May 30, 1968.

R9. Canfield, D. T., and J. H. Bowman: "Business, Legal, and Ethical Phases of Engineering," 2d ed., McGraw-Hill Book Company, New York, 1954.

R10. Harding, C. F., and D. T. Canfield: "Legal and Ethical Phases of Engineering," McGraw-Hill Book Company, New York, 1936.

R11. Lunch, M. F.: Focus: The Law, *Am. Eng.*

R12. McCullough, C. B.: "The Engineer at Law," Iowa State College Press, Ames, 1946.

R13. Nord, M.: "Legal Problems in Engineering," John Wiley & Sons, Inc., New York, 1956.

R14. Popper, H.: How Safe Are Your Company's Secrets?, *Chem. Eng.*, vol. 73, pp. 157–164, May 23, 1966.
R15. "Webster's Third New International Dictionary," p. 1286, G. and C. Merriam Company, Springfield, Mass., 1966.
R16. Werbin, I. V.: "Legal Guide for Contractors, Architects, and Engineers," McGraw-Hill Book Company, New York, 1952.
R17. Wilhelm, R. D.: You and the Law, *Daily Pacific Builder*, vol. 77, pp. 1–7, June 27, 1967.

21
Reporting Results

21.1 Presentation counts

When sound conclusions have been reached by extensive effort and research that was carefully planned and results from accurate calculations, engineers like to feel that they become self-evident truths. Yet this is far from a fact. Conclusions must be passed on to others. Presentation counts.

The ability to write and make oral presentations can be an important factor for success in an engineer's career. Engineers have the reputation of being poor writers, but engineers can write good reports if they will recognize the importance of presentation. Indeed, good writing requires organization, at which engineers excel, and confidence, which engineers should have in abundance as their conclusions are based on fact, not opinion.

21.2 Grand plan—scope and audience

An engineer facing the task of writing a report should have an overall plan. This should be based on the *scope* of the report and the *audience* for which it is intended.

Reports have many purposes. They provide a means for communicating information to others; they serve as a historical record, often eliminating the need for duplication later; they discipline the author by forcing him to reduce the project to writing; they serve as a means of promotion, as for profitable ventures; and, most important, they provide others with the tools needed for decision making.

Written reports are prepared on every phase of cost engineering from routine periodic cost and progress reports to economic evaluations of an entire industry. If the report is periodic in nature or does not require too much detail, a form can be used. Indeed, use of a form when possible is highly recommended. Such forms should have a descriptive title and number, be on $8\frac{1}{2}$- by 11-in. sheets, and have adequate designations and space for the information to be reported. A representative form was shown in Table 16.2T1.

A good report must consider the audience for which it is intended. The reader alone will judge the report. What he obtains from the report will determine its usefulness. The writer must put himself in the position of the reader and write to help, not confuse, him. The reader may be busy. He does not want to search through unnecessary details. Many presentations lose effectiveness by including too much or not relegating the borderline material to an appendix.

Courtesy to the reader is a key factor in good writing and corresponds to good manners in conversation. The aim of every written report should be to help the reader, not impress or oppress him. For example, in one report Table X contained 8 columns and 24 lines, or 192 individual figures. When it was written that "the $100,000 value was taken from Table X" since the value $100,000 appeared 12 times in the table, the statement was lazy and imprecise. With little extra effort a clear sentence would have been "the $100,000 value was taken from column 6, line 22 of Table X."

The overall plan involves *what* and *how*. What to include and how to say it become evident from the scope of the report and its audience.

21.3 The outline

Hanging on the wall in the office of one cost engineer is a plaque reading:

In any communication intended to sell or inform

State the purpose of the exercise.
Give some background to set the stage.
Explain the alternatives considered.
Isolate and support the alternative selected.
Describe the action to be taken or recommended.

This outline can be used for any exposition prepared to convince the reader. The *purpose* should always include the benefits the reader may expect. Never keep the reader in suspense about the benefits, or he may not read far enough to discover them. To illustrate how this outline can be effective in even a five-sentence appropriation request, consider the following:

> *Purpose:* The cost-engineering section has requested that they be supplied with two additional desk calculators to improve the efficiency of that section.
> *Background:* Due to staff increases it is now necessary to shift calculators from one office to another causing delays and waste of valuable man-hours.
> *Alternatives:* A survey was made to determine whether calculators could be released from other sections.
> *Alternative selected:* No calculators being available, new ones are needed to permit the staff to operate at maximum efficiency.
> *Recommendation:* An expenditure of $2,000 should be approved for this purpose.

Generally, however, it is necessary to prepare a separate outline for each major report. The commonest error in report writing is attempting to write without an outline. When the outline is completed, the report is half written. The more care devoted to preparing an outline in extensive detail, the easier it will be to fill in the words and the more readable the final result will be. The preparation of an outline separates the enumeration of ideas from the writing itself and removes the initial impediment for writing.

The best and easiest way to prepare an outline is to list on cards at random all ideas as they come to mind. When complete, the cards can be separated into piles according to divisions and subdivisions. As the report is written, it may become apparent that revision and rearrangement are necessary, but it is best to be sure of a final outline before starting to write.

Cost-engineering reports, like all engineering reports, vary widely in content and presentation. No outline can cover all situations. Peters and Timmerhaus [21.9R8] give a general outline for an engineering design report which can serve as a start for preparing a cost-engineering outline. The outline given in Table 21.3T1 is merely suggestive.

21.4 Special considerations

Some special considerations require discussion. Every presentation, particularly if it is more than a few pages in length, should contain a *summary*. More care should be used in preparing the summary than in preparing any other section because it may be the only portion some people read. The summary should be written last but appears early in the report, perhaps first. The summary may include the recommendations, but only in summary form. Details of recommendations should be included in a separate section. The summary must be precise but not be so precise that it can be misleading.

Another important section of a report is the *purpose* or *introduction*, which appears early in the report. Its function is to explain the reason for the report and what it is about. It can serve to give a proper perspective on the subject matter

Table 21.3T1 Organization of a Cost-engineering Report

- A. Title page
    1. Gives title and report number
    2. Shows department responsible for preparation
    3. Includes name of author and approval signatures as required
    4. Gives date
- B. Contents
    1. Lists titles and page numbers of all major sections
    2. Lists charts and tables by number and title
    3. Lists titles and page numbers of appendix items (if lengthy place at beginning of appendix section)
- C. Introduction
    1. Outlines purpose of report and benefits sought
    2. States the nature of the request leading to preparation of report
    3. Acknowledges assistance of those having a part in its preparation
- D. Summary
    1. Abstracts the important facts derived from the engineering study
    2. States concisely the conclusions and benefits to be obtained
- E. Background
    1. Outlines general historical experience within industry or company
    2. Describes previous work on the subject
- F. Approach
    1. Describes methods used
    2. Defines assumptions made
    3. States limitations in scope
- G. Alternatives examined
    1. Describes alternatives examined
    2. Indicates relative advantages of alternatives
    3. Shows charts and tables to illustrate relative costs and economics
    4. Lists intangible benefits of each major alternative
- H. Alternative selected
    1. Gives more detailed description of selected alternative
    2. Presents flow diagrams, sketches, plans for scope definition (if extensive place in appendix)
    3. Shows cash flows, probabilities, risk, and accuracy of calculations
    4. Presents plan and schedule for accomplishment
- I. Conclusion and recommendation
- J. Bibliography
- K. Appendix
    1. Calculations of cost and economic evaluation for selected case
    2. Copies of correspondence referred to in text
    3. Copies of major cost quotations
    4. Flow diagrams, sketches, charts, and tables not included in body of report

in relation to company ramifications. The effect of the recommendations on future developments of the company is a legitimate component of the purpose section. Like the summary, the section should be brief and precise, but no results are included.

Whether as a separate section or incorporated with other sections, some *background information* is usually necessary. It refreshes the memory and can give vital information for making decisions. Care must be taken in deciding how much detail to include.

Alternatives considered is an important part of any cost-engineering report since many alternatives are usually possible. Not all alternatives have to be presented with equal detail. Those with merit should be discussed at sufficient length, accompanied by charts and tables, to establish their relative values. Others with little merit may be mentioned, with only the reason for discarding them. The idea is to show that all reasonable alternatives have been investigated and to allay the fear that some good possibility may have been omitted through oversight.

In explaining the *alternative selected*, the report should go into detail. Besides costs, a major breakdown into components, information about timing, and possible variations should be included.

Reports on cost engineering, like all engineering reports, are based on assumptions; but since they may be much more sensitive to assumptions, all assumptions, and particularly those which are really surmises, should be clarified in such a manner that there can be no misunderstanding.

Similar to assumptions are intangibles. Intangibles include all factors having an influence on a decision which have not been included on a monetary basis (or at most on an insecure monetary basis). Failure to recognize intangibles can easily lead to wrong decisions. Like assumptions, they should be made apparent, if only listed. Moreover, inclusion of the intangible bespeaks thoroughness and adds authority to the report.

Economic evaluations should be made on the basis of more than one criterion for profitability, since no one criterion is an absolute standard; nor are all readers familiar with the same criterion. The evaluations should be qualified by tables or curves showing the sensitivity of the economics to changes occurring in any of the assumed values. When a high degree of sophistication is practiced, they may, in turn, be assigned probabilities, and the resultant overall probabilities stated. An excellent form for summarizing this information is shown in Fig. 21.4F1, which illustrates the advantage of using printed forms whenever possible.

The *recommendation* section is normally one of the shortest but most forceful. Alternative recommendations may have to be made, but the suggestion of hedging or indecision should be avoided.

21.5 Writing style

Everyone has read about extremely complex subjects which were easily understood, but sometimes reading about the simplest subjects seems most complex. The difference is writing style, particularly clarity in writing. Gunning[1] has listed 10 chapter headings of principles of good writing which are particularly applicable

---

[1] R. Gunning, "The Technique of Clear Writing," McGraw Hill-Book Company, New York, 1952.

PROJECT EVALUATION: HIGHLIGHTS

COMPANY UNIT:		PROJECT:	EXHIBIT
PREPARED BY:	DATE:	CASE:	

A. GRAPHICAL HIGHLIGHTS

YEAR →

B. STATISTICAL HIGHLIGHTS

		ITEM	AMOUNT ($ THOUSAND)		DECISION CASE
1	FINANCIAL INDICATORS	DCF RATE OF RETURN (%)			
2		NET PRESENT VALUE @ %			
3		PAYOUT PERIOD (YEARS)			
4		PROJECT LIFE (YEARS)			
5		MAXIMUM CASH EXPOSURE			
6					
7					
8	INVESTMENT (Project total, gross basis.)	NEW PROPERTY, PLANT, AND EQUIPMENT			
9		TRANSFER PROPERTY, PLANT, AND EQUIPMENT			
10		LEASED ASSETS (PRESENT VALUE @ %)			
11		WORKING CAPITAL			
12		TOTAL			
13	OPERATIONS (Annual Average for ____ years 19___ to 19___.)	VOLUME (UNITS:)			
14		SALES AND OTHER INCOME			
15		COSTS AND EXPENSES			
16		INCOME TAXES			
17		NET INCOME			
18		CASH FLOW			
19	OTHER HIGHLIGHTS	DATE OF FIRST EXPENDITURE			
20		DATE OF INITIAL OPERATIONS			
21		PAYOUT DATE			
22		TERMINAL DATE			
23					
24					
25					
26					
27					
28					
29					
30					

Fig. 21.4F1 A form for project evaluation.

to technical writing:

1. *Keep sentences short.*
2. *Prefer the simple to the complex.*
3. *Prefer the familiar word.*
4. *Avoid unnecessary words.*
5. *Put action in your verbs.*
6. *Write as you talk.*
7. *Use terms your reader can picture.*
8. *Tie in with your reader's experience.*
9. *Make full use of variety.*
10. *Write to express not impress.*

Courtesy is one of the key factors in good writing. Nowhere is this more apparent than in writing style. Affectation soon bores and irritates the reader—it is discourteous. A natural style is the best style. An engineer should concentrate on good organization and clarity. Excellent compact books on good grammar are available, such as [21.9R5].

21.6 Physical form

How a presentation looks does not necessarily reflect its quality, but it does have a psychological effect on the reader. Neat reports are easier to read and understand. A professional appearance implies a professional job. An attractive cover adds to the prestige and protects the report in handling. It is recommended except for short presentations on minor projects.

Everything possible should be done to make the report readable and free from annoyances. All reports (except very short ones) should have a table of contents. Long reports should have an index. Charts and tables frequently referred to should be inserted as foldouts. Spacing and margins should be generous (especially make sure that the binding does not cover any of the print).

Typography and format are important. Clarity and availability of information have a tremendous impact. Tables should have clear headings with no unclear abbreviations. Often it is a good idea to number the columns and lines. Charts should be clear and emphatic with enough lines for the purpose. Pages should not be cluttered. Above all there must be good delineation—indenting, subtitling, spacing, use of italics, boldface, and large type—so that the reader knows where he is at all times.

Also important is the method of reproduction. If a report is anything more than a minor memorandum, the typing should be done on a stencil and the work Multigraphed. Pages with diagrams, pictures, or graphs can be photographed and reproduced economically by a photooffset process. Pasted insertions should be avoided. Lettering on charts to be reproduced may be done by typed stickers, mechanical lettering, or professional adhesive lettering. Whatever process is used for reproduction, a smeared and streaked output must be avoided.

Some companies, such as consulting services, sell only reports and are judged entirely on the basis of the reports. Such companies strive for the utmost in presentation by maintaining art and reproduction departments and editorial staffs. Most large companies might do well to copy this technique. The engineers would be required to prepare reports, as before, but the advantages of having competent art and specialized secretarial work available along with editorial assistance is certain to lead to better presentation, and there need be no net increase in cost.

Preparation of a manuscript can be a tedious mechanical job, but it can be simplified by good organization. Most engineers do not have good writing habits, nor do they take advantage of the office and secretarial conveniences available. Notes, tables, and diagrams can be made as the job progresses. The propensity to allow charts and tables to drag to the end for fear that they will require revision should be overcome. Such items should be handled like blueprints in the engineering office, i.e., made, revised, and finally noted "approved for the report." The final report should not be undertaken until all figures and tables are completed, and then the report writes itself. In writing a report an engineer must refer frequently to pages of published articles, books, and company sources. The necessary pages can be copied by the modern copying machines and reduced to a compact file of all the supplementary material.

The manuscript given to the typist should be neat, readable, and uncluttered. Marginal material, inserts, and messy pages are unnecessary. Most typing mistakes are caused by illegibility and crowding. Marginal notes and inserts can be avoided by cutting the page with scissors, inserting the new material, and reassembling the sheet. Stenographer's correction fluid is helpful in avoiding untidy erasures and reducing writing between lines.

The clue to a good report is polish. All writing can be improved by polishing and rewriting where necessary. This is not a tedious or long job if the principles of the preceding paragraph are followed. A poorly written part can be cut out, literally, and rewording inserted. No report should be submitted in an unpolished form because the engineer is pressed for time. After the report is submitted, it is on record as it is with no excuses for imperfection. Reports must be satisfactory as submitted: Like love letters, they can return to haunt the writer.

21.7 Oral presentations

Oral presentation of a report, whether it is the result of engineering studies or a budget appropriation request, often has even greater importance than a written report. A few salient points will be mentioned.

Practice and time the talk in advance. A tape recorder is excellent for the purpose. In the auditorium, speak loud enough to be heard, and if a microphone is necessary, stay with the microphone. Change the pace, use pauses, and rely on inflection to avoid a monotone. The greatest attraction of an audience for a speaker is his enthusiasm: it is contagious.

Use visual aids liberally. They demonstrate preparation and help the lecturer by reducing his reliance upon memory or a script. They may be in the form of view graphs, slides, or flip charts. A good speaker avoids turning his back to the audience by having a duplicate set of slides in front of him.

The choice between view graphs, slides, and flip charts depends on the cost, the size of the audience, and available time. Uniform, carefully applied lettering is essential in visual aids. The minimum height for lettering on the screen in inches readable with 20/40 vision can be determined by dividing by 30 the distance in feet to the back row of seats, but many screens are too small for the room they serve. Always keep the content of charts and slides down to a bare minimum. Tables showing more than two or three columns of four numbers each are taboo. Charts should show only trends or behaviors, not details. Lists must be split into groupings with only one group shown at a time. Show *only* what you are talking lest the audience read ahead and be distracted. Figure 21.7F1 illustrates an excellent slide taken from a paper on economical thickness for insulation.

APPENDIX D
PAY OUT OF SUCCESSIVE INSULATION THICKNESSES

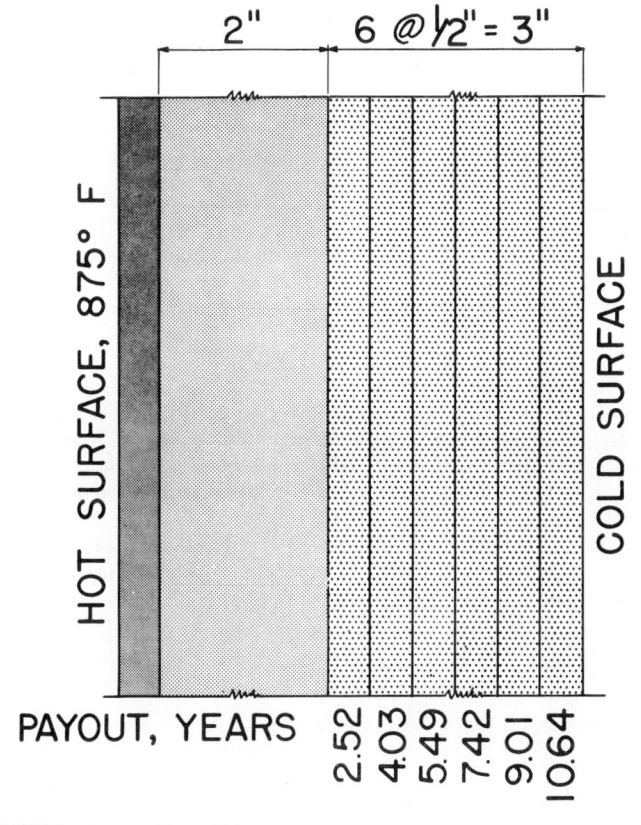

Fig. 21.7F1 An excellent slide.

Discussion following an oral presentation is often the most interesting part of the session. Here are a few hints:

1. Repeat a question to be sure that both you and the audience have heard and understood it.
2. Wait slightly before answering so as to phrase the reply as clearly as possible.
3. If you do not know the answer, admit it or refer it to someone in the audience who does.
4. Do not amplify your reply. Stop when the reply is clearly understood. This is a courtesy to others who wish to discuss another point.
5. Debate, if necessary, but never argue or show annoyance. If you are baited, do not retaliate: The audience will know whom to sympathize with.
6. If the questioner is the only one interested in an extended discussion, ask him to meet with you at the close of the meeting.
7. Be as complimentary and courteous as possible to the intelligence of questions asked or statements made.

Nervousness, even to the extent of shaking, is not easily controlled and is experienced even by some professional speakers. Remember that the audience is with you. All the speaker can do is study the subject thoroughly and polish and practice it in advance. You may find solace, and perhaps calm, in the feeling that the anxiety ends when you are called upon to speak. At that point there is nothing further to do—the die is cast. Arise and stay with your script.

21.8 Questions

Q1. Write an outline for a report on:
   (a) Site surveys for the selection of the location for a new automobile assembly-line plant.
   (b) A study made to determine the best location for a river crossing.
   (c) A study to determine whether maintenance should be carried out by company employees or contractors.

Q2. Write a summary report on one of the subjects of 21.8Q1.

Q3. Write a report on a problem you have worked on.

Q4. Prepare an appropriation request recommending the construction of a lunchroom with vending machines for the use of plant employees. Assume that employee relations dictate provision of eating facilities but stress alternatives and intangible benefits associated with each.

Q5. Prepare a set of flip charts for an oral presentation of the appropriation request prepared in 21.8Q4.

Q6. A client has asked you, as a building contractor, to examine the area at the rear of his home and recommend a design for an enclosed patio. Prepare a written recommendation following the five-step outline presented in this chapter.

21.9 References

R1. DeJen, J.: "Visual Presentation Handbook," Oravisual Co., St. Petersburg, Fla., 1959.
R2. Dubois, W. C.: "Essentials of Public Speaking," Prentice-Hall, Inc., Englewood Cliffs, N.J., 1929.
R3. Eastman Kodak Co.: "Effective Lecture Slides," Rochester, N.Y., 1963.

R4. Gilman, W.: "The Language of Science," Harcourt, Brace & World, Inc., New York, 1961.
R5. Greever, G., and E. S. Jones: "The Century Handbook of Writing," 4th ed., Appleton-Century-Crofts, Inc., New York, 1942.
R6. Gunning, R.: "The Technique of Clear Writing," McGraw-Hill Book Company, New York, 1952.
R7. Nelson, J. R.: "Writing the Technical Report," 3d ed., McGraw-Hill Book Company, New York, 1951.
R8. Peters, M. S., and K. D. Timmerhaus: "Plant Design and Economics for Chemical Engineers", 2d ed., McGraw-Hill Book Company, New York, 1968.
R9. Strunk, W., Jr., and E. B. White: "The Elements of Style," The Macmillan Company, New York, 1959.

Appendix 1
Discrete Compound Interest

Table I. Discrete Compound-interest Table

Discrete compound interest = 2%

	Single payment		Uniform annual series				Uniform gradient series	Depreciation series		
	Compound-interest factor	Present-worth factor	Unacost present-worth factor	Capital-recovery factor	Capitalized-cost factor		Present-worth factor	Sum-of-digits present-worth factor	Straight-line present-worth factor	
	$(1+i)^n$	$\dfrac{1}{(1+i)^n}$	$\dfrac{(1+i)^n - 1}{i(1+i)^n}$	$\dfrac{i(1+i)^n}{(1+i)^n - 1}$	$\dfrac{(1+i)^n}{(1+i)^n - 1}$		$\dfrac{F_{RP} - nF_{SP}}{i}$	$\dfrac{n - F_{RP}}{0.5n(n+1)i}$	$\dfrac{1}{niF_{PX}}$	
	P to S	S to P	R to P	P to R	P to K		G to P	SD to P	SL to P	
n	F_{PS}	F_{SP}	F_{RP}	F_{PR}	F_{PK}		F_{GP}	F_{SDP}	F_{SLP}	
1	1.0200E 00	9.8039E-01	9.8039E-01	1.0200E 00	5.1000E 01		1.0000E 00	9.8039E-01	9.8039E-01	
2	1.0404E 00	9.6117E-01	1.9416E 00	5.1505E-01	2.5752E 01		9.6117E-01	9.7398E-01	9.7078E-01	
3	1.0612E 00	9.4232E-01	2.8839E 00	3.4675E-01	1.7338E 01		2.8458E 00	9.6764E-01	9.6129E-01	
4	1.0824E 00	9.2385E-01	3.8077E 00	2.6262E-01	1.3131E 01		5.6173E 00	9.6136E-01	9.5193E-01	
5	1.1041E 00	9.0573E-01	4.7135E 00	2.1216E-01	1.0608E 01		9.2403E 00	9.5513E-01	9.4269E-01	
6	1.1262E 00	8.8797E-01	5.6014E 00	1.7853E-01	8.9263E 00		1.3680E 01	9.4897E-01	9.3357E-01	
7	1.1487E 00	8.7056E-01	6.4720E 00	1.5451E-01	7.7256E 00		1.8903E 01	9.4287E-01	9.2457E-01	
8	1.1717E 00	8.5349E-01	7.3255E 00	1.3651E-01	6.8255E 00		2.4878E 01	9.3683E-01	9.1569E-01	
9	1.1951E 00	8.3676E-01	8.1622E 00	1.2252E-01	6.1258E 00		3.1572E 01	9.3085E-01	9.0692E-01	
10	1.2190E 00	8.2035E-01	8.9826E 00	1.1133E-01	5.5663E 00		3.8955E 01	9.2492E-01	8.9826E-01	
11	1.2434E 00	8.0426E-01	9.7868E 00	1.0218E-01	5.1089E 00		4.6998E 01	9.1905E-01	8.8971E-01	
12	1.2682E 00	7.8849E-01	1.0575E 01	9.4560E-02	4.7280E 00		5.5671E 01	9.1324E-01	8.8128E-01	
13	1.2936E 00	7.7303E-01	1.1348E 01	8.8118E-02	4.4059E 00		6.4948E 01	9.0749E-01	8.7295E-01	
14	1.3195E 00	7.5788E-01	1.2106E 01	8.2602E-02	4.1301E 00		7.4800E 01	9.0179E-01	8.6473E-01	
15	1.3459E 00	7.4301E-01	1.2849E 01	7.7825E-02	3.8913E 00		8.5202E 01	8.9614E-01	8.5662E-01	
16	1.3728E 00	7.2845E-01	1.3578E 01	7.3650E-02	3.6825E 00		9.6129E 01	8.9055E-01	8.4861E-01	
18	1.4282E 00	7.0016E-01	1.4992E 01	6.6702E-02	3.3351E 00		1.1966E 02	8.7952E-01	8.3289E-01	
20	1.4859E 00	6.7297E-01	1.6351E 01	6.1157E-02	3.0578E 00		1.4460E 02	8.6871E-01	8.1757E-01	
25	1.6406E 00	6.0953E-01	1.9523E 01	5.1220E-02	2.5610E 00		2.1426E 02	8.4255E-01	7.8094E-01	
30	1.8114E 00	5.5207E-01	2.2396E 01	4.4650E-02	2.2325E 00		2.9172E 02	8.1754E-01	7.4655E-01	
35	1.9999E 00	5.0003E-01	2.4999E 01	4.0002E-02	2.0001E 00		3.7488E 02	7.9376E-01	7.1425E-01	
40	2.2080E 00	4.5289E-01	2.7355E 01	3.6556E-02	1.8278E 00		4.6199E 02	7.7101E-01	6.8389E-01	
45	2.4379E 00	4.1020E-01	2.9490E 01	3.3910E-02	1.6955E 00		5.5157E 02	7.4927E-01	6.5534E-01	
50	2.6916E 00	3.7153E-01	3.1424E 01	3.1823E-02	1.5912E 00		6.4236E 02	7.2849E-01	6.2847E-01	

Discrete compound interest = 4%

	Single payment		Uniform annual series				Uniform gradient series	Depreciation series		
	Compound-interest factor	Present-worth factor	Unacost present-worth factor	Capital-recovery factor	Capitalized-cost factor		Present-worth factor	Sum-of-digits present-worth factor	Straight-line present-worth factor
	$(1+i)^n$	$\dfrac{1}{(1+i)^n}$	$\dfrac{(1+i)^n-1}{i(1+i)^n}$	$\dfrac{i(1+i)^n}{(1+i)^n-1}$	$\dfrac{(1+i)^n}{(1+i)^n-1}$		$\dfrac{F_{RP}-nF_{SP}}{i}$	$\dfrac{n-F_{RP}}{0.5n(n+1)i}$	$\dfrac{1}{niF_{PK}}$
	P to S	S to P	R to P	P to R	P to K		G to P	SD to P	SL to P
n	F_{PS}	F_{SP}	F_{RP}	F_{PR}	F_{PK}		F_{GP}	F_{SDP}	F_{SLP}
1	1.0400E 00	9.6154E-01	9.6154E-01	1.0400E 00	2.6000E 01		1.0000E 00	9.6154E-01	9.6154E-01
2	1.0816E 00	9.2456E-01	1.8861E 00	5.3020E-01	1.3255E 01		9.2456E-01	9.4921E-01	9.4305E-01
3	1.1249E 00	8.8900E-01	2.7751E 00	3.6035E-01	9.0087E 00		2.7025E 00	9.3712E-01	9.2503E-01
4	1.1699E 00	8.5480E-01	3.6299E 00	2.7549E-01	6.8873E 00		5.2670E 00	9.2526E-01	9.0747E-01
5	1.2167E 00	8.2193E-01	4.4518E 00	2.2463E-01	5.6157E 00		8.5547E 00	9.1363E-01	8.9036E-01
6	1.2653E 00	7.9031E-01	5.2421E 00	1.9076E-01	4.7690E 00		1.2506E 01	9.0222E-01	8.7369E-01
7	1.3159E 00	7.5992E-01	6.0021E 00	1.6661E-01	4.1652E 00		1.7066E 01	8.9102E-01	8.5744E-01
8	1.3686E 00	7.3069E-01	6.7327E 00	1.4853E-01	3.7132E 00		2.2181E 01	8.8004E-01	8.4159E-01
9	1.4233E 00	7.0259E-01	7.4353E 00	1.3449E-01	3.3623E 00		2.7801E 01	8.6926E-01	8.2615E-01
10	1.4802E 00	6.7556E-01	8.1109E 00	1.2329E-01	3.0823E 00		3.3881E 01	8.5868E-01	8.1109E-01
11	1.5395E 00	6.4958E-01	8.7605E 00	1.1415E-01	2.8537E 00		4.0377E 01	8.4830E-01	7.9641E-01
12	1.6010E 00	6.2460E-01	9.3851E 00	1.0655E-01	2.6638E 00		4.7248E 01	8.3812E-01	7.8209E-01
13	1.6651E 00	6.0057E-01	9.9856E 00	1.0014E-01	2.5036E 00		5.4455E 01	8.2812E-01	7.6813E-01
14	1.7317E 00	5.7748E-01	1.0563E 01	9.4669E-02	2.3667E 00		6.1962E 01	8.1830E-01	7.5451E-01
15	1.8009E 00	5.5526E-01	1.1118E 01	8.9941E-02	2.2485E 00		6.9735E 01	8.0867E-01	7.4123E-01
16	1.8730E 00	5.3391E-01	1.1652E 01	8.5820E-02	2.1455E 00		7.7744E 01	7.9921E-01	7.2827E-01
18	2.0258E 00	4.9363E-01	1.2659E 01	7.8993E-02	1.9748E 00		9.4350E 01	7.8080E-01	7.0329E-01
20	2.1911E 00	4.5639E-01	1.3590E 01	7.3582E-02	1.8395E 00		1.1156E 02	7.6306E-01	6.7952E-01
25	2.6658E 00	3.7512E-01	1.5622E 01	6.4012E-02	1.6003E 00		1.5610E 02	7.2138E-01	6.2488E-01
30	3.2434E 00	3.0832E-01	1.7292E 01	5.7830E-02	1.4458E 00		2.0106E 02	6.8322E-01	5.7640E-01
35	3.9461E 00	2.5342E-01	1.8665E 01	5.3577E-02	1.3394E 00		2.4488E 02	6.4823E-01	5.3327E-01
40	4.8010E 00	2.0829E-01	1.9793E 01	5.0523E-02	1.2631E 00		2.8653E 02	6.1607E-01	4.9482E-01
45	5.8412E 00	1.7120E-01	2.0720E 01	4.8262E-02	1.2066E 00		3.2540E 02	5.8647E-01	4.6045E-01
50	7.1067E 00	1.4071E-01	2.1482E 01	4.6550E-02	1.1638E 00		3.6116E 02	5.5917E-01	4.2964E-01

Table I. (continued)

Discrete compound interest = 6%

	Single payment		Uniform annual series				Uniform gradient series		Depreciation series	
	Compound-interest factor	Present-worth factor	Unacost present-worth factor	Capital-recovery factor	Capitalized-cost factor		Present-worth factor	Sum-of-digits present-worth factor	Straight-line present-worth factor
	$(1+i)^n$	$\dfrac{1}{(1+i)^n}$	$\dfrac{(1+i)^n-1}{i(1+i)^n}$	$\dfrac{i(1+i)^n}{(1+i)^n-1}$	$\dfrac{(1+i)^n}{(1+i)^n-1}$		$\dfrac{F_{RP}-nF_{SP}}{i}$	$\dfrac{n-F_{RP}}{0.5n(n+1)i}$	$\dfrac{1}{niF_{PX}}$
n	P to S F_{PS}	S to P F_{SP}	R to P F_{RP}	P to R F_{PR}	P to K F_{PK}		G to P F_{GP}	SD to P F_{SDP}	SL to P F_{SLP}
1	1.0600E 00	9.4340E-01	9.4340E-01	1.0600E 00	1.7667E 01		1.0000E 00	9.4340E-01	9.4340E-01
2	1.1236E 00	8.9000E-01	1.8334E 00	5.4544E-01	9.0906E 00		8.9000E-01	9.2560E-01	9.1670E-01
3	1.1910E 00	8.3962E-01	2.6730E 00	3.7411E-01	6.2352E 00		2.5692E 00	9.0830E-01	8.9100E-01
4	1.2625E 00	7.9209E-01	3.4651E 00	2.8859E-01	4.8099E 00		4.9455E 00	8.9149E-01	8.6628E-01
5	1.3382E 00	7.4726E-01	4.2124E 00	2.3740E-01	3.9566E 00		7.9345E 00	8.7515E-01	8.4247E-01
6	1.4185E 00	7.0496E-01	4.9173E 00	2.0336E-01	3.3894E 00		1.1459E 01	8.5927E-01	8.1955E-01
7	1.5036E 00	6.6506E-01	5.5824E 00	1.7914E-01	2.9856E 00		1.5450E 01	8.4382E-01	7.9748E-01
8	1.5938E 00	6.2741E-01	6.2098E 00	1.6104E-01	2.6839E 00		1.9842E 01	8.2880E-01	7.7622E-01
9	1.6895E 00	5.9190E-01	6.8017E 00	1.4702E-01	2.4504E 00		2.4577E 01	8.1419E-01	7.5574E-01
10	1.7908E 00	5.5839E-01	7.3601E 00	1.3587E-01	2.2645E 00		2.9602E 01	7.9997E-01	7.3601E-01
11	1.8983E 00	5.2679E-01	7.8869E 00	1.2679E-01	2.1132E 00		3.4870E 01	7.8614E-01	7.1699E-01
12	2.0122E 00	4.9697E-01	8.3838E 00	1.1928E-01	1.9880E 00		4.0337E 01	7.7268E-01	6.9865E-01
13	2.1329E 00	4.6884E-01	8.8527E 00	1.1296E-01	1.8827E 00		4.5963E 01	7.5958E-01	6.8098E-01
14	2.2609E 00	4.4230E-01	9.2950E 00	1.0758E-01	1.7931E 00		5.1713E 01	7.4683E-01	6.6393E-01
15	2.3966E 00	4.1727E-01	9.7122E 00	1.0296E-01	1.7160E 00		5.7555E 01	7.3441E-01	6.4748E-01
16	2.5404E 00	3.9365E-01	1.0106E 01	9.8952E-02	1.6492E 00		6.3459E 01	7.2232E-01	6.3162E-01
18	2.8543E 00	3.5034E-01	1.0828E 01	9.2357E-02	1.5393E 00		7.5357E 01	6.9906E-01	6.0153E-01
20	3.2071E 00	3.1180E-01	1.1470E 01	8.7185E-02	1.4531E 00		8.7230E 01	6.7699E-01	5.7350E-01
25	4.2919E 00	2.3300E-01	1.2783E 01	7.8227E-02	1.3038E 00		1.1597E 02	6.2649E-01	5.1133E-01
30	5.7435E 00	1.7411E-01	1.3765E 01	7.2649E-02	1.2108E 00		1.4236E 02	5.8191E-01	4.5883E-01
35	7.6861E 00	1.3011E-01	1.4498E 01	6.8974E-02	1.1496E 00		1.6574E 02	5.4237E-01	4.1424E-01
40	1.0286E 01	9.7222E-02	1.5046E 01	6.6462E-02	1.1077E 00		1.8596E 02	5.0719E-01	3.7616E-01
45	1.3765E 01	7.2650E-02	1.5456E 01	6.4700E-02	1.0783E 00		2.0311E 02	4.7575E-01	3.4346E-01
50	1.8420E 01	5.4288E-02	1.5762E 01	6.3444E-02	1.0574E 00		2.1746E 02	4.4756E-01	3.1524E-01

Discrete compound interest = 8%

	Single payment		Uniform annual series				Uniform gradient series		Depreciation series	
	Compound-interest factor	Present-worth factor	Unacost present-worth factor	Capital-recovery factor	Capitalized-cost factor		Present-worth factor		Sum-of-digits present-worth factor	Straight-line present worth factor
	$(1+i)^n$	$\dfrac{1}{(1+i)^n}$	$\dfrac{(1+i)^n - 1}{i(1+i)^n}$	$\dfrac{i(1+i)^n}{(1+i)^n - 1}$	$\dfrac{(1+i)^n}{(1+i)^n - 1}$		$\dfrac{F_{RP} - nF_{SP}}{i}$		$\dfrac{n - F_{RP}}{0.5n(n+1)i}$	$\dfrac{1}{niF_{PX}}$
n	P to S	S to P	R to P	P to R	P to K		G to P		SD to P	SL to P
	F_{PS}	F_{SP}	F_{RP}	F_{PR}	F_{PK}		F_{GP}		F_{SDP}	F_{SLP}
1	1.0800E 00	9.2593E-01	9.2593E-01	1.0800E 00	1.3500E 01	1.0000E 00		9.2593E-01		9.2593E-01
2	1.1664E 00	8.5734E-01	1.7833E 00	5.6077E-01	7.0096E 00	8.5734E-01		9.0306E-01		8.9163E-01
3	1.2597E 00	7.9383E-01	2.5771E 00	3.8803E-01	4.8504E 00	2.4450E 00		8.8105E-01		8.5903E-01
4	1.3605E 00	7.3503E-01	3.3121E 00	3.0192E-01	3.7740E 00	4.6501E 00		8.5984E-01		8.2803E-01
5	1.4693E 00	6.8058E-01	3.9927E 00	2.5046E-01	3.1307E 00	7.3724E 00		8.3941E-01		7.9854E-01
6	1.5869E 00	6.3017E-01	4.6229E 00	2.1632E-01	2.7039E 00	1.0523E 01		8.1971E-01		7.7048E-01
7	1.7138E 00	5.8349E-01	5.2064E 00	1.9207E-01	2.4009E 00	1.4024E 01		8.0073E-01		7.4377E-01
8	1.8509E 00	5.4027E-01	5.7466E 00	1.7401E-01	2.1752E 00	1.7806E 01		7.8242E-01		7.1833E-01
9	1.9990E 00	5.0025E-01	6.2469E 00	1.6008E-01	2.0010E 00	2.1808E 01		7.6475E-01		6.9410E-01
10	2.1589E 00	4.6319E-01	6.7101E 00	1.4903E-01	1.8629E 00	2.5977E 01		7.4771E-01		6.7101E-01
11	2.3316E 00	4.2888E-01	7.1390E 00	1.4008E-01	1.7510E 00	3.0266E 01		7.3126E-01		6.4900E-01
12	2.5182E 00	3.9711E-01	7.5361E 00	1.3270E-01	1.6587E 00	3.4634E 01		7.1537E-01		6.2801E-01
13	2.7196E 00	3.6770E-01	7.9038E 00	1.2652E-01	1.5815E 00	3.9046E 01		7.0003E-01		6.0798E-01
14	2.9372E 00	3.4046E-01	8.2442E 00	1.2130E-01	1.5162E 00	4.3472E 01		6.8521E-01		5.8887E-01
15	3.1722E 00	3.1524E-01	8.5595E 00	1.1683E-01	1.4604E 00	4.7886E 01		6.7089E-01		5.7063E-01
16	3.4259E 00	2.9189E-01	8.8514E 00	1.1298E-01	1.4122E 00	5.2264E 01		6.5704E-01		5.5321E-01
18	3.9960E 00	2.5025E-01	9.3719E 00	1.0670E-01	1.3338E 00	6.0843E 01		6.3071E-01		5.2066E-01
20	4.6610E 00	2.1455E-01	9.8181E 00	1.0185E-01	1.2732E 00	6.9090E 01		6.0606E-01		4.9091E-01
25	6.8485E 00	1.4602E-01	1.0675E 01	9.3679E-02	1.1710E 00	8.7804E 01		5.5097E-01		4.2699E-01
30	1.0063E 01	9.9377E-02	1.1258E 01	8.8827E-02	1.1103E 00	1.0366E 02		5.0382E-01		3.7526E-01
35	1.4785E 01	6.7635E-02	1.1655E 01	8.5803E-02	1.0725E 00	1.1609E 02		4.6320E-01		3.3299E-01
40	2.1725E 01	4.6031E-02	1.1925E 01	8.3860E-02	1.0483E 00	1.2604E 02		4.2798E-01		2.9812E-01
45	3.1920E 01	3.1328E-02	1.2108E 01	8.2587E-02	1.0323E 00	1.3373E 02		3.9724E-01		2.6908E-01
50	4.6902E 01	2.1321E-02	1.2233E 01	8.1743E-02	1.0218E 00	1.3959E 02		3.7026E-01		2.4467E-01

Table I. (continued)

Discrete compound interest = 10%

	Single payment		Uniform annual series				Uniform gradient series	Depreciation series	
	Compound-interest factor $(1+i)^n$ P to S F_{PS}	Present-worth factor $\dfrac{1}{(1+i)^n}$ S to P F_{SP}	Unacost present-worth factor $\dfrac{(1+i)^n-1}{i(1+i)^n}$ R to P F_{RP}	Capital-recovery factor $\dfrac{i(1+i)^n}{(1+i)^n-1}$ P to R F_{PR}	Capitalized-cost factor $\dfrac{(1+i)^n}{(1+i)^n-1}$ P to K F_{PK}		Present-worth factor $\dfrac{F_{RP}-nF_{SP}}{i}$ G to P F_{GP}	Sum-of-digits present-worth factor $\dfrac{n-F_{RP}}{0.5n(n+1)i}$ SD to P F_{SDP}	Straight-line present-worth factor $\dfrac{1}{ni}F_{PK}$ SL to P F_{SLP}
n									
1	1.1000E 00	9.0909E-01	9.0909E-01	1.1000E 00	1.1000E 01	1.0000E 00	9.0909E-01	9.0909E-01
2	1.2100E 00	8.2645E-01	1.7355E 00	5.7619E-01	5.7619E-01	8.2645E-01	8.8154E-01	8.6777E-01
3	1.3310E 00	7.5131E-01	2.4869E 00	4.0211E-01	4.0211E 00	2.3291E 00	8.5525E-01	8.2895E-01
4	1.4641E 00	6.8301E-01	3.1699E 00	3.1547E-01	3.1547E 00	4.3781E 00	8.3013E-01	7.9247E-01
5	1.6105E 00	6.2092E-01	3.7908E 00	2.6380E-01	2.6380E 00	6.8618E 00	8.0614E-01	7.5816E-01
6	1.7716E 00	5.6447E-01	4.3553E 00	2.2961E-01	2.2961E 00	9.6842E 00	7.8321E-01	7.2588E-01
7	1.9487E 00	5.1316E-01	4.8684E 00	2.0541E-01	2.0541E 00	1.2763E 01	7.6128E-01	6.9549E-01
8	2.1436E 00	4.6651E-01	5.3349E 00	1.8744E-01	1.8744E 00	1.6029E 01	7.4030E-01	6.6687E-01
9	2.3579E 00	4.2410E-01	5.7590E 00	1.7364E-01	1.7364E 00	1.9421E 01	7.2022E-01	6.3989E-01
10	2.5937E 00	3.8554E-01	6.1446E 00	1.6275E-01	1.6275E 00	2.2891E 01	7.0099E-01	6.1446E-01
11	2.8531E 00	3.5049E-01	6.4951E 00	1.5396E-01	1.5396E 00	2.6396E 01	6.8257E-01	5.9046E-01
12	3.1384E 00	3.1863E-01	6.8137E 00	1.4676E-01	1.4676E 00	2.9901E 01	6.6491E-01	5.6781E-01
13	3.4523E 00	2.8966E-01	7.1034E 00	1.4078E-01	1.4078E 00	3.3377E 01	6.4798E-01	5.4641E-01
14	3.7975E 00	2.6333E-01	7.3667E 00	1.3575E-01	1.3575E 00	3.6800E 01	6.3174E-01	5.2619E-01
15	4.1772E 00	2.3939E-01	7.6061E 00	1.3147E-01	1.3147E 00	4.0152E 01	6.1616E-01	5.0707E-01
16	4.5950E 00	2.1763E-01	7.8237E 00	1.2782E-01	1.2782E 00	4.3416E 01	6.0120E-01	4.8898E-01
18	5.5599E 00	1.7986E-01	8.2014E 00	1.2193E-01	1.2193E 00	4.9640E 01	5.7302E-01	4.5563E-01
20	6.7275E 00	1.4864E-01	8.5136E 00	1.1746E-01	1.1746E 00	5.5407E 01	5.4697E-01	4.2568E-01
25	1.0835E 01	9.2296E-02	9.0770E 00	1.1017E-01	1.1017E 00	6.7696E 01	4.8944E-01	3.6308E-01
30	1.7449E 01	5.7309E-02	9.4269E 00	1.0608E-01	1.0608E 00	7.7077E 01	4.4243E-01	3.1423E-01
35	2.8102E 01	3.5584E-02	9.6442E 00	1.0369E-01	1.0369E 00	8.3987E 01	4.0247E-01	2.7555E-01
40	4.5259E 01	2.2095E-02	9.7791E 00	1.0226E-01	1.0226E 00	8.8953E 01	3.0855E-01	2.4448E-01
45	7.2890E 01	1.3719E-02	9.8628E 00	1.0139E-01	1.0139E 00	9.2454E 01	3.3949E-01	2.1917E-01
50	1.1739E 02	8.5186E-03	9.9148E 00	1.0085E-01	1.0086E 00	9.4889E 01	3.1839E-01	1.9830E-01

Discrete compound interest = 12%

	Single payment		Uniform annual series			Uniform gradient series	Depreciation series	
	Compound-interest factor	Present-worth factor	Unacost present-worth factor	Capital-recovery factor	Capitalized-cost factor	Present-worth factor	Sum-of-digits present-worth factor	Straight-line present-worth factor
	$(1+i)^n$	$\dfrac{1}{(1+i)^n}$	$\dfrac{(1+i)^n - 1}{i(1+i)^n}$	$\dfrac{i(1+i)^n}{(1+i)^n - 1}$	$\dfrac{(1+i)^n}{(1+i)^n - 1}$	$\dfrac{F_{RP} - nF_{SP}}{i}$	$\dfrac{n - F_{RP}}{0.5n(n+1)i}$	$\dfrac{1}{niF_{PK}}$
	P to S	S to P	R to P	P to R	P to K	G to P	SD to P	SL to P
n	F_{PS}	F_{SP}	F_{RP}	F_{PR}	F_{PK}	F_{GP}	F_{SDP}	F_{SLP}
1	1.1200E 00	8.9286E-01	8.9286E-01	1.1200E 00	9.3333E 00	1.0000E 00	8.9286E-01	8.9286E-01
2	1.2544E 00	7.9719E-01	1.6901E 00	5.9170E-01	4.9308E 00	7.9719E-01	8.6097E-01	8.4503E-01
3	1.4049E 00	7.1178E-01	2.4018E 00	4.1635E-01	3.4696E 00	2.2208E 00	8.3079E-01	8.0061E-01
4	1.5735E 00	6.3552E-01	3.0373E 00	3.2923E-01	2.7436E 00	4.1273E 00	8.0221E-01	7.5934E-01
5	1.7623E 00	5.6743E-01	3.6048E 00	2.7741E-01	2.3117E 00	6.3970E 00	7.7512E-01	7.2096E-01
6	1.9738E 00	5.0663E-01	4.1114E 00	2.4323E-01	2.0269E 00	8.9302E 00	7.4944E-01	6.8523E-01
7	2.2107E 00	4.5235E-01	4.5638E 00	2.1912E-01	1.8260E 00	1.1644E 01	7.2507E-01	6.5197E-01
8	2.4760E 00	4.0388E-01	4.9676E 00	2.0130E-01	1.6775E 00	1.4471E 01	7.0194E-01	6.2095E-01
9	2.7731E 00	3.6061E-01	5.3282E 00	1.8768E-01	1.5640E 00	1.7356E 01	6.7995E-01	5.9203E-01
10	3.1058E 00	3.2197E-01	5.6502E 00	1.7698E-01	1.4749E 00	2.0254E 01	6.5906E-01	5.6502E-01
11	3.4785E 00	2.8748E-01	5.9377E 00	1.6842E-01	1.4035E 00	2.3129E 01	6.3918E-01	5.3979E-01
12	3.8960E 00	2.5668E-01	6.1944E 00	1.6144E-01	1.3453E 00	2.5952E 01	6.2026E-01	5.1620E-01
13	4.3635E 00	2.2917E-01	6.4235E 00	1.5568E-01	1.2973E 00	2.8702E 01	6.0224E-01	4.9412E-01
14	4.8871E 00	2.0462E-01	6.6282E 00	1.5087E-01	1.2573E 00	3.1362E 01	5.8507E-01	4.7344E-01
15	5.4736E 00	1.8270E-01	6.8109E 00	1.4682E-01	1.2235E 00	3.3920E 01	5.6869E-01	4.5406E-01
16	6.1304E 00	1.6312E-01	6.9740E 00	1.4339E-01	1.1949E 00	3.6367E 01	5.5306E-01	4.3587E-01
18	7.6900E 00	1.3004E-01	7.2497E 00	1.3794E-01	1.1495E 00	4.0908E 01	5.2390E-01	4.0276E-01
20	9.6463E 00	1.0367E-01	7.4694E 00	1.3388E-01	1.1157E 00	4.4968E 01	4.9724E-01	3.7347E-01
25	1.7000E 01	5.8823E-02	7.8431E 00	1.2750E-01	1.0625E 00	5.3105E 01	4.3992E-01	3.1373E-01
30	2.9960E 01	3.3378E-02	8.0552E 00	1.2414E-01	1.0345E 00	5.8782E 01	3.9328E-01	2.6851E-01
35	5.2800E 01	1.8940E-02	8.1755E 00	1.2232E-01	1.0193E 00	6.2605E 01	3.5482E-01	2.3359E-01
40	9.3051E 01	1.0747E-02	8.2438E 00	1.2130E-01	1.0109E 00	6.5116E 01	3.2273E-01	2.0609E-01
45	1.6399E 02	6.0980E-03	8.2825E 00	1.2074E-01	1.0061E 00	6.6734E 01	2.9563E-01	1.8406E-01
50	2.8900E 02	3.4602E-03	8.3045E 00	1.2042E-01	1.0035E 00	6.7762E 01	2.7252E-01	1.6609E-01

441

Table I. (continued)

Discrete compound interest = 14%

	Single payment		Uniform annual series			Uniform gradient series	Depreciation series	
	Compound-interest factor	Present-worth factor	Unacost present-worth factor	Capital-recovery factor	Capitalized-cost factor	Present-worth factor	Sum-of-digits present-worth factor	Straight-line present-worth factor
	$(1+i)^n$	$\dfrac{1}{(1+i)^n}$	$\dfrac{(1+i)^n-1}{i(1+i)^n}$	$\dfrac{i(1+i)^n}{(1+i)^n-1}$	$\dfrac{(1+i)^n}{(1+i)^n-1}$	$\dfrac{F_{RP}-nF_{SP}}{i}$	$\dfrac{n-F_{RP}}{0.5n(n+1)i}$	$\dfrac{1}{niF_{PK}}$
	P to S	S to P	R to P	P to R	P to K	G to P	SD to P	SL to P
n	F_{PS}	F_{SP}	F_{RP}	F_{PR}	F_{PK}	F_{GP}	F_{SDP}	F_{SLP}
1	1.1400E 00	8.7719E-01	8.7719E-01	1.1400E 00	8.1429E 00	1.0000E 00	8.7719E-01	8.7719E-01
2	1.2996E 00	7.6947E-01	1.6467E 00	6.0729E-01	4.3378E 00	7.6947E-01	8.4128E-01	8.2333E-01
3	1.4815E 00	6.7497E-01	2.3216E 00	4.3073E-01	3.0767E 00	2.1194E 00	8.0758E-01	7.7388E-01
4	1.6890E 00	5.9208E-01	2.9137E 00	3.4320E-01	2.4515E 00	3.8957E 00	7.7592E-01	7.2843E-01
5	1.9254E 00	5.1937E-01	3.4331E 00	2.9128E-01	2.0806E 00	5.9731E 00	7.4615E-01	6.8662E-01
6	2.1950E 00	4.5559E-01	3.8887E 00	2.5716E-01	1.8368E 00	8.2511E 00	7.1814E-01	6.4811E-01
7	2.5023E 00	3.9964E-01	4.2883E 00	2.3319E-01	1.6657E 00	1.0649E 01	6.9178E-01	6.1261E-01
8	2.8526E 00	3.5056E-01	4.6389E 00	2.1557E-01	1.5398E 00	1.3103E 01	6.6689E-01	5.7986E-01
9	3.2519E 00	3.0751E-01	4.9464E 00	2.0217E-01	1.4441E 00	1.5563E 01	6.4343E-01	5.4960E-01
10	3.7072E 00	2.6974E-01	5.2161E 00	1.9171E-01	1.3694E 00	1.7991E 01	6.2128E-01	5.2161E-01
11	4.2262E 00	2.3662E-01	5.4527E 00	1.8339E-01	1.3100E 00	2.0357E 01	6.0035E-01	4.9570E-01
12	4.8179E 00	2.0756E-01	5.6603E 00	1.7667E-01	1.2619E 00	2.2640E 01	5.8056E-01	4.7169E-01
13	5.4924E 00	1.8207E-01	5.8424E 00	1.7116E-01	1.2226E 00	2.4825E 01	5.6182E-01	4.4941E-01
14	6.2613E 00	1.5971E-01	6.0021E 00	1.6661E-01	1.1901E 00	2.6901E 01	5.4408E-01	4.2872E-01
15	7.1379E 00	1.4010E-01	6.1422E 00	1.6281E-01	1.1629E 00	2.8862E 01	5.2725E-01	4.0948E-01
16	8.1372E 00	1.2289E-01	6.2651E 00	1.5962E-01	1.1401E 00	3.0706E 01	5.1129E-01	3.9157E-01
18	1.0575E 01	9.4561E-02	6.4674E 00	1.5462E-01	1.1044E 00	3.4038E 01	4.8173E-01	3.5930E-01
20	1.3743E 01	7.2762E-02	6.6231E 00	1.5099E-01	1.0785E 00	3.6914E 01	4.5500E-01	3.3116E-01
25	2.6462E 01	3.7790E-02	6.8729E 00	1.4550E-01	1.0393E 00	4.2344E 01	3.9840E-01	2.7492E-01
30	5.0950E 01	1.9627E-02	7.0027E 00	1.4280E-01	1.0200E 00	4.5813E 01	3.5326E-01	2.3342E-01
35	9.8100E 01	1.0194E-02	7.0700E 00	1.4144E-01	1.0103E 00	4.7952E 01	3.1667E-01	2.0200E-01
40	1.8888E 02	5.2943E-03	7.1050E 00	1.4075E-01	1.0053E 00	4.9238E 01	2.8655E-01	1.7763E-01
45	3.6368E 02	2.7497E-03	7.1232E 00	1.4039E-01	1.0028E 00	4.9996E 01	2.6140E-01	1.5829E-01
50	7.0023E 02	1.4281E-03	7.1327E 00	1.4020E-01	1.0014E 00	5.0438E 01	2.4015E-01	1.4205E-01

Discrete compound interest = 16%.

	Single payment			Uniform annual series				Uniform gradient series		Depreciation series	
	Compound-interest factor	Present-worth factor		Unacost present-worth factor	Capital-recovery factor	Capitalized-cost factor		Present-worth factor	Sum-of-digits present-worth factor	Straight-line present-worth factor
	$(1+i)^n$	$\dfrac{1}{(1+i)^n}$		$\dfrac{(1+i)^n-1}{i(1+i)^n}$	$\dfrac{i(1+i)^n}{(1+i)^n-1}$	$\dfrac{(1+i)^n}{(1+i)^n-1}$		$\dfrac{F_{RP}-nF_{SP}}{i}$	$\dfrac{n-F_{RP}}{0.5n(n+1)i}$	$\dfrac{1}{niF_{PX}}$
	P to S	S to P		R to P	P to R	P to K		G to P	SD to P	SL to P
n	F_{PS}	F_{SP}		F_{RP}	F_{PR}	F_{PK}		F_{GP}	F_{SDP}	F_{SLP}
1	1.1600E 00	8.6207E-01		8.6207E-01	1.1600E 00	7.2500E 00		1.0000E 00	8.6207E-01	8.6207E-01
2	1.3456E 00	7.4316E-01		1.6052E 00	6.2296E-01	3.8935E 00		7.4316E-01	8.2243E-01	8.0262E-01
3	1.5609E 00	6.4066E-01		2.2459E 00	4.4526E-01	2.7829E 00		2.0245E 00	7.8553E-01	7.4863E-01
4	1.8106E 00	5.5229E-01		2.7982E 00	3.5738E-01	2.2336E 00		3.6814E 00	7.5114E-01	6.9955E-01
5	2.1003E 00	4.7611E-01		3.2743E 00	3.0541E-01	1.9088E 00		5.5858E 00	7.1904E-01	6.5486E-01
6	2.4364E 00	4.1044E-01		3.6847E 00	2.7139E-01	1.6962E 00		7.6380E 00	6.8907E-01	6.1412E-01
7	2.8262E 00	3.5383E-01		4.0386E 00	2.4761E-01	1.5476E 00		9.7610E 00	6.6103E-01	5.7694E-01
8	3.2784E 00	3.0503E-01		4.3436E 00	2.3022E-01	1.4389E 00		1.1896E 01	6.3479E-01	5.4295E-01
9	3.8030E 00	2.6295E-01		4.6065E 00	2.1708E-01	1.3568E 00		1.4000E 01	6.1020E-01	5.1118E-01
10	4.4114E 00	2.2668E-01		4.8332E 00	2.0690E-01	1.2931E 00		1.6040E 01	5.8713E-01	4.8332E-01
11	5.1173E 00	1.9542E-01		5.0286E 00	1.9886E-01	1.2429E 00		1.7994E 01	5.6547E-01	4.5715E-01
12	5.9360E 00	1.6846E-01		5.1971E 00	1.9241E-01	1.2026E 00		1.9847E 01	5.4510E-01	4.3309E-01
13	6.8858E 00	1.4523E-01		5.3423E 00	1.8718E-01	1.1699E 00		2.1590E 01	5.2594E-01	4.1095E-01
14	7.9875E 00	1.2520E-01		5.4675E 00	1.8290E-01	1.1431E 00		2.3217E 01	5.0789E-01	3.9054E-01
15	9.2655E 00	1.0793E-01		5.5755E 00	1.7936E-01	1.1210E 00		2.4728E 01	4.9088E-01	3.7170E-01
16	1.0748E 01	9.3041E-02		5.6685E 00	1.7641E-01	1.1026E 00		2.6124E 01	4.7479E-01	3.5428E-01
18	1.4463E 01	6.9144E-02		5.8178E 00	1.7188E-01	1.0743E 00		2.8583E 01	4.4525E-01	3.2321E-01
20	1.9461E 01	5.1385E-02		5.9288E 00	1.6867E-01	1.0542E 00		3.0632E 01	4.1878E-01	2.9644E-01
25	4.0874E 01	2.4465E-02		6.0971E 00	1.6401E-01	1.0251E 00		3.4284E 01	3.6352E-01	2.4388E-01
30	8.5850E 01	1.1648E-02		6.1772E 00	1.6189E-01	1.0118E 00		3.6623E 01	3.2020E-01	2.0591E-01
35	1.8031E 02	5.5459E-03		6.2153E 00	1.6089E-01	1.0056E 00		3.7633E 01	2.8556E-01	1.7758E-01
40	3.7872E 02	2.6405E-03		6.2335E 00	1.6042E-01	1.0026E 00		3.8299E 01	2.5737E-01	1.5584E-01
45	7.9544E 02	1.2572E-03		6.2421E 00	1.6020E-01	1.0013E 00		3.8660E 01	2.3405E-01	1.3871E-01
50	1.6707E 03	5.9855E-04		6.2463E 00	1.6010E-01	1.0006E 00		3.8852E 01	2.1448E-01	1.2493E-01

Table I. (continued)

Discrete compound interest = 20%

	Single payment		Uniform annual series				Uniform gradient series	Depreciation series	
	Compound-interest factor	Present-worth factor	Unacost present-worth factor	Capital-recovery factor	Capitalized-cost factor	Present-worth factor	Sum-of-digits present-worth factor	Straight-line present-worth factor
	$(1+i)^n$	$\dfrac{1}{(1+i)^n}$	$\dfrac{(1+i)^n-1}{i(1+i)^n}$	$\dfrac{i(1+i)^n}{(1+i)^n-1}$	$\dfrac{(1+i)^n}{(1+i)^n-1}$	$\dfrac{F_{RP}-nF_{SP}}{i}$	$\dfrac{n-F_{RP}}{0.5n(n+1)i}$	$\dfrac{1}{niF_{PX}}$
	P to S	S to P	R to P	P to R	P to K	G to P	SD to P	SL to P
n	F_{PS}	F_{SP}	F_{RP}	F_{PR}	F_{PK}	F_{GP}	F_{SDP}	F_{SLP}
1	1.2000E 00	8.3333E-01	8.3333E-01	1.2000E 00	6.0000E 00	1.0000E 00	8.3333E-01	8.3333E-01
2	1.4400E 00	6.9444E-01	1.5278E 00	6.5455E-01	3.2727E 00	6.9444E-01	7.8704E-01	7.6389E-01
3	1.7280E 00	5.7870E-01	2.1065E 00	4.7473E-01	2.3736E 00	1.8519E 00	7.4460E-01	7.0216E-01
4	2.0736E 00	4.8225E-01	2.5887E 00	3.8629E-01	1.9314E 00	3.2986E 00	7.0563E-01	6.4718E-01
5	2.4883E 00	4.0188E-01	2.9906E 00	3.3438E-01	1.6719E 00	4.9061E 00	6.6980E-01	5.9812E-01
6	2.9860E 00	3.3490E-01	3.3255E 00	3.0071E-01	1.5035E 00	6.5806E 00	6.3678E-01	5.5425E-01
7	3.5832E 00	2.7908E-01	3.6046E 00	2.7742E-01	1.3871E 00	8.2551E 00	6.0632E-01	5.1494E-01
8	4.2998E 00	2.3257E-01	3.8372E 00	2.6061E-01	1.3030E 00	9.8831E 00	5.7017E-01	4.7964E-01
9	5.1598E 00	1.9381E-01	4.0310E 00	2.4808E-01	1.2404E 00	1.1434E 01	5.5211E-01	4.4789E-01
10	6.1917E 00	1.6151E-01	4.1925E 00	2.3852E-01	1.1926E 00	1.2887E 01	5.2796E-01	4.1925E-01
11	7.4301E 00	1.3459E-01	4.3271E 00	2.3110E-01	1.1555E 00	1.4233E 01	5.0553E-01	3.9337E-01
12	8.9161E 00	1.1216E-01	4.4392E 00	2.2526E-01	1.1263E 00	1.5467E 01	4.8467E-01	3.6993E-01
13	1.0699E 01	9.3464E-02	4.5327E 00	2.2062E-01	1.1031E 00	1.6588E 01	4.6524E-01	3.4867E-01
14	1.2839E 01	7.7887E-02	4.6106E 00	2.1689E-01	1.0845E 00	1.7601E 01	4.4712E-01	3.2933E-01
15	1.5407E 01	6.4905E-02	4.6755E 00	2.1388E-01	1.0694E 00	1.8509E 01	4.3019E-01	3.1170E-01
16	1.8488E 01	5.4088E-02	4.7296E 00	2.1144E-01	1.0572E 00	1.9321E 01	4.1435E-01	2.9560E-01
18	2.6623E 01	3.7561E-02	4.8122E 00	2.0781E-01	1.0390E 00	2.0680E 01	3.8561E-01	2.6734E-01
20	3.8338E 01	2.6084E-02	4.8696E 00	2.0536E-01	1.0268E 00	2.1739E 01	3.6025E-01	2.4348E-01
25	9.5396E 01	1.0483E-02	4.9476E 00	2.0212E-01	1.0106E 00	2.3428E 01	3.0850E-01	1.9790E-01
30	2.3738E 02	4.2127E-03	4.9789E 00	2.0085E-01	1.0042E 00	2.4263E 01	2.6904E-01	1.6598E-01
35	5.9067E 02	1.6930E-03	4.9915E 00	2.0034E-01	1.0017E 00	2.4661E 01	2.3816E-01	1.4262E-01
40	1.4698E 03	6.8038E-04	4.9966E 00	2.0014E-01	1.0007E 00	2.4847E 01	2.1344E-01	1.2491E-01
45	3.6573E 03	2.7343E-04	4.9986E 00	2.0005E-01	1.0003E 00	2.4932E 01	1.9324E-01	1.1105E-01
50	9.1004E 03	1.0988E-04	4.9995E 00	2.0002E-01	1.0001E 00	2.4970E 01	1.7647E-01	9.9989E-02

Discrete compound interest = 25%

	Single payment		Uniform annual series			Uniform gradient series		Depreciation series	
	Compound-interest factor	Present-worth factor	Unacost present-worth factor	Capital-recovery factor	Capitalized-cost factor	Present-worth factor	Sum-of-digits present-worth factor	Straight-line present-worth factor	
	$(1+i)^n$	$\dfrac{1}{(1+i)^n}$	$\dfrac{(1+i)^n - 1}{i(1+i)^n}$	$\dfrac{i(1+i)^n}{(1+i)^n - 1}$	$\dfrac{(1+i)^n}{(1+i)^n - 1}$	$\dfrac{F_{RP} - nF_{SP}}{i}$	$\dfrac{n - F_{RP}}{0.5n(n+1)i}$	$\dfrac{1}{niF_{PK}}$
	P to S	S to P	R to P	P to R	P to K	G to P	SD to P	SL to P
n	F_{PS}	F_{SP}	F_{RP}	F_{PR}	F_{PK}	F_{GP}	F_{SDP}	F_{SLP}
1	1.2500E 00	8.0000E-01	8.0000E-01	1.2500E 00	5.0000E 00	1.0000E 00	8.0000E-01	8.0000E-01
2	1.5625E 00	6.4000E-01	1.4400E 00	6.9444E-01	2.7778E 00	6.4000E-01	7.4667E-01	7.2000E-01
3	1.9531E 00	5.1200E-01	1.9520E 00	5.1230E-01	2.0492E 00	1.6640E 00	6.9867E-01	6.5067E-01
4	2.4414E 00	4.0960E-01	2.3616E 00	4.2344E-01	1.6938E 00	2.8928E 00	6.5536E-01	5.9040E-01
5	3.0518E 00	3.2768E-01	2.6893E 00	3.7185E-01	1.4874E 00	4.2035E 00	6.1619E-01	5.3786E-01
6	3.8147E 00	2.6214E-01	2.9514E 00	3.3882E-01	1.3553E 00	5.5142E 00	5.8086E-01	4.9190E-01
7	4.7684E 00	2.0972E-01	3.1611E 00	3.1634E-01	1.2655E 00	6.7725E 00	5.4841E-01	4.5159E-01
8	5.9605E 00	1.6777E-01	3.3289E 00	3.0040E-01	1.2016E 00	7.9469E 00	5.1901E-01	4.1611E-01
9	7.4506E 00	1.3422E-01	3.4631E 00	2.8876E-01	1.1550E 00	9.0207E 00	4.9217E-01	3.8479E-01
10	9.3132E 00	1.0737E-01	3.5705E 00	2.8007E-01	1.1203E 00	9.9870E 00	4.6760E-01	3.5705E-01
11	1.1642E 01	8.5899E-02	3.6564E 00	2.7349E-01	1.0940E 00	1.0846E 01	4.4507E-01	3.3240E-01
12	1.4552E 01	6.8719E-02	3.7251E 00	2.6845E-01	1.0738E 00	1.1602E 01	4.2435E-01	3.1043E-01
13	1.8190E 01	5.4976E-02	3.7801E 00	2.6454E-01	1.0582E 00	1.2262E 01	4.0527E-01	2.9078E-01
14	2.2737E 01	4.3980E-02	3.8241E 00	2.6150E-01	1.0460E 00	1.2833E 01	3.8765E-01	2.7315E-01
15	2.8422E 01	3.5184E-02	3.8593E 00	2.5912E-01	1.0365E 00	1.3326E 01	3.7136E-01	2.5728E-01
16	3.5527E 01	2.8147E-02	3.8874E 00	2.5724E-01	1.0290E 00	1.3748E 01	3.5625E-01	2.4296E-01
18	5.5511E 01	1.8014E-02	3.9279E 00	2.5459E-01	1.0183E 00	1.4415E 01	3.2917E-01	2.1822E-01
20	8.6736E 01	1.1529E-02	3.9539E 00	2.5292E-01	1.0117E 00	1.4893E 01	3.0564E-01	1.9769E-01
25	2.6470E 02	3.7779E-03	3.9849E 00	2.5095E-01	1.0038E 00	1.5562E 01	2.5865E-01	1.5940E-01
30	8.0779E 02	1.2379E-03	3.9950E 00	2.5031E-01	1.0012E 00	1.5832E 01	2.2370E-01	1.3317E-01
35	2.4652E 03	4.0565E-04	3.9984E 00	2.5010E-01	1.0004E 00	1.5937E 01	1.9684E-01	1.1424E-01
40	7.5232E 03	1.3292E-04	3.9995E 00	2.5003E-01	1.0001E 00	1.5977E 01	1.7561E-01	9.9987E-02
45	2.2959E 04	4.3556E-05	3.9998E 00	2.5001E-01	1.0000E 00	1.5991E 01	1.5845E-01	8.8885E-02
50	7.0065E 04	1.4272E-05	3.9999E 00	2.5000E-01	1.0000E 00	1.5997E 01	1.4431E-01	7.9999E-02

Table I. *(continued)*

Discrete compound interest = 30%

	Single payment		Uniform annual series			Uniform gradient series		Depreciation series	
	Compound-interest factor	Present-worth factor	Unacost present-worth factor	Capital-recovery factor	Capitalized-cost factor	Present-worth factor	Sum-of-digits present-worth factor	Straight-line present-worth factor
	$(1+i)^n$	$\dfrac{1}{(1+i)^n}$	$\dfrac{(1+i)^n-1}{i(1+i)^n}$	$\dfrac{i(1+i)^n}{(1+i)^n-1}$	$\dfrac{(1+i)^n}{(1+i)^n-1}$	$\dfrac{F_{RP}-nF_{SP}}{i}$	$\dfrac{n-F_{RP}}{0.5n(n+1)i}$	$\dfrac{1}{niF_{PR}}$
	P to S	S to P	R to P	P to R	P to K	G to P	SD to P	SL to P
n	F_{PS}	F_{SP}	F_{RP}	F_{PR}	F_{PK}	F_{GP}	F_{SDP}	F_{SLP}
1	1.3000E 00	7.6923E-01	7.6923E-01	1.3000E 00	4.3333E 00	1.0000E 00	7.6923E-01	7.6923E-01
2	1.6900E 00	5.9172E-01	1.3609E 00	7.3478E-01	2.4493E 00	5.9172E-01	7.1005E-01	6.8047E-01
3	2.1970E 00	4.5517E-01	1.8161E 00	5.5063E-01	1.8354E 00	1.5020E 00	6.5772E-01	6.0537E-01
4	2.8561E 00	3.5013E-01	2.1662E 00	4.6163E-01	1.5388E 00	2.5524E 00	6.1125E-01	5.4156E-01
5	3.7129E 00	2.6933E-01	2.4356E 00	4.1058E-01	1.3686E 00	3.6297E 00	5.6987E-01	4.8711E-01
6	4.8268E 00	2.0718E-01	2.6427E 00	3.7839E-01	1.2613E 00	4.6656E 00	5.3290E-01	4.4046E-01
7	6.2749E 00	1.5937E-01	2.8021E 00	3.5687E-01	1.1896E 00	5.6218E 00	4.9975E-01	4.0030E-01
8	8.1573E 00	1.2259E-01	2.9247E 00	3.4192E-01	1.1397E 00	6.4800E 00	4.6994E-01	3.6559E-01
9	1.0604E 01	9.4300E-02	3.0190E 00	3.3124E-01	1.1041E 00	7.2343E 00	4.4304E-01	3.3544E-01
10	1.3786E 01	7.2538E-02	3.0915E 00	3.2346E-01	1.0782E 00	7.8872E 00	4.1869E-01	3.0915E-01
11	1.7922E 01	5.5799E-02	3.1473E 00	3.1773E-01	1.0591E 00	8.4452E 00	3.9660E-01	2.8612E-01
12	2.3298E 01	4.2922E-02	3.1903E 00	3.1345E-01	1.0448E 00	8.9173E 00	3.7648E-01	2.6586E-01
13	3.0288E 01	3.3017E-02	3.2233E 00	3.1024E-01	1.0341E 00	9.3135E 00	3.5812E-01	2.4794E-01
14	3.9374E 01	2.5398E-02	3.2487E 00	3.0782E-01	1.0261E 00	9.6437E 00	3.4131E-01	2.3205E-01
15	5.1186E 01	1.9537E-02	3.2682E 00	3.0598E-01	1.0199E 00	9.9172E 00	3.2588E-01	2.1788E-01
16	6.6542E 01	1.5028E-02	3.2832E 00	3.0458E-01	1.0153E 00	1.0143E 01	3.1169E-01	2.0520E-01
18	1.1246E 02	8.8924E-03	3.3037E 00	3.0269E-01	1.0090E 00	1.0479E 01	2.8648E-01	1.8354E-01
20	1.9005E 02	5.2618E-03	3.3158E 00	3.0159E-01	1.0053E 00	1.0702E 01	2.6483E-01	1.6579E-01
25	7.0564E 02	1.4172E-03	3.3286E 00	3.0043E-01	1.0014E 00	1.0977E 01	2.2227E-01	1.3314E-01
30	2.6200E 03	3.8168E-04	3.3320E 00	3.0012E-01	1.0004E 00	1.1069E 01	1.9117E-01	1.1107E-01
35	9.7279E 03	1.0280E-04	3.3330E 00	3.0003E-01	1.0001E 00	1.1098E 01	1.6755E-01	9.5228E-02
40	3.6119E 04	2.7686E-05	3.3332E 00	3.0001E-01	1.0000E 00	1.1107E 01	1.4905E-01	8.3331E-02
45	1.3411E 05	7.4567E-06	3.3333E 00	3.0000E-01	1.0000E 00	1.1110E 01	1.3419E-01	7.4074E-02
50	4.9793E 05	2.0083E-06	3.3333E 00	3.0000E-01	1.0000E 00	1.1111E 01	1.2200E-01	6.6667E-02

Discrete compound interest = 40%

	Single payment		Uniform annual series			Uniform gradient series		Depreciation series	
	Compound-interest factor	Present-worth factor	Unacost present-worth factor	Capital-recovery factor	Capitalized-cost factor	Present-worth factor	Sum-of-digits present-worth factor	Straight-line present-worth factor	
	$(1+i)^n$	$\dfrac{1}{(1+i)^n}$	$\dfrac{(1+i)^n - 1}{i(1+i)^n}$	$\dfrac{i(1+i)^n}{(1+i)^n - 1}$	$\dfrac{(1+i)^n}{(1+i)^n - 1}$	$\dfrac{F_{RP} - nF_{SP}}{i}$	$\dfrac{n - F_{RP}}{0.5n(n+1)i}$	$\dfrac{1}{niF_{PK}}$	
	P to S	S to P	R to P	P to R	P to K	G to P	SD to P	SL to P	
n	F_{PS}	F_{SP}	F_{RP}	F_{PR}	F_{PK}	F_{GP}	F_{SDP}	F_{SLP}	
1	1.4000E 00	7.1429E-01	7.1429E-01	1.4000E 00	3.5000E 00	1.0000E 00	7.1429E-01	7.1429E-01
2	1.9600E 00	5.1020E-01	1.2245E 00	8.1667E-01	2.0417E 00	5.1020E-01	6.4626E-01	6.1224E-01
3	2.7440E 00	3.6443E-01	1.5889E 00	6.2936E-01	1.5734E 00	1.2391E 00	5.8795E-01	5.2964E-01
4	3.8416E 00	2.6031E-01	1.8492E 00	5.4077E-01	1.3519E 00	2.0200E 00	5.3769E-01	4.6231E-01
5	5.3782E 00	1.8593E-01	2.0352E 00	4.9136E-01	1.2284E 00	2.7637E 00	4.9414E-01	4.0703E-01
6	7.5295E 00	1.3281E-01	2.1680E 00	4.6126E-01	1.1532E 00	3.4278E 00	4.5619E-01	3.6133E-01
7	1.0541E 01	9.4865E-02	2.2628E 00	4.4192E-01	1.1048E 00	3.9970E 00	4.2296E-01	3.2326E-01
8	1.4758E 01	6.7760E-02	2.3306E 00	4.2907E-01	1.0727E 00	4.4713E 00	3.9371E-01	2.9132E-01
9	2.0661E 01	4.8400E-02	2.3790E 00	4.2034E-01	1.0509E 00	4.8585E 00	3.6783E-01	2.6433E-01
10	2.8925E 01	3.4572E-02	2.4136E 00	4.1432E-01	1.0358E 00	5.1696E 00	3.4484E-01	2.4136E-01
11	4.0496E 01	2.4694E-02	2.4383E 00	4.1013E-01	1.0253E 00	5.4166E 00	3.2431E-01	2.2166E-01
12	5.6694E 01	1.7639E-02	2.4559E 00	4.0718E-01	1.0180E 00	5.6106E 00	3.0590E-01	2.0466E-01
13	7.9371E 01	1.2599E-02	2.4685E 00	4.0510E-01	1.0128E 00	5.7618E 00	2.8933E-01	1.8988E-01
14	1.1112E 02	8.9993E-03	2.4775E 00	4.0363E-01	1.0091E 00	5.8788E 00	2.7435E-01	1.7696E-01
15	1.5557E 02	6.4281E-03	2.4839E 00	4.0259E-01	1.0065E 00	5.9688E 00	2.6075E-01	1.6560E-01
16	2.1780E 02	4.5915E-03	2.4885E 00	4.0185E-01	1.0046E 00	6.0376E 00	2.4837E-01	1.5553E-01
18	4.2688E 02	2.3426E-03	2.4941E 00	4.0094E-01	1.0023E 00	6.1299E 00	2.2669E-01	1.3856E-01
20	8.3668E 02	1.1952E-03	2.4970E 00	4.0048E-01	1.0012E 00	6.1828E 00	2.0837E-01	1.2485E-01
25	4.4999E 03	2.2223E-04	2.4994E 00	4.0009E-01	1.0002E 00	6.2347E 00	1.7308E-01	9.9978E-02
30	2.4201E 04	4.1320E-05	2.4999E 00	4.0002E-01	1.0000E 00	6.2466E 00	1.4765E-01	8.3330E-02
35	1.3016E 05	7.6824E-06	2.5000E 00	4.0000E-01	1.0000E 00	6.2493E 00	1.2897E-01	7.1428E-02
40	7.0004E 05	1.4285E-06	2.5000E 00	4.0000E-01	1.0000E 00	6.2498E 00	1.1433E-01	6.2500E-02
45	3.7650E 06	2.6561E-07	2.5000E 00	4.0000E-01	1.0000E 00	6.2500E 00	1.0266E-01	5.5556E-02
50	2.0249E 07	4.9385E-08	2.5000E 00	4.0000E-01	1.0000E 00	6.2500E 00	9.3137E-02	5.0000E-02

Table I. (continued)

Discrete compound interest = 50%

	Single payment		Uniform annual series				Uniform gradient series	Depreciation series	
	Compound-interest factor $(1+i)^n$ $P \text{ to } S$ F_{PS}	Present-worth factor $\dfrac{1}{(1+i)^n}$ $S \text{ to } P$ F_{SP}	Unacost present-worth factor $\dfrac{(1+i)^n - 1}{i(1+i)^n}$ $R \text{ to } P$ F_{RP}	Capital-recovery factor $\dfrac{i(1+i)^n}{(1+i)^n - 1}$ $P \text{ to } R$ F_{PR}	Capitalized-cost factor $\dfrac{(1+i)^n}{(1+i)^n - 1}$ $P \text{ to } K$ F_{PK}	Present-worth factor $\dfrac{F_{RP} - nF_{SP}}{i}$ $G \text{ to } P$ F_{GP}	Sum-of-digits present-worth factor $\dfrac{n - F_{RP}}{0.5n(n+1)i}$ $SD \text{ to } P$ F_{SDP}	Straight-line present-worth factor $\dfrac{1}{niF_{PR}}$ $SL \text{ to } P$ F_{SLP}
n								
1	1.5000E 00	6.6667E-01	6.6667E-01	1.5000E 00	3.0000E 00	1.0000E 00	6.6667E-01	6.6667E-01
2	2.2500E 00	4.4444E-01	1.1111E 00	9.0000E-01	1.8000E 00	4.4444E-01	5.9259E-01	5.5556E-01
3	3.3750E 00	2.9630E-01	1.4074E 00	7.1053E-01	1.4211E 00	1.0370E 00	5.3086E-01	4.6914E-01
4	5.0625E 00	1.9753E-01	1.6049E 00	6.2308E-01	1.2462E 00	1.6296E 00	4.7901E-01	4.0123E-01
5	7.5938E 00	1.3169E-01	1.7366E 00	5.7583E-01	1.1517E 00	2.1564E 00	4.3512E-01	3.4733E-01
6	1.1391E 01	8.7791E-02	1.8244E 00	5.4812E-01	1.0962E 00	2.5953E 00	3.9767E-01	3.0407E-01
7	1.7086E 01	5.8528E-02	1.8829E 00	5.3108E-01	1.0622E 00	2.9465E 00	3.6550E-01	2.6899E-01
8	2.5629E 01	3.9018E-02	1.9220E 00	5.2030E-01	1.0406E 00	3.2196E 00	3.3767E-01	2.4025E-01
9	3.8443E 01	2.6012E-02	1.9480E 00	5.1335E-01	1.0267E 00	3.4277E 00	3.1342E-01	2.1644E-01
10	5.7665E 01	1.7342E-02	1.9653E 00	5.0882E-01	1.0176E 00	3.5838E 00	2.9217E-01	1.9653E-01
11	8.6498E 01	1.1561E-02	1.9769E 00	5.0585E-01	1.0117E 00	3.6994E 00	2.7343E-01	1.7972E-01
12	1.2975E 02	7.7073E-03	1.9846E 00	5.0388E-01	1.0078E 00	3.7842E 00	2.5681E-01	1.6538E-01
13	1.9462E 02	5.1382E-03	1.9897E 00	5.0258E-01	1.0052E 00	3.8459E 00	2.4198E-01	1.5306E-01
14	2.9193E 02	3.4255E-03	1.9931E 00	5.0172E-01	1.0034E 00	3.8904E 00	2.2870E-01	1.4237E-01
15	4.3789E 02	2.2837E-03	1.9954E 00	5.0114E-01	1.0023E 00	3.9224E 00	2.1674E-01	1.3303E-01
16	6.5684E 02	1.5224E-03	1.9970E 00	5.0076E-01	1.0015E 00	3.9452E 00	2.0593E-01	1.2481E-01
18	1.4779E 03	6.7664E-04	1.9986E 00	5.0034E-01	1.0007E 00	3.9729E 00	1.8715E-01	1.1104E-01
20	3.3253E 03	3.0073E-04	1.9994E 00	5.0015E-01	1.0003E 00	3.9868E 00	1.7143E-01	9.9970E-02
25	2.5251E 04	3.9602E-05	1.9999E 00	5.0002E-01	1.0000E 00	3.9979E 00	1.4154E-01	7.9997E-02
30	1.9175E 05	5.2151E-06	2.0000E 00	5.0000E-01	1.0000E 00	3.9997E 00	1.2043E-01	6.6666E-02
35	1.4561E 06	6.8676E-07	2.0000E 00	5.0000E-01	1.0000E 00	3.9999E 00	1.0476E-01	5.7143E-02
40	1.1057E 07	9.0438E-08	2.0000E 00	5.0000E-01	1.0000E 00	4.0000E 00	9.2683E-02	5.0000E-02
45	8.3967E 07	1.1909E-08	2.0000E 00	5.0000E-01	1.0000E 00	4.0000E 00	8.3092E-02	4.4444E-02
50	6.3762E 08	1.5683E-09	2.0000E 00	5.0000E-01	1.0000E 00	4.0000E 00	7.5294E-02	4.0000E-02

Table 2.

$F_{PS} = (1+i)^n$ Large i

n	35%	45%	55%	60%	70%	80%	90%	100%
1	1.3500E 00	1.4500E 00	1.5500E 00	1.6000E 00	1.7000E 00	1.8000E 00	1.9000E 00	2.0000E 00
2	1.8225E 00	2.1025E 00	2.4025E 00	2.5600E 00	2.8900E 00	3.2400E 00	3.6100E 00	4.0000E 00
3	2.4604E 00	3.0486E 00	3.7239E 00	4.0960E 00	4.9130E 00	5.8320E 00	6.8590E 00	8.0000E 00
4	3.3215E 00	4.4205E 00	5.7720E 00	6.5536E 00	8.3521E 00	1.0498E 01	1.3032E 01	1.6000E 01
5	4.4840E 00	6.4097E 00	8.9466E 00	1.0486E 01	1.4199E 01	1.8896E 01	2.4761E 01	3.2000E 01
6	6.0534E 00	9.2941E 00	1.3867E 01	1.6777E 01	2.4138E 01	3.4012E 01	4.7046E 01	6.4000E 01
7	8.1722E 00	1.3476E 01	2.1494E 01	2.6844E 01	4.1034E 01	6.1222E 01	8.9387E 01	1.2800E 02
8	1.1032E 01	1.9541E 01	3.3316E 01	4.2950E 01	6.9758E 01	1.1020E 02	1.6984E 02	2.5600E 02
9	1.4894E 01	2.8334E 01	5.1640E 01	6.8719E 01	1.1859E 02	1.9836E 02	3.2269E 02	5.1200E 02
10	2.0107E 01	4.1085E 01	8.0042E 01	1.0995E 02	2.0160E 02	3.5705E 02	6.1311E 02	1.0240E 03
11	2.7144E 01	5.9573E 01	1.2406E 02	1.7592E 02	3.4272E 02	6.4268E 02	1.1649E 03	2.0480E 03
12	3.6644E 01	8.6381E 01	1.9230E 02	2.8147E 02	5.8262E 02	1.1568E 03	2.2133E 03	4.0960E 03
13	4.9470E 01	1.2525E 02	2.9807E 02	4.5036E 02	9.9046E 02	2.0823E 03	4.2053E 03	8.1920E 03
14	6.6784E 01	1.8162E 02	4.6200E 02	7.2058E 02	1.6838E 03	3.7481E 03	7.9901E 03	1.6384E 04
15	9.0158E 01	2.6334E 02	7.1610E 02	1.1529E 03	2.8624E 03	6.7466E 03	1.5181E 04	3.2768E 04
16	1.2171E 02	3.8185E 02	1.1100E 03	1.8447E 03	4.8661E 03	1.2144E 04	2.8844E 04	6.5536E 04
18	2.2182E 02	8.0283E 02	2.6667E 03	4.7224E 03	1.4063E 04	3.9346E 04	1.0413E 05	2.0214E 05
20	4.0427E 02	1.6880E 03	6.4067E 03	1.2089E 04	4.0642E 04	1.2748E 05	3.7590E 05	1.0486E 06
25	1.8128E 03	1.0819E 04	5.7318E 04	1.2677E 05	5.7706E 05	2.4089E 06	9.3076E 06	3.3554E 07
30	8.1285E 03	6.9349E 04	5.1280E 05	1.3292E 06	8.1935E 06	4.5517E 07	2.3047E 08	1.0737E 09
35	3.6449E 04	4.4451E 05	4.5879E 06	1.3938E 07	1.1634E 08	8.6008E 08	5.7066E 09	3.4360E 10
40	1.6344E 05	2.8492E 06	4.1046E 07	1.4615E 08	1.6518E 09	1.6252E 10	1.4130E 11	1.0995E 12
45	7.3286E 05	1.8262E 07	3.6722E 08	1.5326E 09	2.3453E 10	3.0709E 11	3.4987E 12	3.5184E 13
50	3.2862E 06	1.1706E 08	3.2854E 09	1.6069E 10	3.3300E 11	5.8026E 12	8.6632E 13	1.1259E 15

Table 3.

$F_{SP} = (1+i)^{-n}$ Large i

n	35 %	45%	55%	60%	70%	80%	90%	100%
1	7.4074E-01	6.8966E-01	6.4516E-01	6.2500E-01	5.8824E-01	5.5556E-01	5.2632E-01	5.0000E-01
2	5.4870E-01	4.7562E-01	4.1623E-01	3.9063E-01	3.4602E-01	3.0864E-01	2.7701E-01	2.5000E-01
3	4.0644E-01	3.2802E-01	2.6854E-01	2.4414E-01	2.0354E-01	1.7147E-01	1.4579E-01	1.2500E-01
4	3.0107E-01	2.2622E-01	1.7325E-01	1.5259E-01	1.1973E-01	9.5260E-02	7.6734E-02	6.2500E-02
5	2.2301E-01	1.5601E-01	1.1177E-01	9.5367E-02	7.0430E-02	5.2922E-02	4.0386E-02	3.1250E-02
6	1.6520E-01	1.0759E-01	7.2112E-02	5.9605E-02	4.1429E-02	2.9401E-02	2.1256E-02	1.5625E-02
7	1.2237E-01	7.4203E-02	4.6524E-02	3.7253E-02	2.4370E-02	1.6334E-02	1.1187E-02	7.8125E-03
8	9.0642E-02	5.1175E-02	3.0016E-02	2.3283E-02	1.4335E-02	9.0744E-03	5.8880E-03	3.9063E-03
9	6.7142E-02	3.5293E-02	1.9365E-02	1.4552E-02	8.4326E-03	5.0414E-03	3.0990E-03	1.9531E-03
10	4.9735E-02	2.4340E-02	1.2493E-02	9.0949E-03	4.9603E-03	2.8008E-03	1.6310E-03	9.7656E-04
11	3.6841E-02	1.6786E-02	8.0603E-03	5.6843E-03	2.9178E-03	1.5560E-03	8.5844E-04	4.8828E-04
12	2.7289E-02	1.1577E-02	5.2002E-03	3.5527E-03	1.7164E-03	8.6443E-04	4.5181E-04	2.4414E-04
13	2.0214E-02	7.9839E-03	3.3550E-03	2.2204E-03	1.0096E-03	4.8024E-04	2.3780E-04	1.2207E-04
14	1.4974E-02	5.5061E-03	2.1645E-03	1.3878E-03	5.9390E-04	2.6680E-04	1.2516E-04	6.1035E-05
15	1.1092E-02	3.7973E-03	1.3964E-03	8.6736E-04	3.4935E-04	1.4822E-04	6.5871E-05	3.0518E-05
16	8.2160E-03	2.6189E-03	9.0093E-04	5.4210E-04	2.0550E-04	8.2346E-05	3.4669E-05	1.5259E-05
18	4.5081E-03	1.2450E-03	3.7500E-04	2.1176E-04	7.1108E-05	2.5415E-05	9.6036E-06	3.8147E-06
20	2.4736E-03	5.9243E-04	1.5609E-04	8.2718E-05	2.4605E-05	7.8442E-06	2.6603E-06	9.5367E-07
25	5.5164E-04	9.2427E-05	1.7446E-05	7.8886E-06	1.7329E-06	4.1513E-07	1.0744E-07	2.9802E-08
30	1.2302E-04	1.4420E-05	1.9501E-06	7.5232E-07	1.2205E-07	2.1970E-08	4.3390E-09	9.3132E-10
35	2.7435E-05	2.2497E-06	2.1797E-07	7.1746E-08	8.5958E-09	1.1627E-09	1.7524E-10	2.9104E-11
40	6.1186E-06	3.5098E-07	2.4363E-08	6.8423E-09	6.0540E-10	6.1532E-11	7.0771E-12	9.0949E-13
45	1.3645E-06	5.4757E-08	2.7237E-09	6.5253E-10	4.2638E-11	3.2564E-12	2.8542E-13	2.8422E-14
50	3.0431E-07	8.5428E-09	3.0438E-10	6.2230E-11	3.0030E-12	1.7234E-13	1.1543E-14	8.8818E-16

Table 4. Discrete Compound Interest with Negative Rate

$F_{PS,\ p,n} = (1-p)^n$

n	1%	2%	3%	4%	5%	6%	8%	10%	12%
1	9.9000E-01	9.8000E-01	9.7000E-01	9.6000E-01	9.5000E-01	9.4000E-01	9.2000E-01	9.0000E-01	8.8000E-01
2	9.8010E-01	9.6040E-01	9.4090E-01	9.2160E-01	9.0250E-01	8.8360E-01	8.4640E-01	8.1000E-01	7.7440E-01
3	9.7030E-01	9.4119E-01	9.1267E-01	8.8474E-01	8.5738E-01	8.3058E-01	7.7869E-01	7.2900E-01	6.8147E-01
4	9.6060E-01	9.2237E-01	8.8529E-01	8.4935E-01	8.1451E-01	7.8075E-01	7.1639E-01	6.5610E-01	5.9970E-01
5	9.5099E-01	9.0392E-01	8.5873E-01	8.1537E-01	7.7378E-01	7.3390E-01	6.5908E-01	5.9049E-01	5.2773E-01
6	9.4148E-01	8.8584E-01	8.3297E-01	7.8276E-01	7.3509E-01	6.8987E-01	6.0636E-01	5.3144E-01	4.6440E-01
7	9.3207E-01	8.6813E-01	8.0798E-01	7.5145E-01	6.9834E-01	6.4848E-01	5.5785E-01	4.7830E-01	4.0868E-01
8	9.2274E-01	8.5076E-01	7.8374E-01	7.2139E-01	6.6342E-01	6.0957E-01	5.1322E-01	4.3047E-01	3.5963E-01
9	9.1352E-01	8.3375E-01	7.6023E-01	6.9253E-01	6.3025E-01	5.7299E-01	4.7216E-01	3.8742E-01	3.1648E-01
10	9.0438E-01	8.1707E-01	7.3742E-01	6.6483E-01	5.9874E-01	5.3862E-01	4.3439E-01	3.4868E-01	2.7850E-01
11	8.9534E-01	8.0073E-01	7.1530E-01	6.3824E-01	5.6880E-01	5.0630E-01	3.9964E-01	3.1381E-01	2.4508E-01
12	8.8638E-01	7.8472E-01	6.9384E-01	6.1271E-01	5.4036E-01	4.7592E-01	3.6767E-01	2.8243E-01	2.1567E-01
13	8.7752E-01	7.6902E-01	6.7303E-01	5.8820E-01	5.1334E-01	4.4737E-01	3.3825E-01	2.5419E-01	1.8979E-01
14	8.6875E-01	7.5364E-01	6.5284E-01	5.6467E-01	4.8767E-01	4.2052E-01	3.1119E-01	2.2877E-01	1.6702E-01
15	8.6006E-01	7.3857E-01	6.3325E-01	5.4209E-01	4.6329E-01	3.9529E-01	2.8630E-01	2.0589E-01	1.4697E-01
16	8.5146E-01	7.2380E-01	6.1425E-01	5.2040E-01	4.4013E-01	3.7157E-01	2.6339E-01	1.8530E-01	1.2934E-01
18	8.3451E-01	6.9514E-01	5.7795E-01	4.7960E-01	3.9721E-01	3.2832E-01	2.2294E-01	1.5009E-01	1.0016E-01
20	8.1791E-01	6.6761E-01	5.4379E-01	4.4200E-01	3.5849E-01	2.9011E-01	1.8869E-01	1.2158E-01	7.7563E-02
25	7.7782E-01	6.0346E-01	4.6697E-01	3.6040E-01	2.7739E-01	2.1291E-01	1.2436E-01	7.1790E-02	4.0932E-02
30	7.3970E-01	5.4548E-01	4.0101E-01	2.9386E-01	2.1464E-01	1.5626E-01	8.1966E-02	4.2391E-02	2.1601E-02
35	7.0345E-01	4.9307E-01	3.4436E-01	2.3960E-01	1.6608E-01	1.1468E-01	5.4022E-02	2.5032E-02	1.1400E-02
40	6.6897E-01	4.4570E-01	2.9571E-01	1.9537E-01	1.2851E-01	8.4162E-02	3.5605E-02	1.4781E-02	6.0160E-03
45	6.3619E-01	4.0288E-01	2.5394E-01	1.5930E-01	9.9440E-02	6.1767E-02	2.3467E-02	8.7240E-03	3.1748E-03
50	6.0501E-01	3.6417E-01	2.1807E-01	1.2989E-01	7.6945E-02	4.5331E-02	1.5466E-02	5.1538E-03	1.6755E-03

Appendix 2
Continuous Compound Interest

Table I. Continuous Compound Interest

$F_{PS,i,n} = e^{in}$

in ↓ →	.00	.01	.02	.03	.04	.05	.06	.07	.08	.09
0	1.0000E 00	1.0101E 00	1.0202E 00	1.0305E 00	1.0408E 00	1.0513E 00	1.0618E 00	1.0725E 00	1.0833E 00	1.0942E 00
.1	1.1052E 00	1.1163E 00	1.1275E 00	1.1388E 00	1.1503E 00	1.1618E 00	1.1735E 00	1.1853E 00	1.1972E 00	1.2092E 00
.2	1.2214E 00	1.2337E 00	1.2461E 00	1.2586E 00	1.2712E 00	1.2840E 00	1.2969E 00	1.3100E 00	1.3231E 00	1.3364E 00
.3	1.3499E 00	1.3634E 00	1.3771E 00	1.3910E 00	1.4049E 00	1.4191E 00	1.4333E 00	1.4477E 00	1.4623E 00	1.4770E 00
.4	1.4918E 00	1.5068E 00	1.5220E 00	1.5373E 00	1.5527E 00	1.5683E 00	1.5841E 00	1.6000E 00	1.6161E 00	1.6323E 00
.5	1.6487E 00	1.6653E 00	1.6820E 00	1.6989E 00	1.7160E 00	1.7333E 00	1.7507E 00	1.7683E 00	1.7860E 00	1.8040E 00
.6	1.8221E 00	1.8404E 00	1.8589E 00	1.8776E 00	1.8965E 00	1.9155E 00	1.9348E 00	1.9542E 00	1.9739E 00	1.9937E 00
.7	2.0138E 00	2.0340E 00	2.0544E 00	2.0751E 00	2.0959E 00	2.1170E 00	2.1383E 00	2.1598E 00	2.1815E 00	2.2034E 00
.8	2.2255E 00	2.2479E 00	2.2705E 00	2.2933E 00	2.3164E 00	2.3396E 00	2.3632E 00	2.3869E 00	2.4109E 00	2.4351E 00
.9	2.4596E 00	2.4843E 00	2.5093E 00	2.5345E 00	2.5600E 00	2.5857E 00	2.6117E 00	2.6379E 00	2.6645E 00	2.6912E 00
1.0	2.7183E 00	2.7456E 00	2.7732E 00	2.8011E 00	2.8292E 00	2.8577E 00	2.8864E 00	2.9154E 00	2.9447E 00	2.9743E 00
1.1	3.0042E 00	3.0344E 00	3.0649E 00	3.0957E 00	3.1268E 00	3.1582E 00	3.1899E 00	3.2220E 00	3.2544E 00	3.2871E 00
1.2	3.3201E 00	3.3535E 00	3.3872E 00	3.4212E 00	3.4556E 00	3.4903E 00	3.5254E 00	3.5609E 00	3.5966E 00	3.6328E 00
1.3	3.6693E 00	3.7062E 00	3.7434E 00	3.7810E 00	3.8190E 00	3.8574E 00	3.8962E 00	3.9354E 00	3.9749E 00	4.0149E 00
1.4	4.0552E 00	4.0960E 00	4.1371E 00	4.1787E 00	4.2207E 00	4.2631E 00	4.3060E 00	4.3492E 00	4.3929E 00	4.4371E 00
1.5	4.4817E 00	4.5267E 00	4.5722E 00	4.6182E 00	4.6646E 00	4.7115E 00	4.7588E 00	4.8066E 00	4.8550E 00	4.9037E 00
1.6	4.9530E 00	5.0028E 00	5.0531E 00	5.1039E 00	5.1552E 00	5.2070E 00	5.2593E 00	5.3122E 00	5.3656E 00	5.4195E 00
1.7	5.4739E 00	5.5290E 00	5.5845E 00	5.6407E 00	5.6973E 00	5.7546E 00	5.8124E 00	5.8709E 00	5.9299E 00	5.9895E 00
1.8	6.0496E 00	6.1104E 00	6.1719E 00	6.2339E 00	6.2965E 00	6.3598E 00	6.4237E 00	6.4883E 00	6.5535E 00	6.6194E 00
1.9	6.6859E 00	6.7531E 00	6.8210E 00	6.8895E 00	6.9588E 00	7.0287E 00	7.0993E 00	7.1707E 00	7.2427E 00	7.3155E 00
2.0	7.3891E 00	7.4633E 00	7.5383E 00	7.6141E 00	7.6906E 00	7.7679E 00	7.8460E 00	7.9248E 00	8.0045E 00	8.0849E 00

Table I. (*continued*)

$F_{PS, i, n} = e^{in}$

in ↓	.00	.01	.02	.03	.04	.05	.06	.07	.08	.09
2.1	8.1662E 00	8.2482E 00	8.3311E 00	8.4149E 00	8.4994E 00	8.5849E 00	8.6711E 00	8.7583E 00	8.8463E 00	8.9352E 00
2.2	9.0250E 00	9.1157E 00	9.2073E 00	9.2999E 00	9.3933E 00	9.4877E 00	9.5831E 00	9.6794E 00	9.7767E 00	9.8749E 00
2.3	9.9742E 00	1.0074E 01	1.0176E 01	1.0278E 01	1.0381E 01	1.0486E 01	1.0591E 01	1.0697E 01	1.0805E 01	1.0913E 01
2.4	1.1023E 01	1.1134E 01	1.1246E 01	1.1359E 01	1.1473E 01	1.1588E 01	1.1705E 01	1.1822E 01	1.1941E 01	1.2061E 01
2.5	1.2182E 01	1.2305E 01	1.2429E 01	1.2554E 01	1.2680E 01	1.2807E 01	1.2936E 01	1.3066E 01	1.3197E 01	1.3330E 01
2.6	1.3464E 01	1.3599E 01	1.3736E 01	1.3874E 01	1.4013E 01	1.4154E 01	1.4296E 01	1.4440E 01	1.4585E 01	1.4732E 01
2.7	1.4880E 01	1.5029E 01	1.5180E 01	1.5333E 01	1.5487E 01	1.5643E 01	1.5800E 01	1.5959E 01	1.6119E 01	1.6281E 01
2.8	1.6445E 01	1.6610E 01	1.6777E 01	1.6945E 01	1.7116E 01	1.7288E 01	1.7462E 01	1.7637E 01	1.7814E 01	1.7993E 01
2.9	1.8174E 01	1.8357E 01	1.8541E 01	1.8728E 01	1.8916E 01	1.9106E 01	1.9298E 01	1.9492E 01	1.9688E 01	1.9886E 01
3.0	2.0086E 01	2.0287E 01	2.0491E 01	2.0697E 01	2.0905E 01	2.1115E 01	2.1328E 01	2.1542E 01	2.1758E 01	2.1977E 01
3.1	2.2198E 01	2.2421E 01	2.2646E 01	2.2874E 01	2.3104E 01	2.3336E 01	2.3571E 01	2.3807E 01	2.4047E 01	2.4288E 01
3.2	2.4533E 01	2.4779E 01	2.5028E 01	2.5280E 01	2.5534E 01	2.5790E 01	2.6050E 01	2.6311E 01	2.6576E 01	2.6843E 01
3.3	2.7113E 01	2.7385E 01	2.7660E 01	2.7938E 01	2.8219E 01	2.8503E 01	2.8789E 01	2.9079E 01	2.9371E 01	2.9666E 01
3.4	2.9964E 01	3.0265E 01	3.0569E 01	3.0877E 01	3.1187E 01	3.1500E 01	3.1817E 01	3.2137E 01	3.2460E 01	3.2786E 01
3.5	3.3115E 01	3.3448E 01	3.3784E 01	3.4124E 01	3.4467E 01	3.4813E 01	3.5163E 01	3.5517E 01	3.5874E 01	3.6234E 01
3.6	3.6598E 01	3.6966E 01	3.7338E 01	3.7713E 01	3.8092E 01	3.8475E 01	3.8861E 01	3.9252E 01	3.9646E 01	4.0045E 01
3.7	4.0447E 01	4.0854E 01	4.1264E 01	4.1679E 01	4.2098E 01	4.2521E 01	4.2948E 01	4.3380E 01	4.3816E 01	4.4256E 01
3.8	4.4701E 01	4.5150E 01	4.5604E 01	4.6063E 01	4.6525E 01	4.6993E 01	4.7465E 01	4.7942E 01	4.8424E 01	4.8911E 01
3.9	4.9402E 01	4.9899E 01	5.0400E 01	5.0907E 01	5.1419E 01	5.1935E 01	5.2457E 01	5.2985E 01	5.3517E 01	5.4055E 01
4.0	5.4598E 01	5.5147E 01	5.5701E 01	5.6261E 01	5.6826E 01	5.7397E 01	5.7974E 01	5.8557E 01	5.9145E 01	5.9740E 01
4.1	6.0340E 01	6.0947E 01	6.1559E 01	6.2178E 01	6.2803E 01	6.3434E 01	6.4072E 01	6.4715E 01	6.5366E 01	6.6023E 01

$F_{PS,i,n} = e^{in}$

in ↓	.00	.01	.02	.03	.04	.05	.06	.07	.08	.09
4.2	6.6686E 01	6.7357E 01	6.8033E 01	6.8717E 01	6.9408E 01	7.0105E 01	7.0810E 01	7.1522E 01	7.2240E 01	7.2966E 01
4.3	7.3700E 01	7.4440E 01	7.5189E 01	7.5944E 01	7.6708E 01	7.7478E 01	7.8257E 01	7.9044E 01	7.9838E 01	8.0640E 01
4.4	8.1451E 01	8.2269E 01	8.3096E 01	8.3931E 01	8.4775E 01	8.5627E 01	8.6488E 01	8.7357E 01	8.8235E 01	8.9121E 01
4.5	9.0017E 01	9.0922E 01	9.1836E 01	9.2759E 01	9.3691E 01	9.4632E 01	9.5583E 01	9.6544E 01	9.7514E 01	9.8494E 01
4.6	9.9484E 01	1.0048E 02	1.0149E 02	1.0251E 02	1.0354E 02	1.0458E 02	1.0564E 02	1.0670E 02	1.0777E 02	1.0885E 02
4.7	1.0995E 02	1.1105E 02	1.1217E 02	1.1330E 02	1.1443E 02	1.1558E 02	1.1675E 02	1.1792E 02	1.1910E 02	1.2030E 02
4.8	1.2151E 02	1.2273E 02	1.2397E 02	1.2521E 02	1.2647E 02	1.2774E 02	1.2902E 02	1.3032E 02	1.3163E 02	1.3295E 02
4.9	1.3429E 02	1.3564E 02	1.3700E 02	1.3838E 02	1.3977E 02	1.4117E 02	1.4259E 02	1.4403E 02	1.4547E 02	1.4694E 02
in ↓	.0	.1	.2	.3	.4	.5	.6	.7	.8	.9
5.0	1.4841E 02	1.6402E 02	1.8127E 02	2.0034E 02	2.2141E 02	2.4469E 02	2.7043E 02	2.9887E 02	3.3030E 02	3.6504E 02
6.0	4.0343E 02	4.4586E 02	4.9275E 02	5.4457E 02	6.0185E 02	6.6514E 02	7.3510E 02	8.1241E 02	8.9785E 02	9.9227E 02
7.0	1.0966E 03	1.2120E 03	1.3394E 03	1.4803E 03	1.6360E 03	1.8080E 03	1.9982E 03	2.2083E 03	2.4406E 03	2.6973E 03
8.0	2.9810E 03	3.2945E 03	3.6410E 03	4.0239E 03	4.4471E 03	4.9148E 03	5.4317E 03	6.0029E 03	6.6342E 03	7.3320E 03
9.0	8.1031E 03	8.9553E 03	9.8971E 03	1.0938E 04	1.2088E 04	1.3360E 04	1.4765E 04	1.6318E 04	1.8034E 04	1.9930E 04
10.0	2.2026E 04	2.4343E 04	2.6903E 04	2.9733E 04	3.2860E 04	3.6316E 04	4.0135E 04	4.4356E 04	4.9021E 04	5.4176E 04

Table 2. Continuous Compound Interest: Value of

$$F_{SP,in} = e^{-in}$$

in ↓	.00	.01	.02	.03	.04	.05	.06	.07	.08	.09
0	1.0000E 00	9.9005E-01	9.8020E-01	9.7045E-01	9.6079E-01	9.5123E-01	9.4176E-01	9.3239E-01	9.2312E-01	9.1393E-01
.1	9.0484E-01	8.9583E-01	8.8692E-01	8.7810E-01	8.6936E-01	8.6071E-01	8.5214E-01	8.4366E-01	8.3527E-01	8.2696E-01
.2	8.1873E-01	8.1058E-01	8.0252E-01	7.9453E-01	7.8663E-01	7.7880E-01	7.7105E-01	7.6338E-01	7.5578E-01	7.4826E-01
.3	7.4082E-01	7.3345E-01	7.2615E-01	7.1892E-01	7.1177E-01	7.0469E-01	6.9768E-01	6.9073E-01	6.8386E-01	6.7706E-01
.4	6.7032E-01	6.6365E-01	6.5705E-01	6.5051E-01	6.4404E-01	6.3763E-01	6.3128E-01	6.2500E-01	6.1878E-01	6.1263E-01
.5	6.0653E-01	6.0050E-01	5.9452E-01	5.8860E-01	5.8275E-01	5.7695E-01	5.7121E-01	5.6553E-01	5.5990E-01	5.5433E-01
.6	5.4881E-01	5.4335E-01	5.3794E-01	5.3259E-01	5.2729E-01	5.2205E-01	5.1685E-01	5.1171E-01	5.0662E-01	5.0158E-01
.7	4.9659E-01	4.9164E-01	4.8675E-01	4.8191E-01	4.7711E-01	4.7237E-01	4.6767E-01	4.6301E-01	4.5841E-01	4.5384E-01
.8	4.4933E-01	4.4486E-01	4.4043E-01	4.3605E-01	4.3171E-01	4.2741E-01	4.2316E-01	4.1895E-01	4.1478E-01	4.1066E-01
.9	4.0657E-01	4.0252E-01	3.9852E-01	3.9455E-01	3.9063E-01	3.8674E-01	3.8289E-01	3.7908E-01	3.7531E-01	3.7158E-01
1.0	3.6788E-01	3.6422E-01	3.6059E-01	3.5701E-01	3.5345E-01	3.4994E-01	3.4646E-01	3.4301E-01	3.3960E-01	3.3622E-01
1.1	3.3287E-01	3.2956E-01	3.2628E-01	3.2303E-01	3.1982E-01	3.1664E-01	3.1349E-01	3.1037E-01	3.0728E-01	3.0422E-01
1.2	3.0119E-01	2.9820E-01	2.9523E-01	2.9229E-01	2.8938E-01	2.8650E-01	2.8365E-01	2.8083E-01	2.7804E-01	2.7527E-01
1.3	2.7253E-01	2.6982E-01	2.6714E-01	2.6448E-01	2.6185E-01	2.5924E-01	2.5666E-01	2.5411E-01	2.5158E-01	2.4908E-01
1.4	2.4660E-01	2.4414E-01	2.4171E-01	2.3931E-01	2.3693E-01	2.3457E-01	2.3224E-01	2.2993E-01	2.2764E-01	2.2537E-01
1.5	2.2313E-01	2.2091E-01	2.1871E-01	2.1654E-01	2.1438E-01	2.1225E-01	2.1014E-01	2.0805E-01	2.0598E-01	2.0393E-01
1.6	2.0190E-01	1.9989E-01	1.9790E-01	1.9593E-01	1.9398E-01	1.9205E-01	1.9014E-01	1.8825E-01	1.8637E-01	1.8452E-01
1.7	1.8268E-01	1.8087E-01	1.7907E-01	1.7728E-01	1.7552E-01	1.7377E-01	1.7204E-01	1.7033E-01	1.6864E-01	1.6696E-01
1.8	1.6530E-01	1.6365E-01	1.6203E-01	1.6041E-01	1.5882E-01	1.5724E-01	1.5567E-01	1.5412E-01	1.5259E-01	1.5107E-01
1.9	1.4957E-01	1.4808E-01	1.4661E-01	1.4515E-01	1.4370E-01	1.4227E-01	1.4086E-01	1.3946E-01	1.3807E-01	1.3670E-01
2.0	1.3534E-01	1.3399E-01	1.3266E-01	1.3134E-01	1.3003E-01	1.2873E-01	1.2745E-01	1.2619E-01	1.2493E-01	1.2369E-01

$F_{SP,in} = e^{-in}$

in	.00	.01	.02	.03	.04	.05	.06	.07	.08	.09
2.1	1.2246E-01	1.2124E-01	1.2003E-01	1.1884E-01	1.1765E-01	1.1648E-01	1.1533E-01	1.1418E-01	1.1304E-01	1.1192E-01
2.2	1.1080E-01	1.0970E-01	1.0861E-01	1.0753E-01	1.0646E-01	1.0540E-01	1.0435E-01	1.0331E-01	1.0228E-01	1.0127E-01
2.3	1.0026E-01	9.9261E-02	9.8274E-02	9.7296E-02	9.6328E-02	9.5369E-02	9.4420E-02	9.3481E-02	9.2551E-02	9.1630E-02
2.4	9.0718E-02	8.9815E-02	8.8922E-02	8.8037E-02	8.7161E-02	8.6294E-02	8.5435E-02	8.4585E-02	8.3743E-02	8.2910E-02
2.5	8.2085E-02	8.1268E-02	8.0460E-02	7.9659E-02	7.8866E-02	7.8082E-02	7.7305E-02	7.6536E-02	7.5774E-02	7.5020E-02
2.6	7.4274E-02	7.3535E-02	7.2803E-02	7.2078E-02	7.1361E-02	7.0651E-02	6.9948E-02	6.9252E-02	6.8563E-02	6.7881E-02
2.7	6.7206E-02	6.6537E-02	6.5875E-02	6.5219E-02	6.4570E-02	6.3928E-02	6.3292E-02	6.2662E-02	6.2039E-02	6.1421E-02
2.8	6.0810E-02	6.0205E-02	5.9606E-02	5.9013E-02	5.8426E-02	5.7844E-02	5.7269E-02	5.6699E-02	5.6135E-02	5.5576E-02
2.9	5.5023E-02	5.4476E-02	5.3934E-02	5.3397E-02	5.2866E-02	5.2340E-02	5.1819E-02	5.1303E-02	5.0793E-02	5.0287E-02
3.0	4.9787E-02	4.9292E-02	4.8801E-02	4.8316E-02	4.7835E-02	4.7359E-02	4.6888E-02	4.6421E-02	4.5959E-02	4.5502E-02
3.1	4.5049E-02	4.4601E-02	4.4157E-02	4.3718E-02	4.3283E-02	4.2852E-02	4.2426E-02	4.2004E-02	4.1586E-02	4.1172E-02
3.2	4.0762E-02	4.0357E-02	3.9955E-02	3.9557E-02	3.9164E-02	3.8774E-02	3.8388E-02	3.8006E-02	3.7628E-02	3.7254E-02
3.3	3.6883E-02	3.6516E-02	3.6153E-02	3.5793E-02	3.5437E-02	3.5084E-02	3.4735E-02	3.4390E-02	3.4047E-02	3.3709E-02
3.4	3.3373E-02	3.3041E-02	3.2712E-02	3.2387E-02	3.2065E-02	3.1746E-02	3.1430E-02	3.1117E-02	3.0807E-02	3.0501E-02
3.5	3.0197E-02	2.9897E-02	2.9599E-02	2.9305E-02	2.9013E-02	2.8725E-02	2.8439E-02	2.8156E-02	2.7876E-02	2.7598E-02
3.6	2.7324E-02	2.7052E-02	2.6783E-02	2.6516E-02	2.6252E-02	2.5991E-02	2.5733E-02	2.5476E-02	2.5223E-02	2.4972E-02
3.7	2.4724E-02	2.4478E-02	2.4234E-02	2.3993E-02	2.3754E-02	2.3518E-02	2.3284E-02	2.3052E-02	2.2823E-02	2.2596E-02
3.8	2.2371E-02	2.2148E-02	2.1928E-02	2.1710E-02	2.1494E-02	2.1280E-02	2.1068E-02	2.0858E-02	2.0651E-02	2.0445E-02
3.9	2.0242E-02	2.0041E-02	1.9841E-02	1.9644E-02	1.9448E-02	1.9255E-02	1.9063E-02	1.8873E-02	1.8686E-02	1.8500E-02
4.0	1.8316E-02	1.8133E-02	1.7953E-02	1.7774E-02	1.7597E-02	1.7422E-02	1.7249E-02	1.7077E-02	1.6907E-02	1.6739E-02
4.1	1.6573E-02	1.6408E-02	1.6245E-02	1.6083E-02	1.5923E-02	1.5764E-02	1.5608E-02	1.5452E-02	1.5299E-02	1.5146E-02

Table 2. *(continued)*

$F_{sp,in} = e^{-in}$

in →	.00	.01	.02	.03	.04	.05	.06	.07	.08	.09
4.2	1.4996E-02	1.4846E-02	1.4699E-02	1.4552E-02	1.4408E-02	1.4264E-02	1.4122E-02	1.3982E-02	1.3843E-02	1.3705E-02
4.3	1.3569E-02	1.3434E-02	1.3300E-02	1.3168E-02	1.3037E-02	1.2907E-02	1.2778E-02	1.2651E-02	1.2525E-02	1.2401E-02
4.4	1.2277E-02	1.2155E-02	1.2034E-02	1.1914E-02	1.1796E-02	1.1679E-02	1.1562E-02	1.1447E-02	1.1333E-02	1.1221E-02
4.5	1.1109E-02	1.0998E-02	1.0889E-02	1.0781E-02	1.0673E-02	1.0567E-02	1.0462E-02	1.0358E-02	1.0255E-02	1.0153E-02
4.6	1.0052E-02	9.9518E-03	9.8528E-03	9.7548E-03	9.6577E-03	9.5616E-03	9.4665E-03	9.3723E-03	9.2790E-03	9.1867E-03
4.7	9.0953E-03	9.0048E-03	8.9152E-03	8.8265E-03	8.7386E-03	8.6517E-03	8.5656E-03	8.4804E-03	8.3960E-03	8.3125E-03
4.8	8.2297E-03	8.1479E-03	8.0668E-03	7.9865E-03	7.9071E-03	7.8284E-03	7.7505E-03	7.6734E-03	7.5970E-03	7.5214E-03
4.9	7.4466E-03	7.3725E-03	7.2991E-03	7.2265E-03	7.1546E-03	7.0834E-03	7.0129E-03	6.9431E-03	6.8741E-03	6.8057E-03
	.0	.1	.2	.3	.4	.5	.6	.7	.8	.9
5.0	6.7379E-03	6.0967E-03	5.5166E-03	4.9916E-03	4.5166E-03	4.0868E-03	3.6979E-03	3.3460E-03	3.0276E-03	2.7394E-03
6.0	2.4788E-03	2.2429E-03	2.0294E-03	1.8363E-03	1.6616E-03	1.5034E-03	1.3604E-03	1.2309E-03	1.1138E-03	1.0078E-03
7.0	9.1188E-04	8.2510E-04	7.4659E-04	6.7554E-04	6.1125E-04	5.5308E-04	5.0045E-04	4.5283E-04	4.0973E-04	3.7074E-04
8.0	3.3546E-04	3.0354E-04	2.7465E-04	2.4852E-04	2.2487E-04	2.0347E-04	1.8411E-04	1.6659E-04	1.5073E-04	1.3639E-04
9.0	1.2341E-04	1.1167E-04	1.0104E-04	9.1424E-05	8.2724E-05	7.4852E-05	6.7729E-05	6.1283E-05	5.5452E-05	5.0175E-05
10.0	4.5400E-05	4.1080E-05	3.7170E-05	3.3633E-05	3.0432E-05	2.7536E-05	2.4916E-05	2.2545E-05	2.0400E-05	1.8458E-05

Table 3. Continuous Compound Interest: Value of

$$F_{Rp,\,i,n} = \frac{1 - e^{-in}}{in}$$

in ↓	.00	.01	.02	.03	.04	.05	.06	.07	.08	.09
0	1.0000E 00	9.9502E-01	9.9007E-01	9.8515E-01	9.8026E-01	9.7541E-01	9.7059E-01	9.6580E-01	9.6105E-01	9.5632E-01
.1	9.5163E-01	9.4696E-01	9.4233E-01	9.3773E-01	9.3316E-01	9.2861E-01	9.2410E-01	9.1962E-01	9.1517E-01	9.1074E-01
.2	9.0635E-01	9.0198E-01	8.9764E-01	8.9333E-01	8.8905E-01	8.8480E-01	8.8057E-01	8.7637E-01	8.7220E-01	8.6806E-01
.3	8.6394E-01	8.5985E-01	8.5578E-01	8.5175E-01	8.4773E-01	8.4375E-01	8.3979E-01	8.3585E-01	8.3194E-01	8.2806E-01
.4	8.2420E-01	8.2037E-01	8.1656E-01	8.1277E-01	8.0901E-01	8.0527E-01	8.0156E-01	7.9787E-01	7.9420E-01	7.9056E-01
.5	7.8694E-01	7.8334E-01	7.7977E-01	7.7622E-01	7.7269E-01	7.6918E-01	7.6570E-01	7.6224E-01	7.5880E-01	7.5538E-01
.6	7.5198E-01	7.4861E-01	7.4525E-01	7.4192E-01	7.3861E-01	7.3531E-01	7.3204E-01	7.2879E-01	7.2556E-01	7.2235E-01
.7	7.1916E-01	7.1599E-01	7.1284E-01	7.0971E-01	7.0660E-01	7.0351E-01	7.0044E-01	6.9739E-01	6.9435E-01	6.9134E-01
.8	6.8834E-01	6.8536E-01	6.8240E-01	6.7946E-01	6.7654E-01	6.7363E-01	6.7074E-01	6.6787E-01	6.6502E-01	6.6218E-01
.9	6.5937E-01	6.5657E-01	6.5378E-01	6.5102E-01	6.4827E-01	6.4554E-01	6.4282E-01	6.4012E-01	6.3744E-01	6.3477E-01
1.0	6.3212E-01	6.2949E-01	6.2687E-01	6.2427E-01	6.2168E-01	6.1911E-01	6.1655E-01	6.1401E-01	6.1149E-01	6.0898E-01
1.1	6.0648E-01	6.0400E-01	6.0154E-01	5.9909E-01	5.9665E-01	5.9423E-01	5.9182E-01	5.8943E-01	5.8705E-01	5.8469E-01
1.2	5.8234E-01	5.8000E-01	5.7768E-01	5.7537E-01	5.7308E-01	5.7080E-01	5.6853E-01	5.6627E-01	5.6403E-01	5.6181E-01
1.3	5.5959E-01	5.5739E-01	5.5520E-01	5.5302E-01	5.5086E-01	5.4871E-01	5.4657E-01	5.4445E-01	5.4233E-01	5.4023E-01
1.4	5.3815E-01	5.3607E-01	5.3400E-01	5.3195E-01	5.2991E-01	5.2788E-01	5.2587E-01	5.2386E-01	5.2187E-01	5.1988E-01
1.5	5.1791E-01	5.1595E-01	5.1401E-01	5.1207E-01	5.1014E-01	5.0823E-01	5.0632E-01	5.0443E-01	5.0255E-01	5.0068E-01
1.6	4.9881E-01	4.9696E-01	4.9512E-01	4.9329E-01	4.9148E-01	4.8967E-01	4.8787E-01	4.8608E-01	4.8430E-01	4.8253E-01
1.7	4.8077E-01	4.7903E-01	4.7729E-01	4.7556E-01	4.7384E-01	4.7213E-01	4.7043E-01	4.6874E-01	4.6706E-01	4.6539E-01
1.8	4.6372E-01	4.6207E-01	4.6043E-01	4.5879E-01	4.5716E-01	4.5555E-01	4.5394E-01	4.5234E-01	4.5075E-01	4.4917E-01
1.9	4.4760E-01	4.4603E-01	4.4448E-01	4.4293E-01	4.4139E-01	4.3986E-01	4.3834E-01	4.3682E-01	4.3532E-01	4.3382E-01
2.0	4.3233E-01	4.3085E-01	4.2938E-01	4.2791E-01	4.2645E-01	4.2501E-01	4.2357E-01	4.2213E-01	4.2071E-01	4.1929E-01

Table 3. (continued)

$$F_{RP, \, i, n} = \frac{1 - e^{-in}}{in}$$

in ↓ \ →	.00	.01	.02	.03	.04	.05	.06	.07	.08	.09
2.1	4.1788E-01	4.1647E-01	4.1508E-01	4.1369E-01	4.1231E-01	4.1094E-01	4.0957E-01	4.0821E-01	4.0686E-01	4.0552E-01
2.2	4.0418E-01	4.0285E-01	4.0153E-01	4.0021E-01	3.9890E-01	3.9760E-01	3.9631E-01	3.9502E-01	3.9373E-01	3.9246E-01
2.3	3.9119E-01	3.8993E-01	3.8868E-01	3.8743E-01	3.8618E-01	3.8495E-01	3.8372E-01	3.8250E-01	3.8128E-01	3.8007E-01
2.4	3.7887E-01	3.7767E-01	3.7648E-01	3.7529E-01	3.7411E-01	3.7294E-01	3.7177E-01	3.7061E-01	3.6946E-01	3.6831E-01
2.5	3.6717E-01	3.6603E-01	3.6490E-01	3.6377E-01	3.6265E-01	3.6154E-01	3.6043E-01	3.5932E-01	3.5823E-01	3.5714E-01
2.6	3.5605E-01	3.5497E-01	3.5389E-01	3.5282E-01	3.5176E-01	3.5070E-01	3.4964E-01	3.4859E-01	3.4755E-01	3.4651E-01
2.7	3.4548E-01	3.4445E-01	3.4343E-01	3.4241E-01	3.4140E-01	3.4039E-01	3.3939E-01	3.3839E-01	3.3740E-01	3.3641E-01
2.8	3.3542E-01	3.3445E-01	3.3347E-01	3.3250E-01	3.3154E-01	3.3058E-01	3.2963E-01	3.2868E-01	3.2773E-01	3.2679E-01
2.9	3.2585E-01	3.2492E-01	3.2400E-01	3.2307E-01	3.2215E-01	3.2124E-01	3.2033E-01	3.1943E-01	3.1853E-01	3.1763E-01
3.0	3.1674E-01	3.1585E-01	3.1497E-01	3.1409E-01	3.1321E-01	3.1234E-01	3.1147E-01	3.1061E-01	3.0975E-01	3.0890E-01
3.1	3.0805E-01	3.0720E-01	3.0636E-01	3.0552E-01	3.0469E-01	3.0386E-01	3.0303E-01	3.0221E-01	3.0139E-01	3.0057E-01
3.2	2.9976E-01	2.9895E-01	2.9815E-01	2.9735E-01	2.9655E-01	2.9576E-01	2.9497E-01	2.9419E-01	2.9341E-01	2.9263E-01
3.3	2.9185E-01	2.9108E-01	2.9032E-01	2.8955E-01	2.8879E-01	2.8803E-01	2.8728E-01	2.8653E-01	2.8578E-01	2.8504E-01
3.4	2.8430E-01	2.8357E-01	2.8283E-01	2.8210E-01	2.8138E-01	2.8065E-01	2.7993E-01	2.7922E-01	2.7850E-01	2.7779E-01
3.5	2.7709E-01	2.7638E-01	2.7568E-01	2.7498E-01	2.7429E-01	2.7360E-01	2.7291E-01	2.7223E-01	2.7154E-01	2.7086E-01
3.6	2.7019E-01	2.6951E-01	2.6884E-01	2.6818E-01	2.6751E-01	2.6685E-01	2.6619E-01	2.6554E-01	2.6489E-01	2.6424E-01
3.7	2.6359E-01	2.6294E-01	2.6230E-01	2.6166E-01	2.6103E-01	2.6040E-01	2.5976E-01	2.5914E-01	2.5851E-01	2.5789E-01
3.8	2.5727E-01	2.5665E-01	2.5604E-01	2.5543E-01	2.5482E-01	2.5421E-01	2.5361E-01	2.5301E-01	2.5241E-01	2.5181E-01
3.9	2.5122E-01	2.5063E-01	2.5004E-01	2.4945E-01	2.4887E-01	2.4829E-01	2.4771E-01	2.4714E-01	2.4656E-01	2.4599E-01
4.0	2.4542E-01	2.4485E-01	2.4429E-01	2.4373E-01	2.4317E-01	2.4261E-01	2.4206E-01	2.4150E-01	2.4095E-01	2.4041E-01
4.1	2.3986E-01	2.3932E-01	2.3878E-01	2.3824E-01	2.3770E-01	2.3717E-01	2.3663E-01	2.3610E-01	2.3557E-01	2.3505E-01

$$F_{\overline{BP}, in} = \frac{1 - e^{-in}}{in}$$

in	.00	.01	.02	.03	.04	.05	.06	.07	.08	.09
4.2	2.3452E-01	2.3400E-01	2.3348E-01	2.3297E-01	2.3245E-01	2.3194E-01	2.3143E-01	2.3092E-01	2.3041E-01	2.2991E-01
4.3	2.2940E-01	2.2890E-01	2.2840E-01	2.2791E-01	2.2741E-01	2.2692E-01	2.2643E-01	2.2594E-01	2.2545E-01	2.2497E-01
4.4	2.2448E-01	2.2400E-01	2.2352E-01	2.2304E-01	2.2257E-01	2.2209E-01	2.2162E-01	2.2115E-01	2.2068E-01	2.2022E-01
4.5	2.1975E-01	2.1929E-01	2.1883E-01	2.1837E-01	2.1791E-01	2.1746E-01	2.1700E-01	2.1655E-01	2.1610E-01	2.1565E-01
4.6	2.1521E-01	2.1476E-01	2.1432E-01	2.1388E-01	2.1344E-01	2.1300E-01	2.1256E-01	2.1213E-01	2.1169E-01	2.1126E-01
4.7	2.1083E-01	2.1040E-01	2.0998E-01	2.0955E-01	2.0913E-01	2.0870E-01	2.0828E-01	2.0787E-01	2.0745E-01	2.0703E-01
4.8	2.0662E-01	2.0621E-01	2.0580E-01	2.0539E-01	2.0498E-01	2.0457E-01	2.0417E-01	2.0376E-01	2.0336E-01	2.0296E-01
4.9	2.0256E-01	2.0216E-01	2.0177E-01	2.0137E-01	2.0098E-01	2.0059E-01	2.0020E-01	1.9981E-01	1.9942E-01	1.9904E-01
	.0	.1	.2	.3	.4	.5	.6	.7	.8	.9
5.0	1.9865E-01	1.9488E-01	1.9125E-01	1.8774E-01	1.8435E-01	1.8108E-01	1.7791E-01	1.7485E-01	1.7189E-01	1.6903E-01
6.0	1.6625E-01	1.6357E-01	1.6096E-01	1.5844E-01	1.5599E-01	1.5361E-01	1.5131E-01	1.4907E-01	1.4690E-01	1.4478E-01
7.0	1.4273E-01	1.4073E-01	1.3879E-01	1.3689E-01	1.3505E-01	1.3326E-01	1.3151E-01	1.2981E-01	1.2815E-01	1.2654E-01
8.0	1.2496E-01	1.2342E-01	1.2192E-01	1.2045E-01	1.1902E-01	1.1762E-01	1.1626E-01	1.1492E-01	1.1362E-01	1.1234E-01
9.0	1.1110E-01	1.0988E-01	1.0868E-01	1.0752E-01	1.0637E-01	1.0526E-01	1.0416E-01	1.0309E-01	1.0204E-01	1.0101E-01
10.0	9.9995E-02	9.9006E-02	9.8036E-02	9.7084E-02	9.6151E-02	9.5235E-02	9.4337E-02	9.3456E-02	9.2591E-02	9.1741E-02
11.0	9.0908E-02	9.0089E-02	8.9284E-02	8.8494E-02	8.7718E-02	8.6956E-02	8.6208E-02	8.5469E-02	8.4745E-02	8.4033E-02
12.0	8.3333E-02	8.2644E-02	8.1967E-02	8.1300E-02	8.0645E-02	8.0000E-02	7.9365E-02	7.8740E-02	7.8125E-02	7.7519E-02
13.0	7.6923E-02	7.6336E-02	7.5757E-02	7.5188E-02	7.4627E-02	7.4074E-02	7.3529E-02	7.2993E-02	7.2464E-02	7.1942E-02
14.0	7.1429E-02	7.0922E-02	7.0422E-02	6.9930E-02	6.9444E-02	6.8965E-02	6.8493E-02	6.8027E-02	6.7568E-02	6.7114E-02
15.0	6.6667E-02	6.6225E-02	6.5789E-02	6.5359E-02	6.4935E-02	6.4516E-02	6.4103E-02	6.3694E-02	6.3291E-02	6.2893E-02
16.0	6.2500E-02	6.2112E-02	6.1728E-02	6.1350E-02	6.0976E-02	6.0606E-02	6.0241E-02	5.9880E-02	5.9524E-02	5.9172E-02
17.0	5.8824E-02	5.8480E-02	5.8140E-02	5.7803E-02	5.7471E-02	5.7143E-02	5.6818E-02	5.6497E-02	5.6180E-02	5.5866E-02
18.0	5.5555E-02	5.5249E-02	5.4945E-02	5.4645E-02	5.4348E-02	5.4054E-02	5.3763E-02	5.3476E-02	5.3191E-02	5.2910E-02
19.0	5.2632E-02	5.2356E-02	5.2083E-02	5.1813E-02	5.1546E-02	5.1282E-02	5.1020E-02	5.0761E-02	5.0505E-02	5.0251E-02
20.0	5.0000E-02	4.9751E-02	4.9505E-02	4.9261E-02	4.9020E-02	4.8780E-02	4.8544E-02	4.8309E-02	4.8077E-02	4.7847E-02

Table 4. Continuous Compound Interest: Value of

$$F_{SDP,\,i,n} = \frac{2}{in}\left(1 - \frac{1 - e^{-in}}{in}\right)$$

in → ↓	.00	.01	.02	.03	.04	.05	.06	.07	.08	.09
0	1.0000E 00	9.9668E-01	9.9337E-01	9.9007E-01	9.8680E-01	9.8354E-01	9.8030E-01	9.7707E-01	9.7386E-01	9.7066E-01
.1	9.6748E-01	9.6432E-01	9.6117E-01	9.5804E-01	9.5492E-01	9.5182E-01	9.4873E-01	9.4566E-01	9.4261E-01	9.3956E-01
.2	9.3654E-01	9.3353E-01	9.3053E-01	9.2755E-01	9.2458E-01	9.2163E-01	9.1869E-01	9.1576E-01	9.1285E-01	9.0995E-01
.3	9.0707E-01	9.0420E-01	9.0135E-01	8.9851E-01	8.9568E-01	8.9287E-01	8.9007E-01	8.8728E-01	8.8451E-01	8.8175E-01
.4	8.7900E-01	8.7627E-01	8.7355E-01	8.7084E-01	8.6814E-01	8.6546E-01	8.6279E-01	8.6014E-01	8.5749E-01	8.5486E-01
.5	8.5225E-01	8.4964E-01	8.4705E-01	8.4446E-01	8.4189E-01	8.3934E-01	8.3679E-01	8.3426E-01	8.3174E-01	8.2923E-01
.6	8.2673E-01	8.2425E-01	8.2177E-01	8.1931E-01	8.1686E-01	8.1442E-01	8.1199E-01	8.0957E-01	8.0717E-01	8.0477E-01
.7	8.0239E-01	8.0002E-01	7.9766E-01	7.9530E-01	7.9297E-01	7.9064E-01	7.8832E-01	7.8601E-01	7.8371E-01	7.8143E-01
.8	7.7915E-01	7.7689E-01	7.7463E-01	7.7239E-01	7.7015E-01	7.6793E-01	7.6572E-01	7.6351E-01	7.6132E-01	7.5914E-01
.9	7.5696E-01	7.5480E-01	7.5264E-01	7.5050E-01	7.4837E-01	7.4624E-01	7.4413E-01	7.4202E-01	7.3992E-01	7.3784E-01
1.0	7.3576E-01	7.3369E-01	7.3163E-01	7.2958E-01	7.2754E-01	7.2551E-01	7.2349E-01	7.2148E-01	7.1947E-01	7.1748E-01
1.1	7.1549E-01	7.1351E-01	7.1154E-01	7.0958E-01	7.0763E-01	7.0569E-01	7.0375E-01	7.0183E-01	6.9991E-01	6.9800E-01
1.2	6.9610E-01	6.9421E-01	6.9233E-01	6.9045E-01	6.8859E-01	6.8673E-01	6.8488E-01	6.8303E-01	6.8120E-01	6.7937E-01
1.3	6.7755E-01	6.7574E-01	6.7394E-01	6.7214E-01	6.7036E-01	6.6858E-01	6.6680E-01	6.6504E-01	6.6328E-01	6.6153E-01
1.4	6.5979E-01	6.5806E-01	6.5633E-01	6.5461E-01	6.5290E-01	6.5120E-01	6.4950E-01	6.4781E-01	6.4613E-01	6.4445E-01
1.5	6.4278E-01	6.4112E-01	6.3947E-01	6.3782E-01	6.3618E-01	6.3455E-01	6.3292E-01	6.3130E-01	6.2969E-01	6.2808E-01
1.6	6.2648E-01	6.2489E-01	6.2330E-01	6.2172E-01	6.2015E-01	6.1859E-01	6.1703E-01	6.1547E-01	6.1393E-01	6.1239E-01
1.7	6.1085E-01	6.0933E-01	6.0781E-01	6.0629E-01	6.0478E-01	6.0328E-01	6.0179E-01	6.0030E-01	5.9881E-01	5.9733E-01
1.8	5.9586E-01	5.9440E-01	5.9294E-01	5.9149E-01	5.9004E-01	5.8860E-01	5.8716E-01	5.8573E-01	5.8431E-01	5.8289E-01
1.9	5.8148E-01	5.8007E-01	5.7867E-01	5.7728E-01	5.7589E-01	5.7450E-01	5.7312E-01	5.7175E-01	5.7039E-01	5.6902E-01
2.0	5.6767E-01	5.6632E-01	5.6497E-01	5.6363E-01	5.6230E-01	5.6097E-01	5.5964E-01	5.5833E-01	5.5701E-01	5.5570E-01

$$F_{SDP,\,i n} = \frac{2}{in}\left(1 - \frac{1-e^{-in}}{in}\right)$$

in	.00	.01	.02	.03	.04	.05	.06	.07	.08	.09
2.1	5.5440E-01	5.5310E-01	5.5181E-01	5.5052E-01	5.4924E-01	5.4797E-01	5.4669E-01	5.4543E-01	5.4416E-01	5.4291E-01
2.2	5.4165E-01	5.4041E-01	5.3916E-01	5.3793E-01	5.3669E-01	5.3547E-01	5.3424E-01	5.3302E-01	5.3181E-01	5.3060E-01
2.3	5.2940E-01	5.2820E-01	5.2700E-01	5.2581E-01	5.2463E-01	5.2345E-01	5.2227E-01	5.2110E-01	5.1993E-01	5.1877E-01
2.4	5.1761E-01	5.1646E-01	5.1531E-01	5.1416E-01	5.1302E-01	5.1188E-01	5.1075E-01	5.0962E-01	5.0850E-01	5.0738E-01
2.5	5.0627E-01	5.0516E-01	5.0405E-01	5.0295E-01	5.0185E-01	5.0076E-01	4.9967E-01	4.9858E-01	4.9750E-01	4.9642E-01
2.6	4.9535E-01	4.9428E-01	4.9321E-01	4.9215E-01	4.9109E-01	4.9004E-01	4.8899E-01	4.8794E-01	4.8690E-01	4.8586E-01
2.7	4.8483E-01	4.8380E-01	4.8277E-01	4.8175E-01	4.8073E-01	4.7972E-01	4.7871E-01	4.7770E-01	4.7669E-01	4.7569E-01
2.8	4.7470E-01	4.7370E-01	4.7271E-01	4.7173E-01	4.7075E-01	4.6977E-01	4.6879E-01	4.6782E-01	4.6685E-01	4.6589E-01
2.9	4.6493E-01	4.6397E-01	4.6302E-01	4.6207E-01	4.6112E-01	4.6018E-01	4.5924E-01	4.5830E-01	4.5737E-01	4.5644E-01
3.0	4.5551E-01	4.5458E-01	4.5366E-01	4.5275E-01	4.5183E-01	4.5092E-01	4.5002E-01	4.4911E-01	4.4821E-01	4.4731E-01
3.1	4.4642E-01	4.4553E-01	4.4464E-01	4.4376E-01	4.4287E-01	4.4200E-01	4.4112E-01	4.4025E-01	4.3938E-01	4.3851E-01
3.2	4.3765E-01	4.3679E-01	4.3593E-01	4.3508E-01	4.3423E-01	4.3338E-01	4.3253E-01	4.3169E-01	4.3085E-01	4.3001E-01
3.3	4.2918E-01	4.2835E-01	4.2752E-01	4.2670E-01	4.2587E-01	4.2505E-01	4.2424E-01	4.2342E-01	4.2261E-01	4.2180E-01
3.4	4.2100E-01	4.2020E-01	4.1940E-01	4.1860E-01	4.1780E-01	4.1701E-01	4.1622E-01	4.1544E-01	4.1465E-01	4.1387E-01
3.5	4.1309E-01	4.1232E-01	4.1154E-01	4.1077E-01	4.1001E-01	4.0924E-01	4.0848E-01	4.0772E-01	4.0696E-01	4.0620E-01
3.6	4.0545E-01	4.0470E-01	4.0395E-01	4.0321E-01	4.0247E-01	4.0173E-01	4.0099E-01	4.0025E-01	3.9952E-01	3.9879E-01
3.7	3.9806E-01	3.9733E-01	3.9661E-01	3.9589E-01	3.9517E-01	3.9446E-01	3.9374E-01	3.9303E-01	3.9232E-01	3.9161E-01
3.8	3.9091E-01	3.9021E-01	3.8951E-01	3.8881E-01	3.8811E-01	3.8742E-01	3.8673E-01	3.8604E-01	3.8536E-01	3.8467E-01
3.9	3.8399E-01	3.8331E-01	3.8263E-01	3.8196E-01	3.8128E-01	3.8061E-01	3.7994E-01	3.7928E-01	3.7861E-01	3.7795E-01
4.0	3.7729E-01	3.7663E-01	3.7597E-01	3.7532E-01	3.7467E-01	3.7402E-01	3.7337E-01	3.7273E-01	3.7208E-01	3.7144E-01
4.1	3.7080E-01	3.7016E-01	3.6953E-01	3.6889E-01	3.6826E-01	3.6763E-01	3.6700E-01	3.6638E-01	3.6575E-01	3.6513E-01

Table 4. *(continued)*

$$F_{SDP,in} = \frac{2}{in}\left(1 - \frac{1-e^{-in}}{in}\right)$$

in → ↓	.00	.01	.02	.03	.04	.05	.06	.07	.08	.09
4.2	3.6451E-01	3.6389E-01	3.6328E-01	3.6266E-01	3.6205E-01	3.6144E-01	3.6083E-01	3.6023E-01	3.5962E-01	3.5902E-01
4.3	3.5842E-01	3.5782E-01	3.5722E-01	3.5663E-01	3.5603E-01	3.5544E-01	3.5485E-01	3.5426E-01	3.5368E-01	3.5309E-01
4.4	3.5251E-01	3.5193E-01	3.5135E-01	3.5077E-01	3.5019E-01	3.4962E-01	3.4905E-01	3.4848E-01	3.4791E-01	3.4734E-01
4.5	3.4678E-01	3.4621E-01	3.4565E-01	3.4509E-01	3.4453E-01	3.4397E-01	3.4342E-01	3.4287E-01	3.4231E-01	3.4176E-01
4.6	3.4121E-01	3.4067E-01	3.4012E-01	3.3958E-01	3.3904E-01	3.3850E-01	3.3796E-01	3.3742E-01	3.3688E-01	3.3635E-01
4.7	3.3582E-01	3.3529E-01	3.3476E-01	3.3423E-01	3.3370E-01	3.3318E-01	3.3265E-01	3.3213E-01	3.3161E-01	3.3109E-01
4.8	3.3058E-01	3.3006E-01	3.2955E-01	3.2903E-01	3.2852E-01	3.2801E-01	3.2750E-01	3.2700E-01	3.2649E-01	3.2599E-01
4.9	3.2548E-01	3.2498E-01	3.2448E-01	3.2399E-01	3.2349E-01	3.2299E-01	3.2250E-01	3.2201E-01	3.2152E-01	3.2103E-01
	.0	.1	.2	.3	.4	.5	.6	.7	.8	.9
5.0	3.2054E-01	3.1573E-01	3.1106E-01	3.0651E-01	3.0209E-01	2.9779E-01	2.9360E-01	2.8953E-01	2.8555E-01	2.8169E-01
6.0	2.7792E-01	2.7424E-01	2.7066E-01	2.6716E-01	2.6375E-01	2.6043E-01	2.5718E-01	2.5401E-01	2.5091E-01	2.4789E-01
7.0	2.4494E-01	2.4205E-01	2.3923E-01	2.3647E-01	2.3377E-01	2.3113E-01	2.2855E-01	2.2602E-01	2.2355E-01	2.2113E-01
8.0	2.1876E-01	2.1644E-01	2.1417E-01	2.1194E-01	2.0976E-01	2.0762E-01	2.0552E-01	2.0347E-01	2.0145E-01	1.9947E-01
9.0	1.9753E-01	1.9563E-01	1.9376E-01	1.9193E-01	1.9013E-01	1.8837E-01	1.8663E-01	1.8493E-01	1.8326E-01	1.8162E-01
10.0	1.8000E-01	1.7841E-01	1.7686E-01	1.7532E-01	1.7382E-01	1.7234E-01	1.7088E-01	1.6945E-01	1.6804E-01	1.6665E-01
11.0	1.6529E-01	1.6395E-01	1.6263E-01	1.6133E-01	1.6005E-01	1.5879E-01	1.5755E-01	1.5633E-01	1.5513E-01	1.5394E-01
12.0	1.5278E-01	1.5163E-01	1.5050E-01	1.4938E-01	1.4828E-01	1.4720E-01	1.4613E-01	1.4508E-01	1.4404E-01	1.4302E-01
13.0	1.4201E-01	1.4102E-01	1.4004E-01	1.3907E-01	1.3812E-01	1.3717E-01	1.3625E-01	1.3533E-01	1.3443E-01	1.3354E-01
14.0	1.3265E-01	1.3178E-01	1.3093E-01	1.3008E-01	1.2924E-01	1.2842E-01	1.2760E-01	1.2680E-01	1.2600E-01	1.2522E-01
15.0	1.2444E-01	1.2368E-01	1.2292E-01	1.2218E-01	1.2144E-01	1.2071E-01	1.1999E-01	1.1927E-01	1.1857E-01	1.1788E-01
16.0	1.1719E-01	1.1651E-01	1.1584E-01	1.1517E-01	1.1452E-01	1.1387E-01	1.1322E-01	1.1259E-01	1.1196E-01	1.1134E-01
17.0	1.1073E-01	1.1012E-01	1.0952E-01	1.0892E-01	1.0834E-01	1.0776E-01	1.0718E-01	1.0661E-01	1.0605E-01	1.0549E-01
18.0	1.0494E-01	1.0439E-01	1.0385E-01	1.0332E-01	1.0279E-01	1.0226E-01	1.0175E-01	1.0123E-01	1.0072E-01	1.0022E-01
19.0	9.9723E-02	9.9230E-02	9.8741E-02	9.8258E-02	9.7779E-02	9.7304E-02	9.6835E-02	9.6369E-02	9.5909E-02	9.5452E-02
20.0	9.5000E-02	9.4552E-02	9.4108E-02	9.3669E-02	9.3233E-02	9.2802E-02	9.2374E-02	9.1951E-02	9.1531E-02	9.1115E-02

Appendix 3
Probability

Table I Cumulative Probability for Z or Less for Standard Normal Distribution*

Z	0	1	2	3	4	5	6	7	8	9
0.0	0.0000	0.0040	0.0080	0.0120	0.0160	0.0199	0.0239	0.0279	0.0319	0.0359
0.1	0.0398	0.0438	0.0478	0.0517	0.0557	0.0596	0.0636	0.0675	0.0714	0.0754
0.2	0.0793	0.0832	0.0871	0.0910	0.0948	0.0987	0.1026	0.1064	0.1103	0.1141
0.3	0.1179	0.1217	0.1255	0.1293	0.1331	0.1368	0.1406	0.1443	0.1480	0.1517
0.4	0.1554	0.1591	0.1628	0.1664	0.1700	0.1736	0.1772	0.1808	0.1844	0.1879
0.5	0.1915	0.1950	0.1985	0.2019	0.2054	0.2088	0.2123	0.2157	0.2190	0.2224
0.6	0.2258	0.2291	0.2324	0.2357	0.2389	0.2422	0.2454	0.2486	0.2518	0.2549
0.7	0.2580	0.2612	0.2642	0.2673	0.2704	0.2734	0.2764	0.2794	0.2823	0.2852
0.8	0.2881	0.2910	0.2939	0.2967	0.2996	0.3023	0.3051	0.3078	0.3106	0.3133
0.9	0.3159	0.3186	0.3212	0.3238	0.3264	0.3289	0.3315	0.3340	0.3365	0.3389
1.0	0.3413	0.3438	0.3461	0.3485	0.3508	0.3531	0.3554	0.3577	0.3599	0.3621
1.1	0.3643	0.3665	0.3686	0.3708	0.3729	0.3749	0.3770	0.3790	0.3810	0.3830
1.2	0.3849	0.3869	0.3888	0.3907	0.3925	0.3944	0.3962	0.3980	0.3997	0.4015
1.3	0.4032	0.4049	0.4066	0.4082	0.4099	0.4115	0.4131	0.4147	0.4162	0.4177
1.4	0.4192	0.4207	0.4222	0.4236	0.4251	0.4265	0.4279	0.4292	0.4306	0.4319
1.5	0.4332	0.4345	0.4357	0.4370	0.4382	0.4394	0.4406	0.4418	0.4429	0.4441
1.6	0.4452	0.4463	0.4474	0.4484	0.4495	0.4505	0.4515	0.4525	0.4535	0.4545
1.7	0.4554	0.4564	0.4573	0.4582	0.4591	0.4599	0.4608	0.4616	0.4625	0.4633
1.8	0.4641	0.4649	0.4656	0.4664	0.4671	0.4678	0.4686	0.4693	0.4699	0.4706
1.9	0.4713	0.4719	0.4726	0.4732	0.4738	0.4744	0.4750	0.4756	0.4761	0.4767
2.0	0.4772	0.4778	0.4783	0.4788	0.4793	0.4798	0.4803	0.4808	0.4812	0.4817
2.1	0.4821	0.4826	0.4830	0.4834	0.4838	0.4842	0.4846	0.4850	0.4854	0.4857
2.2	0.4861	0.4864	0.4868	0.4871	0.4875	0.4878	0.4881	0.4884	0.4887	0.4890
2.3	0.4893	0.4896	0.4898	0.4901	0.4904	0.4906	0.4909	0.4911	0.4913	0.4916
2.4	0.4918	0.4920	0.4922	0.4925	0.4927	0.4929	0.4931	0.4932	0.4934	0.4936
2.5	0.4938	0.4940	0.4941	0.4943	0.4945	0.4946	0.4948	0.4949	0.4951	0.4952
2.6	0.4953	0.4955	0.4956	0.4957	0.4959	0.4960	0.4961	0.4962	0.4963	0.4964
2.7	0.4965	0.4966	0.4967	0.4968	0.4969	0.4970	0.4971	0.4972	0.4973	0.4974
2.8	0.4974	0.4975	0.4976	0.4977	0.4977	0.4978	0.4979	0.4979	0.4980	0.4981
2.9	0.4981	0.4982	0.4982	0.4983	0.4984	0.4984	0.4985	0.4985	0.4986	0.4986
3.0	0.4987	0.4987	0.4987	0.4988	0.4988	0.4989	0.4989	0.4989	0.4990	0.4990
3.1	0.4990	0.4991	0.4991	0.4991	0.4992	0.4992	0.4992	0.4992	0.4993	0.4993
3.2	0.4993	0.4993	0.4994	0.4994	0.4994	0.4994	0.4994	0.4995	0.4995	0.4995
3.3	0.4995	0.4995	0.4995	0.4996	0.4996	0.4996	0.4996	0.4996	0.4996	0.4997
3.4	0.4997	0.4997	0.4997	0.4997	0.4997	0.4997	0.4997	0.4997	0.4997	0.4998
3.5	0.4998	0.4998	0.4998	0.4998	0.4998	0.4998	0.4998	0.4998	0.4998	0.4998
3.6	0.4998	0.4998	0.4999	0.4999	0.4999	0.4999	0.4999	0.4999	0.4999	0.4999
3.7	0.4999	0.4999	0.4999	0.4999	0.4999	0.4999	0.4999	0.4999	0.4999	0.4999
3.8	0.4999	0.4999	0.4999	0.4999	0.4999	0.4999	0.4999	0.4999	0.4999	0.4999
3.9	0.5000	0.5000	0.5000	0.5000	0.5000	0.5000	0.5000	0.5000	0.5000	0.5000

* If Z is negative, use 0.5000 minus value shown; if Z is positive, use 0.5000 plus value shown.

Table 2. Random Numbers: The First 1,000 Decimal Places of π

14159	26535	89793	23846	26433	83279	50288	41971	69399	37510
58209	74944	59230	78164	06286	20899	86280	34825	34211	70679
82148	08651	32823	06647	09384	46095	50582	23172	53594	08128
48111	74502	84102	70193	85211	05559	64462	29489	54930	38196
44288	10975	66593	34461	28475	64823	37867	83165	27120	19091
45648	56692	34603	48610	45432	66482	13393	60726	02491	41273
72458	70066	06315	58817	48815	20920	96282	92540	91715	36436
78925	90360	01133	05305	48820	46652	13841	46951	94151	16094
33057	27036	57595	91953	09218	61173	81932	61179	31051	18548
07446	23799	62749	56735	18857	52724	89122	79381	83011	94912
98336	73362	44065	66430	86021	39494	63952	24737	19070	21798
60943	70277	05392	17176	29317	67523	84674	81846	76694	05132
00056	81271	45263	56082	77857	71342	75778	96091	73637	17872
14684	40901	22495	34301	46549	58537	10507	92279	68925	89235
42019	95611	21290	21960	86403	44181	59813	62977	47713	09960
51870	72113	49999	99837	29780	49951	05973	17328	16096	31859
50244	59455	34690	83026	42522	30825	33446	85035	26193	11881
71010	00313	78387	52886	58753	32083	81420	61717	76691	47303
59825	34904	28755	46873	11595	62863	88235	37875	93751	95778
18577	80532	17122	68066	13001	92787	66111	95909	21642	01989

Appendix 4
Learning Curve

Table I. Values for Exponential Learning-curve Function

n	90% learning ratio $E(N)$	$\Sigma E(N)$	$\Sigma E(N)/N$	80% learning ratio $E(N)$	$\Sigma E(N)$	$\Sigma E(N)/N$	70% learning ratio $E(N)$	$\Sigma E(N)$	$\Sigma E(N)/N$
1	1.0000E 00	1.0000E 00	1.0000E 00	1.0000E 00	1.0000E 00	1.0000E 00	1.0000E 00	1.0000E 00	1.0000E 00
2	9.0000E-01	1.9000E 00	9.5000E-01	8.0000E-01	1.8000E 00	9.0000E-01	7.0000E-01	1.7000E 00	8.5000E-01
3	8.4621E-01	2.7462E 00	9.1540E-01	7.0210E-01	2.5021E 00	8.3403E-01	5.6818E-01	2.2682E 00	7.5606E-01
4	8.1000E-01	3.5562E 00	8.8905E-01	6.4000E-01	3.1421E 00	7.8553E-01	4.9000E-01	2.7582E 00	6.8955E-01
5	7.8299E-01	4.3392E 00	8.6784E-01	5.9564E-01	3.7377E 00	7.4755E-01	4.3685E-01	3.1950E 00	6.3901E-01
6	7.6159E-01	5.1008E 00	8.5013E-01	5.6168E-01	4.2994E 00	7.1657E-01	3.9773E-01	3.5928E 00	5.9879E-01
7	7.4395E-01	5.8447E 00	8.3496E-01	5.3449E-01	4.8339E 00	6.9056E-01	3.6740E-01	3.9601E 00	5.6574E-01
8	7.2900E-01	6.5737E 00	8.2172E-01	5.1200E-01	5.3459E 00	6.6824E-01	3.4300E-01	4.3031E 00	5.3789E-01
9	7.1606E-01	7.2898E 00	8.0998E-01	4.9295E-01	5.8389E 00	6.4876E-01	3.2283E-01	4.6260E 00	5.1400E-01
10	7.0469E-01	7.9945E 00	7.9945E-01	4.7651E-01	6.3154E 00	6.3154E-01	3.0579E-01	4.9318E 00	4.9318E-01
11	6.9455E-01	8.6890E 00	7.8991E-01	4.6211E-01	6.7775E 00	6.1613E-01	2.9116E-01	5.2229E 00	4.7481E-01
12	6.8543E-01	9.3745E 00	7.8120E-01	4.4935E-01	7.2268E 00	6.0224E-01	2.7841E-01	5.5013E 00	4.5844E-01
13	6.7714E-01	1.0052E 01	7.7320E-01	4.3792E-01	7.6647E 00	5.8960E-01	2.6717E-01	5.7685E 00	4.4373E-01
14	6.6955E-01	1.0721E 01	7.6580E-01	4.2759E-01	8.0923E 00	5.7802E-01	2.5718E-01	6.0257E 00	4.3041E-01
15	6.6257E-01	1.1384E 01	7.5891E-01	4.1820E-01	8.5105E 00	5.6737E-01	2.4821E-01	6.2739E 00	4.1826E-01
16	6.5610E-01	1.2040E 01	7.5249E-01	4.0960E-01	8.9201E 00	5.5751E-01	2.4010E-01	6.5140E 00	4.0712E-01
17	6.5008E-01	1.2690E 01	7.4646E-01	4.0168E-01	9.3218E 00	5.4834E-01	2.3273E-01	6.7467E 00	3.9687E-01
18	6.4446E-01	1.3334E 01	7.4080E-01	3.9436E-01	9.7162E 00	5.3979E-01	2.2598E-01	6.9727E 00	3.8737E-01
19	6.3918E-01	1.3974E 01	7.3545E-01	3.8775E-01	1.0104E 01	5.3178E-01	2.1978E-01	7.1925E 00	3.7855E-01
20	6.3422E-01	1.4608E 01	7.3039E-01	3.8121E-01	1.0485E 01	5.2425E-01	2.1405E-01	7.4065E 00	3.7033E-01
25	6.1307E-01	1.7713E 01	7.0853E-01	3.5478E-01	1.2309E 01	4.9234E-01	1.9083E-01	8.4040E 00	3.3616E-01
30	5.9631E-01	2.0727E 01	6.9090E-01	3.3456E-01	1.4020E 01	4.6733E-01	1.7375E-01	9.3050E 00	3.1017E-01
35	5.8250E-01	2.3666E 01	6.7617E-01	3.1836E-01	1.5643E 01	4.4694E-01	1.6050E-01	1.0133E 01	2.8951E-01
40	5.7080E-01	2.6543E 01	6.6357E-01	3.0497E-01	1.7193E 01	4.2984E-01	1.4984E-01	1.0902E 01	2.7256E-01

470

	90% learning ratio			80% learning ratio			70% learning ratio		
n	$E(N)$	$\Sigma E(N)$	$\Sigma E(N)/N$	$E(N)$	$\Sigma E(N)$	$\Sigma E(N)/N$	$E(N)$	$\Sigma E(N)$	$\Sigma E(N)/N$
45	5.6067E-01	2.9366E 01	6.5257E-01	2.9362E-01	1.8684E 01	4.1519E-01	1.4103E-01	1.1625E 01	2.5832E-01
50	5.5176E-01	3.2142E 01	6.4284E-01	2.8883E-01	2.0122E 01	4.0243E-01	1.3358E-01	1.2307E 01	2.4614E-01
60	5.3668E-01	3.7574E 01	6.2623E-01	2.6765E-01	2.2868E 01	3.8113E-01	1.2162E-01	1.3574E 01	2.2624E-01
70	5.2425E-01	4.2871E 01	6.1244E-01	2.5469E-01	2.5471E 01	3.6387E-01	1.1235E-01	1.4738E 01	2.1054E-01
80	5.1372E-01	4.8054E 01	6.0067E-01	2.4397E-01	2.7957E 01	3.4947E-01	1.0489E-01	1.5819E 01	1.9774E-01
90	5.0460E-01	5.3140E 01	5.9044E-01	2.3490E-01	3.0346E 01	3.3718E-01	9.8719E-02	1.6833E 01	1.8703E-01
100	4.9659E-01	5.8141E 01	5.8141E-01	2.2706E-01	3.2651E 01	3.2651E-01	9.3509E-02	1.7791E 01	1.7791E-01
150	4.6690E-01	8.2156E 01	5.4771E-01	1.9928E-01	4.3234E 01	2.8822E-01	7.5900E-02	2.1972E 01	1.4648E-01
200	4.4693E-01	1.0496E 02	5.2482E-01	1.8165E-01	5.2720E 01	2.6360E-01	6.5456E-02	2.5482E 01	1.2741E-01
300	4.2021E-01	1.4820E 02	4.9401E-01	1.5942E-01	6.9663E 01	2.3221E-01	5.3130E-02	3.1342E 01	1.0447E-01
400	4.0223E-01	1.8927E 02	4.7317E-01	1.4532E-01	8.4849E 01	2.1212E-01	4.5819E-02	3.6260E 01	9.0649E-02
500	3.8882E-01	2.2879E 02	4.5757E-01	1.3525E-01	9.8847E 01	1.9769E-01	4.0849E-02	4.0577E 01	8.1153E-02
600	3.7819E-01	2.6711E 02	4.4519E-01	1.2754E-01	1.1197E 02	1.8661E-01	3.7191E-02	4.4468E 01	7.4114E-02
800	3.6201E-01	3.4103E 02	4.2629E-01	1.1626E-01	1.3627E 02	1.7034E-01	3.2074E-02	5.1355E 01	6.4194E-02
1000	3.4994E-01	4.1217E 02	4.1217E-01	1.0820E-01	1.5867E 02	1.5867E-01	2.8594E-02	5.7401E 01	5.7401E-02

Answers to Problems

2.12P1. (a) $20,408; (b) $20,592.
2.12P2. (a) $1,382.4; (b) $1,448 approximately.
2.12P3. (a) 8% per year; (b) 7.3% per year approximately.
2.12P4. 8.24% per year.
2.12P5. $16,530 a receipt.
2.12P6. $5,335.
2.12P7. $7,015.
2.12P8. (a) $1,610; (b) $1,519.
2.12P9. 8.8 years approximately.
2.12P10. 9.4% per year approximately.
2.12P11. 0.23133.
2.12P12. $2,266.
2.12P13. (a) $711.3 per year; (b) $5,970.
2.12P14. $1,081.63.
2.12P15. 4.2% per year approximately.
2.12P16. (a) 12.3% per year; (b) 16.4% per year approximately.
2.12P17. $955,700.
2.12P18. 73.2% per year.
2.12P19. $50,850.
2.12P20. (a) 12.7% per year approximately; (b) 23.1% per year approximately.
2.12P21. Royalty more economical. Unacost $80,000 against $85,400.
2.12P22. Machine B 12 to 13 years. Machine C cannot pay off.

474 ANSWERS TO PROBLEMS

2.12P23. (a) $P_{A,10} = \$57,695$ $P_{B,10} = \$53,029$
(b) $P_{A,4} = \$28,479$ $P_{B,4} = \$26,176$
(c) $R_A = \$8,598$ $R_B = \$7,903$
(d) $K_A = \$107,480$ $K_B = \$98,790$
(e) 4.6 years
(f) 15.5% per year approximately.

2.12P26. $2,547.

2.12P27. $2,140 per year benefit required for type B pipe.

2.12P28. $4,268,000.

2.12P29. 3 years.

2.12P30. Build full-scale plant now. $P_{A,10} = \$3,093,000$ as against $P_{B,10} = \$3,043,000$.

2.12P31. (a) -3.4% per year; (b) $4,035,000 loss.

3.15P1. (a) 10 years; (b) 1.040 MM$ by SF and 0.472 MM$ by DDB.

3.15P2.

Year	Depreciation for year	
	DDB	UP
1	22,500	2,500
2	11,250	10,000
3	5,625	20,000
4	625	7,500

3.15P3. 9.06 years and 4.98 years.

3.15P4. $P = \$8,223$ SL, or $9,413 DDB with switch, or $8,993 SD.

3.15P5. (a) $0.38 million (b) $0.52 million.

3.15P6. $3,900.

3.15P7. $297.1 per year for 3 years.

3.15P8. New floor never pays off.

3.15P9. 3.3% per year approximately.

3.15P10. A is more economical; $R_A = \$4,493.1$, $R_B = \$8,006.1$.

3.15P11. $1,039.2.

3.15P12. Machine B 12 to 13 years. Machine C cannot pay off.

4.12P1. $P = \dfrac{2Q}{(in)^2} [1 - e^{-in}(in + 1)]$

4.12P2. $P = \dfrac{\bar{R}_2 - \bar{R}_1}{i^2 n} [1 - e^{-in}(in + 1)] + n\bar{R}_1 \dfrac{1 - e^{-in}}{in}$

4.12P3. $P = Y \dfrac{1 - e^{-ikn}}{e^{in} - 1}$

4.12P4. $59,292.

4.12P5. i continuous $= 13.2\%$ per year.

4.12P6. i continuous $= 13.8\%$ per year which is better than value for preceding problem.

4.12P7. $32.95 per month.

4.12P8. $4,220.

4.12P9. Machine A is more economical by $6,657 per year before taxes.

4.12P10. i continuous $= 14\%$ per year approximately.

5.16P1.

	A		B		C	
		Rank		Rank		Rank
Discounted cash flow	28%	1	26%	2	23%	3
Present worth at 10%	371	3	394	1	389	2

ANSWERS TO PROBLEMS

5.16P2. (a) Year 1—10.5%; 2—11.7%; 3—13.3%; 4—15.4%; 5—18.2%; 6—22.2%; 7—28.6%; 8—40.0%; 9—66.7%; 10—200%. (b) 16% per year approximately. (c) Year 1—$4,400; 2—5,160; 3—6,040; 4—7,100; 5—8,320; 6—9,770; 7—11,460; 8—13,450; 9—15,780; 10—18,520.
5.16P3. Public utility, petroleum industry, textile industry.
5.16P4. $3,443.
5.16P5. 0% + 111,000; 4% + 24,000; 6% − 2,000.
5.16P6. 5.8% per year approximately.
5.16P7. Retain old machine but decision is close. Present worth of gain is $330.
5.16P8. 40% per year approximately.
5.16P9. Cash proceeds only given. −2 to −1 year = −844; −1 to 0 = −592; 0 to 1 = 60; 1 to 2 = 190; 2 to 3 = 268; 3 to 4 = 345; 4 to 5 = 392; 5 to 6 = 387; 6 to 7 = 381; 7 to 8 = 375; 8 to 9 = 369; 9 to 10 = 363; 10 to 11 = 357; 11 to 12 = 351; 12 to 13 = 345; 13 to 14 = 340; 14 to 15 = 333; end of 15 = 270.
5.16P10. 5.2% per year approximately.
5.16P11. (1) Book rate of return by years: 36.2%, 24.0%, 12.6%, −2.7%, −25.2%. Average rate of return: 16.7%.
(2) 19.5% per year.
(3) DCF rate of return 10.3% per year (5-year life).
(4) DCF rate of return 17.8% per year (5-year life).
(5) Purchase a new blender and review operations in about 2 years.
6.15P1. $R_{existent} = \$11,400$; $R_{displacer} = \$9,623$.
6.15P2. 20% per year approximately.
6.15P3. $R_{existent} = \$5,928$; $R_{displacer} = \$5,705$.
6.15P4. $R_{existent} = \$825$; $R_{displacer} = \$2,979$.
6.15P5. 5 years.
6.15P6. $R = \$2,204$ per year; $K = \$18,368$.
6.15P7. One decreases and the other increases a fixed amount each year.
6.15P9. 13 years.
6.15P10. Minimum at 11 years with $K/C_i = 1.3826$.
6.15P11. 13.9%.
6.15P12. 18.4%.
6.15P13. 284 bulbs per week.
6.15P14. Minimum cost $217 per period by displacing group every third period.
6.15P15. $28,890.
6.15P16. 18.4% per year approximately.
6.16P17. $22,440.
6.15P18. 4.1 years approximately.
6.15P19. Machine B is more economical. $K_A = \$81,489$; $K_B = \$77,927$. Machine B saves $214 per year as of zero-time dollars.
7.10P1. (a) $0.71 per ton; (b) $4.33 per ton.
7.10P2. 55% of capacity.
7.10P3. $460,000. Yes, by affecting profit.
7.10P4. (a) $0.1574/lb at 75%; $0.133/lb at 100%. (b) $0.06 per lb change. (c) -4.88×10^{-6} dollars per lb changed. (d) $0.133 per lb at 100%.
7.10P5. (a) $0.18 per lb; (b) $0.142 per lb.
7.10P6. (a) $40,000; (b) $538,000; (c) $662,000.
7.10P7. (a) $AN - (B + D)N^3 - CN^4 - C_F = 0$.
(b) $A - 3(B + D)N^2 - 4CN^3 = 0$.
(c) $-2(B + D)N - 3CN^2 + C_F/N^2 = 0$.
(d) $3CN^4 + 2DN^3 - C_F = 0$. (e) $4CN^3 + 3DN^2$. (f) $4CN^3 + 3DN^2$.
7.10P8. (a) $100 - 0.02Q$; (b) 50; (c) 2,500 units per period.
7.10P9. (a) $50,000 on labor and $50,000 on materials. Optimum production 6,250 units per period. (b) Optimum $A = 25$, $B = 50$, $Q = 6,250$ units per period.

476 ANSWERS TO PROBLEMS

8.15P1. (a) 1/12; (b) 1/2; (c) 5/12.
8.15P2. 0.433.
8.15P3. (a) 0.1937; (b) 0.0015; (c) 0.3487.
8.15P4. $E(X) = \mu$.
8.15P5. Some values for X and $Pd(X)$ are $-5, 0.0022, -3, 0.0270, -1, 0.1210, 0, 0.1760,$ 1, 0.1994, 2, 0.1760, 3, 0.1210, 5, 0.0270, and 7, 0.0022.
8.15P6. Some values for X and $Pc(X)$ are $-5, 0.0013, -3, 0.0228, -1, 0.1587, 0, 0.3085,$ 1, 0.5000, 2, 0.6915, 3, 0.8413, 5, 0.9772, and 7, 0.9987.
8.15P7. (a) Mean 4; variance 16.
(b) $Pc(X) = 1 - e^{-X/4}$.
8.15P8. 8 hr.
8.15P9. (b) $Y = 0.5X + 4.0$.
9.10P1. 1,321 hr.
9.10P2. 93.5 hr.
9.10P3. (a) 149.2 hr; (b) 100.4 hr.
9.10P4. (a) 165.1 hr; (b) 180.7 hr.

9.10P5.

Lot	Rule of thumb	Geometric mean	True
1	4.67	6.05	5.53
2	27	24.55	26.19
3	60	55.77	59.07
4	90	88.30	90.27

9.10P6. From plot: $E(N) = 2{,}100 N^{-.31}$ approximately. By least squares: $E(N) = 1{,}605 N^{-0.242}$.
9.10P7. Learning ratio, 84.6%.
9.10P8. New learning curve probably will have a smaller slope and will have to be reestablished.
10.19P1. (a) 100 units; (b) $16 per year; (c) 5 units.
10.19P2. (a) 100 units; (b) $16.64 per year; (c) 9 units.
10.19P3. (a) $5.55 per day for $Q = 70$ units. (b) $4.36 per day for $Q = 75$ units.
(c) $6.61 per day for $Q = 70$ units.
10.19P4. (a) $3.89 per day for $Q = 105$ units. (b) $2.81 per day for $Q = 115$ units.
(c) $5.12 per day for $Q = 105$ units.
10.19P5. Start week with zero units on hand.
11.15P1. (a) $0.16/T_s$; (b) $0.01 T_s$; (c) $0.01 T_s + 0.16/T_s$; (d) $T_s = 4$ min per unit for which $C_t = \$0.08$ per min.

11.15P2.

No. of pumps	T_s opt. minute	C_t opt., $/min
2	5.66	0.1132
3	6.93	0.1386
4	8	0.16

11.15P3. (a) $P(0) = 1/2$; $P(1) = 1/4$; $P(2) = 1/8$, etc.; (b) 1; (c) 1/4.
11.15P4. (a) 6.29 hr; (b) $2.28 per hour.
11.15P5. (a) 2.5 units per hour; (b) $11.12 per hour.
11.15P6. 1.52 units per hour.
11.15P7. 6 crews.
11.15P8. *ABDC*.

ANSWERS TO PROBLEMS

12.19P1. 63.0 ft.
12.19P2. 16.8 Mw.
12.19P3. 2.6 in.
12.19P4. Invest $126,000. Additional investment returns less than 17%.
12.19P5. 14,180 parts per batch.
12.19P6. 11,000 parts per batch approximately.
12.19P7. 5.
12.19P8. $X_{opt} = 7.0$-ft diameter approximately. Total cost $40,941.
12.19P9. $0.12.
12.19P10. $N = 2.13$ effects, or 2 in practice.
12.19P11. 55 hr.
12.19P12. (a) $1,886 per hour with $T = 1.47$ hr. (b) 354 jewels per hour.
12.19P13. $112,000 per year for cycle of 3.06 days.
12.19P14. Area divided by base is average height or average efficiency. Yes, it does matter if input to the equipment is not constant.
12.19P15. (a) 434.3 hr; (b) 1,230 sq ft.
12.19P16. (a) or (b) $X = 3.54$, $Y = 3.54$ maximum; $X = -3.54$, $Y = -3.54$ maximum; $X = -3.54$, $Y = +3.54$ minimum; $X = +3.54$, $Y = -3.54$ minimum.
12.19P17. $X = 0.25$, $Y = 0.25$, $Z = 0.50$.
12.19P18. Tabulate Y against X. For $X = 1.54$, $Y = 0.2698$ and a minimum. At $X = 1.54$ and for $A = B = C = 2$, for equal small changes in A, B, or C, raising B will have the greatest effect in lowering Y.
13.13P3. $X_1 =$ hog liver and $X_2 =$ castor oil; thus

$$X_1 + 3X_2 \geq 8$$
$$3X_1 + 4X_2 \geq 19$$
$$3X_1 + X_2 \geq 7$$
$$Z = 50X_1 + 25X_2$$

13.13P4. Plot first three equations of preceding problem as equalities. Feasible region is above and to the right.
13.13P5. Minimum cost is 150 using one unit of hog liver and four units of castor oil (also five units of slack variable X_3).
13.13P6. Same answer as 13.13P5.
13.13P7. Same answer as 13.13P5.
13.13P8. Optimum $5.05 million with $A = 0$, $B = 2$, $C = 1$.
13.13P9. (a) Optimum $4.00 million with $A = 0$, $B = 2$, $C = 0$. (b) Optimum $2.00 million with $A = 0$, $B = 1$, $C = 0$.
13.13P10. Optimal solution *BJIDA*.
13.13P12. Optimum is either 0 item 1, 3 item 2, and 0 item 3; or 2 item 1, 0 item 2, and 0 item 3.
14.14P1. 1.70 to 1.735.
14.14P2. 1.7188 to 1.7578.
14.14P3. $X = 0$, $Y = 0$.
14.14P4. Place $U = 5Y$; thus $Z = X^2 + U^2$.
14.14P5. $X = 0$, $Y = 0$.
14.14P6. Scale of relation is $-A_m + 3A_{(m+1)} - 3A_{(m+2)} + A_{(m+3)} = 0$. Next term of series $36U^7$.
14.14P7. $1/(1 - 3U + 3U^2 - U^3)$.
15.18P1. $758,000.
15.18P2. $166,000.
15.18P3. $42 million.
15.18P4. $13,600.
15.18P5. $7.26 million.

478 ANSWERS TO PROBLEMS

15.18P6. $11.3 million.
15.18P7. $7,880 with allowance for indirect costs.
15.18P8. $49,200.
17.17P1. 1—3—6—8.
17.17P2. Critical path is 1—2—3—5.

	1—2	1—3	1—4	2—3	2—4	2—5	3—5	4—5
Total float	0	6	7	0	9	7	0	7
Free float	0	6	0	0	2	7	0	7

17.17P3. (a) $1,900 total cost; (b) shorten B by 1 day and E by 1 day at extra cost of $150.

Abramovitz, I., 206
Ackoff, R. L., 206, 228
Adams, C. A., 334
Adams, J. K., 169
Alder, H. L., 169
Ali, A. M., 217, 228
Amey, L. R., 100
Anderson, T. D., 312, 336
Antonacci, D. W., 336
Aries, R. S., 350, 353
Arnoff, E. L., 206, 228
Arnold, T. H., 308, 334
Arnold, T. H., Jr., 417, 421
Arrow, K. J., 206
Ayers, F., 41

Bach, N. G., 318, 327, 334
Baker, B. N., 372
Banks, J., 206
Barish, N. H., 41, 150, 228
Barr, J. A., 312, 334
Bates, A. G., 89, 100, 101
Bauman, H. C., 150, 301, 302, 326, 327, 333–335, 337, 345, 353, 372, 373n., 384
Behrens, H. J., 184
Beightler, C. S., 257, 281, 297
Bell, L. F., 404
Bellman, R. E., 273, 280
Berk, J. M., 311, 312, 318, 335
Berry, E. M., 352, 353
Betz, G. M., 413, 417, 418, 421
Beyer, W. H., 169
Bhatia, A., 228
Bianco, R. E., 312, 335
Bierman, S., 100

Birchard, R., 309, 335
Black, J. H., 353
Boas, A. H., 257, 281, 297
Bock, R. H., 372
Bowman, E. H., 228
Bowman, J. H., 413, 421
Bramer, H. C., 406, 421
Brauweiler, J. R., 82, 101
Brownlee, K. A., 157, 169
Buchan, J., 206
Buffa, E. S., 228
Burford, R. L., 169
Butler, W. S., 312, 335

Canada, J. R., 100
Canfield, D. T., 413, 421
Cardello, R. A., 101
Carlson, R. O., 52–54, 63, 101
Carroll, C. W., 293, 297
Charnes, A., 280
Cherry, J. R., 328, 335
Cheslow, R. T., 101
Chilton, C. H., 308, 310, 334, 335, 343, 349, 353, 372
Chrystal, G., 297
Churchman, C. W., 206, 228
Clark, W. E., 336
Clark, W. G., 327, 335
Cooper, W. W., 280
Couch, J. C., 353
Cronan, C. S., 312, 335

Dantzig, G. B., 268, 280
Davis, R. S., 292, 297
Dean, J., 391, 404
De Garmo, E. P., 41, 131

480 Name Index

DeJen, J., 432
Dickey, R. I., 404
Dooley, A. R., 372
Dougherty, W. J., 312, 337
Dreyfus, S., 280
Dryden, C. E., 337
Dubois, W. C., 432
Dybdal, E. C., 336, 347, 353

Edge, C. G., 100
Edmunds, K. B., 302, 325, 335
Eris, R. L., 372

Faber, J. H., 312, 335
Fabrycky, W. J., 41, 131, 150, 184, 206, 228
Fan, L. T., 257
Fetter, R. B., 228
Fiacco, A. V., 293, 297
Fine, H. B., 297
Flagle, C. D., 228
Friedman, I. R., 372
Friedman, M., 289, 297

Gallagher, J. T., 312, 318, 335
Garvin, W. W., 264, 280
Gary, A., 228
Gass, S. I., 280
Gessner, A. W., 257
Ghare, P. M., 131
Gilman, W., 433
Gilmore, J. F., 318, 335
Glazier, E. M., 319, 335
Goetz, B. E., 228
Gonzalez, R. F., 228
Goode, H. H., 228
Gordan, M. J., 404
Grady, P., 388, 391, 404
Grant, E. L., 41, 63, 100, 131, 404
Graybill, F. A., 169
Grayson, C., 100
Green, P. E., 101
Greever, G., 433
Gunning, R., 427, 433

Hackney, J. W., 100, 302, 335, 338n., 350, 353, 372
Hadley, G., 280
Haines, T. B., 347, 349, 353
Hand, W. E., 305, 316, 335
Happel, J., 405, 407, 421
Harding, C. F., 413, 421
Harris, M. M., Jr., 318, 335
Hart, W. L., 41
Haselbarth, J. E., 311, 312, 318, 335
Hausmann, F., 206
Hawkins, H. M., 101

Hazelwood, R. N., 228
Hertz, D. B., 101
Hillier, F. S., 228
Himsworth, F. R., 257
Hirsch, J. H., 319, 335
Hirschmann, W. B., 82, 101, 184
Hoel, P. G., 169
Hoerl, A. E., 292, 297
Hoffman, R. A., 206
Holmes, J. M., 312, 335
Holstein, W. K., 372
Hooke, R., 292, 297
Horngren, C. T., 404
Horton, R. L., 352, 353

Ireson, W. G., 41, 100, 131
Isard, W., 347, 353
Iscol, L., 257

Jackson, J., 100
Jeeves, T. A., 292, 297
Jelen, F. C., 41, 63, 87, 89, 100, 114, 126, 131, 297
Johnson, S. M., 285, 297
Jones, E. S., 433
Jordan, R., 184

Karlin, S., 206
Katell, S., 312, 335
Kaufmann, A., 228
Keating, C. J., 327, 336
Keifer, J., 285, 297
Kellett, J. W., 101
Kelley, J. E., Jr., 367, 372
Kermode, R. I., 257
King, R. A., 411, 421
Kirkpatrick, C. A., 150, 367, 372
Klei, H. E., 304, 336
Kneese, A. V., 406, 421
Knox, W. G., 323, 336
Koenigsberg, E., 206
Kottler, J. L., 184

Lang, J. H., 316, 336
Lapidus, L. E., 257
Lapple, W. C., 336
Lavi, A., 257
Lavine, I., 312, 315, 337
Lee, N. F., 408, 421
Levin, R. I., 150, 367, 372
Lindgren, B. W., 169
Lukk, G. G., 101
Lunch, M. F., 413, 421
Lyon, J. T., 63
Lyvers, H. I., 292, 297

Name Index

McCormick, G. P., 293, 297
McCullough, C. B., 413, 421
McElrath, G. W., 169
Machol, R. E., 228
McLean, J. G., 101
McMillan, C., 228
McNeill, W. I., 372
Malloy, J. B., 94, 100
Martin, O. E., 101
Martino, R. L., 372
Mattiza, D. S., 327, 336
Meig, J. L., 63
Mendel, O., 332, 336
Mickley, H. S., 94, 100
Miller, D. W., 206, 228
Miller, W. E., 96, 100
Moder, J. J., 372
Mood, A. M., 169
Morris, W. T., 150

Naphtali, L. M., 257
Nelson, J. R., 433
Nelson, W. L., 312, 336, 354
Nemhauser, G. L., 280
Neuwirth, S. I., 257
Newton, R. D., 350, 353
Nichols, W. T., 303, 336
Nickerson, C. B., 404
Nitchie, E .B., 372
Noah, L. W., 184
Nord, M., 413, 417, 419, 421
Norton, P. T., Jr., 63

O'Connell, F. P., 354
Ostle, B., 169

Pardo, V. A., 337
Paterson, S. F., 184
Peck, L. G., 228
Perry, J. H., 345, 350, 354, 380, 382, 384
Perry, R. H., 339, 354, 384
Peters, M. S., 257, 336, 354, 384, 425, 433
Phillips, C. R., 372
Popper, H., 417, 422
Prabhu, N. V., 228
Prater, N. H., 336

Rautenstrausch, W., 138, 150
Reed, C. E., 94, 100
Reistad, D. L., 408, 421
Reul, R. I., 89, 100, 101
Roberts, I., 312, 336
Roberts, O. R., 329, 336
Roberts, S. M., 292, 297
Roessler, E. B., 169
Rosenbrock, H. H., 293, **297**

Saaty, T. L., 228
Salmon, R., 312, 335
Samfield, J., 336
Savage, L. S., 289, 297
Sayre, J. S., 367, 372
Scarf, H., 206
Schofield, B. P., 311, 336
Schooler, E. W., 347, 353
Schwartz, C. C., 318, 336
Schweyer, H. E., 100, 135n., 141, 145, 147, 150, 257
Seamster, A. H., 336
Shapiro, E., 257
Shapiro, S., 257
Sharples, L. P., 336
Shellenberger, D. J., 309, 336
Shelton, J. R., 228
Sherwood, P. W., 311, 336
Sherwood, T. K., 94, 100
Shillinglaw, G., 404
Sindt, H. A., 312, 336
Smidt, S., 100
Smith, E. M., 336
Smith, L. C., 336
Smith, R. W., 184
Solomon, E., 84, 100
Sommers, H. A., 312, 336
Sondak, N. E., 292, 297
Specthrie, S. W., 404
Spiewak, I., 312, 336
Starr, M. K., 206, 228
Stasny, E. P., 336
Stevens, R. W., 307, 337
Stillman, R. E., 257
Stokes, C. A., 101
Strunk, W., Jr., 433
Sweet, E. R., 354
Swift, L. L., 337

Taborek, J. J., 257
Takacs, L., 228
Tamborra, J. M., 304, 336
Tao, L. C., 257
Taylor, G. A., 150
Terborgh, G., 63, 87, 100, 116, 131
Thomas, H. R., 354
Thomas, L. D., 52–54, 63, 101
Thorne, H. C., 52–54, 63, 96, 100, 101
Thuessen, H. G., 41, 131, 150
Timmerhaus, K. D., 257, 336, 354, 384, 425, 433
Torgersen, P. E., 131, 184, 206, 228
Trombetta, M. L., 257
Twaddle, W. W., 94, 100

Ullman, J. W., 312, 335

Vajda, S., 280
Vancil, R. F., 101
Van Dyke, H., 312, 337
Van Noy, C. W., 354
Van Slyke, R. M., 372
Verseput, J. P., 354
Vilbrandt, F. C., 337
Vogl, T. P., 257

Walas, S. M., 321, 337
Walker, M. R., 367, 372
Walton, P. R., 354
Warren, A. S., 337
Weaver, J. B., 85, 100, 301, 302, 337
Werbin, I. V., 413, 422

Wessell, H. E., 347, 354
Wheaton, R. M., 336
White, E. B., 433
Whitin, T. M., 206
Wilde, D. J., 257, 281, 292, 297
Wilhelm, R. D., 417, 422
Williams, R., Jr., 310, 337
Wise, D. C., 96, 100
Wixom, R., 404
Wood, R. T., 304, 336
Wroth, W. F., 317, 337

Zellnik, H. E., 292, 297
Zimmerman, O. T., 305, 309, 311, 312, 315, 337

Abandonment, 53, 93
Absorption costing, 399–400
Accounting:
   absorption costing in, 399–400
   balance sheet, 390
   burden rate, 398
   for by-products, 401–402
   chart of accounts, 388
   cost center, 394
   credit in, 388, 389
   debit in, 388, 389
   depreciation in, 403
   differential costs in, 402
   direct cost in, 393
   direct costing, 399–400
   financial, 390
   future-directed cost in, 391
   historical cost in, 391
   indirect cost in, 393
   of inventory, 402
   job-order costing in, 394–395
   joint costs in, 401–402
   journalizing in, 389
   managerial, 390
   nominal account in, 390
   normal volume in, 399
   in operating cost control, 363
   overhead cost in, 396–398
   process costing in, 394–396
   real account in, 390
   standard cost in, 400
   trial balance, 389
   variance, 400
Activity levels in linear programming, 259
Administrative bodies, 418
Administrative expense, 374

Algebraic method in linear programming, 267
Annuity:
   due, 19
   ordinary, 19
Appraising, AACE classification of, 95
Appropriation request:
   in profitability studies, 96
   reports with, 425
Ascent (*see* Steepest ascent search method)

Balance sheet, 390
Basic solution in linear programming, 264
Basis in linear programming, 264
Battery limits, 304, 381
   cost of plants, table, 312
Bid decision, 416
Binomial distribution, 156–157
Black box:
   in dynamic programming, 273
   in linear programming, 258, 263
Book value, 46, 49, 103
Break-even:
   analysis of, 138–145
   point of, 138, 143
Building costs, 322–326
Burden rate, 398
Bureau of Labor statistics in cost indexes, 306
   figure, 308
By-product accounting, 401, 402

Canons of ethics, table, 412
Capital cost estimates, functions of, 303
Capital-recovery factor, 16–17

Subject Index

Capitalized cost, 27–29, 37, 57
  with continuous interest, 75–76
  of delay, 114
  discounted cash flow in, 87
  in displacement, 104
  extended, 126
  factor, 28
  with inflation, 123–125
Cash flow, 87–91, 135–136
Chart of accounts, 380
Chemical Engineering plant construction index, table, 306, 308
COMET, 367
Community relations, 404
Compound interest:
  double, in Hoskold's formula, 19–20
  factor, 12
  law, 12
  with negative compounding, 115
  as operator, 14
  in profitability studies, 90–91
Constraint:
  in dynamic programming, 278
  in search methods, 292–293
  (*See also* Restraint)
Contingencies, 349, 376
Continuous interest:
  capitalized cost with, 75–76
  discounting with, 80
  with flow at exponential rate, 69–70
  with flow straight line to zero, 70–72
  as operator, 65
  with taxes, 76–77
  with uniform flow, 67–68
Contour tangent search method, 292
Contracts, 413, 414
Control of costs, 355–366
  accounting in, 363
  of capital cost, 355–363
  corrective action in, 361–363, 365
  bp critical path method, 365
  of operating cost, 363–366
  project plan in, 357
  project schedule in, 358
  reporting in, 365
  standard costs in, 365
Corrective action, 361–363, 365
Cost:
  accounting: absorption costing in, 399–400
    definition of, 391
    differential cost in, 402
    direct costing in, 399–400
    future-directed costs in, 391
    historical costs in, 391
    joint costs in, 401–402

Cost:
  of administrative expense, 374
  battery-limits, 304
  break-even, 138–145
  capacity factors, 310–311
    for equipment, table, 313–316
    for plants, table, 312
  of contingencies, 376
  corrective action in, 365
  data for: battery-limits plants, 315
    buildings, 322–326
    distribution, 350
    electricity, 346
    equipment, table, 313–315
    heat exchangers, figure, 305
    insulation, 333
    labor, 347
    laboratory, 349
    maintenance, 348
    piping, 326–332
    plants, 312
      table, 320
    raw materials, 344
    refrigeration, 346
    sewage plants, figure, 304
    steam, 346
    supplies, 349
    unit prices for buildings, table, 325
    utilities, 345
    water, 346
  depreciable, 56
    first cost, 43
  direct, 340
  for engineering, 326
  equipment installation cost ratio, 311
    factor, table, 316
  of estimates, 302–303
  fixed, 136, 340
  of general and selling expense, 373–375
  incremental, 142–145
  indirect, 340
  initial, 46
  installed, 311
  in inventory analysis, 189
  irregular, 30, 57
  Lang factors for, 316
  manufacturing, 338
    checklist, table, 343
  marginal, 145–146
  nondepreciable, 30, 60
  offsite, 380–381
  operating, 341–344
    form for, table, 342
    preliminary, 352
  payroll, indirect, 348
  of piping by diameter-inch method, 329

Cost:
    of plants: by analytical procedure, 319–321
    cost ratio for, 316
        table, 318
        table, 312
    in queuing analysis, 191, 212
    ratio factor, 311
        table, 317
    of rentals, 349
    reporting, 359, 365
    representation of, 304
    of royalties, 349
    semivariable, 340
    six-tenths factor rule for, 310–311
    standard, 365, 400
    start-up, 92, 375–378
    sunk, 85, 93, 103
    unit cost factor, 310
    variable, 136, 340
    by volumetric ratio, 323
    (*See also* Cost index)
Cost accounting (*see* Accounting)
Cost-capacity factors, 310–311
Cost center, 394
Cost control (*see* Control of costs)
Cost index, 305–309
    Bureau of Labor data in, 306
        figure, 308
    comparison of, table, 309
    Chemical Engineering plant, table, 306, 308
    Engineering News-Record, table, 306, 307
    highway bid prices, table, 307
    irrigation and hydroelectric plant, table, 307
    Marshall and Stevens, table, 306, 307
    Nelson refinery construction, table, 306, 307
    sewage treatment plants, table, 307
    sewer line construction, table, 307
    water utility plants, table, 307
CPM, 366–370
CRAM, 367
Created response surface technique (CRST), 293
Credit, 388, 389
Critical path method, 366–370
Cumulative-distribution function, 153–156, 159
Cumulative-probability function, 164
Curve fitting, 166–167
Cyclic processes, 234–240

Debit, 388, 389
Decimal ratio of effort (*see* Learning curve)
Declining-balance depreciation, 48, 50, 53
Deflation, 128
Delay value, 113–114
Depletion, 54–55
Depreciable cost, 56
    first cost, 43
    in inflation, 122
Depreciation:
    in accounting, 403
    declining-balance, 48, 50, 53
    as expense, 42–43
    fractional, 43
    group, 52
    present worth of, 296
    sinking-fund, 47, 50
    straight-line, 46, 50
    sum-of-digits, 49, 50, 53
    switch point in, 52
    units-of-production, 49
    tax situation for, 49–52
Descent (*see* Steepest ascent search method)
Diameter-inch method, 329
Diet problem in linear programming, 271
Differential cost, 402
Direct cost, 340, 393
Direct costing, 399–400
Direct search method, 292
Discounted cash flow, 87
    slide rule, 66
Discounting, 14
    with capitalized cost, 87
    continuous, 66, 80
    by discounted cash flow, 87
    with flow declining in straight line to zero, 71
    with improving performance, 72–74
    with uniform flow, 67–68
    in venture worth, 88
Displacement, 102–122
    by groups, 120–122
    (*See also* Replacement)
Displacer, 103
Distribution costs, 350
Distribution function:
    binomial, 156–157
    continuous, 164
    cumulative, 153–156, 159
    with dice, 152–153
    discrete, 151–158
    expectation of, 154, 158
    exponential, 160–161
    mean of, 153, 158
    normal, 162–163
    Poisson, 157–158
    probability density of, 158
    rectangular, 159–160
    standard deviation of, 154

Distribution function:
　uniform, 159–160
　variance of, 153–154, 159
Double-declining-balance depreciation, 48, 50, 53
Double interest rates, 19–20
Dynamic programming (DP), 272, 278
　black box for, 273
　constraints in, 278
　decision variable for, 273
　optimality principle in, 273
　pros and cons of, 278
　state variable in, 273
　transportation example, 276

Economic production chart, 138–145
　with dumping, 141
　nonlinear, 141–142
　above 100% capacity, 139–140
Educational activities, 407
Effective interest rate, 12, 66
Electricity, cost of, 346
Employee relations, 404–405
Engineering, cost of, 326
Engineering News-Record cost index, table, 306, 307
Equipment, cost of: installation factor, table, 316
　ratio factor, table, 317
　table, 313–315
Estimates:
　cost of making, 302–303
　types of, 302
Ethical aspects, 411–413
　canons of ethics, table, 412
Existent, 103
Expectation:
　in inventory, 202
　value of, 154, 158
Exponential distribution, 160–161
Extended capitalized cost, 126
Extreme point in linear programming, 266

Factor:
　capital-recovery, 16–17, 57
　　continuous, 74
　capitalized cost, 28, 57
　compound interest, 12
　　with negative rate, 115
　for continuous compounding, 66
　for declining-balance depreciation, 48, 50
　for discounting flow declining in straight line to zero, 72
　for double-declining-balance depreciation, 48, 50, 53
　equal-payment-series present-worth, 16

Factor:
　present worth, 13
　psi, 56
　single-payment present-worth, 13
　sinking-fund, 17
　straight-line present-worth, 47
　　in depreciation, 57
　sum-of-digits depreciation, 49
　　present worth of, 49, 57
　unacost present-worth, 15
　for uniform flow discounting, 68
　uniform-gradient-series present-worth, 109
　Z, in inventory, 188–189
Fibonacci search method, 285–287
　number, 285
FIFO, 403
Financing, 378
Finite queuing, 219–222
Fixed capital, 301
　(*See also* Capital cost estimates)
Fixed cost, 136, 340
Float, 370
Flow:
　with exponential rate, 69–70
　straight line to zero, 70–72
　uniform, 67–68
Forecasting, 381–382
Fractional depreciation, 46
Future-directed cost, 391
Future worth, 11–14

Gaussian integration, 94–95
General and selling expense, 338, 373–375
Generating function, 294
Geometric-mean method, 180
Geometrical series, 15
Gradient, 108–113, 295
Gradient search method, 289–292
Graphical solution in linear programming, 265
Grass-roots plant, 380–381
Group depreciation, 52
Group displacement, 120–122

Hedge clauses, 414–415
Hemstitching search method, 292
Highway bid prices cost index, table, 307
Hirsch and Glazier method, 319–321
Historical cost, 391
Hoskold's formula, 19–20

IMPACT, 367
Impatient customers, 191–193, 195, 197–199
Incremental analysis:
　for break-even, 142–145
　in inventory, 201
　in multivariable optimization, 247

Incremental analysis:
 in optimization, 234
 return in, 85
Indirect cost, 340, 393
Inflation:
 capitalized cost with, 123–125
 cost-comparisons with, 122–126
 high rates of, 125
 purchasing power of dollar, figure, 305
 technological advancement and, 127–128
 unaburden in, 125–126
 yearly cost with, 125–126
 (*See also* Cost index)
Initial cost, 46
Insulation costs, 333
Interest (*see* specific types)
Inventory:
 cost of placing order, 189
 definitions, 185
 deterministic models for, 185–201
  classification of, table, 187
 expectation used in, 202
 with finite delivery rate, 195–199
 graphical method in, 199
 with impatient customers, 191–193, 195, 197–199
 incremental analysis in, 201
 lead time in, 189
 Monte Carlo method in, 203–205
 with patient customers, 191–195, 197–198
 probalistic models for, 201–205
 reneging in, 191
 reorder level in, 190
 with safety stock, 191, 195
 shortage cost in, 189
 storage cost in, 189
 tabular method for, 199–201
 valuation of, 402
 Z factor in, 188–189
Irregular cost, 30, 57
Irrigation and hydroelectric plants cost index, table, 307

Job-order costing, 394–395
Joint costs, 401–402
Journalizing, 389

Kuhn-Tucker conditions, 292

Labor, operating cost of, 347
Laboratory costs, 349
Lagrange expression and multiplier, 146, 148, 249–251, 292
Lang factors, 316
Lattice search method, 292
Lead time, 189
Learning with discounting, 72–74

Learning curve, 170–183
 cumulative values of, 176–177
 decimal learning ratio in, 173
 decimal ratio of effort in, 173
 in economic evaluation, 177–178
 function, 172–173
 from grouped data, 178–181
 least squares method with, 181–182
 lot equivalent point, 179
 lot midpoint methods: geometric mean, 180
  lot-midpoint, 179
  rule-of-thumb, 179
  true, 180–181
 percentage learning ratio, 173
 from single-unit data, 178
 slope constant of, 171, 173, 175
 tables, development of, 182–183
Lease or buy, 93
Least squares, 166–167
 in learning curve, 181–182
Legal aspects, 413–420
 with administrative bodies, 418
 checklist for, table, 416
 of contracts, 413–414
 of employee's obligations, 415–416
 hedge clauses in, 414–415
 of patents, 417
 of professional registration, 419–420
 proprietary information and, 417
 starter sheets for, 417–418
LESS, 367
LIFO, 403
Linear programming (LP), 258–272
 activity levels in, 259
 by algebraic method, 267
 basis and, 264
  basic solution, 264
  basic variable, 264
  nonbasic variable, 264
 diet problem, 271
 extreme point in, 266
 matrices in, 268, 270
 objective function in, 258, 260, 269
 pivot in, 270
 restraints in, 260, 261, 263
  quality restraint, 262
 row in, 260
 slack variable in, 261
 solutions for: graphical, 265
  simplex method, 268–270
  tabular, 266
 tableau for, 269
 transportation problem, 271–272
Load factor in queuing, 212
LOB, 367

Subject Index

Location in plant studies, 378, 380
Lot equivalent point, 179
Lot midpoint, 179

Machinery and Applied Products Institute (*see* MAPI model)
Maintenance, cost of, 348
Manufacturing cost, table, 343
  (*See also* Operating cost)
Manufacturing progress curve (*see* Learning curve)
MAPI model, 116–120
  discounted cash flow with, 87
Marginal cost, 145, 146
Marshall and Stevens cost index, table, 306, 307
Matrix in simplex method, 268, 270
Mean, 153, 158
Minimax search technique, 282
Monte Carlo method, 164–165
  in inventory, 203–205
  in queuing, 224–226
  random numbers in, 164–166
Multivariable techniques:
  in optimization, 246–251, 253
  in search methods, 288–293

Nelson refinery construction index, table, 306, 307
Network diagrams, 366–370
Nominal rate of return, 12
Nondepreciable cost, 30, 60
Normal distribution, 162–163
Normal volume, 399

Objective function, 258, 260, 269
Obsolescence, 382
Offsite costs, 380–381
One-at-a-time search method, 288–289
Operating cost, 338–339
  control of, 363, 366
  corrective action for, 365
  estimation of, 341–344
    form for, table, 342
    preliminary, 352
    shortcut methods, 351–352
  reporting, 365
  standard, 365
Operator:
  compound interest, 14
  continuous interest, 65
Optimality principle, 273
Optimization:
  of cyclic process, 234–240
    variocyclic process, 244–246
  Lagrange multiplier in, 249–251

Optimization:
  methods for: analytical, 232–233
    graphical, 233–234
    incremental, 234
    tabular, 233, 234
  multivariable, 246–247, 288–293
    two-variable example, 248–249
  with rate of return, 240–241
  with recycle, 241–244
  response analysis in, 251–253
  sensitivity analysis in, 251–253
  of two-step example, 241–244
Oral presentation, 430–432
Ordinary annuity, 19
Outline for reports, 424–426
Overhead cost accounting, 396–398

Patents, 417
Patient customers, 191–195, 197–198
Payout time, 86
Payroll, indirect cost of, 348
PERT, 366
Piping costs, 326–332
  labor requirements for, 330
  relative, table, 332
Pivot in linear programming, 270
Plant cost:
  by analytical method, 319–321
  breakdown of, table, 320
  by component cost ratios, table, 318
  by cost ratios, 316
  table, 312
Plant location, 378–380
Poisson distribution, 157–158
  connection with exponential distribution, 161
  expectation with, 202
Policy in strategic aspects, 409
Present worth, 11–17
  in abandonment, 53
  factor, 13
  after taxes, 55–60
Probability, 151–165
  density, 158
  in inventory, 201
  (*See also* Distribution function)
Process costing, 394–396
Production chart (*see* Economic production chart)
Professional registration, 419–420
Profit, 383
  in break-even analysis, 138, 140–145, 148
  limit point, 143
  in private enterprise, 83
Profitability, 83–96
  cash flow in, 87–91

Profitability:
  with computer, 96
  considerations in, 92
  with continuous interest, 90–91
  displacement problem in, 95
  with flow changing, 94
  forecasting of, 381–382
  guideposts in, 84–85
  incremental return in, 85
  lease or buy and, 93
  methods for: discounted cash flow, 87–88
    payout time, 85–86
    return on average investment, 87
    return on original investment, 86
    venture worth, 88
  project types for, 92–93
  sunk costs in, 85, 93
  tax inclusion in, 89–91
Progress curve (*see* Learning curve)
Project plan, 357
Project schedule, 358
Proprietary information, 417
Psi factor, 56

Queuing, 207–224
  characteristics of models, table, 211
  classification of systems, 208–210
  finite, 219–222
  load factor in, 212
  Monte Carlo method in, 224–226
  servicing and waiting costs for, 212
  by tabular method, 222

Random number, 164
Rate of return:
  effective, 12
  nominal, 12
  after taxes, 56
Raw material:
  cost, 344
  position, 410
Rectangular distribution function, 159–160
Recurring power series, 293–296
Recycle, example with, 241–244
Refrigeration, cost of, 346
Reneging cost, 191
Rental, 349
Reorder level, 190
Replacement, 102–122
  (*See also* Displacement)
Reporting:
  costs, 359
  by oral presentation, 430–432
  results, 423–430
    outline for, 424–426

Reporting:
  results: style in, 427, 429
Response analysis, 251–253
Restraint:
  in linear programming, 260, 261, 263
    quality restraint, 262
  (*See also* Constraint)
Return on average investment, 86
  on original investment, 87
Ridge analysis search method, 292
Royalties, cost of, 349
Rule-of-thumb method, 179

Safety stock, 191, 195
Salvage value, 31, 56, 60, 92, 103–104, 106, 109
Scale of relation, 294
Search:
  comparison of methods, 287
  constraints in, 292–293
  gradient in, 289–291
  interval, 282
  methods: contour tangent, 292
    created response surface technique (CRST), 293
    direct, 292
    Fibonacci, 285–287
    gradient, 292
    hemstitching, 292
    lattice, 292
    one-at-a-time, 288–289
    ridge analysis, 292
    sequential dichotomous, 284–285
    steepest ascent, 289–292
    uniform, 282–283
    uniform dichotomous, 283–284
  minimax procedure, 282
  multivariable, 288–293
  sequential, 284–287
  unimodality in, 282
  univariable, 281–287
Semivariable cost, 340
Sensitivity analysis, 251–253
Sequential search methods, 284–287
Series:
  geometrical, summation of, 15
  recurring power, 293–296
    coefficients in, 293
    general term of, 294
    generating function of, 294
    scale of relation of, 294
    summation of, 293–294
  uniform gradient, 108–113
    summation of, 295
Sewage treatment plants cost index, table, 307

Subject Index

Sewer-line construction cost index, table, 307
Shortage cost, 189
Shortcut methods for operating costs, 351–352
Shut-down point, 145
Simple interest, 12
Simplex method, 268–270
Simulation (*see* Monte Carlo method)
Sinking fund:
   annual deposit for, 17
   depreciation, 47, 50
   factor, 17
   payment, 19–20
   rate, 20
Six-tenths factor rule, 310–311
Slack variable, 261
Slide rule for discounted cash flow, 66
Slope constant, 171, 173, 175
Social aspects, 405–411
   of community relations, 404
   of educational activities, 407
   of employee relations, 404–405
   government and, 408
Standard costs, 365, 400
Standard deviation, 154
Start-up costs, 92, 375–378
Starter sheets, 417–418
Steam, cost of, 346
Steepest ascent search method, 289–292
Stipulated rate, 20
Storage cost, 189
Straight-line depreciation, 46, 50
Straight-line present-worth factor, 47
Strategic aspects, 409–411
   company policy and, 409
   customer relations and, 410
   market position and, 410
   raw material position and, 410–411
Style in writing, 427, 429
Sum-of-digits depreciation, 49–50, 53
   present worth of, 296
Summation of series:
   geometrical, 15
   recurring power, 293–296
Sunk cost, 85, 93, 103
Supplies, cost of, 349

Tableau in linear programming, 269
Tax:
   capital gain, 50
   with continuous interest, 76–77
   cost comparisons after, 55–60
      with inflation, 122–126
   with depletion, 54–55
   depreciation and effect on, 49–52
   in displacement analysis, 103–104

Tax:
   investment credit in, 50
   normal, 50
   in profitability studies, 89–91
   surtax, 80
Technological advancement:
   with inflation, 127–128
   mathematical model for, 114–115
   rate of, 114
   in profitability studies, 95
   (*See also* Learning curve)
Time value conversion relationship, 14
Total product cost, table, 339
Transportation problem, 276
Trial balance, 389
True lot-midpoint method, 180–181

Unaburden, 125
Unacost, 25–27, 37, 57
   cost comparisons by, 25–27
   in displacement, 104, 106, 111–113
   from present worth, 15–17
   present-worth factor, 13
Unaflow, 74–75
Uniform annual amount (*see* Unacost)
Uniform beginning-of-year annual amount, 17, 57
Uniform dichotomous search, 283–284
Uniform distribution function, 159–160
Uniform flow, 67–68
Uniform-gradient series, 108–109
   present-worth factor, 109
   summation of, 295
Uniform search methods, 281–287
Units-of-production depreciation, 49
Utilities, cost of, 345

Variable:
   basic, 264
   decision, 273
   nonbasic, 264
Variable cost, 136, 340
Variable state, 273
Variance:
   in accounting, 400
   of distribution function, 153–154, 159
Variocyclic process, 244–246
Venture analysis (*see* Profitability)
Venture worth, 88
Volumetric ratio, 323

Water, cost of, 346
Water utility plants cost index, table, 307
Working capital, 86, 92, 301–302

Z factor in inventory, 188–189